THE COMPLETE BOOK
OF COMPOSTING

THE COMPLETE BOOK OF

COMPOSTING

by the staff of

ORGANIC GARDENING

AND

FARMING MAGAZINE

J. I. RODALE *Editor-in-Chief*

Robert Rodale, *Editor*

Jerome Olds, *Executive Editor*

M. C. Goldman, *Managing Editor*

Maurice Franz, *Managing Editor*

Jerry Minnich, *Associate Editor*

Compilation Supervised by
M. C. Goldman

RODALE BOOKS, INC., EMMAUS, PENNA.

INTRODUCTION

Compost is the core, the essential foundation of natural gardening and farming. It is the heart of the organic concept.

Composting is not new. Neither in theory nor practice are the basic tenets of returning organic matter to the soil revolutionary or even of comparatively recent vintage. The pages of history are filled with emphatic evidence that nothing is more fundamental to man's prosperity—to civilization itself —than a lasting, productive agriculture. This, the past proves, can stem only from heeding the most primary of Nature's laws—the law of return, the very cycle of life itself.

Wherever a nation has adhered to this principle, there alone has a people survived and a land flourished. Where it has been violated and abused, whether through ignorance or mistaken custom, there has a race perished, a metropolis fallen to ruins, and a country's soil withered and blown to sterile desert.

Here, then, is a significant text, a compilation of material, facts, features, experiences, research, letters, questions and answers about compost that have appeared in *Organic Gardening and Farming* magazine over the past 18 years. Added to these are the findings of United States and world-wide experimental stations, pertinent data from agricultural bulletins, important excerpts from books, pamphlets and treatises—all contributing to our knowledge of this basic process.

It is our earnest hope that this book will serve well all who seek information from it; that it will provide the explanations, details and directions to enable anyone—farmer or gardener, city dweller, suburbanite or homesteader—to make rich, ample quantities of compost quickly and conveniently, and to use this life-giving fertilizer not only effectively, but to the greatest benefit. More than that, it is our fervent wish that this book may bring a better understanding of the world's soil, its care and vital needs to all who choose to look into it; that it may contribute to the urgent awareness of our own need to work with, rather than against, nature; and that it may yield a deeper insight, a stronger inspiration, and a more practical aid for those devoted to bringing this knowledge to others. To all who keep a love for the land in their hearts, minds and deeds, this book is gratefully dedicated.

CONTENTS

Chapter 1

THE HISTORY OF COMPOST

In the soft, warm bosom of a decaying compost heap, a transformation from life to death and back again is taking place. Life is leaving the living plants of yesterday, but in their death these leaves and stalks pass on their vitality to the coming generations of future seasons. Here in a dank and mouldy pile the wheel of life is turning.

Compost is more than a fertilizer or a healing agent for the soil's wounds. It is a symbol of continuing life. Nature herself made compost before man first walked the earth and before the first dinosaur reared its head above a primeval swamp. Leaves falling to the forest floor and slowly mouldering are composting. The dead grass of the meadow seared by winter's frost is being composted by the dampness of the earth beneath. The birds, the insects and the animals contribute their bodies to this vast and continuing soil rebuilding program of nature.

The compost heap in your garden is an intensified version of this process of death and rebuilding which is going on almost everywhere in nature. In the course of running a garden there is always an accumulation of organic wastes of different sorts—leaves, grass clippings, weeds, twigs—and since time immemorial gardeners have been accumulating this material in piles, eventually to spread it back on the soil as rich, dark humus.

Because the compost heap is symbolic of nature's best effort to build soil and because compost is the most efficient and practical fertilizer, it has become the heart of the organic method. The compost heap is to the organic gardener what the typewriter is to the writer, what the shovel is to the laborer and what the truck is to the truckdriver. It is the basic tool to do the job which is to be done. In the case of the organic gardener the job is the creation of the finest garden soil he knows how to build, and compost has proven itself through thousands of years of use to be the best tool for the job.

COMPOST THROUGH HISTORY

The origin of composting has been lost, along with thousands of other age-old practices, in the dim shadows of history. When man first discovered that manure or leaf mold from the forest was good for growing plants, is a matter of speculation. The important thing is that he did discover the benefits of organic matter, and that the knowledge spread throughout the land, and throughout the world.

Probably our oldest existing reference to the use of manure in agriculture is to be found on a set of clay tablets of the Akkadian Empire, which flourished in the Mesopotamian Valley a thousand years before Moses was born. Akkadia was overthrown by Babylon, which in turn fell to Cyrus, but though empires crumbled, the knowledge and practice of organic fertilizing increased.

Compost was known to the Romans; the Greeks had a word for it, and so did the Tribes of Israel. From the first glories of the Garden of Eden to the sombre shadows of the Garden of Gethsemane, the Bible is interspersed with references to the cultivation of the soil. The generic terms dung and dunghill, used by the learned theologians who translated the scriptural Hebrew and Greek into English, have numerous variants in the original, as examination of a Bible concordance will show. Dung was used both as fuel and as fertilizer, but it is only with the latter purpose that we are concerned. Three methods were in use: the manure was spread directly onto the fields; it was composted along with street sweepings and organic refuse, carried through the dung-gate to the dunghill (more correctly compost-pile) outside the city wall; or else straw, its bulk reduced by trampling down, was soaked in liquid manure (literally "in dung-water").

In the parable of the fig tree—Luke 13:8—the gardener pleads for delay until he can dig about it, and dung it. The mode of fertilizing trees was to dig holes about the roots and fill the spaces with manure, a custom still practiced in southern Italy. The Talmud tells us "They lay dung to moisten and enrich the soil; dig about the roots of trees; pluck up the suckers; take off the leaves; sprinkle ashes; and smoke under the trees to kill vermin." From other sources we learn that the soil was enriched by the addition of ashes, straw, stubble and chaff, as well as with the grass and brambles which sprung up in the sabbatical (seventh) year, during which compost was not allowed to be removed from the pile. An exception to this sabbatical year ban was the permission granted under certain circumstances to fold cattle, for the sake of their manure, upon the land in need of fertilizer. Normally sheep were folded within walled enclosures from which their manure was periodically collected.

Another Talmud passage tells us of the use of blood as fertilizer. The blood of the sacrifice, poured out before the altar, drained through an underground channel to a dump outside the city wall. Here it was sold to gardeners for manuring the soil, on payment of a trespass offering, without which its use for common purpose was prohibited, as it retained the sanctity of dedication at the altar.

According to the Hebrew Talmud, raw manure was not even permissible to the truly religious because it was unclean. The "people of the land," those who dealt with unclean matters, dead animals, manure, hides, and other things that required purification according to the old Law, were an exception, and they even failed to abide by the law that required the religious to fallow their lands every seventh year. Thus a Talmud commentator set down the rule for the faithful: "Do not use your manure until some time after the outcasts have used theirs," which is nothing but advocating the use of rotted or composted manure instead of fresh animal matter.

Our short-sighted practice of setting fire to straw and other dry refuse instead of composting it, was equally prevalent in Biblical days, as frequent references to the burning of chaff, straw and tares show. To add insult to injury, the custom was linked by analogy with the hell fire and brimstone future of the wicked.

Much of the agricultural wisdom of the ancients survived the blight of the Dark Ages, to reappear—along with other fundamental scientific knowledge—in the writings of learned Arabs. Ibn al Awam, variously assigned to the 10th and 12th centuries, goes into extensive detail on the processing and use of compost, and other manures, in his Kitab al Falahah or Book of Agriculture. Blood is recommended for its fertilizing properties and the superiority of human blood for this purpose is casually endorsed. Elsewhere in other old manuscripts the manure value of crushed bones, waste wool, wood ash and lime is set forth.

The medieval Church was another repository of knowledge and lore, where, thanks to the efforts of a few devoted monks the feeble flame of truth was kept alive, while the rest of the country gave itself up to internecine pillage and slaughter. Within monastery enclosures sound agricultural practices were preserved and applied, and in some instances taught to the neighboring farmers by the Abbot, acting as a sort of medieval county agent. It is but natural that the charters of two old English Abbeys, St. Albans (1258) and the Priory of Newenham (1388) should enjoin the use of compost for soil fertility.

References to compost in the literature of the Renaissance are numerous, but space restricts us to a few quotations from the works of famous men, plus one or two noteworthy for their context. William Caxton, pioneer 15th century printer, relates ". . . by which dongyng and compostyng the feldes gladeth." Three renowned Elizabethans reveal in their writings that compost was a familiar word. Shakespeare's Hamlet advises ". . . do not spread the compost on the weeds, to make them ranker," and in Timon of Athens, Timon rages "the earth's a thief, that feeds and breeds by a composture stolen from general excrement." Sir Francis Bacon tells in his "Natural History" that plants degenerate by ". . . removing into worse earth, or forbearing to compost the earth." The unfortunate Raleigh, awaiting execution, writes of the soil "He shall have the dung of the cattle, to muckle or composture his land."

The word compost comes from Old French, but in the 16th-17th centuries various spellings are encountered—compass, compess, compast, composture, etc.

A real organic enthusiast was Tusser (1557) who boasts "One aker well compast, is worth akers three" and "Lay on more compass, and fallow again." Detail is given us by Pultenham (1589) "The good gardiner seasons his soyle by sundrie sorts of compost; as mucke or marle, clay or sande . . . bloud, or lees of oyle or wine." Evelyn (1693) defines it "Compost is rich made mold, compounded with choice mold, rotten dung, and other enriching ingredients." A mere 130 years ago Bingley wrote "The neighboring farmers made them (herring) up into compost, and manured their ground with them."

Poetical contributions include:

"The best compost for the lands
Is the wise master's feet and hands"
—Robt. Herrick.

"A cart he found
That carried compass forth
To dung the ground"
　　　　　—John Dryden.

"Turn the clod,
And wheel thy compost home"
　　　　　—Wm. Cowper.

Whitman Tribute

The best poetic tribute to compost was offered by Walt Whitman, the great American 19th century poet. In his *This Compost*, he captures beautifully the drama of the life cycle, the role of compost, and its meaning to man:

"Behold this compost! behold it well!
Perhaps every mite has once form'd part of a sick
　　person—yet behold!
The grass of spring covers the prairies,
The bean bursts noiselessly through the mould in the
　　garden,
The delicate spear of the onion pierces upward,
The apple-buds cluster together on the apple-branches,
The resurrection of the wheat appears with pale
　　visage out of its graves.
What chemistry!
That the winds are not really infectious,
That all is clean forever and forever,
That the cool drink from the well tastes so good,
That blackberries are so flavorous and juicy,
That the fruits of the apple-orchard and the orange-
　　orchard, that melons, grapes, peaches, plums,
　　will none of them poison me,
That when I recline on the grass I do not catch any
　　disease
Now I am terrified at the Earth, it is that calm and
　　patient,
It grows such sweet things out of such corruptions,
It turns harmless and stainless on its axis, with such
　　endless succession of diseased corpses,
It distils such exquisite winds out of such infused
　　fetor,
It gives such divine materials to men, and accepts
　　such leavings from them at last."

13

Early Use in the United States

In the United States, compost has been used ever since white man set foot on Plymouth Rock. Public accounts of the use of stable manure in composting date back to the 18th century. Early Colonial farmers abandoned the fish to each hill of corn system of fertilizing when they discovered that by properly composting two loads of muck and one load of barn-yard manure they obtained a product the equivalent in fertilizing value of 3 loads of manure. By the middle of the 19th century this knowledge was thoroughly ingrained in Yankee agricultural philosophy, and Samuel W. Johnson, Professor of Analytical and Agricultural Chemistry at Yale College, asserted that "this fact should be painted in bold letters on every barn door in Connecticut."

White fish or Menhaden were abundant in Long Island Sound and many New England farmers found it economical to use fish as well as manure in their compost heaps. Stephen Hoyt and Sons, of New Canaan, Conn., made compost on a large scale, using 220,000 fish in one season. Ten or 12 loads of muck to one load of fish was their formula. A layer of muck one foot in thickness would be spread on the ground, then a layer of fish on top of that, a layer of muck, a layer of fish, and so on, topped off with a layer of muck, until the heap reached a height of 5 or 6 feet. This was periodically shoveled over until fermentation and disintegration of the fish (excepting the bones) had been completed. The resulting compost was free of odors and preserved perfectly all the manurial values of the fish. Land well manured with this would keep in heart and improve.

Professor Johnson, in 1856, had written some articles for "The Homestead" which proved to be so thought provoking and excited so much attention among readers of this journal that at the annual meeting of the Connecticut State Agricultural Society in January, 1857, he was invited to address that body on the subject of "Frauds in Commercial Manures."

It was then established that "gross deceits had actually been practiced by parties soliciting the patronage of farmers in Connecticut, and the facilities for perpetrating further frauds were the subject of the lengthened exposition." A few years later, in 1859, Professor Johnson wrote a book (published by Brown and Gross, of Hartford, Conn.) entitled "Essays on Manure," in which, befitting its importance, the

14

subject of composting received prominence and favorable comment. Composting was said to develop the inert fertilizing qualities of the muck itself, and a fermentation which began in the manure extended to and involved the muck, reducing the whole to the condition of well-rotted dung. *Muck* means in these old books all sorts of rich soil, even manure, but usually river bottom soil. It was pointed out that in this process of composting the muck effectively prevented the waste of ammonia or nitrogen.

Relatively small quantities of plant material were composted in these earlier years, as a sufficiency of barnyard manure characterized this motorless era. However, in some sections of the South, cotton-seed was composted with muck. The heap was started with 6 inches of muck, then 3 inches of cottonseed, more muck, more cottonseed, and so on, finished off with a layer of muck. This was turned over, moistened and replied once a month until complete decomposition of the cottonseed had been effected. Considerable watering was a prime requisite.

As America grew older, many of the sons and daughters of the early New England settlers treked westward searching for more abundant and lower-priced land. Some of them found soil so rich in organic matter from buffalo droppings, plants, grasses and animals, all nicely composted into good earth by nature, that little thought was given to composting— and "land-mining" was born. Only a few farsighted settlers in this newly discovered land of plenty continued the composting practices which their fathers had learned the value of while farming under more trying soil conditions.

From "A Philosophical Discourse of Earth," by John Evelyn, published in 1676: "Lands which are cold and dry are to be improved by contraries; namely, by application of composts, which are hot and moist." Evelyn observed that the use of a varied assortment of manures rather than a single type of manure established a better balance in the compost, and advocated the use of mud of ponds and stagnant waters of ditches, shoveled up and well aired before application to the heap. This mud was used especially around the roots of trees. And in watering the compost, it was suggested that, wherever practicable, water be used out of ponds where cattle drank and cooled themselves.

In 1796, Thomas B. Bailey, writing on the necessity and advantages of care and economy in collecting and preserving different substances for manure, invited attention to Saint John's injunction of Divine Wisdom: "Let nothing be wasted." Francis Blaikie, in 1818, in a treatise on the husbanding of farmyard manure, stressed the importance of many kinds of manures in the composts (referred to as "pies") and the value of animal urine in these pies. Arnold Eiloart, in an old book entitled "No Plant Disease," cautions against the use of hot slops containing carbolic or other disinfectant soap, because germs would be killed or checked instead of multiplied in the compost. He favored what he described as the "earth method" (composting) for disposing of wastes, to secure health of plants and health of man. Parmentier, in "The Nature of Manures, and the Manner in Which They Act," reflected that "the scarcity of manures, and their unskilful employment are the principal causes of the sterility of a country."

Our fourth President, James Madison, was also aware of the need to renew the fertility of crop lands, and on May 12th, 1818, in an address to the Agricultural Society of Albemarle, Virginia, stated: "Closely as agriculture and civilization are allied, they do not keep pace with each other. There is probably a much higher state of agriculture in China and Japan than in many other countries far more advanced in the improvements of civilized life. Nothing is more certain than that continual cropping without manure deprives the soil of its fertility. It is equally certain that fertility may be preserved or restored by giving to the earth animal or vegetable manure equivalent to the matter taken from it. That restoration to the earth of all that naturally grows on it prevents its impoverishment is sufficiently seen in our forests, where the annual exuviae of the trees and plants replace the fertility of which they deprived the earth. Where frequent fires destroy the leaves and whatever else is annually dropped on the earth, it is well known that land becomes poorer, this destruction of the natural crop having the same impoverished effect as removal of a cultivated crop. A still stronger proof that a natural restoration to the earth of all its annual produce will perpetuate its productiveness is seen where our fields are left uncultivated and unpastured. In this case the soil, receiving from the decay of the spontaneous weeds and grasses more fertility than they extract from it, is, for the time being, improved. Its improvement may be explained by the fertilizing matter which the weeds and grasses derive from the water and atmosphere, which forms a net gain to the earth. That individual farms do lose their fertility in proportion as crops are taken from them and return of manure neglected is a fact not likely to be questioned. The most logical mode of preserving the richness and of enriching a farm is certainly that of applying a sufficiency of manure and vegetable matter in a decomposed state; in order to procure which too much care cannot be observed in saving every material furnished by the farm. This resource was among the earliest discoveries of man living by agriculture; and a proper use of it has been made a test of good husbandry in all countries, ancient and modern, where its principle and profits have been studied."

George Washington Carver, famed botanist-chemist-agriculturist who lived until 1943, also advised the farmer to compost materials and return them to the land. In an agriculture experiment station bulletin entitled, "How to Build Up and Maintain the Virgin Fertility of Our Soil," Dr. Carver says, "Make your own fertilizer on the farm. Buy as little as possible. A year-round compost pile is absolutely essential and can be had with little labor and practically no cash outlay."

Dr. Carver also stressed the importance of covering the heap to prevent the leaching away of nutrients by rain.

"It is easy to see," he explained, "that our farm animals are great fertilizer factories, turning out the cheapest and best known product for the permanent building up of the soil. In addition to this farmyard manure, there are also many thousands of tons of the finest fertilizer going to waste all over the South, in the form of decaying leaves of the forest and the rich sediment of the swamp, known as 'muck.' Every idle moment should be put in gathering up these fertilizers."

Start of Organic Method

Compost and the organic method of gardening and farming have been working hand in hand since the days of Sir Albert Howard, father of the organic method. Howard, a British government agronomist, spent the years 1905-1934 in India, where he evolved slowly the organic concept. In making compost, Howard found by experiment that the best compost consisted of 3 times as much plant matter as manure, for that is the way he found it when nature made her compost in the field and forest. He devised the Indore method of compost-making, in which materials are stacked in sandwich fashion, then are turned (or are mixed by earthworms) during the decomposition process. A detailed description of the Indore method is given later in the book.

In 1942, J. I. Rodale, pioneer of the organic method in America, began publication of a monthly magazine, *Organic Farming and Gardening,* assimilating the ideas of Howard and adding knowledge of further experimentation. Thus, it can be said that the organic method actually grew out of compost, or at least the organic method was woven around the composting idea. From 1942, the organic method extolled the use of compost and raised considerably its position as a garden necessity. Subsequent developments of the composting idea included adding raw rock powders to the heap, sheet composting, shredding materials for quicker decomposition, digester composting, and numerous other innovations which are discussed further on in the book.

The history of compost is both ancient and new. In its narrow sense, composting has been going on ever since life began, for composting is the necessary transition by which life is renewed. We know also that compost was recognized by man, as early as ancient Rome and probably before, as a transitional force in the life cycle. At this stage, man began actually to make compost for the expressed intent of renewing soil fertility. When, after centuries, man did stray from the natural ideal, depending on chemical fertilizers to replace compost, it was Sir Albert Howard who pointed out the importance of compost as an integral part of the life cycle. At the present time compost is being used to greater advantage than ever before. It is, however, being used by fewer farmers and gardeners than in the days before synthetics came about. Thus compost is in the unique position of being capable of greater things and being called upon to do less than 100 years ago. There has been a revival, however, and the strides made by the organic method in the past 20 years show promise of placing compost into its natural role as a soil builder. The signs of progress are seen in municipal composting projects which turn city garbage into rich compost; in the bulletins from the state agricultural experiment stations, which advise compost making and other organic soil-building practices; and, in the growing popularity of the organic method itself.

Chapter 2

THE BASICS OF COMPOST

Compost has two meanings: First, we give the general definition which is, a *composition, mixture or compound*. The word *compote*, which means fruit stewed in syrup, has the same origin. The way some people make compost, throwing the ingredients together helter-skelter, you can safely call it a *compote*, or stew.

The specialized meaning of the word *compost* as it applies to farming and gardening, according to Webster's New International Dictionary, Second Edition, unabridged, is, *"a mixture for fertilizing or renovating land in which plants are grown; now, especially a fertilizing mixture composed of such substances as peat, leaf mold, manure, lime, etc., thoroughly mingled and decomposed, usually in a heap called a compost heap."* This is not a bad definition, but it is not the best. The important thing is that the material must be decomposed in order to be called *compost*, and it is not to be called compost until it is. There are two basic things about a compost heap. You must have organic materials and there must be the proper conditions to make them decompose. The degree of decomposition may be referred to in terms such as *finished* or *unfinished compost*. In a more or less finished compost the materials would be greatly reduced in the extent of their fibrous appearance.

In an agricultural textbook you may find the following type of definition: "A compost is a fertilizing mixture of partially decomposed organic materials of plant or animal origin, or both, and may include substances such as ash, lime and chemicals."

In the organic method we would exclude the ash, if it is from coal, and would also condemn the addition of the usual fertilizing chemicals.

In review we can see that organic matter is the raw material of the composting process, which process hastens the formation of humus. Composting, then, is a process of making humus.

MAN, THE COMPOSTER

To get nutritious food, man must feed the soil with good compost. He makes it by gathering residue organic materials which, fortunately, are in abundance all about him, and by controlled methods of decomposition, a form of nature magic which puts Aladdin to shame, he transforms it into a rich brown earth.

Man must maintain nature's equilibrium in the soil if he desires to continue to people the earth. Man is *of* the earth and must tend it properly. One man will say, "From whence will come the raw materials with which to make compost?" and go straightaway to the chemist for a bag of something. He thus identifies himself as part of a system of soil banditry —taking, but not giving.

Another man does not question. He knows that God gave an adequacy of everything and that if he seeks he shall find. He goes forth upon the highways and ventures into the byways. He comes home laden with the necessary stuffs, the wherewithal to mix a dish fit for the most savory carrots or the most exotic zinnias. He is weighted down with humus materials, both animal and vegetable, which the unknowing bystander considers trash or worse, but which, like the touch of Midas, will turn into gold under his competent hand.

The searcher after the compostable will go into the strangest places. He will clean out the shop of a butcher in order to retain the sweepings of sawdust saturated with an aroma of meat and entrails which are rich in nitrogen. He will do the same for a lazy neighbor's chicken house if he can exact the chicken droppings as his payment. He will go to a barber for the hair cuttings, to a restaurant for coffee grounds, to a fish market for fish offal. He will all but mow the neighbor's lawn for the grass clippings. He will gather rubbish, trash, refuse, debris, decaying animal and vegetable remains, cast off materials—anything decomposable. He will forget pride, dignity and his delicate sensibilities, so long as he comes into possession of the kind of detritus matter which will turn into a proper compost.

He develops his own way of blending the materials, learning how to mix and season. His hands learn subtle skills and dexterities. And he watches over the heap like a hen with a newly hatched chick. He listens to its breathing and to its

Compost, that "mixture of partially decomposed organic materials of plant or animal origin . . ." is basic to soil fertility and thus to successful gardening or farming. Applied liberally in early spring, it gives crops a stronger start.

vaporous exhalations, feeling its pulse, taking its temperature twice a day and twelve times during the weekend.

When he returns from work he will run to it before kissing his wife. If it gives off an odor of ammonia he knows he is losing nitrogen and will worry about it worse than if his child had the pox. Like as not he will completely disassemble everything and make the heap all over again. He has become a chemist, learning how to figure nitrogen ratios, oxidations and fixations.

He assuages his compost's thirst with water, but, to your ardent, zealous compost-maker any old water will not do. Where he might drink it with chlorine in it, he would not dream of administering such a questionable potion to his compost. He will devise equipment to secure rain water, or will go miles to fetch it from a brook or a pond.

He has become a biologist, acquiring a knowledge of the part that bacteria play in the organic destruction that he wishes to bring about. He has learned that a proper amount

21

of water must be given to the soil organisms, the microscopic wrecking crews who cannot perform their chemical magic without it. They are the yeasts and the ferments—the agents of decomposition.

Given the necessary conditions, these specky bits of things, these motes of vegetable life, these proletariat of the soil, will tear a stalk into shreds, will turn a leaf into mould. The microscopic soil fungi with their interwoven threads, with their delicate network of filamentous mycelia will surround the organic matter and reduce it to life-giving humus.

But the greatest pleasure of all is when our composter stands close to his heap in the gathering twilight, when the day's work is done. His whole being is filled with a sense of creation. He is mysteriously moved by its radiations and emanations. He is stirred by the thought that some vital force is at work which could improve the face of the earth, and he feels a part of and enveloped by a mighty God-force of creation.

Our composter is a marveling witness, a privileged observer of something which is on the other side of life. He sees death and birth, destruction and creation, under his own hands. He witnesses the interplay of powerful, mysterious forces which are part of the cycle of nature's round. He sees the leaf when the breath of its life goes out, when its sap dries up, and observes it mutate into a soft, new, living substance. Dust thou art and to dust thou returneth!

He has watched the miasmic and mephitic change to the fragrant and the aromatic. He has observed the unsavory dunghill transform itself into the means of producing the enchanting rose.

And when he glimpses his compost come to fruition for the first time, he kisses his fingers to his lips. It is like becoming a father to a first-born. He fondly runs his hand through what once was manure and asks, "Can this be?"

What he has produced will turn the clod into soft loam. It will satisfy the hunger of the soil, its cravings for its daily nourishments. It will give the soil sponginess and resiliency. It will improve its structure, and heal its wounds and deficiencies. It will make it teem and be fruitful. It will give tang to his radishes, sweetness to his onions and a superabundance to his harvests. He will know how the Israelites felt in the wilderness when God sent them manna, and his neighbors will say, "What magic is this that we are witnessing?"

He has gained a new goal, a way of life, a culture, something that will make him keep his feet on the ground and not think of methods to reach the moon. He will want to be *of* this earth, and to make it a better place to inhabit.

He will think of the clerk who makes pencil sharpenings, or of the beautiful, marcelled lady on Park Avenue whose fancy table residues wind up in the ash can, and will say to himself, "They must be taught to conserve these valuable substances. They must not be incinerated or sent out to sea." He will think of the clerk's and the marcelled lady's great-great grandchildren and how, what we do to these substances today will be a matter of life and death and survival to them in the not-too-far-distant future. He will think of making a good heritage to pass on to them. He will not be like Esau who lived for the day only.

THE COMPOST MYSTERY

Ask any soil scientist to describe to you what goes on in a square foot of soil and he will admit that he can't. No one really knows *all* that goes on in the soil—what exactly the bacteria, the fungi, the worms and the other soil organisms do—and probably no one ever will know.

The same is true for compost. Compost is basically the concentrated richness of soil, so it can be even more mysterious. If anyone tells you he knows what goes on in a compost heap, he is not telling the truth.

So you can see that you, the average gardener or farmer, are not at a disadvantage when facing up to a soil scientist, for he doesn't know all the answers either. Take the case of a well-known American writer, E. B. White. He wrote that when he first became interested in farming he was enthusiastic about natural methods. Later, he reported, when he realized that he didn't have any scientific training, he adopted orthodox views because he didn't know enough about the soil to go out on a limb in favor of what many people considered to be wild theories.

I feel that the average person shouldn't feel ashamed to work toward becoming an amateur soil expert. The raw materials for your study are all around you, and if you are an active gardener or farmer you can build up a fund of practical knowledge that may put schoolbook experts to shame.

Take the idea of chelation (keelation) for example. It is

a vitally important process that has always gone on in the soil, and in compost heaps, yet soil scientists have just become aware of it. Chelators are substances produced by humus that help make available plant food in the soil. A soil without organic matter has no chelators, so minerals remain locked up in the soil.

Chelating compounds provide plants with needed trace elements. For example, lichens have their own "built-in" chelators, which allow them to live in barren spots. The chelators in the lichens dissolve rocks and provide vital trace metals.

This same action also can make natural rock powders more effective. An experiment has shown that it is the chelating action of manure that explains the greater availability of phosphate fertilizers when added to farm manures.

Perhaps this newly discovered ability of organic matter to feed plants will help clear up the compost mystery—the mystery of why compost and other types of humus are so effective in feeding the soil and plants.

THE MEANING OF ORGANIC MATTER

No discussion of compost is complete without a discussion of organic matter and humus, the two substances which encircle compost in the life cycle. Humus is—at least to the gardener—the end product of compost. He takes organic matter and, by composting, transforms it into humus. But since organic matter is his theoretical starting point in the composting process, we'll begin by discussing this broad topic.

Organic matter is a term applied to both plant and animal matter, alive or dead. But regardless whether it is dead or alive, organic matter is the life of the soil. Plant and animal matter includes the bodies of bacteria, fungi, yeasts, protozoa, etc. Organic matter represents material that has been in living tissue or that has come from it. Examples are manure, plant sap, sawdust, olive oil, etc. It consists of matter that may have been alive as long as hundreds of thousands of years ago, like peat which may be thousands of years old, or coal which may be hundreds of thousands of years of age. (Peat is the first step in the formation of coal.)

Organic matter represents the remains of all kinds of plants, animals and microorganisms in various stages of decomposition. But actually, the expression *organic matter*, as

Leaves, clippings, stems, roots and other plant wastes are grouped as *green matter*, a major classification of organic materials. Available throughout the growing season, these wastes should be collected regularly and added to compost heaps.

we sometimes refer to it, is a misnomer, for it includes both organic and inorganic substances. A corn cob, for example, is usually referred to as representing organic matter. But, if you burn it down to its ash, destroying all the organic matter, there will be an important residue, in that ash, of a significant amount of minerals. In Nature all of what we usually consider organic matter contains some inorganic compounds. So we must be aware of this confusion when we use the term *organic matter*. Perhaps it would be more correct to say that corn

25

cobs are a form of substance which contains both organic and inorganic materials. We might say that it is an organic type of material.

Typical examples of organic matter, in the common usage of the term, are leaves, weeds, grass clippings, manure, the bodies of cows or pigs, the human body, etc. A piece of stone would not usually be referred to as organic matter, although in extremely rare cases rock may be found that does contain some. A piece of cotton or woolen cloth might be termed organic matter, the way we usually use the term, because it comes from a plant and an animal respectively, although it usually has some inorganic minerals included in its make-up. Dirt as swept up from a floor would usually be a combination of organic and inorganic material. Hair is organic. Metallic iron is inorganic. Such substances as calcium, phosphorous, sulphur, etc., are inorganic.

Some organic matter is in a raw state; others are in an intermediary stage of decomposition. That which is in a more advanced state is sometimes referred to as humus, but that is an inaccurate statement, as we shall see later. The raw materials usually placed in the compost heap, except the lime, are referred to as organic matter. To review the terms we might say that *organic matter* is placed in a *compost heap* to form *humus*.

At one time there was no organic matter on earth or in the sky. That was back in the beginning of the earth. Probably the first organic matter was made by certain specialized bacteria capable of using minerals such as sulphur and obtaining their carbon from carbon dioxide in the air. Their bodies contained carbon from the air and hydrogen and oxygen from both air and water.

After these specialized bacteria fixed some organic matter other general-purpose bacteria then could get their energy from this source.

Plants of low forms then came upon the earth. Plants which were green were able to use energy from the sun, carbon from the air, and oxygen and hydrogen from air and water to make organic matter. It is the green plant today on which we depend for the manufacture of organic matter. Animals must depend upon the green plant to furnish organic matter for their energy. Animals are not capable of making organic matter; neither is man. Both man and the animals must have green plants capturing and storing for their use sunshine, air, and water in the form of organic matter. Man and animals could not live a year if plants stopped growing.

Most forms of bacteria in the soil, as well as fungi, earthworms and other soil flora and fauna, are as much dependent upon organic matter for energy as are man and animals. And without this life in the soil, the soil itself would be lifeless and sterile.

Nothing would grow well in a soil without organic matter. What is there about organic matter in the soil which makes it so valuable?

In the first place, organic matter promotes a granular structure which permits a soil to hold more of both water and air. In other words, organic matter increases tremendously the amount of active surface in each square inch of soil. All chemical and physical activity takes place on the surface of each soil particle. This change brought about by more organic matter added to the soil may mean:

1. A more extensive plant root system.
2. More water entering the soil faster.
3. Less water flowing from the land and thus less erosion.
4. Greater aeration.
5. Less blowing of the soil due to a more moist surface.
6. A greater amount of water stored in the soil for use by plants.
7. Less soil baking and less crust formation.

In the second place, an increase in soil organic matter keeps the soil at a more uniform temperature. In winter, soils with an organic mulch are warmer and in summer they are cooler than soils with no such organic blanket.

Thirdly, soils high in organic matter, especially when used as a surface mulch, lose less water by evaporation into the atmosphere.

In the fourth place, soluble plant nutrients which may otherwise leach out of reach of plant roots, are held in place by partly decomposed organic matter (humus). Plant nutrients so held by humus are readily available to growing plants.

Decomposing organic matter is to growing plants what self-feeders are to livestock. This function may be labeled the fifth function of organic matter in soils. Growing plants need a continuous supply of readily available nutrients throughout the growing season. Not only must plants have all 15 essential elements available, but these elements must be in the proper

27

proportion to each other. In addition, sunshine, water and air must be available in the right amounts at all times. Organic matter aids in directly promoting the proper amounts of all of these factors of plant growth except sunshine. And even more sunshine is captured when organic matter is adequate in the soil. Increased plant growth means that more of the energy from the sun has been trapped in the form of plant material. This too, is organic matter. Thus soil organic matter, when properly used, aids in the rapid regeneration of new supplies of organic matter. In other words, life generates life.

The sixth function of organic matter in the soil consists of furnishing to growing plants, certain growth-promoting substances. These substances may be vitamins or minerals whose functions are not well understood by soil scientists. Certain germ killers (antibiotics), such as streptomycin, penicillin, and aureomycin, are derived from productive soils. These antibiotics are produced by certain soil organisms which in turn obtain their energy from soil organic matter. Soils high in organic matter thus appear to be healthier for plants and animals as well as for man.—Roy L. Donahue

CLASSIFICATIONS

There are several classifications of organic matter which are useful to the gardener-composter. *Green matter,* for instance, differs from organic matter in that it includes only plant materials. It is applied to any plant matter, regardless of whether it is freshly cut or actually green. It would consist of fresh or withered lawn clippings or weeds, dry leaves, cured hay or sawdust.

The term *mold* is often used in the expression *leaf mold* and, according to the dictionary, it is a soft, rich soil or an earthy material. The word *molder* means to crumble by natural decay, and that is exactly what happens to leaves that fall and which are not removed by man. They decompose into a form of compost which is called *leaf mold.* In other words, leaf mold is compost composed entirely of leaves. It is organic matter in its second stage.

The term *organic residue* includes a vast array of decomposable materials which are in the category of organic matter (organic and inorganic). They include city garbage, leather dust of shoe factories, cannery wastes, apple pomace of cider

28

mills (skins), spoiled milk, and hundreds of others. Much of this material today is wasted. By proper handling and quick decomposition processes, they can be turned into valuable organic, humus-containing fertilizers.

Sometimes we use the term *total organic matter* to refer to organic materials in general, using the term *humus* for the real organic fraction of it which is realized when the processes of decomposition go into action.

The term *organic* has several meanings. One of them is in the sense that it is something living. It is the *organic* part of the expression *organic matter*. The other one is entirely different. It consists of anything containing carbon. This type of substance takes in carbon compounds. Since all organic matter contains carbon, the organic matter which the gardener and farmer uses must be considered carbon compounds also. But there is another class of carbon-containing compounds which we would not consider a type of organic material usable as a fertilizer. One of them is petroleum. Impregnate your soil with a fair amount of this oil and you will destroy its ability to raise crops for a long time.

There is an entire field of chemistry devoted to the study of this second type of organic substance, or carbon compounds, some of which are known to cause cancer. For a long time a yellow organic color pigment, called *butter yellow,* was used to color butter. It was banned by the Government a few years ago when experiments proved that it caused cancer. Other examples of organic compounds of this type are alcohol, and many coal-tar derivatives such as aspirin, synthetic vitamins, etc. In our consideration of organic materials which are valuable as a fertilizer we must completely exclude these chemical carbon compounds.

HUMUS vs. DECAY

A question which comes up from time to time asks, "Is it organic matter in itself or its decay that is important to soils?" W. P. Martin, head of the Department of Soils, University of Minnesota, answered the question by saying that although organic matter is important in itself, its decay in the soil produces the prime benefits.

Dr. Martin brought out the fact that as soon as organic matter is incorporated with soil or applied to the surface of it, it is immediately attacked by a host of microbes of every

Humus is the term applied to organic matter that has decomposed completely, in other words to "finished" compost. The microorganisms active in humus, and in the decay of materials from which it evolves, are of benefit to the soil.

kind and description. These are the microorganisms that cause the organic matter to decay and be dissipated in a short time under normal garden or field conditions. These microorganisms are so active that any average soil is able to handle easily many times the amount of organic matter usually applied to it.

Since the microorganisms readily attack the organic matter and soon convert it into humus and other decay products, the question comes up of whether it is desirable to have at least some undecomposed organic matter in the soil. "Yes," is the answer to that. The undecomposed organic matter continues to furnish food for the microorganisms. It also acts as a rough conditioner to open up and aerate the soil. It allows rain to soak down into the soil and helps to prevent wind and rain erosion. Hence, it is necessary to keep applying organic matter to soils, regardless of whether they are garden or farm land. And regardless of whether the organic matter is available or not, *it is still needed by soil microorganisms.*

But what about the benefits other than from the rough organic matter? Dr. Martin says there is no question about benefits. Apparently one of the principal benefits is the release of plant nutrients caused by the microbial action, as well as the chelating action of the organic matter. Of particular importance is the nitrogen and phosphorus released during the decomposition of the organic matter. Also, there are the important actions of carbon dioxide and the organic acids from the organic matter. These help dissolve minerals in the soil such as phosphorus, potash, calcium, magnesium and other essential plant nutrients. Chelation effects occurring when the decomposing organic matter comes into contact with the minerals in the soil make iron, copper and other metals available to plants.

Since microorganisms are most active during the period of plant growth due to the warmer temperatures, essential plant nutrients are also made most available during this period. In other words, Nature has arranged for the dynamic life of the soil to be most active when it is most needed.

Dr. Martin also points out that a little-considered effect of the decomposition of organic materials in soil is the production of "auximones" and other growth-promoting substances. Also, there is the production of toxic or antibiotic substances when green manures are added to the soil. But strangely enough, these toxic substances do not harm the growing plants. They appear to be provided by Nature to help in controlling root-rot and damping-off fungi.

The benefits from organic matter, Dr. Martin feels, are due primarily to the activity of the microorganisms which decompose the organic matter and to the products which they form. Emphasis should be placed on the maintenance of a regular supply of actively decomposing organic matter, he says. This can be done by continued applications of organic matter of all kinds, such as crop residues, grass clippings, compost, manure, etc.

BACTERIA — GOOD LITTLE SOIL "WRECKERS"

Were it not for bacteria and other soil life, an apple placed in the soil would never decompose—nor would any other organic material. It is the soil microorganisms which do the actual work of breaking down organic substances into humus. All the work of building the compost heap to certain specifications, turning it, watering it, and following other recommended procedures is directed towards creating a happy home in which microorganisms can do their work. It is important that we understand the role of the miniature soil life, in order that we may create conditions conducive to its productivity—or *destructivity,* if you prefer.

There are many kinds and weights of microorganisms in the surface foot of soil and there are large numbers of each kind. Each kind of organism plays some significant role in the decomposition of plant and animal residues, liberation of plant nutrients, or in the development of soil structure. Many groups are dependent upon each other; consequently one kind may tend to follow another.

According to Nebraska Agronomists T. M. McCalla and T. H. Goodding in their report, "Microorganisms and Their Effects on Crops and Soils," they set up a series of reactions in the soil that follow one another in an organized sequence, The organisms vary in size from forms invisible with the ordinary microscope but visible with the electron microscope to those that can be seen with the naked eye. In shape they vary from tiny dots to weird twisted forms. They have the capacity to digest the materials in the soil because they produce enzymes which in different microbial groups form a gigantic, complex enzymatic system that extends throughout the soil. There are few things in the soil—even such resistant materials as hair and horn—which escape digestion.

Phages and *viruses* are the smallest forms of living matter in the soil. Some investigators do not class viruses as living. These minute organisms are so small that they are in the twilight zone between the living and the non-living materials. The phages cause diseases of bacteria and the viruses in the soil cause diseases of higher plants.

Bacteria are the microorganisms which account for the largest numbers in the soil. There are many different types. In shape they resemble balls, cylinders or corkscrews. Bacteria in the resting stage are resistant to heat, dryness, and other adverse environmental conditions. The spore formers, which constitute about 10 per cent of the soil bacteria, are highly resistant when in the spore or resting stage. Higher plants can combine carbon dioxide and water in the presence of sunlight and chlorophyll to make their own food, but bacteria are much like animals in that most of them must get their energy from carbohydrates, fats, proteins or other compounds synthesized in plants or bodies. In the process of obtaining their food from plant and animal residues, bacteria in the soil bring about the decomposition of these materials.

Some of the important soil bacteria are the ones which convert unavailable nitrogen of the soil organic matter to ammonia and those which convert ammonia to nitrites and then to nitrates. Others are the bacteria in the root nodules of legumes which fix nitrogen. Most of the nitrogen which is returned to the soil from sources outside the soil is fixed by the legume bacteria. Many other bacteria play important roles in the soil. They make nutrients available or unavailable, modify soil structure, and change the air relations of the soil.

Closely related to the bacteria are the *actinomycetes*. These organisms are more complicated in structure than the bacteria. The characteristic odor which is evident in newly plowed soil in the spring is caused by substances produced by the actinomycetes. Some of the organisms belonging to this group produce plant diseases, such as potato scab. Many carry on the essential activities of decomposing organic matter and making mineral nutrients available for higher plants. A good soil may have 100 to 1000 million bacteria in a gram of soil. Five per cent or more of this number are generally actinomycetes. The growth of actinomycetes on a cultural medium in the laboratory is usually of a leathery nature.

Fungi are an essential part of the soil microbial flora. Although fungi may be outnumbered by bacteria per gram of soil, they have a greater mass of growth. These organisms form a maze of tiny threads called mycelium which may enmesh soil particles into granules. Fungi grow best in an aerated soil. Many of them cause plant diseases. However, they decompose organic matter mainly and during the decomposition of plant and animal residues they synthesize some organic matter as cell tissue.

Algae are microscopic plants which form chlorophyll in the presence of sunlight. They are found in surface layers of soil which is moist, and where light is available they grow as green plants. In the absence of light they grow as other soil microorganisms. Algae change carbon dioxide from the air into organic matter in the presence of sunlight. They take their nitrogen and mineral nutrients from the soil. There may be as many as 100,000 algae per gram of soil under optimum conditions. The development of algae may result in the soil turning green at the surface in moist, shady places. This is not injurious to plants.

Protozoa are the simplest animal form of organism. Although they are unicellular and microscopic in size, they are larger than most bacteria and more complex in their activities. Soil may contain as many as 1,000,000 per gram. Protozoa obtain their food from organic matter in the same way as bacteria.

In addition to these microscopic forms there are larger organisms in the soil such as nematodes, earthworms, and insects. All of these play an important part in changing the soil condition and in promoting or hindering crop production.

Many factors in the soil environment influence the number and activity of soil microorganisms. Factors of considerable importance are temperature, moisture, aeration and acidity or alkalinity.

Temperature plays an important part. During a Nebraska winter microbial activity in the soil is largely at a standstill. In the spring, after temperatures reach 50 to 60 degrees, microbial activity begins to pick up. The optimum temperature for a high state of activity is about 85 to 90 degrees. In order for microorganisms to decay plant material and develop nitrates at a rapid rate the soil must be warm. Microbial growth is retarded at high as well as at low soil temperatures. Temperatures higher than 100 degrees retard or stop the activity of many soil microorganisms.

Moisture greatly influences the decomposition of plant and animal residues. When the soil is too dry there is little or no microbial activity. When the soil has optimum moisture the beneficial groups of microorganisms are most active. In a wet soil unfavorable groups such as anaerobic organisms may be active. (Anaerobic refers to microorganisms which grow in the absence of atmospheric oxygen.) They may convert nitrates to gaseous nitrogen sulfates to sulfides, and use up all the oxygen in the soil. Sometimes wet soils are unfavorable for certain plants because of this type of undesirable microbial activity.

Aeration is the third important factor. Generally a well-ventilated soil supports the growth of beneficial microorganisms which convert nutrients to available forms essential for high crop productivity. Soils possessing good structure are usually well aerated. Soil aeration may be improved by good tillage practices. In a soil not adequately aerated, microorganisms compete with each other for the oxygen and some may convert oxidized compounds such as nitrates into a form

34

not available to plants. Sulfates may be converted to a reduced form. Too much moisture may intensify the shortage of oxygen by slowing down the movement of air through the soil.

Soil acidity is the fourth important factor. Certain organisms become inactive in acid soils: the bacteria which occur in the root nodules of legumes and azotobacter which fix nitrogen in an acid soil. Where lime is deficient, nodulation of legumes is often difficult to obtain until lime is added to the soil. In general, fungi are more active in acid soils than are bacteria. In more alkaline soils the actinomycetes become active. Soils which are excessively alkaline may be devoid of the proper kinds of microorganisms or the activity of the microorganisms may be limited or directed along lines which are unfavorable for plant growth.

ROLE OF BACTERIA

As the farmer or gardener works his soil he must be cognizant that it is full of microorganisms. Good tilth and a workable soil structure are the result of the activity of bacteria which exude a gummy substance, a mucus that binds the soil particles together, gluing fine particles into large masses in such a manner as to give it that exquisite quality which you feel when you run your fingers through good earth. In a soil low in bacteria the particles will not "aggregate" as effectively. This good structure of the soil, caused by the activities of bacteria, prevents its washing away by rain. It reduces soil erosion. When the farmer plants his seed he must be aware that without the action of bacteria the roots could not feed properly and he would not secure satisfactory harvest.

But one of the most important functions of bacteria is to break down organic matter. When a crop has completed its task of growing, the bacteria go to work on the old roots which are left in the ground, decomposing them completely, and transforming them into food for the next set of roots which will take their place. The question may be asked, why do not the bacteria attack live, growing roots? Are there electrified fences around them which scare them off? The answer is no. But the way it works is this. There are hundreds of different kinds of organisms in the soil—each for its own specific purpose. For example there is one that can only extract nitrogen from the air. Certain bacteria are sulphur working organisms.

They are purple in color and can only attack sulphur. There are also nitrate-working, cellulose-destroying, sugar and starch-working bacteria. It is like a drama—each actor waiting for his cue to come upon the stage to do his bit, and to retire.

Let us study one type of bacterial function in detail and you will see how skillful is the hand which has created these living specks, and you will marvel at the system under which they live and work. We will look at the nitrogen "metabolism" of the soil but not in connection with the nitrogen which is obtained or "fixed" from the air by certain bacteria. We will deal with the nitrogen which is in the soil or in plant or animal matter. There is an ordained procedure which must be carefully executed, step by step, before the nitrogen which is in an old piece of cornstalk can be transmuted into a form utilizable by plant roots as food.

First it comes off, in the process of decay, as ammonia, a compound, each molecule of which contains one atom of nitrogen to 3 of hydrogen (NH_3). There are special bacteria whose sole function it is to extract this nitrogen from the ammonia, but they have absolutely no power or effect over the hydrogen. They are nitrite working bacteria. Note that at this stage it is *nitrite* not *nitrate*. When each atom of nitrogen comes forth from the ammonia, through the intervention of the nitrite working bacteria, it combines with two atoms of oxygen. The formula for nitrite is NO_2. The "union" will not permit these bacteria to do any other work. This is the only job they are cut out for. But since the plant roots cannot use nitrogen in the nitrite form (it is very poisonous) another type of bacteria has to come into the picture—the nitrate working bacteria. They turn the nitrite into the nitrate form, which means that they push another atom of oxygen into the molecule. Now we have NO_3. That little extra oxygen turns it into a more or less harmless compound and it becomes fit as a plant food.

But under certain conditions the nitrate in the plant becomes unstable—loses one atom of oxygen, and turns back into the nitrite form. This is especially prone to happen in the green leafy vegetables, and the bodies of those who consume too much of it may be harmed. Chemistry is peculiar. Take the case of water. It consists of two parts of hydrogen to one of oxygen. Hydrogen peroxide is one part of hydrogen to one of water. But if you drank peroxide you would not be long for this world.

Now we must come back to the bacteria we were discussing, whose function it is to clear the soil of the old roots. How do they know the exact moment when the roots die so that they can begin to do their work? It's the same old story. There are certain bacteria whose only function it is to break down dead matter. Anything alive is distasteful to them. They are wreckers.

In the soil the saprophytic bacteria decompose the old roots into substances which are worked over by other organisms and transformed into food for the plants. One of the important functions of soil bacteria, then, is to provide plants with food, and if the farmer and gardener can so regulate his methods as to consider the well-being of the microorganisms of the soil, so that they can multiply to abundance, he will be well repaid for his efforts. To illustrate one aspect of the advantage of a bacteria-rich fertility, when a crop of corn is harvested and the heavy stalks plowed under, if there is a lack of bacteria, a temporary indigestion will occur that will reduce the yield of the next crop.

This principle is illustrated by an experiment described in *The Living Soil* (Lady Eve Balfour, Devin Adair Co., N. Y.). Two different soils were taken—one from a field where chemical fertilizers were used, and the other from a soil rich in organic matter, the latter, of course, having a much higher bacterial count. In each batch of soil a piece of cottonwool was dug in. After 4 months the piece of cottonwool in the chemicalized soil had decayed about 10 per cent, but that in the organic-matter-rich pot was over 91 per cent consumed. As you already may have guessed there were many more bacteria in the organically treated soil and it was their work which disintegrated the cottonwool so fast.

WORKING CONDITIONS OF THE HEAP

Any gardener who has made compost for a number of years can pretty well gauge what type of materials to use, and in what proportions, when to turn the heap, and how long it will be until it is ready for use. He may know how to make compost and how to use it, even without understanding its principles—just as a housewife knows how to use an electrical appliance without understanding its workings. In order to gain the full benefits from compost, however, the gardener must combine experience with a basic knowledge of

37

the principles involved. In this way both his theory and practice will reinforce each other to make a clear and comprehensive understanding of the subject.

As we have just discussed, the first thing to bear in mind is that the microbes playing a part in the composting process must be fed properly on food furnished by the manure and green matter of the heap. Manure especially supplies nitrogen for the bacteria to feed on while breaking down the cellulose. They need phosphorus and potash, too, but in much smaller quantities, possibly only ten per cent as much. They get these from both the manure and the green matter.

As soon as the heap is made, a very strong fermentation occurs, and the temperature goes up to about 160 degrees Fahrenheit. It stays at about this point for quite a while and then gradually goes down to 90 degrees. The question is sometimes asked, "If a temperature of 150 degrees or more will kill bacteria, how can decomposition be brought about with bacteria playing such an important part in it?" The answer is that as the temperature varies, different kinds of microbes come into action. There are certain kinds called thermophilic bacteria which can withstand very high temperatures and some groups of actinomyces ray fungi develop when the temperature goes above 150 degrees. At certain stages, especially at the beginning, the fungi take a more prominent share in the work. After the second turn, the bacteria become the most active because the temperature has declined and come into their range. At this stage they are anaerobic, that is, they do not need air. For this reason air holes need not be made in the heap after the second turn.

It is remarkable how versatile nature can be in the processes of the compost heap. At various stages she uses different forms of bacteria and fungi. But very little is known about the exact functions of each and much additional scientific study is needed.

A good deal of thought has been given to methods of stimulating the biologic life of the compost heap. One scheme is to douse the heap from time to time with water rich in soil organisms, which is obtained by soaking rich garden soil. Two pounds of soil is shaken up in 4 gallons of water and then permitted to stand for an hour. This idea will no doubt prove very practical for small gardens. The average farmer, however, will not have time for it.

Average raw stable manure is made of over 20 per cent

Checking the temperature within a newly constructed compost heap is one important means of determining that conditions have been kept favorable. The temperature of a new heap reaches approximately 160 degrees.

bacteria, which comes from the animal's digestive system where they were used to break down food. If fresh manure is used in the heap, that should be a sufficient start. You can also strew some old, finished compost in a new heap as it is being made; the old matter will be full of biologic activity.

If a compost heap is made right it should begin to heat up in a few days. You can stick a metal rod into the heap and then check to see if it is warm when you pull it out. Another sign that the heap is warming up is that vapor will be seen coming out of the aeration holes. This is not a danger sign as some suppose. If you want to be technical about it you can mount a thermometer at the end of a stick and take daily readings.

Within a few days from the start, the temperature should reach about 160 degrees and stay at this point for a few weeks. You can imagine the effect on weed seeds of such intense heat and moisture combined. The proper temperatures are

39

necessary to insure the working of the different microbial elements at the various stages in the process of fermentation. If the temperature conditions are not satisfactory, the biologic routine will get out of kilter and the wrong organisms come in and upset the process.

If decomposition is unduly delayed because of the upsetting of the temperature conditions there may be a loss of nitrogen. In order to assure the quickest initial heating up, fresh stable manure should be used. I have seen cases where old manure was placed in the heap with disappointing results. Where a heap is made principally of very coarse straw there may be too much aeration with not enough heating. On the other hand where material like leaves is packed too thick there will not be sufficient aeration, which will retard heating. Where the temperature gets too high you don't have a biological decomposition and the microbes do not seem to perform their functions properly.

During the first 8 weeks, air is needed in the heap to insure that decomposition is effected by fermentation and not putrefaction. That is why the materials must be arranged loosely, although as stated they should not be too loose. If possible do not stand on the heap as it compacts it too much. Oxygen must be able to get in so that the right kind of microbes can do their work. Without air at this point the right kinds of fungi and other forms of life cannot live and the pile is apt to turn acid. It is extremely important to aerate the heap during the first 8 weeks, so that oxygen can penetrate easily and carbon dioxide escape.

In making aeration holes some people take rye straw, corn stalks or broom sedge and make it into bundles about 4 inches or more in diameter, tied loosely so as not to be too compact and stand one of these in each place a ventilation hole is desired. Those who prefer this method claim that holes made by a crowbar cave in.

After the second turn, as we have noted, aeration is not needed. The fungus stage is over and the material has darkened. From this point on anaerobic bacteria take over. (Those that need no oxygen.)

If the heap doesn't sink in a few weeks it is a sign of poor aeration and that action has slowed down. Another bad sign is an odor of ammonia emanating from the heap which may mean that the heap is too tightly packed. A too wet condition will cause the same thing. It is best in such cases

40

to make the heap over again. Do not allow weeds or grass to grow on compost heaps. Their roots cut off the supply of air.

The water requirements of compost heaps depend upon many factors. If you are in a region of high rainfall you may not need to add water at all. In a dry country or in an excessively dry season you will have to water it from time to time. When watering use a gentle spray so as not to disturb the general arrangement of the heap. During the process of making the heap, water should be applied from time to time, but do not permit it to get waterlogged. It should have the wetness of a squeezed-out sponge. When you see water running away from the base of the pile it is a sure sign of over-watering.

In some regions of excessive rainfall the heap may have to be protected with a grass thatch roof which may be used for a few years and then itself composted. Too much water interferes with aeration and may turn the heap to a black ill-smelling peat instead of humus; this has a much lower fertilizer value. An excellent scheme is to cover the heap with burlap sacking or a heavy mulch of straw.

The failure of the heap to settle is also an indication that it is too dry. If you are checking your temperature carefully and find that it goes over 150 degrees, the heap should be given a thorough wetting. If the heap is allowed to become too dry, fermentation gradually ceases and the compost takes much longer to mature, with the loss of many valuable nutrients. When heaps must be some distance from the water supply, you are, of course, at the mercy of the climate. Excessive dryness also encourages the wrong kind of fermentation. The presence of ants or wood lice is an indication of dryness.

It is a good thing under certain conditions to place a straw mulch over the top and sides of the heap to a thickness of 7 or 8 inches to prevent excessive drying out by the sun. Other advantages are that it does not permit weeds to grow and it catches much more of the rain and keeps the earth moist under the mulch. Earth-covered heaps cake up in dry spells, and when a rain comes, it washes the earth off the heap.

Where rain water is not sufficient the question arises as to the quality of water available. Rain is a saturated solution of oxygen and contains other valuable elements too, such as carbonic acid, nitric and sulphuric acids—all in a beneficial form manufactured by natural forces. Rain picks up dust, microorganisms and many valuable minerals. For many miles inland from the sea, it contains sea-salts and iodine. Therefore, rain water is best for watering compost heaps. Pond water also is excellent unless it happens to be polluted by factory or other wastes. To accumulate sufficient rain water in barrels is a problem. In some cases rain from barn roofs is saved for this purpose.

The small gardener who has to use city water is up against it in many cases where the water is treated with chemicals. Such water lacks oxygen and the other factors of rain water.

There is very little that can be said about turning the heaps except that the dates for turning be adhered to as closely as practicable. The first turn is in 3 weeks, the second is 5 weeks after the first. These dates need not be followed to the minute, and may vary slightly depending on the weather or individual conditions. It is advantageous if the turn is made on a rainy day. It is advisable to have the dates noted on something that is stuck into the heap, especially if you have many of them.

In order to do away with weed seeds, be sure, when making the turns, that all material that has been on the outside, is placed in the middle of the heap, so as to get the higher heat which is generated there. This should dispose of most of the weed seeds. In turning the heap it is not necessary to preserve the arrangement of the material as far as the different layers are concerned. After the first turn, make the aeration holes again, but not after the second turn.

Because of the fact that fermentation brings about an acid condition under which the microorganisms cannot do their work effectively, it is necessary to provide a neutralizing base, something which will counteract acidity. Earth mixed with lime or wood ashes is ideal for such purposes. Where lime and wood ashes are not available, earth alone may be used. It requires a mere sprinkling, not over ⅛-inch thick and the earth should be topsoil rich in bacteria, fungi and humus. The earth helps to bring up the temperature. Without it, a satisfactory temperature will not be attained. Don't use soil from orchards or land where heavy poisonous sprays have been applied. Such earth will probably retard the action of the heap.

Suitable earth may be obtained along ditches and roadsides where topsoil is washed by rains. Soil from the woods

Screened compost is ideal for potting mixtures, for seed-starting mediums, and for transplanting sensitive seedlings. Made by the Indore method developed by Sir Albert Howard, this rich fertilizer is a basic part of gardening success.

is somewhat acid and needs an extra dressing of lime. There is much earth to be got from under chicken houses or where foundations for buildings are being dug out. On farms earth may be secured from lanes and replaced with stones, rakings and coal ashes. In an exceptional case sand may be used, especially if it contains a lime base.

A rich form of earth may be obtained by farmers who have livestock and who bed them on earth. After this earth has been in use for quite a while and thoroughly impregnated with urine, it is removed and used in the compost heap. It is replaced with other soil and the process repeated.

Some old compost may be used in place of earth if none

of the latter is obtainable, but earth is best as a neutralizer
of acidity. The old compost is rich in bacteria, however, and
will aid the biological life of the heap.

MUST LOOK FORWARD

"The test of any process for converting the waste products of agriculture into humus," wrote Sir Albert Howard,
"is flexibility and adaptability to every set of conditions. It
should also develop and be capable of absorbing new knowledge
and fresh points of view as they arise. Finally, it should be
suggestive and indicate new and promising lines of research.
If the Indore (composting) process can pass these severe
tests, it will soon become woven into the fabric of agricultural
practice. It will then have achieved permanence and will have
fulfilled its purpose—the restitution of their manurial rights
to the soils of this planet."

Composting as it has been developed in the organic method
is far more than an accidental farming habit inherited from
the past. It is, thanks to the devoted and unselfish life's work
of men like Howard, a sound and practical program to maintain truly fertile soil, a way of life and of health—and a beacon
of promise in a torn and wasteful world.

Chapter 3

COMPOSTING METHODS
FOR THE GARDENER

The ways of composting are many and varied. Some
gardeners simply throw waste materials on a heap, call it
compost and hope for the best. Others have been carried
away with the scientific composting idea and will spend years
running from method to method, charting secret figures, constructing weird bins, boxes, ventilating pipes and watering
systems, and carefully measuring each bit of material which
is placed just right upon the heap. You can go to either end
of the scale, of course, but somewhere in the middle is a

This compost heap is being made according to Sir Albert Howard's Indore method. A layer of brush serves as a base; then the heap is built in layers— green matter (as weeds, leaves, straw or hay) followed by manure and a sprinkling of rock powders. Layers are repeated until pile is about 5 feet high.

point where you feel the results you obtain from your heap will more than justify the effort you expend constructing it. Most home gardeners take this middle course. They have at least some idea of the basic requirements, follow the standard methods to a reasonable degree, and come out with a pretty good product.

The ordinary methods, though, are often unsuitable for the gardener with special problems. A suburban dweller, for example, with just a small yard area possibly cannot build an open heap because of unsightliness or possible odors. To solve this problem, he may turn to composting under plastic cover, or he may build an enclosed bin or an earthworm pit. Another example is the farmer who would find ordinary methods grossly impracticable for the huge amounts of materials he has to compost. In his case he may well employ sheet composting along with a green-manuring program.

Most of the variations on the Indore composting method—which is the standard method—have been developed to meet special problems of gardeners and farmers.

In this chapter, the most widely used methods are discussed, with one exception. Municipal composting—the composting of town and city wastes—has in the past decade grown to such stature that its exciting story is presented in a chapter of its own.

HOW TO MAKE A COMPOST HEAP

It is not difficult to make a compost heap. Taking a few simple precautions, you can be certain of creating a living compost heap every time. It is not a difficult thing to do, but occasionally you may have to make an effort to get some extra materials to round out the recipe. Most people get in trouble with their compost heaps by trying to make them out of only one ingredient. They make a pile of just leaves, or just weeds, or just grass clippings and are disappointed when nothing happens. A heap of any one of those materials made separately will not be an ideal one, but mix them all together and you will no doubt have an active, productive compost pile.

The first organized plan for composting, perfected by Sir Albert Howard, became so popular and widely used that it generated the organic method itself. His Indore method was successful because it assured that the heap would heat up and not putrefy. Farmers in many countries in the British Commonwealth began using the Indore Method because it enabled them to compost crop wastes which formerly had been burned. Here, briefly, is the formula for the Indore heap. Later on, we shall study it in more detail:

First, place a layer of brush on the ground to provide a base for the heap.

Then, build the heap in layers, using first a 6-inch layer of "green matter" like weeds, crop wastes or leaves. Next comes a 2-inch layer of manure, which is in turn covered by a sprinkling of topsoil and limestone. The layers are repeated until the pile reaches a height of 5 feet or so.

The pile is turned after 6 weeks and again after 12 weeks, to allow air to penetrate all parts of the heap. After 3 months, Sir Albert predicted and demonstrated that the compost would be "finished."

To make sure that the compost heap is properly aerated, some gardeners make use of "ventilating" pipes, such as the one shown above. These ventilators permit a flow of air through the heap, which is important if heap is to compost properly.

The main purpose of the layering in Sir Albert's method is to assure that the proper amounts of the different materials get incorporated in the heap. You can make just as good a heap without layering if you are sure to put in the green matter, manure and earth in the same proportions.

Although still widely used, the Indore Process has been modified and improved on in several important ways. Most important, shredders have been developed that efficiently cut up manure and green matter going into the compost heap. Probably the best description is to say that shredded material makes a better home for microorganisms. The heap is better insulated, has more air and retains moisture easier. In hot weather a shredded heap will stay moist, while an unshredded one will dry out.

Bacteria and fungi react quickly in a shredded heap. Within 24 hours their activity will be so great that the temperature of the heap will increase to 140 degrees or more.

And within 2 to 14 days the heap will have cooled off sufficiently to be regarded as finished and ready for use.

It is possible to put on paper some general principles of composting that, if followed, will insure good results in a minimum of time:

1. Make sure the nitrogen or protein content of your heap is high enough. Manure, grass clippings and young weeds are high in nitrogen.

2. Try to mix together in your heap two or more types of raw material, primarily to provide proper physical conditions. Leaves alone, for example, mat down and decay very slowly, but if mixed with grass clippings they will compost well.

3. Shred your material if possible, using a rotary mower (run it back and forth over the green matter going into the heap) if a more efficient shredder is not available.

4. Keep the heap moist, but not soggy.

5. Turn it with a fork, as often as you care to.

6. If your soil is acid, mix in limestone. No matter what kind of soil you have, mix in phosphate rock and potash rock to increase mineral content.

Requirements for Success

That is the formula for the Indore method of composting. If you follow it reasonably, you will probably succeed in making good compost, and will have done it that simply. To understand the principles behind the Indore method, however, we must go a little more deeply into the physical conditions necessary for a successful heap. In the first place there must be sufficient moisture, for no organisms can live without water, and they grow and reproduce most rapidly when the amount of moisture present is optimum for them. If too much water is added to the compost heap, it becomes sodden or soggy. This sodden condition interferes with proper aeration and the materials in the compost heap are apt to putrefy instead of ferment. Putrefaction is decomposition brought about by anaerobic organisms. Putrefactions are accompanied with disagreeable odors and the formation of decomposition products and gases which cannot be used in the nutrition of higher plants. If the heap has insufficient water, on the other

Composting can be done in winter if sufficient attention is given to insulating the heap. Many gardeners, for example, build a pit 3 or more feet in the ground and layer materials there. Straw placed on top of the pit helps retain heat.

hand, the growth and reproduction of the soil organisms and, therefore, the rate of decomposition of the organic materials in the heap will be diminished or even brought to a stop. It is important, therefore, to get just the right amount of moisture in each layer of the compost heap. The water should be added with a hose or sprinkling can to each layer as the heap is constructed.

Equally as important as water in the compost heap is air. All the beneficial organisms in the soil are aerobic. That is to say, they need the oxygen from the air to live. It is highly important, therefore, that the compost heap be well ventilated. This can be facilitated by putting a lattice of brush on the ground as a longitudinal axis where the heap is to be built. This will permit a free flow of gases longitudinally through the heap. Then when the heap is completed and at

49

intervals of 3 or 4 feet, holes should be punched from the surface to the brush at the base of the heap. This will make possible a free flow of gases from the atmosphere into the heap and from the interior of the heap out into the atmosphere. The rate of activity of the soil organisms can be controlled somewhat by the amount of air that is admitted to the interior of the heap.

A suitable temperature, such as prevails during the summer months, is best for the organisms in the heap. As the average daily temperature decreases in autumn and winter, the decomposition in the heap slows down gradually and almost stops altogether during the coldest parts of the winter. Winter composting can be done in places where the temperature will permit it, as in a greenhouse, basement, or ground cellar. It is even possible to insulate a compost heap outdoors so that the decomposition processes take place during the winter. This may be done by enclosing a compost heap by a larger enclosure and filling the space between the two enclosures with leaves, hay, straw, sawdust, or other insulating plant material. An insulated composter works especially well when earthworms are used instead of bacteria and fungi exclusively for the breaking down processes. Then again, a pit 3 or more feet in the ground will absorb some heat from the earth and thus tend to provide a more favorable temperature in winter than prevails in a heap built directly on the surface of the ground.

For the development of sufficient heat of fermentation to kill weed seeds and any disease-producing fungi that may be present on the plant materials used in building the heap, a compost heap should be at least 4 or 5 feet square and 5 feet high. In large heaps it is not uncommon for the temperature to rise as high as 160 degrees Fahrenheit. Compost subjected to such a temperature will be free from all seeds and all disease-producing fungi. This is not the most important difference between compost and uncomposted manures.

Unfavorable conditions in the heap so far as water and air are concerned can be prevented by taking care that materials are not put in, in such a manner, that they tend to pack into tight layers. This is apt to be the case if large amounts of leaves are used without grinding them or mixing them with other plant materials. By far the most ideal physical conditions in the heap can be provided by grinding the plant materials, or even all the materials, before they are used to

In large compost heaps, as the one pictured above, it is common for the temperature to rise as high as 160 degrees Fahrenheit. This heat kills weed seeds and disease-producing fungi that may be present in the materials used.

build a heap. The finer the particles of matter, the faster they will be broken down.

MORE DETAILS ON THE
INDORE COMPOSTING METHOD

Following is a further discussion of the basic Indore heap—its construction and the changes which take place during the composting process. Although many new methods have been introduced in the past decade, the Indore heap is still most widely used. It has the advantage that compost can be made in a heap or pit which occupies a very small space while all the remainder of the garden space is available for growing food plants. By building the compost heap in the same place year after year, the soil becomes so well inoculated with the composting organisms that the composting takes less time. Then, too, by protecting the heap from drying winds and soaking rains, Indore compost can be made in late fall or early winter so that it is available for spring planting.

51

An Indore heap should be built from 5 to 10 feet wide, 5 feet high, and as long as desired. The heap should be built on a piece of recently dug soil on the south side of a building, wall or fence, or in the shade of a tree. First set wooden stakes or rolls of old chicken wire 3 or 4 inches in diameter and 6 feet long, two feet apart through the longitudinal axis of the heap to be constructed. The vertically placed rolls of wire, or the holes left after pulling the wooden stakes out when the heap has been built, will serve as ventilators in the heap.

The raw materials which may be used for building an Indore heap include all kinds of plant and animal residues as garden residues, weeds, lawn clippings, kitchen wastes, dust-pan and carpet-sweeper refuse, household rubbish, wood ashes from the fireplace, animal manures, sewage sludge, dried blood, hoof, horn or fish meal, pulverized limestone, pulverized phosphate rock, cleanings from roadside ditches, wastes from brewery, grain mill, grocery store, food market, sawdust, and many other kinds of organic materials which vary in different regions but are always available to those who seek for them.

The aeration of the heap will be facilitated if brush or other coarse material about one foot wide and one foot high is first put down as a longitudinal axis of the heap. Then build up the heap on each side of this central, backbone-like axis with plant materials. The heap will now be one foot high. This material should have the moisture content of a squeezed sponge. Now cover the layer of plant materials with a 2-inch layer of manure or a 1-inch layer if poultry manure is used. Substitutes for manure are cottonseed meal, dried manures, commercial composts, blood and bone meal, and sewage sludge. Over the manure or manure substitutes are sprinkled earth and pulverized limestone and phosphate rock. Subsequent layers consisting of 6 inches of plant materials, 2 inches of manure, a liberal sprinkling of earth, and a light sprinkling of pulverized rock are put down until the heap is 5 feet high. The outside of the heap is then tidied up and the whole outer surface lightly pressed to prevent strong winds blowing through the heap and thus cooling and drying it.

If fresh green stuff is used, it must be finely shredded or should be mixed with dried plant materials in the proportion of one part green materials to two parts dry materials.

The fertilizing value of compost heaps can be increased by adding rock phosphate, rock potash, bone meal, granite dust, cottonseed meal, dried blood and other natural materials. Ground limestone can be added to counteract soil acidity.

The plant material should not include more than one-third of "harsh stuff" as straw or dry leaves.

The finished heap should be covered with earth, hay or old sacking to conserve heat and moisture. Provision should also be made to protect the heap from long continued rain. The top of the heap should have a concavity to catch rain when that is necessary to maintain the moisture inside the heap.

A properly made heap will heat up quickly and in 4 or 5 days will have sunk to a height of about 3½ feet. At this time the stakes should be removed unless they were taken out as soon as the building of the heap was completed. The holes and the axis of brush at the bottom of the heap constitute an aeration system throughout the heap.

Changes in the Indore Heap

The conversion of raw organic matter into compost involves a series of decompositions which take place in a definite order. The materials in a compost heap are taken apart by different groups of soil organisms in much the same way as a house might be taken apart by different groups of skilled workmen whose purpose is to salvage the parts to be used in another building. The decomposition products of the compost heap are used again to build new plants and new animals.

1. *The First Change.* The first change in the Indore compost heap is a chemical oxidation with the production of heat as in any form of burning. Since unwilted plants are protected by the epidermis from such oxidation and from the invasion of bacteria it is evident that the epidermis must be destroyed by cutting or drying to facilitate this first change in the heap. The cutting and bruising of the epidermis of plants is most efficiently done by the teeth and stomachs of grazing animals. The same results may be obtained by passing the plant materials to be composted through a shredder which will reduce them to such fine particles that the juices of a large number of plant cells will be spilled and can be oxidized in the heap. If green materials are finely shredded, they need not be wilted before being incorporated in the heap. A heap built of finely shredded materials will heat up most rapidly.

As a result of this first change, chemical oxidation, the heap will be reduced in height from 5 to about 3½ feet.

2. *The Second Change.* The second change in the Indore compost heap is brought about by aerobic fungi which are able to penetrate the protective epidermis of plants once they become established. The cutting and bruising of the plant materials and the heat produced by chemical oxidation greatly facilitate the penetration of the fungi into the plant materials. Everyone knows that a fruit as apple or grape may be stored for a long time if the epidermis is not broken, but rots (decomposes) very quickly after the epidermis is broken or even punctured at only one point. Conditions which favor the growth of these fungi are moisture, warmth, and oxygen from the atmosphere. The moisture is provided by the water added when the heap is built, the warmth is the heat of oxidation that takes place in the first phase already referred to, and the atmospheric oxygen enters the heap through the aerating

54

The rustic container is one of many that can be built to house compost. Such enclosures not only improve the appearance of your compost-making area, but encourage the gardener to "keep the bin filled," thereby making more compost.

system. Fungous growth is retarded or entirely inhibited by cold drafts, hence the covering of lightly compacted earth and/or sacking over the heap. Conditions inside a properly built compost heap are ideal for the growth fungus. Soon the fungi cover all surfaces with a film of white mycelium and other mycelia penetrate and utilize the nutrients in the plant cells. In about 3 weeks the fungi complete their vegetative growth, produce spores and then begin to die off. The second phase in the conversion of plant and animal residues into Indore compost is complete. An examination of the interior of the heap will show the material completely covered with fungous mycelia.

3. *The Third Change.* The fungi in the compost heap are replaced by aerobic bacteria as the decomposing organisms. The bacteria can now penetrate the cells of the plant materials in the heap by following the fungous threads which have previously broken the epidermis, feeding on the dead fungi as they go. In about 3 weeks the aerobic bacteria will

have finished their work of decomposition, and the material will assume a brown color. By this time the heap has lost practically all of its heat.

4. *The Fourth Change.* By the time the third phase in the conversion of raw materials into compost has been completed, the whole mass will have settled down and become somewhat compacted so as to exclude atmospheric oxygen. This favors the fourth change which is brought about by anaerobic bacteria which require very little oxygen but they must have some. This they can get by slow diffusion, provided the heaps are not trampled on or allowed to become sodden. Should their air supply be entirely cut off they will get oxygen by breaking up the nitrates present, allowing the nitrogen to escape as ammonia, a great loss of manurial value. This fourth phase in the composting process takes from 4 to 8 weeks to complete, depending upon the materials of which the heap is built. Cold weather will retard the composting process.

5. *The Fifth Change.* If sufficient lime was used in building the heap to prevent the heap from becoming too acid, the heap will be invaded by the nitrogen-fixing bacteria, *Azotobacter*, which need lime, air and humus for their activities. They will fix appreciable quantities of nitrogen from the atmosphere and thus help in the conversion of the material to humus.

A Suggestion to Save Time

Sir Albert Howard told how to save time making compost if one cannot follow the original method in every detail. He says:

"This can be done by greater care in the original mixture. If great care is taken in assembling a heap, which, we will say, finally settles to a height of about 4 feet, turning could be avoided if the upper two feet were used first and the lower portion used after an interval, because my experience always has been that it is the portion of the heap nearest the atmosphere which ripens first, because air will percolate into a fermenting heap to a depth of about 18 to 24 inches quite easily. The result is the upper portion is ready, but the lower portion is not, so that if the upper portion is shovelled off first and the lower portion is left for another month, we might get very useful results in this way.

"Labor can be saved in compost-making by a careful assembly and mixing of the materials. In this connection you will be interested to know that as the soil becomes fertile its digestive power as regards organic wastes laid on the surface increases very rapidly; a time comes when a fertile soil will eat anything when spread on the surface.

"What I meant about mixing the materials as they go into the heap is this: instead of sandwiching them and keeping the soil, vegetable wastes and animal wastes separated, to mix them as one goes on, so to speak. It can easily be done in this way. If we start with a 6-inch layer of vegetable wastes, put on a 2-inch layer of farmyard manure, and a sprinkling of earth, and then fork up the layers, they get mixed quite a lot and fermentation is very much better and more complete than if the material is left as separate layers. By doing this we need only turn once. In fact, when the New Zealand Box is used, if we mix the material in the box, as I have suggested, all that is needed is to turn out this material into another empty box by the side and let the fermentation complete itself in the second box; then no more manipulation is necessary."

FOURTEEN-DAY COMPOSTING: THE FAST METHOD

One of the major shortcomings of composting had always been that the gardener had to wait months for the slow decomposition process to take place. Many times he could not predict how much compost he would need in a year, and often he was caught short.

For a period of time in the late forties and early fifties, much hope was placed in the benefits of bacterial activators, and gardeners applied commercial packets of special bacterial cultures to speed the process of decay. Experiments showed, however, that bacterial activators had little or no effect on the well-made heap, and that if conditions were not conducive to bacterial activity, introduced bacteria populations could not survive anyway.

When the Sanitary Engineering Department of the University of California set out in 1949 to design a good method for composting municipal refuse, they found a maze of conflicting claims in the semi-technical literature, but very few proven facts. The 18 scientists on their staff set out to clear the air with a broad and basic scientific study of the mechanism of composting. Out of their work evolved the "14-day method." This technique is suitable for garden, farm and municipal use.

57

The keystone of the 14-day method is the grinding or shredding of all material going into the compost pile. Grinding has these effects on compost:

1. The surface area of material on which microorganisms can multiply is greatly increased.

2. Aeration of the mass is improved, because shredded material has less tendency to mat or pack down.

3. Moisture control is improved.

4. Turning of the heap is much easier.

No layering of material is used in the 14-day method. Material is mixed either before or after shredding, then piled in heaps no more than 5 feet in height. After only 3 days, the heap is turned. Turning is continued at 2- or 3-day intervals. After 12 to 14 days, the heat of the pile has dropped, and the compost is sufficiently decayed to use on the soil.

If compost is being made for garden use, turning can be done by hand. Turning a shredded heap is not laborious, because the material is light and fluffy. For larger applications, turning is usually done by a manure loader, or a machine specially designed for turning large compost piles. Several such machines are manufactured.

Shredding the material prior to composting presents more of a mechanical problem than turning, especially for large composting projects. A number of good machines are available for garden use, however. Horticultural shredders made primarily for potting soil preparation can be used as compost material grinders. Small rotary lawn mowers also shred compost efficiently and easily. Weeds, leaves, straw or stable manure to be cut up are piled on the ground and the lawn mower is run over them. It is helpful to do this near a wall which can prevent the cuttings from spreading out too much. Eventually, large grinders may be designed that will shred municipal garbage at high speed.

At the Organic Experimental Farm, tests were conducted which resulted in compost being made in only 10 days. Here is the report of the supervisor of the tests:

"I feel that trying to make compost in a short time can be extremely rewarding, even though you may not care whether your compost is made in 10 days or two weeks. I do know that we have learned many things of importance by trying to speed up the composting process, and I am sure

58

The key to fast composting is the shredding of all materials going into the compost pile. Research has shown that the surface area of material on which bacteria can multiply is greatly increased by shredding; aeration and moisture control are also improved, as shredded matter does not pack as tightly.

that you too can make interesting discoveries and observations by perfecting your compost-making technique.

"Here are some of the more interesting facts we learned:

1. Manure is essential to fast composting. Manure, by supplying nitrogen, performs the wonderful service of heating up a compost heap quickly. Although satisfactory compost can be made without manure, it will take longer to rot up. Dried manure—available in garden stores—will work well as a heating-up agent.

2. Shredding of the material is essential. If a compost shredder is not available, a rotary mower can be used

59

efficiently. We were able to cut up the material for our average test heaps in 30 minutes with a rotary mower.

3. Sufficient moisture in the heap is needed if composting is to take place quickly. If your heap is made of predominantly dry materials, it is good to water it liberally when it is first made. But it is usually not necessary to water it again for 10 days or two weeks (if the heap is made of shredded material).

"Fall is one of the best times of the year for composting. Leaves and dry weeds are available in plentiful supply. And the soil *needs* compost in the fall and winter months to help it rebuild fertility lost during the past growing season. Compost applied in the fall will have plenty of time to work into the soil and will not in any way interfere with growing plants.

"Leaves would be a good basic raw material for you to start with, because most gardeners have not yet learned how to use them properly and will be glad to give you theirs. In a matter of a half hour you can cut up a tremendous pile of leaves with your rotary mower. Use the leaf mulching attachment if you want them cut up in small pieces (which will speed up the composting).

"Leaves alone are quite resistant to decay, because they are relatively low in nitrogen. Mixing in grass clippings will help, but you still should add manure for optimum composting. A good formula is this:

100 pounds of leaves
100 pounds of grass clippings
100 pounds of manure—fresh or dried.

"If you don't have grass clippings, you can substitute weeds, garbage or spoiled hay. But I would recommend that you do not use just leaves and manure. Even though shredded, leaves tend to mat together and need some other material to separate them.

"Shred everything—even the manure—with your compost shredder or rotary mower. We have found that the average well-made mower will wade through lumpy and stringy cow litter with ease, and with no undue wear on the machine.

"Shred a little of each type of material at a time. Pile it together and water the heap as it accumulates. It is not necessary to layer the materials if they are shredded. And do not wait until the pile is complete before starting to water it.

"When you have shredded up everything organic you can get your hands on that you want to put in your heap, there is nothing more that you can do for several days. You probably won't want to put your material in a bin or enclosure, as that will just make turning more difficult. And, after all, your heap will only be around for 10 days.

"The 24-hour period just after your heap is made is the most crucial period in its life. If it doesn't start heating up actively by the second day, there is not much hope for it. You probably have not put enough manure or highly nitrogenous material in it. If your heap doesn't heat up, your best bet is to add more manure or organic nitrogen fertilizer. If you don't, you may have to wait 6 months to a year for decay to take place.

"Three days after you have made your heap of shredded material, it should be turned. Turning will not be difficult, because the heap will be fluffy and easy to handle. Turning should be continued at 3-day intervals, until 10 days have passed. If the weather is hot and your heap begins to dry out, keep watering it. Don't let it get soggy, however.

"If at the end of 10 days your heap begins to cool, you can feel satisfied. You have made compost in the minimum period possible under home gardening conditions.

"When shredding material with a rotary mower, it is best for two people to work together. One moves the mower back and forth over a given spot, while the other feeds material in front of it. If the mower does not have an efficient exhaust chute, it will be necessary to fork the shredded material by hand from the cutting area. In a small garden area, it is helpful to set up a backstop to catch the cuttings as they are ejected from the mower. That way, they will not spread all over your garden.

"The commercial compost shredders will cut up compost material somewhat finer than a rotary mower, and can be used to handle a wider variety of material. The various types of compost shredders and grinders are described in the chapter on Composting Equipment.

"One thing to remember: You can improve the quality of your compost greatly by adding natural rock fertilizers to it as you make it. For every 100 pounds of compost material, you can add several shovels of rock phosphate, colloidal phosphate, granite dust, greensand and/or ground limestone. The intense bacterial activity in the heap will help break down the nutrients in the rock and make them available faster."

18 TONS OF COMPOST IN 8 BY 4 FEET

Yes, it's true. You can make *18 tons* of crumbly compost in 6 months, in a space *8 x 4 feet!* This is enough compost to put a 2-inch layer—an ample annual dosage—over 6,000 square feet of garden area, or a space 75 by 80 feet!

How is it done? Easy—using a shredder or rotary mower with the 14-day composting method, you begin in early spring, making a 4-foot high heap in a space 8 x 4 feet. After three weeks (we have allowed an extra week for possible slow heating), remove the finished compost—110 cubic feet, weighing about two tons—and begin the next pile. By mid-fall— 6 months later—your ninth heap should be finished, giving you a 6-month total of 18 tons.

Here is the basic formula and procedure. This is not absolute, of course, and it may be altered to suit your individual needs and supply of materials.

Day-to-Day to Two-Week Compost

First Day: Your basic material can be one of a number: leaves, spoiled hay, weeds or grass clippings. To this should be added one of the nitrogenous materials (manure is best) and any other material available. In the editorial experiments, equal parts of leaves, grass clippings and manure, with a liberal sprinkling of natural rock powders, were found to work very well. Remember, too, that leaves tend to mat down, slowing the composting process; they should be mixed with other material. Shred everything—including the manure— with a compost shredder or a rotary mower; mix materials together and place in a mounded heap. If your materials are low in nitrogen, be sure to add a sprinkling of dried blood, cottonseed meal or other nitrogen supplement on each series of layers.

Second and Third Days: By now, the heap should have begun to heat up. If not, add more nitrogen. Bury a thermometer in the heap to check temperature. Keep the heap moist, but not soggy.

Fourth Day: Turn heap, check temperature, keep moist.

Seventh Day: Turn it again, check temperature and keep moist.

Tenth Day: Turn it once more. The heap should now begin to cool off, indicating that it is nearly finished.

Fourteenth Day: The compost is ready for use. It will not look like fine humus, but the straw, clippings and other materials will have been broken down into a rich, dark crumbly substance. You may want to allow the heap to decay further, but at this stage it is perfectly good for garden use.

ANAEROBIC COMPOSTING

Anaerobic composting means, simply, composting in an environment free of air. The usual method of anaerobic composting is by use of a digester, an enclosed airless container, usually containing several sections. The Earp-Thomas digester was invented by Dr. G. H. Earp-Thomas. He termed his vertical cylinder the "continuous-flow digester," because it contained 8 sections or floors, fitted internally with rotating booms. The organic waste is introduced to the top section of the digester where it is inoculated with bacteria. Earp-Thomas' work was instrumental in the development of municipal composting, discussed in a later chapter.

One of the questions which mitigated the initial success of anaerobic composting, was: Since disease organisms live without air, won't anaerobic composting present a health hazard?

Our information points to an answer in the negative. The average compost or manure heap which is left unturned for several weeks has many airless patches in it where anaerobic organisms are helping with decomposition. We have never heard of a verified case of infection from a properly made compost heap. Airless composting has been used for many years by several European cities to dispose of garbage. Actually, the chief disadvantage of any anaerobic composting method is that it is slower. But airless composting does have definite advantages in certain instances. The chief advantage is that no turning or grinding is needed.

There are two disadvantages of aerated composting, as opposed to the anaerobic method. First, aerated compost brings about an oxidation which must destroy much of the organic nitrogen and carbon dioxide, the vapors of which waste upward. Secondly, some of the valuable liquids, the essences, the juices of the materials, leach downward and out of the mass into the ground underneath where they are wasted. This can be seen by the gigantic weeds which grow in an empty compost pit with an earth bottom.

The purpose of keeping out the air is to prevent or reduce oxidation (combustion). Combustion of nitrogenous substances is always accompanied by the production of a great quantity of free nitrogen compounds. Manure kept in efficient condition in an open pit loses 40 per cent of the nitrogen originally contained. This loss is relatively small in comparison with the 80 per cent or 90 per cent we would have as a result of improper ways of keeping, but it is also relatively large in contrast to the 10, 5 or even two per cent obtainable with the use of closed pits. In them the fermentation takes place out of contact with air, and the reduction in weight, when matured, is only one-quarter that of the original weight. If we were able to have perfect anaerobic fermentation, no nitrogen losses whatsoever would occur.

One big difficulty has been finding an efficient and simple way to practice anaerobic composting. The latest technique is to enclose the compost in a plastic wrapping. This technique is explained later in the personal experience of Adrienne Bond, a user of polyethylene.

There has been research which tends to prove that an anaerobic fermentation preserves more of the nutrients. Professor Selman R. Waksman and Florence G. Tenny of the New Jersey Agricultural Experiment Station did research comparing the aerobic and anaerobic decomposition of various types of organic matter. The authors reported: "In a study made on the decomposition of immature oak leaves under aerobic and anaerobic conditions, it was shown that when the leaf material was saturated with water, the celluloses and hemicelluloses were decomposed much more slowly than when the material was under aerobic conditions; the fats and waxes were much more resistant to decomposition and the lignins were preserved almost quantitatively, whereas the protein content of anaerobic material was considerably greater than that of the aerobic compost because of the greater decompositions of the proteins and losses of the nitrogen in the form of ammonia in the aerobic compost."

The fact that the anaerobic storing of manure may be desirable is brought out in a recent book issued by the Food and Agriculture Organization of the United Nations entitled

The Efficient Use of Fertilizers, which states: "In Norway, where cattle are stall-fed throughout the winter, the manure is dropped during the daily cleaning through a trap door into a basement extending the length of the cowshed. In this manner it is well protected until used in the spring." Further comments about this method stress that: "Under the efficient methods of storage described above, which are largely anaerobic (free of air) the rate of decomposition of organic matter is slow and the volatilization of ammonia reduced to a minimum. On the other hand, in dry, well-aerated manure piles there is much loss of organic matter and ammonia."

In the study of aerobic conditions against anaerobic, it must be borne in mind that there is one place where conditions must be aerobic and that is in the soil itself. Where land becomes water-logged due to standing water and the anaerobic organisms take over, crops will suffer. But good compost can be made by the anaerobic method and when it is applied to a well-aerated soil, the aerobic organisms will prevail and begin to work on it to good advantage as far as crop yields and health of plants are concerned. (See also Composting Methods for the Farmer—Anaerobic, and Municipal and Commercial Composting—Anaerobic.)

COMPOSTING UNDER A PLASTIC COVER

The most simple and inexpensive method of anaerobic composting for the home gardener is the plastic cover method. To demonstrate the method, we have selected the story of Adrienne Bond, an enthusiastic user of plastic composting. She reported the following:

"It was early spring and our garden was already planted. An application of raw manure would have done it more harm than good; however, we knew that we would have use for it later. The proper thing to do seemed to be to compost the manure and keep it for use in our garden the following season. Before we could do this there were several obstacles to overcome.

"To begin with, we lived in a residential area and the proximity of the garden to our house and those of our neighbors made it impractical to leave it exposed. Both flies and odor would be a problem. We also feared that leaving the manure exposed to the sun and rain for almost a year before using it would allow much of its valuable nutrients to be leached away.

"We were determined to find a way in spite of seeming difficulties, and in Mr. Rodale's books *The Organic Method on the Farm* and *The New Organic Method* we found a plan that seemed to solve many of our difficulties. A method of anaerobic composting had been developed in Italy and it not only solved the problems of odors, insects, and animal pests, but seemed to produce better compost than the exposed methods did.

"We felt that we were on the right track, but there was still one drawback to this method as far as we were concerned. In order to compost in this manner we would need to build a concrete structure to hold the manure. We were renting and could not build a permanent structure even if we had wanted to invest in apparatus that we would have to leave behind when we bought our own home.

"We were on the point of giving up and telling our friend that we could not use the manure when a picture in a magazine gave us an idea about a method of composting that might suit our needs perfectly. The picture showed a farmer putting silage on the ground and spreading a thin sheet of plastic over it to make a temporary silo. Plastic was air and water tight and inexpensive. Why couldn't we construct a simple anaerobic compost 'pit' out of plastic? We began to look into plastics and their characteristics and finally developed the following plan:

"First we had a portion of the garden disked. We had the manure unloaded onto the exposed soil in such a way that it formed a long ridge 5 feet wide and 3 feet high. (The ground should be plowed or harrowed so that there will be no layer of grass between the soil and the manure to set up an acid condition and prevent earthworms from entering the manure.) With a garden hose we soaked the manure thoroughly and covered it with black building paper. Over the building paper we spread a large sheet of plastic and after giving it time to settle we piled a layer of dirt all around the edges of the plastic to make it airtight. Now all we had to do was forget about it and let nature take its course.

"About two and one half months after we had sealed off the manure, we raised the plastic and found a pile of the blackest, crumbliest, sweetest-smelling compost you could hope for. The pile is almost exactly the same size it was before

Composting under plastic covers is being done successfully by many home gardeners. The plastic covering used by Adrienne and Al Bond of Thetford, Vermont, created the conditions necessary for converting fresh manure into compost.

the composting began and although we have no way of being sure we believe that the percentage of nutrients lost is very low indeed.

"This has been the easiest compost we have ever worked with. After the plastic was placed over the manure there was no watering, no turning, and no bother at all. The manure accomplished its metamorphosis by itself under conditions which probably approach the conditions in the soil itself more closely than any other composting method can.

"We have done further research since we started this project and have found that a black polyethylene plastic is available from one of the large mail-order houses which lasts from 2 to 3 times as long as clear plastic. This black plastic is impervious to sunlight so there should be no need for the layer of building paper if this material is used, since the purpose of the building paper was to shield the compost from the sun. We intend to try this on our next batch of compost.

"One word of caution. If you have dogs, goats, children or any heavy animal around with a yen for high places, put up a little fence around the compost pile to prevent accidental tearing. Even more important, the fence will keep children away from possible accidents in getting underneath the plastic."

SHEET COMPOSTING FOR THE GARDEN

There are two basic composting techniques open to the gardener—sheet composting and composting in heaps. Sheet composting possesses advantages which make it most advantageous for use as a permanent method of rebuilding garden soil. Sheet composting means putting manure and other raw organic matter into the soil fresh, and letting it decay for a month or two while no crops are growing. Inasmuch as organic matter is most valuable to the soil while it is decaying, it is important to allow as much of the decay process as possible to take place in the soil. Also, the heap method puts less bulk of organic matter in the soil, as the heap loses stature considerably as it decays. Nutrients can be leached out by rains, so if the heap method is used it is necessary to sufficiently protect the heap to prevent loss from leaching.

In some cases sheet composting is not completely practical either. If you want to make spot applications of organic matter, finished compost is the best method. Some people make compost in heaps simply because they enjoy doing it and observing the remarkable transformation of raw matter into black humus.

Fresh or raw organic material may be applied as such in sheet composting practice. The undecayed material adds more nitrogen to the soil than when it is almost fully decomposed. This may be explained by the fact that in the process of decomposition in a large bin, heap or pit, there is considerable heat generated which vaporizes much of the nitrogen so that it is dispersed in the atmosphere. Also, when applied fresh, organic material releases its minerals more slowly than when decayed.

Cover Crops for Sheet Composting

Green manuring—the growing of cover crops to be turned under—is the most practical way to add substantial amounts

This close-up of rye that has just been disked into the soil illustrates the amount of organic matter that can be returned to the land by sheet composting. This is a practical way of adding humus to large gardens and farmland.

of organic matter to a large garden or homestead land area. The green manure crop—usually one of the legumes—is generally planted after a food crop has been harvested, and is turned under about 6 weeks before the next crop is to be planted.

The most important thing in selecting a green manure crop is to select the one which will produce the greatest amount of organic matter in the time allowed. This may mean growing several stands in one season. Many gardeners with a sizable area rotate food crops with green manure crops, thus building up a healthy soil with little trouble or expense. If you have the room, green manuring should certainly be included as the mainstay in your soil building program. The crops most widely used for green manuring are buckwheat, common sesbania, cowpeas, hairy indigo, red clover, soybeans, sudan grass and sweet clover. Even weeds are better than bare soil, and can add large amounts of organic material when turned under the soil.

Besides cover crops, the gardener should add any other materials readily available: manure, spoiled hay, corn cobs, cannery wastes, seaweed, spent hops, sludge, wood chips or any other organic waste product. The addition of these materials is essential to increase the organic and nutrient content of the soil. Green manure and crop residues will help, of course, but they cannot do the job alone. Supplementary materials should be broken up by passing over them several times with a rotary mower. Then materials are worked into the soil with a rotary tiller.

Left over winter, the material will be greatly decayed by spring. It is a good idea to add limestone, phosphate rock, granite dust or other natural mineral fertilizers along with the other material, because the decay of the organic matter will facilitate the release of the nutrients locked up in these relatively insoluble fertilizers.

GREEN MANURING IN THE GARDEN

For the gardener with at least a little more space than he knows what to do with, green manuring can do the same for him as it does for the farmer. Until the innovation of rotary tillers and garden tractors, green manuring was an awesome, if not impossible task. But now that many gardeners classify power equipment as "indispensable," the practice is becoming more widespread—and for good reason.

Green manure plants are one of the best soil conditioners ever discovered. They cost little, take little time to use and provide the answer to good soil tilth. Aside from the fact that it is sometimes impossible to compost enough material for some larger gardens, green manuring saves hours of hard work and retains soil fertility economically.

Especially in a large garden it is worthwhile to devote a part of the land to build a green manure crop. It's no secret that farmers have been doing it for years and now consider it a very necessary part of the normal farming rotation. The dividends received in the form of soil building are worth far more than the original investment calls for.

Green manuring fertilizes soils deeply, which is something which cannot be accomplished by composting without undertaking an almost impossible task. By far, the most important source of organic matter is plant roots. These roots, penetrating often to considerable depths and decaying year after year, have in the course of time left great stores of organic matter to be broken down into humus. This type of deep fertilization cannot be duplicated in any other form so cheaply and easily.

70

Another advantage of green manuring is that, when these green manure crops are rotated season after season, plant diseases and insects are discouraged. They are not willing to attack a healthy soil and will turn to more susceptible fields.

Green manuring has a certain advantage over usual composting methods in that it supplies the soil with succulent organic matter at the peak of its nutritional benefit. Compost, no matter how carefully tended, will lose some of its nutrients due to leaching and other actions of the elements. But, by careful treatment of green manure, the soil will hold its nutrients (especially the minerals found only deep in the subsoil) until they may be assimilated by the following stands.

Green manure crops decay in the soil fairly quickly. To get the greatest benefit from your crop, take advantage of the new soil fertility soon after decay is completed. In warm weather with moisture present, almost complete decomposition takes place in less than 6 weeks. Young, succulent material decomposes more readily than older plants. The fertility liberated in the process of decomposition should be utilized immediately by growing plants, or some will be lost by leaching or escaping into the air in the form of gases.

Here are some of the more common green manure crops, used by both farmers and gardeners in sheet composting programs:

ALFALFA—deep-rooted perennial legume; grown throughout U. S. Does well in all but very sandy, very clayey, acid, or poorly drained soils. Inoculate when growing it for the first time, apply lime if pH is 6 or below, and add phosphate rock. Sow in spring in the North and East, late summer elsewhere, 18 to 20 pounds of seed per acre on a well-prepared seedbed.

ALSIKE CLOVER—biennial legume; grown mostly in the northern states. Prefers fairly heavy, fertile loams, but does better on wet, sour soil than most clovers. Sow 6 to 10 pounds per acre in spring, or may be sown in early fall in the South.

ALYCECLOVER—annual legume; lower South. Prefers sandy or clay loams with good drainage. Sow in late spring, 15 to 20 pounds of scarified seed per acre.

AUSTRIAN WINTER PEA—winter legume in the South, also grown in early spring in the Northwest. Winter-hardy north to Washington, D. C. For culture, see *field pea*.

BARLEY—annual non-legume; grown in the North. Loams,

71

not good on acid or sandy soils. In colder climates, sow winter varieties, elsewhere spring varieties, 2 to 2½ bushels per acre.

BEGGARWEED—annual legume; South, but grow fairly well north to the Great Lakes. Thrives on rich sandy soil, but is not exacting; will grow on moderately acid soils. Inoculate when not grown before. Sow 15 pounds of hulled and scarified seed or 30 pounds of unhulled seed when all danger of frost is past. Volunteers in the South if seed is allowed to mature.

BERSEEM *(Egyptian clover)*—legume for dry and alkali regions of the Southwest. Usually grown under irrigation. Will not stand severe cold.

BLACK MEDIC — legume; throughout U. S. A vigorous grower on reasonably fertile soils. Sow 7 to 15 pounds of scarified, inoculated seed in the spring in the North, fall in the South. Needs ample lime.

BUCKWHEAT—non-legume; grown mostly in the Northeast. Tops for rebuilding poor or acid soils; has an enormous, vigorous root system, and is a fine bee plant. Sow about two bushels to the acre, any time after frost. Can grow 3 crops, 40 tons of green matter per acre, in a season. Uses rock fertilizers very efficiently.

BUR CLOVER—a fine winter legume as far north as Washington, D. C., and on the Pacific Coast. Prefers heavy loams, but will grow on soils too poor for red or crimson clover, if phosphate is supplied. Sow in September, 15 pounds of hulled seed or 3 to 6 bushels of unhulled seed per acre. Volunteers if allowed to set seed.

COW-HORN TURNIP—non-legume; widely adapted. Its value lies in its enormous long roots that die in cold weather and add much organic matter in the spring. Plant in late summer, two pounds per acre.

COWPEA—very fast-growing annual legume. Thrives practically anywhere in the U. S. on a wide range of soils. A fine soil builder, its powerful roots crack hardpans. Inoculate when planting it the first time. Sow anytime after the soil is well warmed, broadcasting 80 to 100 pounds or sowing 20 pounds in 3-foot rows.

CRIMSON CLOVER — winter-annual legume; from New Jersey southward. Does well on almost any fairly good soil; on poor soil, grow cowpeas first for a preliminary build-up. Sow 30 to 40 pounds of unhulled seed or 15 to 20 of hulled, about 60 days before the first killing frost. Inoculate if not previously grown. Dixie hard-seeded strain volunteers from year to year in the South.

CROTOLARIA—annual legume. For very poor soil in the South and as far north as Maryland. Sow scarified seed in the spring, 10 to 30 pounds, depending on the variety. Makes sandy soil like loam.

DALEA *(Wood's clover)*—legume; northern half of U. S. Still being tested, but shows promise for strongly acid, sandy soils. Volunteers for many years.

DOMESTIC RYEGRASS AND ITALIAN RYEGRASS — non-legume; many areas. Wide range of soils. Sow 20 to 25 pounds in the spring in the North, fall in the South.

FENUGREEK—winter legume; Southwest. Loam soils. Sow 35 to 40 pounds in the fall.

FIELD BROME GRASS—non-legume; northern half of U. S. Widely adapted as to soils. Good winter cover. Hardier than rye. Sow in early spring or late summer, 10 to 15 pounds per acre.

FIELD PEAS—annual legume; wide climatic range. Well-drained sandy to heavy loams. Sow 1½ to 3 bushels, depending on the variety, in early spring in the North, late fall in the South. Inoculate first time grown.

HAIRY INDIGO—summer legume; deep South. Moderately poor sandy soil. Makes very tall, thick stand. Sow in early spring, 6 to 10 pounds broadcast, 3 to 5 drilled.

KUDZU—perennial legume; South to Central states. All but the poorest soils. Commonly allowed to grow for several years before plowing under. Seedlings planted in early spring.

LESPEDEZA—legume; South and as far north as Michigan (Korean and sericea varieties in the North). All types of soil, but sericea is particularly good for poor, sour soils—for these, it's one of the best fertility builders available. Sow in spring, 30 to 40 pounds. Benefits from phosphate rock. Inoculate first time grown. Will volunteer if seed is allowed to set.

LUPINE—legume; Southeast to North. Sour, sandy soils. Blue lupine is a fine winter legume in the South; white and yellow are most often grown in the North. Sow in spring in the North, late fall in the South, 50 to 150 pounds, depending on the variety. Always inoculate.

OATS—non-legume; widely grown. Many soils. Winter oats suitable for mild winters only. Sow two bushels in the spring.

PEARL MILLET—non-legume; as far north as Maryland.

73

Fair to rich soils. Commonly planted in 4-foot rows, 4 pounds per acre.

PERSIAN CLOVER—winter annual legume; South and Pacific states. Heavy, moist soils. Sow in the fall, 5 to 8 pounds. Inoculate. Volunteers well.

QUAKER COMFREY—a new crop currently being tested. Prefers clays, loams and sandy loams. Its huge leaves are generally chopped up for green manure. Rootstocks planted in spring or fall.

RAPE—biennial non-legume; many areas. A rapid grower in cool, moist weather. Sow 5 to 6 pounds per acre.

RED CLOVER—biennial legume; practically all areas, but does not like high temperatures, so is most useful in the North. Any well-drained fair to rich soil; needs phosphorus. Its decay is of exceptional benefit to following crops. Sow early in the spring to allow time for two stands, 15 pounds of seed per acre. Inoculate the first time grown.

ROUGHPEA (caley pea, singletary pea)—winter annual legume; southern half of U. S., and the Northwest. Many soils, but best on fertile loams. Sow 30 pounds of inoculated, scarified seed in the fall. Needs phosphorus. Will volunteer.

RYE—non-legume; grown mostly in the Northeast and South. Many soil types. Sow 80 pounds in the fall. Tetra Petkus is an excellent new giant variety.

SESBANIA—legume; as far north as Washington, D. C. Prefers rich loam, but will grow on wet or droughty land, very poor or saline soils. Very rapid grower in hot weather. Broadcast or drill 25 pounds in the spring.

SOUR CLOVER—winter legume; South and West. Many soils. Sow in early fall, 15 to 20 pounds of scarified, inoculated seed.

SOYBEANS — summer legume; deep South to Canada. Nearly all kinds of soil, including sour soils where other legumes fail. Will stand considerable drought. Use late-maturing varieties for best green manure results. Sow 60 to 100 pounds, spring to midsummer. Inoculate first time grown.

SUDAN GRASS—non-legume; all parts of U. S. Any except wet soils. Very rapid grower, so good for quick organic matter production. Use Tift Sudan in Central and Southeastern states to prevent foliage disease damage. Sow 20 to 25 pounds broadcast, 4 to 5 drilled, in late spring.

SWEET CLOVER—biennial legume; all parts of U. S. Just about any soil, if reasonably well supplied with lime. Will pierce tough subsoils. Especially adept at utilizing rock ferti-

74

lizers, and a fine bee plant. Sow 175 pounds of scarified or 25 pounds of unscarified seed, fall to early spring. Fast-growing Hubam, annual white sweet clover, can be turned under in the fall; other varieties have their biggest roots in the spring of the second year, so turn them under then.

VELVETBEANS—annual legume; South. One of the best crops for sandy, poor soils. Produces roots 30 feet long, vines up to 50 feet long. Sow when the soil is well warmed, 100 pounds, or 25 to 30 pounds in wide rows.

VETCHES—annual and biennial legumes; varieties for all areas. Any reasonably fertile soil with ample moisture. Hairy vetch does well on sandy or sour soils and is the most winter-hardy variety. Hungarian is good for wet soils in areas having mild winters. Sown in the North in spring, elsewhere in the fall, 30 to 60 pounds, depending on the variety.

WEEDS—whenever weeds will not be stealing needed plant food and moisture, they can be used as green manures. Some produce creditable amounts of humus, as well as helping make minerals available and conserving nitrogen.

The Best Conditioners

Recent experiments reveal that after the addition of green manures and other crop residues, the soil bacteria produce materials called polysaccharides. These are the glue-like materials which stick the soil particles into aggregates so essential for a good structure.

The amount of these valuable polysaccharides, produced by decomposing green manures, can be tremendous. For example, agronomists at the University of Delaware report that decaying alfalfa and oat straw produced as much as 5,500 and 4,000 pounds per acre, respectively, of these glue-like materials only one week after they had been added to the soil!

You can't ask for much better soil-conditioning action than that.

HELPFUL HINTS ON COMPOST-MAKING

When to Make Compost

In temperate climate zones, autumn is generally the most suitable time to make compost. Among the reasons for this are:

1. Garden production is completed for the season; time

75

and attention can more readily be given to preparing humus.

2. Plant wastes, leaves and various other organic materials are plentiful and easily available.

3. Either finished or partially decomposed compost can be readied and applied to all sections of the garden with minimum effort or interference and with ample time to replenish the soil well before spring planting.

Compost, however, can and should be made during any part of the year. In sub-tropical climes, any time is best for compost-making. In the North, however, you often have extremely dry summers, when the decaying process is held up. We recently made a pit of compost of very resistant ingredients —shredded corn cobs and leaves—in the middle of the winter, and by July it had been turned into wonderful compost, using earthworms to do the mixing. If the compost is made in a pit, in the winter, the pit-sides keep it warm and accelerate the decay processes. It wouldn't pay to assemble a compost heap in the open, in the winter. In the winter compost can be made during the warm spells, in pits.

For winter composting, pile up the manure with a covering of soil and burlap bags or canvas. Also have available in a protected place topsoil and green matter that are not frozen. Leaves that have been gathered in the fall are excellent.

If you do have to make a compost in the open during winter, choose a protected place, as on the south side of a building or wall. You could also make a protective barrier of corn stalks tied together. An extra heavy layer of soil on top would help, or a very heavy hay or straw-mulch a few feet thick to keep the heap warm.

October and November are excellent for making compost heaps or pits because at no other time of the year are plant materials more abundant for this purpose. Garden wastes, autumnal leaves, roadside weeds, wastes from food-processing plants and other materials are easy to obtain at this time of year. Also by making the compost heap then, the compost will be ready for use at spring garden making time.

What Grinding Does
Grinding is the key to quick composting, as we saw in the 14-day method. What grinding materials actually does is greatly increase the total surface area of the material. The

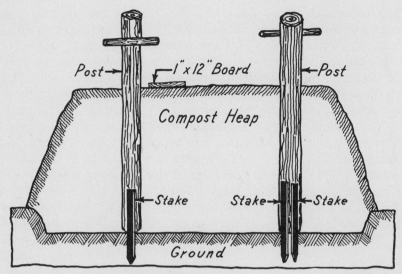

One suggestion for effective ventilation of the compost heap is illustrated in this drawing. After preparation of the pile or pit, common fence posts are set up and held in position by driving 3 small stakes around base of each post.

conversion of raw organic matter into colloidal humus is accomplished by a series of fermentations. These fermentations consume the plant and animal residues like a living fire. The finer the particles, the faster they will be consumed. In breaking up a large particle into smaller particles, the volume decreases so much faster than the surface that in finely ground matter the ratio of surface to volume is very great. It is the large surface and relatively small volume of the fine particles that makes it possible to make finished compost in so short a time as from 3 to 5 days. The same principle applies to the burning of such a substance as charcoal. A large piece of charcoal may burn for hours or even days. If the piece of charcoal is reduced to a fine dust, complete combustion will be accomplished in a fraction of a second with explosive force. The compost made in less time than one week will be even better than that made over a period of months, because there is less time for the dissipation of valuable gases and the leaching out of essential elements.

Ventilating the Heap

It is absolutely essential that the compost heap be well ventilated so that there is a sufficient flow of gases between the atmosphere and the interior of the compost heap. The soil organisms which break down the plant and animal residues and convert them into compost are aerobes, i.e., they must have the oxygen from the atmosphere to carry on their life activities. Here is a suggestion for a simple but effective way of ventilating the heap. As soon as the pits have been dug or the soil has otherwise been prepared for the compost heap, a number of ordinary fence posts are set up and held in position by driving 3 small stakes around the base of each post. The posts are placed where the ventilators are desired. By using chalk or heavy pencil, marks can be made on the posts 8 inches apart to serve as a guide in building the various layers of the heap: 6 inches for plant material, two inches for the fresh manure, a sprinkling of raw ground limestone, and a quarter inch or less of good earth. When the heap has been built to its usual height of 5 feet, the posts are pulled out to form the ventilating chimneys. To facilitate the removal of the posts, a board can be laid on the heap to serve as a walk, and a cross piece nailed near the top of the post to serve as a handle to pull out the post. The size of the ventilator is determined by the size of the post used.

TEN STEPS TO COMPOSTING SUCCESS

1. Where to Make Compost

There are no set rules on the best place to make compost. We know of gardeners with imagination who have set up a composting area on their front lawns in such a way that it added to the overall attractiveness. For the most part, though, gardeners prefer to do their compost-making back of their lots, where the heap can be easily "disguised" in some way.

For example, on our own suburban place, we chose an area behind the fireplace alongside the rail fence at the rear of the property. It's just a few yards from our vegetable patch, so it's a simple procedure to carry weeds, plant wastes, etc., to the pile, as well as take the finished compost to the garden.

Just as important, whenever I'm able to obtain large quantities of waste organic materials, it's a simple job to drive up the alley at the end of the yard and dump the materials directly onto the heap. So in our own case, our composting area has these three advantages:

    1. It fits into our landscaping plan without being an eyesore.

In highly-developed suburban areas, it is often important to keep your compost-making area attractive. This can be done with a variety of bins made of picket fence, bricks, stones or other materials. Hedges make effective screens.

2. It's close to the source of our organic waste materials and to where most of the compost is used.

3. It's little work to bring in outside materials, since they can be dumped directly from a car or truck.

There are a great many ways to improve the appearance of composting areas on your own home grounds. There are wooden bins specially designed for this purpose, where the slats are removable for easy withdrawal of the finished compost. Many gardeners we know use cement blocks—often without mortaring them together—around 2 or 3 sides of the heap. (Hay bales make an excellent "door" on the fourth side.) Still others make use of hedges to "fence off" their home fertilizer factories.

What you decide to do depends a great deal on the size of your grounds. If you have several acres, there's probably little need to think about disguising the heap; your main objective is to choose an area that's accessible and large enough to make all the compost you need.

On the other hand, if you live in a highly-developed suburban area with fussy neighbors, you'll want to be extra careful. Besides the camouflage techniques mentioned previously, you might want to think about making compost in pits.

Here's an idea which John Adamson of East Lansing, Michigan, recently sent in—one that might suggest a solution for your own composting problems.

"I've been trying to come up with a systematic arrangement for making regular use of kitchen and garden refuse. What I have in mind are sunken dual compost heaps, that is, two pits side by side. These are to be dug in the rear of my garden, surrounded by shrubbery for screening and protection. The rectangular depressions are to be about two feet deep, two feet wide, and 4 feet long, with wooden covers to go over them to keep the neighborhood dogs from scattering the contents, and to keep these receptacles from filling up with snow in the winter season.

"In a suburban area, as I live in, it would not be acceptable to try to maintain my compost on top of the ground, even with 3 framed sides. The dimensions mentioned would provide relatively small compost heaps, to be sure, but half a loaf is better than none, and I can get away with this size and also get a more rapid turnover than if they were larger."

The main thing to remember is that in just about every yard, there *is* space for composting.

2. Collecting and Assembling Materials

When it comes to getting materials for your compost heap, the big point is to use imagination and initiative. You'll have a certain amount of waste materials available without moving off your home grounds, such as grass clippings, garden residues, leaves, weeds, kitchen wastes, and so on. If these supply you with enough of the vegetable matter for your composting, that's fine. But don't feel that you are limited to just those sources. If you need more, there are scores of places within a short drive of your home where valuable wastes are available—for the most part *free*. (See chapter on Materials for Composting.)

3. Using Power Equipment

When done correctly, compost can be made according to the Indore method in about 3 months.

Under the method originally devised by Sir Albert Howard, the compost pile is turned after 6 weeks and again after 12 weeks to permit air to penetrate the heap. When materials are shredded, turn the heap twice during the first 4 days.

However, in recent years, various power garden equipment has been developed which cuts down the composting time to as little as 10 days. Foremost among these machines are the grinders and shredders which cut up the green matter and manure going into the compost heap. Shredding materials can also be done with a rotary mower by running it back and forth over a pile of green matter. (See chapter on Equipment for Composting.)

4. Without Power Equipment

While a great many gardeners have access to power equipment of some sort, there are still many who don't. If you're one of the latter group, perhaps you're wondering if you have to give up on the idea of making "speed" compost. This is not the case. We definitely believe that compost can be made quickly without the use of special equipment or chemical activators. Here's how:

When making the compost heap, be sure to mix materials such as grass clippings, vegetable tops, weeds, etc., with materials high in nitrogen (manure, cottonseed meal, dried blood and tankage). All material should be moist to start with, and the heap should be kept wet. A brief watering for the first 3 days should be sufficient.

Turn the heap often. The fastest working bacteria thrive in the presence of air, and turning the heap is the best way to aerate it. Initially, every 3 or 4 days is not too often. It's best not to make the speed compost heaps too large. Remember, a ton of compost occupies a space only 4 feet square and 4 feet high, and will last the average gardener for quite a while.

Adding earthworms to the compost heap has also been found an effective way of hastening decomposition.

5. Improving Value of Compost

Many home-made composts have relatively little plant foods, that is, a low nitrogen, phosphorus and potash content. Yet they accomplish a conditioning effect in the soil which is beyond the power of the most expensive high analysis fertilizer. Besides increasing the soil's water-holding capacity, improving its tilth and aeration, compost also makes plant nutrients already in the soil more available to plants.

However, there are many ways that you can make compost even more valuable. For example, if testing shows that your soil is acid, mix in ground limestone when assembling the materials. Regardless of what kind of soil you have, it will always help to add some rock phosphate and potash, as well as other natural mineral fertilizers. As stated before, manure and other nitrogen-rich materials speed up the compost material, while increasing the N content of the finished compost.

Sufficient water is especially important in the first few days after the heap is made. Build the top of the heap so that it slopes toward the center; then rainwater and water from a hose can seep down and keep the entire heap moist.

6. Watering and Turning

With the standard Indore method, the pile is turned after 6 weeks and again after 12 weeks, to allow air to penetrate all parts of the heap. After 3 months, Sir Albert predicted and demonstrated that the compost would be "finished."

When the materials are shredded in the 10–14 day composting technique, it's relatively easy to turn the heap with a pitchfork, so you can do it as often as time permits. However, the heap should be turned at least twice during the first 4 days.

If the materials are not shredded and you want finished compost as fast as possible, it's best to keep the heaps relatively small so they can be turned often without too much effort.

Regarding watering, it's especially important to have the heap quite moist during the initial days. It's well to have the top of the heap sloping toward the center, so that rainwater and water from a hose will seep down through the heap. A good practice is to check the heap at regular intervals to make sure the heap is always moist.

7. Mistakes to Avoid

Most people get in trouble with their compost heaps by making them of one ingredient. They make a pile of only leaves, or weeds or grass clippings and are disappointed when nothing happens. Last year we made a test heap consisting only of shredded hay. Although we kept this heap moist and turned it frequently, little decomposition took place. It's essential to add some nitrogen-rich material such as fresh or dried manure, dried blood or compost previously made, or even a small amount of rich soil, because the nitrogen in these materials is needed food for the decomposing bacteria.

Just as important as not letting the heap dry up is not keeping it in a perpetually soggy condition.

Difficulties can arise also if the compost heap is too large. Five feet is about the right height, as it allows air to get into every spot, provided that the heap is not too wide either (no more than 10 to 12 feet wide at the bottom, generally not less than 5 feet).

During the winter months, little decomposition usually takes place in the heap because of the cold. Many gardeners get around this by covering the heap with burlap bags or canvas, or by even using soil.

8. How to Tell When Finished

Some people think the finished product of their composting process should be crumbly like old leaf mold, but generally we're satisfied with a compost in which the straw, grass clippings, and more refractory substances such as corn stalks are broken up and have a rich, dark color.

When we apply compost, the mass is crumbly, not soggy; very often, on close inspection, you can determine its origin. Of course, if you're in no rush to use the compost, there's no harm in letting the compost break down into finer material. For ordinary gardening purposes, this is not necessary though,

Compost does not have to be completely crumbly like old leaf mold. Many veteran organic gardeners believe compost is ready to apply when it has cooled off, has a rich dark color and strawy material is broken up.

since the final decay can take place right in the ground. For flower growing, especially potted plants and for starting seedlings, it's good to screen the rougher material or to use the finer material which develops later. (See section on Testing and Judging Condition of Compost which follows this chapter.)

9. When and How to Use Compost

Many gardeners schedule their compost applications about a month before planting, when the materials are decomposed and rather fine. Others "double up" on their composting production by applying it half-finished, or notably fibrous, in the fall, and allowing it to break down right in the soil. In this way, they can make a second compost heap in the same space as the first and have twice as much finished compost by the time spring comes.

For general application, the soil should be turned thoroughly; then the compost is added to the top 4 inches of soil. When adding compost to growing crops, it can be mixed with topsoil and together applied as a mulch, so the roots of established plants will not be disturbed. This procedure is called a top dressing of compost.

Compost should be applied annually—anywhere from 1 to 3 inches in thickness. You can get by with less, but in gardening with small plots, put it on heavily. As a guide, an average figure of weight for one cubic yard of compost is 1,000 pounds.

When composting trees, start about 2 to 3 feet away from the trunk and go to a foot beyond the drip-line at the end of the branches. First cultivate the soil under the tree; then work about an inch or more of compost into the upper two inches annually.

When adding compost to your lawn, make sure that it is finely ground-up, so there's no chance of smothering the grass. An excellent way to improve your lawn is to first use an aerator to slice up the sod; then apply a thick covering of fine compost. As an optional final step, you could use a rotary mower to distribute the surface compost into the crevices. In this way, the compost provides the roots with moisture and nutrients, prevents soil from compacting. (See chapter on How to Use Compost.)

10. Sheet Composting

This discussion would not be complete without mention of sheet composting—making compost right in the soil. By this method, you're converting raw organic matter into humus in the surface layer of the soil.

For some time, this has been considered a more efficient method than composting in heaps, since all the decay occurs in the soil. Although recognized as more efficient, sheet composting also means more work for the gardener who sets out to do the job with manual garden tools. But *power* sheet composting for the home gardener can be simple with the use of rotary tillers and garden tractors. Here's how to go about it:

The vegetables have been harvested from your garden; stalks, leaves, mulch materials still remain. With a rotary mower or mower attachment, make several passes over the garden to cut up much of the surface vegetation. Next spread other materials (weeds, leaves, manure, etc.) over the garden, shredding either before or after applying them. Add any lime, nitrogen fertilizers, phosphate or potash rock powders at this time.

Now let your tiller take over. The object is to work all

of these organic materials into the soil—about 3 to 5 inches deep. It may require several passes with the tiller to bury the surface green matter, but most of today's tillers are powerful enough to do this job well. Incidentally, besides working the material into the soil, the tiller also shreds it somewhat. Therefore, in a month or two, your garden's humus content will be increased accordingly.

Growing green manure and cover crops, then working them into the soil, are closely related to the sheet composting idea. (See section on Sheet Composting for The Garden in this chapter.)

CHANGES DURING COMPOSTING

F. B. Smith and G. D. Thornton, of the Florida Agricultural Experiment Station, got a general picture of changes within the heap during a 4-month period. The percentage of nitrogen (1.3 at the start) was 1.74 by the end of the second month and 2.57 at the end of the fourth; the percentage of soluble sugars plus polysaccharides (31.2) was 25.4 and 22.7 at the same stages. At the end of the first, second, and fourth months molds per gram numbered 5,000, 25,000, and 300,000; the numbers of bacteria were 3,250,000, 2,300,000, and 76,000,000; and the temperature of the heap went from 130 degrees Fahrenheit, to 107 degrees, to 118 degrees.

NUTRIENT CONTENT OF VEGETABLE TRIMMINGS BEFORE AND AFTER COMPOSTING*

Per cent ash	7.6	17.4
Per cent moisture	80.7	85.6
Per cent carbon	41.7	34.5
Per cent nitrogen	1.66	2.45
Per cent phosphorus	0.13	0.27
Per cent potassium	0.80	1.65
Carbon to nitrogen ratio	24.9	14.1

* *Reclamation of Municipal Wastes by Composting*, Table No. 6, published by the Sanitary Engineering Research Project, University of California, Berkeley. Note that the moisture content of the finished compost was higher than that of the raw material. This is not usually the case, but was caused by the fact that this test batch was made under laboratory conditions in a drum.

MISCELLANEOUS METHODS OF COMPOSTING

In organic gardening the fertility of the soil increases so startlingly that sometimes convenience dictates the employment of a method that gives less nutrients but is more adaptable to the needs or preferences of a particular gardener.

The Earthworm Method

In the orthodox method of making compost there are two main disadvantages. One: because of the earth bottom, much valuable liquid containing large amounts of valuable nutrients leaches out from below. Two: because the materials are piled 5 feet high, a strong heat decomposition takes place. Such oxidation destroys nutrients, bacteria, and valuable enzymes. In watching earthworms breeding in our earthworm boxes, I saw that they were turning out a compost of the highest quality. In these boxes the materials are never more than two feet high, and I have never noticed any heating in them. One of the factors preventing this is that we thoroughly mix the various raw organic materials which go into these earthworm boxes. Secondly, the earthworms immediately penetrate into the matter, working it up thoroughly. So there seem to be 3 factors to prevent heating in the way these boxes are constituted:

1. The raw material is not more than two feet high.
2. There is thorough mixing of the raw materials.
3. The earthworm acts as the decomposing agent.

In this method the compost can be made in boxes indoors or in pits on the outside. The boxes should not be more than two feet high, but their width and length are optional. The same applies to the construction of a pit. It can be of any width or length that is convenient, it can be of any shape—square, oblong, or even round. As earthworms do not like light, it is desirable to make a wooden top, one that is not too tight-fitting. When it rains the cover should be removed, for rain water is of great value as a watering agent.

A variety of materials are placed in the pit and thoroughly mixed. The more they are mixed, the less tendency there is to heat up. See that the mass is well watered and put the earthworms in immediately. The more earthworms that are put in, the quicker the composting will take place. In a pit 10 feet square it would be nothing to put in 10,000 earthworms. They breed very fast if you start breeding them indoors. This method itself is practically a method of breeding earthworms which can be used for various purposes, such as feeding to chickens or placing in a mass of raw organic matter used as a mulch. One need not purchase more than a

Pits provide an excellent spot to compost the family garbage as well as garden wastes. Earthworms can be added to walled-in pits to speed up the decomposition process. After the earthworms are added, the pits are generally covered.

thousand or two earthworms, as they will multiply fantastically. (See full instructions in chapter on Earthworms and Compost.)

The action of the earthworms will produce the finest compost you can ever make. Their castings will thoroughly impregnate the mass with a material extremely rich in all the nutrients and trace-mineral elements. It will become darker than compost made by other methods. As soon as the material is assembled and the earthworms placed in it, cover the entire top of the pit with rocks or old boards. Conditions of darkness will make the earthworms work better and the composting time will be greatly reduced. The rocks or boards will also conserve moisture. If the top is not covered, the time element will be increased. Try to find flat stones that would be light to handle. The thinner type of purchased flag-stones would be excellent for this purpose. By this method compost can be made in two months or less.

Such a pit is an excellent place for the family garbage. Coffee grounds are excellent feed for earthworms. They seem to thrive on them. To enable the earthworms to make a better compost, buy some ground whole wheat and mix it in with the materials. You can use other seeds, ground up, such as soybeans, corn, etc. The ordinary garden angleworm cannot be used in this box method as it does not thrive or work under these conditions.

Earthworm Green-Matter Formula

In the boxes a typical mixture would be about 70 per cent weeds, leaves, grass clippings, etc., about 15 per cent manure and 15 per cent topsoil. This can be greatly varied. If no manure is available, parts of your table wastes can be substituted. You can try almost any formula.

One subject which never has been thoroughly studied is that of the enzymes in the composting process. Since enzymes are destroyed at 40 degrees centigrade (104 degrees Fahrenheit), and since compost heaps get up to about 160 degrees Fahrenheit, it would appear that all of the enzymes are destroyed. But in the earthworm boxes the heat would not reach such danger points.

We must also be aware that manures and green matter contain vitamins. One rarely sees mention of this. We are told that in cooking foods much of the vitamin content is destroyed by heat. Therefore, why should this not also be true of vitamins in a compost heap?

Do not put too much water in the boxes or it will create an anaerobic condition, which will impede the earthworms from working properly.

The process takes about 60 days. Then you take out half a box of material and fill it up with the raw materials again. In 60 days the new stuff will be completely composted. It is advisable to feed the earthworms something equivalent to chicken mash, but you can make your own feed, using ground leaves and ground grain seeds such as wheat, barley, corn. This food is sprinkled lightly on top. I have noticed that in the pits where we placed the earthworms less weeds grew on top, which leads me to believe that these little fellows chew up the weed seeds along with the other materials and take the sting out of them. This is terrifically important if true. When the compost is taken out of the pit we leave some of it at the bottom to act as an inoculant for the new material. The earthworms it contains will enter the new heap as soon as the heating has ceased. (See chapter on Earthworms and Composting.)

The Lehigh Compost Box Method

Many gardeners prefer to make compost in pits, wooden boxes, and so forth. Some have used wooden barrels, steel drums, and many other ingenious devices. Here is a method

I worked out—a type of bin which any person can assemble without tools of any kind. The picture gives you the idea. There is not a single nail in the whole thing. You can make it of a size to suit your needs. It is made of 2-by-4's, or heavier lumber if your purse can stand it. Ask the lumberyard to drill ¾-inch holes near each end, unless you are handy and have the tools yourself. Then secure round iron rods, ½-inch in diameter, and force them into the ground for about 6 inches to give rigidity to the bin. The picture will illustrate what I mean.

Such rods are sold in the bigger hardware stores or mill supply concerns. If you want to turn the heap, all you have to do is pull out the rods and the wood pieces will all come apart. You then set the box up close by and shovel the material into it. This way it will be easier to get at the stuff. On the second turn, since the heap has become more compacted, you need use only half or two-thirds of the wood pieces. The increased cost of the wood will be compensated for by its longer-lasting qualities. (See Equipment for Composting chapter.)

University of California Method

I would like to quote from a booklet issued by the University of California, Sanitary Engineering Research Project, entitled *Reclamation of Municipal Refuse by Composting*, issued June 1953 (price $1.00). It is a very interesting method of making compost in only 12 days.

"Two experiments were conducted within the limitations imposed by 'backyard' composting. In these experiments no material was ground, and turning was restricted to a minimum.

"In the first experiment a 3-foot-square bin with a removable front was filled with grass clippings and garden weeds to a depth of approximately 3½ feet. The material was turned every other day. Temperature rise and fall followed a normal course.

"Composting was completed within 12 days and an excellent product rich in nitrogen, phosphorus, and potassium resulted.

"The second experiment involved the use of a wider variety of materials. Grass clippings, entire dahlia plants, whole heads of lettuce and cauliflower, dry garden weeds, dry sycamore leaves, avocado seeds, and some kitchen refuse, were placed in a bin without shredding in any manner. Because of the dry leaves and weeds, the mass was sprinkled at the start to increase the moisture content. The material was turned every other day. The sycamore leaves were slow to break down. However, within 13 days, the process was complete and a very satisfactory product resulted. No initial analysis was made because of the difficulty in obtaining a representative sample.

"These experiments show that even in a fairly small volume, material ordinarily encountered in gardens and in kitchen wastes, excluding paper and large bones, can be composted readily and rapidly without preliminary grinding or any treatment other than turning every other day."

Maye Bruce "Quick-Return" Method

The "Quick-Return" system was devised by Miss Maye E. Bruce of Cirencester, England. Although originally intended for smaller gardens, it has proved quite satisfactory with bulk compost also. The method is highly spoken of by many who have adopted it.

As described in a New Zealand compost booklet by F. H. Billington, it is a simple and effective procedure very suitable for small-scale composting but by no means limited to such, and it has been adopted successfully for bulk compost without the use of bins.

As the name indicates, the object is to produce good quality compost in a minimum time. While adhering to general approved principles, Miss Bruce advocates several notable innovations. Special emphasis is laid upon the following points :

1. Protective walls or bins to ensure retention of heat in small heaps. Half the success of the process is attributed to this one factor.

2. A 3-inch foundation of rubble on which is a ½-inch layer of charcoal—easily obtained by dowsing half-burnt wood with water. Also a spraying with clay-water upon the walls and floor.

3. Alternating layers — about 4 inches deep — of soft green and drier materials, trodden firmly down.

4. A layer of crushed, wet nettles and a sprinkling of soil at each foot of depth.

5. A 2-inch layer of animal manure—except pig—when

the heap is about two feet high: no meat scraps are included.

6. Sprinklings of lime — on the vegetable matter — at intervals of a foot to 18 inches—immediately covered with soil or green refuse.

7. Providing shelter from heavy rain by a rough tent-like cover, and conserving heat by sacks laid on the heap during building and for about a month after the final soil-covering is put on the completed heap.

Naturally, slow-decaying materials are kept out of these "Quick-Return" heaps. Furthermore, the more rapidly they are completed the better—within 2 to 3 weeks if possible.

Compost made as described above will rot down satisfactorily without turning or further attention. The quality is improved, however, and decay greatly hastened by (a) adding liquid manure and; (b) inserting certain "solutions" much in the same way as the Biodynamic "preparations."

Compost treated with the herbal solutions is stated by Miss Bruce to be ready for use in about 6 to 8 weeks in summer and some 12 weeks in winter.

SAVE YOUR COMPOST!

The following is a Colorado gardener's description of an unusual and practical "tub and pail" idea for keeping compost:

"As long as we could remember, the empty lot next door to us raised nothing but weeds—and not too fine a crop of these. So when we 'borrowed' this ground to house our sprawling squash, melons, and cucumbers, we had visions of tons of fertilizer gobbled up by a compost-hungry soil. Instead we decided to make a rich feeding area for each hill—our 'tub and pail method.'

"First, we dug a hole about 3 feet in diameter one full spade deep—something like a tub. In the center of this hole we dug another in the sandy-clay mixture about the size of a pail.

"The next step was to fill the pail part with rich compost, pack it down and soak it with water . . . as much as it would take, while we went on to other tub-and-pail holes.

"To finish the job of filling the holes, a half-and-half mixture of compost and choice topsoil were packed into them and shaped into moats. Hotbed-grown plants were put in after a thorough watering job.

"Now, as well as 2 or 3 times a week throughout the season, we turned the hose into the moat with a slow flow of water. Later we learned to stick an iron rod into the ground to be sure that the water reached the lower roots.

"The plan was quite successful and brought us good crops for a few years. Now, alas, the building shortage has caught up with us and a house is going up in our vine bed. We can only hope that our enterprise has contributed something to the fertility of our new neighbor's yard."

—ORVILLE GRISIER

SINGLE-HANDED GARDEN COMPOST-MAKING

After having made compost for 25 years in other parts of the world and at elevations ranging from sea level to 8,000 feet, with ample local labor and sufficiency of manure, I am now up against the problem that faces so many of us— how to make satisfactory compost single-handed from my own plot of one-third of an acre, and with no manure available.

It is simple to make a compost with wonderful fertilizing properties, but alas! too often it produces such a growth of weeds that one is tempted to go back to the old digging technique and bury it under a spit of soil. That is not the way to use compost; Nature always leaves hers on the surface, and we who have studied her have become chary of unnecessary disturbance of the soil.

We have learned that people do not dig in order to make things grow. Any hedgerow will show that digging is unnecessary for this. They dig to prevent things growing, i.e., by burying all the surface weeds and their seeds under a layer of earth.

The books tell us that digging is necessary in order to get air into the soil. It is a half-truth more worthy of a politician than a farmer. You have got to get air into the soil because by your previous diggings you have upset Nature's way of doing this—the innumerable channels made by earthworms when attracted by a layer of decomposing vegetable matter left on the surface. They also tell us to dig in the autumn and leave the soil rough so that the frost can break up the clods. In other words, you should dig in the autumn to make it easier for you to dig in the spring.

When you dig, you should be quite clear about what you are doing and why. The agelong technique of digging with its inversion of the soil is wonderfully well suited to the job

94

of destroying surface weeds, and provided you do not turn in ripened weed seeds and do not dig too deeply there is not much against it. Of course, if you turn in weed seeds they will simply be well protected ready to start into growth again as soon as your next spell of digging brings them to the surface. If, however, you dig without inverting the soil, there will always be masses of weeds ready to start into growth, so constant hoeing is required: a first-class system of cultivation for anyone who has the time for it.

An alternative way of dealing with weed seeds is to smother them with a thick surface of something that is free of such seeds. Good compost is ideal but the quantity required renders it impracticable except over small areas.

The idea of the necessity of a friable seedbed dies hard. But again, look to Nature. She grows her seeds well enough on undisturbed soil, after having arranged a good layer of her compost on the top. It is obvious, therefore, that if we are to follow her example and use a layer of compost on the surface for our seed beds it must be of such a nature that it will not grow a mass of weeds. Weed seeds will grow and germinate more quickly than those you sow. That is one of the properties that make them weeds.

Small Garden Compost Box

A one-third of an acre plot yields sufficient vegetable trash when combined with all kitchen waste, screened ashes and the compostable refuse of a household, to fill a 4-foot by 4-foot by 3-foot, 6-inch compost box once every month from April to December. Observation of the resulting compost will show that the late summer and autumn stuff is far fuller of troublesome weed seeds than that of the spring and early summer. This points to the advisability of getting your trash on the rubbish heap before it has had time to ripen seeds. You also get a much better heating effect in your boxes if most of your material is wilted green stuff.

In small-scale composting the management of the rubbish heap is most important. It should always be regarded as the initial stage of composting. If a little care is taken much labor is saved later. The heap should be of adequate size and everything put on it should be looked at from the composting angle. All sappy green stuff should be scattered thinly over the whole area so as to wilt thoroughly before being in turn covered. All long stems should be cut into manageable lengths before being put on the rubbish heap. Excess of harsh dry stuff such as autumn leaves and straw should be avoided. When you have a plethora of these they are best dumped in your leaf-mould pit and added to your compost from time to time.

Your weedings should not be shaken too free of adhering earth. You need a considerable quantity of this to neutralize the acidity that results from bacterial action, which if not dealt with inhibits their growth. This is helped by the comparatively small amount of fine ash from the fireplaces. There is never enough of this in a single household to check aeration. Crushed chalk or limestone grit is best of all if available.

The rubbish heap should never be allowed to dry out or all action will cease.

The starting of the composting process in your rubbish heap is much helped if you can give the bacteria and fungi some immediately available food to start on. An occasional sprinkling of dried sludge, for example, works fine.

You can never get a first-class compost without the use of some organic matter as a starter. Urine-soaked litter and manure is, of course, the best. Do not be misled by advertisements of proprietary ones which promise marvellous results. It is the living matter in your compost heaps that does the work and Nature does not take kindly to being hurried.

All vegetable wastes will eventually break down into humus without a starter as you can see in any old neglected rubbish heap. But it takes much longer and you lose a lot of bulk from long continued oxidation. The resulting compost will be quite serviceable for applying as a mulch to growing plants. Once established they can deal with the competition of the weed seeds that spring up, if helped by your own hoeing. It will not, however, do for seedlings. For these you need partially to sterilize your compost.

Most seedbeds can best be sown on the surface of the ground, as in Nature, if they are covered with a layer of compost, well trodden down. If your soil is in good "heart," no digging is necessary before making such a seedbed. Any previous cultivation to destroy weeds is best done with a fairly heavy short-handled hoe with which the weed stems are severed just below the surface. Even the deep-rooted ones succumb to this if done repeatedly. It is best to leave your soft weedings on the surface for awhile. The worms will dispose of most of it before you need to tidy up and put the balance on the compost heap. If you have a pan in your soil, it may be necessary to expose the underspit in order to break up this pan with the fork. But remember that such pans are not formed in Nature, but only as a result of long-continued cultivation without deep-rooting plants in the rotation. Subsoiling once done should not be required again if the necessity of this is kept in mind.

Being compost-minded, you may want to make use of the roadside trimmings that at present are so wastefully burnt. Those of early summer, being soft and sappy, make excellent material for your compost heaps, but the later cuttings are so full of coarse grass and other weed seeds that it is better to use the material as a mulch around your fruit trees.

Experience soon teaches you what to keep out of your rubbish heaps. Thistles and all thorny materials are best avoided since compost is likely to be much handled. Their ashes will of course go in. Any woody prunings thicker than the little finger are best used as a base on which to set up your heap. It will all disintegrate in time.

Some sort of protection from wind such as is given in a box is essential with small-scale work. To get adequate heating in an open heap it needs to be at least 10 feet by 6 feet by 5 feet.

If care is taken to fill your boxes when you have a supply of fresh lawn mowings available, heating up is easier. Enough at any rate to get the fungus stage well started. But don't expect the high temperatures of a large farm pile unless you can get some fresh horse dung.

One of the difficulties met with in small-scale composting is that after long spells of rain the heaps get sodden and do not dry out adequately afterwards in the center. This results in the bacteria having to get their small oxygen requirements by breaking down the valuable nitrates already formed in the heaps. This difficulty can easily be got over if we adapt the method used by primitive peoples to protect their seed grain. Just replace the aerating stake in the center of the heap and tie around it a tick petticoat of long leafy twigs. This will direct much of the rainfall to the outside of the heap where it will evaporate in due course and the center will never get sodden.

—*By* E. FAIRLIE WATSON, O.B.E., A.M.I.M.E.
For the Albert Howard Foundation of
Organic Husbandry, Publication No. 6.

WHY AND HOW TO MAKE COMPOST

The organic gardener who makes compost, and the farmer who values good humus higher than chemicals, have both recently had their methods justified by research in America and England.

Plants, it seems, from radishes to oak trees, are very "choosey" about what they take from the soil, like a girl who picks all the hard centers from a box of chocolates. An experiment with wheat in America showed that the crop took only two per cent of what was in theory available from a dressing of chemical phosphate fertilizer. Yet when the straw from the crop was used to make humus, the next crop took it almost completely. The maximum that can be absorbed as a chemical in a wide range of experiments was 35 per cent; for an organic manure, the figure is in the high nineties. The "soft center" portion of the chemicals washes out of the soil, causes chemical complications like that by which too much phosphorus locks up potash, and lime and sulphate of ammonia waste each other and alter the balance of the soil bacteria on which our crops depend.

Our compost heaps are all "hard centers." Their plant food molecules are selected by plant roots. Therefore, though analysis may show that the plant foods in an organic manure seem low compared with the analysis of a crude chemical, those in the organic manure are a picked team. Those in the chemical *may* do only two per cent of good, and 98 per cent of harm, whereas the organic manures *are* 90 per cent or more good and no harm whatever. This is what good farmers have known for 50 years; science has merely confirmed us in scientific terms that are now locked away in technical reports where farmers and gardeners cannot see them.

If we use an organic manure like fish-meal or bone-meal, the molecules that do the work were selected by the plankton plants or the grass that fed the fish or the cow. Only a plant can choose food for another plant; science can no more tell the molecules apart than they can tell the sex of a pelican, for which the only test is another pelican (as the Ministry of Works informed the House of Commons when America kindly re-stocked St. James's Park after the war).

By passing through animals the plant foods are altered, but in a way that soil bacteria are specialized to change back again. The compost heap gains by using the very least alteration of all; it is a harnessing of Nature to the needs of Man invented early in China, but only recently in the West.

In all vegetable matter, on which all living creatures depend for the chemicals of their bodies and their energy, potassium, as an example, is present as plant-selected molecules of potassium sulphate. A drop of sap on a microscope slide shows the crystals looking like house roofs in an air photograph of a flood. A crystallographer cannot tell the difference between these shapes and those in chemical sulphate of potash. But you can certainly *taste* the difference in potatoes grown with compost, even if your taste buds are dulled by heavy smoking.

When we burn garden rubbish, dead leaves or wood, we are converting (apart from wasted humus, nitrogen and phosphates) these root-selected molecules to an unsorted batch of a different chemical. This is potassium carbonate, which is a powerful alkali that made our soap before the end of the 18th century when caustic soda was invented. Burning the forest made deserts, before chemicals replaced wood ashes as the first "artificial fertilizer." We can reconvert them by bacterial action in the compost heap to potassium nitrate, but they are still unsorted and inferior to the material that was the rootlets' own choice.

Compost is rather like homemade wine—you start by following the book and add your own variations, but stick to a few simple principles that are the heap equivalent to a few raisins and some yeast on a slice of toast. The most common failure, even though you have followed the directions carefully on any system, is the forest of weed seedlings, a frequent beginner's trouble and as easily achieved as an earthy taste of a "Bad Cough Mixture Port Type" for the inexperienced wine maker.

The fault lies not with our failure to follow the book, but because we do not understand that in every compost heap there is a slow and secret bonfire that needs both fuel and air, just as we need fuel and air to produce the energy of our bodies. The fuel supply is one of the few aspects of composting that can be measured accurately, and while there is no need to measure it in the garden, we can take advantage of knowing what has been discovered by research.

Wheat straw is what most farm heaps are made from. It has 120 parts of carbon, that is, starches, sugars and woody matter all of which are fixed from carbon dioxide and hold

99

the energy of the sun just like wood, coal or petrol, to one part of nitrogen which will be linked up with other ingredients as protein. Add an activator, such as old compost or compost water, to give the bacteria some nitrogen they can get at more quickly, (this is not, of course, the whole story), water, and lime to keep the kinds of bacteria that we need thriving, and it will rot down to between 14 to 1 and 10 to 1. This proportion between the two is called the "carbon-nitrogen ratio" and the low ratio at the end is tested in the garden by the fact that the worms arrive and their opinion is both accurate and without charge, for if you want to know when your heap is quite ready, ask the worms. They can be quite "rude" about some chemical activators.

Where has the spare carbon gone? Mostly in producing heat, but some has been spent on fixing more nitrogen (it is not possible to sort out which came in when; the late Sir Albert Howard secured 26 per cent gain on that in activator and material from bacterial action at Indore). A farm heap has plenty of fuel, it can cook all its weed seeds easily, but the gardener has less to spare.

Summer weeds are soft and sappy, they are usually about 20 to 1, their carbon is high in starches and sugars which "burn" as quickly as paper, and though they may look a large pile at the start, this is very largely water. Therefore they are always short of fuel; though they can get very hot quickly it is soon burnt and easily wasted. When the weeds go on with large quantities of soil on the roots and this contains weed seeds, or soil layers in place of lime or ashes are used, there is not sufficient fuel to kill them. To expect the average heap to warm up cold soil lumps to between 130 and 160 degrees that will kill weed seeds in from 2 to 4 days, is like trying to boil a kettle with matches. Killing a root is a matter of 180 to 200 degrees Fahrenheit, like simmering a long, narrow potato, and takes more heat than cooking a relatively small weed seed or killing the spore of some plant disease.

The flower heads on the weeds may get well cooked, and when the heap is turned to bring the air-cooled undecayed sides to the middle, like forking together a burnt, hollow bonfire, you may heat up those which have been in the cold spots around the unwarmed soil, but there will be weed seeds. If you want fewer, knock off more soil from the roots and use lime instead of a soil layer, and keep the perennial weeds for the bonfire; if you make a low temperature heap, it can be just as good humus so long as you are using green material which has a near ratio not a wide one which causes trouble, when too much "fuel" is dug in, as with sawdust.

The best small-scale system, for those who use lawn mowings and weeds plus kitchen waste as it accumulates and can never get enough to make a big heap in one go, is the New Zealand Box. This is like a deep cold frame with one side removable and no glass, but a temporary roof can be put on in winter with a great improvement of quality. It can be used with any system of composting; its action is simply to stop heat loss from the sides, and with this and less soil on the roots, there will be fewer weed seeds or none.

The carbon-nitrogen ratio test does not tell the whole story. If a great deal of the material is cellulose and harder materials like hemicellulose or lignins, it takes a very long time to decay, but leaves a real bulk of humus behind when it does.

The more woody the material, the more nitrogen you need, for it has none of the protein which gives the balance in soft green stuff. Poultry manure is ideal to rot wide ratio material. With weeds and lawn mowings and household refuse, so long as you provide lime layers you can manage with no activator at all at a pinch. The need here is to keep up the air supply, and stop the heap growing acid, for with no activator and no lime you will make silage instead of compost. Lack of air puts the "fire" out, and acid chokes it with "ash" for acid decay, mainly lactic acid from carbohydrates can hold your compost undecayed like pickles in vinegar.

The other methods are modifications of the Indore system. This means a heap built with layers of manure, soil and lime like the cream in a layer cake, with the refuse in the place of the sponge mixture. Some people turn them, and this is advisable if you have time.

Build your heap above ground if you can, a pit holds water in winter and gets the compost too wet. With a New Zealand Box, or one in the open, air from the bottom helps your bacterial fire. You can start with brushwood, but in a garden 2 or 3 double rows of old bricks or brickends set on their flats to leave a channel down the middle will not close with the weight of the heap. They can be dug out and used again and again.

Then pile in an 8-inch layer of garden rubbish, spread flat and add the "activator" which supplies the bacterial food, or rather the nitrogen they need for their increase to the numbers required. This can be horse, cow, pig or any animal manure in a layer about an inch thick. If you are using poultry droppings this can be as thick as 3 inches, but the material wants to be stemmy, and not all soft weeds. On top scatter just a little garden soil, to make sure of a good stock of bacteria, but if there are weeds with soil on the roots this does instead.

In this layer thrust some upright poles, about the thickness of a fork handle. These are drawn out when the heap is finished, and leave air holes. One member has bought 3-foot wide and half-inch mesh wire netting, cut up and rolled on a rake handle into tubes made by hooking the ends round. These go in the middles of the rubbish layers, about 8 to a heap 6 feet square and provide ample ventilation. They have lasted two seasons so far since they were made. Most people do without them, the brick and pole system is usually enough.

On the activator and soil layer spread another 8-inch layer of rubbish, then scatter on about 4 ounces of lime to each square yard of surface, enough to make it really white. Then more rubbish, then more activator and so on. A New Zealand Box makes a cube heap. In the open the shape has to come in to a point, and either it is a long mound or a flat sided cone. Few heaps can be built in one go in the garden, usually one keeps on until it looks big enough, then starts another. Dried poultry manure or fish meal used at about the same rate as the lime or a bit more is an easy organic activator, and both tins can stay in the shed at the bottom of the garden ready for when a barrowload completes a rubbish layer.

Wilted comfrey, especially Bocking No. 14, can replace the manure with a 3-inch layer which is going to add more potash than any of the other activators. Wood ashes can replace the lime, for they contain it, but use twice as much, and those who have wood fires can make these layers two inches thick, for the bacteria take up the potassium carbonate in it and convert it to potassium nitrate, (the process that once made saltpeter for gunpowder) which is better for potatoes, especially on heavy clay that ashes can make sticky.

House refuse should always go in the middle of the heap

because of rats, and be scattered as it can bind solid. Lawn mowings should also be spread, and they are better value as a mulch around bush fruit or in the bottoms of pea trenches than in the heap.

In winter or a wet summer, it pays to protect the heap from rain with a propped sheet of corrugated iron or asbestos. Black polyethylene sheet excludes air, but is a good and cheap winter covering, either nailed on a timber framework or just held down with stones. Make the heap in a sheltered place. It always rots best away from the prevailing wind, and a windbreak of anything temporary and large enough is a help. These are only some of the ways of making compost. The real proof is in the crops it grows, and the weeds it brings to them, for good compost should be weed seed free, and should get nearly as hot as an electric soil sterilizer.

The research carried out in 1955 by the Henry Doubleday Research Association on the farms and gardens of members, the first comparative compost trials yet undertaken, has merely shown the reasons for some of the standard practices of composters, which are, like much traditional lore, based on sound scientific principles. The comparison in terms of analysis merely measures the same things in every case, but it leaves out far more important values which are impossible to measure cheaply.

The wider the ratio the more humus went with the plant foods. The comfrey was by far the richest but there was less of it because it broke down so far.

All heaps compared well with farmyard manure, but good compost is always richer in potash. The gardener's problem is always to get enough material. It is a pity to waste it on making something like an old-fashioned rubbish heap which wastes most of its plant foods, or on a bonfire, because one's last heap "went wrong" like some homemade wines.

—*By* LAWRENCE D. HILLS
Henry Doubleday Research Assn.
from *Compost, Comfrey and Green Manure*

Chapter 4

TESTING AND JUDGING THE CONDITION OF COMPOST

There are many tests and checks by which the various aspects of the composting process and the condition of compost may be judged. From the point of view of the over-all operation and the final product there are 3 groups of tests: (a) tests of the sanitary quality of the operation and of the finished product, i.e., pathogen and parasite destruction and the absence of flies and odors; (b) tests of the fertilizing or agricultural nutrients, nutrient conservation, the C/N ratio, and the compost value as shown by crop returns; and (c) economic tests, i.e., whether the total cost of producing the compost is less than its value as fertilizer plus the cost of disposal by other means, such as incineration or land fill.

The farm, the garden, or the small village compost operator usually will not be concerned with detailed tests other than those to confirm that the material is safe from a health standpoint, which will be judged from the temperature, and that it is satisfactory for the soil, which will be judged by appearance. However, in large-scale municipal composting, tests for the sanitary and agricultural quality of the compost are necessary for marketing, while tests of the process may be necessary for operation control.

Tests for organisms of public-health significance can be made by health organizations and laboratories when it is deemed desirable. Chemical tests for nitrogen in its different forms, phosphorus, potash, and the organic character of the material can be made by standard techniques, and are useful in analyzing the finished product and in determining the effect of different composting procedures. For routine day-to-day operations, temperature, appearance of material, odors, and the presence of flies are the important tests. Cleanliness and the absence of flies at the site, as well as the absence of large numbers of larvae in the piles, are criteria of the sanitary quality of the compost operation. Temperature is the best single indicator of the progress of aerobic composting

Three ways of ascertaining the temperature of the compost heap are: (a) digging into the stack and feeling the material; (b) checking the temperature of a rod after insertion into the pile; and (c) using a thermometer, which is generally most direct and accurate. Research worker is testing small experimental heaps.

and is also the basis for determining whether pathogens, parasites, and weed seeds are being destroyed.

The temperature of the compost can be checked by: (a) digging into the stack and feeling the temperature of the material; (b) feeling the temperature of a rod after insertion into the material; or (c) using a thermometer. Digging into the stack will give an approximate idea of the temperature. The material should feel very hot to the hand and be too hot to permit holding the hand in the pile for very long. Steam should emerge from the pile when opened. A metal or wooden rod inserted two feet into the pile for a period of 5 to 10 minutes for metal and 10 to 15 minutes for wood should be quite hot to the touch, in fact, too hot to hold. These temperature-testing techniques are satisfactory for the smaller village and farm composting operations. For large village and municipal compost operations, long-stem metal thermometers should be provided for observing the temperature of the composting mass at different places. A metal thermometer with a stem about two feet long and with a dial and pointer on the top is the most satisfactory type for temperature determinations, since it is not easily broken.

When aerobic composting progresses in a typical manner there will be a rapid rise in temperature to 55 degrees to 70 degrees centigrade in the first 3 days. In small piles or pits, a pause in the temperature rise often occurs somewhere between about 43 degrees and 50 degrees centigrade, during the transition from mesophilic to thermophilic decomposition. Larger piles or pits, such as might be used in composting on a municipal scale, do not usually show this interrupted temperature rise, owing to the greater insulating qualities and the rapidity with which the thermophilic organisms take over. After the initial temperature rise, a high temperature is maintained for several days during the active decomposition period, provided that aerobic conditions are maintained; then a slow decline of temperature starts as the rate of heat generation falls below the rate of heat radiation of the material. During this period the rate of bacterial activity is dropping faster than the temperature indicates, owing to the insulating qualities of the composted material.

The failure of a compost pile to attain a high temperature in a period of 3 to 6 days indicates that the pile is too small to retain the heat, that the moisture is either excessive or insufficient, or that insufficient organic material and nutrients are present for rapid decomposition.

The conditions within the composting mass, however, cannot be determined by the temperature alone. A temperature drop may result from the development of environmental conditions unfavorable to aerobic thermophiles, either through excessive heat, through the onset of anaerobic conditions, or through the lack of sufficient moisture. In rare instances, not usually encountered in composting municipal wastes, when some acid material has been added a low pH might also cause a lowering of the temperature. Hence other simple criteria than temperature must be used in judging the progress of a compost.

If a thermal kill is responsible for a decrease in temperature, the temperature for a time prior to the decrease will have been appreciably above 70 degrees centigrade. Anaerobic conditions are easily detected by an unpleasant odor, which is especially noticeable when the pile is disturbed. This indicates the need of aeration to maintain active decomposition and high temperatures. Also, when anaerobic conditions develop, the material inside the pile has an easily recognizable, pale green color, faintly luminous, that shows little change from day to day, whereas a properly aerobic compost is characterized by a progressively darkening color. Excess or lack of moisture is likewise easily detected by the experienced compost operator, who soon learns to tell by visual inspection when the compost is too wet or when additional moisture is needed. Within practical limits, a dry compost simply looks dry, and a compost that is too wet will show a tendency for liquid to drain from it and will look wet and soggy. An iron rod may be used to judge the moisture content at different depths of the pile. When inserted into the composting material the rod should become quite moist where it has touched the material.

A compost may be considered finished when it can be stored in large piles indefinitely without becoming anaerobic or generating appreciable heat, and may be put on agricultural land with safety because of its low C/N ratio or the poor availability of its carbon. The material, however, is still slowly active and will "ripen" somewhat in the large stacks.

—H. B. GOTAAS, *Composting*
World Health Organization

THE IDEAL COMPOST

Following are 17 checkpoints with which you can gauge the success of your compost. These points will serve as a standard from which you can determine the efficiency of your composting methods.

1. STRUCTURE: The material should be medium loose, not too tight, not packed, and not lumpy. The more crumbly the structure, the better it is.

2. COLOR: A black-brown color is best; pure black, if soggy and smelly, denotes an unfavorable fermentation with too much moisture and lack of air. A greyish, yellowish color indicates an excess of dead earth.

3. ODOR: The odor should be earthlike, or like good woods soil or humus. Any bad smell is a sign that the fermentation has not reached its final goal and that bacteriological breakdown processes are still going on. A musty, cellar-like odor indicates the presence of molds, sometimes also a hot fermentation, which has led to losses of nitrogen.

4. ACIDITY: A neutral or slightly acid reaction is best. Slight alkalinity can be tolerated. One has to keep in mind that

too acid a condition is the result of lack of air and too much moisture. Nitrogen-fixing bacteria and earthworms prefer the neutral to slight acid reaction. The pH range for a good compost is, therefore, 6.0 to 7.4, 7.0 being neutral. Below 6.0 the reaction is too acid for the development of nitrogen-fixing bacteria. Under certain circumstances, a reaction of 5.5 is required, for instance for potatoes, azaleas, rhododendrons, alpine flowers. In this case, one puts no lime, or very little, in the compost and increases the amount of woods soil and leaves as well as of conifer needles.

5. MIXTURE OF RAW MATERIALS: The proper mixture and proportion of raw materials comprise one of the most important factors. Indeed, it determines the final outcome of a compost fermentation and the fertilizer value of the compost. We have analyzed compost heaps with as low an organic matter content as 8 per cent which is only a little more than that of good humus earth (5 per cent), and we have had heaps with as much as 60 per cent, even 80 per cent, organic matter. In the latter case, frequently a hyper-humus or peat base had been used. On the average, we feel that an organic matter content of from 25 to 50 per cent should be present in the final product. This means that one to two-thirds of the original material ought to be organic matter: leaves, garbage, weeds, manure. The balance should be made up of earth, old rotted compost and lime. As far as the earth used is concerned, good topsoil is preferable. If dead or mineralized soil and subsoil is to be used, that which has frozen out over winter secures better results. Ditch scrapings, or soil from the bottom of a pond, are better frozen and exposed to air for a season, before being incorporated into a compost.

6. MOISTURE: Most of the composting failures we have seen, have resulted from the proper moisture conditions not being maintained. There is one simple rule: maintain a moisture content like that of a wrung out sponge. That is, no water should drip from a sample squeezed in the hand. But, by all means, do not let the compost get dry. This stops fermentation. No bacteria and earthworms can live without moisture. Too dry a condition leads to heating up, mold formation, to losses of nitrogen and finally to a complete cessation of fermentation.

7. POTASSIUM: The potassium content depends upon the original content of the earth used as well as of that of the

How well a compost fermentation and the fertilizer value of the final product turn out are determined by such major factors as the proper mixture and proportion of raw materials. Finished compost should have an organic matter content of from 25 to 50 per cent in order to provide a rich, well-balanced fertilizer.

plants used in the heap. Up to 5 per cent of the mineral content of plants consists of potassium. The more organic matter one uses in a heap the more potassium one will have. However, potassium is easily soluble and can be washed out by rain. The original material should not be scattered around, exposed to the weather, but incorporated in the heap at once. If the heap itself is exposed to drenching rains it will lose potassium. Fresh cow manure contains 11 pounds of potassium per ton. We take this as a guide and use the following specifications: 14 pounds per ton, very high; 12 pounds per ton, high; 8 pounds per ton, medium; two pounds per ton, low. Most of the samples received have been in the medium range. If potassium is low we advise increasing the organic matter content. Liquid manure is very rich in potash.

8. LIME: Usually there is not too much natural calcium in the original material, except when bone meal is used. Lime is added. A difficulty in the analytical procedure is that of sampling. Sometimes the composts contain lumps of lime which we discard, accounting only for the "digested" or absorbed fraction of lime. Nitrogen bacteria need lime, but not lumps, which are too alkaline (when coming in touch with moisture). Frequently, such lumps will lie inert in the soil afterward, too. The use of finely powdered lime and its distribution over the heap so that no lumping occurs are important.

Cow manure contains about 10 pounds, sheep manure 17 pounds, and poultry manure up to 55 pounds of lime per ton. Our scale for compost is: above 20 pounds per ton, extremely high; 15 pounds per ton, very high; 10 pounds per ton, high; 5 pounds per ton, medium; below 5 pounds per ton, low. The average compost contains 5 to 10 pounds per ton. Considering the fact that about 8 to 10 tons of compost are applied per acre, the 50 to 100 pounds of lime contained in the compost would not represent a complete lime supply for fields according to the average rule of one ton of lime per acre. But it is enough to give the nitrogen-fixing bacteria a stimulant.

9. MAGNESIUM: Many soils are low and even deficient in magnesium. The soil fraction of a compost earth is, therefore, low. Most of the magnesium derives from green leaves, for here magnesium is combined with the chlorophyll. The use of green garbage and leaves in a compost heap is thus important as a magnesium supply. Also the use of dolomite in place of lime would increase the magnesium content. Cow manure contains on the average two pounds per ton of magnesium, horse manure 3 pounds per ton, sheep manure 4 pounds per ton, poultry manure up to 16 pounds per ton. Our scale is: Above 4 pounds per ton, very high; two pounds per ton, high; one pound per ton, medium; below one pound, low. On the average, composts do not have too high a magnesium content, except when dolomite, sheep or poultry manure is used. Most of the samples we have tested were medium to low.

10. NITRATES: These are derived partly from the decomposition of proteins, from the use of good topsoil, from the addition of manure and—if everything goes well—from the

A frequent cause of composting failure is the lack of maintaining proper moisture conditions. To avoid this, adhere to one simple rule: Keep your compost's moisture content like that of a wrung-out sponge. A sample squeezed in the hand should have no water drip from it; yet it must never become dry.

activity of nitrogen-fixing bacteria during the fermentation. The latter work only at the described slightly acid to neutral reaction, and if the fermentation is aerobic and the heap does not heat up. As long as there is a hot fermentation no fixation takes place. Sometimes older heaps with well-rotted material still increase in nitrogen content. Cow manure contains 7 pounds per ton of total nitrogen (nitrates and ammonia), horse manure 13 pounds per ton, liquid manure 6 pounds per ton, sheep manure 19 pounds per ton, and chicken manure up to 34 pounds per ton. Our scale for nitrate nitrogen is: Above 18 pounds per ton, extremely high; 14 pounds per ton, high; 6 pounds per ton, medium; below 3 pounds per ton, low.

To maintain or increase the nitrogen by bacterial action: this is the ART of composting.

11. AMMONIA: Under unfavorable conditions, the ammonia fraction is higher than the nitrate fraction, especially in the beginning of composting and if fresh manure is added. Ammonia nitrogen is frequently lost and we, therefore, do not favor a high ammonia count. Little or no ammonia is preferred in a good compost heap. Too much lime and too great an

111

alkalinity favor the losses of nitrogen via ammonia. Putrefaction instead of fermentation also increases free ammonia. The heap has a typical smell which tells the composter at once that something is wrong. Our scale is: little or no ammonia in a good compost.

12. PHOSPHATES: A distinction must be made between available (soluble) phosphates and unavailable phosphates. In general, we determine only the available fraction. The "total" phosphate would also contain the unavailable fraction, but one does not know how much of this will really be used for plant growth. In order to receive a quick result from compost application only the available fraction counts. If the material is rich in colloidal humus and clay, it is possible that the unavailable fraction is stored and made available to plant growth in the course of time. The presence of calcium with phosphates is a means to balance the available fraction together with a rather neutral fraction. According to the rule calcium and phosphate should balance, but in practice we frequently find an irregular proportion of calcium and phosphate. Cow manure contains 6 pounds per ton phosphoric acid, sheep manure 15 pounds per ton, liquid manure very little (except where phosphates are used on the barn floor and in the gutter), chicken manure up to 34 pounds per ton. Our scale is: Available phosphate 15 pounds per ton, extremely high; 10 pounds per ton, very high; 6 pounds per ton, high; 4 pounds per ton, medium; below two pounds per ton, low. Many composts we have analyzed were medium to high.

13. MANGANESE: Manganese might be present in soils and plants. However, most of the soils we have had were low or deficient. Without the addition of manganese to the compost we doubt that a high manganese content can be had. When we speak of "high" here, of course, a trace is meant. The same is true for other trace elements, such as zinc and boron. The contents of these are usually expressed in parts per million, and 30 parts per million would already represent a respectable count. One must bear in mind that trace elements are beneficial to plants only as "traces," not in bulk. 30 ppm of boron in a soil already borders on the dangerous content. Since compost is not used straight, but is distributed over a wide acreage, 10 tons per acre for instance, a content of 300 ppm would not be objectionable in a compost.

14. SULPHATES: Free sulphates in connection with acidity

Nitrates, the nitrogen-rich factors of compost, are produced partially from the decomposition of proteins, from the use of good topsoil, from the addition of manure, and from the activity of nitrogen-fixing bacteria during the fermentation process. Nitrate nitrogen content of 14 pounds per ton is high.

mean the presence of sulphuric acid, which by all means should be avoided. The sulphate content, therefore, means one thing if the reaction is neutral, and quite another thing if the reaction is acid. Usually very little if any sulphates are found in compost.

15. NITRITES: These are the expression of an unfavorable breakdown of organic matter (protein) and should be avoided if the compost is to turn out well. The nitrite nitrogen is usually lost. With proper composting methods we have rarely encountered nitrites.

16. CHLORIDES: These come in only with sea water, heavily chlorinated water, or sewage water, and are usually not found in compost.

17. IODINE: No information has been obtained as to the presence of iodine in compost. It is possible that rain in the neighborhood of the seashore may contain iodine. Plants do not contain iodine, but manure may. Where milk

113

residues or water from whey is used in compost, some iodine might be present.

COMPOST FEVER CHART

Following is a report on composting experiments conducted by R. J. Emmons: "Three years ago I built a pen about 15 feet square, using steel posts and 48-inch woven wire. Into the pen went all kinds of organic surplus from our 4½ acres. The largest bulk of material was a mixture of red clover, timothy and blue grass mowed before seeds had matured enough to grow. With it was a wide variety of weeds and garden plants. In reducing the size of my active garden, the rye cover crop on the unused area was allowed to grow and mature. When ripe it was 6 feet high. It was mowed and tied into bundles using a band of straw, just to see whether I could remember how to do it. The bundles were shocked until winter and then taken one at a time into the edge of the woods and placed in a low tree crotch. After the pheasants cleaned out the grain, the straw went into the compost pen.

"Some of the partly rotten compost was used for mulch in the garden after the first and second winter and more fresh material added to the pen. Leaves, sweet corn stalks and some garbage added their bit of special flavor.

"I bought a shredder and adapted it for use with a tractor. A small experimental pile of compost, after being turned at 3 or 4-day intervals, was ready for use in about 3 weeks. It was full of the biggest, fattest earthworms I ever saw.

"In May a pile about 8 feet by 4 feet by 4 feet was shredded around a 4-inch diameter post and the post pulled out to provide a center chimney. The pile was composed of partly rotted organic material, small amounts of earth, finished compost, rotted cow manure and ground limestone. Old sunflower stalks were used to push the material into the shredder, since they added satisfactorily to the compost and did not damage the shredder as sticks might have done. Forty-eight hours after shredding, the temperature of the pile was taken by inserting a laboratory thermometer into the pile about 12 inches down in the center chimney.

"Two days after the first temperature was taken, the pile was turned and again piled around a 4-inch post. The

114

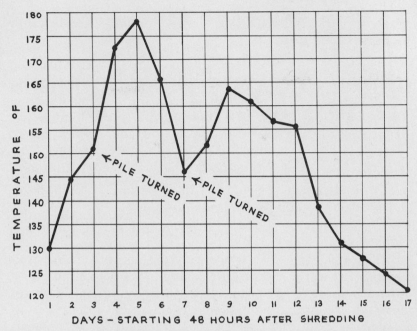

Chart of composting experiment conducted by R. J. Emmons shows rise of temperature from start of heap through fifth day, then drop until second turning on seventh day, followed by two-day increase, and finally a gradual change to finished compost in 17 days. Material was dark and well-decomposed.

post was again removed to provide center ventilation. The rapid temperature rise after this turning, to the maximum of 178 degrees Fahrenheit indicates aerobic bacteria predominate at this stage of composting. This is further indicated by the second abrupt temperature rise after the second turning 4 days later.

"The temperature chart shows how the temperature gradually dropped off until by the seventeenth day the earthworms had started moving into the cooler parts of the pile. By this time the compost was well decomposed, granular in texture and dark brown or black in color. I find it is excellent for use in the garden, flower beds and around the shrubs and fruit trees."

Chapter 5

GARDEN COMPOSTING IN VARIOUS SECTIONS OF THE COUNTRY

Certain areas of the country present gardeners and farmers with special problems in making compost and using it to full advantage. Principally, the adverse soil composition and hot, arid weather conditions prevalent in the Southwest and in portions of Florida cause particular difficulties for composting in these sectors.

The following discussions of the soils and composting methods for warm and dry areas, and of successful examples of overcoming the handicaps where these conditions exist, are aimed at bringing a better understanding and practical suggestions to those who live there. Also included is a personal-experience report from a Maine gardener showing how he adopted the rich natural materials available along the coastline to his composting and garden's benefit. Further details for various sections will be found in the chapters on How to Use Compost and The Results of Composting.

COMPOSTING IN SOUTHERN, WARM AND DRY CLIMATES

Dry, warm climates present quite a few problems which are different from those encountered in moderate and northern climates. Drought counteracts bacterial action and earthworm growth, for all the microlife of the soil needs moisture. Then too, warm soils, which heat up easily, weather away very quickly under prolonged, intensive sun radiation. Under such conditions, even granite rock gets brittle and swiftly weathers into a sandy, gravelly soil. Such granite decomposition soil, in the South and Southwest, is very fertile as long as the rains and natural moisture support plant growth. Without moisture it can remain desert. Chemical analysis reveals a high percentage of available minerals, potassium and phosphate, for instance, and less calcium. If there is some organic matter present, then with the rains a high nitrate

116

content might be found. But, without organic matter, these soils wash out very easily and lose their high chemical rating.

The washed-out products together with clay and soluble humic acids are then deposited in the valley bottoms. There they may cake into a hard pan, the so-called adobe soils of Southern California, which make excellent material for adobe building bricks, but are exasperating to cultivate. These soils thus fall under two extreme categories, the hard-caked variety, just mentioned, and the very loose, crumbly type on the slopes. The latter, with alternate, increasing washing and burning, become unfertile, eroded and gullied unless there is a plant cover.

The amount of clay present determines whether a soil will hold its own or lose out. Clay is a colloid which absorbs and retains moisture. When drought sets in, the clay soils hold out longer, thus enabling soil life to establish itself over a longer period and to form humus. Once humus forms, and is not lost again, the situation is fairly secure. The soils with humus hold and lend themselves to successful cultivation. As long as there is moisture, rain, even mist, and/or irrigation these soils will be extremely fertile. However, humus is broken down under intensive sun radiation and conditions of drought. Shading, with cover crops or mulching, is extremely important.

If these soils are constantly watered, and do not dry out, then a natural balance between precipitation and evaporation can be maintained and a most beautiful humus soil will develop, even without the addition of organic matter, compost or manure, chiefly by means of the microlife naturally present. It is then up to man to maintain the fertility and ideal conditions by cover crops, avoiding excessive irrigation which would cake the soil, and by proper crop rotations which balance exhausting crops (corn, cabbage, beets) with restoring crops (legumes, or plants and trees) which shade the soil. In summing up, one can say that the control of moisture, shade and humus decides whether such soils will hold or be lost.

Rules for Dry-Area Composting

This behavior of soils can give us leads for the development of proper composting methods in a hot, dry climate. The most important rule: Never let your compost pile dry out. Eighty per cent of all the compost piles which the writer saw in California in recent weeks were too dry. When such material is spread on a dry or caked soil it will not be absorbed, even when plowed or harrowed under. It will lie inert and have little value until the rain comes. Much valuable time is lost. It is *this* time which counts in the improvement of the soil and *not* the time which is spent in attending properly to compost practices. The composting which is done *right* will pay.

Bulky material such as dried-out, tall weeds, the leaves of orange, avocado, and eucalyptus trees, even sage, can be composted if shredded. Many of the compost heaps contained these materials but they were dry with lots of air spaces and dry soil in between. No fermentation could take place. It is best, therefore, to place a compost heap under the shelter of trees to help against its drying out. (Contrary to general belief, eucalyptus trees do no harm when used for wind protection. If they grow too tall, top them and sever the roots which tend to spread out too far into the orchard or field.)

If there is no natural shelter available a simple shed can be built to take its place. Set a few upright posts; these need not be high, just tall enough to enable you to work the heap easily. Then use some perforated material as a cover (tin, for instance) which will give enough shade yet let the rain through. Slant this roof so that the rain can still run onto the heap. A chicken-wire screen covered with large leaves, Spanish moss, or weeds also makes an adequate shelter. If you have irrigation at hand, lead a ditch or pipe near the heap. Build the heap up in a pit, about two feet in depth, and let the water soak through from underneath and around the heap. In the first stages you can let the water run on the material. It is very important that all dry material be wet down thoroughly while building your heap.

After shredding, mix the organic material with earth, and never forget to cover the whole heap as soon as it is completed. If you do not have enough earth for this cover then use leaves, old sacking, plants, anything which does not seal it up yet still provides a skin for it. Under the warm conditions prevalent there in the South fermentation will be much more rapid than in the North. Well built heaps are often ready after two months. And the writer has seen heaps in fine condition, described as considerably less than two months old, where the pit system was used with the addition of earthworms.

118

A completely rotted compost should be used up quickly. Of course, as long as it is kept sponge moist and covered, it will keep for many months, maybe more than a year. But if it is allowed to dry out it will lose a great deal, particularly nitrogen. It should be worked into the surface right with the planting of the crops.

A half-rotted compost of coarse material is best for mulching on top of the soil, covering the interspaces between plants or trees. It is only necessary to mulch between the rows in groves of full grown orange and avocado trees, or of young walnut trees.

For most young trees mulching nearer to the trunk is advisable, unless one uses cover crops. But a ring, one to two feet in width, should be left free around the trunk. Sometimes one sees the compost or mulch piling up against the tree trunks. When this happens, the air bark is covered and rots, is given over to infections and pests which hide underneath the loosened bark. When the area around the trees builds up too high through mulching, it should be leveled out again. One often sees trees in gardens which are too deeply "buried." If you dig out such a tree you will see old roots growing horizontally and downward, while the young roots grow upward. This might cause disturbances in the circulation of the sap, resulting in the gum bleeding of apricots, almonds and peaches.

In connection with the humus management, the right handling of irrigation is also important. Basin irrigation, where the water stands for a long time until it soaks in, crusts the soil and produces a hardpan underneath. Caked surfaces resist irrigation and lead to water losses. Mineralized soils, without absorbing humus, also behave in this way. The cultivated surface is best for irrigation; so is the furrow system. Here, one allows just enough water to run down the furrow to reach the other end.

So often one hears complaints about the lack of water and then sees people wasting great quantities through wrong practices on caked soils. The most ideal conditions for absorption are present just after a mulch cover has been worked in or removed. After irrigating orchards or gardens, one might mulch again to hold the moisture. This is easily done in small gardens, but large areas present difficulties.

Agriculture in extreme climatic conditions such as those of Florida or California tends toward onesidedness. The diversified pattern has been lost. The fact that one can make a living by growing a few specialized crops on small acreages has produced such phenomena as the "farmer" or "orchardist" who has *only* beans, or artichokes, or lettuce, or oranges, or avocados. These partial or complete monocultures draw upon the soil resources in a onesided way. Mineral and trace mineral deficiencies occur, plants gradually get weaker, a very specialized, monotonous microflora develops and the farmer is surprised that plant diseases and pests increase. In order to survive, he takes the labor and expense of spraying insecticides in his stride. When balancing organic methods are mentioned the objection is raised that they are too complicated and involve too much labor. Old orange growers tell us that in their youth, maybe 40 or 50 years ago, no pests or diseases were encountered. In those times, manure and mulching was the order of the day. They changed to modern methods. It is so easy to call up the nearest airport and have a plane come and spray insecticides. The changes of quality in foods and soils which result are not taken into consideration. The general public is not yet quality and health conscious. People still judge by size, packaging and labeling.

It is difficult to introduce a balanced, diversified system in a situation as onesided as a citrus growth or a vegetable farm which produces only one or two kinds of crops. It may be necessary to compromise, for example, by using as many different kinds of materials as possible for compost (garbage, leaves, weeds, etc.) in order to add something "different" to the soil.

In California, alfalfa hay is considered by the old timers to be the ideal mulch for fruit trees. One of these men told us that he used it as long as it was cheap and never had any trouble with his trees. Nowadays it is too expensive, but organic composting methods could take its place. This same man told us that were one of his groves to die off, he would plant alfalfa to rejuvenate the soil and sell the hay for mulch. He felt that this would be more profitable. Twenty years ago, it took 125 oranges to fill a box, now it takes 185 to 225 to fill the same size box. The harvest of a successful grower, two decades ago, was 1100 boxes per acre. From the same land, he now harvests 800 boxes.

Were I in possession of an orange grove or a truck garden monoculture, I would try to grab any and every possible organic material from outside plus small amounts of manure and apply it to my land. As a matter of fact, I observed in many of the small 1 to 3-acre lots and gardens that, with the lush and fast growth of trees in these Southern climates and sufficient irrigation, such large masses of organic matter can be grown that they more than suffice for the fertilizer needs of the land. In one two-acre garden of mixed fruit trees and vegetables a two years' supply of compost was collected in one year. In fact, it was necessary to advise the owner to step his production down a bit. In this particular situation it will come true that compost will be a natural cash crop.

It is the small lot which can be intensively developed, while with increasing size the problems grow. This again should stimulate consideration of a possible future development: Subdivision in mixed cultures which can be handled by one man, instead of large monocultures. Pests dwindle away in such small controlled areas. California, at present, is considered by man to be the new frontier. She has a weekly influx of thousands of people who seek a better future in a favorable climate. Large monocultures will not be available to nourish and supply such an increasing population with work. The small, diversified grower could make a living and survive. The trend in population, the soil, and health conditions favor the natural, organic, self-sustaining unit. These alone will be able to absorb the increasing population and make possible its survival.

—Dr. Ehrenfried Pfeiffer

FALL COMPOSTING IN FLORIDA

Fall is spring in South Florida. Now's the time gardeners plant annual crops and start boosting perennials and fruit trees into full production.

After summer's searing heat and tropical rains have leached the porous soil, growers must get busy restoring fertility. The smart ones know that what their sandy land needs most is organic material to reduce pH, supply nutrients, and hold moisture. October is compost time for them.

Some, like Mrs. Elsie Picot of Miami, start a compost heap each fall to use the following year. Others follow the mulch-composting method of her neighbors, the Raymond Underwoods. A visit with these successful organic gardeners proves that both methods work.

Mrs. Picot makes compost in old garbage cans. She layers leaves, builders' sand, and cleanings from her parakeet cages. (In case you're wondering how anyone could salvage enough material from parakeets to make compost, Mrs. Picot breeds the birds and each of her outdoor cages is almost as big as a living room.)

One-third compost and two-thirds garden soil is the proportion Mrs. Picot likes for October seed beds.

Some of the compost also goes into the potting mixture she makes each fall. This mixture is excellent for carrying house plants through the winter, and Elsie Picot gives it credit for helping her win many blue ribbons for her begonias, African violets, and seedling orchids. Here's her formula:

3 parts peat moss
1 part sand
1 part dried sheep manure (use part sieved chicken manure when available)
1 part charcoal
1 part compost or leaf mold
¼ part bird gravel
⅛ part bone meal

Peat moss should be wet. Mix ingredients thoroughly.

The Raymond Underwoods haven't made a compost heap in years, but they are enthusiastic about their compost grinder. They actually make compost right on top of their garden soil. About once a week they shred leaves and cuttings from their own and neighborhood yards. These they spread as mulch.

"We don't cultivate or hoe, just mulch," says Mrs. Underwood. As the mulch decays it feeds the soil and attracts earthworms which aerate it. Their garden is an example of what this kind of program can do.

In a highly alkaline area where citrus are supposed to curl up and die, they have a glossy-green orange tree, a tangelo, and a grapefruit. The trees keep them supplied with fruit most of the year.

Their fig tree, so loaded with fruit they ask friends to help them eat it, flourishes in contradiction to local experts who say root knot nematodes are supposed to kill figs in South Florida.

A Hayden mango furnishes bushels of succulent fruit each spring, and an avocado tree bears so heavily the branches must be propped up. Red Ceylon tropical peaches and Key limes also contribute their share of vitamins and delicious eating.

But the Underwood yard, an average-size city lot, isn't cluttered in spite of its abundance. There's room for a velvety expanse of lawn. Secret of the thick, green lawn is cottonseed meal.

"Cottonseed is cheap in the fall and we spread it around almost everything," say the Underwoods. "We used it on the grass in '48 and '49 and haven't used any fertilizer at all since. Yet we're told grass must be fertilized several times a year down here. We wish more gardeners would try cottonseed meal this fall. They'll have a pleasant surprise."

—JEANNE O. WELLENKAMP

COMPOST FOR THE WEST COAST

An excellent authority on the use of the rich compost concentrate from garden composting bins on growing fruit and vegetables is Mrs. E. A. Turlington, 1335 Appleton Way, Venice, California. Mrs. Turlington has a large backyard laid out as a heavily-producing garden, with some two dozen fruit trees—citrus, plums, peaches—scattered along fences and throughout the garden. She averages 75 dollars a month towards the family food budget, and has practically reared a large family on the organic fruit and vegetables she produces in her year-round gardening activities.

"I have two big compost bins," says Mrs. T. "All the weeds, grass clippings from the lawns, bean vines, corn stalks, vegetable trimmings from the kitchen, and all other plant waste go into the bins. During our winter (rainy season) I also put in egg shells, all meat and fish scraps. I sometimes gather a load of fresh or dried seaweed from the beaches and pile this into the bins. Occasionally I water down the bins. They are rich with earthworms.

"During warmer weather 3 to 4 months are required to reduce the material in the bins to usable compost. During cold seasons more time is required. Using this rich soil compost made by bacterial and earthworm action is the base of my gardening work and soil rehabilitation," she continues. "In advising the new gardener who has a good supply of rich compost in his bins and wants to know how to use it, I say use this on all producing vegetables, fruits and flowers.

123

"In the late fall, when my fruit trees have gone into the dormant period, I put buckets of compost around base of trees out to the drip line. Scatter it right on top of the mulch, rake it on lightly. Then I let the winter rains and snow filter its goodness down to the tree roots. I put perhaps a half dozen buckets (35–50 pounds) to the tree. It works wonders.

"In the spring work up the soil where you are going to plant vegetables. Lay out rows, then scatter compost along tops of rows, about a bucketful to 10 row feet, rake in lightly. Then plant the seeds or plants, water down well. This is my method that I have used to produce bumper vegetable crops for 15 years in my present garden.

"Everything in the garden loves this composted soil concentrate from my compost bins. Pole beans, cucumbers, sweet corn, squash, radishes, lettuce, carrots, tomatoes, green peppers, berries—boysen, logan, and black. Compost-feed your berries in fall when you cut back dead canes. Rake in a water bucket of compost to two row feet of cane berry row. Don't work this compost in, just let the rains and snow filter it down. I also use good steer manure—scatter profusely along base of vines during the dormant season."

Mrs. Turlington says plants use the rich food of compost slowly. It's not a shot-in-the-arm feeding like chemical fertilizers. You put back into the soil what you take out. Use of compost mellows the soil, according to Mrs. T. It develops plants and flowers that are healthier, more resistant to insects and disease. Garden products fed on compost taste better, she insists. Composting adds humus, bacteria, earthworms to gardening soil. Compost-fed soil doesn't dry out.

—GORDON L'ALLEMAND

MAINE COAST COMPOSTING

For years I had thought the idea of compost was simply to throw all the trash and garbage in one spot until it could be buried in the garden in the spring.

Then I bought a farm and now I know as well as you do that there are scientific reasons and methods of composting.

Our farm is about 100 acres of beautiful shoreline property on the coast of Maine, about half of it woodland.

This is not a tale of poor soil brought back to life. Most of it was good when we took over. A commercial truck farmer had owned it for 6 years. I suppose he used commercial fertilizer. In fact I noticed a definite lack of earthworms, which I attribute to this cause. Before the truck farmer, a fisherman had lived on the farm for years and had raised cattle for meat. Whatever had happened to the earth, it still seemed in fine condition. We did nothing to it the first spring, and the fields flourished with clover and timothy.

Soon I realized that we were ideally situated for compost farming at no cost beyond transportation. That was a big item, though, that first year. My first successful compost pile was built with a wheelbarrow and two bushel baskets.

The first thing I did was to build a box, 6 by 12 feet on sodless ground. Then I took to the woods with my wheelbarrow to get a good quantity of rich black humus for the bottom of the compost pile. I reasoned this would be full of bacteria and make a good "starter."

When we started to clean up the farm, I decided to clear out a lovely birch grove for a picnic ground. I cut out all the small bushes with pruners and saved them to pile between the rows of my future raspberry patch. I had often noticed that raspberries grew wild in and close to piles of slash left from lumbering operations. I raked all the leaves into a pile and a third pile was devoted to dozens of birch limbs that had been left lying on the ground where someone had trimmed a firewood tree years before. It was so rotten that I could break 3 inch limbs by stamping on them.

These, I decided, could go into the compost pile. After spreading them about 6 inches deep in the driveway, I drove the passenger car back and forth over them until they pulverized so fine I could scoop them up with a shovel. It is recommended that leaves be chopped before composting as they mat together. I had no way to do this, no chopper, grinder nor even a hammer mill. Therefore I thinly sprinkled my leaves, mixed with the fine birch wood, between layers of my most precious ingredient—*rockweed,* a coarse family of seaweeds which grows attached to rocks.

This rockweed was a constant joy. It washed ashore after every storm. Three of our beaches are accessible by car, and load after load of rockweed was transferred from shore to compost box. Rockweed is comprised largely of air cells which cause it to float. Due to this it shrinks more than anything else I have used but it is also the easiest to collect.

I gathered mine at first in bushel baskets. It weighed 30

pounds to the bushel when green. A garden fork or pitchfork is fine for handling it, although I used my bare hands at first. After I had picked up all that I found lying at the high water mark, I could go down to the ledges at low tide and cut it off the rocks.

Hay on the farm had not been mown for years. As a precaution against fire we raked out as much as possible of the old dead hay. It couldn't have had much value in that condition, yet it would add lightness to the soil and it all went between heavy layers of rockweed.

When our apples started to ripen we made an unhappy discovery. A whole apple, in the compost, would be preserved a remarkably long time. We found it necessary to let the windfalls begin rotting on the ground, or to smash them to a pulp before adding them to the heap.

One day the children brought some crabs from the shore. I was requested to cook the lifeless things. Instead I relegated them to the compost heap. Three days later I discovered, with a tinge of horror, that the creatures had revived and were thriving in the top layer of seaweed.

I learned that crabs, all fish in fact, were fine fertilizer, and local fishermen offered to get them for me if I would pick them up at the wharves. Of course it was a nuisance for the fisherman, so I didn't accept too many, but I did arrange to place one layer of dead crabs for every 12 inches of compost.

The available livestock manure was pretty poor stuff. The price was cheap and so was the product. It was so dry that even flies seemed uninterested in it. Although I used a little, I fear it added little except bulk. With the ocean products, though, manure seemed unnecessary.

I allowed myself one extravagance. Fishermen buy bait, pure fish scraps from the canning factories, at $1.50 a bushel. I purchased two bushels. (You can find it in the dry form under the name of fish meal in most garden supply shops.)

I did not use lime in my compost. We used an old wood range for cooking and all the wood ash was sprinkled over the compost regardless of which layer I happened to be working on. On calm days I sifted the ashes directly on to the pile with an ordinary kitchen sieve. This not only made an even distribution but was necessary to remove old nails, as we burned a lot of old used lumber.

When the town mowed the roadsides I asked the workmen to give me the grass and weeds instead of taking them

126

to the town dump. Within a reasonable distance of our farm, they brought me all the rakings, saving a lot of extra hours and gas for the town. The staggering heap made my little compost box look silly. Needless to say the town hay never got composted, but the following year it turned out to be dandy mulching material.

Our land also receives two direct treatments. Depending upon the crop. One year it is mulched with sawdust. The next year a dressing of poultry manure is added and the whole plowed under. I use more than the recommended amount of poultry manure as I feel that the decaying sawdust will compensate for the extra nitrogen. I have had no burned crops.

The sawdust is free at the local sawmill. Our neighbor, a chicken farmer, gives me the dressing in exchange for cleaning out the pens. He used to bed with wood shavings, but I offered to share bedding expenses with him if he would change to peanut hulls and sugar cane. The land seems rich enough now to handle these raw applications.

Until recently I haven't had enough equipment to make compost for our entire acreage. We composted what we could. I made an interesting observation. While plowing, I have noticed that the poorer land wouldn't hold an even plow depth. At spots the plow even skidded to the surface and required extra weight to "bite in." The plot that received my first amateur composting efforts takes a plow beautifully to a depth of 12 to 14 inches. I noticed last fall that I had a fine colony of earthworms, and I now feel that my soil is in excellent physical condition, has an abundance of bacteria, and will continue to yield good crops.

—J. B. Ames

Chapter 6

MATERIALS FOR COMPOSTING

With very few exceptions, any organic material is a potential candidate for the compost heap. Any vegetable or animal matter, and even some minerals, can be returned to the soil through composting. Taking a look around you, then, you can easily discredit the oft-heard complaint, "I just can't find enough material for compost." Around the home grounds you can see weeds, grass clippings, kitchen garbage, leaves, garden residues and other organic matter. If this material is not enough, you can probably go to nearby farms and buy spoiled hay, manure and other wastes. Another great source of compost material, often untapped, lies in the various industries nearby.

Here's a system used successfully by many gardeners: First, page through the classified section of your telephone directory; make a list of a few promising firms (lumber companies, mills, meat packing houses, quarries, dairies, leather tanneries, city park departments, riding stables, wholesale food companies, etc.). Then you are ready to embark on a most rewarding collection trip. If you can't borrow a pick-up truck or small trailer, you most likely can rent one for a few hours at a nominal charge. Or else, you can always use the trunk of your car to haul materials back to your garden.

A NEW ENGLANDER'S EXPERIENCE

Here is the experience of Betty Brinhart, which is typical of many organic gardeners who have gone on material finding trips. Her experience is further proof that materials are readily available, and that only a little time and effort are needed to seek them out:

"Hampshire County, Massachusetts, like so many other counties in the United States, is chuck full of hidden sources of organic fertilizers. And, if an organic gardener would only take the time to seek them out, he would find that most of these fertilizers are free for the asking. Free to take home, and, with them, rebuild his present soil condition to its height of productivity.

"The work it takes to locate these free organic fertilizers, to bring them home, and to apply them to our soil is little compared to the enjoyment of good eating and splendid health that comes only from working in the open air and eating organically grown fruits and vegetables.

"Organic methods of gardening, I well know, are not as widely practiced as they should be. For this reason many organic gardeners may hesitate in approaching different concerns for their organic wastes. May I truthfully say, 'Have

A variety of garden waste materials can be returned to the soil through composting. Typical items might include weeds, plant residues, lawn clippings and leaves. Household wastes, such as kitchen garbage, should also be used.

no fear.' Although these people do not garden organically, down deep in their hearts, they know that organic gardening is best by far.

"When I approached several of these different concerns in the county, and asked if they would be so kind as to give their organic wastes to interested gardeners to use as fertilizer, most of them replied, 'Yes,' immediately. At one poultry farm, I politely stood by and listened for half an hour while the farmer explained why all soils should be rebuilt organically. Although he is not an organic gardener completely, he certainly believes in the sound method.

"I visited and phoned many different business establishments throughout the county in search of sources of free organic wastes for all gardeners in the area who might be interested. Wherever I went, I was greeted with a smile when the purpose of my visit was explained. Not one person turned a cold shoulder. Most were very interested in the cause, and were glad to help.

"Many a small business, that heretofore had placed a slight charge on their wastes, decided to eliminate it completely where gardeners were concerned.

"As for sources of sawdust and wood shavings, you might have found that lumber yards charge slightly for these two products. But, if you were to take the time and visit the lumber mill up in the hills, you would find that you can take all of the sawdust and shavings you like, and, at the same time, be thanked for moving it.

"If you are a sincere organic gardener, you know the great wealth in mulching with shredded brush trimmings. This valuable material is not as difficult to obtain as one might think. Early spring, or late fall, utility companies send their crews out to trim all branches overhanging electric or telephone wires.

"These crews all have shredders that chop the branches up fine enough so that the material can be used for mulching. After talking with the head of one such crew, I learned that anyone in the area where the crew is working may have this material free. You need only to approach the crew and tell them where you want it dumped. I am sure other such crews throughout the country will do the same for interested gardeners and farmers.

"So hike up your trousers, or tie your apron strings tighter, and go out after some of this free organic fertilizer. The world is really on your side, so don't be afraid to state your purpose for wanting organic wastes. Be wise, economize, and rebuild your soil's fertility with good, free, organic wastes!"

ENRICHING COMPOST

Beside the basic materials, the quality of the heap can be boosted considerably by the addition of lime, if needed,

In many places, you can get sawdust without charge—all you have to do is haul it away. Used as a mulch and soil conditioner, sawdust can increase the productivity of any garden. It's also a useful addition to the compost heap.

and rock powders and other special materials for bringing the nutrient content of the heap up to par. If an acid compost is wanted, lime must not be added. If a distinctly acid compost is needed for such acid-loving plants as rhododendrons, camellias and blueberries, acid peat may be used instead of soil. For compost which is to be used for plants which prefer neutral or slightly alkaline soils, a sprinkling of pulverized limestone should be added to each layer of the heap. The limestone will neutralize the acids and tend to prevent the escape of volatile fermentation products which would otherwise diffuse into the atmosphere. Pulverized dolomite instead of ordinary limestone which is a calcium-magnesium lime may be used in making the heap. Other forms of calcium which are recommended for the compost heap are pulverized oyster and clam shells and egg shells.

If the soil to be treated with compost is known to be low in phosphorus, raw pulverized phosphate rock should be used in alternate layers with the pulverized limestone. Other deficient elements may likewise be added by using different

131

rock powders such as granite dust and potash rock. These rock powders will probably have to be purchased, but it is possible that you can find a way to gather native rocks and have them crushed by a local processor.

Deficient elements can be added in other ways, especially by adding to the compost heap plants which contain them. Seaweeds, such as the kelps, are rich in such elements as iodine, boron, copper, magnesium, calcium, phosphorus and many others and should be used in the compost heap if available locally. The water hyacinths which grow so abundantly in the rivers of the South are especially rich in many of the elements which are apt to be deficient in the soil. Autumn leaves, which will be discussed more thoroughly later, are a teeming source of trace minerals which are not found in upper layers of soil; they should constitute a major part of every compost heap.

PERCENTAGE COMPOSITION OF VARIOUS MATERIALS

Material	Nitrogen	Phosphoric Acid	Potash
Alfalfa hay	2.45	0.50	2.10
Apple, fruit	0.05	0.02	0.10
Apple, leaves	1.00	0.15	0.35
Apple pomace	0.20	0.02	0.15
Apple skins (ash)	....	3.08	11.74
Ash from Cana tree	....	....	15.65
Banana skins (ash)	....	3.25	41.76
Banana stalk (ash)	....	2.34	49.40
Barley (grain)	1.75	0.75	0.50
Bat guano	6.00	9.00	....
Beet wastes (roots)	0.25	0.10	0.50
Beet wastes	0.40	0.40	3.00
Bloodmeal	15.00	1.30	0.70
Bone meal	4.00	21.00	0.20
Brewer's grains (wet)	0.90	0.50	0.05
Brigham tea (ash)	....	....	5.94
Ground bone, burned	....	34.70	....
By-product from silk mills	8.37	1.14	0.12
Cantaloupe rinds (ash)	....	9.77	12.21
Castor-bean pomace	5.50	2.25	1.13

(*Continued*)

Seaweed and river grasses (being hauled from the St. Lawrence River) are excellent for enriching compost with many trace minerals as iodine, boron, copper, magnesium, calcium and phosphorus. Use these materials when available.

Material	Nitrogen	Phosphoric Acid	Potash
Cattail reed and stems of water lily	2.02	0.81	3.43
Cattail seed	0.98	0.39	1.71
*Cattle manure (fresh)	0.29	0.17	0.10
Coal ash (anthracite)	....	0.125	0.125
Coal ash (bituminous)	....	0.45	0.45
Cocoa shell dust	1.04	1.49	2.71
Coffee grounds	2.08	0.32	0.28
Coffee grounds (dried)	1.99	0.36	0.67
Corncobs (ground, charred)	....	....	2.01
Corncob ash	....	....	50.00
Common crab	1.95	3.60	0.20
Corn (grain)	1.65	0.65	0.40
Corn (green forage)	0.30	0.13	0.33
Cottonseed	3.15	1.25	1.15
Cottonseed meal	7.00	2.50	1.50
Cottonseed-hull ashes	....	8.70	23.93
Cotton waste from factory	1.32	0.45	0.36
Cowpeas, green forage	0.45	0.12	0.45
Cowpeas, seed	3.10	1.00	1.20

(*Continued*)

Material	Nitrogen	Phosphoric Acid	Potash
Crabgrass (green)	0.66	0.19	0.71
Cucumber skins (ash)	....	11.28	27.20
Dog manure	1.97	9.95	0.30
Dried jellyfish	4.60	....	....
Dried mussel mud	0.72	0.35	....
*Duck manure (fresh)	1.12	1.44	0.49
Eggs	2.25	0.40	0.15
Eggshells (burned)	....	0.43	0.29
Eggshells	1.19	0.38	0.14
Feathers	15.30	....	....
Field bean (seed)	4.00	1.20	1.30
Field bean (shells)	1.70	0.30	1.30
Fire-pit ashes from smokehouses	....	....	4.96
Fish scrap (red snapper and grouper)	7.76	13.00	0.38
Fish scrap (fresh)	6.50	3.75	....
Fresh water mud	1.37	0.26	0.22
Garbage rubbage (New York City)	3.50	0.80	3.25
Garbage tankage	1.50	0.75	0.75
Greasewood ashes	....	....	12.61
Garden beans, beans and pods ..	0.25	0.08	0.30
Gluten feed	4.50	....	....
Greensand	....	1.50	5.00
Grape leaves	0.45	0.10	0.35
Grapes (fruit)	0.15	0.07	0.30
Grapefruit skins (ash)	....	3.58	30.60
Hair	14.00	....	....
Harbor mud	0.99	0.77	0.05
*Hen manure (fresh)	1.63	1.54	0.85
Hoofmeal and horndust	12.5	1.75	....
*Horse manure (fresh)	0.44	0.17	0.35
Incinerator ash	0.24	5.15	2.33
Kentucky bluegrass (green) ...	0.66	0.19	0.71
Kentucky bluegrass (hay)	1.20	0.40	1.55
King crab (dried and ground) ..	10.00	0.25	0.06
King crab (fresh)	2.30	....	....
Leather (acidulated)	7.50	....	....
Leather (ground)	11.00	....	....
Leather, scrap (ash)	....	2.16	0.35

(Continued)

| | | Phosphoric | |
Material	Nitrogen	Acid	Potash
Lemon culls (California)	0.15	0.06	0.26
Lemon skins (ash)	....	6.30	31.00
Lobster refuse	4.50	3.50	....
Lobster shells	4.60	3.52	....
Milk	0.50	0.30	0.18
Mussels	0.90	0.12	0.13
Molasses residue in manufacture			
of alcohol	0.70	....	5.32
Oak leaves	0.80	0.35	0.15
Oats, grain	2.00	0.80	0.60
Olive pomace	1.15	0.78	1.26
Olive refuse	1.22	0.18	0.32
Orange culls	0.20	0.13	0.21
Orange skins (ash)	....	2.90	27.00
Pea pods (ash)	....	1.79	9.00
Peach leaves	0.90	0.15	0.60
Peanuts (seed or kernels)	3.60	0.70	0.45
Peanut shells	0.80	0.15	0.50
Peanut shells (ash)	....	1.23	6.45
*Pigeon manure (fresh)	4.19	2.24	1.41
Pigweed (rough)	0.60	0.16	....
Pine needles	0.46	0.12	0.03
Potatoes (tubers)	0.35	0.15	0.50
Potatoes (leaves and stalks) ...	0.60	0.15	0.45
Potato skins, raw (ash)	....	5.18	27.50
Poudrette	1.46	3.68	0.48
Powderworks waste	2.50	....	17.00
Prune refuse	0.18	0.07	0.31
Pumpkins, fresh	0.16	0.07	0.26
Pumpkin seeds	0.87	0.50	0.45
Rabbit brush ashes	....	....	13.04
Ragweed, great	0.76	0.26	....
Red clover, hay	2.10	0.50	2.00
Redtop hay	1.20	0.35	1.00
Residues from raw sugar	1.14	8.33	....
Rockweed	1.90	0.25	3.68
Roses (flower)	0.30	0.10	0.40
Rhubarb stems	0.10	0.04	0.35
Rock and mussel deposits			
from sea	0.22	0.09	1.78

(Continued)

Material	Nitrogen	Phosphoric Acid	Potash
Salt-marsh hay	1.10	0.25	0.75
Salt mud	0.40	....	....
Sardine scrap	7.97	7.11	....
Seaweed (Atlantic City)	1.68	0.75	4.93
Sewage sludge from sewer beds	0.74	0.33	0.24
*Sheep manure (fresh)	0.55	0.31	0.15
Shoddy and felt	8.00	....	....
Shrimp heads (dried)	7.82	4.20	....
Shrimp waste	2.87	9.95	....
Siftings from oyster shell mound	0.36	10.38	0.09
Silk worm cocoons	9.42	1.82	1.08
Sludge	2.00	1.90	0.30
Sludge (activated)	5.00	3.25	0.60
Soot from chimney flues	5.25	1.05	0.35
Spanish moss	0.60	0.10	0.55
Starfish	1.80	0.20	0.25
String bean strings and stems (ash)	....	4.99	18.03
Sunflower seed	2.25	1.25	0.79
Sweet potato skins, boiled (ash)	....	3.29	13.89
Sweet potatoes	0.25	0.10	0.50
*Swine manure (fresh)	0.60	0.41	0.13
Tanbark (ash)	....	0.34	3.80
Tanbark ash (spent)	....	1.75	2.00
Tankage	6.00	5.00	....
Tea grounds	4.15	0.62	0.40
Tea leaves (ash)	....	1.60	0.44
Timothy hay	1.25	0.55	1.00
Tobacco leaves	4.00	0.50	6.00
Tobacco stalks	3.70	0.65	4.50
Tobacco stems	2.50	0.90	7.00
Tomatoes, fruit	0.20	0.07	0.35
Tomatoes, leaves	0.35	0.10	0.40
Tomatoes, stalks	0.35	0.10	0.50
Waste from hares and rabbits ..	7.00	2.40	0.60
Waste from felt hat factory ...	3.80	....	0.98
Waste product from paint manufacturer	0.02	39.50	....
Waste silt	9.50	....	....
Wheat, bran	2.65	2.90	1.60

(*Continued*)

| | | Phosphoric | |
Material	Nitrogen	Acid	Potash
Wheat, grain	2.00	0.85	0.50
Wheat, straw	0.50	0.15	0.60
White clover (green)	0.50	0.20	0.30
White sage (ashes)	....	....	13.77
Wood ashes (leached)	....	1.25	2.00
Wood ashes (unleached)......	....	1.50	7.00
Wool waste	5.50	3.00	2.00

* Dried manures contain amounts up to 5 times higher in nitrogen, phosphoric acid and potash.

ACTIVATORS

A compost activator is any substance which will stimulate biological decomposition in a compost pile. There are organic activators and artificial activators. Organic activators are materials containing a high amount of nitrogen in various forms, such as proteins, amino acids and urea, among others. Some examples of natural activators are manure, garbage, dried blood, compost, humus-rich soil, etc.

Artificial activators are generally chemically-synthesized compounds such as ammonium sulfate or phosphate, urea, ammonia, or any of the common commercial nitrogen fertilizers. These materials are not recommended in the organic method.

There are two areas in which an activator can possibly influence a compost heap:

1. Introduction of strains of microorganisms that are effective in breaking down organic matter; and

2. Increasing the nitrogen content of the heap, thereby providing extra food for microorganisms.

Claims have sometimes been made that special cultures of bacteria will hasten the breakdown of material in a compost heap, and will also produce a better quality of finished compost. Products are manufactured which are reported to be effective in improving the action of a compost heap.

Experiments conducted at the University of California, Michigan State University, and Kyoto and Tokyo Universities in Japan have indicated that there is no benefit to be gained from the use of an activator which relies only on the introduction of new microorganisms to a heap. In addition, experiments with activators at the Organic Experimental Farm showed that activators were not effective in improving the action of the heap; that is, none of the trials indicated that a bacterial activator will increase the speed or degree of composting.

On the other side of the question, a project undertaken at Dacca University in East Pakistan showed that a bacterial activator made from well-rotted manure *did* speed up composting. The University recommended that a compost plant using the inoculation treatment be set up. The final product of the Dacca project was 10 times richer than manure in nitrogen and potassium and 3 times richer in phosphorous.

Here is the report of the trials undertaken at the Organic Experimental Farm, giving results and recommendations:

". . . In order to gain data on this question (whether bacteria cultures activate compost) we made the following compost heaps in the greenhouse at the Experimental Farm:

Activated heap
20 pounds wheat straw (shredded)
¼ pound lime
2 pounds dried blood
1 pound phosphate rock
8 pounds earth
1 pound bacterial activator

Standard heap
20 pounds wheat straw
¼ pound lime
2 pounds dried blood
1 pound phosphate rock
9 pounds earth

Both heaps were watered equally and were turned on August 13, two days after being made. Temperature readings were made of both heaps daily, until August 25. At no time was there a variation in temperature between the two heaps. On August 11 the temperature of both heaps was 99 degrees Fahrenheit. On August 13 the temperature of both heaps had risen to 113 degrees. By August 15 they were up to 131 degrees. On August 25 both heaps had returned to 95 degrees, close to their original temperature.

Temperature of compost is considered a good judge of the bacterial activity of the heap, because the temperature is generated by the action of microorganisms in breaking down

It's always a good practice to add vegetable remains to the compost heap. For example, the gardener above is collecting the foliage of snap beans which have finished bearing. The high nitrogen content encourages quick decomposition.

the compost materials. Since both heaps generated equal temperatures, it was concluded that the activator was not effective in improving the action of the heap. No difference in the quality or odor of the two heaps could be observed. In the course of the experiment several series of similar compost heaps were made in order to be certain that the results were accurate. None of the other trials indicated that a bacterial activator increased the speed or degree of composting.

From a theoretical point of view, there seems to be little basis for the use of strictly bacterial activators. All the raw materials that are used in compost heaps are rich in the types of microorganisms that cause decay. There should be little or no value in adding more.

Nitrogen Activators

It has been our experience that the cause of most compost heap "failures" is a lack of nitrogen. Almost invariably, a heap that doesn't heat up or decay quickly is made from material which is low in nitrogen. Nitrogen is necessary as a source of energy for the bacteria and fungi that do the work of composting.

In order to demonstrate the value of adding a nitrogen activator to compost, 3 compost heaps with varying amounts of nitrogen added were made at the Organic Experimental Farm. Here are the ingredients of the heaps:

#1:
    20 pounds of ground wheat straw
    1 pound phosphate rock
    ¼ pound lime
    9 pounds earth
    1 pound blood meal activator

#2:
    20 pounds of ground wheat straw
    1 pound phosphate rock
    ¼ pound lime
    8 pounds earth
    2 pounds blood meal activator

#3:
    20 pounds of ground wheat straw
    1 pound phosphate rock
    ¼ pound lime
    7 pounds earth
    3 pounds blood meal activator

The piles were made by first putting down a 5-pound layer of straw, then wetting it down with two gallons of water. Next a 3-pound layer of blood meal and earth mixture was added, followed by two more gallons of water. This process was repeated until there were 4 layers. Daily temperature readings were taken by placing a thermometer 12 inches below the surface of the pile. The highest temperatures occurred between the third and fourth day. The pile with the most nitrogen activator reached a peak temperature of 170 degrees Fahrenheit, while the low-nitrogen pile reached a temperature of only 125 degrees Fahrenheit.

It can be concluded from this experiment that it is definitely advisable to add a nitrogen supplement or activator. Blood meal, tankage, manure, Agrinite, bone meal and cotton-seed meal are all good nitrogen activators. Just how much you will have to add depends on the nature of the material you are composting. Low-nitrogen materials like straw, saw-dust, corn cobs and old weeds should have at least 2 or 3

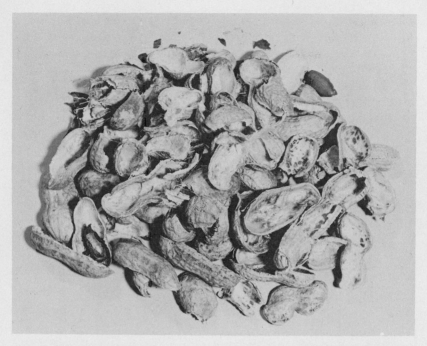

The hulls and shells of many materials, such as peanut shells shown above, are commonly used as a fertilizer, mulch or for addition to the compost pile. They are typical of many organic "wastes" that can improve soil condition.

pounds of nitrogen supplement added per 100 pounds of raw material. If plenty of manure, grass clippings, fresh weeds and other high-nitrogen materials are available to be mixed in with the compost, no nitrogen supplement will be necessary.

Some of the commercial compost activators that are sold are high in nitrogen, and it is probably this nitrogen value which accounts for their effectiveness. We feel that there is a need for a packaged compost activator that would be very rich in nitrogen in organic forms. Phosphate rock, granite dust, lime and other natural mineral fertilizers might also be included in such an activator. Then organic gardeners would have available a complete compost additive that would bring the nitrogen level up and would add natural minerals too.

LIST AND VALUE OF MATERIALS

Apple Pomace

Apple pomace decays readily if mixed with material that provides for proper aeration. Its value in the wet state is not high, since the nitrogen content is only one-fifth of one

141

per cent. But when analyzing the ash content of apple skins, it appeared that they had over 3 per cent phosphoric acid. Since apple pomace can be had in quantities, a goodly amount of phosphoric acid may be obtained from it at the cost of the hauling. The potash content is, of course, much higher, amounting to about 12 per cent of the ash, which corresponds to three-quarters of one per cent of the pomace. It would seem best to use apple pomace for mulching in the orchard whenever feasible, possibly mixed with straw to permit penetration of air.

In the compost heap, apple pomace should be used in thin layers because heavy layers tend to become compact and, as a result of this, fail to break down. When heavy applications of metallic sprays are used, the apple skins may contain not inconsiderable amounts of poison residues that will in time endanger the soil. Care should be taken to prevent the formation of those "toxic orchard soils" which make future growing of food crops impossible. Heavily sprayed apple residues had best not be used for food crops, but for growing chemurgic crops.

As apple pomace contains large amounts of seeds and as seeds are storage organs which contain valuable nutritive substances, especially phosphorus and nitrogen, the fertilizer value of the seed part is to be considered, too, as of value to organic farming.

Banana Residue

Analyses have shown that banana skins and stalks are extremely rich in both phosphoric acid and potash, rating from 2.3–3.3 in phosphoric acid and from 41 to 50 per cent in potash, on an ash basis. The nitrogen content is not given in the literature, but must be relatively high, because these residues decompose very readily and must therefore offer an almost complete diet for bacteria. When available in quantity, it would be thoroughly practical to utilize banana residues for gardening purposes. Table cuttings and kitchen refuse containing banana skins are valuable also for the reason that these materials contain large amounts of bacteria which effect quick break-down and act as activators for the rest of the compost material.

Basic Slag

An industrial by-product, basic slag results when iron ore is smelted to form pig iron. The ore contains, in addition

142

to iron, small amounts of such elements as silicon, aluminum, sulphur, manganese, chromium, titanium, and traces of many other elements. In smelting the iron ore, large amounts of limestone and dolomite are used. The impurities unite with the limestone to form a sludge which rises to the surface of the molten mass and is poured off. In its cold, hard form this sludge is called slag.

The chemical composition of slag varies according to the ore which is used and with variations in the mixtures. The average ranges in the major constituents expressed in terms of the compounds indicated, are shown in the accompanying table.

Material	Compound	Per Cent		
Lime	CaO	38	to	45
Magnesia	MgO	4	to	9
Silica	SiO_2	33	to	39
Alumina	Al_2O_5	10	to	14
Manganese oxide	MnO	0.2	to	1.5
Iron oxide	FeO	0.2	to	0.7
Sulphur	S	1.0	to	2.0

Spectographic studies of slag indicate that it also contains traces of boron, sodium, molybdenum, tin vanadium, copper, zinc, titanium, potassium, strontium, chromium and zirconium. It is because of the presence of so many kinds of essential nutrient elements that slag may be used as a soil builder.

For agricultural purposes, slag must be very finely pulverized. When slag is used in the soil, its efficiency varies directly with its degree of fineness. It is best known as a liming agent. It provides crop plants with calcium and magnesium. In comparative studies it has been found to be better than lime. This is doubtless due to the fact that it contains some of the trace elements which are so important in plant nutrition.

Slag is alkaline in action. It does best on moist clays and loams, and on peaty soils deficient in lime, but can be used in some light soils if a potash mineral is used with it.

It should be applied to the soil in autumn and winter. Slag is especially adapted to the needs of such leguminous crops as beans, peas, clovers, vetches and alfalfa.

Ordinary iron and steel slags contain practically no phosphates but do contain other fertilizer constituents. Before

143

using a slag for agricultural purposes, make sure that it contains soil-building constituents and especially the trace elements. Avoid slags which contain excessive amounts of sulphur.

Since slag is made up of finely pulverized but insoluble particles, it can be applied at any time and at any rate without injuring the plants. An average application is from one to several tons per acre. Basic slag may also be used in the composting program, in liberal amounts.

Beet Wastes

In the sugar beet growing regions, wastes are easily available. Much of that material can be used for ensiling or feeding, but plenty could be composted. Numerous analyses of beet roots showed that their potash content varied from .7 to 4.1 per cent; the variation in nitrogen is less pronounced, and an average might be .4 per cent, while phosphorus ranges from .1 to .6 per cent. Astonishingly enough, the leaves are not very different in their make-up, although their content in calcium and magnesium far exceeds that of the roots.

Where beet wastes can be used for feeding, the sound farmer will do so, since he will in the end obtain valuable manure, besides having saved on energy food and pasture; where for some reason, such as labor costs or contracts with processors, feeding is impossible, the beet residues should be returned to the land, either as part of sheet compost, dressed with manure, or as part of composting by the heap or pit methods.

Bird Cage Cleanings

One of the out-of-the-way materials which are often found by alert gardeners is the cleanings from bird cages. Fred M. Packard, Executive Secretary of the National Parks Association, reports that "The manager of the Annandale Pet Shop, in Virginia, had 6 large cages where several hundred parakeets and canaries provided enough waste seed (mixed with droppings) to fill half a dozen burlap sacks every week or so. She was delighted to let me have it without charge, and in return I cleaned her cages when I called for the seed. Half an hour's work gave me an excellent base for compost."

Small amounts of this material will help to activate a compost pile, generating tremendous heat in a short time.

144

Like sawdust and other wood wastes, these chipped tree branches are useful in the garden. They have a higher nutrient content than sawdust and do a good job of aerating soil. Chips can be obtained from tree-trimming crews in your area.

Blood Meal

Blood meal (dried blood), collected from slaughterhouses, has a nitrogen content of 12 per cent or over. There are different grades, all of which are used mainly for feeding purposes. The dried blood that finds its way to the fertilizer dealer or mixer is a small quantity. There is often a considerable amount of phosphorus in dried blood, ranging from 1 to 5 per cent; this is often not indicated on the bag, but may increase the value of the material considerably.

Dried blood can be used directly in the ground or may be composted. Because of its high nitrogen content, a sprinkling of it suffices to stimulate bacterial growth, and it is advisable either to soak the plant matter thoroughly before applying such a sprinkling or to apply the dried blood in moist form after a soaking or even to combine both methods.

145

Sources of dried blood and similar bagged fertilizers are the mail order houses, seed dealers, fertilizer plants and dealers, and the feed supply houses.

Bone Meal

Along with rock phosphate, bone meal is the major source of phosphorus for the garden. Bones have been used for centuries as a fertilizer, their value recognized first in England. They have long been recognized as an excellent source of phosphorus as well as nitrogen (phosphorus 21 per cent, nitrogen 4 per cent). In the early days of farming in this country, great amounts of buffalo bones were collected on western plains for use as fertilizer. Now the main source of bone meal comes from the slaughterhouses. Consisting mostly of calcium phosphate, the phosphorus and nitrogen content in bone fertilizers depends mainly on the kind and age of the bone. According to Prof. G. H. Collings of Clemson Agricultural College, young bones generally contain less phosphorus and more nitrogen than older bones. The percentage of fluorine in older bones is considerably higher than in younger bones.

Raw bone meal generally contains between 2 to 4 per cent nitrogen, 20 to 25 per cent phosphoric acid. Because of the fatty materials found in raw bone meal, decomposition is somewhat delayed when it is applied to the soil.

Steamed bone meal is the most common of the bone meal fertilizers sold. This type is made from green bones which have been boiled or steamed at high pressure to remove the fats. Its removal causes a slight loss in nitrogen content, but a relative increase in phosphorus. When the bones are steamed, they can be ground more easily and are considered to be in better condition for the soil; steamed bone meal is almost always finer than raw bone meal. Steamed bone meal contains 1 to 2 per cent nitrogen and up to 30 per cent phosphorus.

Another bone fertilizer is bone black, which is charred bone, with a nitrogen content of about 1.5 per cent, a phosphoric acid content over 30 per cent, and many trace elements.

Although bone meal is often applied alone to soils, best results are obtained when it is applied in conjunction with other organic materials, as in compost. Its effectiveness is increased because of its nitrogen content. In general, bone meal acts more quickly when applied to well-aerated soils.

146

Because of its lime content, bone meal tends to reduce soil acidity.

Buckwheat Hulls

Buckwheat hulls are seldom used in the compost pile, not because they are not a suitable material, but because they make such an effective and attractive mulch. The hulls are disc-shaped, very light in weight, and after a rain they have the appearance of rich loam. When applied about 1½ inches deep, they will not blow away, but slither into place. After they have served as a mulch, buckwheat hulls can be worked into the soil to provide organic material for sandy soils and to help break up soils of clayey texture.

Castor Pomace

After the oil has been extracted from the castor bean, a residue is left that is widely used as an organic fertilizer in place of cottonseed meal, because the latter is valuable also as feed. The nitrogen analysis of castor bean pomace is the decisive factor. It varies from 4 to 6.6 per cent, while phosphoric acid and potash analyze from 1 to 2 per cent, with greater variation occurring in the phosphorus content.

Where animal matter is unavailable and where plant matter alone is present, compost could be easily made with castor pomace, especially if it were first moistened and spread over the green matter in semi-liquid form. The finer the plant matter to be broken down, the more intimate the contact between the plants and the pomace, and consequently the quicker the bacterial action.

Castor pomace is handled by fertilizer dealers in various parts of the country. Recent studies have indicated that castor pomace is fully comparable to cottonseed meal, if used on an "efficiency" basis. This means that 160 pounds of nitrogen in castor pomace will have the same crop-producing effect as 200 pounds of nitrogen in cottonseed meal. For farm practices, castor pomace may be substituted, pound for pound, for cottonseed meal.

Citrus Wastes

Citrus wastes are most easily composted, and there is no danger to the soil in their oils and resins, because these disintegrate in the composting process. The fact that some citrus peels may have spray residues on them need not be overestimated, since such residues are small and will not likely harm the soil after the material is broken down into compost. Orange skins and citrus skins of all kinds are richer in nitrogen if the skins are thick; their phosphoric acid analysis shows about 3 per cent of the valuable element in orange skins, while the potash content of the ash is surpassed only by banana skins; the former analyzing about 27 per cent, while banana skins have almost 50 per cent in potash. Lemons, as a rule, have a lower potash, but a higher phosphorus content than oranges; grapefruits seem to hold the middle between the extremes: 3.6 per cent phosphoric acid and 30 per cent potash. Whole fruits, so-called culls, are also useful, though their fertilizer value is necessarily lower than that of the skins, because they contain great amounts of water.

The skins will decompose more quickly if shredded, mixed with other green matter, and inoculated with a nitrogen- and bacteria-rich material.

Coal Ashes

Although coal ashes will lighten heavy soils, there is serious danger of adding toxic quantities of sulphur and iron from this material. Some ashes do not contain these chemicals in toxic quantities, but the coals from various sources are so different that no general recommendations can be made. The safest procedure is to regard all coal ashes as injurious to the soil.

An analysis of 32 samples of soft coal ashes showed from 4 to 40 per cent iron oxide and from 0.3 to 10 per cent sulphur trioxide. When water is added to sulphur trioxide, sulphuric acid is formed in such amounts as to destroy all vegetation. Hard coal ashes have lesser amounts of iron and sulphur, but it is best to play safe and not use them to lighten heavy soils. It is much better to lighten the soil by adding compost or plain sand. It is probable that the addition of coal ashes to the compost would have similar harmful effects.

Cocoa Bean Shells

Coarse cocoa shells are rarely used in the compost heap, because they are much better put to use as a mulch. If available in large quantities, however, they make a fine addition to the heap because of their relatively high nutrient value. It must also be remembered that the terms "mulch" and "compost" are not unrelated, and that most mulches, when

148

Mostly used as a mulch, cocoa bean shells will increase the mineral content of compost piles; nitrogen, phosphorus and potash content is usually two per cent or more. A one-inch covering around plants is attractive, conserves moisture.

allowed to remain on the ground surface for some time, will decompose gradually, thus becoming compost.

Cocoa shell dust analyzes rather high in nitrogen for a product of this woody kind, namely one per cent. The phosphorus content is about 1.5 per cent, the potash content approximately 1.7 per cent. Usually theobromine and caffine are first extracted from the shells, and the residues analyze 2.7 nitrogen, .7 phosphoric acid, and 2.6 potash. The raw, untreated shells are slightly higher, but must of course be finely ground to be useful as fertilizer material. Cocoa pressed cake has also been sold for fertilizing purposes, but the analyses vary according to treatment. As a rule, this cake is rather high in nitrogen, but lower than the shells in potash, while the phosphorus content is close to .9 per cent.

The chocolate factories have begun to market cocoa shell wastes which have been freed of the oil and the theobromine. In the extraction process, lime is used. The finished product is without odor, weed seeds and acids, and therefore is useful for mulching soils in acid regions, because the lime content will balance the acidity of the soils while the organic matter of the residue acts as a fine water-storage medium.

When the shells are spread on the ground about one inch in depth, they furnish fine protection against drought. At the same time, rain will remove a great deal of the soluble plant food contained in the shells. During the winter months, they afford excellent protection against the damages caused by alternate freezing and thawing of seed beds and roots.

Cocoa bean shells can also be applied on lawns and when used in landscaping, they provide a very colorful, light even-brown color around shrubberies and evergreens as well as flower beds.

Coffee Wastes

The average gardener has usually access only to coffee grounds. These, like other kitchen wastes, may be applied to the compost heap. They may also be applied directly to plants.

As a seed, the coffee bean has some nitrogen. Coffee grounds have up to two per cent nitrogen in them, a third of one per cent phosphoric acid, and varying amounts of potash. Drip coffee grounds are richer than grounds that have been boiled, but the potash content is still below one per cent. Coffee grounds sour easily because they preserve moisture well and seem to encourage aceticacid-forming bacteria. If mixed with lime and applied to the compost heap or fed to earthworm cultures they are by no means negligible additions to the fertilizer resources of the average family. Being acid, they are good for blueberries, evergreens, and all acid-loving plants. When using on plants that like lime, mix some ground limestone with the grounds before using as a mulch. They seem to have a remarkable effect on stimulating the growth and health of certain plants. Chemical analyses show that the grounds contain all sorts of minerals including trace elements, carbohydrates, sugars, and even some vitamins. They also have some caffeine present.

A waste product from coffee manufacturing, coffee chaff seems to be an excellent material for use in home gardens as well as farms. Over two per cent in both nitrogen and potash, chaff also appears very suitable for use as a mulch material, where its dark color is an asset.

Corn Cobs

Corn cobs are an excellent material for making compost, but they should be first cut up with an ensilage cutter, shredder, or grinder that will break it down; otherwise it will take years for the material to compost.

The cobs mixed with leaves prevent the latter from caking and impeding aeration. Corn cobs can be left to weather in the open for a few months. They will then break down much finer in the shredder.

Corn cobs are a valuable ingredient for the compost heap and should be carefully preserved, rather than burned up as many farmers do. Tests show that the cob, in nutrient value is equivalent to two-thirds that of the corn kernel. This is amazing when one considers how sinfully the cobs are disposed of.

If gardeners or farmers will contact the mills in their community that shell corn, they will find mountains of cobs free for the taking.

Because of its moisture-holding properties, corn cobs are regarded as one of the best mulches available. Used as a mulch, they should be applied to a depth of 3 or 4 inches.

Cottonseed Meal

An excellent by-product organic fertilizer, cottonseed meal is made from the cotton seed which has been freed from lints and hulls and deprived of its oil. Since cottonseed cake is one of the richest protein foods for animal feeding, relatively little finds its way for use as fertilizer. The special value of cottonseed meal lies in its acid reaction which makes it a valuable fertilizer for acid-loving specialty crops. The meal is used mainly as a source of nitrogen, of which it contains varying amounts, usually around 7 per cent. Phosphoric acid content is between 2 and 3 per cent, while potash is usually 1.5 per cent.

While cottonseed meal is usually applied directly to the soil, it can be a valuable addition to the compost heap, providing the nitrogen necessary for rapid decomposition.

Dolomite

Dolomite, a rock similar to limestone, is interchangeable with limestone for uses in which physical properties are the determining factor. Limestone is composed of the mineral calcite, calcium carbonate, whereas dolomite rock is composed of the mineral having the same name which chemically is a double carbonate of calcium and magnesium. Theoretically pure dolomite contains 45.73 per cent magnesium carbonate, and 54.27 per cent calcium carbonate.

Earthworms

The earthworm is a valuable addition to the compost heap. These creatures can help to mix materials, aerate the heap, and hasten decay of organic materials. The addition of earthworms in the heap makes unnecessary the laborious turnings which were once required to mix materials in the Indore composting method. A comprehensive discussion of the earthworm, and its place in composting methods, will be found in another chapter of this book.

Felt Wastes

Hatteries have a certain amount of hair and wool wastes, which may analyze as high as 14 per cent nitrogen. The same that is true of hair and wool applies to felt wastes. If included in a compost that is teeming with bacteria, hair and feathers as well as felt wastes break down rather easily, provided the heap is kept moist enough. It is always wise to mix some manure or other high-protein material in with dry refuse, such as felt wastes, in order to supply bacterial life from the outset and to hasten the decomposition process.

Fish Scrap

Fish scrap is often available locally; its nitrogen and phosphorus value is high, frequently about 7 per cent for each and over, computed on a dry basis. While dried ground fish is free from fats, fish scrap contains much fish oil and may thereby attract fat-eating ants, besides being slower to break down. In tropical regions where citrus or banana wastes are easily available or near canneries where refuse is obtainable, composting of fish refuse with plant refuse can be easily undertaken on a large scale, because those plant residues supply good amounts of potash while the fish scrap contains the other two major plant nutrients besides such minor elements as iodine. In warm regions the outside temperature hastens furthermore the breakdown of the material. But care must be taken to have the heaps well covered with earth and in a good state of moisture to secure quick action and absence of odors. The pit method is recommended. By sinking trenches about 3 feet deep, the composter will still supply enough air surface to stimulate aerobic bacterial growth, especially if the plant material is bulky. In the small garden, fish scrap can hardly be used successfully; but on a farm scale, the inclusion of wastes from fish markets or canneries in the compost is by no means impossible, and in the Northeast as well as Northwest cannery wastes of fish material could profitably be used for making sheet compost.

Where much fish material has to be disposed of, it may be advisable to use the drastic method of sprinkling the fish with quick lime. After some period has elapsed, the resulting substance should be ready for inclusion in a compost heap. We do not otherwise recommend the use of quick lime, but suggest for all other purposes agricultural lime or ground limestone.

Garbage

Garbage is a neglected source of compost material which is particularly rich in nitrogen and other nutrients essential to soil building and plant growth. The individual gardener should compost his kitchen wastes whether he lives in a rural area or a suburb. In either case, animal-proof bins should be used to avoid the committing of nuisances. If the gardener lives in a comparatively densely settled community, local statutes should be consulted.

Commercially-built anaerobic bins are available to the suburban gardener. These are moderate in cost and are designed to hold 6 months' garbage, producing a good quality compost.

If the local situation permits, the gardener can build his own compost bin. It need not be anaerobic but it should be animal-proof. To start his joint garbage disposal-composting program, he merely dumps his garbage in it daily. It is advisable to add a little soil, spoiled hay or straw to the garbage, covering each day's layer of kitchen waste.

Some gardeners bury their garbage on next year's planting sites, thus rotating their garden and leaving some land "resting" in anticipation of next year's crop. They take the precaution of burying the kitchen waste deep enough to escape detection by scavenging animals.

Still another course is open to the homesteader. He can build an enclosure of cement blocks, high and strong enough to be animal-proof. Here he can dump his garbage, permitting it to break down partially. From time to time he removes some of this highly nitrogenous material, adding it to new compost heaps composed mostly of vegetable manures. In this way he is assured of a steady supply of activating material for his composting program.

The European method of garbage trenching may be used to advantage where more garbage is available than can be used in the compost heaps, or where compost heaps cannot be built, as in some towns.

A trench about a foot deep is dug across the garden in spring, and the soil left heaped up beside it. (The trench and heap of soil may both be temporarily covered with mulch, to prevent drying.) As the trench is filled with garbage, starting at one end and working toward the other, the heap of soil is pulled over it, and again mulched. The entire row is left unplanted during the entire season, to permit bacterial action below ground to be completed.

The relatively recent innovation of municipal composting techniques has returned to the soil much garbage which formerly was incinerated. This aspect of garbage treatment is discussed fully in the chapter on municipal composting.

Gin Trash

The disposal of gin trash (wastes of the cotton plant) had been an expensive burden on the cotton industry, until in 1952 the processors stopped burning gin trash and began to compost it. Now, gin trash has joined the growing list of waste industrial materials which are being returned to the soil.

The Texas State Department of Health, in cooperation with commercial bacteria breeders, has developed a process of composting gin trash into a "manure" which returns everything to the soil except the seed and blossoms of the cotton plant. Within 21 days after a pile of gin trash—burs, stems and dust which normally is destroyed in a bur burner—is injected with a special breed of bacterial culture, the farmer or ginner has a compost equivalent to leaf mold or well-rotted manure. The cost approximates one dollar per ton and appears to be a low-cost answer to reclamation of fertility-mined soils of the South.

The TSDH entered the gin trash research field during its search for a substitute for improper incineration, which,

154

since the origin of cotton gins, has been a source of smoke nuisance complaints. Soil nutrient conservation, which also has tremendous public health significance, was a secondary motive.

The significance of the reclaimed organic matter is readily seen. For each bale of cotton harvested from one acre of land, the soil loses about 25 pounds of potash, two pounds of phosphate, and 4 pounds of nitrogen, along with varying quantities of trace elements. Portions of those elements go into the seed and fiber of the plant, but the major portions are in burs and other waste blown into the bur burners. In Texas, the amount of gin trash produced each year exceeds 2½ million tons. If all this waste had been composted and returned to the soil, the vast amount of minerals and organic matter lost from the soil as a result of cropping would have been replaced.

Studies observed by the department show that the composted trash exceeds in value an application of commercial fertilizer, plus the decomposed residue of a green manure crop. The best effect of applying this humus to the land is the friability which it produces. Normal application rates are 2 to 3 tons per acre. In a comparative per-acre study, 300 pounds of 16-20-0 formula fertilizer supplied only 48 pounds of nitrogen, 60 pounds of available phosphoric acid, no potash and no organic matter. On the other hand, 3 tons of the gin trash compost supplied 60 pounds each of nitrogen, available phosphoric acid, and potash, plus 5,820 pounds of organic matter. The fertilizer effects of the gin trash will be noticeable for several years after the application.

Alert gardeners can obtain composted gin trash for nominal amounts, and can often get uncomposted material free. Both make valuable additions to the compost heap.

Granite Dust

Granite dust or granite stone meal is a highly recommended natural source of potash. Its potash content varies between 3 and 5 per cent, and often more.

One of the first researches showing the value of granite dust to plants took place at the Connecticut Experimental Station. Tests there showed that the potash in granite rock is available to a growing crop of tobacco, a plant which needs a liberal quantity of potash for optimum growth. The opinion popularly held by most agriculturists is that only the chemical fertilizers, such as the sulfate or muriate compounds, contain potash in an economically available form.

This work in Connecticut definitely shatters that idea. The experiment was written up by the Connecticut Agricultural Station in a booklet entitled *Granite Stone Meal as a Source of Potash for Tobacco,* Bulletin 536, April 1950. The work was done by T. R. Swanback, of the Tobacco Laboratory, Windsor, Connecticut.

The value of using potash rock, such as granite dust, over the chemical form is that it is cheaper and leaves no harmful chemical residues. It also contains valuable trace mineral elements. There are sources of granite and other rocks that contain potash all over the country and these sources are being uncovered gradually to make natural rock powders available to all gardeners.

Here are some excerpts from the Connecticut report: "An 'ideal' form of potash-bearing materials is the potash carried in the organics, which are widely used in fertilization of Connecticut tobacco. However, the organics (cottonseed meal, castor pomace, etc.) are mainly used as carriers of nitrogen and only a limited quantity of potash is derived from that source.

"The common sources of commercially available potash, such as sulfate, nitrate, carbonate of potash and ashes, all have limitations in their usage. Too much sulfate of potash should not be employed because of its sulphur content. This element is commonly known to affect adversely the burn of tobacco and also, in excess, may impair the grading (quality) of the finished product. Nitrate of potash is limited because of the restricted usage of nitrate nitrogen in tobacco fertilizer. The general use of carbonate of potash and ashes is unsatisfactory because of their alkaline effect on the soil.

"Recently, experiments were started with a type of granite stone meal with an unusually high content of total potash, obtained from granite quarries in Massachusetts.

"The potash-bearing minerals in granite are the potash feldspars and the micas, of which the latter contain the most easily released potash.

". . . Granite stone meal used in the experiment carried a total potash content of at least 8 per cent. In addition, the material contained small amounts of trace elements.

"An application of two tons of stone meal per acre, combined with the usual amount of nitrogen and phosphoric acid, produced fully as good a yield and quality as a standard 6-3-6 formula."

Granite dust is a fine source of adding potash to the compost, and should be used in liberal quantities. It can also be used as a top dressing, worked directly into the soil, or used when establishing a cover crop. In the garden, suggested rates of application are 10 pounds to 100 square feet, 100 pounds to 1,000 square feet; on the farm, the recommended application rate is two tons to the acre. Some brands of granite dust now being marketed are Hybrotite, Soil-Con and Super Gran-its.

Grape Wastes

The prunings of grape vines, when shredded and composted, return much of the organic matter and nutrient content lost by cropping. Vine prunings must be cut into pieces 3 to 6 inches long if they are to pack sufficiently closely for successful composting. The amount of water required depends upon the rate of evaporation and hence upon the local climate. The water content of the mass, if the prunings are to be composted alone, should be from 70 to 80 per cent, indicated by the development of fungus mycelium on the surface. Excessive water is harmful, as fermentation cannot proceed in a water-logged medium. Some added nitrogenous fertilizer is desirable to stimulate bacterial activity.

The process should be completed in about 6 months, and the finished product resembles ordinary garden compost.

It has been objected that the compost, because of its nature to fungus activity, will predispose the vines to mildew infection. This is not the case; in fact, the fungi responsible for forming the compost secrete substances which attack and destroy the vine mildews.

Shredded prunings, of course, are valuable additions of green matter to the ordinary compost heap, and should be treated as any other green matter. Although the nutrient content of grape wastes is not very high, the material will add the organic matter necessary to maintain soil health.

Grass Clippings

One of the materials most easy to obtain, grass clippings are valuable to the compost heap. Many people, feeling that clippings should not be taken from the lawn, do not use them in compost or as mulch. It is true that clippings are valuable when left on the lawn, but they may also be used in other garden areas.

There are many reasons why grass clippings can play an important role throughout other parts of the garden and in a number of soil-improving steps. First of all, a good lawn doesn't need as much enrichment, added organic matter or mulching as do the more heavily cropped plots. As such a rich source of nitrogen, these clippings can most often be better used elsewhere. They can be a valuable fertilizer in the vegetable garden, a helpful addition in all mulches, and a major aid in converting leaves and other low-nitrogen wastes into best-quality compost.

Then, too, collecting grass clippings is one way to curtail unwanted weed growth in the lawn, since doing this helps to remove the weed seeds. Also, periodic collection of the clippings promotes better appearance, aids in keeping a neater lawn.

We don't recommend that *all* grass clippings be removed. Some can and should be left as occasional replenishment for the lawn itself.

Grass clippings, freshly cut, contain a very large percentage of nitrogen. That is why grass is such a good soil builder. Perhaps, too, few gardeners are aware of this fact. As proof of that statement, if cut grass is allowed to remain undisturbed on a pile for two days, extreme heat will build up within the very center of the heap. If not moved, the grass will soon turn into a slushy, brown muck. This heat and reaction are caused by the rapid release of nitrogen as the grass decays.

Because green grass clippings are such a wonderful source of nitrogen, they should be utilized to the utmost. There are 3 excellent ways in which they can be put to work in the garden and flower beds: They may be used as a mulch; they may be turned in as green manure; and they may be used in the compost heap to create the necessary heat for good decomposition.

As a mulch, lawn clippings surpass most others. They are easy to handle; will remain in place nicely; will fit in the smallest spaces with no trouble, and when dried, will give your rows and beds a very neat appearance. Of course you will not have enough mulch for your entire garden from the first cutting, but mulch as much as you can each week. In a short time, all of your rows will be mulched. It is a good idea to mulch first those vegetables that mature early, then work on the others.

Freshly-cut grass clippings contain a high percentage of nitrogen, will decompose rapidly especially when mixed with some manure. Apply directly in your vegetable or flower garden as mulch, or "turn them in" as green manure.

Because it is so finely chopped, these clippings disappear completely into the soil by fall. The mulch may be replenished in late summer, but it is not necessary. For some reason, grass does not like to grow in areas covered with decayed clippings.

Green mulch, such as this, may temporarily rob the soil of available nitrogen, including both ammonia and nitrates. But this condition is so short-lived that it can, in no way, stunt the rapid growth of the plants.

Later in the season, you may have a surplus of grass clippings on your hands. The garden has all been mulched. What to do with them now? Don't throw them away, by any means, or add to other mulch where it is not necessary. If you are not planting a second crop in your pea patch, or in

159

the section where the lettuce or string beans have been, scatter a few inches of the green clippings over the entire area. Turn these in immediately as green manure along with the mulch previously applied. You can work a small plot at a time, depending upon the amount of excess clippings on hand. Later, you may remulch the entire area and allow it to remain thus until the following spring.

When green vegetation is mixed with the soil under favorable conditions of temperature and moisture, decomposition immediately begins. This rapid decomposition is brought about by many species of bacteria and fungi found in the earth. These microorganisms require a source of energy such as nitrogen, which green grass supplies in abundance. Because of this large amount of nitrogen in grass, these hungry bacteria and fungi will tend to draw from it, instead of robbing the soil of its necessary supply. In no time, the grass is digested into humus, and the soil made many times richer for plant growth. The nitrogen in the earth has, also, been stepped up, which will cause plants to become stronger and greener.

If you care to turn in green grass clippings as green manure before planting a second crop in a vacant plot, you may do so. Give the section a week or 10 days to return to normal, then plant as before. Many times, if the plot has thus been treated, the second crop surpasses the first. This, of course, makes the effort worthwhile.

When used as green manure, grass clippings greatly improve the physical condition of heavy-textured soils. But to all, they give the much-needed humus and nitrogen. If acidity is a factor, a small amount of limestone may be applied with the clippings.

The third use of grass clippings is incorporating them into the compost heap to create the necessary heat for proper decomposition. The best principle to follow here is to use two-thirds grass clippings and one-third stable manure.

Greensand

Glauconite greensand or greensand marl is an iron-potassium-silicate that imparts a green color to the minerals in which it occurs. Being an undersea deposit, greensand contains traces of many if not all the elements which occur in sea water. Greensand has been used successfully for soil-building for more than 100 years. It is a fine source of potash.

A fine natural source of potash, greensand is surface mined in southern New Jersey and elsewhere in the United States. This glauconite potash mineral may be applied on surface of soil in sheet composting or added to compost heap.

Greensand is commonly called a glauconite potash mineral, because it contains from 6 to 7 per cent of plant-available potash. The best deposits contain, in addition to the potash, 50 per cent of silica, 18 to 23 per cent of iron oxides, 3 to 7.5 per cent of magnesia, small amounts of lime and phosphoric acid, and traces of 30 or more other elements, most of which are important in the nutrition of higher plants.

The factors underlying the immediate response of grasses to greensands seem to be the following:

1. Absorb and hold large amounts of water in the surface layer of the soil where the plant roots feed.

161

2. Round up and feed to the grass roots the nutrient elements which are already in the soil.

3. Provide an abundant source of plant-available potash which stimulates photosynthesis and rapid growth of grasses.

4. Contain the trace elements which may be deficient in the soil or in the surface layer of the soil in which the grass roots feed.

Greensands are so fine that they may be used in their natural form with no processing except drying if the material is to pass through a fertilizer drill. An application consists of about one-quarter pound of greensands per square foot of soil. It may be applied at any time without danger of injuring plants. In gardens and fields it may be applied when the soil is prepared for planting or to growing vegetables and crop plants. It may be applied on the surface with the organic materials in sheet composting, or used in the compost heap to stimulate bacterial action and to enrich the compost.

Hair

Hair, in common with wool and silk, has a high nitrogen content. If the sweepings from a barber shop were regularly applied to a compost heap, an enormous amount of nitrogen could be saved, since 6 to 7 pounds of hair contain a pound of nitrogen or as much as 100 to 200 pounds of manure. If kept in a well moistened heap, hair will disintegrate as easily as feathers.

Experiments with 32 varieties of roses by William Stafford, of Austin, Texas, indicate that human hair used around the roots of bushes produce longer stems, larger buds and deeper color tones.

The chemical constituents of human hair are nitrogen, hydrogen, oxygen, carbon and sulphur, approximately the same as bone meal which is a popular rose food.

Stafford experimented with hair at the base of plants, found it accelerated growth—but slowly—since it took a long time for the hair to decay. It seemed to work best on roses, also.

He wanted the hair to decay faster and worked out a recipe for a compost material which chemically decays the hair more rapidly.

His recipe—enough for 50 rose bushes:
10 pounds of hair clippings (should be clipped to ¾-inch lengths to prevent matting).
20 pounds of cottonseed meal to help hold moisture and encourage decomposition.
1½ yards of leafmold.

Mix the ingredients together; then wet down well. Keep in a compost pit 30 to 60 days, turning it until it is all rotted, then put about 3 quarts around each bush. Water frequently the first 10 days and keep watering until results show.

Hair used alone will get the same results, but takes longer. Spread the hair around the surface as a mulch and water until it decays. Keep the hair on the surface. It is good insulator for the roots of all tender plants in severe cold and Stafford has a blue ribbon as proof it helps roses bloom longer in winter.

Hoof and Horn Meal

There are many grades of hoof and horn meal; the granular material breaks down with some difficulty unless kept moist and well covered; it also tends to encourage the growth of maggots because it attracts flies. The finely ground horn dust, which gardeners use for potting mixtures, is on the other hand quite easily dissolved. In fact, it can be smelled clearly which shows that small particles break off all along. The nitrogen content is from 10 to 16 pounds per 100 pound bag or as much as a ton of manure or more, while the phosphoric acid value is usually around two per cent. If available, this is a very handy source of nitrogen for flower growers and gardeners with small compost heaps, because it can be easily stored, is pleasant to handle, and is relatively less costly than other forms of bagged organic nitrogen.

Hops

Spent hops (the residue after hops have been extracted with water in the brewery) is another industrial by-product valuable to the gardener. In their wet state, they are 75 per cent water, .6 per cent nitrogen, and .2 per cent phosphorus. Moisture content varies considerably, and the analysis expressed on the dry matter is the most satisfactory figure. On this basis the nitrogen ranges from 2.5 to 3.5 per cent and the phosphoric acid about one per cent. Spent hops in their natural condition are to be regarded mainly as a source of nitrogen. In many areas, gardeners and farmers have been successfully using the hops in their natural condition, spreading it in the same way as farmyard manure. Many other growers have been composting the hops before applying to the soil.

Another brewery waste often available is the material left over from the mashing process, composed of grain parts. This wet brewer's grain, which decays readily, has been found to contain almost one per cent of nitrogen.

Spent hops have been used as a mulch with excellent success. For the owner of the small garden, however, they have their disadvantages because of the very strong odor, but this disappears in a short time.

Used in larger areas, where the odor is not seriously objectionable, spent hops prove to be a very effective mulch.

Like other mulches, it conserves the soil moisture, raises the soil temperature in the late fall and early spring, and aids bacteria in their work in the soil. Spent hops, direct from the brewery, are very wet and have a pH of about 4.5. One 6-inch application about a plant will last at least 3 years and sometimes longer. Stirring the material once or twice during the growing season aids in keeping down any of the weeds that may have grown up through it.

Two of the most important characteristics of this material are that it does not blow away when dry and does not burn if a lighted match or cigarette butt is thrown into it. Many other mulch materials burn easily.

Because of the tremendous amount of water in them, fresh hops heat very readily in the compost pile, serving as an activator for other materials. This same property may be harmful to young plants, however, if fresh hops are used as a mulch; it is best to keep them at least 6 inches away from any young stems.

Incinerator Ash

Incinerator ash, if easily available, is a fine source of phosphorus and potash for the compost heap. Its phosphorus content, depending upon the particular content, runs around 5 or 6 per cent, and its potassium content is from 2 to 3 per cent. Often, it can be obtained from municipal incinerators or from large apartment dwellings.

Leather Dust

Leather dust makes an excellent fertilizer material, high in nitrogen. The nitrogen content varies from 5.5 to 12 per

Experts have estimated that the leaves from a single large shade tree can be worth as much as 15 dollars in terms of plant food and humus. Because trees are deep-rooted, their leaves absorb minerals, making them especially valuable for autumn composting. New tools speed up the job of leaf-collecting.

cent, and the material also contains considerable amounts of phosphorus. Leather dust may be added to the compost pile or may be applied directly to the soil. It is available in commercial form, but may often be secured from leather processing plants.

Leaves

The leaves of one large shade tree can be worth as much as $15 in terms of plant food and humus. Pound for pound, the leaves of most trees contain twice as many minerals as manure. For example, the mineral content of a sugar maple leaf is over 5 per cent, while even common pine needles have 2.5 per cent of their weight in calcium, magnesium, nitrogen and phosphorus, plus other trace elements.

Since most trees are deep-rooted, they absorb minerals

from deep in the soil and a good portion of these minerals go into the leaves. See the accompanying chart for an analysis of the nutrient elements in fallen leaves.

Actually these multi-colored gifts from above are most valuable for the large amounts of fibrous organic matter they supply. Their humus-building qualities mean improved structure for all soil types. They aerate heavy clay soils, prevent sandy soils from drying out too fast, soak up rain and check evaporation.

A lawn sweeper is a good machine to use for collecting leaves. Using a sweeper is much faster than hand raking, and a better picking-up job is done. Neighbors will be happy to have you sweep up their leaves—and you will add to your supply of leaves.

Some people complain that they have no luck composting leaves. "We make a pile of our leaves," these people say, "but they never break down." That is indeed a common complaint.

There are two things you can do that will guarantee success in composting leaves:

1. Add extra nitrogen to your leaf compost. Manure is the best nitrogen supplement, and a mixture of 5 parts leaves to 1 part manure will certainly break down quickly. If you don't have manure—and many gardeners don't—nitrogen supplements like dried blood, cottonseed meal, bone meal and Agrinite will work almost as well. Nitrogen is the one factor that starts a compost heap heating up, and leaves certainly don't contain enough nitrogen to provide sufficient food for bacteria. Here is a rough guide for nitrogen supplementing: add two cups of dried blood or other natural nitrogen supplement to each wheelbarrow load of leaves.

2. The second thing to do to guarantee leaf-composting success is to grind or shred your leaves. We will deal with this in detail later on, but let me tell you right now that it will make things simpler for you in the long run. A compost pile made of shredded material is really fun to work with, because it is so easily controlled and so easy to handle.

A compost pile can be made in almost any size, but most people like to make rectangular-shaped piles, because they are easier to handle. It is a good idea to put the material in the heap in layers. Start with a 6-inch layer of leaves, either shredded or not shredded. Then add a 2-inch layer of other organic material that is higher in nitrogen than leaves. Try to pick something from this list: manure, garbage, green weeds, grass clippings or old vines from your garden. You *can* add low-nitrogen things like sawdust, straw, ground corn cobs or dry weeds *if* you put in a nitrogen supplement such as described above. It is important to mix leaves with other material both to supply nitrogen and to prevent the leaves from packing down in a dry mat. Keep the heap moist, but not soggy.

Turn the heap every 3 weeks, or sooner if you feel up to it. If you can turn it 3 or 4 times before late spring comes, you will have fine compost ready for spring planting use.

You can make compost out of leaves in as short a time as 14 days by doing these things:

1. *Shred or grind the leaves.*

2. *Mix 4 parts ground leaves with 1 part manure or other material liberally supplemented with nitrogen.*

3. *Turn the heap* every 3 days. *Turning a heap made of shredded leaves is not difficult, because the compost is light and fluffy.*

One more tip: Why not experiment with covering your heap with a plastic sheet? It will keep the warmth in, and prevent the heap from getting too wet or too dry. And you might also want to add a package of earthworms after the heap cools down. You can order them by mail.

Leaves can be used much more conveniently in the garden if they are ground or shredded. Leaves in their natural state tend to blow away or mat down into a tight mass. If shredded they turn into compost or leaf mold much faster, and make a much better mulch.

If you have a leaf and compost shredder, your leaf-shredding problems are solved, as long as you have a model large enough to do the volume of work you have.

If you don't have a shredder, there are various other devices you can adapt to leaf shredding, or make yourself. Many people use a rotary mower for shredding leaves and even for weeds. A mower that is not self-propelled is best, as it is easiest to control. Two people can work together very nicely. One person piles up leaves in front of the mower and the other operates the mower back and forth over the pile. A leaf-mulching attachment placed on the mower will cut the leaves up finer, but sometimes it is not necessary. You will be surprised how much leaves you can shred this way in a half-hour or so, even with only one person working by himself.

Of course, some people use a mower with a mulching attachment to cut leaves up right on the lawn. That is fine, if you don't want to use the leaves for compost or mulch somewhere else. Most gardeners need leaf mold more on their gardens and beds than on their lawn.

A hammer-knife mower, made by either Mott or Henderson, is fine for cutting up leaves and other things for compost. The swinging bars dig right in and make mincemeat of whatever they hit. These mowers are safe to use, too, because they are well guarded.

If you have so many leaves on your place that you can't compost all of them—or if you just don't have the time to make compost—you can make leaf mold. Leaf mold is not as rich a fertilizer as composted leaves, but it's easier to make and is especially useful as mulch.

A length of snow fencing makes the best kind of enclosure for making leaf mold. You can make a circular bin. A bin made of wood or stones can be used if you don't have a fence.

Gather your leaves in the fine fall days and tamp them down in the enclosure—after wetting them thoroughly. Leaves have a slight acid reaction. If your plants don't need an acid mulch, add some ground limestone to the leaves before tamping them down.

Over the winter, these leaves will *not* break down into the black powder that is the leaf mold you find on the forest floor. But they will be in a safe place, secure from the winter winds, where you can pull them out next spring and summer for use as mulch. By then they will be matted down and broken up enough to serve as a fine mulch. Some people keep leaves "in cold storage" like that for several years. Nurserymen who require fine potting soil sometimes do that. Then, when they come for their leaves, they find really black, crumbly humus.

You can shred your leaves with a compost shredder or a rotary mower before putting them in your bin. Then they will break down a lot more over the winter.

Leaf mold is ordinarily found in the forest in a layer just above the mineral soil. It has the merit of decomposing slowly, furnishing plant nutrients gradually and improving the structure of the soil as it does so.

The ability of leaf mold to retain moisture is almost miraculous. Subsoil can hold a mere 20 per cent of its weight; good, rich topsoil will hold 60 per cent, but leaf mold can retain 300 to 500 per cent of its weight in water.

Freshly fallen leaves pass through several stages from surface litter to well-decomposed humus partly mixed with mineral soil. Leaf mold from deciduous trees is somewhat richer in such mineral foods as potash and phosphorus than that from conifers. The nitrogen content varies from .2 to 5 per cent.

If you keep poultry or livestock, use your supply of leaves for litter or bedding along with straw or hay. Leaf mold thus enriched with extra nitrogen may later be mixed directly with soil or added to the compost pile.

Oak leaf mold is particularly effective, reports Earle Dilatush, of Robbinsville, N. J., when worked into an enriched compost. Where the soil is "very poor" he uses the following leaf mold compost: "to every ton made up of two parts oak leaf mold and one part well-rotted cow manure, add 400 pounds of cottonseed meal and 200 pounds of crushed tobacco stems. If your ground is very sour, hardwood ashes can be used in place of the tobacco stems."

Nutrient Elements in Fallen Leaves

Name	Cal-cium	Magne-sium	Potas-sium	Phos-pho-rus	Nitro-gen	Ash	pH
Red maple	1.29	0.40	0.40	0.09	0.52	10.97	4.70
Sugar maple ...	1.81	0.24	0.75	0.11	0.67	11.85	4.30
American beech.	0.99	0.22	0.65	0.10	0.67	7.37	5.08
White ash	2.37	0.27	0.54	0.15	0.63	10.26	6.80
White oak	1.36	0.24	0.52	0.13	0.65	5.71	4.40
E. hemlock	0.68	0.14	0.27	0.07	1.05	....	5.50
Balsam fir	1.12	0.16	0.12	0.09	1.25	3.08	5.50

Leaves can be used as an activator, also, in place of manure. Many gardeners keep a pile of leaves on hand, then use the bottom layer, which is dark and moist, as a regular addition to the compost heap. After each layer of green matter is added to the heap, a layer of these partially decomposed leaves is put on top. The swarming bacteria from the leaves spreads quickly through the other green matter, hastening its decay, and the moisture of the leaves helps to maintain optimum condition in the heap.

When raw leaves are used in the compost heap and are piled in too thickly, they tend to impede the aeration. That is why we recommend that where leaves are used, they should be used sparingly along with the other green matter, and should be aged somewhat.

Limestone

Ground limestone is the form in which lime is best applied to soil to provide lime in a beneficial form which will be available over a long period of time. In order to be of use immediately and to continue to break down for gradual use over a period of years, limestone should be ground fine enough to sift through a 100-mesh screen. In this form the lime will be exposed to water in the soil in sufficient quantities to dissolve slowly, but the entire application will not have dissolved for several years. Lime is particularly valuable in the compost heap, as many materials used are acid in nature, and should be neutralized by this alkaline material.

Lime is seldom used as a fertilizer, although its calcium content is very important to plant life as it is to animals. However, most soils contain enough calcium in one compound or another to supply all that plants need.

The primary use for lime in the garden or farm is as an alkalizer, to raise the pH factor of the soil or compost. It is important that certain plants requiring an acid soil do not receive too much lime, or that alkaline-loving plants receive enough. The soil and compost pile should be tested for pH (as well as for NPK) annually.

The following garden plants prefer soils which are approximately neutral: abelia, alyssum, anemone, arborviate, aster, barberry, begonia, clematis, columbine, coreopsis, cosmos, dahlia, deutzia, forsythia, larkspur, lilac, mock orange, narcissus, pansy, peony, poppy, bell flower, box, bittersweet, butterfly bush, calendula, canna, carnation, chrysanthemum, geranium, gladiolus, hibiscus, honeysuckle, hyacinth, hydrangea, iris, ivy, primrose, privet, rose, spirea, tulip, violet, wisteria and zinnia.

Some plants which prefer slight to medium acidity are: some varieties of aster, bunchflower, fir, heather, holly, huckleberry, juniper, lily, lily-of-the-valley, magnolia, red oak, phlox, pine, spruce, creeping willow and wintergreen.

Medium to strongly acid soils are required by the following: arethusa, arnica, azalea, most varieties of ferns, galax, gardenia, orchid, ladyslipper, pitcherplant, rhododendron, rose pogonia, sandmyrtle, sundew, trailing arbutus, and wild calla.

Most vegetables prefer lime, and dislike acidity. Carrots and tomatoes are only slightly affected by acidity, but only potatoes, radishes, and watermelons positively dislike lime. Fruits which prefer acid soil are blackberry, blackcap raspberry, blueberry, cranberry, huckleberry and strawberry.

The only field crops which prefer acid are flax and velvet bean, while flint corn, millet and rye are only slightly affected by it. All others prefer limed soils.

Leguminous crops—peas, beans, vetch, clover—increase their yield to a remarkable degree in the presence of sufficient lime. Beans, sown in the open field, have been known to yield 10 times as much as formerly after the field was limed. The reason for this is that nitrogen-fixing bacteria, which live in the root tubules of legumes, thrive in alkaline soils.

Lime has a physical as well as a chemical effect upon soil. When spread upon clay soils, lime flocculates the clay, i.e., it causes particles to gather in groups to make larger physical units in the soil. Water and air more easily penetrate such a soil than a soil composed of fine clay particles. On the other hand, in a sandy soil lime has the effect of holding the particles more closely together, so that water is held for a longer period.

One other function of lime in the soil is to release some of the phosphorus and potash from their insoluble compounds, making them available for plant use. Thus, though lime is not itself a fertilizer, it has the effect of increasing the fertility of the soil.

Lime may be applied either to the compost heap or, as is more common, directly to the soil. General advice recommends the application of about one ton of ground limestone per acre every 3 or 4 years. On most soils, this rate will be effective, although soil testing is always advised to avoid unnecessary liming. Since ground limestone becomes available slowly, dangers of overliming are lessened. For the garden, the rate would be about 50 pounds for 1000 square feet every 3 or 4 years, unless tests indicate differently. Fall or early spring applications are satisfactory. Liming is usually done on freshly cultivated soil, preferably on a windless day. Make sure that the lime is spread evenly and thoroughly to avoid skipping areas. Unlike fertilizers, lime does not spread itself over adjacent areas, but works itself down into the soil.

Tons of Ground Limestone Needed to Raise pH

Soils of warm-temperate and tropical regions:	From pH 3.5 to pH 4.5	4.5 to 5.5	5.5 to 6.5
Sandy and loamy sand	0.3	0.3	0.4
Sandy loam	...	.5	.7
Loam	...	.8	1.0
Silt loam	...	1.2	1.4
Clay loam	...	1.5	2.0
Muck	2.5	3.3	3.8
Soils of cool-temperate and temperate regions:			
Sandy and loamy sand	.4	.5	.6
Sandy loam	...	.8	1.3
Loam	...	1.2	1.7
Silt loam	...	1.5	2.0
Clay loam	...	1.9	2.3
Muck	2.9	3.8	4.3

Manure

One of the basic components of the compost heap has always been manure. Man learned early that dung was to be returned to the soil, and he has been returning it ever since. Tradition has it that King Augeas was the first in ancient Greece to make use of manure, and that Hercules introduced the practice into Italy. M. Varro assigns the first rank for excellence to the dung of thrushes kept in aviaries, and praises it as being not only food for land, but excellent food for oxen and swine as well. Columella gives the second rank to pigeon manure, and third rank to poultry manure. Next to these, the dung of swine was highly esteemed. Dungs rated less in quality were, in order, goats, sheep, oxen, and last of all, beasts of burden. The ancients also doubtless composted their manures in some regions, for we read, ". . . In some of the provinces, too, which abound more particularly in cattle, by reason of their prolific soil, we have seen the manure passed through a sieve like so much flour, and perfectly devoid, through lapse of time, of all bad smell or repulsive look, being changed in its appearance to something rather agreeable than otherwise."

Varro believed that corn (small grains) land should be manured with horse-dung, that being the lightest manure of all, while meadow land, he said, thrives better with a manure of a more heavy nature, and supplied by beasts that have been fed upon barley.

The rise of chemical fertilizers in the 20th century has led to a decrease in the amount of manure utilized by world agriculturists. This wasteful misuse of natural fertilizer is often rationalized by farmers and agriculturists, who allege that the supply is not adequate for the need for fertilizers. This faulty reasoning is shown by the fact that in 1889 there were 13,663,000 horses in the United States and 50,331,000 head of cattle. Today there are fewer horses—about 3 million total—but almost 100 million head of cattle. There has also been a subsequent rise in the number of other livestock. The total farm animal population today is just a little under 200 million, compared with 180 million in 1900. And to this must be added a chicken and turkey population of about 450 million. The total manure produced in one year in the United States, is over one billion tons—about 7 tons per head of population. This is plenty for fertilization purposes. The problem is not one of scarcity, but of misuse.

It has also been calculated that a farmer by wise management of his animal manures can return to the soil 70 per cent of the nitrogen, 75 per cent of the phosphorus, and 80 per cent of the potash which was taken out by the home-grown plants his animals eat. This is a considerable saving when it is realized that a dairy cow gives 27,000 pounds of manure annually and a horse, 18,000.

Actually, only a small fraction of the potential crop-producing and soil-conserving value of manure is used. Approximately half of the excrements from farm stock is dropped on pastures and uncultivated ground. Vast amounts of manure in stockyards, piggeries, poultry farms, and other animal industries are considered worthless wastes and are dumped on uncultivated lands. On most farms the manure is so badly handled that it suffers enormous losses of nitrogen through improper fermentation and drying, and of nutrients due to the draining off of the urine and leaching of the solid portion of the manure by rain and surface water. Fermented manure loses ammonia if allowed to dry on the field before it is worked into the soil. There is also a loss as a result of the inefficient use of manure as, for instance, when it is not applied at the season, in the manner, at the rate, or to the crop which would give the greatest return. In view of these facts it is safe to assume that only from a third to a quarter of the potential value of the manure resource of the country is now realized. The present wasteful and inefficient methods of using manure seen in all sections of the country are sufficient evidence that many farmers do not understand the true nature of manure, the perishable character of its most valuable constituents, and the direct money loss incurred through its improper treatment. This situation is doubtless due in large part to the increased use of artificial chemical fertilizers during the past 50 years.

The most common domestic animals which are a source of manure are horses, cattle, goats, sheep, pigs, rabbits, and poultry. The dung consists of the undigested portions of the foods which have been ground into fine bits and saturated with digestive juices in the alimentary tract. It also contains a large population of bacteria which may make up as much as 30 per cent of its mass. Dung contains, as a rule, one-third of the total nitrogen, one-fifth of the total potash, and nearly all of the phosphoric acid voided by the animals. It is because of the large bacterial population, rather than the nutritive elements, that manure is so valuable in the compost heap. The addition of manure provides the necessary bacteria which will break down other materials (grass, plants, etc.) in short order.

The urine contains compounds from the digested portion of the foods and secretions from the animal body. The urine usually contains about two-thirds of the total nitrogen, four-fifths of the total potash, and but very little of the phosphoric acid voided by the animal. Because they are in solution, the elements in the urine are or become available as plant nutrients much more quickly than the constituents found in the dung.

The value of animal manure varies with the food eaten by the animal, the age of the animal, the products yielded (as milk, wool, or meat), and the physical condition and health of the animal. The richer the food is in the elements which are essential to plant growth, the more valuable will be the manure. The manure of animals fed on wheat bran, gluten meal, and cottonseed meal, for instance, will be much richer in nutrient elements than from animals fed with straw or hay without grains.

The manure of young animals, which are forming bones and muscles from their foods, will be poorer in nutrient elements than the manure of mature animals.

The value of the manure varies also according to the animal products which are made, as milk which contains considerable amounts of nitrogen, phosphorus, and potassium; wool which contains a large amount of nitrogen; and beef which contains practically all the elements necessary for plant growth.

Sometimes cattle are grown in regions with mineral-rich soils and fattened in regions where carbonaceous foods are abundant and cheap. The manure from mature animals which are being fattened is relatively rich in minerals, as fat contains little or no minerals.

Unfortunately the values of manure and fertilizers in general have been, in the past, based on the relative amount of nitrogen, phosphoric acid, and potash which they contain. While these are major elements and doubtless affect the values of manure to a greater extent than the proportion of any other constituents, it is misleading to make a direct comparison between farm manures and artificial chemical fertilizers on the basis of the relative amounts of N, P and K. Soil needs organic matter to keep it converted into humus, and humus plays an important role in making the nutrient elements in the soil available to the higher plants.

The average composition of farmyard manure, based on many analyses made at the Experiment Station, Amherst, Massachusetts, was found to be water, 67.7 per cent; nitrogen, 0.465 per cent; phosphoric acid, 0.326 per cent; and potash, 0.485 per cent.

It has been estimated that 80 per cent of the manurial constituents found in the food of milk cows will be voided in the excrements. In fattening cattle and hogs, as much as 90 per cent of the nutrient elements in the food are voided. By keeping these percentages in mind, it is not difficult to calculate the amount of nitrogen, phosphoric acid, potash, and other elements in the manure when the composition of the feeds is known.

As a rule, horse manure is more valuable than the manure of other farm animals. This doubtless varies with the amount of grain which is included in the diet. Grains are relatively high in all plant nutrients. Horse manure is richer in nitrogen than either cow or hog manure and is much more prone to fermentation. For this reason it is frequently referred to as *hot manure*. Another hot manure is that of sheep which is generally quite dry and quite rich. Cow manure and hog manure are relatively wet and correspondingly low in nitrogen. Because of their high water and low nitrogen content, these manures ferment slowly and are commonly regarded as *cold manures*.

It is worth noting that the urine of most animals contains more nitrogen and more potash than the solid excreta. Unfortunately farm manures are handled in such ways that most of the urine is carelessly allowed to escape into drains which lead it off the farm. Urines are especially valuable as activators in converting crop residues into humus.

Assuming that fresh manure is a normal mixture of urine and feces and that conditions have been controlled, fresh manure differs from rotted manure in composition as follows:

1. Rotted manure is richer in plant nutrients. This is a result largely of the loss in dry weight of the manure. One ton of fresh manure may lose one-half its weight in the rotting process.

2. The nitrogen in the composted manure has been fixed by microorganisms while nitrogen in fresh manure is mostly soluble. These organisms build the soluble nitrogen compounds into their own bodies. The nitrogen in the urine is used in the formation of complex proteins during the decomposition of the manure.

3. The solubility of the phosphorus and potash is greater in the composted manure. If leaching can be prevented, there is no change in the total amount of phosphorus and potassium. Precautions must be taken to prevent the loss of nitrogen in the composting process.

Manure can be handled in several ways other than composting, although composting is an excellent way to make use of it, since it will hasten the decomposition of other organic materials in the heap. Manure can be hauled out directly to the fields or garden as it is received, or it can be stored. In city and suburban gardens, of course, manure will have to be composted because of odor problems. One of the best ways of handling it in this situation is by the plastic cover method, discussed earlier.

176

On the farm, if it is spring or summer and there is a proper place for it in a field, it should be applied directly, and then disked or plowed right in. *If even one day goes by between applying the manure and disking it in there is a great loss which will be reflected in a lower yield.* Experiments were conducted where manure was left lying on the soil for about a week before being plowed under and the resultant yield of the plant went down by almost one-half. Organic matter is closely tied in with the general process of the release of nitrogen in the soil and the more organic matter is properly applied to the soil, the more nitrogen will be available to the growing crop and the greater the yield.

Some farmers haul their manure out to the fields daily and, during the winter, put on top of snow. Especially on a farm that has rolling land there will be disastrous losses where this method is followed.

Unless manure can be properly stored and protected without loss through oxidation and leaching, it should be spread on the land, winter and summer, as soon as possible. In no case should it be applied on land with a considerable slope so that it is washed off during the winter months.

The methods by which manures are stored and kept affect their value to a greater degree than any other one factor. It is almost impossible to prevent loss of nutrients entirely. Sources of loss are (1) escape of the natural drainage occuring in manure, (2) leaching caused by soaking of water through the manure, and (3) losses of the gases of fermentation into the air. Perhaps the best storage is in watertight, covered pits. If stored in the open, manure should be heaped on a level or slightly concave place with a clay base to prevent seepage of the juices into the soil. The heap should be made so high that rain will not soak through from top to bottom, and the top of the heap should be slightly concave to catch rain water. It is well also to cover the heap with a thin covering of topsoil if it must stand for a long time.

In the enclosed pit, the manure soon becomes impregnated and completely enclosed by an atmosphere of carbon dioxide having also a relatively high humidity. Under these conditions manure breaks down semi-anaerobically to form a product that is unusually high in the important nutrient elements. There seem to be very little or no losses of nitrogen or other elements when manures are fermented in a properly constructed enclosed pit.

The conditions which affect the fermentation or other decomposition of manures are temperature, degree of compactness of the manure, degree of moisture, and the composition of the manure itself. It is especially important to prevent the manure from drying out. When too dry the manure turns white and is said to be "fire-fanged." In this condition manure has lost a considerable portion of its nitrogen, and some of its organic matter which has escaped into the air as carbon dioxide.

The amount of manure that can be produced by various animals can be determined by multiplying the dry matter consumed in the foods by an appropriate factor. For the horse, multiply the weight of the dry matter consumed by 2.1; for the cow, the factor is 3.8; for the sheep the factor is 1.8; and for poultry, the factor is 1.6. To the product of each of these weights, add the weight of the bedding or litter to determine the total amount of manure that will be made.

In addition to the loss of the nitrogen and potassium, which has been discussed earlier, other losses occur as the result of leaching, scattering and volatilization. Commonly manure is thrown in the barnyard or other exposed place where it is unprotected from rain. Not infrequently the rain water from the barn roof drains into the manure. If the manure is thrown in small, loose, open piles and exposed to rains, it may, in the course of 6 months, lose more than half of its fertilizing value. Leaching losses include the nitrogen, phosphorus, and potassium from the solid portion as well as from the urine.

Organic matter and nitrogen in some volatile form are lost by passing into the air in gaseous form. In the decomposition of the manure, the ammonia produced combines with carbonic acid to form ammonium carbonate and bicarbonate. Losses may be prevented or reduced by the direct hauling of the manure to the field or by protecting it from the various factors which are responsible for the losses. Manure spread on the land and worked into the soil is perhaps in its safest place. The soil has the capacity to rapidly fix large quantities of the plant nutrients carried in the manure. Very little loss as a rule occurs when manure is hauled directly to the field, except when it is spread on hillsides or on frozen ground, where it may be washed down the slope. In any case, it is better to have the liquid go into the soil where plants are to be grown than to allow it to be absorbed by the barnyard soil or to be washed away in surface drainage.

Leaching by rain may be even more serious, as the total soluble matter is thus removed. A single heavy rain of 1½ inches is equivalent to about one gallon of water which will percolate through manure in shallow piles and remove a large part of the soluble material in doing so.

The amounts of fresh excrements produced by farm animals are subject to wide variations, being governed by the kind of animal, age, amounts of food, activity, and other factors. How much is produced annually is given in the following table:

Annual Excrement Per 1,000 Pounds Live Weight

Kind of Animal	Total Excrements Pounds	Solid Pounds	Liquid Pounds
Horse	18,000	14,400	3,300
Cow	27,000	19,000	8,000
Pig	30,500	18,300	12,200
Sheep	12,000	8,300	4,200
Hen	8,500		

In the compost heap, a definite series of decomposition processes take place. These may be outlined briefly as follows:

1. Decomposition of urinary nitrogen. The first change is the formation of ammonia in urine which is lost unless the manure is kept moist and compact.

2. Decomposition of insoluble nitrogen. Next the insoluble nitrogen contained in the solid parts of the excrement undergoes putrefactive changes with the formation of ammonia.

3. Conversion of soluble into insoluble nitrogen. The ammonia and other soluble compounds of nitrogen are used in considerable amounts as food for the bacteria in the manure and are stored in their bodily substance in insoluble form. This nitrogen becomes available when the bacteria die and undergo decomposition.

4. Formation of free nitrogen. Under certain conditions ammonia and nitrates are decomposed with the formation of free nitrogen which escapes into the atmosphere and is thus lost permanently.

5. Decomposition of nitrogen-free compounds. The fibrous parts of the manure which are made up largely of cellulose, lignin, and other complex carbohydrates are eventually broken down with the escape of the carbon into the atmosphere in the form of carbon dioxide, and hydrogen in the form of water. These elements, carbon and hydrogen, escape in such amounts that from $\frac{1}{4}$ to $\frac{1}{2}$ of the original dry matter in the manure is lost. This is the reason for the great shrinkage in bulk during decomposition.

Percentages of Nitrogen, Phosphate and Potash in Different Manures

Kind of Animal Manure	Per Cent Nitrogen	Per Cent Phosphate	Per Cent Potash
Rabbit	2.4	1.4	0.6
Hen	1.1	0.8	0.5
Sheep	0.7	0.3	0.9
Steer	0.7	0.3	0.4
Horse	0.7	0.3	0.6
Duck	0.6	1.4	0.5
Cow	0.6	0.2	0.5
Pig	0.5	0.3	0.5

Scientists Kevorkov and Pchelkin report in a foreign technical journal that additions of 5 to 10 per cent limestone improves manure. The limestone increases biological activity and decreases loss of nitrogen. Manure composts made with limestone had a superior effect on grasses as compared to composts made without limestone. Ground natural limestone should be used. Add to fresh manure at the rate of about one shovelful to every 15 to 20 shovelfuls of manure.

Searching for Manure

The average gardener may have difficulty in obtaining manure for his compost heap. But, as with all materials, manure can be found if a little ingenuity is used, and if a thorough search is made. Here, in the words of Jerome Fisher, is how one gardener found the search for manure interesting and quite rewarding:

When I get all steamed up to build myself a good-sized compost pile, there has always been one big question that sits and thumbs its nose at me: Where am I going to find the manure? I am willing to bet, too, that the lack of manure is one of the reasons why your compost pile is not the thriving humus factory that it might be.

A few years ago I was able to get a good load of cow manure from a nearby farmer for $8.00. You don't have to be an intellectual giant to figure out why that farmer is no longer in business. He sold out his cows last year and got himself a job on the roads.

As a matter of fact I am still able to buy cow manure—from a chap named Joe. He's in the trucking business and is very cagey about where the manure comes from. But the catch is that it costs me $14.00 a load—a scant cord. I bought one load at that figure, but for 6 months could not get up the nerve to incorporate it into my compost pile. At that price I just wanted to stand and look at the golden nuggets—or have my picture taken standing proudly beside my precious pile. No, so far as I'm concerned manure at that figure is a luxury I can't afford.

When I had finally convinced myself that cow manure was out, I said to myself: What about horse manure? The trick seemed to be to find a chap who owned a horse but who for some strange reason was not a gardener. And it was a whole lot easier than I had expected it would be.

I remembered that occasionally I had seen a couple of fellows all decked out in Texan riding gear trotting past my place on Sunday afternoons. The next time I caught sight of them through the lindens down the driveway, I jumped into the car and took after them. One of the riders turned out to be my iceman who I had never learned before was an enthusiastic horseman—and no gardener! Not only that but he had over the past few months accumulated a good pile of manure that he would very much like to get rid of.

It is costing me $6.00 to have that load delivered, and I have made arrangements to channel all of my iceman's horse manure right into my compost pile.

Just about this time a new neighbor moved in down the road a ways. The young son of the family, I was quick to see, was the owner of a Shetland pony. I found that the new neighbors were mighty pleased when I promised to keep their manure pile whittled down. I don't get much there, of course, but the pony is a mare. And she's expecting very soon.

If you, too, are finding that cow manure is out of the picture, investigate the horse situation in your neighborhood.

And if you see a group of horseback riders hitting the trail, take after them, thar's gold in them manure piles.

—JEROME L. FISHER

Poultry Manure

Despite the fact that poultry manure is richer in plant nutrients than stable manure, it is often shunned by gardeners who believe it is detrimental to growing plants.

"Poultry manure burns plants." "Poultry manure must be used with caution." "Poultry manure gives off foul odors." These libels have been repeated so often in speech and in print that even poultrymen have repeated and believed them. As a result of believing such misstatements, they have wasted and misused their valuable product.

In some poultry-producing sections used litter and manure from chicken houses are given away for the hauling; in some places quantities of manure are dumped into holes in the ground, such as unworked quarries, as if it were so much trash to be gotten rid of.

I do not believe we should lower our appraisal of poultry manure even to the extent of calling it a by-product. We who have gained the organic concept of soil fertility realize that growth is but one half of the "wheel of life" pictured by Sir Albert Howard; decay is the other and equally essential half, and in this half manure and so-called waste products are essential helpers.

A poultryman, however small his flock, becomes through commerce a world figure. When he buys mash or grain from his feed dealer, he is drawing upon fertility of soils far away. Perhaps these fields lie in the wheat or corn belts of the United States, perhaps in some other country of the world. After he feeds the grain to his flock, some part of it becomes human food in form of eggs and poultry meat. Another part becomes poultry manure, which as continued production requires, should be returned to the soil.

Into specialized poultry-producing areas pour millions of bushels of grain annually, representing fertility drawn from a vast area of land. A great deal of this potential soil fertility is lost or wasted through poor methods of use. In the eastern United States we often find specialized poultry regions where manure is literally dumped out not far from truck-growing regions where soils need them badly, but the latter imports fantastic quantities of commercial fertilizer.

It is definitely to the interest of the poultry industry, as well as to the interest of crop farmers of all kinds, that they use these wasted resources. Their business depends upon its use; upon its use also depend the health, welfare, and ultimate survival of people. Perhaps we can expect advances in methods of handling poultry manure. Poultrymen in specialized areas may cooperate to prepare their product and market it as compost. Poultrymen, who are also general farmers, are learning to use manure more economically. Those who operate combination poultry and truck farms stand in an ideal position to profit immediately by applying the organic method in handling their manure.

Why has poultry manure acquired an unsavory reputation? What can poultrymen do to realize its full possibility? As a starting point toward answers to these questions, let's compare plant nutrient contents of poultry manure with those of ordinary or "average" stable manure.

Plant Nutrients	Poultry Manure	Stable Manure
Nitrogen	2.12%	0.5%
Phosphoric acid	1.21%	0.3%
Potash	0.6%	0.5%

The higher nitrogen content of poultry manure is a part of the story. This explains why fresh, undigested poultry manure, if applied to plants, produces unbalanced growth and sometimes a withering condition described as "burning." This higher nitrogen content also gives rise to ammonia gas and its unpleasant odor from a pile of manure lying exposed to rain and sun. The odor of ammonia sometimes is stifling inside poultry houses, causing discomfort to people and promoting disease among chickens.

Whenever you get a smell of ammonia gas around a manure pile or stable, you may assure yourself that nitrogen is escaping beyond the reach of plants. Such an odor stands as an undeniable symptom of wasted plant nutrition.

Still another bad result from mishandling this high nitrogen content may be seen where fresh poultry manure is spread on growing grain. Wherever the manure spreader drops a bit of its cargo, grain stalks collapse before harvest. Lush but unbalanced growth resulting from the too-rich and undigested nitrogen content of the manure, has produced stalks too weak to support their own weight.

Certain practices in the poultry house keep down nitrogen losses and prevent ammonia fumes. Sprinkling ground phosphate rock and ground dolomitic limestone into the litter will help. These materials aid in keeping litter dry as well as combining with nitrogen to form a relatively involatile compound. Composting of poultry manure can actually be started on the poultry house floor.

In selecting litter for the poultry house, first consideration should go to its water-holding capacity. Cutting straw by running it through a roughage mill doubles its capacity to hold moisture. Dry ground corn cobs absorb a large amount of moisture, and may be used in combination with chopped straw. Finely shredded corn stalks also have large absorptive capacity. These home-grown products are available to many poultrymen. Commercially produced peat moss and dried shredded stalks of sugar cane may be bought from supply houses.

Since the making of compost in heaps requires more labor than most of us care to spend, and valuable nutrients are often washed out of the heap, it is most practical to spread the manure right in the field. However, certain precautions must be taken. If manure is exposed to the sun and air for several days before being disked or plowed in, it will lose most of its value.

We also find that good results with poultry manure are obtained by applying a light sprinkling of the manure on fields carrying a heavy plant cover, such as a field of sod. The heavy sod supplies enough carbon to produce a balanced decay with the nitrogen and other nutrients carried in the manure.

Since sod is not always available, crops may be planted and grown for the specific purpose of supplying plant material to balance the high nitrogen content of poultry manure and to aid in field composting. Small grains, thickly sown corn, sorghums, Sudan grass, soy beans and other quick growing annuals are well adapted to sheet composting. Sprinkled lightly with poultry manure, then worked into the soil, these crops improve soil structure and result in increased fertility and improved yields.

If, for some reason, it is not possible to grow a special crop to receive the manure, fresh plant matter can be mixed with the poultry droppings and spread on the fields to be fertilized as a mulch. Or, this mixture of manure and green matter can be disked into the soil. The general farmer has plenty of plant residues in the farm straw, low-quality hay, or corn stalks, but the specialized poultryman may be hard pressed to find enough. As suggested earlier in this article, the solution of this problem requires cooperation between poultrymen in specialized areas in preparing their product into compost. Specialist poultrymen may also be able to work out cooperatives with crop and truck farmers for their mutual benefit.

In having an unbalanced material with which to work, the specialized poultryman stands in a position somewhat similar to that of the specialized grain farmer who produced the grains which went into the chicken feed. The grain farmer, of course, has an excessive amount of straw, the decay of which is difficult because he lacks enough material of nitro-genous content to balance with it. They stand at opposite ends of an economic line, and are often separated by many miles, possibly thousands of miles, but sometimes they may be within a reasonable distance of each other.

For further discussion on manure handling, see the chapter on Animal Manure in Composting.

Olive Residues

The analysis of olive pomace is given as 1.15 nitrogen, 0.78 phosphoric acid and 1.26 potash, while some olive refuse showed 1.22 nitrogen, 0.18 phosphoric acid and 0.32 potash. It is not known how olive pits would show up from a fertilizer standpoint, but there is little doubt that they too should be used for adding fertility to the soil, since they not only contain phosphorus and nitrogen in higher amounts than mere refuse, but also lignin. Olive residues should be thoroughly composted, mixed with other materials, before using.

Pea Wastes

Pea wastes are of several kinds, mainly available in quantities in the cannery regions. Apart from the high feeding value of any legume crop, pea shells and vines should be returned to the land in some form. If they can be fed and thus be used as manure residue, they are best employed. If they show diseases, they can be burned and the ashes used for fertilizing. Pea pod ash contains almost 3 per cent phosphoric acid and 27 per cent potash. They can be composted with great ease since their nitrogen content, which is highest in green pods and vines, tends to produce a quick breakdown.

Peat Moss

Peat moss is the partially decomposed remains of plants accumulated over centuries under relatively airless conditions. It is a highly valuable organic material for soil building. Peat moss loosens heavy soils, binds light soils, holds vast amounts of water, increases aeration, aids root development, stops nutrients from leaching away. It can be added to the soil, used as a mulch, or used as a composting material.

When dry, it will absorb up to 15 times its weight of water. Its effect on soils is to make a "crumb" structure that holds much more water because of the increased surface area of the soil particles. This fact becomes important when we realize that for every pound of dry matter or actual solids in a plant, there must be taken from the soil from $\frac{1}{4}$ to $\frac{1}{2}$ ton of water.

Soil-held moisture is not only vital in preventing drought damage, but it is also necessary to carry in solution the nutrients the plant must have to grow. Proper amounts of moisture also aid the soil organisms to break up the organic compounds into usable forms.

Peat moss has a very open, fibrous texture, permitting free development of even tiny hair roots. It improves aeration, too, letting the soil "breathe deeply." The ground is kept loose and friable, without crusting or compacting, and it does not dry out rapidly. Drainage is also improved in heavy clay soils, and in light, sandy ones, plant nutrients are prevented from leaching away. Peat moss contains no weed seeds, no plant disease organisms, no insect eggs or larvae. It is biologically sterile.

Like other organic materials, peat acts as a buffer against toxic substances. It will clear up unbalanced soil conditions, as when a soil is overloaded with alkalis or the residues of certain chemical fertilizers. Large applications of peat have restored many such soils to production.

Finally, its effects last many years. Tests at Pennsylvania State Agricultural College showed that 70 per cent of its organic content was still in the soil after 10 years.

For all its good points, peat moss should not be regarded as a miracle soil amendment. While some sedge peats do contain as high as 3 per cent nitrogen, this is released slowly,

The wide open, fibrous texture of peat moss, which is illustrated above, permits free development of the tiniest root hairs. Peat moss is commonly used to improve soil aeration, keep ground loose and friable, and make compost acid.

over many years. Compost, or materials like leaf mold, are preferable to peat moss if easily procurable, because they have more nutrients and in a more readily available form.

Because of its low nutrient content, and because peat often is rather expensive to purchase, it is not generally used in compost. If, however, a distinctly acid compost is wanted for certain plants, peat can be substituted for soil in the heap and lime should be omitted. Peat compost is used for camellia, rhododendron, azalea, blueberries, sweet potatoes, watermelons, eggplant, potatoes, tomatoes, many perennial herbs and most shrubs and trees—all acid loving plants.

Phosphate Rock

Phosphate rock is an excellent natural source of phosphorus for fertilizer use. Phosphate rock varies somewhat in its composition dependent upon its source; however, the

187

general constituents are as follows: Calcium phosphate or bone phosphate of lime composes 65 per cent of the total (equivalent P_2O_5—30 per cent). Phosphate rock contains other compounds and mineral elements, many of which are essential for plant growth; included are calcium carbonate, calcium fluoride, iron oxide, iron sulphide, alumina, silica, manganese dioxide, titanium oxide, sodium, copper, chromium, magnesium, strontium, barium, lead, zinc, vanadium, boron, silver and iodine.

The phosphate rock sold on the market today is different from that of a few decades ago. Phosphate rock today has been much more finely ground. In the old days the machinery for grinding the raw phosphate rock into a powder was quite crude so that ground-up particles were coarse and did not break down too easily in the soil. However, today there is such elaborate machinery available that the rock can be ground finer than talcum powder, thus a sufficient part of it is immediately available to the plant because the particles are so tiny that the organic acids and carbon dioxide produced by the plant roots and bacteria in the soil can break them down quickly.

Many of the minor elements found in phosphate rock are inactivated in the superphosphate process. Such elements as boron, zinc, nickel, iodine and others are available in rock phosphate but not in superphosphate.

Phosphorus may be added to the compost heap and to the soil in the form of raw pulverized phosphate rock or as bone meal. The soil acids will make these relatively inert forms of phosphorus soluble in sufficient amounts to meet the needs of the plants.

Superphosphate. The difference between superphosphate and rock phosphate is that superphosphate has been treated with an equal amount of sulphuric acid to make it more soluble. This results in mono-calcium-phosphate, a slowly water soluble phosphate and calcium sulphate, a highly soluble neutral salt. One disadvantage of sulphur, among many others, is that it causes sulphur reducing bacteria to multiply which work on it to reduce it. But these sulphur reducing bacteria have to feed, and part of their diet is a certain fungus whose function is to break down cellulose in the soil. It becomes a vicious cycle. Sulphur multiplies a bacteria which destroy certain badly needed fungi. The use of superphosphate, therefore, causes an imbalance in the microbiological population of the soil.

Rock phosphate, on the other hand, is not highly water soluble and is lost in the soil only through cropping. The beneficial effects of rock phosphate far outlast those of superphosphate. Rock phosphate, when finely ground is available to the plant as it needs it. Plant roots give off carbon dioxide and certain organic acids, which in contact with the rock phosphate in the soil, make it available for plant use. Thus, that rock phosphate which is not made available by the action of plant roots remains unchanged in the soil until roots develop in its vicinity.

Humus and Phosphate. In his article, "Organic Matter . . . The Key to Phosphate Availability," Dale H. Sieling, Dean of the University of Massachusetts School of Agriculture, wrote that additions of chemical phosphate "usually have only a very temporary beneficial effect because the action of certain soil components changes the phosphate into forms not readily available to plants. In fact, some experiments with radio-active phosphorus have shown that only 5 to 10 per cent of the phosphate added to acid soils reaches the crop for which it was intended."

He recommends following the procedure of "practical farmers (who) have long observed that loss of organic matter in soils caused phosphate deficiency and consequent crop failure. Others have found that management practices which traditionally included the addition of large amounts of barnyard manure were adequate for great crop production, even though the manure was known to be low in phosphate."

Profitable. Reports also point out the added profit in using rock phosphate, since it is actually less expensive than superphosphate. A. L. Lang, professor of Agronomy at the University of Illinois, reports on the lasting quality of rock phosphate. "Laid down once in a rotation, rock phosphate will have plenty of reserve plant food at the end of 4 or 5 years." As an example of this permanence, he cites a demonstration plot in Urbana, Illinois, where 1,500 pounds of rock phosphate per acre were applied in 1935 on land which was continually cropped without the addition of any other fertilizer except limestone until 1949. At the end of these 15 years the gross returns over limestone amounted to $129.67 an acre, or $8.65 for each dollar invested. In the same experiment an equal amount of money spent for superphosphate

189

returned only $4.90 per dollar invested during the same period.

Professor Lang concludes, "This is the kind of return which makes us feel here in Illinois that rock phosphate is a good investment and that it will make a good investment in any part of the country where there is a phosphorus deficiency, particularly in the acid soils of the South."

In most grain growing areas, the limiting factors in production are poor physical structure and inadequate amounts of phosphate, nitrogen and water. Limestone and rock phosphate, states Professor Lang, have been used to eliminate these confining factors. This is done by applying them not to the grain crop but to the legume and grass in the rotation in large enough quantities to insure immediate response and maximum growth. The legumes supply the soil with nitrogen and, together with the grasses, add active organic matter which improves the physical structure of the soil and increases its water holding capacity. In many sections of the country rock phosphate use is on the recommended list of conservation practices for which the Production and Marketing Administration will contribute about half of the cost.

Application Rate. Phosphate rock is often added to the compost pile. A light sprinkling applied with each series of layers (in the Indore heap) will be sufficient to supply phosphate to maintain a healthy soil. For vegetable and flower gardens, phosphate rock may be applied alone; generally, one pound for 10 square feet is enough for 3 to 5 years. The same application is usually recommended for lawns. The other major source of phosphorus for the garden is bone meal.

Potash Rock

Potash rock, a naturally-occurring rock containing a high percentage of potassium, is the material used most often for a potash source in the compost heap. It is readily available in most parts of the country and is inexpensive. Modern machinery can pulverize rock materials to such fineness that nutrients become available for plant assimilation in relatively short periods of time, dependent upon the condition of the soil to be treated.

Potash rock, in addition to being incorporated directly into the compost pile, may be used alone. Usually, one-half ton per acre, or 2-1/3 pounds per 100 square feet, is the recommended application. It may be used on most any type of soil, contributing a wide variety of minerals without danger of overdosage. The mineral elements are readily available, when organic matter is added to soils, by multiplying the bacteria and also gives mild organic acids which take care of most deficiencies.

Potato Wastes

The potash content of tubers is usually around 2.5 per cent. Dry potato vines contain approximately 1.6 per cent potash, 4.0 per cent calcium, 1.1 per cent magnesium, and considerable amounts of sulphur and other minerals. Potato skins are usually put on the compost with other kitchen wastes. Their nitrogen content has been found, even when the skins were reduced to ashes, as high as .6 per cent. Tubers are storage organs and therefore abound with trace minerals.

Rice Hulls

Often considered a waste product, rice hulls have been found to be very rich in potash and decompose readily when worked into the soil, thereby increasing humus content. The hulls make an excellent soil conditioner and a worthwhile addition to the compost heap.

Gardeners in the Texas-Louisiana Gulf Coast area will be able to get ample amounts of this material from rice mills, which often deliver it free in order to dispose of it. Some mills make a practice of burning the hulls, and the residue from this operation contains a high percentage of potash, making it especially valuable as a composting material.

The hulls are especially suited for mulching material; they are long-lasting and will not blow away.

Sawdust

Sawdust is a useful addition to the compost heap, although it is better used as a mulch. Some gardeners who have access to large quantities use it for both with equally fine results. In most areas, lumber yards will give away sawdust without charge, and the gardener has only to come and haul it.

Sawdust is becoming more and more widely recommended for use in gardening and farming. It is a fine natural mulch and soil conditioner that can be used to bring about improvement in soil structure.

Sawdust is low in nitrogen, containing about one-tenth of one per cent in its total make-up. One of the objections against using sawdust is that it may cause a nitrogen deficiency. However, many gardeners report fine results applying sawdust as a mulch to the soil surface without adding any supplementary nitrogen fertilizer. If your soil is of low fertility, watch plants carefully during the growing season. If they become light green or yellowish in color, side-dress with an organic nitrogen fertilizer as cottonseed meal, blood meal, compost, manure or tankage.

Some people are afraid that the continued application of sawdust will sour their soil, that is, make it too acid. A very comprehensive study of sawdust and wood chips made from 1949 to 1954 by the Connecticut Experiment Station reported no instance of sawdust making the soil more acid. It is possible, though, that sawdust used on the highly alkaline soils of the western United States would help to make the soil neutral. That would be a very welcome effect.

Plentiful quantities of wood chips, as well, are becoming available in many sections of the country and are being widely used by gardeners and farmers. In some ways wood chips are superior to sawdust. They contain a much greater percentage of bark, and have a higher nutrient content.

The general verdict on sawdust and wood chips is that both materials are safe and effective soil improvers. They do a fine job of aerating the soil and increasing its moisture-holding capacity.

Seaweed

Seaweed has been in use in England, Scotland and Wales for many years and is a well-valued fertilizer. There are different types of seaweed. The most important ones are laminaria, also called driftweed or kelp. This plant has a stem and a broad flat lamina or leaf. It grows immediately below low water mark. Its stems are higher in moisture, but also they have a very high percentage of potash, while the leaves are somewhat drier and have a lower percentage of potash. The dry stems have about 10 to 12 per cent potash, the dry leaves or fronds, 5 per cent. Another seaweed is fucus, this is also known as bladder wrack or cutweed and grows between tide marks. Its potash content is low, when dried it does not contain more than 2 to 4 per cent. But fucus grows very well in sheltered waters, inlets, where not so many laminaria can be found. Then too, it can be cut from the rocks at low tide. Laminaria on the other hand must be washed

Every seaside gardener should make use of the abundant seaweed washed up along the shoreline. Roughly comparable to barnyard manure in organic matter and mineral content, seaweed can be collected by hand or by machine.

ashore. Another one is ulva, also called sea lettuce. It is washed ashore in great quantities in quiet bays and inlets. This weed is very rich in nitrates. The content of ulva in bays and inlets, where sweet water rivers carry a lot of mud, is much higher in nitrogen than one grown in pure sea water.

Seaweed in general, that is a mixture of all of those which can easily be found on the shore, contains on the average, per ton 7 pounds of nitrogen compounds, 2 pounds of phosphoric acid, 22 pounds of potash, 36 pounds of sodium chloride, and about 400 pounds of organic matter. Barnyard manure, for comparison, may contain per ton 11 pounds of nitrogen, 6 pounds of phosphoric acid, 15 pounds of potash, and 380 pounds of organic matter. Of course, there is no sodium chloride in manure. Fresh seaweed, therefore, is rather similar in its organic matter content as compared with ordinary farmyard manure. It is, however, poor in nitrogen and poor in phosphate, but much richer in potash. Wherever it can be collected easily, with not too much labor and expense, it is one of the most ideal materials for fertilizing and composting. In the old world it has been used before and after potatoes and, in particular, for broccoli, lettuce, peas and cabbage, also for root crops, mangels. For cabbage and root crops it is

193

best to have the seaweed well-rotted, while for potatoes it could be plowed under in November or December. The plowing under of fresh seaweed is more easily done when well-rotted. However, if it is to be plowed under, it should be done immediately after collecting, that is, while it is still wet and green, and early enough so that the salt which adheres to it can be washed out by rain and does not poison the soil. On the Island of Jersey, it has been used for early potatoes, and then about 40 tons of freshly collected seaweed were used on sandy soils. It also has been used after the harvest of potatoes for the next crop. When it had dried about 14 tons per acre were used. The difficulty with drying seaweed is that it deteriorates, and if it is rained on, then many of the minerals, particularly the easily soluble potassium salts, are washed out and lost. If dried, it should, therefore, be dried on a platform or a floor through which the moisture cannot run away, and should also be protected from rain. It is better to dry it relatively quickly and in the dried state it can be spread directly, but we would advise adding it to the compost heap.

It could, however, be composted in the green state. The observation has been made that if composted with manure, particularly manure which is very rich in litter, it makes an ideal mixture and aids a speedy decay of the straw. This is carried out in such a way that very little nitrogen is lost and all the other substances are preserved. Its decay is very rapid. The washing out of potash in the case of composting is less of a danger. It is not quite as well balanced as manure, but we believe that in cases of compost, where there is a shortage of potassium, as we have frequently observed in analyzing compost samples, it would be a very good substance to use for balancing compost. For this reason seaweed is excellent for potatoes, which need a lot of potassium. Its content of salt might be a certain disadvantage, but composting, or applying it late in fall, or in winter, might compensate for the salt. Barley responds particularly well to it, besides the other crops mentioned already, especially on light sandy soils.

It should not be allowed to rot in large heaps in the open, without protection, or without proper composting methods. The other way of preserving it is drying as described. A third way is to burn it and use the ashes, as is done with kelp. The ashes, of course, are much richer in minerals in per-

194

centage, than the original seaweed, because through the burning and eliminating of water and organic matter, there is a concentration of salts. The potash content in such a case might run up to 12 per cent. In burning seaweed one should take care that it is not heated up too violently, otherwise more volatile substances and trace elements which are present in seaweed might be lost. The potash content of the ashes of laminaria, for instance, is 28 per cent, while of fucus, it ranges between 12 and 18 per cent. The nitrogen content of the fresh material ranges between 0.2 to 0.38 per cent, as a dry seaweed between 1.1 to 1.5 per cent. The organic matter of the fresh seaweed ranges between 12 to 25 per cent, of the dry seaweed, from 64 to 79 per cent. Its particular value for the root crops and sugar beets has suggested that in cases where the seashore is not near enough to collect the material one should try to get the dry seaweed, have it pressed in bales like hay, or use the ashes as an addition to compost and manure, which is used for root crops. Either in bales or the ashes could be shipped relatively easily.

Seaweed is also rich in iodine, in fact the burning of seaweed in Normandy and Brittany and in England was one of the important sources of iodine. On a recent visit to Rhode Island we picked up several varieties of seaweed and analyzed them in our laboratory. The figures found there confirm the figures quoted about this in the literature. In composting it will be best to underlayer it with earth and other composting material, especially if wet, fresh seaweed is used. Dried seaweed would be composted just as one does hay, or grass cuttings. The ashes would be sprinkled into the compost heap like thin layers of lime, as they are usually applied. Besides sugar beets, asparagus is a plant which responds very well to seaweed. There the fresh seaweed could be used as well as the ashes, and the sodium chloride content would even be beneficial, for asparagus is a plant which grows much better when a teaspoon of salt is given to each plant. Dry seaweed could also be used as a mulch around asparagus. While its use might not be in question for the inland farmer, it is certainly a very welcome supplement for the farmer and gardener near the seashore.

Straw

Although straw will add little nutrient value to the compost heap, it is used widely because it bulks up the heap

Straw is among the most common materials used for composting. It is easily obtainable, supplies bulk as well as organic matter and plant food to the heap. Bales of spoiled hay and straw can often be bought from local farmers.

quite a bit, adding considerable organic material, and large quantities are readily available. Most farmers can offer bales of spoiled hay to gardeners at nominal costs.

The fertilizer value of straw is, like that of all organic matter, twofold: first, carbon material is added to the compost; second, plant food is added. The carbon serves the soil bacteria as energy food, while the plant food becomes released for growing crops. Where much straw is available, it is advisable to incorporate considerable amounts of nitrogen, preferably in form of manures, so that the bacteria which break down the straw into humus do not deplete the soil of the nitrogen that is needed by growing plants.

It is also recommended that the straw be cut up if used in quantities. If mixed with other materials that hold water, or if composted with ample amounts of barnyard manure, long straw offers no trouble, though heaps cannot be turned easily. Straw compost must therefore be allowed to stand longer. Quicker action is secured by weighing down the material with a thicker layer of earth. This also preserves the moisture inside the heap.

If a large straw pile is allowed to stay outside in the field where deposited by the thresher, it will, with the help of rain and snow, in time decay at its bottom into a crumbly substance. Such predigested material is excellent for compost-making and mulching. Some of the fungi are of the types that form mycorrhizal relations with the roots of fruit trees, evergreens, grapes, roses, etc., and a straw mulch will therefore benefit these plants not only as a moisture preserver but as an inoculant for mycorrhizae.

The nitrogen value of straw is not negligible, but so small that it need not be accounted for in composting. The mineral value of straw depends on the soils where the crops were grown. Typical analyses of straws, computed by Kenneth C. Beeson of the U. S. Department of Agriculture, are here given in per cent:

	Calcium	Potash	Magnesium	Phosphorus	Sulphur
Barley	.4	1.0	.1	.1–.5	.1
Buckwheat	2.0	2.0	.3	.4	?
Corn stover	.3	.8	.2	.2	.2
Millet	1.0	3.2	.4	.2	.2
Oats	.2	1.5	.2	.1	.2
Rye	.3	1.0	.07	.1	.1
Sorghum	.2	1.0	.1	.1	.2
Wheat	.2	.8	.1	.08	.1

Sewage Sludge

The use of sewage sludge by gardeners and farmers throughout the United States has been climbing upward in recent years. The fertilizer value of the sludge produced depends largely on which processing method is used.

Activated sludge: This kind is produced when the sewage is agitated by air rapidly bubbling through it. Certain types of very active bacteria coagulate the organic matter, which

197

settles out, leaving a clear liquid that can be discharged into streams and rivers with a minimum amount of pollution.

Generally, activated sludge is heat-treated before being made available to gardeners and farmers; its nitrogen content is between 5 and 6 per cent, phosphorus from 3 to 6 per cent. Its plant food value is similar to cottonseed meal—a highly recommended organic fertilizer and a good material for the compost heap.

Digested sludge: This type of residue is formed when the sewage is allowed to settle (and liquid to drain off) by gravity without being agitated by air. The conventional anaerobic digestion system takes about 10 to 14 days from the time the sewage reaches the sedimentation tank until the digested solids are pumped into filter beds, often sand and gravel, for drying. The final step is removal of the dry material, either to be incinerated or used for soil improvement.

Digested sludge has about the same fertilizer value as barnyard manure. Nitrogen varies from 2 to 3 per cent, phosphorus averaging about two per cent.

In putting sludge into a compost heap, it must be thoroughly broken up, otherwise it will not be able to aerate itself, and it should be applied in very thin layers, not more than one inch at any one place. Complete breakdown can be assured through the use of manure, good soil and earthworms in the heap.

Suggestions to Organic Gardeners — Practically every superintendent of a sewage treatment plant will allow a gardener to haul all the sludge he can use. The air dried sludge cake or the filter cake makes excellent compost material.

Some plants have a sludge disintegrater to pulverize the sludge cakes, in which case the pulverized sludge cake can be mixed with the garden soil without any further preparation. Some people may object to the use of sludge on lawns and gardens because of a slight odor from the sometimes insufficiently digested sludge.

The compost gardener, however, can use the sludge cakes as they come from the sludge drying beds or sludge filters in his compost heaps. The small garden owner will not have any lack of compost material, as he can get all the sludge he desires—for the hauling.

In building his compost heap, he can use instead of water-waste activated sludge, an odorless liquid with a high nitrogen content (6 per cent and more). This activated sludge is available, of course, only in sewage treatment plants using the activated sludge process.

The question has been raised as to whether or not industrial wastes in the sewage are harmful for plants. As a reasonably safe rule, it may be stated that if the sewage treatment plant uses a biological process for purification (sand filter, trickling filter, activated sludge) the sewage sludge can be considered harmless, because biological treatment is not possible if toxic industrial wastes are to be treated with domestic sewage. Furthermore, the superintendent of a plant usually knows the type of wastes treated in his plant and quite often has an analysis of the sewage sludge produced.

As previously mentioned, most sewage treatment plants are glad if they can get rid of the sludge or filter cakes without any expense. If the sludge would be offered in a pulverized form—which could be done by an inexpensive machine—the sludge would be more easily accepted. However, to the organic gardener the unpulverized sludge cake should be a welcome compost material which will be easily broken down with the other material of the compost heap.

For a more complete discussion on the value and use of sludge, see the chapter on that subject.

Soil

An important ingredient in the compost heap is soil. Besides being layered along with the other materials in the Indore heap, the heap itself should be built directly on freshly dug earth. The site of the heap should be leveled and the soil loosened. Each layer of the heap included 6 inches of plant material, two inches of fresh manure, and one-eighth of an inch of soil. This is an exceedingly thin layer and it will not be possible to spread it as evenly as a layer of cement, for example. But enough soil can be added to each layer to be the equivalent of a layer one-eighth of an inch thick.

The soil in the compost heap acts as a base for absorbing the volatile substances produced in the process of fermentation and thus prevents them from being lost to the air. Fertile soil also contains billions of the soil organisms which do the work of breaking down the plant and animal residues and converting them into compost. The soil contains the minerals which are necessary for the life processes of the soil organisms which grow and reproduce rapidly in the compost heap.

After the heap has been built it is covered with an outer

layer of soil to prevent excessive evaporation of water and to conserve the heat of fermentation in the heap. This outer encasing layer of soil should be about two inches thick.

One need not hesitate to take top soil from the garden or field for building a compost heap as it will be returned again and in manifold measure. When the heap is turned, the outer layer of soil can be carefully removed and used again over the rebuilt heap.

For hastening the composting process, old compost may be added to the new heap in place of soil. When this is done, the composting may be completed in approximately one-third of the time that is ordinarily required.

The outer layer of soil on the side of the heap can be dispensed with if a suitable enclosure is used. Compost may be made in a pit dug in the ground in which case the earthen walls of the pit form the enclosure. In some cases the sides of the pit are lined with bricks or cement blocks, but the bottom must never be anything but the soil.

For making peat compost, the soil is replaced by peat in making the successive layers of the heap and in the outside or top casing of the heap. Peat compost is especially recommended for blueberries, azaleas, camellias, and other acid-loving plants.

Many gardeners consider soil as the compost ingredient most difficult to obtain in sufficient quantities. Especially if he is a small-lot gardener, he may have trouble finding sufficient quantities of soil unless he is fortunate enough to haul some away from an excavated site for new homes, or unless he purchases topsoil from a local nursery. Another way of getting soil is to take a shovel and a small truck or station wagon, and go into the country to find good loam (always get the landowner's permission, and don't take more than 4 or 5 inches of earth from any one spot in the woods). Silt from ponds, streams and ditches, soil from new roads and paths (replaceable with coal ashes and stones), hills to be graded, and unplanted spaces in front of buildings, all provide additional sources that gardeners may tap in the soil search.

Mud from ponds, lakes or streams (if not chemically contaminated) should be spread out for aeration in flat heaps not over 6 or 7 inches in height, with straw, hay and leaves mixed in to break it up, before using in the compost material. Add plenty of ground limestone or wood ashes, as the mud will probably be quite acid. It would be a mistake to directly apply this mud to the land as this would cause the same trouble usually experienced when raw manure is incorporated in the land or a green manure cover crop is plowed under.

The overflow from the Nile River in Egypt contains a fine sediment that makes unnecessary the application of other fertilizers. The Chinese have been adept in utilizing the sediment of streams, but include it in compost heaps instead of directly adding such sediment to the land. River bottoms and washed down soil from floods and overflows provide excellent composting material.

In the average compost pile, earth comprises only about 5 per cent of the bulk of the heap; but here, as in many things in life, quality and utility outrank quantity. In successive layers in the compost heap appear 6 inches of plant material, two inches of manure, and one-eighth of an inch (just a mist-like sprinkling, to which compost is a valuable amendment as an activator) of earth (with a touch of lime), until a 5 foot height is attained, when a two-inch blanket of earth will be needed. A corner of a barn or cellar, or a pit (like that which is used for storing root crops) dug below the frost line and walled in with straw, might be utilized. Mix some straw or hay with the earth and cover the heap of earth with a thick layer of straw, to lessen the danger of freezing. If no earth has been saved and you have a lot of manure, leaves and other materials ready for composting in the wintertime, extra quantities of lime must be used in the inside sandwich layers of the heap and the outside blanket normally of earth should be of at least two feet of straw. Any type of earth excepting sterile sand may be used in a compost heap, but the more "life" or bacterial activity present, the better.

Sugar Wastes

In sugar manufacturing, several wastes accumulate; the greatest quantity is the filter material, often made of bone transferred into charcoal, which is filled with residues from the sugar and sold as bone black. Its phosphorus content is above 30 per cent, its nitrogen value around two per cent, and its potassium content varies. Raw sugar wastes show a content of over one per cent nitrogen and over 8 per cent phosphoric acid.

Tanbark

Tanbark is the residue, resulting from the process of tanning leather. In past years, it was made up of the bark from hemlock, oak and chestnut trees. For the most part, this tanbark was strictly a waste product, to be piled in huge mounds near the tanneries, similar to the large waste piles near coal mines.

The tanbark being used today represents the waste materials from wattle, mangrove, myrobalans and valonia—plants used in modern tanning methods and imported from South America, Africa, India and Asia Minor.

In the tanning process, these materials are made up into batches of two tons—consisting of equal parts of the imported ingredients. These materials are then placed into an autoclave (steam pressure cooker) and "cooked" for two hours under 70 pounds steam pressure.

This cooking extracts the tannins—used to tan the leather. The waste material is dumped into trucks and hauled to a hammermill where it is ground through a ½-inch screen.

The ground material is made into piles from 5 to 6 feet high, 10 to 12 feet wide and 300 feet long. These heaps are inoculated with 4 different types of bacteria. After the bacteria has worked on the material for two weeks, it is turned over by a bulldozer and allowed to work for another week or 10 days.

At the end of 3 weeks, the material looks and smells like virgin soil. It is being packaged in half bushel and 3 bushel bags, and is sold in bulk at $10 per ton. The product is distributed under the trade names of Elkorganite for the screened material and Soil Naturalizer for the screenings.

Laboratory tests have given the following analysis of the material: nitrogen 1.7 per cent; phosphorus 0.9 per cent; potash 0.2 per cent and trace minerals of aluminum, calcium, cobalt, copper, iron, lead, magnesium, manganese, molybdenum, zinc and boron.

Many gardeners have long been enthusiastic about tanbark as a mulching material. Generally it varies in size from crumbs to large peagravel and has a good dark color. Beds mulched with this material appear for long periods as if they have just been cultivated. Because of its attractiveness, tanbark is a favorite for use as a mulch around flowers.

Other characteristics: material is heavy and not conducive to blowing away; wets easily and holds up to 100 per cent of its own weight in water; pH slightly more acid than peat moss.

Tankage

Tankage is the refuse from slaughterhouses and butcher shops other than blood freed from the fats by processing. Depending on the amount of bone present, the phosphorus content varies greatly. The nitrogen content varies usually between 5 and 12.5 per cent; the phosphoric acid content is usually around two per cent, but may be much higher.

Tankage, because it is usually so rich in nutrient value, is especially valuable to the compost pile. It is one of the few sources of animal matter available. Tankage is usually given away free to anyone who will bring a container for it. However, the gardener should make inquiry before going for it, as each slaughterhouse handles this waste product differently and the product is usually available only at certain times.

Tea Grounds

Useful as a mulch or for adding to compost heap, one analysis of tea leaves showed the relatively high content of 4.15 per cent nitrogen, which seems exceptional. Both phosphorus and potash were present in amounts below one per cent.

Tobacco Wastes

Tobacco stems, leaf waste and dust are good organic fertilizer, especially high in potash. The nutrients contained in 100 pounds of tobacco wastes are 2.5 to 3.7 pounds of nitrogen, almost a pound of phosphoric acid, and from 4.5 to 7 pounds of potassium.

After the tobacco leaves are stripped for market in the late fall, thousands of tobacco stalks are left on nearly every farm. Some of these the farmer uses to fertilize his own fields, chopping the stalks up and disking them into the soil in which he will raise grains and legumes. Some of these stalks are available for gardeners, however, and tobacco processing plants bale further wastes for shipment to gardeners.

These wastes can be used anywhere barnyard manure is recommended, except on tobacco, tomatoes and other members of the tobacco or potato family, because they may carry some of the virus diseases of these crops, especially tobacco mosaic virus.

Compost tobacco wastes, or use them in moderation in mulching or sheet composting mixed with other organic materials. They should not be applied alone in concentrated amounts as a mulch—the nicotine will eliminate beneficial insects as well as harmful ones, and earthworms and other soil organisms. For the same reason, nicotine insecticides are not recommended, and in addition they may contain even more harmful hydrated lime and sulphur compounds which can damage foliage.

Water Hyacinth

Southern composters who lack sufficient green matter for the heap can often find quantities of the water hyacinth *(Eichhornia crassipes)* which grows with such profusion in the streams of the South. This plant has been considered a serious menace to agriculture, fisheries, sanitation and health in the South and other parts of the world where it grows with remarkable rankness. It has become such a menace to the sanitation and health of rural Bengal, for instance, that the Bengal Department of Agriculture suggested the possibility of utilizing the plant as a source of manure to meet, to some extent, the deficiency of nitrogen in the soils of India and Pakistan. With a view to obtaining information regarding the course of decomposition of water hyacinth in compost and soil, A. Karim of Dacca University undertook an investigation of the microbiological decomposition of water hyacinth and reported his results in an issue of *Soil Science*. The researcher found that fungi, rather than bacteria, played the major role in the decomposition of the plant, but when composting was controlled, the resulting product was of high manurial efficiency. A comparison of water hyacinth compost with horse manure indicated almost equal manurial efficiency of the two.

Although water hyacinth is readily decomposed by fungi, it does not appear to be a satisfactory source of energy for nitrogen-fixing bacteria. The soil experiments indicated that water hyacinth, if allowed to decompose in the soil, offers definite promise as a nitrogen-carrying manure. Home gardeners in the South will find this plant to be a readily available source of green matter for the compost heap, especially when shredded and mixed with partially decomposed "starter" material, such as soil or manure.

Weeds

Weeds can be put to use in the compost pile. Their nitrogen, phosphorus and potash content are similar to other plant residues, and their large quantities can provide much humus for the soil. Weed seeds will be killed by the high temperatures in the compost pile, and any weeds which sprout from the top of the heap can merely be turned under. Weeds can even be used in the green manuring program, as long as they will not be stealing needed plant food and moisture. Some produce creditable amounts of humus, as well as helping make minerals available and conserving nitrogen. In any case, one should not burn weeds any more than he would burn leaves; both are humus sources and should be utilized.

Wood Ashes

Here is a valuable source of potash for the compost heap. Hardwood ashes generally contain from 1 to 10 per cent potash, in addition to $1\frac{1}{2}$ per cent phosphorus. Wood ashes should never be allowed to stand in the rain, as the potash would leach away. They can be mixed with other fertilizing materials, side-dressed around growing plants, or used as a mulch. Apply about 5 to 10 pounds per 100 square feet. Avoid contact between freshly spread ashes and germinating seeds or new plant roots by spreading ashes a few inches from plants. It is not recommended to use wood ashes around blueberries or other acid-loving plants, since they are alkaline. Added directly to the compost heap, wood ashes lend potash enrichment and can take the place of lime as an acid neutralizer.

Like sawdust and other wood wastes, wood chips are useful in the garden. They have a higher nutrient content than sawdust, and do a fine job of aerating the soil and increasing its moisture-holding capacity.

Following is a summary report by Herbert A. Lunt of the Connecticut Agricultural Experiment Station on the use of wood chips:

Studies were conducted over a five-year period to determine the effectiveness of wood chips (and sawdust) for soil improvement. In most cases the chips were applied only once and worked into the soil, with and without extra nitrogen.

Crop yields or plant growth was measured and various tests made on the soils. The work was done in greenhouse pots, in outdoor soil frames, and on field plots.

These studies show that wood chips (or sawdust) :

1. Had no appreciable effect on soil acidity nor were they toxic to plants aside from the temporary nitrogen deficiency.

2. Chips had a modest but generally favorable effect on soil structure, organic matter content, and associated soil properties.

3. When fresh, chips almost invariably reduced first crop growth, and were not consistent in their effect on succeeding crops.

4. When supplemented with sufficient nitrogen or when composted before applying, chips did not decrease first crop yields, and they generally increased yields of succeeding crops.

5. Chips are probably more effective on sandy soils than on loams, although very coarse-textured soils may become excessively loose and open the first year or two, unless the chips are first composted.

6. Birch chips decomposed more rapidly than either oak or pine and would require the most nitrogen to prevent deficiencies. Pine decomposition was slowest of the 3 and required the least amount of nitrogen. In general, pine chips were more effective than oak or birch in improving the soil.

It is concluded that wood chips, sawdust, or other types of wood fragments are beneficial to the soil, particularly where the texture is sandy loam or coarser. (Their effects on fine-textured soils have not been studied in this work but there is evidence from the literature of marked improvement in porosity and friability as a result of sawdust or shavings applications.) Repeated use of chips every few years, in conjunction with good soil management, would undoubtedly result in appreciable and permanent soil improvement.

Generally the incorporation of fresh chips has no detrimental effect on the crop if sufficient nitrogen is present or provided. A safer practice, however, is to apply the chips ahead of a green manure crop, preferably a legume, or in any event to allow about a year interval between application and seeding or planting of the main crop. Other good ways to use wood fragments which may be preferable under some conditions are: (a) as bedding in the barn followed by field application of the manure; (b) as a mulch on row crops, eventually working the partially decomposed material into the soil; or (c) after adequately composting the chips with other organic materials. Naturally well-rotted pure chips or sawdust is safe material to use under almost any condition.

A complete description of the use of all wood waste materials in soil appears in the chapter, Composting Industrial Wastes.

Wool Wastes

Wool wastes, also known as shoddy, have been used by British farmers living in the vicinity of wool textile mills since the industrial revolution in the early 19th century. The wool fiber decomposes when in contact with moisture in the soil, and in the process, produces available nitrogen for plant growth. Generally, the moisture content of the wool wastes is between 15 and 20 per cent. It analyzes from 3.5 to 6 per cent nitrogen, 2 to 4 per cent phosphoric acid, and 1 to 3.5 per cent potash.

NITROGEN CONTENT OF ORGANIC SUBSTANCES

The following is a list of representative classifications of organic matter and typical analyses with respect to their nitrogen content:

MEAL

Bone Black Bone Meal	1.5
Raw Bone Meal	3.3 to 4.1
Steamed Bone Meal	1.6 to 2.5
Cottonseed Meal	7.0
Corn Fodder	.41
Oats, Green Fodder	.49
Corn Silage	.42
Gluten Meal	6.4
Wheat Bran	2.36
Wheat Middlings	2.75
Meat Meal	9 to 11
Bone Tankage	3 to 10

MANURES

Cattle Manure (fresh excrement)	0.29
Cattle Manure (fresh urine)	0.58
Hen Manure (fresh)	1.63
Dog Manure	2.0
Horse Manure (solid fresh excrement)	0.44
Horse Manure (fresh urine)	1.55
Human Excrement (solid)	1.00
Human Urine	0.60
Night Soil	0.80
Sheep Manure (solid fresh excrement)	0.55
Sheep (fresh urine)	1.95
Stable Manure, mixed	0.50
Swine Manure (solid fresh excrement)	0.60
Swine (fresh urine)	0.43
Sewage Sludge	1.7 to 2.26

ANIMAL WASTES
(Other than manures)

Eggshells	1.00+
Dried Blood	10 to 14
Feathers	15.3
Dried Jellyfish	4.6
Fresh Crabs	5
Dried Ground Crabs	10
Dried Shrimp Heads	7.8
Lobster Wastes	2.9
Shrimp Wastes	2.9
Mussels	1
Dried Ground Fish	8
Acid Fish Scrap	4.0 to 6.5
Oyster Shells	.36
Milk	.5
Wool Wastes	3.5 to 6.0
Silkworm Cocoons	10
Silk Wastes	8
Felt Wastes	14

PLANT WASTES

	% Nitrogen
Beet Wastes	.4
Brewery Wastes	1.0
Castor Pomace	4.0 to 6.6
Cattail Reeds	2.0
Cocoa Shell Dust	1.0
Cocoa Wastes	2.7
Coffee Wastes	2.0
Grape Pomace	1.0
Green Cowpeas	.4
Nut Shells	2.5
Olive Residues	1.15
Peanut Shells	3.6
Peanut Shell Ashes	.8
Pine Needles	.5
Potato Skins	.6
Sugar Wastes	2.0
Tea Grounds	4.1
Tobacco Stems	2.5 to 3.7
Tung Oil Pomace	6.1

LEAVES

Peach Leaves	.9
Oak Leaves	.8
Grape Leaves	.45
Pear Leaves	.7
Apple Leaves	1.0
Cherry Leaves	.6
Raspberry Leaves	1.35
Garden Pea Vines	.25

GRASSES

Clover	2.0
Red Clover	.55
Vetch Hay	2.8
Corn Stalks	.75
Alfalfa	2.4
Immature Grass	1.0
Blue Grass Hay	1.2
Cowpea Hay	3.0
Pea Hay	1.5 to 2.5
Soybean Hay	1.5 to 3.0
Timothy Hay	1.19
Salt Hay	1.06
Millet Hay	1.22

SEAWEED

Fresh Seaweed	0.2 to 0.38
Dry Seaweed	1.1 to 1.5

Phosphate Sources

(Other than Phosphate Rock or Bone Meal)

Material	Phosphoric Acid Per Cent
Marine products	
Shrimp waste (dried)	10
Dried ground fish	7
Lobster refuse	3.5
Dried blood	1–5
Tankage	2
Hoof and horn meal	2
Wool wastes	2–4
Cottonseed meal	2–3
Raw sugar wastes	8
Rape seed meal	1–2
Cocoa wastes	1.5
Castor pomace	1–2
Silk mill wastes	1.14
Activated sludge	2.5–4.0
Manure	
Poultry, fresh	1–1.5
Poultry, dried	1.5–2.0
Goat and sheep, fresh	0.6
Goat and sheep, dried	1.0–1.9
Hog, fresh	0.45
Horse, fresh	0.35
Horse, dried	1.0
Cow, fresh	0.25
Cow, dried	1.0
Wood ashes	1–2
Pea pod wastes (ashed)	3
Banana residue (ashed)	2.3–3.3
Apple pomace (ashed skin)	3
Citrus wastes (orange skins, ashed)	3

NATURAL SOURCES OF POTASH

MATERIAL	Potash Content (K_2O)
Wood ashes (broad leaf)	10.0%
Wood ashes (coniferous)	6.0
Molasses wastes (curbay)	3.0 to 4.0
Flyash	12.0
Tobacco stems	4.5 to 7.0
Garbage (NYC analysis)	2.3 to 4.3
Water Lily stems	3.4
Cocoa Shell residues	2.6
Potato tubers	2.5
Dry potato vines	1.6
Vegetable wastes	1.4
Castor pomace	1.0 to 2.0
Rapeseed meal	1.0 to 3.0
Cottonseed meal	1.8
Olive pomace	1.3
Beet wastes	0.7 to 4.1
Silk Mill wastes	1.0
Wool wastes	1.0 to 3.5

HAY MATERIALS

	Potash Content (K_2O)
Vetch hay	2.3
Alfalfa hay	2.1
Kentucky blue grass hay	2.0
Red clover hay	2.1
Cowpea hay	2.3
Timothy hay	1.4
Soybean hay	1.2 to 2.3
Salt hay	0.6
Pea forage	1.4
Winter rye	1.0
Immature grass	1.2
Garden Pea Vines	0.7
Weeds	0.7

LEAVES

	Potash Content (K_2O)
Apple leaves	0.4
Peach leaves	0.6
Pear leaves	0.4
Cherry leaves	0.7
Raspberry leaves	0.6
Grape leaves	0.4
Oak leaves	0.2

NATURAL MINERALS

	Potash Content (K_2O)
Granite dust	3.0 to 5.5%
Greensand marl	7.0
Basalt rock	1.5

STRAW

Millet	3.2
Buckwheat	2.0
Oats	1.5
Barley	1.0
Rye	1.0
Sorghum	1.0
Wheat	0.8
Corn Stover	0.8

MANURE

Cow (fresh excrement)	0.1
(dried excrement)	1.5
(fresh urine)	0.5
Horse (fresh excrement)	0.3
(dried excrement)	1.6
(fresh urine)	1.5
Hog (fresh excrement)	0.5
(fresh urine)	0.8
Goat and Sheep	
(fresh excrement)	0.3
(dried excrement)	3.0
(fresh urine)	2.3
Chicken (fresh)	0.6 to 1.0
(dried)	1.2
Pigeon (fresh)	1.0
Duck (fresh)	0.6
Goose (fresh)	0.6
Dog (fresh)	0.3

ASHED MATERIAL

Banana residues (ash)	41.0 to 50.0
Pea pods (ash)	27.0
Cantaloupe rinds (ash)	12.0

Chapter 7

EQUIPMENT FOR COMPOSTING

Today, equipment for composting is becoming increasingly ingenious, varied and useful. Organic gardeners, farmers and manufacturers are producing new tools and machinery in a growing stream. As the trend towards utilizing all organic wastes for rebuilding the soil grows, so too does the range of implements available for this vital purpose.

Those who practice organic gardening or farming, or produce compost for commercial purposes, can now purchase an enormous variety of tools and machines to make composting easier and more efficient. Shredders, grinders, rotary tillers, power mowers, and hand implements in all sizes and types are sold in ever-increasing quantities and ever-better quality. Homemade compost boxes and bins, shredders, containers for gathering compost materials and all sorts of other helpful devices developed by amateurs, add to the list.

By taking full advantage of this equipment, the organiculturist reduces his chores while growing health-laden crops and building the soil.

EQUIPMENT FOR THE GARDENER

Devices for Carrying Compost Materials

Baskets, bags, sacks, carts and wheelbarrows—all of these are extremely handy and useful for gathering and transporting organic materials to the composting site. Many gardeners utilize containers originally meant for other purposes, such as laundry sacks or duffel bags.

A simple carrier for leaves or other materials can be made by opening burlap bags to form rectangular pieces of burlap. These are then sewn together, the size of the "leaf sled" being determined by the number of bags used.

After the bags have been fastened together, nail them to pieces of wood to form the front and back end of the sled. Attach to the front wooden crosspiece a rope to be used in

211

pulling the sled. Leaves or other materials can be easily raked or dumped on the sled for pulling to the compost heap.

Composting in Plastic Bags

Isabelle Moore suggests a novel means of making compost for city gardeners or others whose space is extremely limited:

"As a child, the 'compost detail' was mine each evening. It was one of the cardinal sins in our family to throw away anything that could go back to the soil.

"When I moved to the city and had no spot for a compost heap, I was troubled. Every garbage day I felt guilty, thinking of all the wonderful compost I was throwing away. I tried digging a small hole behind a shrub and making a miniature one. The cats, dogs, mice and neighbor's children soon fixed that idea!

"Now I fill the plastic bags that peat moss comes in, alternating the green material used, with dirt, fertilizer, some moisture and hang these in the garage. On good days, I hang these bags outside to dry out a bit. I do get some compost material. My borders are beginning to show results in the soil. It is much more workable, the flowers are huskier and I'm even beginning to get some worms!"

Wire Walls for Compost Heaps

Here is a quick, neat, and almost moneyless method of caring for compost. Obtain a length of woven wire fencing. At the site of the compost heap, bring both ends of the fencing together to form a circle. The diameter of this wire cylinder will be the size of the compost heap. The length of fencing to get for any desired diameter is obtained by multiplying the desired diameter by 3.1416.

The ends of the fencing are held together by 3 or 4 small chain snaps obtainable at any dime or hardware store. Simply slip the snaps over any two end wires.

Start building the compost heap inside of this wire enclosure. When it is half-full drive a wooden or steel stake through the center and into the earth beneath. Be sure that the top of the stake is as high as the pile is intended to be. Fill to desired height with compost material.

When ready to start a second heap, simply remove the

snaps holding the ends of the fencing together. Pull the fence away from the completed heap. Erect again at site of new heap. It takes less than a minute to remove these snaps and they can be used countless times. With the fencing removed, the compost pile presents a symmetrical appearance. The stake through the center prevents caving or falling apart.

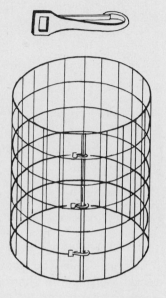

If only one compost heap is to be kept, remove fencing when ready to turn. Set up the fencing again near the compost heap within easy shovelling distance. Pull the stake out of the center. Now start turning by slicing downward on the outside of the compost heap. Toss this into the waiting wire retainer. Continue carving around until the entire heap is finished.

A pair of such retainers will make it possible to make any number of compost heaps of uniform size, one retainer being used to build full heaps, the other to be used when the heaps are being worked over. When weather remains dry for long periods, it will be wise to dig out a fair-sized depression in the top of each heap into which water may be poured. The post will not interfere with forming the depressions. Instead, water will find it easy to follow the post through the center of the heap.

Woven wire fencing, held together by several small chain snaps, makes the quickest and most economical compost bin.

Use of Poultry Netting

Organic gardener Edward P. Dorsey has come up with a variation on this idea. He says, "Thirty feet of poultry netting (one-half inch mesh), about thirty tomato stakes (one inch square) and about 60 feet of soft iron baling wire will make a container for about 150 cubic feet of compost. Corrugated cardboard pieces, placed inside the enclosure, will keep the wind from drying out the compost, and it will allow for proper drainage in the event of heavy rains or melting snow.

Poultry netting, tomato stakes, about 60 feet of soft iron baling wire—that's all you need to make a container that can hold about 150 cubic feet of compost. Corrugated cardboard, placed inside netting, keeps compost from drying out.

"To construct, first mark off a rectangle about 10 feet by 5. Then drive the tomato stakes, along the edge of this rectangle, placing them about a foot apart. The stakes that I used were about 3½ feet long. If driven 6 inches into the ground that will hold them erect and secure. The baling wire should then be looped around the top of each stake and continued around to the starting point. It isn't necessary to wrap this wire too tight, as the purpose is merely to keep the stakes from falling.

"The poultry wire is then placed inside the stakes and held in place by inserting small pieces of soft wire through the loops along the top edge of the poultry wire and then around the post with just a light twist of the thumb and forefinger.

"Short lengths of baling wire were used across the top of the container to keep the stakes from spreading when the compost is placed in the container. These cross bracings looped over alternate pairs of stakes, allow ample space between them for easy loading of the composting material. This material pressing outward against the poultry wire and the stakes will pull the soft bailing wire bracings tight all around.

"The cardboard, if used, can be pieces of boxes, flattened out, or odd pieces of various sizes, plain or corrugated. This

214

is placed inside the poultry wire before filling the container. I used cardboard and only two cross bracing wires, instead of having them at alternate pairs of stakes. Next time I'll use more cross bracing to prevent sides from bulging.

"In preparing the compost, I followed this recommended arrangement: 6 inches of organic waste material—stalks, old hay, straw, flower and vegetable leaves, etc.—then two inches of barnyard manure, one inch of soil and a sprinkling of lime. The poultry wire was 3 feet high, so I piled up 4 layers.

"I prepared my compost pile at the end of the gardening season, utilizing every available bit of organic waste material, instead of burning it. At the end of 5 weeks, when it was time to turn the compost, the small wires holding the poultry wire to the stakes were removed. Then the cross bracing wires, and the long wire, that had been looped over the stakes, was taken off.

"After pulling out the wooden stakes, the poultry wire was rolled away carefully and a nice solid pile of compost was ready for turning. As soon as the stakes, poultry wire, bailing wire and cardboard were rebuilt into a new container, this compost was forked over into its winter location, just a few feet away.

"I then removed the back seat from my car, placed plenty of newspapers inside to protect the floor and upholstery, and found out that 3 metal ash barrels fitted snugly, where the seat had been. A few cardboard boxes were added, as I set out for a public park, about a mile from home.

"When I returned, these were tightly packed with oak leaves and securely tied. These oak leaves were placed on top of the compost pile and a few pieces of cardboard and some sticks added, to hold the leaves down, against winter's breezes. Oak leaves were used, because they are less acid.

"As we have had an open winter in southern New England, up to mid-January, I have had a chance to check the condition of the compost. After several years experimenting with the organic method, I will now have some excellent compost to bolster up the clay soil in my flower and vegetable garden.

"While there may seem to have been a lot of work involved in the preparation of this compost container, I didn't find it to be either tiring or time-consuming. The flower and vegetable beds had to be cleaned up anyway, and this proved to be an easy and satisfactory way to save garden wastes

An insulated compost bin will help you make compost right through the coldest months of winter. Insulating material can be made up of leaves, straw and burlap—all held in place by poultry netting fastened to the 4 wooden posts.

and convert them into worthwhile compost for next summer's garden."

Insulated Bin Protects Earthworms

An "insulated composter" was developed by R. A. Caldwell so that his earthworms could continue to do their composting work all through the winter:

"One 'wrinkle' we have found effective in keeping leaves, dried lawn clippings and other vegetative waste from being blown around over the place, and at the same time keep in a convenient form for use in making up compost beds, is to set up 4 posts, surrounded with poultry netting. We build a small compost pile in this, supplying ventilation as usual. Around this, and at a distance of a foot and a half to two feet, we set up another 4-cornered enclosure of wire. Into this outside enclosure we dump our excess of leaves, grass, weeds, vines and other waste, until it is as high as the inner compost pile. We then place earthworms on top of the inner compost pile, cover the entire outfit with a thick covering of leaves sloping to a peak at the center, lay on some burlap bags sewed together roughly, as a sort of tarpaulin, weight or tie them around the edges and forget the whole matter until spring.

"When opened by taking the wire loose from a post and laying back, there are your leaves partly broken down, ready to be used in new piles. The center pile is composted and

Block or brick bin is easily constructed with concrete blocks or bricks, laid without mortar. Blocks are laid to permit plenty of aeration spaces. This bin is sturdy, durable, easily accessible with its open end, can be built to match a brick house.

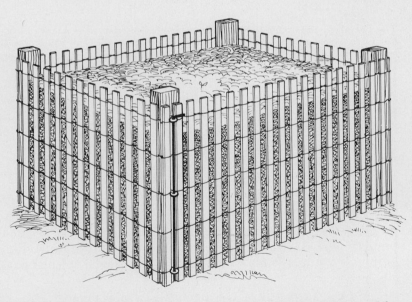

Picket fence bins have always been popular because of their simplicity, satisfactory appearance, and ease of building, moving and storing when not in use. To build a picket bin, buy sections of prefab fencing and fasten in a square, as shown.

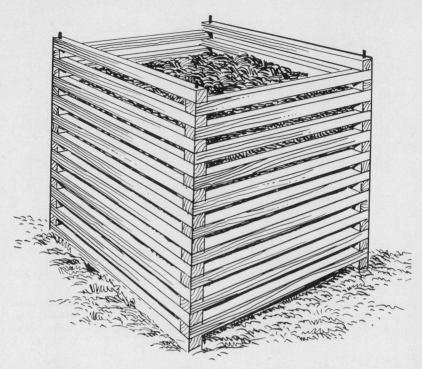

The Lehigh-Keston compost bin, designed by J. I. Rodale over ten years ago, has been extremely popular. Made of wooden slats, the bin can be easily constructed and taken down, as well as moved from place to place in the backyard.

full of worms ready to go to work under your trees, vines and plantings; in addition you have thousands of them scattered all through the stored leaves, as they multiply rapidly in a pile that has been surrounded by a sort of 'Insulation Overcoat,' keeping them warm enough to work all winter long."

Other Materials for Enclosures

Common furring strips, obtainable at lumberyards and building supply dealers, and sections of prefabricated picket fence, are some of the other materials used to make compost enclosures. In devising these simple enclosures, the gardener is limited only by his own ingenuity and the materials available.

He can also utilize the Lehigh-Keston Compost Bin, an efficient slat affair invented by J. I. Rodale, which has been extremely popular. The Lehigh-Keston is easy to erect and to disassemble. It is adjustable in size, attractive, portable, long lasting, and ideal for proper ventilation and protection.

Planned by a California organic gardener, front of the above box has movable planks that can be lifted out when working on the compost. Concrete bottom slopes toward front so compost water can run off into sunken cans.

COMPOST BINS AND BOXES

Gardeners who are not satisfied with composts in heap fashion have come up with a great variety of bins, boxes, pits, and other containers. These structures make composting easier and can improve the appearance of the compost. They also protect the compost from washing rains and baking sun. The type of container you select for your home grounds depends on your personal taste, the amount of labor you wish to expend, and the materials you have on hand.

Wood strips are inexpensive, and provide an easy-to-build bin that is efficient, looks good and allows a desirable maximum of air-circulation in the compost. Utilizing a fence or wall, you can erect a handy 3-sided bin of these slats readily. Many enterprising gardeners have constructed bins of this type that are detachable, which may be moved, stored and put up quickly as needed, and which permit a gradual increase in size as the organic matter is accumulated.

Other very suitable building materials include brick, which is quite sturdy and good looking, cement or Hollywood blocks, various stone forms and metal drums.

Fred Seitz of Burlingame, California, tells of a redwood

Many gardeners who prefer the "well-groomed" bin make use of a long, 3-compartment brick enclosure with wooden roofs. Fresh organic matter is placed in the first compartment and as this decomposes, the material is turned and placed in the second bin. The third bin is reserved for finished compost.

composting box he built: "I live in the city with limited space for gardening and have devised a compost bin which is unobtrusive to even the nearest neighbor. It is built on level ground with 2 by 6-inch redwood planks. The back, two sides, and middle partition are nailed together. Against the side of the 3 front posts are nailed 2 by 1-inch strips upright, two inches apart. They form grooves into which the front planks can be slipped in and lifted out when working on the compost.

"The bottom of the bin is concrete, and slanted towards the front and also towards the middle partition. On each bottom near the middle partition is a gutter so the surplus liquid can run off. In front of the bin I dug a pit and lined it with boards so that it would not cave in. It is large enough to hold 3 gallon cans. This pit is covered with boards. The liquid caught in the cans is used in the garden or thrown back over fresh compost in the bin. It seems to me that thereby the disintegration is speeded up as the new pile will become heated in two days.

"For covers I nailed boards together to fit within the bins. They are made in two parts for each bin, so they are not too

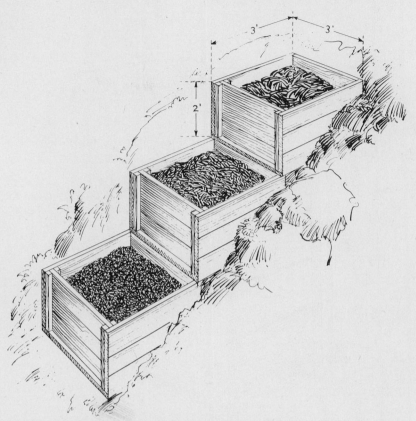

The above design may appeal to gardeners having a hillside location. Fitting into the slope, the bins are directly below one another; the top bin is filled first, and when the material is ready for turning, it is merely dropped into the bins below.

heavy to handle. As the compost in the bin settles, these covers sink with it. I have no trouble with flies or odor.

"I use the rollers from the grinding disks of an old mill to crush all trimmings from hedges, bushes, etc., before putting them into the compost bin."

Provide for Drainage

Bins should not have a concrete flooring unless a drainage system is provided which will drain off excess moisture to a sunken barrel which can later be siphoned off and used as liquid manure or, more specifically, liquid compost. Normally, compost bins utilize the soil surface as the flooring and this actually aids in decomposition of the organic matter. The top few inches of this flooring soil, too, may be removed when the bin is emptied and makes a nutrient-rich material.

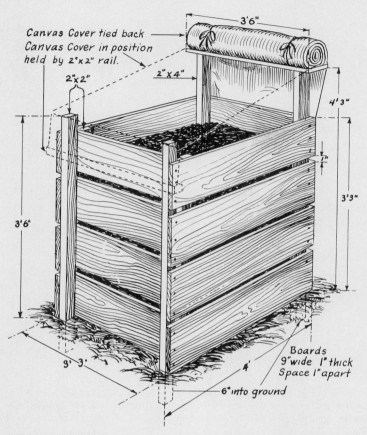

Canvas Cover tied back
Canvas Cover in position
held by 2"x 2" rail.

3'6"

2"x 2"

2"x 4"

4'3"

1"

3'3"

3'6"

3' 3'

4'

6" into ground

Boards
9"wide 1"thick
Space 1"apart

Removable front allows for free access for turning material while open sides permit good air circulation. The simple roll-back canvas cover, such as the one shown on the above bin, will protect the compost from the sun and heavy rainfall.

No matter what the type of bin finally constructed, it should protect the material from both rain and sun. The former would cause nutrients to leach away, and the latter would dry out the heap too rapidly.

Those bins made with removable front boards have much in their favor for it is then easier to turn the compost as well as to add fresh organic matter. Normally the entire heap should be well turned every 3 weeks so that the decaying process may be uniform and the heat generated will destroy any weed seeds.

The long 3-compartment bin utilizes the first bin for

222

fresh organic matter and, as this decomposes it is turned and put in the second bin, and the same rotation as in the hillside compost bin, described below, continues.

An unusually and attractive bin which will doubtless appeal to gardeners having a hillside location. An excavation is made to provide space for a series of bins to fit into the hillside or slope. Each bin should be placed immediately below another, each has a lid and a sliding panel in front. The top bin obviously is filled first and, when the contents are ready for turning, it is a simple matter to draw the contents forward with a curved fork and drop it, turned, into the next lower bin, repeating the performance to the third bin when the freshly filled top bin is ready to be emptied into the second bin. While we have suggested an easy size, this will of course be increased by those gardeners who have large grounds and require a lot of compost.

As an alternative to a wooden lid or one of tar paper on a frame, we have included a suggested design in a canvas cover which can be rolled back. This "roof" is light in weight and can easily be handled by a child.

The New Zealand Box

Another simple, efficient box is the New Zealand Box, developed by the Auckland Humic Club of New Zealand.

There are many variations of this box but the simplest one is a wooden structure 4 feet square by 3 feet high with neither top nor bottom. The wooden sides consist of pieces of wood 6 inches wide by one inch thick. As they are nailed on, one-half inch air space is allowed between each board so that air may penetrate into the heap from all sides. The box is movable. The boarding in front slides down between two posts so that when it is desired to empty the box these slides may be pulled upward and taken out, one by one. The framework is held together by 2 x 4's.

The preferred method in filling the box is as follows: Mix the green matter, soil, lime and manure thoroughly, eliminating the layers of material. Make one air hole in the center of the box all the way down to the ground with a crowbar. If you turn the mixture twice, no air hole is needed after the second turn.

Cover the top with burlapping, or make a burlap frame with ½ inch mesh wire, for use as a cover. When the material in the box is turned over, it has to be taken out of the box in

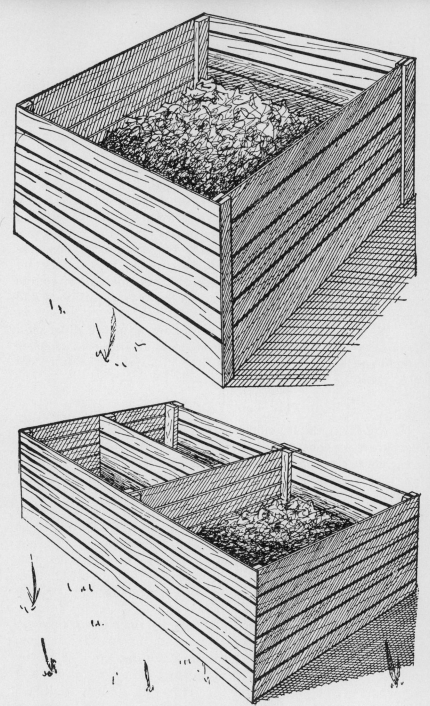

The New Zealand Box is a simple wooden structure 4 feet square x 3 feet high without any top or bottom layers. Front boards slide down between two posts, so the compost can be more easily turned or removed. Framework is 2 x 4's.

224

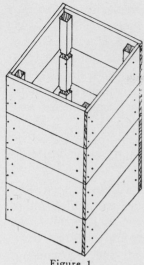

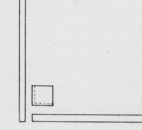

Figure 1.   Figure 2.

Figure 1 shows box sections assembled to a height of 4 feet. Note the relationship of the 4 x 4 corner posts to the section levels. Figure 2 indicates the 4 identical 2 x 12 x 30-inch pieces and the 4 x 4 corners which are used for more support.

a pile and then put back again. This double operation may be saved by building a double-sized box 8 by 4 feet square with a partition in the center. The material is forked from one into the other and a new batch is then placed into the first section. This makes it a continuous process where only one turn is given. Where two turns are used, a 3-section box can be made which is 12 by 4 feet. It is started in section A. When A is turned into B, a new batch is made in A. When B is turned into C, then A is turned into B, and a new batch is made in A. The process is continuous. We have used a 3-section box and it gives good results.

The 4 x 4 box will produce about a ton of compost. If the quantity of wastes available warrants, a larger size box may be used, 6 x 6, 3 feet high.

A California Design

Lloyd K. Rosenvold describes his "Yucaipa Garbage Disposal and Compost Box," which he named after the community in California in which he lives:

"The sides of each section are constructed of 4 pieces of 2 by 12 inch lumber, each measuring 30 inches in length. The

225

corner posts are lengths of 4 by 4-inch material sawed ½ inch shorter than the height of the side pieces. These parts are assembled as shown in the accompanying diagrams. The 4 by 4 corner pieces are preferred to smaller ones because they permit the use of large spikes and thus add stability to the sections. The corner posts are allowed to protrude about ¾ inch below the bottom of the section and because they are shorter than the height of the side pieces, there will always be adequate clearance between the corner posts of one section and those of another. Thus particles of dirt, etc., will not prevent a tight assembly.

"Because it is impractical to expect absolute accuracy in constructing the box sections and because water may cause warping and sticking of the sections at a later time thus interfering with assembly and disassembly of the box, a small portion of the outer surfaces of the protruding portions of the 4 by 4's is removed by means of a saw and chisel. Except for this minor procedure the gardener needs only hammer and nails for assembly for the lumber yard will gladly cut the lumber in the two standard sizes needed.

"The lowermost section is placed on a square foundation of bricks laid end to end on levelled ground. The dirt floor remains in the center. The box is then filled in layers (6 inches vegetable matter and garbage, two inches manure, a sprinkling of wood ashes or lime and an inch of soil) and sections are added as needed. Since the box is so small the average family should be able to complete each 6-inch layer of green matter in 1 to 3 days by adding weeds, leaves, hay, etc., to the garbage. I filled my first such 4-foot box with ease in about two weeks. It only takes a few minutes each day or two to construct a compost layer in order not to leave garbage exposed to flies too long. To further discourage flies, a tightly fitting screened cover may be constructed if desired.

"When a height of 4 feet is reached another section is added and this is filled with about a foot of leaves. The latter discourage weed growth, keep out the flies and keep the moisture in. After one month the top layer of leaves is pushed aside and several cubic feet of earthworm culture, including egg capsules as well as adult worms, are added to the process and the leaves replaced as cover. By this time the box contents will have decreased in volume so that one or more of the sections may be removed and utilized in another compost box assembly. Herein is brought to light one of the advantages of

Improvised from storm windows and discarded blinds, this experimental compost frame provided Alden Stahr of Mt. Bethel, Pa., a workable winter composting arrangement. Glass lid, hay insulation, and manure mixed with organic materials raise temperatures enough for bacterial action to continue throughout the winter.

the sectional box. In a solid box or pit much lumber stands idle above the level of the shrinking compost mass after the first 2 to 4 weeks, whereas, in the Yucaipa box less lumber stands idle. When the compost is ready for use at the end of about 4 months, the box may be emptied layer by layer with ease, by prying the box sections off one at a time.

"I am now in the process of constructing a series of larger sections 40 inches square in order to study their feasibility. In the use of 2 by 12 inch boards, that is probably the largest size practicable because of their weight. Undoubtedly boxes of greater square surface area could be built if 2 by 8 inch lumber were used. Small homes or gardens might be able to use 24 inch square sections made of one inch lumber for the sides and 2 by 2 inch stock for the corners. Another advantage of the Yucaipa sectional box is that the organiculturists with little land (I only have ⅔ of an acre) can place his boxes at the most desirable location and is able to move his composting area if his needs so require. However, the Yucaipa box was primarily designed to facilitate garbage disposal. It is obviously not usable on a farm scale for general composting but belongs to those of us who do gardening on a relatively small scale in addition to its use in garbage disposal."

Winter Composter

Alden Stahr, Mt. Bethel, Pa., was frustrated for 15 years in his desire to continue composting activities in cold winter months. Finally, one frigid morning, he thought of an idea that would allow bacteria to make compost for him right through the winter.

He rigged up an experimental compost frame, constructed very simply of 4 old blinds once used on his house, and two storm windows which he placed to slant toward the south to pick up the long, low rays of the winter sun. Old bales of hay were stacked around the sides to serve as insulation. The glass lid kept out cats, dogs and wild animals, and prevented excessive rains or snow from over-soaking the heap, and high winds from drying it out. To help the heating process, Mr. Stahr mixed in manure with kitchen wastes.

The idea worked. The material had decomposed greatly by early spring, when it was transferred to the regular heap. One cold January morning, Mr. Stahr found a 50-degree difference between the inside and outside temperatures. "I could just feel the billions of happy bacteria," he said, "hard at work in the warm interior making black gold to spur the seeds in spring."

Built-in Compost Beds

J. J. Bartlett has a unique system he calls "built-in humus beds." He combines a simple box, garbage, manure, green matter and earthworms, and makes his compost right in his flower beds.

The first step is to build or find a box (no bottom or top). It can be any size, but Mr. Bartlett has found that a long narrow one is more suited to inconspicuous placement along fences, in front of hedges, in borders, and other small spaces. His boxes are 4 feet long, one foot high and one or two feet wide.

Next, pick a spot and dig a rectangular hole about 18 inches deep and just slightly smaller in dimensions than the box, so that the box will rest firmly on the ground above the hole. After this is done, you are ready to begin composting. The hole is filled in layer style—kitchen garbage, manure

Rough stone enclosure as one shown above with an open side makes an attractive, informal appearance, is easily accessible for piling materials for composting. A bin of this type makes a fine camouflage for the suburban gardener's compost heap.

and green matter, in that order. Mr. Bartlett has found kitchen garbage to compost faster when run through a meat grinder, but this is not essential. He keeps a bag of pulverized manure and a pile of shredded green matter at the side of the box, and each time garbage is introduced he follows immediately with the other two layers. After each addition, he covers the pit with a burlap bag and wets it down, then places a board on top of the box. In this way there is absolutely no odor, nor any pest problem.

In about 3 weeks when the bottom layers have decomposed to a great extent, introduce about 500 earthworms. You may have to buy these, but they will be the only ones you'll ever have to buy; you'll soon have thousands, to use all around the garden. These little composters will work through successive layers which you add to the pit, mixing and breaking down the heap for you. Be careful, though, not to introduce the earthworms during the terrific heat of the initial breakdown. Heat of successive layers won't bother them, because they'll remain below until the above layer cools.

Continue this layering process until the pit is filled all the way to the top of the box. Then allow it to decompose for

5 or 6 more weeks, keeping it moist. In the meantime you can start another box.

After the first pit is fully composted, remove the compost down to soil level, place it in several cone-shaped piles on a large board or tarpaulin, and leave it exposed to the sun for one or two hours. The worms will have balled up at the bottom of each pile, and can be easily removed and introduced to the second pit. The finished compost piles may be sifted and bagged for future use. Meanwhile, you have just created the richest 18-inch-deep flower bed in town, which you can use as is, or tempered down with soil—any way you like.

Now you may begin pit number 3, using the box you have just emptied. Using this system, you'll have a new load of compost each sixth week, you'll be able to make rich humusy flower beds from the worst clay or sand; you'll be raising thousands of earthworms for general garden use; and you'll have done it with little trouble or expense in a small space, with no odor or pest problem.

Bricks, Stones and Concrete Blocks

A brick or concrete block bin is easily constructed and may be made in any convenient size. Lay the bricks or blocks with spaces between them to permit plenty of aeration, and leave one end open for easy access to the compost. No mortar is used.

For a rustic, informal appearance, field stones can be heaped up in the same way, again leaving one end open. Or you can use logs similarly to make a rough but handsome enclosure of this kind.

Organic gardener John H. Mahan built his pit of cinder blocks. He says, "I decided to build a pit 44 inches wide by 9 inches long by 40 inches deep, in a part of our garden called the work area. A partition across the middle would divide the pit into two compartments each 3 feet by 4 feet, big enough to get down in and use a fork and just deep enough to still allow lifting the compost over the top easily. In one compartment I could put the materials to start breaking down into compost, and later toss them over into the second compartment, to finish their breakdown. Then I could start a new batch of green material in the first compartment. By this time the material in the second compartment would be sufficiently converted into compost to use it extensively in the garden, for pots, flats, etc. Over the top of the pit I planned to put a slat lid, divided in two, for easier access to either compartment. Later I became interested in earthworms and decided to propagate enough to add to the pit. They could do the digesting of the materials and I would be saved the labor of tossing the materials from one compartment to the other.

"No sooner did I start digging the hole than it started raining. This went on week end after week end. Each time, before I could go ahead with the job, I would have to rig up the garden hose as a siphon and drain the pit—then quickly dig out some more dirt. Finally the hole was dug to a depth of 40 inches.

"As the bottom of the compartments were to be left plain dirt a cinder fill was used as a drainage footing for the walls.

"One hundred and four cinder blocks 4 inches thick by 16 inches long by 8 inches high were purchased. Eighty-four were hollow blocks and 20 solid. The cinder footing was tamped down and leveled. Then a batch of mortar was mixed and the lining cemented in place. The joints were staggered with each course and common red brick used to fill the shortest spaces. The four lower rows or courses of blocks were hollow—the fifth and top course of solid cinder blocks. When it was finished the top rim was several inches above ground level to keep out surface water. The front and back of the top edge were notched out to receive the battens which would be used to hold the slat top together. A smooth coat of cement was laid all around the top and wet burlap bags placed on top to keep the cement from cracking as it dried. The bottoms of the compartments were leveled off and a number of boards laid down, with wide spaces between them, simply to mark the bottom level each time I would be digging down later to empty the pit. The pit was now ready to be filled.

"Remembering the details of compost making that I had read I put in a 6 inch layer of green materials, then not having any fresh manure I put in a one inch layer of soil with a top dressing of ground limestone, repeating this process until both compartments were filled. On some layers I also added a generous coating of wood ashes or bone meal. Later, after the earthworm population had increased sufficiently from my propagating efforts, I added at least 500 worms to each compartment. Two sections of slat top were constructed, and later painted woodland green. Once the top was in place the pit was practically inconspicuous and we could walk right across it to tend our flower beds in back. It has also been used as a place to put flats of seeds being started.

"All of our make-up soil for the garden now comes from the pit. We work first on one side then the other. I screen out the coarse material and always keep a box of prepared compost on hand. The soil which came out of the hole originally was screened and saved. Together with a constant stream of garden refuse, we feed this material back into the pit and so keep up our compost supply."

Concrete, Wood and Earthworms

Dr. Parley W. Monroe of Brewster, New York, built a compost pit of poured concrete to handle his garbage. First he sank a shaft in the semi-shade of an old maple tree that flanked his large garden. The spot was not too far from the kitchen.

In the bottom of this excavation he erected forms for a concrete pit 6 feet long, 4 feet wide and 4 feet deep. In the cemented bottom, he fixed a drainage grill similar to that installed in many basements to carry off excess water.

When completed, the sturdy structure looked like the foundation for an over-sized doll's house. The walls were 8 inches thick and the top projected about 18 inches above the ground. The hollow oblong square now was ready to be capped with a flat roof.

This roof was built, not of concrete, but of wood—tongued-and-grooved boards nailed to well-seasoned 2 by 4s firmly braced inside the structure. Part of this roof or top was cut to form a small door on hinges that could be lifted to receive garbage and then closed tightly again. The whole business was hinged at one side so that it could easily be tipped back to allow cleaning of the pit.

The new garbage-disposal unit was fly-tight and animal-tight. Its worth, however, was yet to be proved. Would Nature co-operate by taking over the job of garbage man?

In all his planning, the doctor was counting heavily on earthworms. Now he was to learn whether that marvel of creation was as amazing a helper of mankind as he had always believed.

He selected a fine array of the red wrigglers and placed them in a sizable quantity of earth at the bottom of the new pit.

Now he began chucking in his first kitchen wastes from

which all tin cans, bottles, jar rings and similar insolubles had carefully been screened. Then he sat back and waited, feeling a little like an inventor who is reasonably certain his contraption will work but who also knows there's many a slip between theory and practice. It wouldn't be long now until he knew the best—or the worst.

But the worms, who had never had it so good, did not let him down. Dining on green-grocer largess, the like of which a bountiful Nature never before had provided, they flourished mightily and produced more and more of their kind.

The pit quickly teemed with so many tiny but ravenous "disposal units" that kitchen wastes were being digested long before they could decay to the odor stage.

Even the optimistic inventor was not fully prepared for what happened. He expected the pit to fill rapidly and need frequent cleaning. But the close watch he kept on it soon showed him there was a convenience angle he had not suspected. The worms kept bulk down so well that the pit needed no attention to speak of.

Not until 3 years had gone by—with regular contributions of garbage all that time—did the doctor consider cleaning of any kind called for. The worms seemed to sense they had a job to do and did it without fuss of any kind.

And at that, the first clean-out could have been put off for at least another year. However, the doctor was curious and decided it was time to do a little research on what had been going on.

And that research was richly rewarding. The top was propped back and two men descended. First, they pushed aside the newest garbage. Beneath it, they struck pay dirt, rich black stuff that looked like the prime topsoil that erodes from badly used but prime farm land. It was friable like leaf mold and richly rewarding when wheelbarrowed onto the garden.

What impressed the doctor was the absence of odor. Only the most recently decomposing materials had any smell and resembled well-rotted cow manure.

The whole converted-garbage-to-topsoil was squirming with healthy earthworms. Enough of these were left in the pit, along with a generous supply of compost, to act as a starter for the next cycle of garbage conversion. Then the hinged top was dropped back and the pit was ready for another 3 or 4 year spell of work.

The worms that went out onto the garden with the

compost did not have to look far for their food. Like cattle turned out to pasture, they thrived on their change of diet. This new "pasturage" was rotting leaves that had been carefully raked onto the garden as a winter cover the previous autumn.

Now, in the springtime, those leaves provided just the menu that a garbage-jaded worm might enjoy gobbling in celebration of his or her return to the wide-open spaces.

Added to the garbage compost, the worm casts from these leaves, made the garden bloom amazingly well.

The doctor long had felt that leaves never should be burned and his beliefs had been confirmed by experts of the United States Department of Agriculture.

Combined with garbage compost, these leaves make a plant food that enables the doctor to grow things that are the envy of his friends and neighbors as well as fellow-members of The Harlem Valley Garden Club.

The doctor disclaims all the credit for the rich garden product he makes from his garbage. Most of the real work is done by the worms and they should come in for the lion's share of attention. All he does is to bring worms and garbage together under the right conditions and step back out of the way.

One important condition is to build the pit in semi-shade. Direct sunlight, the doctor feels, would build up heat inside so intense that the worms might die.

Flue Lining for Closed Pit

An inexpensive enclosed pit can be made by digging a section of flue lining into the soil. The upper rim of the flue lining should be an inch or two above the surface of the ground. To prevent the plant juices from escaping into the soil at the bottom of the pit, pour a thin layer of cement to serve as a floor, or tamp a layer of clay to seal the bottom. Because of the small size, it is not necessary to provide a drainage pit for discharging the plant juices which are formed as a by-product of the fermentation processes.

The flue linings come in different sizes and can be obtained from a building supply dealer. A flue lining two feet square and two feet deep is recommended.

The pit should be covered with a close-fitting board or metal cover. The cover need not be air-tight but should fit

234

closely enough to prevent the escape of the carbon dioxide which is formed as a by-product of fermentation. This cover will also prevent the loss of moisture so that the pit will have a humid atmosphere rich in carbon dioxide. This atmosphere is especially favorable for earthworms.

The covered pit is hidden from view by planting around it creeping plants such as nasturtiums, squashes or ornamental vines.

Inexpensive Tile Pit

An inexpensive rodent-proof pit can easily be constructed of terra cotta tiles. Dig a hole of the dimensions the pit is to have and two feet deep. Fit a piece of wire netting (hardware cloth) in the bottom of the pit to prevent rodents from digging into the pit from below. Line the sides with tiling which should extend a foot or more above the level of the ground. Now fit wire screening across the top to exclude rodents from that approach. The pit may be made in the form of a twin, as shown in the illustration, so that the compost heap may be started in one side. Then after 3 weeks, the heap is turned by transferring the material to the other side of the pit. After 5 weeks more when the heap is ready for the second turning, the compost is returned to the side in which it was originally made where it will remain until it is finished.

After the second turning, a new compost heap may be started in the empty side of the pit at such time that the finished compost will be ready to be taken out by the time the new heap is ready for its first turning. If the heap in the pit is properly moistened and aerated, it will be free from odor at all times. This gadget can be an attractive structure in the back yard, especially if tied into the back yard by suitable landscape plantings.

The "Wishing Well" Pit

A really handsome compost pit was built by gardener P. H. Parrott, who made a "wishing well" structure that is a real decorative asset to his garden. He says, "If you have a garden, but wish it were a better one, why not build yourself a 'wishing well' like ours and help make your wish come true? For years I watched our lawn clippings and other valuable garden waste go into the rubbish can, paid to have it carted away, and paid for fertilizer to replace it—simply because we thought we had no space on our 50 by 100 foot lot for a compost heap which, we thought, though useful, would be unsightly.

"Then I solved the problem by building the simple structure pictured here. The heavy plank base makes a box 4 by 6 feet and 4 feet high; this is veneered with brick except for an opening across the bottom of the front that enables us to remove the compost from the bottom of the heap or turn the pile over by taking from the bottom and throwing it back on top.

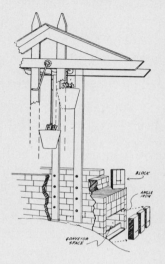

"To close the opening at other times, I made 4 plugs, each of 3 vertical bricks on a horizontal one cemented together and with a wire handle in front. Four 7-foot high 2 by 4 inch uprights support a windlass and two redwood and cedar buckets on a white rope; also a waterproof plywood roof attached to the house and painted red and white.

P. H. Parrott devised this "wishing well" composter; uprights support windlass and buckets.

This makes an open, but sheltered, bird feeding station, and the birds repay us by contributing their droppings to compost below. A fair exchange, we think, just as the whole affair combines aesthetic attractiveness and practical usefulness."

Compost Cabinets and a "Drum Composter"

A number of companies are making and selling compost cabinets, in sizes for the garden and for larger operations. These will handle all types of organic materials and usually are equipped with a grid or screen that lets the finished compost drop down into the lower part of the cabinet for easy removal. The organic materials are put in at the top and a bacterial activator or earthworms are generally added to speed up the composting process. Fine quality compost is produced in as little as 30 days in these cabinets.

Ralph Poe of Canton, Illinois, developed his own "drum composter" that is very successful. Like compost cabinets, it is ideally suited to small gardens where space is at a premium.

236

Anyone handy with tools can easily build a composter of this type, and it may be kept indoors or outdoors.

The compost maker is made from one complete steel drum and ⅓ of another. The complete drum forms the container for the ingredients making up the compost.

He first cuts out the end of the drum that has no openings, cutting it about two inches from the edge with a special cutting tool he devised. A chisel or other tool that will cut heavy sheet metal may be used for this. This end of the drum is the top of the container.

He then cuts out the other end of the drum which contains the two openings. This is cut about an inch from the edge. The piece cut out is used for the lid of the container, the smaller opening being utilized to accommodate the handle for raising and lowering the lid. The lid is attached to the top of the container by a hinge.

Mr. Poe then cuts off a third of a second drum just above a crease. He places some roofing cement around the inside of the crease, sets the container in this and pounds the top edge in around the drum. This effectively seals the two together. This bottom part is used as a reserve chamber to store garden soil or partially-made compost.

He then cuts out a 6 by 8-inch piece from the side of the container at the bottom of the drum and directly below it in the reserve chamber an 8 by 10-inch piece. This piece cut out is used to form a door for the 6 by 8-opening above. The chamber opening is left open. However, if bothered by rats getting in, a door may be made for this.

A ½ inch steel rod is placed across the top of the container by punching a hole through either side through which the rod is placed. A 3-inch conductor pipe, with a wire hook at the top to hook over the rod, and long enough to reach to the bottom of the container, is perforated with ¼ inch holes for air to reach the composting material.

A lattice work grate is made the diameter of the container from ¾-inch wood strips ¾-inch thick. This is placed in the bottom of the container, being supported by the one-inch portion of the end of the drum left for that purpose.

Folded newspapers are put on top of the grate and the container is now ready for the composting materials.

The chamber below is partly or completely filled with garden soil or partially-made compost.

To start the compost maker, a few shovelfuls of the

garden soil or partially-made compost are placed in the container on top of the newspapers. On top of this are placed the materials to be composted. Mr. Poe always has a pile of leaves and in summer some weeds or grass are available. A mixture of these is made with the kitchen garbage. He uses a discarded 5-gallon paint bucket in which he places the materials to chop and mix. He puts a wooden bottom made from two-inch board in the base of the bucket, first putting in some roofing cement, enough so that when the wooden bottom is pressed down in it, some of it will squash up around the sides and seal it. A spade or similar tool is used to chop the materials.

To secure quick action of the bacteria to form the compost from the raw materials, he uses a powder-form activator, two teaspoonfuls to a bucket of garbage, mixing it in as the garbage is chopped. There are also other activators, both powder and liquid, that may be used. One concern makes an activator that is extensively used in large city garbage plants to break down the garbage.

When the garbage has been chopped and mixed, it is put in the container on top of the soil previously put in and a little more of the soil put over it. From now on, the rest is achieved by the action of the bacteria contained in the activator, which breaks down the materials into compost. As a usual thing, this is accomplished in 2 to 4 weeks.

The compost is removed from the bottom through the 6 by 8-inch door. Mr. Poe has a hook attached to a wooden handle which he uses in pulling it out into some kind of a container. As it is pulled from the bottom, that above it settles down so it can be removed. If the ingredients have not been entirely decomposed to form a uniform mass, they are replaced for further breakdown.

The process is a continuing one. As long as there is room in the container, new garbage can be added at any time. Also, removal can be made at the bottom as fast as the process of decomposition is complete.

Partially-completed compost is better than soil to have in the reserve chamber as the bacteria already in it hastens the process.

The activator used by Mr. Poe forms a gas that repels flies and absorbs odor so the compost maker does not smell. In the summer, he keeps the composter outdoors, but in the

238

Designed, assembled and tested in the Organic Gardening Experimental Farm Workshop at Emmaus, Pa.

Many mechanical-minded gardeners have made their own efficient shredders by converting a reel-type lawn mower. As illustrated, the cutting bar is mounted in a vertical position, flush with bottom of the "feeding trough" of a wood table.

winter keeps it in the basement. The bacteria work best in a temperature of around 70 degrees.

Because the composter is odorless and may be kept in the basement, the process of composting is carried on the entire year. It takes only a few minutes a day or week to take care of the kitchen garbage and a nice lot of fertilizer is secured which works wonders in the vegetable and flower gardens.

SHREDDING AND GRINDING EQUIPMENT

Since organic materials decompose into humus much more rapidly when they are shredded or ground up fine, this type of machinery is receiving increasing attention today.

Using Rotary Mowers

If you own a rotary mower, you have an excellent tool for grinding up materials like straw, weeds and leaves. First, pile up the materials. For mowers with side exit ports, use a carton or fence as a backstop. Then depress the handle and push the machine forward until the blades are positioned directly over the pile. Lower the machine gradually into the pile. If at any time it seems about to stall, merely depress the handle. The shredding is done quite rapidly, a couple of bales of hay, for example, being reduced to fine shredded material in a few minutes.

Rotary mowers, incidentally, today have special baffles that deliver the grass clippings on the uncut area for further chopping. This eliminates "windrowing," and the clippings are reduced for quicker decomposing on the lawn as you mow.

Alden C. Utton of Wilder, Vermont, devised a frame to hold his mower when using it for shredding. A simple wooden frame on which the base of the mower rests with the wheels over the edge, plus a "filler chute" to feed the materials into the blades, makes up the device. Mr. Utton says, "I shoveled all of last year's compost through it this fall so it took a lot of weight and abuse. When the rotor is set up at high speed the stuff goes through pretty fast, so look out for your hands. It will chew up 4 or 5 corn stalks at a time in a hurry."

Converting a Reel Mower

A reel lawn mower can also be converted into an efficient shredder by making a suitable frame for it. Either remove the handle and braces of your regular lawn mower, or purchase an old one at a sale for a small amount of money. Mount the lawn mower in such position that the cutting bar is in a vertical position and flush with the bottom of the feeding trough of the wooden table that can be constructed of waste lumber. This should be a table of convenient height and well braced with stout boards. The feeding trough should have sides 3 or 4 inches high and a bottom which will permit easy feeding of the plant material into the machine. For easy feeding of the plant material into the machine, line the feeding trough with bakelite or galvanized metal.

The machine may be operated by hand, as shown in the drawing, or with a motor mounted on a platform attached to a leg or frame of the machine. For hand operation, drill a small hole halfway between the center and edge of one wheel and attach a handle with a bolt and nut. To operate with a motor it is necessary to attach a pulley to the wheel. The pulley on the motor should be relatively small while that on the lawn mower wheel should be much larger so that the machine is not turned too rapidly and does not choke up easily.

For feeding the plant material into the machine, use a rectangular piece of board with a handle attached to one side so that it can be used as a "pusher." While the machine is operated with the right hand, the material is fed into the machine with the left hand just fast enough to allow the material to be cut without jamming the cutting knives against the cutting bar.

Meat Grinder for Small Quantities

Isabelle Moore recommends a meat grinder for shredding small amounts of garbage. "This method is of inestimable value for the tiny-patch gardener whose space is at a premium. Not having a spot for an honest-to-goodness compost pile and no room at all for a real shredder, I find this a good substitute. I attached an old meat grinder to the garage wall and run through kitchen waste that makes good compost. This material takes up very little room at the back of one of the flower borders—and shredded this way, composts much more rapidly."

Wire Mesh Shredder

A simple box on legs plus some wire mesh makes a good leaf shredder. An old apple box can be used, or construct a box of any available scrap lumber. Replace the bottom with ½-inch wire mesh and add two strips of wood on the bottom to act as legs to provide clearance for the finished material to fall through.

Leaf Chopper from License Plates

Boyd E. DeLamater devised a leaf chopper of old license plates. "September, the leaf falling season, was at hand. I still had not devised a method for pulverizing leaves. For over a year I had tried to figure a way to do this. My garden was in need of humus to loosen the soil and also of the enrichment which the leaves would furnish.

"One Sunday morning I wandered out into the back yard, through the garden and finally into the garage. A few leaves were falling from nearby trees. Now, I thought, another year will go by and I still will have done nothing about chopping leaves for the garden. It was then that I noticed hanging on the inside garage wall some of my old automobile license plates. They might be used for a chopper.

"Before the day was over I had my chopper. I took two of the plates, each 12 inches in length and 5 inches in width, flattened the bottom crimp, and filed to a sharp edge. Then I bent each ½ inch off center and to a 90 degree angle. This resulted in a 6½ inch length one way and a 5½ inch length the other and provided for a one-inch overlap for the attachment of the plates to the squared end of a broom stick which I found I could use for a handle.

"I then fastened the two bent plates to the broom stick with 3 small bolts, placing the broom stick ½ inch above the bottom edge of the plates. The result was a 4-blade chopper measuring 12 inches across each way.

"Since the chopper was somewhat light in weight, I fastened a 5-inch length of one-inch diameter pipe over the lower portion of the broom stick handle, using two bolts to hold it in place. Then, not having a box into which I could place the leaves for chopping, I searched the basement and came up with an 18-inch rectangular corrugated cardboard container, which I used temporarily.

"Not many leaves had fallen and those that had were still somewhat green. I found, however, that I could chop them in the container to whatever degree of fineness I cared to, depending on how much effort I wished to expend. By the end of that September Sunday I had a small pile of pulverized leaves.

"Sometime later I made another chopper similar in design and size but this time of 1/16 inch steel 4 inches in width. I also constructed a box 18 inches by 18 inches with a height of 20 inches. I lined the bottom of the box with cardboard.

"During the months of October and November I gathered and chopped leaves. During this period there occurred about 3 weeks of dry weather and I was able to gather leaves that were dry and brittle. This made the chopping much easier. Furthermore, in a nearby city park, I found leaves of small texture. These chopped even easier.

"In the process of chopping, about 50 per cent of the leaves were reduced to near powder."

Power Added to Reel-Mower Shredder

Oregon gardener J. A. Starkweather made a motorized shredder from a reel mower. He says, "An inexpensive leaf shredder can be made from an old lawn mower. Choose one with ball bearings. The old timers often have better steel in the blades and the cutter plate than the newer ones.

"The wheels and handle are removed. Inside the frame, place sides of ⅜-inch waterproof plywood or other ⅜-inch lumber, making the holes on each side to match the rods and the wheel axles. The side pieces are 16 inches high and 12½ inches wide. The width is, of course, determined by the lawn mower. Place ¾-inch boards or waterproof plywood to fit front and back.

"The side pieces are held in place by rods. First: the main brace rod on the mower. Second: a rod through the axle where wheels were taken off. Third: a piece of electrical pipe chosen to fit over the metal ends used for holding the wooden roller in place. The rods were threaded back far enough so that a nut could be placed inside the wood box to hold the sides to the frame.

"The bottom screen was made of ⅝-inch mesh hardware cloth, 16 inches by 18 inches. It was fastened to fit fairly close to the cutting blades from the front frame rod to the rod which replaced the wooden roller.

"A 6-inch pulley was attached to the cutter shaft. The cutter shaft rod was pushed to the left so as to allow room for the pulley to be attached. It was necessary to cut ⅛-inch off each end of each of the 5 blades by a sand blast cutter so that the blades could turn without rubbing the sides. This might not be necessary in some other mower.

"A hopper was built on top of the first enclosure of the mower of sheet metal and wood. It could be constructed entirely of wood by making the back and sides 11 inches higher than described above. The front piece has a slanting bottom running from the wheel axle rod to the front at an angle of 45 degrees. All wooden parts were fastened with screws so that the whole thing could be taken apart easily.

"A second hand ¼-horsepower washing machine motor with a 2-inch pulley was fastened to a suitable board and attached to the frame with an old strap hinge so that, in use, the motor weight kept the belt tight.

"The support frame was 19 inches wide by 28 inches long and made of odd pieces of 2 by 4 and 4 by 4. The mower is set with the cutting edge up and leaves are fed in a way similar to which the grass would be cut, except that the leaves move and the mower is stationary.

"This machine will cut dry leaves at a rate of a bushel

every few minutes into pieces about ½ inch square and finer, although some leaves come through only partly cut. The product is ready to spread on the ground as a mulch. The machine will cut wet leaves also; however, they will not drop through, but must be pulled out with a stick. Be careful about sticks and stones. The motor runs on a 15 ampere fuse which will blow out if too heavy materials are put in.

The cost:

Second hand ¼ hp. motor	$ 5.00
Six inch pulley	3.35
Hardware cloth	.50
Rubber belt	.85
Shortening cutting blades	.50
Total cost	$10.20

The wood used was scrap lumber picked up, with consent of the builder, from waste around cement and wood buildings in process of construction."

POWER SHREDDERS

Shredders Are Three-Way Tools

More organic gardeners and farmers are shopping for a compost shredder than for any other piece of garden equipment. The reason for this intense interest in shredding is the tremendous popularity of the new "speed-composting" techniques.

There is another factor about the compost shredder which appeals to the hard-working gardener—it's a tool that you can bring to the work. This is a real boon to the compost-maker who wants to have several heaps piled up in his garden where he will need them. The movable shredder makes this easy because it can go to work wherever the ground is reasonably level.

Compost shredders are designed to do 3 big garden jobs for you. First they can speed and ease your task of preparing mulches. Today it is widely known that cut up and macerated leaves, weeds and other similar material make much better mulch than the rough raw product because they hold moisture better and form a thicker blanket which chokes off the weeds.

The shredder is a real friend in need when you are getting

244

Compost grinders and shredders do a fine job of cutting up materials, shortening the time necessary for decomposition of organic materials. Equipped with interchangeable cutters and screens, the machine saves much time and effort.

ready to build your compost heap. Again, it will take the raw stock and chew it into the kind of shape that eases the job of the bacteria in your pile.

A third use which contributes to the shredder popularity today is the grinding and pulverizing job it can do with finished compost. The fine compost that can be achieved is ideal for potting soil and for use on lawns, flowerbeds, in greenhouses and in other "high-quality" jobs.

The important, business part of the shredder is a series of teeth or knives set in a revolving roller which is belted or geared to an engine or motor, usually gasoline powered. There is a hopper above the grinding or cutting chamber and an exhaust chute under the blades.

Partially rotted hay or compost goes through the machine much more quickly than dry hay or straw. If you leave raw compost material out in the weather for several weeks or months prior to use, shredding will be facilitated. Dry corn cobs are difficult to shred, but if they are allowed to soak up water for a week they go through very easily.

We are a machine-minded people today, used to working with power tools and getting results with them. But it is still

245

Most shredders are highly portable, and the heavy-duty ones will handle both light and coarse materials ranging from straw to branches and wood chips. It only takes a few minutes to shred the straw bales shown above, yet the cut-up material will compost in as short a time as 10 days compared with several months for uncut straw.

good to keep an extra-alert, inquisitive, experimental attitude when working with the shredder and to maintain a great deal of respect for the tool and what it can do to you as well as that material you are feeding into its hopper. Also, keep the children a good distance away when the machine is going.

Don't use a heavy, rigid stick or club to push material into and through the hopper—use a light, flexible stick. The latter will break or give way if caught up by the whirling blades, but the heavy stick will jam the machine or, with bad luck, injure or bruise the operator.

In general, you will find it harder to work with wet material than dry. But, again, a little experimentation will show that you can mix damp or even wet materials with dry and get highly gratifying results.

A few trials will probably convince you that the compost shredder helps you do a better gardening job and lightens your chores as well. But remember to keep that experimental attitude working overtime. This machine can modify your entire gardening technique and you can learn a lot from it.

246

Most definitely, the compost shredder has won a place in the gardening scheme of things. Once you adjust your work habits to its productive possibilities, you will wonder how you got along without it. It will give you lots and lots of compost and mulch, and it will cut down on your work hours and efforts.

Versatility is the keynote of the new shredders constantly being developed. At least one, for example, has both a set of shredding bars and a grinding screen which are interchangeable with each other so that the user can process his material in the proper manner. Most organic matter being processed for composting must be shredded, but some material such as dry leaves, hard manure, phosphate rocks, cotton bolls, small bones and fruit pits must be ground to process properly.

Most of the shredders are highly portable, and the heavy-duty ones will handle both light and coarse materials ranging from straw to branches and wood chips. Prices are quite low, some models selling for under $100 without power (they may be equipped with either an electric motor or gasoline engine). Large units which allow the materials to be fed into the machine by conveyor belt, are also available.

A Home-Built Shredder

R. A. Hill of Detroit, Michigan, has designed and built his own shredder. He describes its construction: "The main part of the shredder, the grid, is made of a 44-inch piece of $\frac{1}{8}$ inch by $1\frac{1}{2}$ inches by $1\frac{1}{2}$ inches angle iron, cut and bent to make a frame 11 inches by 11 inches and welded at one corner to form a square. Twelve pieces of $\frac{1}{8}$ inch by 1 inch by 11 inches cold rolled steel are spaced inside this frame $\frac{3}{4}$ inch apart, using a $\frac{3}{4}$ inch square piece of metal as a spacer. These cross-bars are electric-welded in place (electric welding produces less heat than gas welding or brazing and thus prevents warping.

"For the cutter bars use 12 pieces of the same material as the grid cross-bars. Bore a $\frac{1}{2}$ inch hole in the center of these cutter bars. It's best to make a jig for this by locating the hole position carefully in one bar; then bore a small hole. Bore the small hole in all the bars first, then enlarge the holes to $\frac{1}{2}$ inch.

"As spacers for the cutter bars you will need 10 pieces of one inch round cold rolled steel $\frac{3}{4}$ inch long with a $\frac{1}{2}$ inch hole in each.

"The shaft is made of a 15 inch piece of $\frac{1}{2}$ inch cold rolled steel. Place the shaft upright in a vise and slip on one

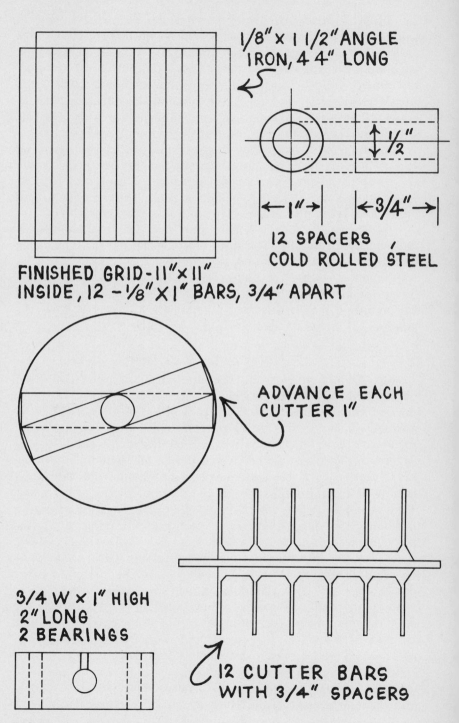

1/8" × 1 1/2" ANGLE IRON, 4 4" LONG

1/2"

←1"→ | ←3/4"→

12 SPACERS, COLD ROLLED STEEL

FINISHED GRID-11"×11"
INSIDE, 12 – 1/8"×1" BARS, 3/4" APART

ADVANCE EACH CUTTER 1"

3/4 W × 1" HIGH
2" LONG
2 BEARINGS

12 CUTTER BARS
WITH 3/4" SPACERS

of the cutter bars, making sure that it is square with the shaft. Then slip on one of the round spacers and tack weld it to the cutter bar (use arc welding). Put another cutter bar, advancing the front edge about one inch.

"Complete the cutter bar assembly by putting on the bars with a spacer between each. When all the bars are in place, move the front edge of each bar so that they are staggered to complete a circle. This is done so that the load will not come on the motor all at two spots, as would happen if the bars were placed in line. Tack weld all the bars in place, then place the assembly on its side and weld on both sides of each bar as well as on the outside of the first and last bar. Make a good job of these two welds or your cutter bar assembly will slip on the shaft.

"The bearings for the shaft are made from two pieces of cold rolled steel $\frac{3}{4}$ inch by 1 inch by 2 inches long. Drill and ream a $\frac{1}{2}$ inch hole—a running fit for your round shaft. Drill an oil hole on top and a $\frac{5}{16}$ inch hole near each end.

"Now you had better brush up on your carpenter work: The frame is made of two pieces of 2 inches by 4 inches about 48 inches long. Slip the grid in between these, placing it in the center. Then add 4 crosspieces of 2 inches by 4 inches to make a frame. Board over the top to the grid on each side.

"Place the cutter bar over the grid and put the bearings in place. Then bore the 4 $\frac{5}{16}$ inch holes through the angle iron and through the wood frame pieces. Bolt the bearings in place with 4 $\frac{5}{16}$ inch bolts, using good-sized washers on the underside. To keep the cutter bars in place so that they revolve in the center of the spaces in the grid, use a $\frac{1}{2}$ inch collar outside of each bearing.

"Add 4 legs on a slant, bracing both ends with cross braces and flat pieces of metal.

"The sides of the hopper are made of two pieces of $\frac{3}{8}$ inch or $\frac{1}{2}$ inch plywood. Use waterproof marine plywood and cut to shape with a notch to slip over the shaft. Note that the circular part of the top, made of galvanized iron, is hinged for cleaning out and oiling. The bottom part of the hopper is also made of galvanized iron. Punch holes for nailing the iron on the reverse side with a slim nail set large enough to take a good-sized nail.

"Do not try to improve the hopper by placing it upright. When placed upright the wind from the blades will blow leaves and other light material out as fast as you can put it in.

"A ¼-horsepower electric motor belted up 2 to 1, and the job is complete."

Tractor-Powered Grinder

Dr. Howard G. Laskey also designed and built his own compost grinder. Although he uses the power from his farm tractor, a motor could easily be attached to the grinder to make it self-powered. Dr. Laskey tells about his grinder:

"It cost me about $15.00 to make. It is powered from a belt-pulley on my farm tractor. The grinder is most efficient at moderate speed, and will grind materials fine enough for seed flats. Wet strawy manure is shredded to a very fine consistency.

"Take a cord-wood saw mandrel which weighs about 48 pounds and costs $10.50 and weld two steel disks, 10 inches in diameter, to the shaft. To the disks weld 4 steel bars. Each steel bar carries 7 teeth welded in position.

"Next, make a simple wooden stand and attach the rotor to it. A wooden box cover with an open end rests over the rotor. The cover has a hatch into which materials to be shredded are thrown. A steep chute carries this material to the rear of the rotor teeth. The material falls on the revolving teeth at a level of 9 o'clock on the rotor.

"A large stone thrown into the machine causes the unattached box top to elevate itself. The stone is ejected through the front without damage to the machine and without injury to the operator. The box top then falls back into position again.

"This machine is light enough to be carried by one man. During operation it should be bolted to heavy skids. This prevents the drag of the 6-inch belt-power from easing the unit out of line."

ROTARY TILLERS AND TRACTORS

In the past few years, interest in rotary tillers and small tractors for the garden has grown by leaps and bounds. Costing almost nothing to operate, they prepare ground for planting, tend the plantings, mow the lawn, and do just about any job around the grounds.

For soil preparation they are tops. Mixing in organic material, the rotary tillers plow, disk and harrow in one operation, then they can be used to cultivate, weed and mulch. They insure good soil structure with proper drainage and

Heavy-duty rotary tillers are useful as "power sheet composters" as they chop and uniformly mix in humus-making cover and green manure crops, as well as mulches, lime, and natural fertilizers. These qualities have made them popular.

aeration, and let you incorporate organic materials into your soil in Nature's way. "Power sheet composters," they chop and uniformly mix in humus-making cover and green manure crops and mulches along with lime, rock and other natural fertilizers. Thus one small, maneuverable machine can do all your tillage and soil-feeding jobs, with enormous benefit to your soil.

Although it is not a matter of absolute necessity for the average home-owner to own a rotary tiller, these digging machines have soil-building values which have made them particularly popular with organic gardeners. Basically their popularity stems from this cause: the rotary tiller makes the most efficient use of horsepower of all power soil-working machines. For example, a two-horsepower tiller will do a more satisfactory job of seed bed preparation than will a two-horsepower garden tractor.

This maneuverable tiller will improve soil fertility. Comments one California gardener: "Any weeds, green manures or other organic materials are shredded and mixed with air and soil in such a way that they decompose rapidly."

Why should the soil-working ability of the tiller be of particular interest to organic gardeners? The answer is that the tiller is a machine that helps the soil build itself. You can help the soil rebuild itself by tilling it and growing green manure, and the small tiller is the most practical machine that gives the gardener the ability to do this.

Of course, there are Ruth Stout and many of her followers who say that they never work their soil at all—just mulch it very heavily. It is a fine way to garden with a minimum amount of labor and weed problems. But most gardeners are not able to get enough mulch to cover more than just their kitchen garden area, so any way at all to help the soil rebuild itself is certainly welcome. And many soils are so tight and hard that they require the aeration of some kind of tilling periodically.

Says Jim Stout of Santa Rosa, California: "Properly done,

rotary tillage can improve soil fertility. Any weeds, green manures or other organic materials are shredded and mixed with air and soil in such a way that they decompose rapidly. Lime, rock powders, compost and other material can be put where they do the most good."

Over the years we've asked a great many tiller owners if the machines have helped increase the humus content of their soils. The answer in almost every case has been yes. One Newburyport, Mass., gardener reported: "I was greatly surprised to see how a layer of leaves, seaweed and chicken manure disappeared last spring after working it in the previous fall." A New York grower plows crops of rye and oats into the soil between rows of nursery plants, while a Texas woman uses a tiller to turn under the first crop of young weeds and prepare her garden for planting.

Power Equipment in the Garden

Power garden equipment has made the benefits of green manure plants, one of the best soil conditioners ever discovered, more available to gardeners. Fertility-building crops such as rye, clover and buckwheat can be fitted into the garden rotation schedule. The practice is especially worthwhile in large gardens, where at little cost, time or effort, a great amount of organic matter is returned to the soil.

Green manuring is an idea and a method that has long been used by farmers to build soil—but has been largely overlooked by gardeners. Tests that we recently conducted on the Organic Experimental Farm showed us that by taking advantage of garden-scale power equipment we could do as good a green manuring job as any farmer. We were able to work into the soil a green manure crop that soon decayed and turned into fertile humus.

Sheet composting—one of the foundations of the organic method—is merely an advanced form of green manuring. Sheet compost is made by spreading extra organic material over a green manure crop. Then both the crop and the extra material are worked into the soil.

For several years, this has been considered a more efficient method than composting in heaps, since all the decay occurs right in the soil. Organic matter is especially valuable to the soil while it is decaying, so you can readily see the big advantage in the sheet composting process.

Sheet Composting with Power

Although recognized as more efficient, sheet composting also means more work for the gardener who sets out to do the job with manual garden tools. But *power* sheet composting is a relatively simple task.

The secret behind fast sheet compost is rotary tilling. That's what tests at the Organic Experimental Farm have shown. In order to make these tests we got together 7 rotary tiller machines—typical of the various types on the market today.

We found that sheet compost was easily made with the rotary tillers. For example, suppose at the end of the summer, you have several good stands of flowers, which you ordinarily gather and put in a compost heap. Unless shredded, they can take anywhere from 3 to 6 months to decompose. But with rotary tillers, you can mulch them in to a depth of 3 or 4 inches, and—at the end of little more than 15 days—you will not find a trace of the plants left. Instead there will be only a more fertile soil.

But the point we liked best about the rotary tillers was that they opened up new spheres of activity. You could do in the garden with a rotary tiller what a farmer needs 3 or 4 machines to do in a larger area.

The potentials of this phase are exciting. Throughout the nation agricultural experiment stations are coming up with discoveries that mean new ways of soil building for the farmer. Very often the discovery is in the form of a new green manure crop which is more effective in producing organic matter than previously known plants.

Taking advantage of research like that would be out of the question for a home gardener . . . unless he has use of a rotary tiller. Then he's just as able to seed and till in a cover crop as any of the most mechanized farmers in the United States. This was the observation that fascinated us most about power tilling equipment.

Test of Hand vs. Power Tilling

In order to make an accurate comparison, we first dug in a rye cover crop over an area 5 by 10 feet. The rye was about 8 inches high. We made certain that the entire crop was turned under, but we were unable with the tools used to break up the material to any degree.

Next we rotary tilled the rye crop in a similar sized section, making several passes over the area. One point to bear in mind—until you become fairly adept at handling the machine, a rotary tiller is no toy. (For that matter, practically every machine will give an operator—expert or not—quite a workout.) It takes some experience to handle the machines properly, so don't get discouraged in the beginning.

After some practice, we began to really appreciate the job the rotary tillers were doing. The rye was being shredded somewhat and at the same time it was being worked into the soil to a depth of about 3 to 5 inches.

Weather conditions for fast composting were not ideal, as the late fall climate made things too cool. However, the difference in breakdown of the rye crop at the end of only 4 weeks time was clearly visible between the area worked in by hand and by the rotary tillers.

On plot A—done by hand—the rye was still primarily in a fresh and undecayed condition. It certainly would have decomposed eventually, but at that time little breakdown was evident.

On the other plots—worked over with the tillers—a lot of decomposition had already taken place at the end of 4 weeks. This was undoubtedly due to the fact that the rye had been partially shredded and tilled deeper more uniformly than plot A. With better weather conditions—more sunshine and rain—we are sure that power compost can be made right in the soil in only several weeks.

At time of turning under, it's a good practice to spread natural rock fertilizers, as well as nitrogen-rich material like bone meal, manure or dried blood, over the crop. In case the crop is too high or dense for the tiller to handle readily, go through the area with a rotary mower. Several passes with the tiller may be necessary to get the material into the soil.

Generally, most gardeners find that they can successfully plant about a month to 6 weeks after tilling under the green manure crop. Therefore winter cover crops, as rye and wheat, can be worked in about late March or April.

Avoid Over-Tilling

One caution in using a tiller to prepare soil: it is necessary to be careful not to pulverize the soil too thoroughly (especially soil that is low in organic matter). If that is done, the tilth of the soil can be harmed and packing will result. Pulverizing can be prevented by using the slowest efficient tine speed. Also, the soil should not be too wet or too dry when tilling is done.

As an organic gardener, you may find it most profitable to buy a tiller equipped with mower and other attachments. One company puts out a tiller that has the following attachments: a reel mower, sicklebar mower, gang mowers, a roller, hauling cart, riding sulky, plow, harrow, hay rake, seeder, fertilizer spreader, circular saw, chain saw, snow blower and posthole digger! Another will give you everything from a buzz saw and water pump to an air compressor and electric generator.

Aside from what they can do for the soil, tillers are additionally valuable for what they do for the *gardener*. It seems that the gardener who either owns or borrows a tiller never runs short of organic material. He knows he has a machine to build his soil, and this knowledge somehow serves to increase his supply of the materials he needs to build with. He watches out for sources of humus; local factories, parks and farms become economical fertilizer suppliers. And the net result is that his garden becomes a better one—both inside and out.

MISCELLANEOUS EQUIPMENT FOR GARDEN COMPOSTING

Black Plastic: Several years ago, a gardener came upon the idea of sealing his compost heap in plastic. This simple invention solved the perennial problem of compost odor, provided a simple way to discourage insects and rodents, and gave the home gardener a wonderfully simple and inexpensive way of composting anaerobically (without air). Now the suburban gardener can freely accept manure for his heap without fear of sanitation officials knocking on his door. He simply covers the compost heap with a large sheet of black polyethylene plastic (preferable to the transparent type), seals the bottom with a layer of soil, and forgets about it. No odors, no flies, no rats. And the anaerobic compost is finished in a shorter time than exposed heaps.

Composting under plastic is not only faster than regular methods, but it is easier, too. There is no turning, no watering, no extra work of any kind—except perhaps keeping the cover in place. First the ground is tilled, to loosen the soil and expose bacteria. The heap is then built upon this soil in the usual manner. It is watered down once, then covered with a sheet of polyethylene.

A Compost Ventilator: The question of the best ventilator has many composters puzzled. While it is easy to place poles in a heap and to remove them after building, leaving a hole for air to get in, poles are often not so easy to find nowadays. Making an opening with a rake handle has been found satisfactory, especially in wet regions, because the holes can be made from the side, thus keeping them from becoming waterlogged. But a very practical suggestion comes from a reader who advises a chimney made with chicken wire rolled twice.

A Compost Sifter: Organic gardeners are an ingenious lot. If something can be done at all, they're never satisfied until it can be done faster and easier. Leon R. Horsted of Waunakee, Wisconsin, felt that way for years about his problem of screening compost. By his old method, he spread out finished compost to dry in the sun, then sifted it through wire mesh by hand. Then, one day, he hit upon an idea which he hoped would speed up the process.

"I came up with a simple rotary screen affair," says Mr. Horsted, "using hardware cloth (wire mesh) as the screen. Old-timers may remember such an affair that was used atop a barrel, to separate unburned coal from ashes. The finer compost is placed in a pile to further decompose until used the following spring. The coarser compost is piled by itself to further decompose, or it is used around shrubs and small trees."

Fertilizer Spreaders: These make it easy to distribute finished compost, or such fine-textured materials for sheet composting as dried manure or rock powders. Some of the newer models are combination seed and fertilizer spreaders— ideal for green manuring—others are also garden carts or lawn sweepers.

Hand Tools: Even the basic hand tools have uses in various aspects of composting. For gathering compost materials, for example, you can get rakes not only in the old steel-tooth design, but also in bamboo, flexible metal and rubber, and even one that has special teeth to reach under the branches of crabgrass and sheer off the entire head. Weeders come in all sizes and styles, many designed to go down deep to cut the tap roots of weeds. Hand-powered wheel hoes are useful for sheet composting on small areas. Grass catchers that capture the clippings as you mow conserve these for the compost heap.

Power Tools: Electric hedge trimmers, power scythes, chain saws—these are handy on the larger place for such jobs as pruning, trimming and mowing heavy growths of grass or weeds, all of which result in materials usable in composting. Lawn trimmers and edgers fall into the same category. For cutting heavier growths of brush, you can use a sickle-bar mower, unless you have one of the heavy-bladed rotaries equipped with a circular saw. These are excellent for heavy trimming work and land clearing. Most of them come as attachments for garden tractors.

With ingenuity, the organic gardener can adapt many old tools and gadgets, or invent new ones, that will make his composting operations easier and more efficient. The wise gardener is always on the lookout for ideas for better composting. So are the equipment manufacturers, who are eager to produce new tools or machines, often at great monetary advantage to the gardener who designs them. (See also chapters on Composting Methods for the Gardener, How to Use Compost, and The Earthworm's Role in Composting.)

EQUIPMENT FOR FARM COMPOSTING

In some respects, equipment for composting on the farm differs from that used in the garden only in size. Heaps and pits, for example, will be larger, as will shredding, mowing and spreading equipment. Where the gardener aims to make perhaps a few tons of compost a year, the farmer's purpose is to produce this vital material in the hundreds or even thousands of tons annually.

While sheet composting is generally the mainstay of farm soil building, many farmers do considerable composting in heaps, bins and pits. The materials suggested for these structures in the previous section on garden composting equipment are equally suitable for making their larger counterparts on the farm. Bricks, concrete or cinder blocks, and tiles are most commonly used. Sometimes a cement floor is used, as well as a wooden roof. The floor can be slanted to one side, with drainage pipes in that side that carry liquid from the compost into a smaller cemented pit for collection and application to the soil. Pits are usually dug into the ground from 18 to 24 inches.

Anaerobic Digesters

Farm-sized anaerobic digesters, such as described in the chapter on Composting Methods for the Farmer, have been in use in India, France, Germany, Algeria, England and the United States since about 1945. These installations generally consist of one or more air-tight pits with a capacity of 4 to 5 cubic yards, and a tank for collecting gas with a capacity of two or more cubic yards. The slow reduction of the carbon in manure and litter produces sufficient gas to make practical an investment of about $1,500 in such a unit. They are most economical in areas which do not have gas or electric service, and which have a mild climate. Prolonged freezing weather requires extra attention to prevent freezing of the digester and its contents.

The gas tank is similar in construction to the large gas tanks used to hold gas for city use. It rises and falls as the supply of gas increases or decreases. Gas digesters are becoming especially popular in areas in which manure is used for fuel, as they enable both fuel and humus to be obtained from the manure. After several months, the manure in the digester tank is expended and it can be removed and used on the soil. Pathogenic organisms have been killed by the prolonged anaerobic digestion, making it practical to use human wastes if desired. Gasoline engines, gas furnaces and stoves can be run on methane gas.

Shredders and Mixers

Large shredders which will handle as much as 150 cubic yards of compost material per hour are on the market today. Most of these are designed to be fed by hand shovel, conveyor or tractor bucket. They are finding increasing acceptance for compost preparation on farms, nurseries, sewage treatment works and similar operations.

An unusual one has recently been developed by a British firm. Tests show that the machine can convert straw and other waste vegetation to finished compost in from two to three weeks. It's called the Standen-Hawkomatic Compost Mixer; here's how it works:

The dry material used for composting (straw, weeds, etc.) is forked onto a feeder conveyor which throws the material into a revolving drum where water is sprayed as required. The action of the revolving drum soaks the material with the proper amount of water and helps break it up.

As the wetted material passes from the drum onto another conveyor, rock phosphate and potash, limestone or nitrogen-rich organic fertilizers can be added from a hopper mounted immediately behind the drum. They can be added at the rate

Developed by an English equipment company, this "Compost Mixer" is described as capable of converting straw and other waste vegetation to finished compost in from 2 to 3 weeks. Machines like this can improve farm composting methods.

of 7 pounds to several hundred pounds per ton of raw material and are also damped down by a fine spray of water.

A third conveyor takes the mixture into a spinner mechanism, which breaks up the material further and aerates it. From the spinner, the material is thrown onto a pile until it is about 6 feet high. If necessary, the entire process may be repeated a second time at varying intervals, adding more water and organic fertilizers to produce the type of compost desired in as short a time as possible.

Mounted on wheels, the Standen-Hawkomatic Compost Mixer is driven by a 3-hp. electric motor, is 15 feet 3 inches long, 4 feet 2 inches wide, 7 feet 10 inches high, and weighs about 2,000 pounds. Readers interested in learning more about this machine should write to Mr. F. A. Standen, F. A. Standen & Sons, Ltd., St. Ives, Hunts, England. Here's what Mr. Standen wrote us:

"We are in full production of the machine and a good number are now in use in Great Britain. We're looking forward to receiving inquiries from growers in the United States."

Manure Loaders and Spreaders

Manure loaders and spreaders can be used to mechanize the handling of not only manure, but also sawdust, corn cobs and other organic materials. They are among the most basic tools of an organic farmer.

Alden Stahr tells how he built his own inexpensive loader: "Several hundred dollars was more than I could spare for the amount of time I use a loader. But faced with a 50-ton pile of chicken manure and little time, something had to be done, so I went to see a friend who is handy with a welding outfit.

We got a couple of lengths of 1½-inch galvanized pipe and cut a piece of steel for the scoop out of an old milk cooler. The pipe should have been two inches, but the lack of strength of the 1½ inch was compensated for by extra bracing. We wanted used pipe, but since none was available we bought new. A couple of pulleys, 25 feet of cable and an emergency brake from an old Plymouth made up the balance of the material except for assorted bolts, etc.

The pipes were anchored to the tractor at support points for the cultivators and braces welded in place. At first we used simple pulley wheels without bearings, but these soon jammed under the weight and wouldn't let the scoop come down. Next we tried a two-and-one block and tackle, but the bearings burned out in an hour of use. Finally my friend made a double pulley with good bearings out of two auto fan pulley wheels and got a single steel block for the scoop. The reason for the double and single pulleys is to slow down the lift and to put less strain on the motor when throttled down.

The belt pulley was taken off the tractor and a reel made for it, with a drum to fit the Plymouth emergency brake. The brake is rigged with a spring to stay on all the time except when the lever is pulled to allow the scoop to descend or to be pulled up. The cable runs through a 3-foot piece of ¾-inch galvanized pipe to prevent snaring the operator's leg.

Although my tractor has a hydraulic lift, the thrust was not sufficient to get a 7-foot lift with the scoop, so we settled on the mechanical lift as being our best expedient. The scoop is 30 inches wide and picks up several hundred pounds of manure at a time, so it's a great back saver even though it may not be as "purty" as factory-made rigs. And after you've loaded a few tons of wet manure, you can't tell whether a loader was made in a factory or not. The parts cost about $30. Since I don't do welding I had to pay for that to be done, but even at that the loader cost me less than half the factory price.

Wood Chippers

The farmer with a fairly extensive woodlot, or with access to thinnings or slash—the limbs, tops and defective material left after a logging operation—from any woodlands, may find a wood chipper an excellent buy. Several manufacturers are marketing chippers, costing as low as $600, which convert forest thinnings and slash up to 6 inches in diameter into coarse or fine chips for bedding, mulching or direct application to the soil. Operating costs run from $2 to $5 per ton of chips produced, considerably less expensive than many other purchased organic materials.

EQUIPMENT FOR LARGE-SCALE SHEET COMPOSTING

Plows have been used since the earliest days of history, but in recent years the ancient soil practice of plowing has become a controversial subject. Here are the basic reasons for the growing anti-plowing attitude:

The plow turns manure and crop residues under and buries them where very little decomposition takes place. Turning the soil "wrong side up" exposes the bare, unprotected ground to the hot rays of the sun in summer and to unnecessary freezing in winter. The soil is also subjected to wind and water erosion. A hard, driving rain soon loosens the bare soil particles and seals over the surface of the land. Critics describe the moldboard plow as a good tool with which to exploit the land, but one of the poorest machines to build back fertility.

With the growing trend to sheet composting to maintain soil structure and fertility, methods have been developed to replace plowing. Disking, rotary tillage, chisel plowing and a system of mulch farming are among the practices now recommended.

Disk Tilling

Disking will slice and stir up the soil, leaving organic materials on the surface. Notched disks are used for trashy ground, allowing the organic matter to compost rapidly under

Disking down crop residues, such as sunflowers, is a basic part of the sheet composting program on the farm, which consists of (1) always having soil covered; (2) mixing surface growth into the soil surface and (3) replacing humus.

aerobic conditions in the upper level of soil. Large, heavy disks have entirely replaced the moldboard plow in many areas.

Organic farmer John Moyer tells why he puts his faith in the disk: "If more farmers were using disk plowing, or disk tilling methods, their soil and water would remain on their farms and the rivers would not overflow their banks every time a prolonged heavy rain occurred. Furthermore, the quality and quantity of the crops would be higher than they are now.

"Of course no tillage method can be much better than another unless the essentials of basic soil fertility are first met. One requirement is an abundance of vegetable matter available to mix into the surface of the topsoil. Along with plenty of organic matter, of course, proper crop rotations are a must. Soybeans, sweet clover, or alfalfa mixed into the soil will certainly put new life into all soils not having had such previous treatment. If this is done every third year or so, depending on the type of farming and particular soil conditions, excellent fertility will result.

"Thorough knowledge of soil and experience are the best guides as to how to till. In many cases, disking will cover the

263

Disking, rotary tillage, chisel plowing and "mulch farming" are practices that will help build up the soil's organic matter content. Many organic farmers prefer disking to other tillage methods since it leaves organic materials on the soil surface.

organic matter rather deeply. However, disks leave the surface in a rough condition, which is desirable.

"Personally, I prefer to use an offset disk to mix in the organic matter. Then, when it is necessary to have a deeper seed bed I follow with a field cultivator, such as the Graham-Hoeme or Ferguson. Both implements till the soil without burying the organic matter, especially the undecayed matter. The same procedure is followed with disk plowing as in using the moldboard plow, following with a disk harrow for final preparation. However, when disking with a heavy duty disk tandem or perhaps an offset such as I use, certain tricks can be used to advantage.

"When disking in a cover crop, such as sweet clover or soybeans, a good cutting angle should be allowed so that the disk will penetrate 3 to 5 inches in depth, depending on soil conditions. A slow forward speed should be used. A disk works best when traveling slowly. The better the job of cutting the disk does the first time over, the easier it will be later on to finally prepare the seed bed. The second time over the same area, it should be disked in the same direction as the first disking. This is important because at least one disking, especially where a heavy cover crop is involved, can be saved by being particular about this point. The vegetation has a tendency to nap under more easily when the same direction as the first disking is followed.

"One can easily cut in a 3 to 4-foot growth of sweet clover with 4 diskings, when properly done. The diskings should be spaced 4 to 7 days apart, depending on weather and soil condition. Weather conditions have much to do with it. One cannot till in a heavy cover one day and plant the next. A reasonable time must be given for decomposition.

"I am not necessarily trying to sell anyone on disking or disk plowing. Any implement that will mix undecayed cover crops into 3 to 4 inches of topsoil is a good tool. I have adopted the offset disk simply because it is most economical to operate. Seldom are any repairs involved.

"I have found that, when properly done, disking takes less man and horsepower hours than any other method. When I first used this method it took me twice as long as it does now to prepare an acre of seedbed, because through previous use of the moldboard plow the humus had been gradually depleted and the soil had become heavier and harder.

"Any soil that requires chemical fertilizers and poison sprays to grow a crop is an unbalanced soil. Improper tillage damages it further by depleting the humus more rapidly than the plants can profitably use it. It is to eliminate some of these problems that I have turned to disking."

Combined Method

Herman W. Hostetler finds shredding, disking and chisel plowing works well for him: "Natural methods go hand in hand with natural materials. In '53, I did my first chisel plowing with a two-tractor-tandem pull of one 14-foot Graham-Hoeme plow. In '54, I didn't plow a single furrow. My method in corn, for instance, was this: First, I went over the field with a good cornstalk shredder with companion sharp wheel disk. Secondly, I chisel plowed to a depth of 10 inches, an operation I could handle alone at 5 miles an hour with the tandem hitch. Finally, I went over the field with disk and harrow. *After only 3 steps,* the field was again ready to plant. According to my time-study and cost-accounting figures, it takes no more than 45 minutes per acre at the outside to get a field ready for planting by this method. Most farmers using the old method consider two hours per acre to be 'good time.' I feel that the natural method described here is not only cheaper and faster, but it is also more effective in getting the soil ready for planting without disturbing the organic cycle going on within it.

"Is my soil exceptional? By no means. I am farming 352 acres of a 400-acre farm in Bureau County near Tampico, Illinois. Approximately 200 acres are peaty loam, 60 acres are deep peat, 110 acres are yellow-grey sandy loam, 10 acres are black mixed loam, and 20 acres are largely dune sand. Any farmer will readily agree that this analysis indicates only 'an average farm.' "

ROTARY TILLAGE

In 1911, the Swiss invented the rotary tiller, whose whirling tines replace the plow, disk and harrow in preparing a seedbed. But rotary tillage has another advantage: it provides a better means of incorporating crop residues and other organic matter into the soil than the plow-disk-harrow combination. While plowing tends to bury organic matter too far below the soil surface to allow optimum decay and breakdown by microorganisms, rotary tillage mixes it into the soil evenly through the full tillage depth.

Farm-scale rotary tillage is steadily growing in popularity, but it has so far failed to be adopted by the great majority of farmers. The major implement firms have not yet added rotary tillers to their lines. There are a number of reasons why farmers have tended to stay with their old practices. Larger tractors able to pull 4 and 5 bottom plows have become common and have made plowing more rapid an operation. Tillers are more difficult to operate in rocky ground. Perhaps most important, some farmers have felt that tillers require a larger initial investment and greater maintenance expense. By contrast, the plow is one of the simplest tools used by man and has been tested and proven in field use for thousands of years. Any new implement coming along to challenge the supremity of the plow must undo those centuries of ingrained acceptance of a traditional tool.

However, tillers have become extremely popular with organic gardeners and farmers, primarily because of their efficient handling of soils with heavy plant cover. Often a rotary cutter or heavy mower is first run over the land to chop up plant material for tilling. For farm-scale tilling, the rotary cutter is almost a necessity.

Organic farmer Alfred Moon of Star City, Indiana, is really "sold" on rotary tillage. Alfred aims for high yields by tilling his land to get the following results:

1. Leave the land ready to absorb moisture and air.
2. Kill weeds just prior to planting.
3. Mix organic matter uniformly into the soil.
4. Avoid compacting the soil.
5. Prevent erosion or standing water.

To accomplish these results, Moon relies entirely on but two tillage tools—a sub-soiler and a Howard Rotavator. He first became interested in rotary tillage when under certain dry conditions he could not get his plow to scour. He also felt that without working organic material evenly into the soil, tillage methods were not doing the job. Many farmers, he feels, realize that the plow is wrong—that plowing "seals" the ground so water can't penetrate and even stands on top of the soil.

Rotary tilling, Moon found, is quicker. The first time over he can cover an acre per hour; second time, 2 to 3 acres in an hour; third time, 3 to 4 acres per hour. He's using the method for the third season now, and feels there will be continued improvement in the condition of his soil and that it will require even less time for tillage.

Besides the time factor, rotary tillage benefits the soil in many ways, according to Alfred Moon. "Erosion from water is no problem," he states. "My corn stood the cold, wet weather this spring better in the Rotary-tilled field." You can even help the weather with this system, he adds, because rotary-tilled land absorbs water, holds it, and doesn't dry out. In this way, the soil stores up moisture for the dry periods ahead.

Moon prepares for corn by rotary tilling shallow, 2 to 3 inches deep, in the clover, wheat stubble or corn stalks in second gear behind his tractor. This he does in the fall to break up the stalks and mulch them into the soil.

In the spring, he rotary tills deep (6 or 7 inches) in very low gear as early as he can get into his fields—earlier than it is possible to plow. This soil is ideal for seed germination.

Then just before planting, he tills shallow, in third gear, to kill weeds that have come up. The shallow pass does not go deep enough to bring additional weed seeds up to sprout later, and has left some of his fields so clean that Moon feels it may not be necessary to cultivate his corn even once.

To prepare what he considers the perfect seed bed for wheat, Moon simply goes once over land that had been in sweet corn. This is done with his Rotavator set at a 5 or 6-inch depth, which the standard first gear of his tractor will handle.

For beans following corn, Moon's first tillage is 2 to 3 inches deep (second gear), in the fall as soon as he can get into the fields following corn picking. His second pass, in first gear, is deeper but not as deep as for corn. The shallow weed-killing pass can be made in third gear.

"In ground where formerly I could not get my plow to scour, the land is now loose, easy to work, and sweet smelling," contends Moon. Rotary-tilled soil keeps an even temperature and seems to warm up much deeper without getting so baked on top. There is seldom a crust of any kind on it, and if there is one, it's so thin it cannot prevent water soaking into the soil.

Getting sufficient organic matter into the soil and leaving it in condition to absorb rainfall so that it can be stored in the subsoil cannot be overemphasized, according to Alfred Moon.

Sheet-Compost Farming with a Rotary Tiller

Floyd Drauden concurs in these ideas. He says, speaking from his own experience, "In my own farming operation I have junked the moldboard plow. Not only that, I now use a disk less each year, having found that it loses its effectiveness in sheet-compost or mulch farming. The drag or harrow, too, should be changed or modified to be useful in this type of agriculture. I now use the finest soil-building tools with which a farmer could be blessed—the rotary tiller and the chisel plow.

"No other machine can do the same job of mixing organic matter, crop residue, or manure into the soil as a rotary tiller. It reminds me of a mix-master a woman uses to blend the ingredients of a cake together. In fact a woman would never put flour, sugar, butter, milk and flavoring in a baking pan without mixing them and then thrust this pan of separated material into the oven expecting it to come out a delicious cake. About the same results are obtained when material is plowed under with the moldboard plow. Ingredients are not mixed and at best are put in the ground in chunks or in layers.

"With the rotary tiller all organic matter is mixed uniformly with the soil; you might say it is homogenized. Fast decomposition takes place without the addition of any chemical nitrogen. The organic matter at the top is constantly attacked by a weathering action. The rest is never buried so deeply that there is no air. Therefore, the material from the top of the ground to tiller depth is continuously exposed to oxidation plus the action of all the soil microorganisms.

"When weeds are tilled with a tiller they are killed, not transplanted. I have tilled weeds 3 feet high during the summer and left the ground untouched for two weeks. Nothing had started to grow at that time and decomposition had taken place to such an extent that one more tilling would have made a seed bed fit for any garden crop. Farmers for centuries have dreamed of *weedless* farming. I think it can be achieved by the use of the field chopper, rotary tiller, chisel plow, good farming practices and a high state of soil fertility.

"Farmers the world over realize fertile ground and good soil structure make weed control much easier. Moldboard plowing buries the weed seeds where they lie dormant for long periods of time. These seeds when plowed up and exposed to sunlight and warm weather, sprout and grow. Rotary tilling and chisel plowing keep weed seeds closer to the soil surface, where they either grow or rot. It has been said, and I will agree, that during the first 2 or 3 years of this kind of tillage there will probably be more weeds to contend with, but if kept under normal control during this early period there will be little use for the hoe or spray in the succeeding years.

"Rotary tillage is the soil-working method of the future. Not only is it efficient, but it enables farmers and gardeners to build up the wealth of their soil."

Chisel Plow Analysis

Mr. Drauden also analyzes the chisel plow:

"The chisel plow was born when Fred Hoeme of Hooker, Oklahoma, pulled a road scarifier across one of his fields in the fall. A road scarifier is a machine with big, tough, heavy teeth. It is used to tear up gravel or black-top roads. The following spring, Hoeme noticed the wheat on that scarified strip was better than anywhere else; so he bought some old steel rails, welded on some strong, curving teeth, and mounted this contraption on wheels. It was not a perfect tool, but it worked. Bill Graham, another Texas farmer, some miles down the road, heard about this strange implement. He became interested and with Hoeme, worked out several additional features. Later they obtained a patent on the machine. That was the beginning of the Graham-Hoeme plow. It has already captured the Southwest and is fast moving into the Corn Belt. Graham later purchased Hoeme's interest and is now manufacturing the plow at Amarillo, Texas, and Pueblo, Colorado.

"This is the best and most fool-proof machine ever made available to the American farmer. If the tractor operator goes to sleep and runs into the neighbor's fence, the only thing that happens is the neighbor is minus a fence. The machine is indestructible. It is made of I-beams and built like a battleship. There is no place to grease, practically nothing to break; the only wear is on the chisels and heel sweeps or shovels. This chisel and the rotary tiller plus clover, alfalfa, and grasses is the complete answer to all our erosion problems. The late Louis Bromfield found by using these tools in addition to legumes and grasses on the hill farms of Ohio, which he acquired to rehabilitate, he could eliminate contour farming completely and still have no erosion. After large amounts of organic matter had been worked into the soil for a few years and the ground had been chiseled down to from 14 to 18 inches, the rain that fell stayed on the hills and did not run off. Springs at the foot of the hills that had been dry for a 100 years began to flow the year around.

"The chisel plow, like the rotary tiller, is a humus tool. It is no miracle machine that will cure the ills of poor crop rotation and constant land exploitation. Ripping the ground open from 12 to 20 inches will not improve soil structure or texture unless organic matter is present, although it will temporarily promote better drainage. Good results can be expected only when there is a relationship between the depth of chiseling and the organic matter to be worked in. During the first year of mulch farming, chisel penetration of 8 or 9 inches should be enough. As the organic matter and humus is built up, deeper chiseling should be attempted, going down an extra inch or so each year. *The chisel depth should be governed by the amount of organic material available.*"

The Field Chopper

Floyd Drauden goes on to evaluate the field chopper:

"The field chopper is as important to me in mulch farming as the rotary tiller and chisel plow. It reduces heavy windrowed straw, or green standing hay crops to small pieces and distributes them evenly on the ground. Fast decomposition takes place as soon as this material is mixed with the soil.

270

"The first actual forage harvester was built in the 1920's, but it was not until 1936 that the conventional field chopper was produced and introduced to the American farm market, which could chop from the windrow, either field cured hay or green hay for grass silage. They were, and still are, called forage harvesters. They were built and used to take a crop *from* the field. It has been only recently that a few farmers thought of using them to chop a crop of straw or hay *back on the field*.

"The conventional forage harvester has different heads that fit on the base machine. These heads can be changed quickly and consist of a pick-up with revolving fingers for windrowed straw or hay, a sickle bar and reel for cutting standing green hay crops, and a sickle with gathering chains for cutting row crops. The material is delivered to the cutting knives. Some choppers, such as Fox, have an independent cutting head. A blower, attached behind the cutting head, delivers the chopped material to the wagon or truck. Machines such as Gehl, Papec, Case, and others have the cutting knives on the fan blades and the cutting and blowing is done at one time.

"The regular field, or stalk chopper uses two different ways to chop material. Some machines are the flail type having swinging knives, hammers, or chains. Others have horizontal revolving blades traveling just above the ground. When these machines were first produced, they were designed to chop material and spread it in the field, but now they have attachments which make it possible to harvest crops, so I guess they too may be classed as forage harvesters. All these choppers have proved they can successfully harvest a forage crop. In this report, we are not interested in its harvesting abilities, but rather in the possibilities of the field chopper as a conservation and soil-building implement.

"The field chopper is a *must* in sheet-compost or mulch farming. The chopper in converting bulky crop residue into tiny particles not only makes it possible for the rotary and chisel plow to work at maximum efficiency, but also helps the soil bacteria make organic matter into humus, or plant food, faster. Almost anyone knows that a piece of straw, stem of alfalfa, or corn stalk will decompose much more quickly if cut into pieces. The demands that crops put on land today call for an abundance of humus to be present all during the growing season. To chop organic matter helps accelerate its decomposition and provides the aerobic bacteria with raw material which they process into humus at a terrific rate.

The Mulch Till Planter

A machine has recently been developed that can plant through a mulch, fertilize deeply, and—its manufacturers say —*can make a soil-building crop out of corn*. This machine is the McCormick 4M-21 mulch till planter, made by the International Harvester Company.

The mulch till planter prepares the seedbed, plants two rows of corn or other row crops directly in corn, oat, soybean, wheat stubble or sod. It leaves a protective mulch on the soil surface and at the same time can apply a deep and a shallow application of fertilizer.

According to company officials, this once-over operation saves 7 to 8 tractor manhours per acre over the conventional method of seedbed preparation and planting.

From the photograph of the mulch till planter, you can see that the soil-working and deep fertilizer applicator units are forward-mounted on the tractor. The colter on each front unit slices through the ground and cuts any stalks or trash.

In direct contrast with the mulch planting method, current practices for growing corn have the reputation of "soil destroyers." Soil Conservation Service experts have stated that over 70 per cent of all corn land is slowly eroding. Most legume rotations leave land bare over winter at least half of the time. With conventional plowing and clean cultivation, all corn land is bare in the spring, when much erosion takes place.

Another important feature of the new corn-growing technique is to let weeds come up along with the crop instead of practicing clean cultivation. When weeds are grown in soil that is rich in minerals and nutrients, they can be almost as important as any other cover crop in increasing fertility and stopping erosion.

Following this is the top sweep, 36 inches wide, which works about two inches below the surface of the ground. It breaks up but does not invert the soil. Roots of live vegetation are sheared off below the surface of the ground.

The combination of soil and residues thus formed has exceptionally high water absorbing and holding capacity. This protective mulch prevents pelting raindrops from puddling and sealing the surface of the soil.

Underneath the surface sweep is a second sweep, 18 inches

wide, equipped with knife blades. This sweep can be set to work to a maximum of 9 inches below the surface. Its purpose is to aerate and till the soil.

Besides planting through a mulch, the McCormick machine also has a deep fertilizer spreader. This is desirable because:

1. The fertilizer is placed in the row below the seed for maximum benefit to the growing crop;

2. Deep placement of fertilizer encourages growth of a strong, deep root system. This helps in sustaining plant growth during periods of temporary drought; and

3. Fertilizer is not wasted in stimulating weed growth because the placement is such as to favor the corn.

Mulch planting is especially advantageous in sloping fields where conventional methods of seedbed preparation, planting and cultivation result in water runoff and soil erosion. In fact, mulch planting on the contour has been found to practically eliminate the costly soil erosion that so often results from clean-tilled row crop production under such conditions.

Development of the mulch planter is indicative of the progress that can be made in modern farming methods through better machines. As the trend toward large-scale farm composting on the soil continues to grow, we can expect to see more and even better machines designed for this purpose. (*See also chapters on* COMPOSTING METHODS FOR THE FARMER, ANIMAL MANURES IN COMPOSTING, APPLYING COMPOST ON THE FARM, MUNICIPAL AND COMMERCIAL COMPOSTING.)

COMPOSTING EQUIPMENT SOURCES

The following is a list of manufacturers of a wide range of tools, power machinery, attachments, bins, boxes, screens and other equipment designed for many aspects of both garden and farm-scale composting. While thorough, the listing is not all-inclusive. Concerns the nation and world over are constantly adding mechanical and other devices, improvements, etc., that help make composting and its application easier, more practical and efficient.

By writing any of the firms under the equipment categories in which you are interested, you can secure descriptive material, details and recommendations to fulfill your own requirements.

Tillers and Tractors

S. L. ALLEN & COMPANY, INC.
5th & Glenwood Avenue
Philadelphia 40, Pennsylvania

AMERICAN FARM MACHINERY CO.
Garden Tractor Division
1060 33rd Ave., S. E.
Minneapolis 14, Minnesota

ARCO IRON WORKS
410 E. 4th Street
Topeka, Kansas

ARIENS COMPANY
Brillion, Wisconsin

AUTO-HOE, INC.
De Pere, Wisconsin

BAIRD MACHINE CO.
Stratford, Connecticut

BOLENS PRODUCTS DIVISION
of Food, Machinery & Chemical
Corp.
Port Washington, Wisconsin

BREADY TRACTOR & IMPLEMENT CO.
Solon, Ohio

CHARLES MACHINE WORKS
P. O. Box 66
Perry, Oklahoma

CIZEK MFG. CO.
Glutier, Iowa

CONSOLIDATED EQUIP. CO., INC.
P. O. Box 2216
Wichita, Kansas

COPAR, INCORPORATED
21 Avondale Street
Laurel, Maryland

COUNTRY SQUIRE TRACTOR CO.
P. O. Box 107
Muskegon, Wisconsin

CULTILLER MFG. CO.
162 Church Street
New Brunswick, New Jersey

DETROIT HARVESTER CO.
2750 Guardian Blvd.
Detroit 26, Michigan

EASTERN TRACTOR MFG. CORP.
36 St. James Street
Kingston, New York

ENDLESS TREAD TRACTOR CORP.
P. O. Box 807
Cumberland, Maryland

ENGINEERING PRODUCTS CO.
915 Niagara Court
Waukesha, Wisconsin

CHESTON L. ESHLEMEN CO.
109 Light Street
Baltimore 2, Maryland

FARM-CRAFT CORPORATION
Cleveland 27, Ohio

FARM-ETTE
Tom Moore Tractor, Inc.
Mantua, Ohio

FORD MOTOR COMPANY
Tractor & Implement Division
2500 E. Maple Street
Birmingham, Michigan

GARDEN PAL CORPORATION
2011 N. Columbia Blvd.
Portland 17, Oregon

GEORGE GARDEN TOOLS
811 S. Hamilton Street
Sullivan, Illinois

GILSON BROS., CO.
Plymouth, Wisconsin

GLENCOE MFG. CO., DIV.
Glencoe, Minnesota

GREAT LAKES TRACTOR CO.
Rock Creek, Ohio

HAHN, INCORPORATED
1825 W. Franklin Street
Evansville 12, Indiana

HOWARD ROTAVATOR, INC.
Box 26
Harvard, Illinois

JARI PRODUCTS, INC.
2938 Pillsbury Avenue
Minneapolis 8, Minnesota

MERRY MFG. COMPANY
Edmonds, Washington

MITCHELL MFG. CO., INC.
Monett, Missouri

PACIFIC MACHINE MFG. CO.
7107 S. E. 65th Avenue
Portland 6, Oregon

PIONEER MFG. CO.
1910 S. 81st Street
West Allis 14, Wisconsin

PIONEER-MIDLAND CO.
1200 Rawson Avenue
S. Milwaukee, Wisconsin

POWER KING TRACTOR CO.
9246 W. Appleton Avenue
Milwaukee 18, Wisconsin

QUICK MFG. INC.
3240 E. Main
Springfield, Ohio

ROTO-HOE & SPRAYER CO.
Newbury, Ohio

ROTOTILLER, INC.
102nd Street & 9th Avenue
Troy, New York

SEAMAN-ANDWALL CORP.
13050 W. Bluemound Road
Milwaukee, Wisconsin

SHAW MFG. CO.
372 Dublin Avenue
Columbus 15, Ohio

SIMPLICITY MFG. CO.
336 S. Spring Street
Port Washington, Wisconsin

SOUTHERN SAW WORKS, INC.
Power Implement Div.
Atlanta, Georgia

SPEEDEX GARDEN TRACTOR CO.
Ravenna, Ohio

STANDARD MFG. & SALES CO.
Lebanon, Indiana

TIGER TRACTOR CORPORATION
Keyser, West Virginia

UNIVATOR, INC.
805 Gilman Street
Berkeley, California

WAGNER IRON WORKS
1905 S. First Street
Milwaukee 11, Wisconsin

WHEEL-HORSE PRODUCTS, INC.
51467 U. S. 31st Street
South Bend, Indiana

YARD MARVEL MFG. CO.
5509 Market
Spokane, Washington

YUBA POWER PRODUCTS, INC.
800 Evans Street
Cincinnati 4, Ohio

Rotary Lawn Mowers

BALCO EQUIPMENT CO.
7055 Olive Boulevard
St. Louis 5, Missouri

BLAIR MFG. CO.
312 Birnie Avenue
Springfield 7, Massachusetts

COOPER MFG. CO.
411 S. First Avenue
Marshalltown, Iowa

THE ECLIPSE LAWN MOWER CO.
Div. of Buffalo-Eclipse Corp.
Prophetstown, Illinois

FOLEY MFG. CO.
3300 Fifth, N. E.
Minneapolis 18, Minnesota

FOX-HOWARD CORPORATION
3500 W. Touhy Avenue
Skokie 45, Illinois

GOODALL MFG. CORP.
438-444 E. Market
Warrensburg, Missouri

HEINEKE & COMPANY
1900 S. Eighth Street
Springfield, Illinois

JACOBSEN MFG. CO.
747 Washington Avenue
Racine, Wisconsin

KING O'LAWN, INC.
South Gate, California

LAWN-BOY
Division of Outboard Marine Corp.
Lamar, Missouri

LAZY BOY LAWN MOWER CO., INC.
1315 W. 8th
Kansas City, Missouri

MOTT CORP.
Brookfield, Illinois

ROOF MFG. CO.
Pontiac, Illinois

SENSATION MOWER, INC.
7577 Burlington Street
Ralston, Nebraska

SHAWNEE MFG. CO.
1947 N. Topeka Avenue
Topeka, Kansas

SPEISER ENGINEERING CO.
1601 W. Main Street
Stroudsburg, Pennsylvania

SUNBEAM CORPORATION
5600 Roosevelt Road
Chicago 50, Illinois

WOOD BROS. MFG. CO.
Box 148
Oregon, Illinois

YARD-MAN, INC.
1410 W. Ganson
Jackson, Michigan

YAZOO MFG. CO.
Livingston Road
Jackson 6, Mississippi

Bins & Boxes

ANDERSON BOX CO.
700 W. Morris
Indianapolis 6, Indiana

BENNETT MFG. CO.
E. Home & Penn. R. R.
Westerville, Ohio

HOME GARDEN PRODUCTS
159 Pine Ridge Road
W. Medford 55, Massachusetts

KESTON ORGANIC PRODUCTS
Owensboro, Kentucky

NEW IDEA, DIV. AVCO MFG. CO.
Coldwater, Ohio

Chippers

ASPLUNDH CHIPPER CO.
505 York Road
Jenkintown, Pennsylvania

R. N. BAILEY & CO.
9 W. 42nd Street
New York, New York

CARTHAGE MACHINE CO.
1941 Thomas Street
Carthage, New York

FITCHBURG ENGINEERING CORP.
Fitchburg, Massachusetts

MITTS & MERRILL
67 McCoskry
Saginaw, Michigan

D. J. MURRAY MFG. CO.
104 Murray Boulevard
Wausau, Wisconsin

THE PORTLAND COMPANY
60 Fore
Portland, Oregon

SUMNER IRON WORKS
Everett, Washington

Manure Loaders

ALLIS-CHALMERS MFG. CO.
Farm Equip. Div.
Milwaukee 1, Wisconsin

AMERICAN TRACTOR EQUIP. CO.
9131 San Leandro Boulevard
Oakland 3, California

BURCH PLOW WORKS
Evansville 7, Indiana

J. I. CASE CO.
Racine, Wisconsin

CASWELL MFG. CO.
Cherokee, Iowa

COCKSHUTT FARM EQUIP. LTD.
Brantford, Ontario, Canada

JOHN DEERE & CO.
Moline, Illinois

276

DUMP MASTER CO.
Sioux City, Iowa

FRAZER FARM EQUIP. CO.
York, Pennsylvania

HOLT EQUIP. CO.
Independence, Oregon

H-S ENGINE CO.
Billings, Montana

JOHNSON HYDRAULIC EQUIP. CO.
515 W. 78th Street
Minneapolis 23, Minnesota

LO-BOY, INC.
Markesan, Wisconsin

NEW IDEA FARM EQUIP. CO.
Coldwater, Ohio

SCHWARTZ MFG. CO.
Lester Prairie, Minnesota

SHAWNEE MFG. CO., INC.
Topeka, Kansas

ULRICH MFG. CO.
Roanoke, Illinois

WYATT MFG. CO.
Saline, Kansas

Sheet Composting Equipment

Disk Tillers

ADAMS HARD-FACING CO.
Guymon, Oklahoma

J. I. CASE CO.
Racine, Wisconsin

COUPLAMATIC, INC.
Morrison Implement Sup.
Lyman, Nebraska

CRUCIBLE STEEL CO. OF AMERICA
Oliver Building
Pittsburgh, Pennsylvania

R. HERSCHEL MFG. CO.
Peoria, Illinois

INGERSOLL PRODUCTS DIV.
Borg-Warner Corp.
Chicago 4, Illinois

LOVE MFG. CO.
Eau Claire, Michigan

NOLL BROS.
Milwaukee, Wisconsin

STOCKER & SON
Elmont, L. I., New York

Chisel Plows

AGRICULTURAL IMPLEMENT DIV.
Lincoln Steel Works
Lincoln, Nebraska

CHENEY WEEDER CO.
Spokane, Washington

COOK DISC & IMPLEMENTS
Clovis, California

GLENCOE-PORTABLE ELEVATOR
MFG. CO.
Bloomington, Illinois

GRAHAM PLOW, INC.
Amarillo, Texas

GRAY'S MFG. CO.
Modesto, California

JEOFFROY MFG. CO.
Amarillo, Texas

KIRKENDAHL PLOW CO.
Newkirk, Oklahoma

KRAUSE CORP., INC.
Hutchinson, Kansas

LONE STAR TRAILER & MFG. CO.
Amarillo, Texas

MINNEAPOLIS-MOLINE CO.
Minneapolis 40, Minnesota

NEAL-WAY MFG. CO.
Lebanon, Tennessee

OLIVER CORPORATION
Chicago 6, Illinois

SCHAFER PLOW CO., INC.
Pratt, Kansas

SOIL MOVER CO., INC.
Columbus, Nebraska

SUPERIOR MFG. CO.
Amarillo, Texas

TALBOT MFG. & SALES
Modesto, California

TENNESSEE IMPLEMENT CO.
Athens, Tennessee

277

YONKERS & JOHNSON, INC.
Palos, California

YUMACHISEL-
Columbus, Nebraska

Carts, Wagons, etc.

ACORN EQUIPMENT CO., INC.
Stevens Point, Wisconsin

BRINDERSON FARM SUPPLY, INC.
Chino, California

COUNTRYMAN'S CART
Box 702
Hinesburg, Vermont

GILSON BROS. CO.
Plymouth, Wisconsin

GIRTON MFG. CO.
Millvale, Pennsylvania

HEDLUND MFG. CO.
Boyceville, Wisconsin

H. D. HUDSON MFG. CO.
Chicago 11, Illinois

JAMES MFG. CO.
Fort Atkinson, Wisconsin

LOUDEN MACHINERY CO.
Fairfield, Iowa

THE NORMAGREX CO.
Walden 48, Massachusetts

OLSON MFG. CO.
Albert Lea, Minnesota

PATZ COMPANY
Pound, Wisconsin

SHAWNEE MFG. CO.
Topeka, Kansas

STANDARD EQUIPMENT, INC.
Bel Air, Maryland

Shredders & Grinders

ALGOMA FOUNDRY & MACHINE CO.
Algoma, Wisconsin

AUSCO
St. Joseph, Michigan

B-M-B COMPANY
Holton, Kansas

BARRENTINE MFG. CO., INC.
Greenwood, Mississippi

BEARCAT-WESTERN LAND ROLLER
CO.
Hastings, Nebraska

BENNETT & SON, INC.
Lenox, Iowa

JOHN BLUE CO.
Huntsville, Alabama

BRADY MULTI-CROP—Brady
Mfg. Corp.
Des Moines, Iowa

BRILLION IRON WORKS, INC.
Brillion, Wisconsin

BROOKS ORGANIC WASTE REDUCTION
Box 507, Rt. #1
Miami 44, Florida

L. BROWNLEE CO., INC.
Mokena, Illinois

BROWN MFG. CO.
Ozark, Alabama

BUSH HOG MFG. CO.
Selma, Oklahoma

E. I. CALDWELL & SON
Corpus Christi, Texas

CASTAGNOS CANE LOADER CO., INC.
Donaldsonville, Louisiana

CLEVIDENCE MACHINE WKS.
Caruthersville, Missouri

CONTINENTAL BELTON CO.
Belton, Texas

CORSICANA GRADER & MACH. CO.
Corsicana, Texas

W. F. COVINGTON PLANTER CO., INC.
Dothan, Alabama

EDWARDS EQUIPMENT CO.
Yakima, Washington

DANUSER MACH. WKS., INC.
Tulsa, Oklahoma

DEALER ASSOCIATES, INC.
Minden, Louisiana

ERNST BROS. MFG. CO.
Bakersfield, California

Farmhand Co.
Hopkins, Minnesota

Philip Hartigan
P. O. Box 283A
Honesdale, Pennsylvania

Haynes Mfg. Co.
Livingston, Texas

Hoffco, Inc.
Richmond, Indiana

International Harvester Co.
Chicago 1, Illinois

Kemp Mfg. Co.
1027 E. 29th Street
Erie, Pennsylvania

Lindig Mfg. Co., Inc.
1875 W. County Road
St. Paul 13, Minnesota

Lockwood Graders
Gering, Nebraska

Roof Mfg. Co.
Pontiac, Illinois

Royer Foundry & Machine Co.
158 Pringle Street
Kingston, Pennsylvania

Standard Mfg. Co.
Wellington, Missouri

Taylor Machine Works
Louisville, Mississippi

Tormey's "New Era" Co.
Box 428
Temple City, California

Wood Bros. Mfg. Co.
Oregon, Illinois

W-W Grinder Corp.
2957 N. Market Street
Wichita, Kansas

Chapter 8

WHEN TO USE COMPOST

Your compost is finished. After carefully following the recommended steps for turning the year's bounty of organic materials into rich, mellow humus, you want to be certain that it's used right—that it benefits your soil most and helps to insure a natural abundance and health in your coming crops.

It is not possible to stress too heavily the "soil bank account" theory of fertilizing. The real purpose of the organic method is to build permanent fertility into the soil by adding to its natural rock mineral reserves and to its humus content. Practically all the natural fertilizers are carriers of insoluble plant food. They start working quickly, but they don't drop their load of food all at once, as does a soluble fertilizer. An insoluble fertilizer will work for you for months and years.

So you can see that—as an organic gardener or farmer— you are not adding fertilizer to supply only immediate plant food needs, but also to build up the reserves that future crops will draw upon.

WHEN TO APPLY

The principal factor in determining when to apply compost is its condition. If it is half finished, or noticeably fibrous, it could well be applied in October or November. By spring it will have completed its decomposition in the soil itself and be ready to supply growth nutrients to the earliest plantings made. Otherwise, for general soil enrichment, the ideal time of application is a month or so before planting. The closer to planting time it is incorporated, the more it should be ground up or worked over thoroughly with a hoe to shred it fine. A number of garden cultivating tools and machine equipment offer an excellent time-and-labor-saving hand in accomplishing this. Several will help spread it evenly and mix it thoroughly with the soil.

If your compost is ready in the fall and is not intended to be used until the spring, it should be kept covered and stored in a protected place. If it is kept for a long period during the summer, the finished compost should be watered from time to time.

USE OF UNFINISHED COMPOST IN FALL

According to F. C. Gerretsen of the Holland Agricultural Experiment Station, "Investigations have shown that the use of incompletely decomposed compost in the fall gave better results than the use of decomposed compost in the spring. The reason is that the presence of considerable quantities of paper forces the bacteria of the soil to utilize the nitrogen of the soil for the decomposition of the cellulose and to fix that nitrogen in their bodies. In this way the nitrogen is preserved through the rains and snows during the wet period of the winter despite the work of erosion and leaching, and in the spring, after the decomposition of the bacteria, it is again available to the plants."

APPLY FERTILIZER DURING SLACK PERIODS

A report put out by the College of Agriculture, University of Illinois, Urbana, stresses the points to consider when applying fertilizer and compost to the soil. One of these is the time of year.

For organic farmers and gardeners, it's not at all a bad idea to make applications of fertilizer either in the fall or winter or in the early spring. The big advantage here is that application at such a time helps to equalize the workload. Usually this time of year is the least crowded with busy schedules, and the farmer or gardener can devote more time to doing a good job without interfering with the rest of the crop program. Also, there is less chance of damaging the soil or of injuring crops.

Just before the spring plowing is a particularly good time to apply fertilizer. Then when the plowing is done, the fresh organic matter can be worked down into the soil to supply food for the spring soil organisms. These organisms are what give life to the spring soil. They become active and start to grow at about freezing temperatures. However, soil temperatures must rise to 50 degrees F. before they really take on the dynamic action that so characterizes a living organic soil.

Thus, the addition of organic fertilizers in the spring just before the soil is plowed is an especially good time. The organic material can be worked into the soil at this time. Also, the temperature is just about to rise to the level where the vital soil organisms can make use of it.

There is no better carrier for plant nutrients than organic matter. This is because organic matter already has plant nutrients closely combined in the form that Nature has found best for the crops of the fields and the plains and the forests. How can man improve on Nature, other than to give Nature a better chance to work its own wonders?

Nature doesn't resort to the strewing of bags of chemicals over forest and field. Nature uses the nutrients already present in the materials that have grown on the land. That which has been taken from the soil is returned to the soil. This is the natural process, and the one that the wise gardener follows.

The chemical gardeners have never really heard of or understood all of the advantages of the natural process. The same goes for the chemical farmers. For example, suppose there is an extra heavy rain in the spring. Chemicals dissolve in the water and wash away. The chemical gardener or farmer pours his dollars into the muddy ditch of water that runs across his land and on down the river to the ocean.

On the other hand, the organic gardener by applying his fertilizer in the organic form, as compost or green manure, is actually doing much to prevent this erosion as well as nutrient loss. For the organic matter not only holds the plant nutrients combined in the form of chelates closely tied up in the plant residues, but each piece of organic material acts as a tiny dam to prevent erosion. His land does not wash away in streams of muddy water. And even wind erosion is slowed down. For, again, the tiny bits of organic matter slow down the force of the wind over the soil, and prevent its blowing away the particles.

Suppose that the soil is a tight clay. Then organic matter helps to loosen up the soil. It does this by opening up spaces which go down into the soil. These spaces carry air and water down into the soil like so many little tunnels. And this air and water are vitally important for crop growth the rest of the year. Otherwise, a tight clay soil will shed the water almost like a duck's back. And it is so tight that air can't get down to the roots of the plants. Yet the plants must have this air for best growth. The addition of the organic matter not only adds the nutrients, but also adds the air to the soil that the plant roots must have.

And, of course, the water that comes down the little tunnels penetrates into soil, opening it up and causing nutrients to dissolve. And as the water level rises in the soil there is less danger from drought, because plants can draw from this extra supply of water. Then, too, when plenty of organic matter is added to the soil, it acts just like a sponge. It soaks up the water during the rainy season, and then turns it loose during the drier times of the year. Thus, plants in the organic garden live on and thrive while plants in the chemical garden wither and die in the heat and drought of summer.

—CHARLES COLEMAN

A SOIL-BUILDING PROGRAM FOR FALL

The following reports from different sections of the country will give you an idea of how to use compost and other organic soil-building materials in autumn.

"Fattening Up" Soil in Michigan

A healthy diet the year round will make any garden do better work for its owner.

Food production pulls more value from the soil than we can replace during the growing months, so the fall and winter months are the time to "fatten up" the soil for the next growing season. That's why we've adopted fall fertilizing.

Our two-part fall feeding plan doesn't overwork us, because preparations are started months ahead, as we build our balanced-blend compost and accumulate materials for the winter "blanket." Our compost isn't just a random tossed-salad mixture, but is composed of the elements we think the soil needs most. We have two composters—one the bottom of an old concrete silo in which we "ripen" the bulkier refuse, and the other a compost cabinet situated nearer the house.

To the usual compound of garbage, leaves, twigs and stems, cut up in our shredder, we add an occasional sprinkling of powdered rock phosphorus, a few shovels of barn or poultry manure, several hundred earthworms, crushed eggshells, and cut-up fish. If we find any tomato worms, we add those; but we seldom find more than 5 or 6 of these green creatures in a season, which leads us to the conclusion that our organic tomatoes are just too rich for their weak stomachs.

Most families like fishing expeditions and it's real fun to go fishing for the compost beds. (Remember how the Indians planted a fish with each hill of corn?) Carp, bullheads, suckers —any kind is good for compost balancing. Or you may have kept some in your freezer too long to taste good on the table. That happened to us, last spring, and some overripe seafood went into the compost cabinet. If you don't use many eggs, ask a local hatchery for some shells. They'll be glad to get rid of them.

The addition of earthworms came when we discovered fluid leaking from the bottom of the cabinet. We threw in 150 earthworms and in two days the dripping had stopped completely. Now we add them frequently, in both composters— about 200 at a time in the large silo base.

As soon as we harvest a vegetable, we spread at least two inches of compost over the ground. With the garden tractor, we mix this "food" into the soil, to a depth of about 4 inches. Then we cover the space with its winter blanket, 3 to 4 inches deep. This year we are using mostly poultry litter with a straw base, for the covering; but other materials are just as satisfactory. Sometimes we use woodchip poultry litter, or straw cut up in our shredder. Any of these work into the soil easily, in spring.

Fall fertilizing is an important step in our soil replenishment routine, we are convinced. We first tried it on a small piece of idle ground that we had worked up for a potato patch. The soil was light and the first crop wasn't worth harvesting. We applied the fall-feeding treatment and when spring came we found our little earthworm friends busily tilling the soil and enriching the hungry plot. This year, we grew some really good potatoes there; and next spring we plan to give this spot the sunflower treatment. From then on, we feel sure it will keep pace with the rest of our garden, if we continue to keep it well-fed.

—ELLEN PERRY

Fall Program for Adobe Soil

We are not soil scientists, but we know that fall is the time when the leaves drop from the trees, when grasses die or die down, when plants give themselves back to the soil whence they came. In short, fall is the season when Nature begins making *her* compost, when she starts reconditioning the soil for the coming spring. That would seem reason enough for the good gardener to do likewise.

Organic fertilizers, of course, are relatively slow to take effect. In compensation, they are long-lasting. Applying them in the fall allows them time to seep down to varying levels so that roots of different lengths can later find them. It allows the beneficial winter's moisture and its alternate freezings and thawings to act on whatever organic matter may have been only partially decomposed (or even quite raw) when first introduced.

The fall application of organic soil enrichers is particularly convenient in a vegetable garden. The waste materials of the past season are then most easily available. You must dig up the garden in the fall. You must do something with these "waste" materials. Why not combine the two operations and so turn waste into wealth?

We live in a part of the arid Southwest where the soil is chiefly adobe clay, rich in minerals of many sorts but deficient in phosphorus (or rather, sufficiently alkaline to make the phosphorus unavailable), largely lacking in humus, heavy, and given to the "hard bake" when irrigated. Our problem is to make that soil friable and capable of retaining moisture.

In the fall we leave all but the heaviest plant materials in the garden and dig them in. Then we fill a garden cart with successive loads of a mixture composed of approximately 1/3 rotted or dried manure to 2/3 finished compost into which we have previously incorporated ground phosphate rock instead

284

of the lime needed by more acid soils. We spread this perhaps an inch thick over the surface of the soil, then dig it in, leaving the surface of the garden rough and cloddy so that winter may best do its work.

When, in the spring, the garden is again dug and this time raked, the old plant material has miraculously "vanished" —it has become humus, of course—and the soil is teeming with happy earthworms, descendants of two small packets of pellets which we planted some years ago in a once wormless earth.

This process is used throughout the garden in the fall. Special treatment needed for individual crops comes at planting time. Thus, peas must be planted here in January or early February (another reason for fall conditioning is that several vegetables must be seeded very early) and when we dig our planting trenches we line the bottoms with compost. Squash and melon hills receive a generous extra dose of old manure and compost at planting time, tomatoes plenty of compost, perhaps some bone meal, and so on according to the needs of each. This is a simple matter, once the over-all conditioning has been taken care of, for it's the conditioning that most concerns those of us who must garden in adobe.

We are fortunate in having a source of several different types of manure. We try to vary the "makings" of our compost sufficiently so that the finished product is likely to be well-balanced. The final step, and one of the most important, is the mulching. For this we use chiefly oat straw (it's weed-free and inexpensive) supplemented by native grasses cut before they've gone to seed. When fall comes, the mulch, too, is dug in to make better soil for another year.

And the result? We haven't got a show place (we're not full-time gardeners), but after 5 years of following this simple plan we have porous, fertile soil on which, in a very small area, we grow asparagus, peas, broccoli, tomatoes, corn, beans, squash, melons, chard, onions, lettuce, cucumbers, strawberries, and a dozen kinds of herbs; but the soil outside the rabbit fence is still heavy adobe that bakes in the sun and sheds water (when there is any) like a duck's back. We think fall conditioning pays.

—ELIZABETH RIGBY

Fall Fertilizing and Landscaping

Fall feeding of evergreens, lawns, and ornamental shrubs begins in October. And what better natural fertilizers can any gardener use than manure, bone meal, compost, and peat moss? These fertilizers are very effective, easily available and inexpensive. We have been using them for years with gratifying results—especially manure, which comprises over one-half of all the fertilizer we use.

Because we like our evergreens to quickly absorb the excellent plant food contained in the manure we apply, we feed it to them in liquid form. This fertilizer is made by placing 5 to 8 pounds of dehydrated manure in a burlap bag, and soaking it in about 20 gallons of water. The bag is punched with a rod until the water turns brown. Each evergreen is then fed 4 gallons of this liquid manure.

The following day, 5 handfuls of bone meal are scattered around each tree, and worked into the soil. Then 4 inches of peat moss is applied to ward off heavy frosts. Evergreens thus fed survive the winters better, and emerge in spring stronger, healthier, and more beautiful. Manure-fed evergreens take on a darker green color and their foliage becomes denser each season.

Lawns, too, thrive beautifully on manure. If you have access to a large amount of aged manure, crumble and scatter it evenly over your lawn. Melting snows and spring rains will carry the food down to the roots in time for growth.

If such manure is not available, you may use our method with equally good results. With a fertilizer spreader, we feed 4 pounds of dehydrated manure or screened compost to every 100 square feet of lawn. The amount used may be increased or decreased depending upon the condition of the lawn. Dehydrated manure, because it is so finely ground, blends quickly with the soil to produce a rich, dark loam vital to good lawns. In early spring, an all-organic fertilizer may be applied to add extra fertility to your soil. We have fed manure and organic fertilizer to our lawn for 3 years. The turf is now as thick and soft as a Persian rug.

Ornamental shrubs, too, should be fed manure in the fall to bloom their best in spring. We combine manure and compost with excellent results. When feeding, we loosen the top few inches of soil around each shrub, and apply ½ bushel of compost per bush. This is worked into the soil, then mulched with ½ bushel of manure-clumps that are well aged. By spring, water will soak all of the available food down to the hungry roots.

In landscaping, the thing to remember is that fall feeding

is all important. Use compost, manure, peat moss, and bone meal generously. Your efforts will be repayed in vigorous, robust evergreens, thick, green lawns, and beautifully blooming shrubs.

Start Sheet Compost in Fall

Autumn is the time when cultural practices must be instituted to insure a productive garden in the year ahead.

One of the most important cultural practices to begin now is that of the cover crop, the basis of the sheet composting program. Cover crops increase soil organic matter which in turn will increase absorptive activity and stimulate biochemical processes.

In addition, cover crops prevent soil erosion. They bring leached nutrients back to the surface where these will be available for the new planting.

Choices among cover crops are many. A good cover crop should make as large an amount of growth as possible in the shortest possible time. To assure good growth, the crop must be adapted to climate and soil.

To facilitate soil preparation it is advisable to choose a crop that is easy to incorporate into the soil.

In making a decision in the choice of a cover crop, the considerations will dwell with the use of legume or non-legume. Here it should be noted that the legume has an added advantage in supplying extra nitrogen as well as organic matter. Among the individual crops which have cool temperature requirements the legumes include crimson clover and vetches. The non-legumes encompass rye, oats, wheat, buckwheat and rape. Those with warm temperature requirements in the legume group are cowpeas and soybeans. The non-legumes are millet and Sudan grass.

Soybeans are an excellent green manure crop for the heavier soils of the North. Rye, although difficult to turn under, is one of the best recommended since it can be planted from August 1 to October 15. If sown by the latter date, rye will make enough growth to be turned under in November.

The actual planting of these crops can be accomplished at vegetable harvest time or somewhat earlier by planting between the vegetable rows. Planting should not be done so early that it may compete with the main crop.

Two other sources of important consideration for the addition of organic matter to your garden are weeds and crop residues. Weeds are an excellent source of organic matter and can be grown without expense. To prevent weeds from becoming troublesome, timely plowing is recommended to stop the spread of weed seeds.

Crop residues are also important in helping to maintain soil fertility. However, they are usually not in great enough quantity to accomplish the job singly. One of the exceptions is sweet corn which returns a sizable amount of plant material to the soil.

In putting under these materials, whether they be cover crop or soil improving crop, it is best to work them under while they are still succulent. Where weeds and crop residues are concerned the control of weed seeds, insects and diseases should be considered.

Fall plowing where severe freezes occur may destroy many insects by exposing the larvae or adults. Plowing at this time may also have beneficial effects on the soil if alternate thawing and freezing occur. By plowing in the fall, the garden can be prepared earlier in the spring. Water will also enter the soil more readily in winter because there is a larger exposed surface resulting from the fall plowing.

With all the advantages of fall plowing, care must be taken in certain cases to prevent erosion. This is especially true if the soil is not frozen during winter rains.

—STEPHEN PATRONSKY

For Better Lawns and Shrubs in the Northwest

What does a gardener think about in the fall? How his garden is going to look next year, of course! It is nice to sit and dream about that subject, but a little more important is to get down to the business at hand of making that dream become a reality.

Here is what the writer has done, and will do again. Sometime in the fall, preferably after the rains start in the Pacific Northwest, we applied rock phosphate to the entire lawn. This application will stay in the ground and be supplying the roots of the grass for 5 years and will not have to be applied again within that period. On our lawn, of about 3,000 square feet, we put 80 pounds. This could vary some, but in our area, the rock phosphate is put up in 80 pound sacks and it was convenient.

Each year in the fall an application of bone meal (raw) is a life-giver to lawns. This was applied at the rate of a 100 pound sack for the lawn of 3,000 square feet. The bone meal may be mixed with the rock phosphate, if desired. If you want a beautiful lawn, it has to be fed, and this is an easy way to do it. A good healthy lawn is an inspiration and really easier to care for than one with ugly, dry bare spots or patches of moss.

The third step in the plans for a lovely lawn for next year is the top-dressing. Here is a good place to use a lot of compost to good advantage. You can use it straight or mix it with loam or leaf mold, but be sure it is a flowing mixture and not sticking together in clumps. This top-dressing can be applied over the entire lawn any time in the fall, but take particular care to keep it from smothering any of the grass plants. The blades of grass must show through and be able to get the sunshine. Pay particular attention to filling in any holes or depressions in order to make your lawn level. We always sift our compost through a coarse grating, thus keeping out any bones, sticks, whole leaves, or clods of earth. This makes a compost easy to handle and suitable for applying.

We have had many compliments on our lawn and the care hasn't seemed especially difficult. After this fall treatment it grows so lush in our wet Northwest springs that my husband always falls back on that old joke about putting cement down in place of a lawn. It could be painted green and save him the trouble of mowing!

We are able to get, from one of the members of our Organic Gardening Club, deep litter from the house where he raises chickens for the market. He uses sawdust, built up to about 3 feet deep. After several months under the chickens, it is a lovely brown sawdust which is dry and is wonderful for mulch. This is excellent material to put around under shrubs. It gives a neat appearance to the ground and protects it from the winter rains, as well as working slowly into the soil for further enrichment. This can also be used as top-dressing for the lawn, but it would be preferable to mix it with the compost to give it more body. Other mulches can be used around the shrubs, as well, depending on what you have, but try to use something! This mulch should give protection to the ground all winter and more can be applied next year when it begins to disappear. —ELEANOR McCONNELL

ORGANIC APPLICATIONS IN SPRING

While I dig my compost in at the time I do my fall spading, I have sometimes an excess over the bushel per square yard that I use in the garden every year. This I use in spring with the more demanding crops, especially tomatoes, cucumbers, watermelons, squash or pumpkin, peppers, and scarlet runner beans.

The plants which grow fast, that is, the warm-weather crops which go out only after the frosty period is definitely over, can take more compost than slow-growing crops. An extra addition of nutrients supplies ample growth food which produces quick pick-up and therefore tender vegetables: In early spring, you may therefore give an extra dressing to head-lettuce. Spinach, beets, snap bush beans as well as the various members of the cabbage family, such as radish, kohlrabi, cauliflower, cabbage, savoy, Chinese cabbage, are not so demanding and can get along on smaller amounts. If you have enough compost to make another dressing, mulch around the warm-weather crops.

With many root crops, I find that a top-dressing of compost does not benefit them much, the exception being only the knob celery or celeriac. But even this delicious vegetable had better be given the extra compost in the planting hole or row. Its roots will even go after green matter or leaves dug under in spring.

Carrots, rooted parsley, parsnip, rutabagas are much less exacting, though they do not make a very satisfactory growth if overfed with nitrogen. They respond favorably to bone meal or rock phosphate and to potash in form of wood ashes, well dug in so that the roots do not have to forage and fork out for it. The wood ashes from the fireplace that you have collected and saved in winter can now be used as a sprinkling over the garden, but may also be dug in. Bone meal, horn dust, phosphate rock or colloidal phosphate, on the other hand, should be left on the surface, but dug in at spring spading or at least cultivated into the ground with a hoe or at least a rake, cultivator or other suitable instrument, such as a wheel-harrow. The reason for the difference in treatment is that potash fertilizers are soluble; wood ash dissolves rapidly and drains into the ground where the roots can reach it. Phosphorus, on the other hand, does not "move" much in the soil and must be put within the zone where the main roots are formed. Otherwise, the application may stay in the upper inch of the soil without doing much good to the growing plant.

In making compost, gathering material as it accumulates, I suggest that the phosphorus fertilizer, preferably horn dust

In transplanting warm-weather vegetables or flowers into the garden after all danger of frost has passed, use a liberal compost application. Such crops as lettuce, tomatoes, cucumbers, watermelons, squash, pumpkins and runner beans are heavy-feeders, need more early-season nutrients than the slower-growing root crops.

and hoof and horn meal or bone meal, the former two being also especially rich sources of nitrogen, the latter mainly of phosphorus, be added as sprinklings over the green matter. While they cannot altogether replace fresh manure, they may be suitable substitutes where manure is scarce or lacking.

Of the bagged manures, especially goat, sheep, poultry and rabbit manure are valuable, since their nitrogen content is frequently higher than that of dehydrated cow manure, thus supplying the bacteria with growth food and producing better heating and breakdown of the compost material. When organic sources of phosphorus in form of bone and horn products are not available, rock and colloidal phosphate are needed. On a farm scale, they are the only ones that can be applied in sufficient quantities. All experiments have shown that rock phosphate is best when applied to the manure in the process of composting. It remains longer available or only becomes available when mixed with organic matter. The more alkaline the soils, the more important it is to supply rock phosphate together with organic matter.

Neither wood ashes nor phosphatic material should be

used in excess. True, some vegetables thrive on ashes, especially lettuce seems to like wood ashes. But on the whole a thin sprinkling is enough. We might add in this connection that coal ashes are not recommended at all.

If you have not done fall spading which in the cold regions is always preferable because it allows the winter freezes to break up the soil particles and to untie the minerals in the soil, especially if the beds are left in the rough and not smoothed out, then spring spading is the only way out. But even then, I do not recommend too fine a seedbed unless you can be sure that no major rains will follow. If they do come and hit a very smooth bed, finely raked, then the upper part will crust and make it difficult for young seedlings to push through, however much compost you may have incorporated. Compost loosens the soil, but it takes many years of composting until heavy spring rains are absorbed without forming a crust on the top.

In laying out the garden, keep also in mind that you need not sow everything at once, that it is better always to have a small bed of crisp fresh radishes and a long succession of lettuce than a sudden surplus. Also keep in mind that in July or August some crops may be sown again, for instance cabbages, turnips, rutabagas, radish, and storage crops, including beets. In the warmer regions the need for fall planting of vegetables is even greater than for spring sowing. Still, in the cooler regions with relatively short growing seasons, the 2 or 3 months between taking off spring crops and the arrival of fall frosts are important. You now want to provide for compost to dig in during the second crop season. And then you want to provide that real amount of compost which you need for spading in during the fall months when the beds become gradually cleared. This spading process starts when spinach is off and when the first radishes are harvested; it continues, as the bush beans are finished; it is followed by the beds that have yielded beets, carrots, early cabbage, etc. To provide for the large requirements of compost, make use throughout the year of all sources and build up an ample supply. Thus composting becomes part of the ordinary garden work. As you throw out refuse and gather wastes, partly for cleaning-up purposes, partly because you need compost, you do not have to encounter any great waste of time. You have to dispose of the material anyhow, you might as well have the additional plant food ready which should go into the heap.

Hoof and horn meal, cotton seed meal, cotton gin wastes, and all the other organic matter that is rich in nitrogen and usually in other fertilizer materials can sometimes be had for little; sometimes they cost considerable sums. But a bag of horn dust may contain as much as fifteen and more pounds of nitrogen, which is always costly. When you compare it with another bag, that contains perhaps 1.5 per cent of nitrogen, you may easily compute which is the less expensive source of this indispensable plant food. In this connection we should perhaps also think of the growing amount of refuse blood available from small slaughtering outfits. If this can be hauled home and put in the compost pile, it will add valuable fertility, which would be lost if it were let down the drain. But when you use it, make a heavier sprinkling of earth over your heap in order not to attract flies.

A gardener recently wrote, and many others before him have said the same: "When I became compost-conscious I soon found that it wasn't so hard to get the necessary materials. Once you put your mind to it you can usually find what you want, often at little cost. I cleaned out under a shoe-maker's shop and hauled away hundreds of pounds of leather dust. This worked fine with my compost." Others will find other substances, but they will find them and thus put back in the land what the crops have taken out. Plan for it as the season starts and you will not only get a better garden this year, but also better soil for the future in which you will get healthier plants and more beautiful flowers in years to come.

The treatment of lawns with compost is more and more becoming the rule. Give your lawn a thin top-dressing when the grass resumes active growth, and you will not only get a lusher turf, you will also get a spongier soil which retains moisture better and cuts down on watering. If compost is not available, use at least hyperhumus, possibly mixed with a thin sprinkling of chicken manure or the like. By saving leaves when you can again do so, you will furthermore improve your chances at organic gardening. The treatment of flowers with compost is a special question which we shall take up some other time. A bushel a square yard is just as good for the annuals as it is for the vegetables. But evergreens should not be given too much compost, and broad-leaved evergreens should especially not be overfed with nitrogen in any form. They thrive best with raw humus derived from raked-up leaves.

—H. MEYER

BUILD SOIL THROUGH THE SUMMER, TOO

Most gardeners and farmers are tied to the spring and fall theory of fertilizing. If they use chemical methods, they have good reason to avoid fertilizing in summer and winter, but organic methods know no such limitation.

First of all, you don't have to worry about "burning" your plants when you apply compost or natural rock fertilizer. Second and equally important, natural fertility will stay put in the soil until it is needed by crops. Truly, when you fertilize by organic means there is no closed season on building soil. That fact itself is a tremendous advantage for organic gardeners and farmers.

In summer, plants take more nutrients from the soil than they do in any other season. Everyone knows that. But perhaps you didn't realize that in summer the soil has more nutrients available to give to plants than at any other time of the year.

Primarily, the increased activity during the summer of bacteria and other soil microorganisms is responsible for the abundance of plant food. That is quite significant to what we are talking about, *because microorganisms are one of the primary forces that act on organic and natural rock fertilizers to make them available to plants.* Isn't it a good idea, then, to apply these natural fertilizers when the activity of microorganisms is greatest?

Summer then, can be a fine time to apply compost and the natural rock fertilizers—rock and colloidal phosphate, greensand, granite dust and diabase dust. Organic fertilizers of all types are needed even more in the summer, because they hold moisture in the soil and stimulate the bacterial activity that takes place during the warm months. You will get a fast return on your money, and the added fertility will quickly transform itself into strong roots and tops. And the fertility you add in the summer will continue to do good for your plants next year and the year after.

HUNGER SIGNS IN THE GARDEN

Plants are just like humans. If they don't get the right things to eat, they get sick from malnutrition.

And, of course, sick plants are not the most healthful to eat. They are deficient in some of the nutritional elements needed by humans for the best health and vigor.

Sick plants are also more susceptible to attack from

insects and plant diseases. The produce from sick plants sometimes brings lower prices on the market, since something is obviously wrong with it.

Like sick humans, sick plants exhibit to the trained eye of the plant doctor certain symptoms which are characteristic of specific nutritional deficiencies.

With a little keen-eyed observation you can diagnose many hunger symptoms in the plants in your garden. Once you have done this, treatment of the condition is easy with the proper organic fertilizer.

Nitrogen Deficiency

Nitrogen is especially important for vegetables of good quality since it is essential for the synthesis of natural proteins. Plenty of nitrogen gives a good normal deep-green color to foliage and stems. In general, a nitrogen deficiency is characterized by slow growth, slender fibrous stems, and foliage and stems that fade to yellow in color.

Tomatoes: Tomatoes deficient in nitrogen exhibit very slow growth at first. This is followed by the green of the leaves becoming lighter. This starts at the tip of the leaves at the top of the plant. The leaves remain small and thin, and the veins may become purple. The stems are stunted, brown, and die. Flower buds turn yellow and shed, and the yield is reduced.

Cucumbers: When deficient in nitrogen, cucumbers exhibit stunted growth. The green of the plant turns to a yellow color. Roots turn brown and die. Nitrogen deficiency is also what causes cucumbers to point at the blossom end. These market as low-grade produce.

Radishes: Radishes deficient in nitrogen are retarded in growth. The leaves are small, narrow, thin, and yellow in color. The stems are slender and weak. And the edible roots are small and imperfectly developed. They have a faded reddish color.

Corn: The most prominent symptom for corn that is deficient in nitrogen is the yellowish-green of the plants rather than the normal deep-green color.

While these are specific examples they indicate the general symptoms exhibited by most vegetables for deficiencies in nitrogen.

TREATMENT FOR NITROGEN DEFICIENCY: Use compost or any organic fertilizer high in nitrogen. Some of the best products available commercially are blood meal (15 per cent nitrogen), hoof meal and horn dust (12.5 per cent nitrogen), and cottonseed meal (7 per cent nitrogen). These products could be mixed with compost in ample quantities and applied to the soil in fall, or in very early spring. Always allow at least 6 weeks for complete decomposition of organic materials in the soil.

Phosphorus Deficiency

In general, plants which are deficient in phosphorus are slowed in growth. The underside of leaves assumes a reddish-purple color, and the plants are slow to set fruit and mature.

Tomatoes: A phosphorus deficiency causes a reddish-purple color to develop on the underside of leaves, and the whole foliage eventually assumes a purplish tinge. The leaves are small, and the stems are slender and fibrous. The plants are late in setting fruit.

Radishes: The leaves of radishes deficient in phosphorus may be a reddish-purple on the underside.

Celery: Celery deficient in phosphorus exhibits poor root development and slender stalks.

Corn: Corn deficient in phosphorus has a yellowing of leaves similar to nitrogen starvation. After the ears set with kernels, check them to see if all the rows are filled, and if the kernels fill out to the end of the ear. If they don't, this is a sure sign of phosphorus starvation.

TREATMENT FOR PHOSPHORUS DEFICIENCY: Use either phosphate rock (30 per cent phosphorus) or bone meal (21 per cent phosphorus) applied either directly to the soil or mixed with your compost. The amount you apply depends on how much your soil needs. A soil test would be very helpful in determining the correct amount of any fertilizer to apply.

Potassium Deficiency

General symptoms of potassium deficiency show up in plants that are reduced in vigor, have poor growth and poor yield, and are more susceptible to disease. Ashen-gray leaves are observed instead of the good normal deep-green color. The leaves develop brown edges and crinkle or curl. Later they become bronzed.

Tomatoes: Tomatoes deficient in potassium grow slowly, are stunted, and have a low yield. The young leaves become crinkled. The older leaves turn ashen-grayish green at first, developing a yellowish-green along the margins. This progresses further into bronze-colored spots between the longer veins. These may become bright orange in color and brittle. Leaves turn brown and die. The stems become hard and woody and fail to increase in diameter. Roots are not well developed and are brown in color. Fruit may ripen unevenly, that is, a tomato sliced across may show traces of green on one side while being red-ripe on the other. The fruit may lack solidity.

Cabbage, Brussels Sprouts: The leaves become bronzed on the border and the color spreads inward. The leaf rim parches and brown spots appear in the interior of the leaf.

Carrots: Carrots exhibit the first symptoms of potassium deficiency in curled leaves. The rim of the leaf becomes brown, the inner portion grayish-green, and finally bronzed.

Cucumber: Leaves of cucumbers deficient in potassium exhibit a bronzing and dying of the leaf margin. The fruit has an enlarged tip. This is just the opposite symptom of nitrogen starvation where the fruit has a pointed tip.

Radishes: Radishes which are deficient in potassium have leaves which are dark-green in the center while the edges curl and become pale yellow to brown. Extreme deficiency is indicated by deep yellow color of leaves and stems. The leaves may become thick and leathery. The roots are more bulbous than normal.

Beets: Beets deficient in potassium develop long tapered roots rather than the preferred bulbous type.

TREATMENT FOR POTASSIUM DEFICIENCY: By placing 6 inches of green matter to every two inches of stable manure in your compost heap, you supply adequate amounts of potassium for gardening purposes. Once the moisture of green plants is eliminated and the material is broken down, a great percentage of the solids consists of potassium. If your soil is particularly low in potassium, add potash rock, granite dust, wood ash, or some other potassium-rich organic material to the compost— or apply these materials directly to the soil.

Heavy mulching also seems to help maintain the potassium supply. At Purdue University, Clarence E. Baker found that mulching with manure, straw, and soybean hay eliminated symptoms of potassium deficiency in a peach orchard. Check trees, which received no mulch, did not recover.

Calcium Deficiency

In general, plants exhibiting calcium deficiency are retarded in growth and develop thick woody stems.

Tomatoes: The upper leaves appear yellow in color. This distinguishes the deficiency from that of nitrogen, phosphorus, or potassium where the lower portion of the plant has discolored leaves, while the upper leaves and stem remain more or less normal. The plants are weak and flabby and lacking in firmness. The terminal buds die and the nearby stem becomes spotted with dead areas. The roots are short and brown in color.

Peas: Red patches appear on the leaves near the center and spread out. The healthy green of the leaves changes to a pale green, then white. Growth is slow and the plants are dwarfed.

Corn: Corn deficient in calcium exhibits the most startling symptom of all plants. The tip ends of the leaves are stuck together as if they had been glued.

TREATMENT FOR CALCIUM DEFICIENCY: Use any good grade of ground natural limestone. About 60-mesh is a good grind.

Magnesium Deficiency

Magnesium deficiency is widespread. Plants deficient in magnesium are, in general, late to mature, and do not mature uniformly. They have poor market quality. They exhibit a characteristic lack of green color with the lower leaves being affected first. The areas between the leaf veins turn yellow, then brown, while the veins remain green.

Tomatoes: Tomatoes deficient in magnesium have brittle leaves which curl up. A yellow color develops in the leaves. This is deepest further from the vein. The older leaves of mature plants are the ones which most commonly show the symptoms. There is little effect to be observed on stems or fruit.

Cabbage: Mottled light-colored spots appear on the leaves of cabbage deficient in magnesium. The lower leaves pucker. The edge of the leaves may turn white or very pale yellow. These may turn brown and die. If only magnesium is deficient, the entire leaf becomes mottled with dead areas. If nitrogen is also deficient the entire leaf turns a light-green color, then yellow, and finally develops a mottling of dead areas. Potas-

298

sium deficiency, which is sometimes confused with lack of magnesium, can be distinguished by the bronzing which occurs before the dead areas appear.

Turnips: The leaves of turnips deficient in magnesium develop brown areas around the rim. These dry up and drop out. The inner areas are mottled with light-colored spots.

Carrots, Cucumbers, Squash and Lima Beans: These show the typical characteristics of mottling and then browning of foliage.

Corn: Magnesium deficiency is very easy to tell in corn plants since they develop a yellow striping or white streaks only on the older leaves.

TREATMENT FOR MAGNESIUM DEFICIENCY: If obtainable, add a quart of sea water to each 100 pounds of compost. Or, use Dolomite limestone since this contains quite a bit of magnesium.

Boron Deficiency

A deficiency of boron in plants causes plants to grow more slowly. Severe deficiency causes crop failures, since plants die. Unlike the other nutrient elements which produce general changes in most truck crops, boron deficiency produces more specific changes in different vegetables. Beets and turnips develop cork-like areas in the edible root, and a hollow stem develops in cauliflower, while celery cracks. The leaves may be stunted and twisted with dark spots on the tips of young leaves which grow larger as the leaves mature.

Celery: Celery deficient in boron develops a brownish mottling of the leaf. The stems become brittle and have brown stripes. Crosswise cracks appear in the stem, and the tissue curls back and turns brown. Roots turn brown and die.

Beets, Turnips, and Other Root Crops: These, when affected by boron deficiency, develop what is commonly known as brown-heart disease. Dark-brown water-soaked areas appear in the center of the roots. Sometimes a hollow, discolored center results. The roots do not grow to full size and may have a rough, unhealthy, grayish appearance. The surface may be wrinkled or cracked. The plants are stunted, the leaves smaller, twisted and less numerous than normal. Leaves sometimes develop yellow and purplish-red blotches, and the stalks may show splitting.

Tomatoes: Blackened areas appear at the growing point

299

of the stem, and stems are stunted, and terminal shoots curl, then turn yellow and die. The plants have a bushy appearance, and the fruit may have darkened or dried areas.

Lettuce: Lettuce deficient in boron exhibits malformation of the more rapidly growing leaves, and spotting and burning of leaves.

Cauliflower: Deficiencies of boron cause discolored, water-soaked areas in the stem of cauliflower. These may spread. The leaves around the curd may be stunted and deformed.

TREATMENT FOR BORON DEFICIENCY: Use plenty of manure or compost.

Iron Deficiency

Iron deficiency in plants is characterized by spotted, colorless areas developing on young leaves. Yellow leaves appear on the upper parts of plants. The growth of new shoots is affected and plant tissues may die if the deficiency is severe. Too much lime causes iron deficiency to develop.

TREATMENT FOR IRON DEFICIENCY: Plenty of manure, compost and crop residues, dried blood and tankage are the best methods for correcting iron deficiencies.

Copper Deficiency

Copper deficiency is usually confined to peat or muck soils. Plants deficient in copper exhibit slow growth or complete cessation of growth. Leaves become bleached-looking, and leaves and stems are flabby. Normal bright color is lacking.

Tomatoes: Tomatoes deficient in copper have stunted shoot growth, and very poor root development. The foliage may be a bluish-green, and the leaves curled. There is an absence of flower formation, and leaves and stems are flabby.

Lettuce: Leaves become bleached-looking. The stems and the rim of the leaf are affected first.

Onions: Onions which are deficient in copper have an abnormally thin scale which is pale yellow in color rather than the usual brilliant brown. Growth may be stunted or fail entirely.

TREATMENT FOR COPPER DEFICIENCY: Use plenty of manure or compost.

Zinc Deficiency

Zinc deficiency occurs in peat soils. It is particularly characterized in plants by leaves which are abnormally long and narrow. The leaves may also turn yellow and be mottled with many dead areas.

Squash, Mustard, Tomatoes, Beans: These plants usually are the first to exhibit the typical symptoms of zinc deficiency as described above.

Corn: Corn deficient in zinc exhibits older leaves which are dead, while yellow striping appears between the veins on the newer leaves.

TREATMENT FOR ZINC DEFICIENCY: Use plenty of manure or compost.

Manganese Deficiency

Plants deficient in manganese are slow to grow, and mature late and unevenly. The areas between the veins of leaves become yellow, then brown, while the veins remain green.

Tomatoes: Leaves have a typical lightening of green color which gradually turns to yellow farthest from the major veins. Dead areas appear in the center of the yellow areas and spread. Growth is stunted, and there are few blossoms and no fruit.

Spinach: Spinach deficient in manganese exhibits a loss of color at the growing tips. This spreads in towards the center of the plant. The normal green color gradually changes to a golden yellow. White, dead areas eventually appear.

Beets: The leaf takes on a deep red to purple color which gradually becomes yellow. Dead areas finally appear between the veins. The growth of roots and tips is stunted.

Snap beans: Whole leaves turn a golden yellow and small brown spots appear between the veins.

Cucumbers, Cabbage, Peppers: These plants when deficient in manganese have small, slender and weak stems. The leaves turn yellowish white while the veins and midribs remain green. The blossom bud may turn yellow.

TREATMENT FOR MANGANESE DEFICIENCY: Use plenty of manure or compost.

Although, at first glance it may appear somewhat difficult to diagnose the problem in a garden where the plants are sick, it is easy if you pick out one vegetable and concentrate on that.

301

For example, if cucumbers are pointed at the end, then the soil is deficient in nitrogen. If cucumbers are narrow at the stem and bulging at the flower end, then the soil is deficient in potassium. In just a few minutes you can tell what your garden's soil is deficient in.

In general, it can be stated that plenty of manure, or good quality compost made with kitchen scraps and a wide variety of plant materials such as weeds, grass clippings, etc., will correct all soil deficiencies. At the same time, manure and compost will tend to neutralize an unfavorable soil pH, and will also reduce the harmful effects of previous applications of toxic chemicals, whether of the fertilizer or the weedicide or pesticide type. Whenever there is doubt concerning the cause of sick-looking plants, it is recommended that heavy applications of manure or compost, or both, be used.

After becoming well-versed in applying the powers of observation, you can state rather definitely what causes plants to be sick. Then, being able to prescribe organic methods for their recovery, there's no reason why you can't become the first "organic plant doctor" in your neighborhood. You can help out your friends' and neighbors' gardens as well as your own.

—CHARLES COLEMAN

Deficiencies in Fruit Trees

Deficiencies in fruit trees can cause new twig growth to die back, abnormally twisted leaves and blotchy fruit.

Possibly your trees have symptoms of mineral deficiency. Potash or phosphorus may be low or your soil may be too alkaline to allow certain minerals like iron and aluminum to become available. The following list can perhaps solve your problem. These symptoms apply for all deciduous fruit trees.

NITROGEN DEFICIENCY: Examine the leaves on the old branches. With a lack of nitrogen, these older leaves turn a yellowish-green, working toward the tips. You may also notice reddish or reddish-purple discolorations. If nothing is done to relieve the deficiency, leaves become very small, and the twigs slender and hard.

PHOSPHORUS DEFICIENCY: The young twigs develop a ghost-like hue; stems show purple coloring; leaves are abnormally small and dark green. Old leaves become mottled with light and dark green areas. Occasionally bronzed leaves will show up on mature branches.

POTASH DEFICIENCY: The key to potash deficiency is purplish discoloration and scorching of leaf edges. The dead spots will be found on mature leaves, but under continued deficiency, even very young leaves are affected. Peach foliage often becomes crinkled and twigs are unusually slender.

MAGNESIUM DEFICIENCY: The large, old leaves will display flesh-colored patches of dead tissue, not restricted to the leaf edges. Watch for dropping of leaves, first on old branches, then on twigs of the current season. Defoliation may be so severe that only tufts or "rosettes" of thin, small leaves are left.

ZINC DEFICIENCY: Both zinc and magnesium deficiencies are very much alike. Each of them can cause rosettes of leaves in the advanced stage. But without zinc, crinkled leaves are common, which are also chlorotic (rather washed-out yellow in color). In peach trees this is very true. With citrus fruit, very small, smooth fruit and pointed leaves are the symptoms. There may also be striking contrasts in leaf patterns—dark green veins and yellow tissue.

CALCIUM DEFICIENCY: Calcium and boron shortage will show up first on young twigs rather than the mature branches. Dead areas are noticeable on the young, tender leaves at the tips and margins without calcium. Later, the twigs will die back and roots are injured.

BORON DEFICIENCY: Immediately coming to mind should be internal cork of apples, which is the commonest boron deficiency problem. Early in the season, hard, brown spots with definite margins form inside the fruit. As the season progresses, the spots soften, become larger, and lose their definite outline. The leaves may be entirely unaffected.

In other cases, the young leaves can become very thick and brittle, then cause dieback of twigs. Some trees may also form wrinkled, chlorotic leaves.

IRON AND ALUMINUM DEFICIENCY: With an overdose of lime comes an unavailability of certain minerals like iron and aluminum. These minerals may be right in the soil, but are held insoluble when the acidity is low. Look for yellow leaves with brown patches, and loss of flavor in the fruit.

DEFICIENCY CORRECTIONS

Nitrogen—apply compost, cottonseed meal, dried blood, tankage, raw bone meal, fish wastes, legume hay, or one of the organic nitrogen commercial products now on the market.

Phosphorus—raw or colloidal phosphate rock, bone meal, fish wastes, guano, or raw sugar wastes.

Potash—granite dust, glauconite marl (greensand), wood ashes, seaweed, or orange rinds.

Magnesium—dolomitic limestone or raw phosphate rock.

Zinc—raw phosphate rock.

Calcium—raw pulverized limestone.

Boron—raw phosphate rock (avoid lime, add manure and acid organic matter like peat moss, sawdust, or ground oak leaves).

Iron and Aluminum—glauconite marl (avoid lime, use the acid organic matter recommended under boron).

YEAR-ROUND COMPOST CALENDAR

The following is a season-by-season listing of composting activities for gardeners throughout the United States:

North and East

WINTER

To get a head start, sow in flats snapdragons, delphiniums, penstemons, asters, ever-blooming begonias, Shasta daisies, canterbury bells, and many other annuals. For seeds sown indoors, use prepared potting soil or bring in some mature compost, mix it with an equal part of leaf mold, and add plenty of sand. Some people use straight compost, and some use only leaf mold. Repot non-blooming house plants; don't let them get potbound. Bulbs in storage should be looked over for possible rotting. Place unusable ones deep in the compost pile.

SPRING

Flower and Vegetable Garden. Work compost into top 4 inches of soil about one month before planting. Spread compost over the perennial borders to give them a good start. Rock fertilizers, including greensand, will add vital nutrients and trace elements to the compost, the benefits of which will be noticed for a long time to come.

Top-dress lawns with compost. If there is moss on the lawn, there is a lack of nutriments; spread on a liberal application of screened compost over the effected areas or over the entire lawn. When reseeding bare spots, feed a lawn mixture of screened compost and rock powders. Top-dress all bush and cane fruits with compost, fortified with pulverized rock phosphate and, where easily accessible, granulated seaweed.

Since peonies are heavy feeders, give them a top-dressing of bone meal or well-rotted manure mixed with compost. Water hydrangeas with liquid manure or compost while they are in bud to increase the size of the blossoms. A heavy dose of acid compost will provide blue flowers. Seeds of biennials and perennials for flowering next year may be planted the latter part of May. Work compost into the soil together with pulverized potash and phosphate rock.

Beans, corn, cucumbers, melons, potatoes and squash may be safely planted in open ground in mid-May, assuming the ground is not too cold. If the season is mild, early corn may be planted during the first week. Add plenty of compost and a pound each of pulverized phosphate rock and potash rock to every 10 square feet of soil.

In June, cultivate rose beds thoroughly, watering them with liquid manure or liquid compost. Preparation of beds where perennials are to be sown should include mixing in a good mixture of compost, bone meal and, if necessary, lime.

SUMMER

Make sure the mulch is in place. If you have a plentiful supply of compost, consider using as mulch. August is a good time to set out strawberries. When planting runners, work plenty of compost deep into soil. Remember compost can be applied as top-dressing to growing plants throughout the summer.

FALL

September is the time to plant bulbs, narcissus, hyacinth and crocus. These should be planted about 4 inches deep in well-spaded soil that has had a little compost placed about two inches below the bulbs. This will give them a good start in the spring. Chrysanthemums can be boosted by an application of compost water.

The compost pile should be building up with waste materials from the garden. In case of a dry Indian summer, be sure to keep the heap moist.

Give rhubarb and asparagus a liberal application of compost. Clean-up is important in the fall season, to destroy weeds and control pests and diseases. All this material should be added to the compost heap. Use a rotary mower or shredder if available to cut up woody stalks before composting. Sanitation should be practiced under the trees.

November is when to incorporate compost and green matter to the soil. It's a good practice to rotary till the material into the garden soil and allow the soil to stay in a rough condition until spring. Apply the winter protective mulching materials around plantings now.

South

WINTER

Many vegetables such as beets, broccoli, cabbage, carrots, cauliflower, endive, lettuce and radishes can be seeded in the South as early as February. The soil where these plants are to be sown should have applications of compost. Cucumbers respond to heavily-composted soils, doing away with fusarium wilt and being free from insect pests. Make a hole the depth of a shovel, and a foot or more in diameter, and fill with compost. Mix fine soil and compost deep enough to cover the seed. Allow about 3 plants to the hill.

SPRING

March is the big planting month in the South. Give gardenias a dressing of compost to prepare them for the enormous quantity of blooms that begin opening up in May. In April, dahlias may be planted. Tubers left in the ground all winter should be taken up, divided and replanted immediately, before sprouts begin to show. Use a knife to divide, taking care to have a portion of the stem on each division, to be sure to have an eye or bud from which the sprout comes. Tubers that break off without an eye will not sprout. After preparing the hole with compost in the bottom, set stake firmly for later support. It's a good idea to supply a generous sprinkling of granite dust to the compost in order to strengthen stalks. Magnolias like a deep rich soil with lots of acid compost and plenty of water. In April, also feed bulbs, roses and shrubs and the lawn using compost and the rock powders. Give pansies an application of compost and peat moss at this time.

May is the time to plant most summer crops. Be generous with compost and when plants are 4 to 5 inches high apply a mulch at least 3 inches deep. Cut okra pods before they mature so the plants will continue to bear all season. Plant in wide rows with stalks every 2 or 3 feet, using compost liberally.

SUMMER

June is a good time to feed roses, dahlias and chrysanthemums working compost into the upper inch of the soil. When iris has finished blooming, large clumps may be dug, separated and replanted any time from now until fall. Inspect carefully for borers and cut out and remove from the bed any damaged or rotted parts. Use compost, well-mixed, in the iris bed and plant rhizomes just under the surface.

Take care of the compost heap in June, watering it if it is dried out and continue adding materials. Warm weather is breakdown time, but the bacteria cannot do their work in dry material.

In August, give all flowers a mid-summer boost by applying liquid compost. A shovelful of compost mixed in a pail of water should do for each plant.

FALL

In September apply compost around each rose bush, dahlia and chrysanthemum plant, keeping them watered to encourage large full blooms. Be sure the plants are mulched as well.

Plant as many greens this month as needed. They like rich soil so apply plenty of compost.

In October, place liberal helpings of compost below plantings of Madonna lilies and peonies. After frost, asparagus tops can be placed on the compost heap. Apply heavy feeding of well-rotted stable manure or compost and a good mulch to the asparagus plants.

Southwest

WINTER

January is a fine time for planting azaleas and camellias. Use leaf mold or acid compost instead of peat.

In warm sandy soil, potatoes may be planted. Spread well-prepared compost over the area before planting.

Make the last turning of sheet-composted material preparatory to spading under for the February plantings. Mulch winter vegetables and flowers with unsifted compost. It will keep down winter weeds, conserve heat and provide nourishment.

In case humus is lacking in the sun-baked soils, spread plenty of compost in rows before planting. Start new bins or fill old ones immediately. Generally speaking, it is not necessary to add lime to the compost, since most Southwest soils are high enough in pH.

Make good use of the lush growth of winter wheats before

they go to seed. They may be spaded under along with other cover crops. The waste from winter crops, which are now waning, furnishes more good material. Save lawn clippings for either mulch or for adding to the compost heap. Spade in cover crops and sheet composting materials early in the month.

SPRING

Feed deciduous bulbs with compost and bone meal until the leaves have turned brown. Never cut off leaves while still green. These two precautions will insure blooms for the next year. Feed azaleas and camellias with compost and leaf mold, do not let them dry out at any time. Camellias are slow growers in poor soil, but being such stunning plants they are worth a little care.

The heat-loving vegetables, as lima beans, summer squash, peppers, eggplants and tomatoes, should be planted in deeply composted holes.

Water spring bulbs until the leaves die down and feed with a mixture of bone meal and compost. Mulch heavily and water lightly during the summer. Bird-of-Paradise, one of the most exotically beautiful of all ornamentals, is making its chief growth in June; be sure to water and feed freely with compost. When planting such vegetables as tomatoes, eggplants and peppers, put compost in the bottom of the holes and sink water down before planting.

SUMMER

July is a crucial "mulch month" in the Southwest. Be sure to keep a covering of organic materials over your plants. The lower layers of the mulch break down and it means that your garden has in effect a "constantly-rotting compost pile" over it. Here again you can give your plants a summer boost with an application of compost water.

September marks the beginning of the "second spring" in the Southwest. So, it's another important time to apply compost to your garden before setting out winter vegetables and winter-blooming annuals.

FALL

Plan to sheet compost any unused areas of the garden this fall. Use waste raw materials such as dried grass, straw, spoiled hay and vegetable refuse. Add manure for nitrogen insurance.

308

Northwest

WINTER

Gardeners who seeded the ground to rye and vetch for green manure should turn it over in February and prepare at least that strip which is to be seeded to early peas. (Washington's birthday is the date on which the peas are sowed in the Pacific Northwest.) Turn the compost heap, and "feed it" with table scraps to stimulate activity of the earthworms and bacteria.

In March fertilize bulb beds, violets, pansies and primroses. Liquid compost or fish emulsion may be used. Continue to feed primroses once a week during blooming season.

SPRING

Never plant seeds in poorly prepared soil. Make sure the compost is well worked in, the seedbed raked over, and the surface pulverized.

In general, if the ground is friable and ready for use, these vegetables may go out in the open by April: Cabbage and broccoli plants, seeds of turnips, beets, lettuce, carrots, chard, potatoes, spinach, parsnips, radishes and salsify. Partially fill the seed furrow with compost containing a small amount of manure to furnish a little warmth.

The winter compost pile should be ready to yield some returns now. Turn the top layer over into a new heap and sift the well-rotted compost out of the remainder. Place the residue on the new heap for tne decomposition.

Prepare the vegetable garden well with standard organic methods. The reward will come, as a large humus content of the soil keeps the garden from drying out, the mulch keeps the weeds down and the compost furnishes the food needed.

In June continue mulching to control weeds. The warm weather is just right for the bacterial action in the compost heap. Give the bacteria a chance by keeping the heap moist.

June is the time to grow the following year's stock of rock garden plants. The ideal soil for them is a mixture of sand, compost and peat.

SUMMER

August is a busy time in the flower garden. Clip dead rose blooms to prevent mildew, adding them to the compost pile. Fall and winter bulbs, starting with the crocus, can go in the ground in mid-August and on into the fall. Continue top-dressing gladiolus with compost. Now is also a good time to add many materials to the compost heap. When strawberries are finished bearing, it's a good idea to seed the patch generously with a mixture of compost, and phosphate and potash rock to give the plants a good start next year. When transplanting peonies, put at least a bucketful of compost and a cup of bone meal in the bottom of each hole.

FALL

Prepare the garden in October where lilies are to be planted in November. Put plenty of bone meal and compost with the soil. Clean out all plant residues and throw them on the compost pile. Now is the time when the heap should be built up for next year's use. Grass clippings, leaves and any other organic matter can help.

When transplanting fruit, ornamental trees and shrubbery, be sure that the holes are wide enough to take the root-spread without twisting. Compost, well-rotted manure, or other organic fertilizer should be worked into the bottom, as well as the soil, which is to act as the fill. Spread compost on any vacant beds and spade in later.

Chapter 9

HOW TO USE COMPOST

Gardeners have found compost excellent for everything from starting seedlings to curing sick trees. On the following pages, you'll find just how compost can be used for a variety of jobs.

GENERAL RULES OF APPLICATION

Try to figure on applying at least ½ inch to 3 inches of compost over your garden each year. There is little if any danger of burning due to overuse, such as is always the case with the chemically concocted fertilizers. You can apply compost either once or twice a year. The amount would depend,

The compost you add to your garden soil will improve its structure as well as its fertility level. Rotary tillage equipment is excellent for mixing finished or half-finished compost into the top 4 inches of the soil either in fall or early spring.

of course, on the fertility of your soil originally and on what and how much has been grown in it. Incidentally, an average figure of weight for one cubic yard of compost (27 cubic feet) is 1,000 pounds. There would be variations depending on the materials used and the length of time composted.

When applying either half-finished or finished compost to your soil, turn over the soil thoroughly and mix it in with the top 4 inches. If you have a rotary tiller, you can simply spread the compost on the soil surface and go over it a couple of times to work it in.

To quickly improve the structure and fertility of poor soil, give it a thorough compost treatment in the fall. Spade it up 12 to 18 inches deep and mix in all the half-rotted compost you have. Then leave the surface rough and cloddy so that the freezing and thawing of winter will mellow it (or plant a green manure crop that will add more fertility when it is dug or tilled under in the spring).

Putting compost down deep in the soil, by the way, will

311

Here compost is being placed in trenches before gladiolus bulbs are to be planted. When mixed well with the soil, compost provides the bulbs with food and good drainage throughout the season as the gladiolus plants grow and begin blooming.

give your plants built-in protection against drought. Having humus down in the lower levels of your soil means that moisture will be held there where plant roots can get all they need in dry weather.

Too, this moisture will prevent the plants from *starving* to death in drought—their roots can only pick up food when it is in liquid form.

The Vegetable Garden

To enjoy superbly delicious, healthful vegetables, apply compost, compost, compost. Dig it in in the fall, bury it in trenches, put it in the furrows where planting and in the holes when transplanting. After the plants start shooting up, mix it with equal amounts of soil and use it as a top-dressing, or mulch them heavily with partially rotted compost or with such raw compost materials as hay, straw, sawdust, grass clippings, shredded leaves and the like.

One hint: the rule when mulching is, the finer the material, the thinner the layer.

You can make good use of compost in the vegetable garden by mixing it with equal amounts of soil and using it as top-dressing around growing plants. This treatment will produce rich, good-textured soil capable of yielding top-quality vegetables.

This kind of treatment will give you a rich, loamy, friable soil that will grow big yields of all kinds of vegetables, without fear of drought, disease or insect troubles. And the vegetables will taste better and keep better than any you have ever bought or grown before. They'll be higher in vitamins and minerals, too.

For sowing seeds indoors or in a cold frame, put your compost through a ½-inch sieve, then shred it with a hoe or even roll it with a rolling pin to make it very fine. Then mix it with equal amounts of sand and soil. The ideal seeding mixture is very mellow and tends to fall apart after being squeezed in your hand.

The Flower Garden

Finely screened compost is excellent to put around all growing flowers. Apply it alone as an inch-thick mulch to control weeds and conserve moisture, or top-dress it mixed with soil. In the spring, you can loosen the top few inches of soil in your annual and perennial beds and work into it an

Many gardeners prefer screening compost before applying it around plants in the flower garden. It can be applied as a one-inch mulch to save soil moisture and keep down weeds, top-dressed, or worked into the ground before planting in spring.

equal quantity of compost. And use compost generously when sowing flower seeds.

Compost watering is an excellent way to give your flowers supplementary feeding during their growing season. Fill a watering can half full of compost, add water and sprinkle liberally around the plants. The can may be refilled with water several times before the compost loses its potency.

Plenty of compost has been found to keep the moisture level of the flower bed too high for ants, thereby discouraging them.

Your Lawn

Want a lawn that stays green all summer, has no crabgrass and rarely needs watering?

Then use compost liberally when making and maintaining it. You want a thick sod with roots that go down 6 inches, not a thin, weed-infested mat laying on a layer of infertile subsoil.

In building a new lawn, work in copious amounts of compost to a depth of at least 6 inches. If your soil is either

Finished compost that has not been screened makes a very good mulch around newly planted trees in spring or fall. When fertilizing trees with compost, use the "ring" method: start a foot or two from the trunk, ending beyond drip-line.

sandy or clayey (rather than good loam), you'll need at least a two-inch depth of compost, mixed in thoroughly, to build it up. The best time to make a new lawn is in the fall. But if you want to get started in the spring, dig in your compost and plant Italian ryegrass, vetch or soybeans, which will look quite neat all summer. Then dig this green manure in at the end of the summer and make your permanent lawn when cool weather comes.

To renovate an old, patchy lawn, dig up the bare spots about two inches deep, work in plenty of finished compost, tamp and rake well, and sow your seed after soaking the patches well.

Feed your lawn regularly every spring. An excellent practice is to use a spike tooth aerator, then spread a mixture of fine finished compost and bone meal. Rake this into the holes made by the aerator. You can use a fairly thick covering of compost—just not so thick it covers the grass. This will feed your lawn efficiently and keep it sending down a dense mass of roots that laugh at drought.

315

When applying compost by the "ring" method, you can work in from an inch to several inches into the soil surface. Some gardeners pile a variety of organic materials around fruit or shade trees, adding more as the material decomposes.

Trees and Shrubs

"A $5 hole for a 50 cent plant"—that's the rule experts follow. A good job of planting new trees and shrubs will pay off in faster-growing, sturdier specimens every time.

Always make the planting hole at least twice the size of the root ball in all directions. The best planting mixture is made up of equal parts of compost, topsoil and peat moss or leaf mold. Fill this in carefully around the plant, tamping it down as you put in each spadeful. Soak the ground well, then spread an inch or two of compost on top. A mulch of leaves, hay and the like will help keep the soil moist and control weeds.

Established shrubs should be fed yearly by having a half bushel of compost worked into the surface soil, then mulched.

The "ring" method is best for feeding trees: start about two feet from the trunk and cultivate the soil shallowly to a foot beyond the drip-line of the branches. Rake an inch or two of compost into the top two inches.

When hilling up the soil around your rose bushes for

House plants will thrive on a two-week feeding of compost "tea" made by suspending a cheesecloth bag of compost in water and using the liquid when it is a weak tea color. Compost can be added to potting mixtures as one-fourth of the total.

winter protection, mix plenty of compost with it—they'll get a better start next spring.

Fruit Trees

The ring method is ideal for fruit trees, too. You can work in as much as 3 or 4 inches of compost, then apply a heavy mulch, which will continue to feed the trees as it rots. Some gardeners merely pile organic materials as deep as two feet around their fruit trees, adding more material as the covering decomposes. You can even add earthworms to speed the transformation to humus. Berry plants may be treated the same way, with lower mulches, of course, for low-growing varieties.

Another good trick for pepping up old fruit trees is to auger holes a foot apart all around the tree, and pack these with compost.

House Plants

Lots of humus means extra-good moisture retention and air circulation in house plant soil. A good potting mixture is composed of equal parts of loam, sand and compost, the

317

Sifted, finished compost makes an excellent mulch in the flower boxes around your garden and house. Place at least two inches thick and do not firm down with your hand. When it rains, the plants will be fed nutrients contained in the compost.

latter put through a ¼-inch mesh. Leaf mold compost makes a fine, loose soil, while for acid-loving plants like azaleas, pine-needle or oak leaves compost is best. Feed your house plants every two weeks with compost "tea," made by suspending a cheesecloth bag of compost in water and using the liquid when it is a weak tea color. In general, compost can be added to potting mixtures as one-fourth of the total.

To rejuvenate the soil in window boxes, tubs and indoor plant boxes, scratch an inch or so of compost into the surface twice a year. Occasional light top-dressings of compost are also excellent for the soil in greenhouse benches. All of these will benefit from regular feeding with compost tea.

Soil-Compost Mixture for Starting Seedlings

Make a mixture of two parts good garden loam, one part fine, but sharp sand, and one part compost. Mix well and put 8 inches of it into the hotbed, cold frame or flat. It's a good idea to let this mixture age for several months before seeding. Sift the soil mixture through a ¼-inch mesh screen to get it in

In late fall or early spring, be sure to put a generous supply of compost into your cold frame and mix well with the soil. A mixture of two parts good garden loam, one part fine, but sharp sand, and one part compost is often used for starting plants.

condition for planting. When screening the mixture, place coarse screenings in the bottom of the flats to provide better drainage.

There is enough plant food in this mixture without adding manure or other organic fertilizers high in nitrogen. Used too soon, these often cause the young plants to grow too rapidly, unbalancing their natural growth.

When starting plants in flats, some gardeners prefer using sphagnum moss in the bottom quarter to half of the flat.

319

You'll stand a better chance of getting earlier yields from your seedlings if you feed them with a starter solution made from compost or manure. A solution of this type, applied while plants are still in frame, provides immediately available food.

Then after the seed has been placed in the rows, finely screened compost is sifted over. When the seedlings are ready for transplanting to another flat, the new flat may have a small amount of compost mixed with the loam and sand. The theory is that if the roots must seek further for food, they will build a strong healthy root system, which is more important than height of stem at this point in their growth.

Starter Solution for Plants

Starter solutions made from compost or manure can be a big help in the growing of vegetable plants. The home gardener as well as the commercial grower will benefit from the rapid and unchecked growth of his plants, if such a solution is used before they are moved to the field from the greenhouse, hotbed or cold frame. According to Oregon's Ralph Clark, extension horticulturist specialist, greenhouse operators have long made use of this method to bring their crops to a rapid and profitable production. Earlier yields have also been reported in the field.

The main benefit received from these solutions is that of providing the plant with immediately available plant food. This stimulates leaf and root growth, giving the plant a quick pickup after transplanting. These solutions are used especially on young lettuce, tomatoes, celery, peppers, melons, eggplant, cabbage, cauliflower, and all kinds of transplanted plants.

Here is a recommended starter solution making use of compost:

Fill barrel or other container one-quarter full of compost. Continue to fill container with water, stirring several times during next 24 to 48 hours. In using, dilute liquid to a light amber color with water. Pour one pint around each plant when setting out or later as necessary to force growth. Liquid compost can be used at 10-day to 2-week intervals especially when soils are not high in fertility.

Tests have shown that seeds sprout more than twice as well when soaked in a solution of this kind. In the wild, practically all seeds depend upon the moisture which seeps to them through a layer of Nature's compost. In soaking the seed flat, place it in a large container holding an inch or two of starter solution. Allow the flat to soak until its sandy surface shows signs of dampness.

Seed flats containing mature compost and handled in this way seldom suffer loss from the "damping-off" of the seedlings.

Preventing Damping-Off

Damping-off is a name given by gardeners to the wilting and early death of young seedlings usually soon after they emerge from the soil. The fungus attacks the seedlings at the ground line and causes them to break over at that point.

Damping-off may be caused by different organisms which live in or near the surface of the soil. Conditions which favor damping-off are: (1) crowding of seedlings due to sowing the seeds too freely, (2) high humidity, and (3) lack of sufficient aeration. Remedial measures consist in proper ventilation, drying off the soil in which the seedlings are growing and sprinkling on the soil powdered charcoal or finely pulverized clay which has been heated in an oven.

Damping-off can be prevented by providing seed flat with proper drainage, sowing the seeds in a mixture of compost and

321

sand (equal parts), covering the seeds with pulverized, heated clay, keeping the young seedlings in a well-ventilated, well-lighted, cool place so that the tissues of the stem become well differentiated.

Improving Seed Germination

You can be almost certain of good germination if you will sow seeds in a mixture of equal parts of compost and sand. When the seedlings are large enough to be transplanted, transplant them into a seed flat filled with one part compost, one part sand, and two parts leaf mold.

Compost and Rotation

Rotation in the vegetable and flower garden is one of the essentials of a good growing program, just as it is on the farm.

Plants are classified, according to their needs and their groups. The *heavy feeders* (1), needing generous fertilizing, include corn, tomatoes and cabbage. Next the *legumes* (2), to help the soil following the heavy demands of those crops, especially in poorer soils. In a live humus soil, legumes may go in third place if desired. The last group, *light feeders,* (3) include root vegetables, bulbs, herbs, etc. When in doubt about a plant, put it in this group.

FLOWERS: A flower garden probably contains both annuals and perennials, which complicates rotation, as we cannot shift perennials every year. However, we can keep these principles in mind when they do need moving, meanwhile treating them to the kind of fertilizing they like.

In *Group 1* belong flowers in the cabbage family—arabis, cheiranthus, rocket, aubrietia, alyssum, candytuft, etc. If cabbage is often followed by cabbage, the inevitable result is club foot (the immediate result of not rotating crops) and all such diseases, as well as the cabbage butterfly, cabbage worm and other pests. Here perennials as well as annuals need frequent change of location, besides good manuring. In this group is the ranunculus or buttercup family with many garden favorites—peony, delphinium, larkspur, monkshood, columbine, nigella, clematis, anemone, meadow rue, helleborus, adonis.

LEGUMES: The legumes in *Group 2* form one of the largest and most important of plant families, distinguished by its

322

Good germination and protection against damping-off are other reasons for providing your plants with compost. When seedlings, such as the onions shown above, are transplanted, put them in a row that has received compost application.

ability to "breathe in nitrogen" whereas other plants "breathe it out" of the soil. Because they are so beneficial in or around a garden, we list here the more commonly known, be they trees, shrubs or garden flowers—sweet peas, lupines, scarlet runner beans, kudzu vine, bush clovers, lotus, coral tree, baptisia, amorpha, false indigo, lead plant, pea tree, robinia, false acacia, yellow wood, Japanese pagoda tree, colutea, sainfoin, coronilla, licorice, wisteria, gorse, golden chain tree, laburnum, Scotch broom, red bud, cassia or senna, honey locust, mimosa, acacia. Although not in this family, all the flaxes are soil benefactors and for cultivation purposes may be classed here. Their fine root structure has an excellent soil-loosening effect.

LIGHT FEEDERS: *Group 3,* the light feeders, include the lilies and all bulbous plants, those with fleshy roots such as iris, and plants with delicate growth and high aromatic quality like most herbs. Some of these may grow naturally under rather poor conditions, but remember that under cultivation unusual demands are made on them while they also give up their naturally chosen habitat and companions. Fertilizing, though lighter, is not less essential, with well-decayed compost.

323

One family belonging here has special interest in that its members are helpful companions to delicate, warmth-loving plants. This spurge family has between 700 to 1,000 species, most having a milky juice, many being fleshy, desert plants or native in warm climates. Best known are snow-on-the-mountain, poinsettia, crown of thorns and castor bean. They seem to radiate a certain warmth into the soil around them that helps plants which need a little coddling, perhaps because they, too, are far away from their native tropics.

—EHRENFREID PFEIFFER

Compost and Clean-Up

Your compost heap can help you keep the garden neat-looking and "clean." Piles of decaying plant materials scattered throughout the vegetable and flower garden can harbor a surprising number of destructive organisms. Weeds, fallen bark, fallen fruit, etc., should be promptly removed to the compost pile.

How to Use Compost Water

The juices of compost can be the best part. Often, some of the valuable nutrients in compost are dissolved in water quite readily, and in solution these nutrients can be quickly distributed to needy plant roots.

Since plants drink their food rather than eat it, the use of compost water makes quite a bit of sense, particularly during dry periods when plants are starved both for food and water.

Many problem plants and trees can be nursed back to health by treating them with compost water. You can use it on bare spots on your lawn, on trees that have just been transplanted and on indoor plants that need perking up. You can even use it on vegetables in the spring to try to make them mature earlier. Compost water is really good in greenhouses, where finest soil conditions are needed for best results.

It is really no trouble to make compost water on a small scale. For treating house plants or small outdoor areas, all you have to do is fill a sprinkling can half with finished compost and half with water, stir gently 10 or 12 times, and pour. Nothing could be easier than that. The compost can be used several times, as one watering will not wash out all its soluble nutrients. The remaining compost is actually almost as good as new, and should be dug into the soil or used as mulch. It takes the action of soil bacteria and plant roots to extract the major value from compost.

Your garden will benefit much more from properly-made compost heaps than from scattered rubbish piles. Weeds, fallen bark or fruit, etc., should be promptly removed to the compost pile. Sanitation is an important aid to insect control.

Developing a continuous way to make compost water for the home grounds requires a little more ingenuity and mechanical skill.

One method is to weld hose connections on a metal can with a lid that will stand up under normal water pressure. We used an ordinary 5 gallon paint drum. The water intake was located at the bottom of the can, and the exit at the top. Therefore, the water has to circulate up and through the compost before it can get out of the can. Although the large lid on the paint drum allowed compost to be placed in it easily, it did not provide a perfectly tight water seal. A can with a screw type lid would be better, even though the loading and unloading of the compost would be more difficult.

The operation of this compost watering can is simple. You attach the water supply to the intake connection, and the hose or sprinkling device to the exit connection. The can can be carried to different parts of your garden, and one charging of compost lasts for about 15 minutes of watering. A screen placed over the exit hole on the inside of the can prevents solids from escaping and clogging sprinkling heads.

325

Tricks for Heavy Soils

Sometimes you've got to work deep in the ground to make it produce, especially if your soil is heavy. J. E. B. Maunsell is a noted English organic gardener and one of his special methods is what he calls "disturbing" the soil. Here is what he says in his book *Natural Gardening Methods:*

"I 'disturb' the soil to a depth of 12 inches because I am greedy enough to want two crops a year, and I could never get these with shallow cultivation. I feed the land for those two crops by doubling the amount of compost because the presence of humus will insure continuous fertility."

Maunsell "disturbs" the soil of his garden plot in this manner: First, all the clumps of weeds are cut off at ground level and composted. A 4-tined 12-inch fork is used for the disturbing, not a spade. It is pressed into the ground for its full length, and then pressed back until the subsoil can be felt cracking. The fork is then returned to its upright position and pulled straight upward without turning or disturbing the soil strata. After the soil is broken up in that way, an inch of compost is spread over the surface without trampling the bed.

The advantage of "disturbing" the soil, as Maunsell describes the process, is that drainage is greatly improved and roots are able to spread out vigorously in the mineral-rich subsoil. You must realize, though, that Maunsell and other English gardeners are using this method on vegetable and flower garden beds that have been in use for a number of years and are rich in humus. Their soil is in such fine shape that "disturbance" is all that is necessary to prepare a seedbed. If your soil is in similar condition, you may want to give "disturbance" a try.

"Double digging" is another English method that has long been practiced by old-time gardeners who give more than just a passing thought to what is going on below the topsoil. It is a procedure that is hard on your back muscles, but it is not going too far to say that double digging deserves credit for much of the magnificent beauty of English gardens. Telling you how to do it is easy. Just dig away the topsoil from your flower bed or vegetable plot and place it to one side. Then get down in the trench and thoroughly spade the subsoil—or till it with your tiller. Finally, put the topsoil back in place and cover the bed with compost.

Roses benefit greatly from double digging. No other

ground preparation technique is as sure of supplying to roses the tremendous amount of fertility they need. Root crops benefit from double digging, and in fact every garden plant is likely to thrive in a loosened subsoil that has been double dug.

Place Compost Deep

An important idea recently developed is the concept of the deep placement of fertilizer. Particularly in regions where the soil is poor or there is scarcely enough rainfall during the growing season for proper growth, deep placement is most effective.

The whole concept of deep placement is based on the placing of fertilizers deep down at the very bottom of the root system of plants. If this is done, the roots of the plant work themselves deep down in the soil to reach the nutrients. This means that the plants will become especially well-rooted. When there is a shortage of rainfall, the plants thus well-rooted will be able to stand up under the drought conditions. Plants that are inadequately rooted in the shallow topsoil will dry up and die when the topsoil dries out.

Another important reason why deep-placement of organic fertilizer is better than chemical fertilizer is water retention. A good compost has billions of pores and absorptive plant cells per cubic yard. Chemical fertilizers have few and will retain no water except what little is held by the surface wetting of the chemicals. Good compost is like a sponge taking up water. It soaks it up when there is plenty of rainfall and releases it to the growing plants when there is insufficient rainfall.

COMPOST FOR BEAUTIFUL LAWNS

One of our greatest prides is our thick, green turf. There was a time, however, when it was patchy, dried off completely in summer, and consisted mostly of weeds. Through careful study with experts in the field, and with the help of the Department of Agriculture, we finally managed to build it up to its present state. Our turf, as a whole, is now thick, healthy, a heavy green, and almost weed free. I'd like to let you in on a few secrets we have learned in good lawn care to show you how simple it is to come by a soft, green lawn.

Cleaning up after a long winter is as important a step as any other in lawn care. Remove leaves, trash, old grass and

Excellent for lawns, screened compost can be spread with an ordinary fertilizer spreader. You can distribute a thin layer over your entire lawn every spring and fall, making sure that layer is thin enough to permit tender shoots to come through.

litter by raking every inch of the lawn with a bamboo leaf rake. Add this material to the compost heap.

If you have gravel or sandy soils, you know that they will not support grass unless fortified with organic matter. At least 4 inches of enriched topsoil is necessary to produce a thick turf.

Screened compost is excellent for lawns. Use a fertilizer spreader to distribute a thin layer over the entire lawn every spring and fall. Be careful, however, not to apply too thick of a layer, or it may suffocate the tender shoots about to come up.

If you have a troublesome slope from which rains wash the grass, rework the entire area down to 8 inches, mix organic matter, such as peat moss, muck, manure or compost, well into the soil, rake smooth, then roll with a roller half filled with water. Loosen surface slightly with an iron rake then reseed with good seed. Rake seed lightly into the soil, then roll with empty roller.

Because we have found that commercial lawn fertilizers

When reseeding lawn areas, cultivate soil deeply, mixing in large quantities of organic matter like peat moss, manure or compost. Loosen soil surface slightly with a rake. After spreading grass seed, rake it lightly into the ground; water and mulch.

leach out far too quickly, and all too often seriously burn the grass, we have switched to all-organic fertilizers, namely compost and dried manures. They not only do not burn, but are slower acting, which means greener lawns longer.

We give our lawn 3 feedings a season. The first—an all-organic lawn fertilizer high in nitrogen—is applied in spring after all clean-up, rolling and repair work is finished. The second is given in June, and consists only of dehydrated cow manure. It manages to keep the grass green throughout the hot, dry months. The third feeding of the all-organic fertilizer is in September. This conditions the turf for next season.

To keep that fresh look on your lawn, pick up all grass clippings until mid-summer. At that time adjust the mower to leave two inches of grass, and allow all clippings to remain to protect the roots and to retard rapid evaporation of moisture. These clippings will also decay and add humus to your soil. Pick up the clippings again in fall; and use them in constructing a new compost heap.

Grass, like any other plant, must be well fed if it is expected to do its best. Manures of all kinds are excellent for building thick, green turf. They should be well rotted before using, however. Give your lawn the care and attention you do your garden. In a few years the grass will be so thick that your mower will have trouble getting through it.

—BETTY BRINHART

Starting a New Lawn

Fall is a good time of year to do this work because the weather is settled, which means your ground is neither too wet nor too dry. Don't work with wet soil or soil that is powdery; if you do, you'll be defeating yourself at the start. Seeding is best done in the fall also since the new grass has less competition from weeds.

Hard, packed soil that won't let water through and restricts root growth is probably the most common cause of lawn failure. So right at the very beginning, make sure you do everything you can to aerate the soil and improve drainage. The best way to do this is to work in organic materials as you break up the clods of earth. This will speed and ease the job of making a proper grade also. You'll find that a rotary tiller makes this job a lot easier.

Spread, mix and get your organic fertilizers right into the topsoil while you are in the topping-off phase. Spread and mix from opposite directions at right angles to insure uniformity.

When using compost, 100 pounds per 1,000 feet will add two pounds of nitrogen to the soil.

Work it into the topsoil thoroughly. Your soil should be well mixed and loose to a depth of 6 to 10 inches.

Be sure the ground is fairly dry when you roll and follow this operation by a light raking until the surface is very smooth and quite fine in texture. This should be done almost immediately before sowing so that rain will not interfere to cake the surface. If this happens, rake the surface again and then sow.

Sheet Composting for Lawns

If you've just moved into a new home and the grounds are lacking topsoil, consider a sheet composting program before seeding a permanent lawn.

Here's how it's done: sow a green manure cover crop right into your subsoil after you have enriched it with compost, sludge, cottonseed meal, tobacco stems, bone meal, etc.

This is the common sense advice of Thomas H. Everett,

A landscape you can be proud of—that's the result of an organic fertilizing job. Many new homeowners, faced with the task of starting a lawn and establishing foundation plantings, have learned that compost is the first step to garden beauty.

Curator of Education and Horticulturist, New York Botanical Garden. In his handbook on lawns, Mr. Everett makes this sound suggestion: after liming and fertilizing the subsoil, sow two quarts of winter rye to each 1,000 square feet of soil or the same quantity of Canada field peas.

"Green manuring (and sheet composting) means growing cover crops especially for the purpose of turning them under and converting in the soil to humus," notes Mr. Everett, adding that "humus is formed by the decay of the extensive root systems as well as the tops . . . When top growth is 6 to 12 inches tall, spade the cover crop under or bury it with plow or rotary tiller and immediately refertilize and sow another cover crop. Don't turn the last of the cover crops under later than 6 weeks before sowing the permanent grass seed." In other words, give the cover crop at least 6 weeks to decay and form humus.

To this sound counsel to lawn builders who are willing to build their own topsoil from scratch, we should like to add this word to residents of the Deep South. The fall is an excellent time to plant crimson clover, hairy vetch, winter rye or ryegrass. Here, again, you are providing excellent green

331

manures which you can turn under prior to your spring lawn planting. At this time, you can also add other organic materials to your soil. These crops also provide a cover for the soil during the fall and winter.

Controlling Crabgrass in Your Lawn

Here is a program which will show results:

1. First, if you have a lawn sweeper, use it after several midsummer mowings to pick up crabgrass seeds that will sprout the following year. Put the clippings in your compost heap.

2. Aerate your soil as much as possible, using either a hand aerator or an aerating attachment for a tiller or garden tractor. Don't be afraid to really shake up your soil, because air and moisture are needed below the surface to give encouragement to good grass roots.

3. Spread on your soil liberal amounts of phosphate rock, potash rock and lime, if needed. For an average soil, apply these amounts:

Phosphate and potash rock—10 pounds per 100 square feet.

Lime—5 to 10 pounds per 100 square feet, depending on soil pH. (Larger amount for acid soils, less for those nearer neutral pH.) If soil is alkaline, do not apply lime.

Bone meal is also an excellent mineral supplement for lawn soils. Apply in the same proportions as the ground rock fertilizers.

These natural mineral fertilizers will make sure that the good grass you want to grow has ample mineral food.

4. Now comes the most important step—the creation of a good soil structure. It is hard to get across how much can be accomplished in producing a good lawn by improving soil tilth and structure. And the only practical way to do this is to pack plenty of compost, humus, leaf mold, peat or other organic material into your lawn soil.

You should not be concerned about nutrients in the materials you use, because in promoting good growth of grass, nutrient value is secondary to tilth. You have to be a little cautious about spreading sawdust or chopped straw on your lawn (they are low in nitrogen content), but small amounts of those things can be spread without harm.

Spread your "structure builders" in installments that will

There's no reason why any garden soil cannot be made to grow lovely flowers. Heavy and moist soils can be made lighter by adding a good quantity of sharp sand or well-rotted compost; organic materials will also improve structure in sandy soils.

give the grass a chance to grow a little between spreadings. Basically, what you are doing is *mulching* your lawn, but you still want to encourage the grass to grow through the mulch. Peat moss is one of the best materials for this type of work. Compost is excellent, but it should be ground or shredded before application.

Other organic fertilizing materials that will go a long way in boosting lawn growth include dried blood, cottonseed meal and soybean meal. These 3 are especially rich in growth-promoting nitrogen, and should be applied as liberally as needed and available.

The result of this program will be a vigorous lawn with a minimum of crabgrass and other weeds.

COMPOST FOR THE FLOWER GARDEN

Preparing the Annual Flower Bed

Most annuals do best in an open, sunny location, that has had large amounts of compost worked into the soil.

The preparation of the permanent bed should be given

333

careful attention to make the best out of the planting. Before digging the flower bed, mark out the dimensions, using the spade to get a clean-cut edge. Any good garden soil will usually produce a fine array of flowers if spaded to the proper depth and broken up to make a fine seedbed. Heavy and moist soils can be made lighter by adding a good quantity of sharp sand. It will greatly help to spade well-rotted compost into the soil. The compost should be well rotted, since the heating effect of fresh organic materials can interfere with the growth of most seeds.

In composting the ground, spread a layer of well-rotted compost evenly over the surface, 2 or 3 inches thick, and then spaded into the soil so that it is entirely covered. The depth to spade depends on the thickness of the good topsoil. Usually 6 inches is deep enough. While spading the ground, break up the large clumps. After spading, use a steel rake to give a fine, smooth surface to the seedbed. Stones and other coarse material must be raked out, as they interfere with the sowing.

In many cases the seedbed is used for raising seedlings which later are transplanted to their permanent place in the garden. The purpose of the seedbed is to provide an ideal location for the germination and early growth of the seedling. A corner of the garden thoroughly spaded, with the top layer of soil enriched by compost, will make a suitable bed.

Rotating and Fertilizing Perennials

A rich soil, not too heavy, is best for practically all perennials. It should be light and crumbly, well-drained but moisture-retaining, amply supplied with humus.

The best way to provide this is to dig at least 18 inches deep and work in a 3-inch layer of leaf mold or peat moss, plus a one-inch layer of rotted manure or compost; increase these amounts if your soil is poor to start with.

Mulching in late fall is recommended, even though the plants are hardy. After frost has penetrated the ground an inch or so, apply a mulch 3 to 6 inches thick, depending on the severity of your winters. It should be a light mulch, such as compost, strawy manure, pine needles, fresh or partly decayed leaves, peat moss or salt hay. Be careful not to smother any plants that have evergreen leaves. Mulch under these, and use evergreen boughs to protect their upper portions. Many growers believe in leaving a 2- to 3-inch mulch under their perennials all year round.

If long-lived perennials such as iris or chrysanthemums are grown in one spot for a long time they will deplete the soil. They will continue to grow, but their health will suffer. They may be top-dressed or side-dressed with compost, but some perennials do not want too much cover. It may be impossible to give them enough food to prevent rust and other infestations. The only way to treat them is to move them to new and more fertile positions.

A heavy dressing of manure, compost and possibly leaf mold may be given the spot from which an old perennial has been moved, and it may be given a rest during the winter. In the spring, after an application of wood ashes, phosphate rock, or bone meal the spot will be ready to receive a different kind of perennial.

Often the gardener fails to observe that the rains of several seasons tend to lower the soil level considerably, washing earth off into the paths or down into the deeper spots of the garden. This means that the volume of earth from which growing plants in the higher spot could draw nourishment is somewhat reduced, if not largely depleted. To counteract this, especially with peonies and other plants that stay put for many years, nothing is better than to make a top-dressing of plain garden soil, possibly enriched a little with compost. New earth is thus added and the nutrients in it are washed down to feed the plants and give more profuse bloom the following season.

How do different flowering plants stand in regard to compatibility? There are for example acid-loving evergreens that need very little nitrogen, no rich compost, just leaf mulches and occasionally some bone meal. Likewise there are lilies that like humus and a deep mellow shaded soil; these two can go together. But will a lime-loving plant, like the campanulas grow next to them? Theoretically this looks like a real puzzler. The inexperienced gardener thinks that he should prepare different subsoil and make for himself a great deal of extra work. Practically, the matter is not serious at all. Many hundreds of thousands of gardens grow both azaleas and columbines; both campanulas, foxgloves, coreopsis, carnations and rhododendrons. It seems, indeed, as if the question of acidity were overemphasized. Organic matter in the ground will act as a buffer against extremes and enable the plants to seek with their roots what they need, lime as well as acid humus. But since the acid-loving shrubby plants will usually be in the background, more leaves may be left there, while in the foreground, where carnations and tulips may be planted a slight sprinkling of lime is made in fall.

Daffodil

Daffodils are hungry plants and thus fast growers. Before planting, spade the soil to about 12-18 inches and incorporate generous amounts of compost and well-rotted manure. Peat moss or leaf mold may be used generously in sandy soil, and heavy clay soils should be loosened by working in sand and humus material, such as compost. These bulbs are very intolerant of raw manure, so be sure it is well composted.

Fern

A woodsy location, with shade, moisture and an organic soil high in leaf mold is perfect for the majority of ferns. Dig a fairly deep hole and put in a mixture of leaf mold, sand and loam. Oak leaves and compost are good substitutes for the leaf mold. If the soil is acid, a little limestone is advisable, and a mulch of organic materials is always recommended.

The popular maidenhair is easy to establish in any compost-rich, well-drained soil. The hardy climbing fern, however, likes acid soil and grows well among mountain laurel and blueberry bushes. A heavy mulch of oak leaves will keep it thriving. For limestone sites, walking fern (its thread-like frond tips "walk" to root and form new plants) spreads to a tangled mat over mossy rocks in the shade.

For indoor-fern planting, give them a dim light—too strong illumination yellows the fronds; a north window with two hours or less sun a day is good—plus rich organic soil with good drainage, and a temperature range of 50 to 70 degrees; a large number of ferns will thrive in the home.

Ferns do not like a heavy soil; one composed of 4 parts of a sandy loam, one part sand, and one part compost, will give good results. For most of the ferns a little leaf mold may be added. Pack the soil fairly firm about the roots but do not make it hard. The soil in which ferns are growing must never become dry, neither must it become water-logged. It is a common assumption that, because ferns grow naturally in damp places, they cannot be over-watered, but while the soil in which ferns thrive outdoors may be very damp it is always well drained and aerated.

Annual repotting is necessary only for young ferns, and

Since daffodils are relatively heavy feeders, spade the soil deeply before planting bulbs; compost or well-rotted manure should be generously applied. Since daffodil bulbs are very intolerant of raw manure, always make sure it's well composted.

monthly feedings of dilute compost "tea" will keep all of them healthy and vigorous for years. Never use chemical fertilizer —ferns are extremely sensitive to its unbalanced formulations.

Geranium

Geraniums are not difficult to raise. They need only a moderate amount of water, a fairly cool, well-drained, moderately rich (but not too rich) soil, and plenty of sunshine. In the northern regions of the country, they should be planted in full sun, but in the South and Southwest, half a day's exposure should be enough to make the plants bloom freely without burning. An annual top-dressing of decayed manure or rich compost should be ample stimulation for geraniums. The fact that geraniums are fairly drought-resistant makes them a popular cultivated plant of the Southwest.

A recommended mixture for potting geraniums is two parts garden loam, one part leaf mold or compost, and one part sharp sand. Some gardeners recommend including one part well-rotted manure, and some add a teaspoonful of bone meal to a 5-inch pot when planting. If the soil in your outdoor beds is heavy, it should be lightened with leaf mold and sand. And although geraniums may be planted directly in the earth, it is sometimes better to sink them in clay pots for easier removal.

Gladiolus

All garden soil that has good drainage, and is rich in organic matter, is excellent for gladiolus culture. Plant the corms in small, circular beds among other flowers for summer color, or plant in rows in the garden for a steady supply of cut flowers.

When planting in flower beds, dig a round hole 8 inches deep and 12 inches across. Loosen soil in the bottom, and add one quart of old manure, or a pint of dehydrated manure, two fistfuls of an organic fertilizer that is balanced, and a fistful of lime if the soil is acid. Work the fertilizer well into the soil, cover with an inch of dirt, then set in 6 large corms spaced two inches apart in all directions.

Refill the hole, leaving a slight depression to catch water. The earth should be firmed only enough to eliminate air pockets.

If planting in rows in the garden (which, by the way, produces the largest flowers), work the soil well to a depth of 12 inches. Turn in any organic matter you have on hand such as compost, aged manure, leaf mold or green manures. Rake area smooth, then make trenches 8 inches deep about two feet apart.

Since gladiolus are such heavy feeders, some organic food should also be incorporated into the bottom of each trench for immediate use. We like to mix old manure equally with compost, and apply two inches deep in each trench. Then we give each furrow a good dusting of bone meal. All of this is then worked into the soil, and covered with an inch of dirt.

When plants are 8 inches tall, loosen soil between rows, and apply a compost high in phosphorus. This early feeding determines the bud count on each spike and its final length. Water in fertilizer with a fine spray. When ground has dried sufficiently, hill each row to a height of 6 inches for later support.

Gloxinia

Gloxinias thrive best in a soil rich with compost and may be grown from mature tubers, young potted plants, leaf cuttings, or seed.

Iris need plenty of rich soil as well as good drainage to attain utmost loveliness. In early spring, apply mixture of compost, bone meal and lime, using equal parts of each. Evenly distribute the mixture, which will be washed into soil by spring rains.

A good potting mixture is one-third part each of sand, peat moss or leaf mold and good garden loam soil. The main thing to remember is that gloxinias like the potting mixture to be rich and fibrous.

Ground Cover

Soil rich in organic matter holds moisture and prevents leaching on slopes, besides aiding a quick, dense plant growth that refuses to give weeds a chance.

Dig to a depth of at least 8 inches, removing all weeds and foreign material. Mix in a 2 to 3-inch layer of organic material such as compost, peat moss, rotted manure or aged sawdust. Soak well a few hours before planting.

Iris

When planting iris, lift the entire clump with a spade and tear the clump apart into small divisions. Choose only the largest and healthiest looking ones for transplanting. Let the hose run gently over these while you spade the soil deeply for the new plantings. Sprinkle bone meal over the spots and spade in. Irises demand plenty of rich soil so mix in a generous portion of rotted manure or compost. Good drainage is a must, too.

In the middle of March give the beds a dressing of compost, bone meal and lime, using equal parts of each. This mixture should be distributed evenly and thickly. The heavy spring rains—or March snow—will carry this down into the ground to feed the plants.

During July the first dying leaves of the bearded iris will droop. Remove these. They will be a good addition to the compost pile, while if left on the plant they will shut out the sunlight from the rhizomes, and give the plant an unkempt appearance, too.

The following rules may be of help in controlling the troubles which sometimes attack irises:

1. Avoid excess watering and rich nitrogen fertilizers for the Tall Beardeds. Lush growth can sometimes encourage disease and follow-up borers.

2. When replanting, examine each plant carefully, throwing diseased specimens and leaves into the compost heap. Constantly pick off diseased foliage. Cut away any borers found.

3. Keep the soil supplied with compost.

Lily

Lilies, with their fleshy open bulbs, must have good drainage above all else. If water is allowed to settle among the scales of the bulb, which in some cases are as loose as leaves of an artichoke, the bulb will rot, and the plant die. A bed on a hillside, where good drainage is assured, is safest for most varieties. In addition, some gardeners make a practice of tilting the bulbs slightly when planting them, to allow water to run out away from their centers. Exceptions are *L. canadense* and *L. superbum*, which thrive in damp situations.

While the bulb must be kept well drained, it must also be kept cool and moist. A bed deeply prepared with compost, mixed with a large percentage of sand, is ideal. No manure should be permitted to come in contact with the bulbs, but manure may be used in the mulch over the top of the soil, if it is sufficiently decayed. A deep mulch of leaf mold over the lily bed will be appreciated during the hot weather. Or the lilies may be planted among low-growing annuals or shrubs which will keep the soil shaded. All lilies prefer slightly acid soil, and few will tolerate lime.

Feeding Lily Ponds

Rotted compost placed near the bottom of the tub, is a very good fertilizer for water lilies. Be sure to put it near the bottom to prevent the manure from turning the water green. A ration of 3 parts soil to one part manure is recommended. Chemical fertilizers are especially dangerous to fish and other water life in your pond. Cow manure will do the job very adequately. Also, in the spring, it would be well to add ground blood to each tub. Small pots require one tablespoonful, while large 3-foot tubs require one full pint.

Narcissus

When planting in groups, spade the soil deeply to allow for plenty of root action in the spring. Work in plenty of compost or rotted manure throughout the planting area until the soil assumes a good, crumbly structure. A light application of bone meal and wood ashes will give the bulbs a good potassium and phosphorus balance for a good spring start. Remove about 6 inches of the soil to form a trench. Then mix the bone meal and wood ashes with the soil you removed and set the bulbs in a one-inch layer of sand. Apply more sand until the bulbs are covered up to their necks. Then replace the soil you removed. The bulbs should be about 3 inches below the surface and at least 6 inches apart.

Pansy

Pansies are quite hardy, withstanding temperatures down to 15 degrees if given a light covering of salt hay, dry leaves or strawy manure through the winter. They want cool, moist soil and a rich mulch, for they are gluttons. Use manure, compost, woods soil, leaf mold, or sawdust and shavings mixed with sheep or poultry manure. The mulch feeds them richly— they are surface feeders—and keeps the roots cool in summer, warm in winter.

New plants are easily rooted from cuttings made from the side shoots in August. Set the cuttings out and treat them the same as seeds. Feedings of compost or manure water will make them grow fast and healthy.

Primrose

Primroses grow best in a soil well supplied with organic matter which is retentive of moisture. A liberal addition of leaf mold or thoroughly rotted manure or well-decomposed compost should be spaded in where they are to be planted. Unlike many woods natives, primroses do not want too much acid. Their preference is a pH between 6.0 and 8.0. Yearly top-dressings of compost or rotted manure may be lightly dug in around them.

Rock Garden

A loam, sandy loam or peat soil is most suitable for a rock garden. Avoid a heavy clay soil at all costs, or be prepared to renovate it with large amounts of organic matter.

Usually it is a good idea to make your own soil mixture: dig out the site to a depth of 18 inches, and replace the existing soil with a mixture of equal parts of loam, sand and leaf mold or compost.

Where alkaline-loving plants are to be grown, add 5 to 10 per cent of limestone chips, pulverized clean clam, oyster or eggshells, or ground limestone. To create acid conditions, use oak leaf or pine needle mold, acid, peat or compost.

Some rock gardeners cover the soil after planting with a stone mulch made of crushed rock the size of peas. This helps to keep the moisture in and the heat out, and also prevents winter heaving. A mulch of compost, evergreen boughs, salt hay or leaves also make good winter protection for most rock garden plants.

Sweet Pea

In preparing the soil for planting sweet peas, dig a trench 1½ to 2 feet deep, fill the bottom foot with good soil and well rotted manure, or compost, and the remainder with fertile topsoil to which has been added one pound of bone meal to 15 feet of row. If the soil is acid, apply lime at the rate of ½ pound to 15 feet of row.

Tulip

Tulip bulbs grow best in well-drained, light loam. The soil should be deep and enriched with plenty of well-rotted manure or compost to insure good plant growth and large flowers over a period of several years. Fertilizers such as

342

bone meal, dried and shredded cow or sheep manure or compost are excellent dressings.

Wild Flower Garden

Some of the rarest wild flowers require very acid soil, with a pH of 4.0 to 5.0. Unless the garden site is in a pine woods, the chances are against its having soil near this extreme of acidity. Many other wild plants need slight acidity, and a still larger number, among them the commonest wild flowers, will grow in neutral soil, or are indifferent to slight acidity or alkalinity.

Very acid soil is composed largely of partially decomposed leaves, bits of bark and branches, and toppled dead trees rich in tannic acid. These are most commonly hemlock, pine, or oak. Forests in which these trees predominate will have a floor of extremely acid soil. On the other hand, woods which are made up of maples and other sweet-wooded trees will be carpeted with soil which is neutral or nearly so. Native vegetation which may be found growing under these two types of forests may be used as an index of the acidity. In the acid soil blueberries, wood anemone, and star grass may grow. Poison ivy and goldenrod are an indication of little or no acidity in the soil.

By mixing soil from a very acid area with neutral soil, a slightly acid layer may be produced in which some of the plants needing only slight acidity may grow. But to achieve a very acid soil in a neutral soil area, it may be necessary to plant some of the acid-producing trees first. Temporary soil acidity may be manufactured by use of acid mulch and compost, but unless a permanent supply of such mulch and compost is planted on the spot, the wildlings dependent on it will eventually die out.

Soil texture may be altered more easily than the pH factor to suit specific plants. Plants like alpines which require a gritty soil may be accommodated by spreading a fine rock-chip mulch over the soil surface. Damp meadow conditions may be simulated by laying perforated water pipes below the surface of the soil. A chopped leaf compost mixed with plenty of rotted manure or cottonseed meal has approximately the texture and nutrients of rich woods soil. If acid spring water is available on the site, a planting of sphagnum moss in it will make a fine bed for pitcher plants or bog orchids.

ROSES, SHRUBS AND VINES

A Compost "Trench" For Foundation Plantings

Do you have trouble digging holes in your yard to plant trees and shrubs? Does the shovel bounce back in your face and a pick have to be used?

This is surely a problem common to tens of thousands of new homeowners in heavy clay soil regions. For when the area is stripped and leveled by the bulldozers, the subsoil becomes very much impacted. Even though topsoil is put back by the contractor, it is often true that when you go out to dig a hole the first few inches are easy—but after that it is like iron.

Flowers planted in this mess often do poorly to put it mildly. While the soil may be improved by organic compost and eventually made good, this takes time. Many new home owners dream of a brave showing of flowers the first year that they move in. If you are dreaming of a flower border with a deep organic soil that you can sink a trowel into with ease in midsummer . . . soil that will grow prize flowers . . . why not try a trench garden?

Let us say that you plan a 3-foot-wide garden along the border for 50 feet. After marking this out with string, the topsoil may be shoveled out on all sides to form a rectangular dike. Dig until you hit the impacted subsoil, then fill the trench with water and let it sink in overnight. When it has dried enough this impacted subsoil will dig a little easier than usual . . . at least for a layer or so.

By picking and digging away off and on over a period of a few days you should reach a depth of perhaps a foot and a half. The impacted subsoil is best wheelbarrowed away and used to level some ground nearby. Then into the trench with the dike topsoil and any manner of compost that you have on hand.

In a new home you probably will have to buy material for much of the trench. A good method is to fill the trench about halfway with builder's sand or sandy topsoil (usually available at low cost). The rest of the trench should be filled with good rich compost. Thoroughly spade up the resultant mixture, wet it down and plant your flowers. Three times the growth and beauty is not uncommon as compared to the same flowers planted a few feet away in the thin topsoil of many housing developments.

When making a flower bed for the first time, add plenty of compost and mix it well with the soil. Deep cultivation and heavy applications are essential, especially in clay soil areas where the impacted subsoil will keep plant roots from developing.

Evergreens, shrubs and trees also will benefit from large holes prepared in the same manner as the trench. (Substitute acid leaf mold for broadleaf evergreens.) When the digging is as hard as I have described, it is certainly a temptation to "cheat" on the size of the hole.

However, there seems to be no substitute available for the hard work necessary to dig a hole large enough to give a tree root room to grow. Asking a tree to send roots out into an inhospitable, dry, iron-hard layer of pounded earth is just too much. No wonder we see so many unhappy trees in new housing developments.

As a nurseryman I cannot help being distressed by the gummy clay or hard, packed soil that we so often find when planting evergreens around new homes. It is of course caused by modern methods where bulldozers dig the cellar excavations and then level the ground, packing it hard as sheet steel in the process, then shoving back any kind of gummy subsoil that happens to be handy. Of course, where the soil is sandy the problem is not great. But so many more homes are built on heavy soil than upon light soil!

How much more fun it is to work around the foundations of old homes that were dug by horse and man-power. For in those days the soil was filled in by hand or slow-moving equipment, and the man who built the house knew that he and his wife would be planting that ground and made sure it was halfway decent to dig in.

If you live in a heavy clay soil region, the result usually is that you have some very gummy or hard soil right next to the house where you wish to plant expensive evergreens.

We have found that when you try to mix leaf mold with the heavy gummy clay the result is not really "natural" or satisfactory. There are lumps of gook in the leaf mold and that is about all. It is as though you tipped a can of nails into the mashed potatoes. The potatoes are good to eat but the nails obviously aren't. Evergreens apparently often feel the same way about gumbo clay in their leaf mold. It seems to work out in our own experiences as nurserymen that when you have a sandy soil or a light soil it mixes very well with organic materials and gives good results. But when you have a heavy clay soil it often does not mix well with the organics and better results are had by using pure organics or bringing in sandy loam and mixing it with the organic materials, throwing out the heavy clay soil altogether in the area of planting.

If you have a heavy clay fill around your home we believe the best solution is to dig a trench all the way around the house (where you wish to landscape) to a depth of a foot and a half or two feet. Remove the clay mess, using it to fill some waste land nearby. The width of the trench can vary with the pattern that you plan for your foundation planting. As previously explained, the trench should then be filled about halfway with sandy topsoil (make sure that you do not get "clayey topsoil").

The top half of the trench should be filled with leaf mold (or acid compost) from a nearby woods or nursery. This organic material should be spaded over and mixed somewhat with the sandy topsoil underneath. Now you have a planting area that will grow holly, azalea, rhododendron, andromeda, laurel, wildflowers, shrubs and any cultivated flowers that like acid soil. Anytime that you wish to go out and plant a new evergreen or fern or flower you will find a soft "easy-to-dig" bed equal to a nurseryman's growing area. With watering and

occasional organic fertilizer you should be able to grow evergreens that are the envy of the neighborhood.

—TOM DILATUSH

Evergreen

These plants thrive best in an acid soil. The soil should
be rich in humus and provided with good drainage.

An occasional top-dressing of well-rotted compost can be
given, but if the soil is well supplied with humus and if a
plentiful leaf mulch is maintained, any special feeding is best
done with fertilizers of an acid-forming nature.

After the plants have become established, the soil surrounding them should be disturbed as little as possible, for
the roots are very near the surface. It is known that there is
a definite mycorrhizal association between the feeder roots of
most of the evergreen plants and shrubs and certain fungi.

Sometimes a balanced organic food or one rich in nitrogen
is given to stimulate growth. This should be dug into the soil,
and the area well watered; or it may be applied in solution or
in crow-bar holes driven at two-foot intervals down to the
feeding roots, starting the holes at least 18 inches from the
trunk.

Excellent materials for mulching are acid compost, evergreen boughs, threshed rye straw, salt hay, oak leaves, peat
moss, grass cuttings, and coconut fiber. They should be applied
in a layer not in excess of 3 inches and extending a little
beyond the natural spread of the roots.

Holly

American holly may be delicate in more northerly locations unless it is given large quantities of acid humus, such
as oak leaf mold. They do best in rich, well-drained soil; the
evergreen holly types prefer a partly shady location. Of all
the leaf molds, oak seems the best in character and richness.
Most any woods leaf mold is good, other than maple, which
tends to be sweetish and not much to the liking of hollies.

The top surface of the woods consists of fresh leaves and
the leaf mold itself is permeated by the rootlets of trees and
shrubs. Men must go out and gather it by hand, scraping off
the top fresh leaves, spading out the layer of leaf mold and
roots, avoiding the poor subsoil beneath. By dint of shaking
out the roots, the rich brown oak leaf mold remains. Composting can yield the same product from home-gathered leaves,
and the use of a shredder will hasten the process.

The yearly care of hollies is both easy and simple. They love water and should be thoroughly soaked once every week or two during the growing season, for summer rains are rarely heavy enough to please a holly. Waterings by hose or bucket are well repaid by more beautiful growth. Aside from the yearly surface mulch of well-rotted oak leaf compost or woods leaf mold, hollies are benefited by a blanket of tobacco stem mulch placed over the root area underneath the entire branch spread of the tree. Tobacco stems are rich in nutrients and perhaps are also detrimental to insects. Hollies respond with darker green leaves and more berries when fed with a yearly mulch of tobacco stems.

Lilac

Lilacs need full sun. They acquire mildew very easily in a shady site. Incidentally, this unsightly affliction of the lilac does not seem to do it permanent harm. The soil should be loamy and well drained. Never allow a lilac to have wet feet.

Since it is a heavy feeder, a course of fertilizing is called for every other year at least. In the spring spread a 6-inch layer of well-rotted compost around the bush and out far enough to take in most of the branch spread. Dig this in well, being careful not to injure the roots, and cover with a mulch of hay or leaves, wood ashes, or pine needles if the soil is not acid enough. Lilacs, like most shrubs, grow best in slightly acid soil. If it is too acid, an application of agricultural lime is recommended. In the late fall, work this mulch into the soil and remulch with leaves or grass clippings for the winter. This will prevent heaving of roots when the ground freezes and thaws.

Unless your winters are very severe, it is best to transplant a well started shrub in the fall. Dig a hole two feet deep. Layer the hole with a mixture of compost and topsoil, and again, bone meal, setting the roots on this. Fill in the hole with the same mixture and water generously.

Mock Orange

In planting these shrubs prepare the ground well for them. Dig the hole 3 times as deep and wide as the ball of roots. They thrive in a sandy loam. In the bottom of the hole place some well-pulverized compost and mix with good soil. Set the shrub in the center of the hole and be sure it is straight. Fill in around the ball of roots and when the hole is

¾ full of soil, run water in to settle it, being sure to give enough water to reach down below the roots. Fill in with more soil and make a basin around the shrub to hold water.

During the hot days of summer it is well to use a mulch 3 to 4 inches thick. Put it on after a thorough watering. Different materials may be used for this purpose. Well decomposed vegetable matter from the compost pile, manure or leaf mold, will be suitable. As it is washed into the soil, a fresh application has to be applied. Although some mulches are at the same time top dressings, these two preparations are applied for different purposes. Mulches are used primarily to prevent over-rapid evaporation, and the aim of the top dressing is to enrich the soil and furnish new food for the shrub. Top dressings are used to augment the plant food supplied by manure at time of planting, or when it is not feasible to disturb plants so that manure may be dug in.

Roses

For successful rose growing, nothing is more important than organic matter in the soil. According to one secretary of the American Rose Society, "compost of plant and animal refuse is the best soil conditioner for roses."

Here is that advice of one organic gardener, Charlotte Hoak, on the best ways of growing roses: "It is an excellent plan to prepare the soil a month or two before you plant. Our preparation consists of adding compost and composted manure to the soil and incorporating it thoroughly to the depth of at least 18 inches. It's not necessary to spade over the entire ground, but dig good roomy holes and fill them with your soil mixture. If manure is used, be sure to keep these filled holes moist so that it will be thoroughly decayed by planting time."

Mrs. Genevieve Thompson describes her year-round rose program as follows:

"After frost danger is past the mulch is removed and only the dead wood pruned from the roses. The ground is raked and cleaned thoroughly, every leaf picked up. Then the plot lies naked for the sun to bake and sterilize the soil. This entire treatment is to safeguard against black-spot, which lives over the winter in the soil and straw.

"When new shoots appear it is time to mulch. If we are going to use manure (we don't every year) it is applied. Wheelbarrow load after wheelbarrow load of beautiful black compost is scattered on the rose bed. After that the heavy mulch is applied.

"We buy the material most easily available and cheapest. Usually that is wheat or oat straw. With it we mulch heavily (half knee deep when newly put on and 4 to 6 inches after packing down). This is put on in the spring and remains until the next spring. When it is removed (as a sanitary measure) it is spread between the raspberry rows where it remains for good.

"We believe there is something in the mulch, perhaps some chemical reaction, which discourages pests. And we feel sure the strength and health of the bushes makes them resistant to both disease and insects.

"That is about all of it. Here in the Mid-west we have killing hot weather and the last 3 years have had a severe drought. Our roses are in full sun all day until about 4 in the afternoon. When the temperature hits one hundred degrees and over, day after day, they are hard put to hold up their heads. But their roots go deep because they are *never* shallow watered. Once a week, *only if it has not rained,* the hose, minus the nozzle, is pushed under the mulch and they are watered for 2 or 3 hours. One of the best ways to invite mildew and blackspot is to sprinkle roses, especially in the evening when the foliage cannot dry off before nightfall."

A Rose-Compost Program

Most gardeners grow a few roses, often without too much success. Their best plants are poor specimens when compared with the flawless plants produced by the rose growing experts. How do these expert rose growers obtain such fine results?

First, let us see what the average gardener does when he plants a few roses. He knows that roses require a good deep loam, rich and well drained, so he digs out the bed to a depth of about 3 feet, breaks up the subsoil with a pick, and lays down broken stones, bricks, etc., to a depth of about one foot. Over this he places a layer of well-rotted horse manure. If the roses he wishes to plant are Teas he knows that they will require a rather light, sandy soil. He knows that Hybrids do best in soil containing some clay. Therefore, he usually pulverizes the removed soil and sods and mixes with them some sand and leaf mold to lighten the mixture—or clay to make the mixture heavier, as the case may be—adds some well-rotted horse-manure to the mixture, and fills in the bed so that it will be level after it has settled; in the meantime, of course, setting out the plants. More often than not his roses are mediocre and afflicted with plant disease.

What method does the successful rose grower follow? He takes care of drainage and builds his bed in much the same manner. But his materials differ. He usually begins by composting certain substances. He has very definite ideas about what these substances should be.

In his composting the rose expert aims at getting very definite results. He believes that soil for rose culture should be clayey but friable enough to be easily pulverized. So he selects good heavy clay turf, often stripped from a rich meadow. He has found that when this material has been broken down by composting, it produces a humus that is open and porous enough for easy root action.

He builds his compost heap by arranging alternate layers of sods and cow manure, two parts of clay turf to one part of cow manure. He hates to have to substitute horse manure, but will do it if necessary. The heap is moistened during dry weather. Be sure to correct acidity by applying a medium sprinkling of lime with the compost. Not much emphasis is placed upon heating or fermentation although the heap is occasionally turned. From the organic gardening viewpoint his method of composting is rather inefficient. The material is broken down rather slowly. But it is a step in the right direction. If climatic conditions allow, the rose expert likes to arrange his compost in the winter; he believes that newly formed but properly matured compost humus—not over 6 months old—is best.

Where the ordinary gardener simply pulverizes the soil removed by digging, mixes it and returns it to the bed, the expert discards the removed material altogether and replaces it with specially composted humus. This is a point worth noting, for upon it depends much of the success of the expert.

Often the expert also uses several other types of composted materials, each formed for a different and specific purpose. His methods of composting may not be perfect but he has a deep understanding of the true value of compost humus. The humus which he is to use in his greenhouse benches, hotbeds, flats, etc., is made for that purpose. For this he secures rich turf and stable manure. Here again he follows the alternate layer plan of composting but carefully varies the amounts. For example, he uses about 3 parts of horse manure to one part of sods to produce a humus suitable for fast growing, succulent plants, but greatly reduces the amount of manure if he wishes to produce a humus suitable for stocky, slow-growing plants such as cabbage, etc.

The rose experts' methods are a big improvement over those of the ordinary gardener. They are methods worked out through generations of practice. They have deep significance for the organic gardener. And considering the expert, the ordinary gardener will discard all soil, sods, removed at planting time and replace it with properly composted humus. Just why does this method tend to promote healthy plant growth?

To begin with, it surrounds the roots of the plant with an easily penetrated humus, rich in natural plant nutrients. It offers exactly the right condition for proper growth. Not only is root growth encouraged but the mycorrhizal association is also encouraged without which the roots system is unable to ingest much valuable nutrient material.

The rose expert seldom cultivates his plants unless the bed has been badly trampled, even then the cultivation is as shallow as possible to avoid root injury. He prefers to mulch the plants. Here he often turns again to composted material. During periods of drought he increases the depth of the mulch after applying a mixture of cow manure and water.

Plant disease sometimes bothers even healthy roses. Black spot, caused by a fungus, is most destructive during summer months. The infection overwinters in fallen leaves. A thorough cleaning up in the late fall will often do much to prevent serious attack the following summer. Pruning is often helpful. Strong plant growth may be brought about by cutting back and in persistent cases it is sometimes necessary to cut the plant back and force it to start over again with new clean foliage.

Powdery mildew is prevalent wherever roses grow. This fungus produces grayish or whitish spots on leaves and buds. Its spread is encouraged by sour soil, poor air drainage, matted growth, overlapping leaves, and "soft" foliage. This condition usually calls for a thorough pruning and the encouraging of open sunshine and currents of cool fresh air which tend to harden the foliage and bring about a certain amount of mildew resistance. It is because rose experts have found

352

that artificials cause rapid growing "soft" foliage that they seldom use them.

Roses are also much subject to attack from nematodes (eelworms). However, these seldom worry either the rose expert or the organic gardener because nematodes do not thrive in soils rich with composted organic humus.

—ROGER W. SMITH

Vines

In planting, careful preparation of the soil is rewarding. The plants will make quicker and healthier growth if planted in ground that is well prepared. The soil around the foundation of buildings is often of poor quality. Make the hole 3 times deeper and wider than the ball of roots, and open up the bottom of the hole to ensure good drainage, for this is important to the future well-being of the plant.

Then put in 2 or 3 spadefuls of well-decayed composted material, and two of top soil; mix thoroughly together. Mix compost with soil to fill in around the ball of roots. Tamp down the soil mixture in the hole, putting in enough so that when the plant is placed on it, the top of the ball of roots will be level with the ground. In time it will settle a little. Fill in with soil around the roots. When the hole is nearly filled, run a slow stream of water in from the hose, letting it run until the water is down below the roots. This will settle the soil and fill up any air pockets. Fill in with soil and finish planting by making a well around the the vine to hold water. Tie the vine to its support.

The decayed vegetable matter in the soil will make a soft run for the roots to penetrate, and will put humus in the soil, so necessary for healthy growth. During the summer months cover the ground over the roots with a good mulch, which always has to be renewed every little while, as it breaks down and gets washed into the ground.

Perennial vines need feeding in early spring. Work some compost and a little rotted manure lightly into the ground around them and water well to carry nourishment down to the roots, then mulch.

Shrub Requirements

Soil requirements differ with various shrubs, but generally evergreens need an acid soil rich in humus, but with not too high a nitrogen content, while deciduous shrubs need richer soil, and may be given top-dressings of compost or rotted manure. A leaf mulch under most shrubs will replenish organic matter in the soil. Unless fungus disease is a problem, leaves should be left where they fall, and should be supplemented by liberal mulching with grass clippings, peat, corncobs, straw, composted sawdust, or leaf mold. Bone meal may be added, and wood ashes are also beneficial if extreme acidity is not necessary to the species. Evergreens which are overfed become weak and spindly, and do not bloom too well. Most deciduous shrubs are grateful for nitrogen, and the more rapidly they grow, the more hungry they are for it.

Compost for Propagating Shrubs

Air layering is a method of propagation used on certain woody plants, usually, which have become too "leggy," that is, too tall and gangly, with a few leaves growing at the end of the long stem. Its purpose is to produce shorter, stockier, more robust looking, and better foliaged plants.

Another object is to increase the number of shrubs and trees in the home landscape at practically no cost.

When tree branches have been damaged, either intentionally or by accident, the bark and the cambium soon begin the process of healing the wound, by gradually growing over the exposed wood. Here then is Nature's secret to successful propagation by air-layering—taking advantage of the efforts of the branches to continue to live.

One of several layering techniques, air-layering is a method often used in England. Select a twig or branch about the size of a pencil in circumference, and with a sharp knife, make an incision in the branch center and continue the cut upwards for about two inches. This cut should be made just below a dormant bud situated not more than 12 inches from the tip of the branch. Now, carefully bend open the incision or open it with the aid of your knife and keep it open until you have inserted in the incision, a tiny pebble or stone, or better still a small piece of sphagnum or other moss. The object of this is to prevent Nature from healing the wound by contact.

You now envelop this incision with a good-sized handful of sphagnum moss or compost—all of which must be moistened—preferably in rain or pond water—to the consistency of a squeezed-out sponge. To keep the material properly moist,

Peat moss or compost is used in propagating plants. Above it is applied in air layering—a technique used to produce shorter, healthier and better-foliaged plants. Moistened compost is placed around stem cut and held in place by plastic shroud.

cover with a wrapping of polyethylene film or aluminum foil, completely enclosing the moistened moss and securing each end of the "shroud" with string, tape, etc. In 4 or 5 weeks, depending on the type of plant you are air-layering, roots should develop.

The importance of the "shrouds" and their proper application to the location of the incision or removal of bark is so important that it must be emphasized. It is the "shroud" which prevents the rapid evaporation of the essential moisture and once you have properly moistened the enveloping materials in which the roots actually will form, the materials will thereafter be kept properly moist and there will be no need to add additional moisture at any time the roots are forming.

APPLICATIONS FOR VEGETABLES AND FRUITS

The following chart will give you an approximate idea of the nutrient requirements of vegetables. You can increase the nitrogen, phosphorus or potash content of your compost by applying any of the materials rich in those elements.

COMPOST APPLICATION GUIDE FOR VEGETABLES

Nutrient Requirements

EH = Extra Heavy   M = Moderate
H = Heavy   L = Light

Vegetable	Nit.	Phos.	Pot.	pH factor
Asparagus	EH	H	EH	6.0-7.0
Beans, bush	L	M	M ·	6.0-7.5
lima	L	M	M	5.5-6.5
Beets, early	EH	EH	EH	5.8-7.0
late	H	EH	H	same
Broccoli	H	H	H	6.0-7.0
Cabbage, early	EH	EH	EH	6.0-7.0
late	H	H	H	same
Carrots, early	H	H	H	5.5-6.5
late	M	M	M	same
Cauliflower, early	EH	EH	EH	6.0-7.0
late	H	H	EH	same
Corn, early	H	H	H	6.0-7.0
late	M	M	M	same
Cucumbers	H	H	H	6.0-8.0
Eggplant	H	H	H	6.0-7.0
Lettuce, head	EH	EH	EH	6.0-7.0
leaf	H	EH	EH	same
Muskmelons	H	H	H	6.0-7.0
Onions	H	H	H	6.0-7.0
Parsnips	M	M	M	6.0-8.0
Parsley	H	H	H	5.0-7.0
Peas	M	H	H	6.0-8.0
Potatoes, white	EH	EH	EH	4.8-6.5
sweet	L	M	H	5.0-6.0 or 6.0-7.0
Radishes	H	EH	EH	6.0-8.0
Rutabaga	M	H	M	6.0-8.0
Soybeans	L	M	M	6.0-7.0
Spinach	EH	EH	EH	6.5-7.0
Squash, summer	H	H	H	6.0-8.0
winter	M	M	M	6.0-8.0
Strawberries	M	M	L	5.0-6.0
Tomatoes	M	H	H	6.0-7.0
Turnips	L	H	M	6.0-8.0

Planting Vegetable Seeds

The following practices give good results. For peas and beans of all kinds, draw flat trenches with a hoe, slightly deeper than usual; then cover the bottom with compost, sow the seeds directly on the compost and cover with soil. For radishes and other plants belonging to the mustard family, make drills rather deeper than usual, fill with compost, and sow on it.

356

Onions and leeks can also be sown on compost in drills, but these like a top-dressing after thinning. Sweet peas thrive on compost, as do all annuals. Peas sown in compost germinate several days earlier than those without and, as a rule, the crop matures quicker.

Seeds of shallow-rooted plants, such as lettuce, are best sown on soil with a layer of compost underneath.

Cantaloupe

The cantaloupe, like all the melon family, does best in somewhat sandy soil. It should not be grown in heavy clay, as melons thrive best in humus-rich, well-drained soil. Another essential is frost-free, warm and sunny weather. Cool temperatures and prolonged cloudiness, even where no freezing occurs, are hard on these sensitive plants. For this reason, melons should not be planted until the soil has thoroughly warmed in the spring—which for the northeastern states usually means June.

Before planting, an application of well-rotted compost or manure to the soil is advisable. Seed should be sown in hills 4 feet apart each way. To prepare a hill, dig out two shovelfuls of soil, insert one shovelful of rotted manure, and cover with 6 inches of well-firmed soil. Plant about 6 to 8 seeds per hill and cover with ½ inch of soil. Keep seeds two inches apart and each hill at least 12 inches in diameter. One ounce of seed will plant 20 hills. In about two weeks, the seed should germinate and plants appear. When these are 3 to 4 inches high, thin out to 3 strongest plants per hill.

Compost and Organic Corn

For best results, dig in well-rotted compost about two weeks before planting your rows of corn.

The organic raising of corn under a heavy layer of mulch has the advantage of ending between-row cultivation in the hottest time of the year. Early objections that corn needs direct sunshine and will not thrive in mulch have not been borne out by results.

Mulching and composting corn will appeal to the organic gardener on the basis of obtaining produce of superior nutritional value. There is the added benefit of eliminating unnecessary between-row cultivation. Finally, building up the soil structure by the gradual addition of slowly decomposing organic matter as the mulch breaks down is essential organic practice.

Because corn takes relatively large amounts of nitrogen out of the soil, it is advisable to fertilize heavily. Using weathered compost or animal manures plus a concentrated nitrogen source such as cottonseed or soya meal while planting is gaining acceptance. There is no possibility of burning the tender shoots because the organic fertilizers are slow-acting.

The organic fertilizer goes directly into the planting site. A mixture of one part aged animal manures plus one part cottonseed or soya meal is recommended. If the ground is somewhat heavy a third part of ground rock powder may be added.

Mulching with straw or hay between the rows immediately after planting will keep the weeds down from the start. Mulching between the young stalks of corn along the row should be done when they are 6 to 8 inches high.

Side-dressing corn during the growing season is practiced on many organic homesteads. The two-part mixture of compost plus the cottonseed or soya meal is again recommended.

Results appear to justify the mulching and composting technique. The corn is remarkably insect-resistant, ears are full while the kernels are tender and flavorful.

The mulch should be left on the ground at the end of the season. If necessary, it should be reinforced with an extra supply of straw, hay or other vegetable matter to act as a ground cover during the winter. If plowing or rotary tillage is practiced, a winter cover crop of vetch or clover should be sown. In this case, the partly decomposed mulch can be turned under and the cover crop sown.

Eggplant

The soil prepared for transplanting should be particularly rich. A good combination for it will be: two parts of rotted sod and one part of compost in which a small amount of sand has been mixed. Later on in the garden, eggplant will flourish in almost any type of soil, provided it is well fed. Someone has expressed it, "the best soil for eggplant is that which is very fertile as the result of long-continued good treatment."

This "good treatment" consists first of all, in not using fresh manure, but in nourishing the bed with well-rotted manure or compost. Apply these at the rate of about one bushel of either to each square foot of soil.

358

When transplanting endive, work a layer of compost into the surface soil. Many gardeners grow endive in the same area where lettuce grew earlier in the spring, thus making use of second plantings which can "double" your garden harvest.

Given good drainage and a very fertile soil, the eggplant tract will require moisture equal to about one inch of rain a week. In very dry weather this must be given with watering by hand. Do not forget at such times when this is necessary, that it is always better in the vegetable garden to give the ground a good soaking once a week, than to sprinkle it every day.

When the ground is thoroughly warmed in the spring, and the young plants are putting forth new growth, one may know the time has come to give the necessary adjunct—a mulch. Use hay or straw for this, laying it about two inches thick.

All mulches are valuable, but one is especially so for the eggplant with its necessarily unhampered development. Besides smothering the weeds, it will help to conserve a uniform supply of moisture which in turn will enable the roots to feed on the top, moist two inches of soil with which they are surrounded.

By the middle of July, your eggplants will be in need of extra food. This is best given as a side-dressing of compost or other natural fertilizer.

It is generally conceded that warm, sandy soils are best adapted to eggplants. This crop is seldom grown in clay soils, except under the most favorable climatic conditions. It is important that the soil be deep, rich and well drained. A liberal amount of compost is essential to the largest yields.

Manure may be applied heavily for an early crop, like lettuce or radishes, to be followed by eggplants.

Endive

An excellent plan for success in endive growing is to use the same area where lettuce succeeded early in the spring. A thin layer of compost lightly dug in along the lines where the rows of endive are to grow will insure success.

Seed should be thinly sown, covered with not more than ⅓ inch of finely sifted, mature compost, clean sand, or a mixture of the two. To make easier the job of sowing, seed, sand, and compost may be well-mixed first in a suitable container and the mixture spread in a narrow ribbon along the bottom of a shallow trench formed by drawing the corner of the hoe along a line indicated by a tight string stretched across the garden. The rows should be placed about one foot apart and the plants early thinned to stand one foot apart in the row.

Grapes

A good fertilizer program for home planting of grapes is to apply for each vine 2 to 3 pounds of finely ground granite rock in the fall and about ½-pound of some good source of organic nitrogen in the spring. Spread evenly over an area of from 6 to 8 feet in diameter from the base of the vine. Grape vines have long roots that extend as much as 8 feet from the base of the vine. Most of the feeder roots are from 3 to 6 feet from the base so much of the benefit will be lost if the fertilizer is placed next to the trunk.

If available, it is a good plan to place some bone meal, compost or ground granite rock in the hole. Set the vine so that the two buds left on the top are just above the soil level. Either mulch or cultivate the first year.

Kale

Kale can make good use of both rotted manure or compost at planting time, and a side-dressing of organic nitrogen—

about ⅓ of an ounce to a foot of ground—at intervals of 3 weeks during the summer. Lime is essential for all members of the cabbage family. A liberal application of crushed calcium limestone or shell limestone should be applied to the area at the time of preparing the ground to assure good growth and make the plant food supplied by the previously applied compost readily available.

When preparing the row for seeding, dig in small amounts of lime, and liberal amounts of well-decomposed manure or other types of organic matter. Once they are in the ground, cover the seeds lightly by raking the soil over them. When the sprouts are two or more inches high, scatter humus lightly along the sides of the row, and around the individual plants, but do not allow it to go nearer than 3 inches from the stems of the plants.

It will bear repeating that, like all other members of this cabbage family, one cannot expect to obtain top quality in kale if the growth of the plants is hindered by lack of nutrients and water, and so are unable to make the rapid growth necessary for their highest development. If this growth appears to be slow, side-dress the plants with the following application: Dissolve two teacupfuls of manure or compost in 12 quarts of water and let the solution stand for 24 hours. At the end of this time, make a narrow furrow, also 3 inches away from the plants, and pour into it one cupful of the liquid for each foot of the row. Two weeks later, make a similar application, this time placing the solution 6 inches away from the plants.

Mushroom

Mushrooms grow in organic material containing carbohydrates such as sugar, starch, cellulose or lignin, as well as the nitrogen required by all green plants. However, mushrooms cannot manufacture these products the way other plants do because they have no green color in their tissues. They develop their full root system, a network of fine white threads called mycelium, before any part of the plant appears above the soil. Fresh strawy horse manure is excellent for mushroom growing. It should be composted by turning it every 4 or 5 days, shaking thoroughly and watering well each time. Keep it moist, but not saturated. After 3 or 4 turnings, it should be a rich dark brown, with no odor. It can then be put in trays of any convenient size and allowed to "sweat out"—heat to 140 degrees. After about a week, this should be ready for planting.

Many growers do not use horse manure as their special mushroom compost, but instead find it more practical to make compost using materials more readily available. Here is how to do it:

Mix together in a heap about 100 pounds of corn fodder or finely ground corn cobs and an equal amount of straw. Water and firm this well and let it stand a few days. Then mix in thoroughly 20 pounds each of leaf mold or peat moss, tankage, and either greensand or granite dust. Some well-rotted compost can be added to aid decomposition. About 30 pounds of whole grains completes the mixture.

After a good watering, let it stand 5 or 6 days before turning. A second turning a week or so later should be enough before setting in the trays and planting. Plant the spawn as soon as the temperature of the beds reaches about 75 degrees.

When the entire bed is cropped out, the compost will make a fine garden fertilizer. Most gardeners don't try to grow mushrooms during the summer—it's too hard to maintain a 60 degree temperature—so you can set up a profitable schedule: fall preparation of compost, winter cropping, and spring fertilization of your garden with the used compost.

Okra

Thorough preparation of the soil before planting okra is very important, although it will do very well in any kind of ground. These woody plants can take on all the food that can be given them. Because okra is very rapid growing, nitrogen is particularly needed. Poultry manure is splendid material for the okra beds, but as it is very strong only about one-tenth as much as other animal manures can be used. Compost, leaf mold, peat moss and wood ashes can be used to advantage to improve poor soil in the garden. Peat moss and leaf mold are usually acid and a slight amount of lime should be used along with either of these two materials. These soil builders should be plowed under in the winter awaiting the planting time, or in a small home garden can be spaded under in the early spring.

Parsley

Any ordinary garden soil which does not dry out too rapidly and is not excessively alkaline is suitable for parsley. Parsley requires large quantities of nitrogen, and this is best

362

supplied in two ways: Before planting the seed, a trench about 3 inches deep should be dug where the row is to stand. Fill the trench with sifted compost to which has been added some well-rotted manure. Sow the seed, firm and water. Later in the season a side-dressing of sifted compost should be applied.

Pea

The pea-grower must regulate his planting according to the particular soil with which he is working. Heavy soil calls for shallow seeding, while a light soil calls for deep planting. On a heavy clay soil, if the peas are planted too deeply, heavy rain may fall before the plants are up. In this case, a hard crust will form and make it difficult for the peas to break through. The best way to prepare a seedbed in heavy soil is to work the soil rather deeply and produce a tilth which is quite flaky.

Should the ground be hard and dry, deep planting is essential in order to get down far enough to provide the necessary moisture to germinate the seed. Plenty of organic matter in the soil will greatly lessen the dangers of hardening. Weeds, old leaves and grass clippings are wonderful organic materials to work into the soil.

A good manure such as cow manure is a great help in growing peas. In using such a manure, if the garden has not been manured the previous fall, only well-rotted manure should be applied. If a fresh manure is used, it will prove too hot and as a result, will endanger the crop.

FERTILIZERS: The pea, being a legume, absorbs its supply of nitrogen from the air. This process does not, however, take place until after germination. Bone meal is a fine source of nitrogen. It has a slow action in the soil and cannot harm any crop. Dried blood, usually obtained from slaughter houses, is another good fertilizer. Basic slags and ground phosphates supply phosphoric acid which helps in final crop production. From 4 to 6 per cent potash is found in ordinary wood ashes. A suggested organic fertilizer for peas consists of one part of dried blood, one part of bone meal, and one part of greensand potash mineral or granite dust. This fertilizer should be applied at the rate of from $\frac{1}{4}$ to $\frac{1}{2}$ pound per square foot of soil area.

Potato

Fresh manure must never be used on potato land and even if well-rotted manure is used, it should be plowed or raked well under the topsoil in the autumn before the spring planting. For a 100 foot row, 10 wheelbarrow loads of rotted manure will pay dividends. But never touch the planted tubers with it. It may burn them and thus ruin chances for a successful crop.

An excellent green manure crop to use before the potato crop is soybeans, according to R. G. Atkinson and J. W. Rouatt. They recommend that soybeans be sown for several years in soil heavily infested with scab, as a control measure. Scab, they discovered, can only live in neutral or slightly alkaline soil. Soybeans turned under as green manure acidifies it. It has long been an accepted fact that green manure, whether soybean or Japanese millet, which is also recommended, will help to control scab by rapidly decaying and fostering rival soil organisms, beneficial to the potatoes and antipithetic to scab.

Insufficient potash in soil can result in potatoes which become soggy when cooked. Ample potash produces mealy potatoes. A potash deficiency can be corrected by adding to the soil about ¼ pound per square foot of a natural potash mineral such as greensand, granite dust, or pulverized feldspar. These natural minerals also contain the trace elements which are so essential to normal healthy growth, and which may be lacking in the soil.

A good fertilizer for potatoes may be made by mixing one part cottonseed meal, one part dried fish meal, one part bone meal, two parts greensand, and two parts ground phosphate rock.

One organic gardener has reported growing potatoes successfully on leaves with a cover of mulch, but without planting in soil. Leaves are piled over the potato patch the previous fall to a depth of 3 feet and left there for the winter. By spring they have packed down and earthworms are working through them. Potatoes are planted by laying the pieces directly on the leaves, in rows where they are to grow. The seed is then covered with 12 to 14 inches of hay or straw. More mulch is added later, if tubers appear through the first. When harvest time comes the mulch is pulled back, and potatoes are picked up and put into their sacks, with no digging necessary. No potato bugs have ever visited this bed, according to the grower.

Organic matter goes a long way in controlling plant disease. Several organic growers report they successfully con-

Potatoes can be successfully grown on top of the ground—one organic gardener even planting her "patch" right on top of leaves. Others report laying seed potatoes on top of the ground, and covering each potato with a handful of compost.

trolled potato scab when their soil was treated with plenty of compost. After vines have already been infected with disease, one might pull them up and add them to the compost heap.

Potato Growing

Humus functions as a buffer in the soil. Garden and crop plants are far less dependent upon a specific pH in the soil when there is an abundant supply of humus. For instance, potatoes require a distinctly acid soil when the humus content is low. In less acid or neutral soils low in humus, potatoes are highly susceptible to potato scab. In practical potato growing it often is desirable to follow potatoes by crops which will not tolerate soils that are too acid, as cabbage, cauliflower, and Brussels sprouts. According to organic gardener Hugh A. Ward with the application of compost and the accompanying low soil acidity (pH 6.0 to 6.8), it becomes possible to follow early potatoes with cauliflower or Brussels sprouts which are transplanted in the fields in late July or early August for harvesting in October and November. If it is not desirable to grow these other vegetable crops after potatoes, the pH of the soil is favorable for such legumes as vetch and cowpeas for increasing the nitrogen content of the soil. Mr. Ward also reported that he can grow potatoes free from potato scab in a soil having a pH as high as 7.2 when he has plenty of compost in the soil. This observation emphasizes the importance of soil pH on the occurrence of plant diseases in general, and also the need for compost and humus in the soil.

Sweet Potatoes

For sweet potatoes start preparing ground during April. Make a furrow long enough to accommodate the plants you need (they should be spaced 12 to 18 inches). Place an inch or two of well-rotted compost or manure in the furrow. Then ridge up the soil on top of this band of humus. Ridge height is important—it should be at least 10 inches to prevent roots from growing too deep for easy growth and harvesting.

Rhubarb

Rhubarb requires a good rich soil so the more compost and rotted manure you give them the better they like it. Before planting the divisions, enrich the ground; then regular feeding from year to year is required if good-sized stalks are to be grown. A good plan is to heap compost, manure, or both, around the plants in the fall and to dig it in when spring comes.

Fall or spring planting may be done. Many prefer fall planting in September as the plants are well established and in the spring you may have some to harvest. By the second and third years you can expect a full harvest. Dig the soil thoroughly and incorporate plenty of organic fertilizer before planting the rhubarb divisions. Set the roots 3 or 4 inches deep and allow 3 or 4 feet between plants. Be sure to firm the soil well around each crown.

Squash

Regardless of the condition of the garden, greater success in growing squash will be assured if you dig in a few shovelfuls of compost per hill. Any spot in the garden where more than one plant is to grow in a group is called a hill.

The soil should not only be enriched by the addition of good humus, it should be as carefully prepared as you can make it.

It will pay you to keep in mind the idea that the squash

Autumn is a good time to apply compost or manure to your future strawberry site—as much as 500 pounds for each 1,000 square feet of strawberry plantings. Leaves and lawn clippings, fortified with natural fertilizer materials, will also aid plants.

plants will have to be so vigorous that they will succeed in reaching maturity and developing their fruits before insect enemies and diseases can cut them down.

Strawberry

Strawberries may be grown in any soil which is not too alkaline, too dry, or in need of drainage. Best soil is a light rich loam with plenty of humus and a pH factor between 5.0 and 6.0.

If strawberries are to be planted in the spring, they will profit by being put into a bed which was prepared the previous fall. Site for the plot should be soil which has been cultivated preferably two years before strawberries are planted. This will be free of the beetle grubs and wire worms which may infest soil in which sod has recently been turned.

A site which slopes slightly, toward the south if possible, is best for perfect drainage. Water must never be allowed to stand on a strawberry patch during the winter. A southern slope will encourage earlier blossoming and earlier fruit. This may not be desirable in areas where late frosts often nip the flower buds, unless protection can be given the beds during such emergencies. (Frost-bitten blossoms may be distinguished by their darkened centers.)

Compost or manure may be turned under in fall at the rate of 500 pounds to each 1000 square feet of proposed strawberry patch. At the same time, leaf mold may be stirred into the top layer of soil. Or if no manure is available, leaves and lawn clippings may be worked into the soil at the rate of 5 or 6 bushels to each hundred square feet, accompanied by liberal dressings of cottonseed or dried blood meal, ground phosphate rock, and bone meal. Limestone should be avoided unless the soil is very acid—below pH 5.0.

Strawberries may be grown in holes in the sides of a barrel, if garden space is limited, although the yield will naturally be small.

Various improvements on the strawberry barrel may be added. A perforated pipe may be incorporated down the center of the barrel, through which water of liquid manure may be fed to the plants. The whole barrel may be mounted on a small wheeled platform, to permit it to be turned so that plants on all sides will get sun. A perforated pipe filled with manure may be placed in the center of the barrel, and water applied through the manure, to leach out its nutrients into the barrel.

Indoor Fruit Growing

Growing fruit indoors can be a lot of fun, and more often than not, you harvest a reward for your gardening efforts. But to grow fruit, or anything else, indoors with the maximum success, you must apply the same gardening know-how that you use in your outdoor gardening.

First, remember that potted plants cannot send their roots very far in search of food; it must be brought to them. This is done by potting in compost-enriched soil. (Use acid-type soil for acid-loving plants, alkaline for the others.) Be sure to incorporate generous amounts of compost in the soil to be used for repotting; or, if repotting is not indicated but a "boost" is, wash out the top inch of soil and replace it with a humus-rich material.

Vegetables in Compost Heaps

From time to time, gardeners have reported amazing results growing vegetables in or near a compost pile. Follow-

This young man from an upstate New York farm is mighty proud of the huge pumpkins which "sprung up" right in one of the numerous compost heaps located on his grandfather's land. A great many organic gardeners report fabulous yields from plants which have grown (often by accident) in or near compost piles.

ing is a report from H. F. Walbridge about an experience he had with cabbages:

"I recently had another convincing demonstration of the truth about compost gardening. My next-door neighbor gave me a dozen cabbage plants (which I didn't want as I was never able previously to raise any in Pennsylvania due to the "club root.") Having no other spot in the garden, I stuck them in the edge of last year's compost heap and promptly forgot them until several weeks later. I was amazed, surprised, also delighted to see the pep and vigor of the young plants. They seemed to say, 'We are perfectly satisfied here in this spot— this is it.' There were no weeds of any account, no bugs or worms, the taste was superior to that in the market. We were using our cabbage when our good neighbor's plants were half grown although they were from the same batch of plants that he gave to us. Our neighbor uses commercial fertilizers mostly, but I want no more of it. Every cabbage head in our garden weighed 3 pounds within an ounce more or less.

"Although mute and speechless, these cabbage heads standing in an arching row around the edge of an old compost

369

heap have taught me much about the importance of humus in soil fertility and the importance of living soil to the growing of plants that are relatively free from all diseases and pests— plants that are rich in health-promoting substances."

Cucumber Culture with Compost

Here is another example of harvesting results from "compost heap" plantings as told by L. C. Lemmon:

"It has been our habit to return kitchen wastes to the soil day by day rather than give them to the county garbage collection. This we have done by various methods. To handle this disposal one fall, I dug a hole near my compost heap. This hole was 4 feet square and 3 feet deep, and the earth removed was put in a pile close by.

"After I had completed my digging I noticed a large pile of raspberry canes which I had pruned from my bushes during the summer and was reluctant to burn. The thought occurred to me that here was the opportunity to incorporate such woody stuff into the soil as it would be deep enough not to hinder cultivation.

I reasoned that if this woody material were chopped into short lengths, it would pack much more closely but still be absorbent enough to take up much of the watery waste during freezing weather. I threw the canes into the hole and went to work on them with a mattock. After a half hour's chopping I had the hole half filled with nicely broken canes and ready to receive kitchen refuse.

"A large heap of autumn leaves was kept close at hand to cover the daily deposit and to prevent any possible nuisance or unsightliness. From time to time when the weather permitted, a shovelful of earth was scattered over the contents of the hole.

"As we had been raising domesticated earthworms for some time in our basement, I decided to add a box of them and their castings to the contents of the hole. This was done before freezing weather set in and to make sure the worms would stay near the surface I added a bushel of horse manure at the same time.

"By spring much of the earth which I had excavated had been returned to the hole along with kitchen waste and leaves. At this time we decided to close the hole and add our refuse to the compost heap which, with its millions of worms, was able to transform this waste to good soil in a week or two, in warm weather.

"Having no further need of our little hole, we drew the remaining local earth into it, and added a few bushels of woods earth and levelled it off with the rest of the garden.

"From then on the kitchen refuse was added to the compost heap and the hole was forgotten in the rush of gardening activities until it remained the only unplanted area in the garden. This little square area quite naturally suggested cucumbers, so a small packet of hybrid seed was put into the ground and fifteen healthy seedlings came up. They were all so vigorous that we never had the heart to thin them.

"Before very long my cucumbers had grown so vigorously I had to do something to protect my other crops. I drove tomato stakes into the ground and led some of the vines into the air; the remainder I directed towards my compost heap. These latter were permitted to range all over as much of the heap as they could cover. As my heap had a base measuring 12 feet x 20 feet, the reader can get some conception of the extent of these vines when I say that they covered half of this area with a tent of green. I have never before seen so few vines cover so much territory in such a short time.

"Seeing so much vine develop we were a bit apprehensive as to whether there would be any fruit. As it turned out, we needn't have been. Before the season was over this magnificent hill had produced 178 excellent cucumbers, 144 of which weighed one pound or more.

"During this period of vigorous growth not a blemish of any kind was to be found on leaf or vine, and the phenomenal thing about all this was the fact that every day for a period of at least 4 weeks we could find striped and 12 spotted cucumber beetles on the raspberries and tomatoes just a few feet away. I'm confident they were not eating the leaves of either of these plants, nor were they disturbing the cucumber. Perhaps they wanted to be near for any sign of weakness. This would seem to bear out the theory of Mr. Rodale and others that our so-called garden pests may not care for the taste of a healthy plant, preferring rather to feed upon one which is undernourished or otherwise unfit for survival.

"Nothing was done to side-dress or fertilize these vines as is recommended by most authorities. In spite of this negligence they held their initial vigor until 140 large crisp fruit had been borne.

371

"The first indication that the vines were not so strong as formerly, was the evident diminishing size of the fruit. Having reached the zenith of their powers they had begun the descent. Then we began to see the beetles on the vines. Leaves would be eaten and withered and the good dark green gave way here and there to pale green and then to yellow.

In spite of these difficulties the hill continued its production, and before we decided to pull up the vines they had produced 20 more pounds of nice cucumbers.

"This experience has taught me several important lessons: 1. Organically grown plants can be so healthy that garden pests will not attack them during their most productive period; 2. Lack of vigor precedes depredations from disease and insects; 3. The health of the soil is the first and most fundamental interest of the farmer or gardener."

Compost Water for Beans and Tomatoes

Using compost water for vegetable plants has meant excellent results for Blanche Fewster.

The following is her planting method: set 4 poles so that they are 8 feet above ground. Set them deep so a wind or weight of bearing will not unbalance them. Scoop soil out in a circle making a dam of it in a ring around pole. Refill the hole with compost, almost full. Put on a thin layer of sand and plant bean seeds, finish filling with compost and press down. This refill should be slightly lower than the circle of soil around pole. Mulch with lawn clippings when beans push through the ground.

Just as the beans begin to set, give each a good drink by filling the circle around each pole with compost water. The dam will hold the water until it sinks in deep and the grass clippings will prevent evaporation. The watering from then on depends on the weather. This last season I watered only once—as beans began to set. I picked beans from the stepladder and had more than I could possibly use or give away; both as green and shell until frost.

I find that a large metal container such as the one used as a garbage can makes a splendid tank for making compost water. The lid eliminates any objectionable odors or chance of anything falling in. I use rain water whenever possible with which to fill it. The compost is tied into a gunny sack and set to soak. After a refill of water is used, the compost is added to whatever particular plant that is in favor and the process

Fruit trees will get off to the best start if fed a steady diet of compost. Humus is important if trees are to be productive, disease-free and fast-growing. Use your compost as a mulch as well as a steady source of nutrients to your growing trees.

is repeated. If the compost gets a week's soaking, I dilute the water, judging by the color of the water as to how much.

Here is my system for growing tomatoes:

First I spade the whole patch. Second, set foot high stakes deep where I expect the tomatoes to come in the rows. Third, dig hole around said stake and refill with compost. Four, set tomato plant—deep. Over the entire plot I put a 4-inch layer of straw. The plants grow as they like. Just as the blossoms begin to set, I pull out the stakes, leaving the hole. Into this hole, once a week, I pour a quart fruit jar full of compost water. The straw has kept the fruit up off the soil and I have not had any rot, scorch, blight, or bugs using this method.

USING COMPOST FOR TREES

Start right from the very beginning. Use compost to start and nourish your tree. We cannot recommend commercial, chemical fertilizers which do not add humus to the soil. You must add organic matter to the soil if you want productive, disease-free trees. Soil that is well supplied with humus retains moisture and has good drainage and aeration.

As humus decomposes, it releases a continuous supply of plant food in contrast to the "flash" action produced by chemical fertilizers. It encourages the existence of beneficial bacteria and earthworms. It fights erosion and over-compactness of the soil.

Every tree grower must have a compost pile. Use your compost as a mulch around each tree. Your trees need nitrogen, phosphorus and potash and your compost pile should contain these nutrients in good proportion.

When organic expert Herbert Clarence White of Paradise, California, plants a tree, he doesn't even glance at the little instruction sheet that the nursery sent with the stock. He proceeds to plant the tree using an unusual method handed down to him by his grandmother years ago. Grandma White's method has worked so well for Herbert over the years that he has used it to plant hundreds—possibly even thousands—of trees. He has seen fruit trees planted by Grandma White's method show 3 or 4 feet of new growth in a year, and start bearing crops in only a couple of seasons.

You start out by digging a hole 3 feet wide and 3 feet deep in which to plant your young tree. That size hole is much bigger than is usually recommended, but a big hole is the heart of Herbert's method and he insists on it. Separate the topsoil from the subsoil that is dug from the planting hole. In the bottom of the hole place a couple of pieces of 4-inch drain tile and plug up the ends with stones. Fill up the bottom foot of the hole with a mixture of equal parts of topsoil, peat moss and finished compost, plus about five pounds of phosphate rock or colloidal phosphate.

The top 12-inch layer—consisting of a mixture of compost, thoroughly soaked peat moss, leafmold, colloidal phosphate and rich topsoil, is most important. This is the immediate "seedbed" where the tender young feeder roots will be working. No *raw manure* or chemical fertilizer should ever contact this area. Such materials will seriously burn the roots, and perhaps even kill the tree outright. Even raw manure, used as a mulch at the top has often proved disastrous to newly planted trees. *So go slow* on the manure!

On top of that mixture place a layer of small rocks. The next one-foot layer consists of pure topsoil. Now put into the hole a large stone. Spread the roots of the tree over that stone, then fill the rest of the hole with the compost-topsoil-peat-phosphate-rock mixture. As mulch over the planting,

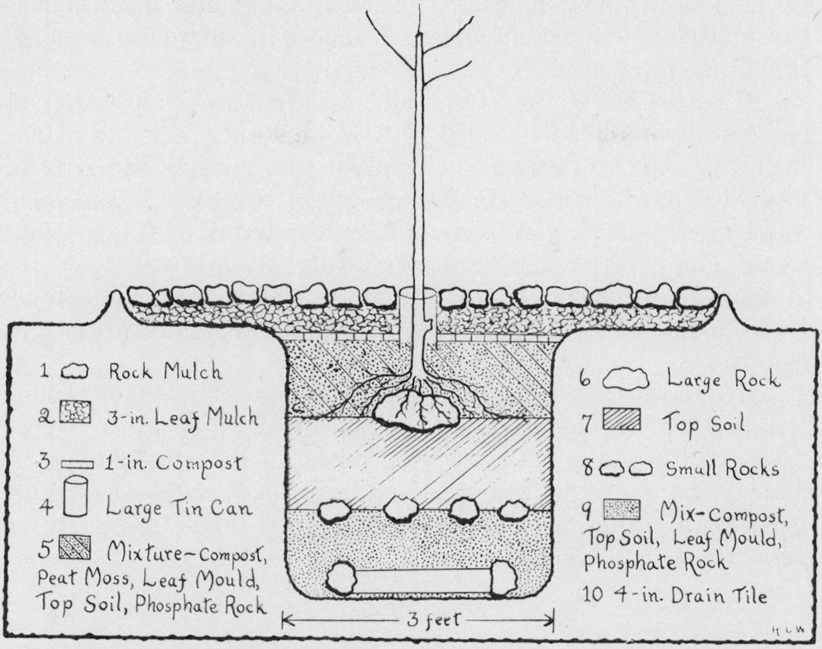
1 Rock Mulch
2 3-in. Leaf Mulch
3 1-in. Compost
4 Large Tin Can
5 Mixture-Compost, Peat Moss, Leaf Mould, Top Soil, Phosphate Rock
6 Large Rock
7 Top Soil
8 Small Rocks
9 Mix-Compost, Top Soil, Leaf Mould, Phosphate Rock
10 4-in. Drain Tile
3 feet

Here is the "Grandma White" method for planting trees. Start out by digging a hole that is 3 feet wide and deep, separating topsoil from subsoil. Place drain tile, stones at bottom, filling hole with topsoil, compost, peat moss and mineral powders.

place one inch of compost, 3 inches of leaves, plus a layer of stones if desired. White also advises putting 250 to 500 earthworms in the top compost layer, and adds this postscript to the description of his method:

"Does all this sound too weird and grotesque? Too utterly fantastic? If so, far be it from me to try and convince you. But if you are just a wee bit interested in watching a miracle, just try it out on one little tree—following the planting plan as indicated in the diagram carefully—and it will be hard for you to believe your own eyes when that baby tree starts growing."

In treating a sick tree, or one which has failed year after year to produce a crop, use the same formula as used in planting a baby tree. In other words, make a "blend" or mixture consisting of: ½ yard (12 bushels) topsoil; 2 bushels compost (completely decomposed); 2 bushels leaf mold (completely broken down); 20 pounds colloidal phosphate (or rock phosphate); and 20 pounds of rock potash. The above formula will be sufficient for a young tree of from 2 to 6 years of age that has shown little vitality and below average growth. This enriched earth will be used to fill the 20-inch holes that encircle the young tree. (Dig 8 holes, 8 inches in diameter and 20 inches deep, around the tree at the drip line.)

The next step in "treating" a sick tree is to level off the land around the trunk a little beyond the drip line of the branches, and to build a sturdy dike just outside the ring of 20-inch holes. Ten pounds of each of the two above-mentioned minerals should then be spread from the trunk of the tree out to the rim of the basin, and worked lightly into the soil with a rake. One inch of compost and leaf mold (mixed) should then be added to the area within the basin, and spread out evenly.

If domesticated earthworms are to be used in this "health-building" program, they should be spread over the compost (from 500 to 1,000) and covered with a 3-inch leaf mulch. A little corn meal or coffee grounds spread on the compost before spreading the leaves would help to give the worms a good start in their new environment.

Pine Trees

If pine trees have not grown on your soil in a long time, it helps to bring in some soil or humus from a pine forest, mix it with some compost, and spread a handful or so around each newly planted tree. That will inoculate your soil with the mycorrhiza fungus, an organism that normally grows on pine roots and helps take up nutrients from the soil. Experiments show that mycorrhiza—if present or introduced —will double the growth rate of young trees.

Nitrogen for Fruit Trees

Available from various organic sources, nitrogen may be used in the form of, say $2\frac{1}{4}$ pounds of dried blood or $4\frac{1}{2}$ pounds of cottonseed meal or about 15 pounds of compost to the tree, if the winter is not too severe. It should be applied several times in the spring when the frost is well out of the ground, and a good 3 weeks before the time when the trees will be in blossom. The actual amount of nitrogen given in the form of dried blood or cottonseed meal, or any of the other basic materials from which nitrogen is released, will depend on the type of mulch which has been used on the young trees, as well as on the age of the trees, plus the nature of the soil.

One-half the amount recommended above may well be

sufficient for young trees grown in a cover crop which is later used as a mulch around their base. For instance if apple trees are grown in sod and mulched with nonlegume hay, obviously they will obtain little nitrogen under those circumstances and the dosage of dried blood or other material will have to be increased. Similarly, with each recurring season, the amount would have to be increased depending on the condition of the trees, reaching a maximum application of two pounds of nitrogen when the trees are 7 or 8 years old.

Irrespective of the amount of nitrogenous material, it should be applied in a circle about 3 feet wide under the outer extremities of the branch spread.

A deficiency of nitrogen will show up in the tree by the leaves being small and yellowish; the remedy has already been suggested. If the foliage rolls and scorches, though, that indicates a lack of potassium in the soil. A liberal mulch of compost or a clover mulch to which lime has been added, mixed with from 400-500 pounds of potash rock applied to the acre, will adjust the potassium deficiency.

—MILTON JOHNSON

Compost and Tree Disease

The following experience of Regina Jones illustrates the effectiveness of compost in treating a tree disease, gummosis, which causes cracks in the tree bark. "A few years ago we bought an acre ranch on the outskirts of town here in Visalia, California. A young orchard ran in single file down each side and across the back of the acreage. The first year we lost 3 trees on the south; the soil was strongly alkali. Two of them were plum trees, and early in the season a gummy substance began to form on the trunks and limbs. At this time we did not know too much about gummosis, or what caused it; however, I noticed that the trees seemed to be slowly dying of what appeared to be rot.

"One of the transplanted trees was a healthy, young apricot that had begun to bear. We had moved it in December. Early in March the buds on it began to swell and soon burst into an abundance of bloom. But alas, our gratification was short-lived. Scarcely had the blooms dropped, when I noticed the same sticky gum forming on the trunk and branches. I was heartsick. It was the only apricot tree we had. It was also a very fine variety. I rushed to the telephone and called our neighborhood nursery, and asked if they could tell me what was causing the formation of the gum, and if there was any way I could save the tree.

"The owner of the nursery came to the telephone, and promptly stated that there was no known cure for gummosis or, in other words, the brown rot that was causing the formation of the gum. He added that as far as they could determine, it was caused by something in the soil, or the condition of it. He said I might as well dig the tree up and cast it into the fire.

"I set my jaw. I won't give up—not yet, I said to myself.

"I picked up a hoe, cut all the grass and weeds growing nearby, and loosened up the hard soil around the tree. This done, I turned to a large pile of compost on my garden plot. It consisted of sand, sawdust and steer manure, scrapings from big cattle trucks. I dumped two wheelbarrow loads of it around the tree, covering a circle of 3 feet in circumference.

"As the hot summer days passed, I kept lovingly pulling the gum from the dying tree; adding fresh compost and grass clippings; cutting away the limbs as they died. By autumn, the soil was soft and loamy, alive with earthworms, but the trunk and the main limb of the tree was all that was left. All winter, it protruded from the mellow soil like a lonely sentinel.

"Then one day in February I decided that I might as well take it up, and plant another one. I bought another tree, and the next day, with shovel and new tree in hand, went out to carry out my decision. A few feet from the sick tree, I stopped —and gazed at it as if I were seeing things.

"Across the fence, my neighbor was working in her garden. I looked at her, and cried out with delight, Look! I guess I have proved that trees, as well as people, are what they eat!

"What she saw was the one brown limb shooting forth green branches in every direction.

"That was less than two years ago, and the tree attained more than its former size, and is entirely free of the gum."

Restoring Old Trees

Here's some general advice when trying to bring new life into old, neglected trees:

Cut out old wood and prune heavily to strong, new growth; remove all suckers that are not necessary to replace the top; prune out interlacing branches to open the trees to light and the circulation of air; break up the soil around the tree, working in a great deal of compost, manure and other organic materials; apply organic nitrogen such as dried blood, cottonseed meal or nitrogen-rich sludge or compost—about 25 to 35 pounds per tree; mulch heavily. Do this regularly for several seasons.

Fertilizing Citrus Trees

Similar to other fruit trees, citrus trees require well-drained, well-aerated, and fairly fertile soils. Excellent drainage is particularly important. Therefore cover cropping, sheet composting and the addition of organic fertilizers are vital to the success of every citrus grower, if soil structure is to be improved.

The time cover crops are grown usually coincides with the period of heaviest rainfall. In California practically all of the rain occurs during the winter, and so cover crops that grow in cool weather are started in the fall just before the rains stop. In Florida, most of the rain takes place in the summer; cover crops are started in the spring and worked into the soil in fall—usually just before the harvest season.

To get an idea of how to fertilize your citrus trees, let's take a look at how Will Kinney of Vista, California, handles his 24-acre orange grove. When he was first building up the soil, Kinney used 20 tons each of natural limestone and gypsum, plus 30 tons of a rock phosphate mixture that included many trace elements such as cobalt, zinc, boron, molybdenum, iron and magnesium. Comments orange grower Kinney: "Seventy tons of this material on 24 acres is a very heavy application. However, this sheet composting program will be continued, with some changes, for several more years to bring the grove into maximum production of maximum food value fruit.

"Each month throughout the year, the permanent cover crop is chopped at the rate of 6,000 pounds per acre. These chopped plants return a high-nutrient green manure residue to the soil. I have been using grasses and clovers for cover crops, and they produce an abundance of organic matter for our soils. In addition, I've been able to add hundreds of tons of cow manure, which is an excellent organic nitrogen carrier."

Recently more and more reports have been issued about the decline in citrus production, especially in Florida. To a great extent, the cause seems to be excessive use of concentrated chemical fertilizers. In general, California growers have been making better use of organic nitrogen fertilizers, such as manure, alfalfa hay and straw, than orchardists in Florida, where only a small percentage of the nitrogen is derived from organic sources.

Growing Figs

Like all fast-growing semi-tropical plants, the fig responds quickly to fertilizer. There is danger in overfeeding, however, as lush tender growth is easily damaged by cold. A slow, mature growth is preferred to a fast one. A heavy mulch in the summer to retain moisture, and in the winter to protect against the weather, plus a spring application of good compost, will usually guarantee even growth. A tree treated like this needs no cultivation.

Orange Trees and Compost

The following illustrates the tremendous role of compost in growing orange trees:

"When we first planted our citrus trees some 35 years ago we thought little of the humus content of the soil. We applied chemical fertilizers and thought the ideal condition was clean cultivation. The trees soon began to show that all was not well.

"The next step was to plant leguminous crops between the trees and plow them in at the end of the wet season. This helped considerably but the ground remained bare for some time after this plowing in.

"The next advance was to use the disk harrow instead of the plow which turned in some of the cover crop but left some of it on the surface as a mulch. This was a real step forward, as we now know that this mulch provided cover and allowed bacteria of the *Azotobacter* class, and others, to get to work and more rapidly to decompose the organic matter so that atmospheric nitrogen could be fixed.

"Then we found that applications of farmyard manure, old grass and any other organic trash we could collect, all helped. In fact the more vegetable waste we added the more the soil seemed able to assimilate.

"Then gradually the compost era dawned and we found that if we could afford to scatter 3 or 4 boxes of compost round the trees under the drip there was a quick response. Now, as we cannot possibly make enough compost for all our trees, we mix it with the trash and it probably has an action something like a starter. Just as we mix raw rock phosphate with our compost material in making the heaps so we scatter compost among the trash or on the soil.

"In the old days our fruit was inclined to be coarse: now with plenty of organic phosphorus in the soil the quality is much finer and the skins are thinner.

"In a climate like Southern Rhodesia the soil never reaches a temperature low enough to let the bacteria rest so that the burning up of humus continually goes on. Round some trees, dry grass was heaped up inside the drip to a height of 18 inches and pressed down. A little compost had been put on the surface of the soil first. In less than two seasons all trace of the grass had gone. Meanwhile it had hastened its own decomposition and assimilation by providing shelter for the aerobic bacteria to get to work, at the same time keeping the surface moist."

—J. M. MOUBRAY

HOUSE PLANTS

The window box and flower pot must be regarded as miniature, portable gardens. In addition to holding the soil, these containers must be of such nature and construction as to provide adequate drainage and aeration so that the soil will be a favorable environment for the plant roots and the micro-organisms which live in the soil and play important roles in the plant's nutrition.

Some house plants, such as Bromeliads and Cacti, thrive in a soil that would prove to be inadequate for most other plants; others, like the Chinese Evergreen, can get along very well for long periods on just plain water and air; but most of them require a soil high in humus and rich in minerals.

Soils for the window garden are formulated by mixing together in suitable proportions such ingredients as loam, sand, pulverized rocks, and organic matter in the form of compost, leaf mold, muck, and peat. Some suggested potting mixtures are given below:

1. *General Potting Mixture*
   2 parts good garden loam.
   1 part compost, leaf mold, or other fermented organic matter.
   1 part clean coarse sand.
   To the above mixture, add pulverized phosphate

rock and potash rock (granite dust or greensand), each at the rate of a tablespoon for each potful of mixture.

2. *Potting Mixture for Seedlings*

1 part good garden loam.
1 part compost, leaf mold, peat, or other form of humus.
2 parts clean coarse sand.

3. *Potting Mixture for Humus-loving Plants*

1 part good garden loam.
2 parts compost, leaf mold, peat, or other form of humus.
1 part coarse, clean sand.
To this mixture should be added pulverized phosphate rock and potash rock (granite dust or greensand) at the rate of one tablespoon of each for each 6-inch pot of mixture.

4. *Potting Mixture for Cacti*

1 part good garden loam.
2 parts of coarse, clean sand.
1 part broken pots, coarse gravel or small stones.
To this mixture may be added pulverized rock phosphate and potash rock (granite dust or greensand) at the rate of one tablespoon of each for each 6-inch potful of mixture.

These potting mixtures represent various soil types which must be considered in the window garden. Potting mixture 1 will best meet the requirements of many house plants, and particularly those which occur naturally in mineral rather than in organic soils. For woodland plants, as ferns, African violet, primroses, and azaleas in the window garden, use potting mixture 3. The potting mixtures given above may be modified in one way or another to still better meet the requirements of special plants. In the case of acid-loving plants, for instance, acid peat may be added to give the soil an acid reaction, and lime may be added to make a soil mixture neutral or slightly alkaline.

By adding compost and such insoluble but plant-available minerals as phosphate rock and potash rock, the soil in the window box and flower pot will have the capacity of supplying the essential plant nutrients for a relatively long period of time, or until the plant needs to be repotted. This makes unnecessary the feeding of the plants in the window garden with manure water which gives off an unpleasant odor or with soluble chemical salts which usually make the plants susceptible to insects and diseases.

The best forms of humus in making up the potting mixtures are compost and oak leaf mold. If compost is not available, use the leaf mold. This can be collected in almost any woodland, or it can be made from autumnal leaves. If the leaves are shredded and then put in heaps mixed with a small amount of soil, leaf mold can be made in a comparatively short time.

DRAINAGE: One of the most important things to provide for in a soil is drainage. This is best secured by adding sand. Use a clean, sharp sand such as a mason would use for making mortar. If sand from the seashore is used, get it from the shore side of the sand hills, and wash it thoroughly before using in order to remove any salt. If the plants are to stay for a year or so in single pots without repotting (as is the case with palms), charcoal is a distinct advantage, not only because of the better drainage it affords, but also because it prevents the soil from souring.

It is very important to have on hand at all times the ingredients necessary to make up a good potting soil, so in an out-building away from the weather, or in the cellar, have bins in which a 6 months' (if not a year's) supply of the articles just mentioned can be stored. Even manure may be stored in the cellar, if it is well decayed, without the least inconvenience.

Mix the soil thoroughly before planting. The best way to do this is to layer the component parts together and then throw the mass over to make a new pile. Always shovel from the bottom of the pile, and always throw the added matter on the apex of the new pile so that the soil can roll down the sides. If this is done, and the pile turned 3 or 4 times, the soil will be thoroughly mixed.

Before mixing the soil determine whether it is sufficiently moist. This may be told by taking a handful of the soil and pressing it firmly in the hand. If water can be squeezed out, the soil is too damp, and ought not to be worked over until enough dry soil has been added to take up the surplus moisture.

If, after having been pressed in the hand, the soil remains

together, but will break upon being lightly touched, it contains the proper amount of moisture. If it will not remain in a lump but breaks up immediately the pressure is released, it needs more water. Add it by means of a watering pot; the amount necessary can be judged better from experience than by any rules which may be laid down.

Caring for African Violets

When potting African violets, the soil should be a loose, friable one consisting of one-third good garden soil, one-third sand, and one-third peat or leaf mold. To this mixture add one teaspoonful of bonemeal for each quart of mix. The soil should be slightly acid, about pH 6.5. For the beginner and the inexperienced gardener, it is advisable to use one of the well-prepared organic soil mixes on the market. These mixes are complete and especially prepared for violets by experts.

When potting, remember that the roots are delicate and the fine root hairs absorb the nourishment, so care must be taken to pot loosely, gently firming the soil about the roots. The potting mixture should be moist, not wet.

Place a piece of broken flower pot over the drainage hole of a large pot, then ¼-inch layer of chicken grit (or crushed oyster shells or flower pot chips), followed by a wad of sphagnum moss and the potting soil. Just enough potting soil is placed in the pot so that when the root ball is set on it, the crown of the plant is ¼ to ½ inch below the rim of the pot. Now fill in the sides of the pot, tapping gently to settle the soil and prevent air pockets.

(Omit the drainage material and just cover the drainage hole with broken pot chips, if pots are to be watered from below.)

Here is a formula which has been used successfully. It includes no chemicals but only organic ingredients.

    1 pint natural ground phosphate rock
    1 pint natural ground potash rock
    ½ pint natural ground limestone rock
    ½ pint bone meal
    1 pint dehydrated cow manure
    1 pint fine charcoal
    5 pints fine builder's sand
  15 pints coarse baled peat moss, soaked, excess water squeezed out
    2 tbsp. bacterial activator

The advice is to "mix the ingredients thoroughly, keep moist and do not use for at least two weeks; the longer it composts, the better."

Foliage Plants

Foliage plants require less care than flowering plants. They need less sunlight, will stand higher temperatures; many are not injured easily by drying—the main cause of failure with flowering plants. Furthermore, there are fewer insect and disease troubles with foliage plants.

A mixture of one part compost and one part good garden loam is a fine potting mixture for most foliage plants. Other than that, they should need no food at all, except for annual changing of potting soil.

Gardenia

Gardenias demand a very acid soil, with a pH of 4.5 to 5. This may be supplied in well-composted sawdust or oak leaves. Leaves which fall from the plant, as well as its own faded flowers, may be placed on top of the soil to form a self-mulch. In addition, if the foliage shows a tendency to turn yellow, a handful of rotted manure or of cottonseed meal may be mixed with the top layer of soil.

Orchids

All orchids need good drainage and an abundance of air about their roots. For this reason, the most commonly used potting medium is osmunda fiber, the coarse roots of the osmunda ferns. This loose material provides both the correct measures of aeration and drainage, and also feeds the orchids as it decays, making fertilization unnecessary.

In recent years, there has been a trend toward planting orchids in bark, either fir, cedar or pine. Orchids root well in this medium, but it has virtually no food value. This is a big drawback, for little is known about the exact nutrient requirements of many orchids, and a hit-or-miss feeding program can easily ruin the chances of bloom. Diluted manure water and organic fish fertilizer, however, seem to work out well. Bark also dries out more quickly, making more frequent watering necessary.

Other mediums, such as charcoal, vermiculite and certain gravels, have also been tested, but nothing has been found that is all-around better than osmunda. It is inexpensive and meets all the needs of the plants.

Terrestrial orchids are best potted up in mixtures of osmunda, woods soil or leaf mold, sand and manure. Compost can be substituted for the manure, and peat moss for the leaf mold. Brown osmunda, a more aged form, is usually considered better than regular osmunda, and terrestrial orchids are sometimes planted in it alone. In any case, the medium must be very fluffy and porous, like that offered by the forest floor where most of these orchids grow.

With all indoor orchids, the bottom third of the pot should be filled with gravel or broken crock to insure good drainage. Most orchids need repotting every two years.

A good potting mixture for the orchid cactus is one which contains a more moist and richer soil than required by desert types of cacti. A suggested ideal composition consists of two parts loam, two parts leaf mold, one part sharp sand, and half part dried rotted manure, plus a pint of bone meal to each bushel. This soil should be kept rich in humus but porous. Shade well from all strong sunlight.

After the first year some feeding is necessary. Diluted compost and bone meal several times a year are recommended. If a dry fertilizer, such as well-rotted steer or rabbit manure is used, it is not necessary to feed so often. Just before and after the bloom season will do for the balance of the year. Blooming time is from the last of April to the middle of June.

Chapter 10

IS TOO MUCH COMPOST HARMFUL?

Thus far practically nothing can be found in the literature of organic gardening which throws light on the question of a possible overuse of organic matter. Very few, if any, have given much thought to the possible dangers inherent in over-stocking the soil with humus. It is a common belief that we should pile organic matter into our gardens until the earth turns black, and it is the unquenchable ambition of every organiculturist not to rest until that color is attained. But

I wonder if this is desirable! Are we overdoing a good thing and are we plaguing ourselves with unnecessary work?

Some years ago, I received a sample of the soil of the Hunza country in India, sent to me by their mir, or ruler. The citizens of Hunza are an extremely healthy people because they are very conscientious farmers, realizing that their well-being is related directly to soil fertility. I was expecting a dark soil but was greatly surprised to see a greenish tinge to it. It had a powdery aspect, giving it a feeling of finely crumbled rock. Looking at it, you would imagine that it contained no organic matter whatever. We do know that organic matter is scarce in Hunza. Yet there is a sufficient quantity in the soil to give the Hunzukuts wonderful health, because of the quality of food it produces. A good soil today must contain a considerable portion of minute rock particles to make it a proper medium for growing plants and to give it the necessary mineral content. Organic matter contains some minerals but it is also a source of vitaminlike substances of which rock is completely void. Rocks are the main mineral suppliers. To be good, a soil must contain some organic matter, but its physical structure and lack of mineral elements in the rock may militate against producing good crops.

Dr. Ehrenfried Pfeiffer attempted to determine the maximum amount of compost that would be effective in giving the optimum yield on a crop such as peas. He set up an experiment a few years ago, using varying amounts of compost in order to determine whether the use of more would create greater yields. The results indicated that in peas there was an increase in yield up to the use of 5 tons per acre of compost, but beyond that it remained the same. For a gardener, 5 tons per acre is an extremely small amount—about one pound for every 4½ square feet.

Radish Experiments

In the early days of the organic method, I decided to find out how the use of extremely large quantities of compost would affect the growing of radishes. Therefore I set up 3 little plots. In number one no compost was added. In number two a liberal amount was put in, and in number 3 we dug in an amount equivalent to 100 per cent compost. Number two, with its reasonable amount of compost, gave the best radishes, from both the standpoints of size and quality of structure. In the all-compost radishes the insides were coarse-looking.

Let us look at Nature and the way in which she handles her organic matter. In many forests there is a comparatively thick growth of huge trees, but the organic matter of their soil comes from a thin annual layer of fallen leaves. Surely this is a much smaller amount of fertilizer than the average organic practitioner places in his soil. Yet the trees thrive. Think of the gigantic sequoia of California—their size, health, and age. They live off that small amount of fallen leaves, which turns to leaf mold. Of course there is some subtle alchemy that goes on in the soil because of its natural condition, and because of the presence of certain bacteria and other organisms which extract diverse things from the air and make that little go a long way. It used to be thought that the soil organisms get only nitrogen from the air. There is now evidence that they also do the same thing in regard to phosphorus. Who knows? Before all the results are in, it may be discovered that soil bacteria extract even trace minerals from the atmosphere.

Chandler, at Cornell University, in a series of studies, found that mixed hardwood trees on a Lordstown silt-loam soil produced annually 1¼ tons of dry-leaf material per acre. On other soils (Ontario silt loam), it was 1½ tons. In France the figure for beech trees was 1½ tons of organic matter to the acre annually. In a crop of oats amounting to about 40 bushels to the acre, the dry matter in the grain and straw was about the same amount. These are reasonable amounts. But some gardeners put into their soils the equivalent of 100 tons to the acre per annum.

In the field, also, Nature is not too liberal in giving sustenance. Frugality seems to be her watchword. Here organic matter is doled out sparingly. In the tropics, however, where the humus burns out more rapidly, the growth of plants is lush and more abundant, so that its decay furnishes more humus than in more temperate climates. It is amazing how, in Nature, the requirement for sustenance thus automatically adjusts itself. When a tree is young, and its food requirements little, there is a small amount of leaf fall. As it grows and its requirements increase, the leaf fall goes up accordingly. Is there something we can learn from this?

Of course we have the problem of getting a "yield," but if the necessary research could be done, we might find, like Pfeiffer did, that the amount of organic matter required to obtain an optimum crop is nowhere near what present thinking imagines it is.

Leafage vs. Fruit

One of the dangers of using too much organic matter is that in many crops there would be too much development of leaf because of the nitrogen in the humus. The latter seems to be a good provider of nitrogen, and this element is very effective in producing vegetative growth. I distinctly remember a small apple tree to which we gave so much compost that a visiting agricultural professor, seeing it, remarked, "What wonderful leaves!" They were the thickest he had ever seen. But he wasn't there a few months later to observe the poor fruit that formed. Too much of the sustenance had gone to the leaves.

I wrote to Stark Bros. Nurseries, famous growers of fruit trees in Louisiana, Missouri, asking their opinion of the effect of too much nitrogen. They replied, "In our experience the most obvious results from the use of an excess of nitrogen on apple trees are later maturity and less red color in the skin. In the case of late fall and winter apples, there is a reduction in the sugar in the fruit and some varieties never develop a satisfactory flavor."

Dr. Selman A. Waksman, the recent Nobel prize winner and a world authority on humus, says in his book *Humus:* "Too much organic matter, especially from legumes (high in nitrogen), may not be very desirable, because it favors excessive vegetative growth of the trees."

Flower gardeners may also have noticed that bulbs and some root crops may be damaged in soils too high in organic matter content. There are some flowers that do not do well on too much compost. Here, for example, is a list of flowers which Mandeville and King suggest require a poor soil: alyssum, bachelor's-button, calliopsis, candytuft, celosia, clarkia, cosmos, 4-o'clock, godetia, kochia, nasturtium, California poppy, Shirley poppy, portulaca and verbena. Alyssum, candytuft, nasturtium and California poppy especially give best results if grown in a poor soil.

Is it possible, also, that too much compost produces oversucculence which entices the insect? There is some evidence that overcomposting may be one of the agents in drawing insects. We saw it in our own experience with the Mexican bean beetle. This is one insect that we do not seem to be able to control in our gardens. One year, however, when we grew beans on some new ground that had received compost for the first time, the beans were far less infested with the Mexican beetle than a batch of beans growing on a soil not far away which had received compost every year for about 10 years. That experience first led me to consider whether there wasn't some harm in overdoing composting.

Insects and Lushness

The insect is not here by accident. It is part of Nature's scheme to keep things in order. She used the insect to destroy unwanted vegetation. If a growing plant is unbalanced in its nutritional content by reason of artificial methods of fertilization, if it is grown on the wrong kind of soil, as potatoes on clay with little organic matter, if an acid-loving plant is growing on an alkaline soil, if it becomes sick for any reason at all, the insects will come to attempt to destroy it. Then there is war. It is man with his spray guns against the winged enemy. There is much evidence of this role of the insect, and it is reflected in writings about the organic method. A bug, with a few exceptions, rarely comes to attack a healthy plant which is growing under the proper conditions and in the right place.

Now, if a plant is growing on a soil which has been overcomposted, it may become a candidate, from Nature's point of view, for a visit from her tiny winged policemen. There might be something about such a plant which is not quite right. Perhaps it is an oversupply of nitrogen.

We receive letters from time to time from readers who complain that although they do everything we tell them to, they still have some trouble with their vegetables. This type of letter does not come too often, but it baffles me. A gardener writes that his tomato vines produce only small tomatoes, or none at all. Could it be due to an overcomposting, the excess of nitrogen going all to leaf, leaving little for the fruit itself?

I recall reading in one of Alexis Carrel's books that a plant which grows too fast is not a healthy plant. He states that a slow, steady growth makes for the best conditions of health. We know that on the average those people who eat frugally live the longest. There is the classical case of Luigi Cornaro, who lived in Italy in the fifteen hundreds, and who was given up by his physician in his forties, because of poor health. He worked out a diet so small in quantity that it seemed almost starvation. But he lived to be close to 100. Medical literature is replete with experiments which prove that animals on diets of less food have less cancer. In Europe the austerity conditions and food shortages brought about by the war showed up very favorably in the mortality and health statistics. There was less disease. Today, with all their food difficulties and starvation diets, the English have a longer life span than we do. Statistics kept by the life-insurance companies show unquestionably that obesity, which is due to overconsumption of food, causes earlier deaths. Should we consider a plant growing in an overcomposted soil which shows an excellent growth and size as obese rather than succulent?

Dr. J. K. Wilson's Work with Nitrogen

There is some proof that too much nitrogen may be a hazard to health, and since humus is the principal agent that furnishes nitrogen in the soil, we have another worry now to consider. The late Dr. J. K. Wilson of Cornell wrote in the January, 1949 issue of the *Agronomy Journal* that nitrites could cause poisoning through combination with the blood. He shows that possibly in rural regions nitrates from fertilizer seep into wells and cause a disease in babies drinking such water. This disease is called methemoglobinemia, or blue-baby disease. In 1947 in Illinois alone there were 33 cases, with 5 deaths. Dr. Wilson found that there was danger from the overconsumption of leafy plants which may contain too much nitrite and recommended that the following should not be overconsumed: broccoli, cabbage, cauliflower, and rhubarb. In other words, if our soil is overcharged with nitrogen through applying too much compost, there might be a danger of our leafy vegetables taking up too much of it. Dr. Wilson sums up the subject as follows: "Leafy vegetables, frozen foods, and prepared baby foods were analyzed for their content of nitrate. From the findings it is suggested that the nitrate in such foods may contribute to hemoglobinemia found in infants and may produce certain toxic, if not lethal, conditions in adults. The high content of nitrate in the foods may be attributed in many instances to the application of nitrogenous fertilizers, especially nitrate of soda, to the growing crops."

The point brought up by Dr. Wilson may not apply to organically produced vegetables, but can we be certain of it without thorough research into the subject? According to his article, it is a question of the stability of the nitrogen compound. In the form of nitrates, the nitrogen is not harmful, but due to instability some of the nitrate turns to nitrite, and it is only the latter form that is lethal. Is the nitrate in organically grown vegetables more stable? That is something which has not been proven.

There is a vast amount of research that proves unquestionably that too much nitrogen in a plant opens it up to a host of diseases and conditions. One writer refers to how plants may go on a "nitrogen jag." He describes an experiment with rabbits which were given an opportunity to eat grasses treated with varying amounts of nitrogen. They always avoided grass that was grown with too much nitrogen, leaving it to the very last and consuming it only to avoid starvation.

There is evidence that a large amount of nitrogen encourages the production of soft, succulent tissue which bruises more easily and is susceptible to the attack of disease —mildew, verticillium wilt, virus infections, etc. The evidence is too conclusive to be ignored.

In conclusion, on this point of too much compost, you might ask: "Are you attempting to break down the organic method?" I would reply, "No. I am attempting to strengthen it by maintaining an open mind." This is merely an exploratory bit of writing. I am not going to take too definite a stand on the subject. Let us check and observe and decide later. Why kill yourself by lugging too much organic matter for your compost heap? Bear in mind that as the store of humus in your soil rises there will be an increase of the earthworms and soil microorganisms. They will do part of the job for you. Let us not overdo a good thing.

Chapter 11

COMPOSTING METHODS
FOR THE FARMER

METHODS FOR INDIVIDUAL FARMS

Most farmers appreciate the value of animal manure as a fertilizer, and many have found that the composting of organic materials such as straw, weeds, leaves, sawdust, and other types of litter is economic as well as important in maintaining the fertility of their soil at a high level. However, very often little attention is given to utilizing the most efficient techniques for effecting sanitary treatment, maximum reclamation of nutrients, and production of good-quality compost.

Composting by correct techniques will: (a) produce a humus which has a C/N ratio satisfactory for application to the soil; (b) effect maximum conservation of nitrogen, phosphorus, potash, and other nutrients; (c) destroy weed seeds in the organic litter and pathogenic organisms and parasites in the manures; (d) reduce fly-breeding on the farm; and (e) provide a means for the sanitary disposal of farm wastes. Composting in stacks and pits is the most satisfactory way of controlling, processing and storing farm manures and wastes.

Building of Stacks and Pits

The stabilization of manure and organic litter can be effected in pits or on a slab on the ground surface. It is seldom that a farm has sufficient manure and litter to permit the building, at least once a week, of an individual compost stack which is sufficiently large to maintain high temperatures. Therefore, stacks to which material is added as it becomes available over a period of several weeks must generally be used. Handling and stacking of manure and litter will usually be done by hand labor with pitchforks. However, the use of machinery for conveying the material to the stack and loading the final humus on to carts or trucks may be economical on large stock and dairy farms.

Cattle manure supplies the greatest amount of material for the composting operations of many farms. Properly made compost conserves the nutrient value of manure, and makes useful organic materials which might otherwise be destroyed.

The size and number of pits or stacks to be used depends on the amount of manure and wastes available. Farms with 1 to 4 animals should provide for only one pit or stack, which should be of sufficient size to contain the manure for a period of approximately 5 to 6 months in cold climates, and 3 to 4 months in warm climates. Farms which stable a larger number of animals will find it more satisfactory to have two or more pits or stacks, so that one can be finishing composting during the period when the other is being filled. One horse or cow which is stabled will produce 10 to 16 tons of manure per year.

A compost pit can be built of concrete or masonry. The area should be such as to provide the desired volume when the pile of material to be composted is 4 to 5 feet high. The walls of the pit should be about two feet high, and the pit may either be sunk in the ground or placed on the surface. The walls prevent surface drainage from entering the stack and leaching out valuable nutrients, and also permit the retention of any liquid drainage from the manure, which contains large concentrations of dissolved nutrients. An

394

Equipment is all-important to farm composting operations. Since manure contains a fairly large amount of nitrogen, it's important to add organic litter. Another recommended practice is to place a layer of coarse cellulose material at the bottom.

outlet may be placed in the corner of the pit to permit the drainage to flow into a concrete or masonry sump. The walled pit also helps to control fly-breeding and prevents pieces of manure and litter from being scattered around the ground by chickens.

The sides of the manure piles can be nearly vertical when there is sufficient straw and litter in the manure to allow stacking. The top should be slightly rounded to turn rain water and prevent seepage through the stack.

The urine from the stable should be drained either to the sump of the compost pit or to a separate sump, constructed, in the same manner as the pit-drainage sump, at an appropriate place to intercept it. If there is insufficient straw and other organic litter available to provide adequate absorption and retention of the liquid drainage from the manure pile and the stable urine, a large liquid-tight sump of 200 gallons capacity, or larger, depending on the number of animals and the rainfall, should be used to collect and contain all the liquid manure. The liquid from the sump should be removed as necessary and sprayed on the land. Since this liquid contains large concentrations of chemical nutrients it should not be wasted. Absorption of the liquid by litter waste

395

is usually more satisfactory from the standpoint of maximum conservation of nutrients and development of soil humus; however, most of the nutrients can be recovered from the liquid by spraying it on the fields.

The size of the stack is determined by the amount of organic waste material available and the time the material will remain in the stack, as described above for the compost pit. It is desirable to have a concrete or masonry slab under the stack and a sump for catching the drainage. If the cost of a slab is too great, a reasonably satisfactory base for the stack can be made by packing the ground surface and, if possible, placing on top a layer of packed clay, which will be relatively impervious. The ground should be sloped so that any drainage from the stack can be caught in a small sump, filled with straw or other litter to absorb the nutrients.

If the manure is placed on a concrete or masonry slab, a 6-inch deep channel can be made in the slab around the edges of the manure stack to trap fly larvae and pupae which move to the outer edges of the stack to escape the high temperature. The inside edge of the channel should be raised about one inch so that drainage from the stack will flow to the sump and not enter the channel. The channel is kept filled with water in which the larvae are trapped. The channel is not effective as a larvae trap, however, unless it is cleaned and refilled frequently; as this is usually neglected by the farmer, its provision in the slab is of questionable value.

Addition of Litter to Manure Piles

The placing of a layer of straw, cane stalks, or other coarse cellulose material on the bottom of a compost stack is very important for the retention of nutrients and development of humus. The layer should be at least 12 to 18 inches deep so that it will pack to no less than 3 or 4 inches when subjected to the weight of the stack. This porous layer of cellulose material will provide some air for composting and will absorb a considerable amount of the manure drainage. Since this type of cellulose material has a low content of nitrogen and other nutrients and the manure and urine have a high one, it will absorb excess nutrients and decompose into a rich humus. The provision of this layer on the bottom is particularly important when the compost pile is built directly on the ground.

Since most manure contains large amounts of nitrogen,

Above you see compost heaps being turned at the Organic Experimental Farm. No artificial nitrogen or other mineral fertilizers have been used, yet the soil there is so fertile and productive that no such artificial application is needed for crops.

some of which may be lost in composting, any type of organic litter can be added satisfactorily to the manure pile and composted. The resulting humus will be very satisfactory for use as fertilizer, the amount of humus will be increased, and the nitrogen loss will be decreased. A manure pile can be a repository for weeds, live fence or hedge trimmings, and waste organic materials which might otherwise be burned with a resultant loss of nutrients and humus.

To minimize fly-breeding, droppings from the sides of the stack or pit should be picked up immediately and placed on the stack. Feces and garbage are most attractive to flies, whereas organic litter is not very attractive. Hence, placing the manure which contains large amounts of fecal material on the inside of the pile and the manure which contains more straw and litter on the top and sides will help to reduce fly-breeding. More information on manure handling appears in the chapter on that subject.

—H. B. GOTAAS, *Composting*, World Health Organization

SHEET COMPOSTING FOR THE FARM

The development of sheet composting was a boon to the organic farmer, as well as to the gardener with space to spare. In sheet composting the raw organic material, instead of being processed on the compost heap, is incorporated directly into the surface layer of soil, where it is quickly decomposed. The obvious advantage of this method is that of saving time and effort in building heaps and transporting materials. Most gardeners, however, find sheet composting unsatisfactory because they are seldom willing to take a section of the garden out of production for several months.

Sir Albert Howard maintained that subsoiling, the reform of the manure heap and sheet composting are 3 of the most important agricultural practices. The raw materials for sheet composting he described as: "(1) vegetable residues in the form of the stubble and roots of crops like cereals; (2) temporary pastures due for plowing up, which must always contain deep-rooting plants and herbs; and (3) green-manures, catch crops and weeds."

In his mind, sheet composting was merely a supplement to the practice of composting in heaps. It was a device to keep the land actively producing humus at all times and to prevent the loss of nitrogen, which leaches and escapes when organic matter is not decaying in the soil, or when a legume is not growing.

But with the advance of organic farming the compost heap has been largely left behind as too cumbersome and wasteful. Since it is well known that organic matter is valuable to the soil only while decaying, why not let all the processes of decay take place in the soil itself? That thought above all others has been responsible for the current popularity of sheet composting.

Here are the basic principles underlying sheet composting:

1. Always have the soil protected by a crop of some kind, or by weeds if no crop is growing. Vegetable matter must always be being produced by the soil. Only by such continual growth will the full energy of the sun be harnessed for the benefit of the soil.

2. Whenever possible, hasten the soil's production of humus by mixing what is growing into the surface of the soil, by any tillage method you find convenient or practical.

Together with subsoiling and improved heap composting methods, the adaptation of sheet composting is regarded as one of the most important agricultural practices. Modern equipment incorporates organic material directly into the surface layer.

3. *Help the soil produce humus yourself by replacing that organic matter that is taken off by cropping.* Only by so doing can the permanent fertility and productivity of the soil be maintained.

The practical methods by which these goals can be reached are many and varied. Each change in climate and crop grown and method of production makes necessary a new approach to sheet composting.

A farmer who lives in a lumbering region and has plenty of sawdust available has his problems solved. He can load up his manure spreader with sawdust every chance he gets and so supply to the soil the organic matter his crops take from it. So many farmers are doing that today, at the urging of the state experiment stations, that sawdust is becoming a scarce commodity in many places.

But the first step to be taken is the growing of a green manure crop. Although the green manure crop is not the whole answer, it is the backbone around which the sheet composting program revolves.

Growing of a cover crop is the first step in the sheet composting program. The photograph shows a cover crop prior to being tilled into the soil when it has reached full growth. Sheet composting is an excellent method of returning humus.

To do a decent job of sheet composting, land must be taken out of production for at least a half-year or a year. When you consider that once you begin farming organically you no longer have to spend money for chemicals, you can well afford that period of rest and recuperation for your soil. The best time for a green manure crop to reach plowing-in time is, of course, late spring or early summer. It is then possible to compost a second time by sowing another cover or green manure crop on the sheet composted land.

Another advantage of the late spring schedule is the fact that by that time you have the benefit of a winter's accumulation of manure from your animals. For before the green manure crop can be plowed in it is very necessary that the soil be given a supplementary covering of organic matter— the return of that which has been taken from her by crops.

Manure is ideal. Spoiled hay, corn cobs, cannery wastes, seaweed, wood chips and even straw all add that extra spark which benefits the soil all out of proportion to what you would expect. Green manuring is merely a replacing of organic matter. To add to what has been depleted from your soil that only answer is the extra tonic of organic wastes. Experiments have shown that the plowing in of a green manure crop every year will merely *prevent the depletion* of organic matter.

400

Manure is an ideal combination with green matter in the sheet composting program. Above you see manure being loaded into a spreader prior to distribution. Application rate is from 3 to 5 tons per acre, often mixed with rock powders.

If your soil does have a normal amount of organic matter and your objective is to increase quickly its mineral content, then plow in your green crop when it is in the young stage. If your main need is to increase the humus content of your soil, then wait until the green manure crop has reached its maximum growth.

One of the most important values of sheet composting is the fact that while the composting process is taking place the soil's nitrogen supply is being held in readiness for use by the following crop. There is a definite relation between the amount of organic matter in the soil and its content of nitrogen. So close is this relationship that you can predict accurately the amount present of one by the soil's content of the other.

It is always recommended that a cash crop not be planted immediately after a piece of land has been sheet composted, as the soil's nitrogen supply is being tied up by the bacteria that are breaking down the raw organic matter. The nitrogen is most certainly there, but a seed placed in the soil would not benefit by it until the composting process has progressed for a month or two. If a leguminous cover crop is plowed in at the

401

time the soil is sheet composted, the soil's nitrogen supply will be greater and the time lag before a crop can be planted will be shorter.

Here is another fact about soil nitrogen and sheet composting that should be realized. After your soil has been treated organically for some time it will be so rich in organic matter, bacteria and nitrogen that it will be able to take all kinds of mistreatment and still produce a fine crop. Such a soil can be seeded almost immediately after sheet composting and no ill effects will be noted. In an organic-rich soil the nitrogen forming bacteria operate the same way they do in a compost heap—constantly pulling nitrogen from the air into the soil.

No artificial nitrogen fertilizers have ever been used on the soil of The Organic Experimental Farm, yet the soil there is so rich in nitrogen that no more is needed. For a comparison talk to a farmer who has used chemicals for years and has therefore unbalanced the bacterial life in his soil. He will tell you that the chemical nitrogen that he puts on his soil just doesn't seem to last. Contrast those two conditions and decide which you would like to have on your farm.

The organic method is not a package deal, like the use of chemical fertilizers. The chemical farmer can in one application put on his soil what he is told is a complete source of nutrients for his plants. And that is that. His obligation to the soil for that year is over.

But the organic farmer can never rest. True, he can purchase a balanced diet of rock fertilizers—phosphate rock, greensand, granite dust and limestone—but to a successful organic farmer they can only ever be a supplement to the sheet composting method. The organic matter in the soil must be maintained, and doing that is a never-ending challenge to the wits of the individual farmer.

He must be able to analyze his climate, the crops he can grow and his sources of organic matter. He must choose his green manure crops carefully. Soybeans, kudzu, reseeding crimson clover, white clover, alfalfa and vetch are excellent, but in some areas one will work better than the other.

The factors involved in sheet composting are basically identical to those of the Indore method. For best results, all factors must be favorable and must act together.

Green matter, for instance, instead of being carried to the heap, and then carried back to the soil, is grown and

After spreading manure, lime and rock fertilizers over the cover crop, farmers will then work these materials into the soil surface. Rotary tillers, plows (no deeper than 5 inches), disks—these are some suitable tools for digging in organic matter.

reinvested into the soil at the same place—saving two time-consuming and laborious steps in the composting process. Recommended cover crops are kudzu beans, sweet clover, other clovers, alfalfa, soy and other beans, crotolaria, vetch and other legumes, brome and other grasses; and for soils lower in fertility, rye and buckwheat. The growing of these cover crops requires no special equipment. They are worked into the soil with manure and lime to form compost.

Manure can be applied in the regular way with a manure spreader at the rate of from 3 to 5 tons per acre. The raw limestone which has been pulverized to colloidal particles may be applied with the manure, or may be drilled in the field with a regular lime drill.

After the manure and lime have been spread over the cover crop, all these materials must be incorporated into the surface layer of the soil. It matters little with what equipment this is done, so long as the organic matter is near enough the surface of the soil where there is sufficient oxygen from the air to enable the aerobic organisms to break down the organic matter and convert it into humus. If the plow is used, do not plow deeper than 4 or 5 inches. Other suitable equipment include the disk, rotary tillers, and other types of tillers.

The moisture necessary for the composting process is inherent in the green matter and the soil, and is renewed from time to time by the precipitation of water out of the atmosphere. The moisture factor is important, and must be just right if humus manufacture in the soil is to succeed. It should not be attempted in regions where sufficient water is not available in the form of rain or irrigation water. The rate of composting will vary also with the temperature, and will proceed most rapidly when aeration, moisture, and temperature all are optimum for the organisms of decomposition.

As soon as the organic materials have been worked into the soil and to the extent that environmental conditions are favorable, decomposition begins. The soil organisms secrete digestive enzymes which digest the carbohydrates: sugars, starches, celluloses, and lignins; the proteins; and the fats in the soil in much the same way as the digestive juices in the intestinal tract of an animal break these substances into simpler water-soluble compounds. The composting process begins slowly but increases rapidly just like a fire which consumes a brush pile or other organic matter.

During the time the soil organisms are consuming the organic matter in the soil, they often use the available plant nutrients for their own use. It is for this reason that a soil cannot grow a crop at the same time humus is being made in it. The soil will invariably give preference to the making of humus.

The time required for the complete transformation of raw organic matter into humus depends upon the nature of the soil, the amount of organic matter involved, and the conditions which favor the activity of the soil organisms. Any farmer can, by digging into the soil, determine how the decomposition is progressing, and when it is complete. This is no more difficult than checking a baking potato or a fowl in the oven by the housewife. Some kinds of plant material will break down more rapidly than others. Cellulose breaks down more rapidly than lignin. Leguminous plants break down much more rapidly than the straw of wheat and other grains. Accordingly leguminous cover crops lend themselves especially well to the sheet composting method of fertilization.

When the organic matter has been more or less completely

By digging into the soil and exposing a cross section, the farmer can determine the progress of decomposition of his sheet-composted material. Leguminous plants break down more rapidly than other grasses or grains, allow planting sooner.

converted into humus, the crop may be planted. With some crops, as Indian corn, the seeds may be planted before the sheet composting process is entirely complete because the corn kernel contains sufficient food to feed the corn seedling for two weeks or more. But humus formation in the soil should be completed by the time the fibrous roots develop from the base of the young plant and reach out for nutrients for the growing corn plants.

How Organic Matter Penetrates Soil

A good idea of how organic matter penetrates down into the soil and improves soil structure is found in the results obtained by Remé Bétrémieux and Lucien Turc, French scientists, as a result of some pertinent research they have been doing on the evolution and migration of organic matter in the soil and its influence on soil structure.

The scientists found, on making soil tests 6 months after the addition of lucerne to the soil, that about $\frac{1}{8}$ of the free organic matter had penetrated down to a depth of two inches. And about $\frac{1}{17}$ of the free organic matter had penetrated down as far as the 4 inch depth.

Soil analysis showed that about $\frac{1}{5}$ of the carbon and nitrogen added to the soil in the lucerne was fixed in the soil

COVERCROP CHARACTERISTICS

Compiled by B. A. MADSON
Agronomist, California Extension Service

Crop	Density of growth	Soil	Type of growth	Cost of seed	Rate of seeding (pounds per acre)
Legumes					
Common vetch	Moderate	Loam	Succulent	Moderate	60-75
Purple vetch	Moderate to heavy	Loam	Succulent	Moderate to low	50-65
Hairy vetch	Moderate to heavy	Sand loam	Succulent	High	40-50
Calcarata vetch	Moderate	Loam to heavy	Succulent	High	30-50
Monantha vetch	Moderate	Loam to heavy	Succulent	Moderate to low	50-60
Hungarian vetch	Moderate	Loam to heavy	Succulent	Moderate to low	60-75
Bitter vetch	Moderate	Loam to heavy	Stemmy	High	35-50
Horse beans	Moderate to heavy	Loam to heavy	Stemmy	High	125-175
Tangier peas	Heavy	Loam to heavy	Succulent	High	80-110
Wedge peas	Light	Loam to heavy	Succulent	High	80-110
Field peas (Canada)	Moderate	Loam to heavy	Succulent	Moderate	75-100
Field peas (Aus. winter)	Moderate	Loam to heavy	Succulent	Moderate	70-90
Fenugreek	Light	Loam to heavy	Stemmy	Moderate	35-45
Bur clover	Light	Loam	Succulent	Moderate	20-30
Nonlegumes					
Mustards	Heavy	Loam to heavy	Stemmy	Moderate	15-20
Wheat	Moderate	Loam to heavy	Succulent	Moderate	60-90
Barley	Moderate to heavy	Loam to heavy	Succulent	Moderate	60-90
Oats	Moderate to heavy	Loam to heavy	Succulent	Moderate	60-90
Rye	Moderate to heavy	Sandy to heavy	Succulent	Moderate	60-90

organic matter giving an increase of about 50 per cent. There was also a slight increase in the carbon to nitrogen ratio.

One of the more important points that the scientists noted was that the decomposition of the lucerne caused a marked increase in the water stability of soil aggregates. This was particularly noticeable in the layer of soil which was 2-4 inches below the surface.

GREEN MANURE CROPS FOR TRACE ELEMENTS

Right in your own backyard—or lower "40"—that's where you'll find your trace element fertilizers. Just as he can grow or find the major plant food materials right on his own land, so can the organic farmer find these rare and mysterious elements, the micronutrients.

There are plants that have the ability to *collect trace minerals from the soil*. They can store up in their tissues up to several hundred times the amount contained in an equal weight of soil.

The horsetail plant, for instance, can seek out and blot up as much as 4.5 ounces of gold per ton, 600 times the gold content of the surrounding soil. Loco weeds, the pea-like herbs that poison cattle, concentrate in their leaves and stems 300 times as much selenium as is found in the soil around them.

This is equally true, with many plants, for the trace minerals found to be vital for crops and animals.

The wide-awake farmer will find this a definite advantage. It gives him a means of overcoming trace element deficiencies without resorting to the use of harmful chemicals. These deficiencies are widespread today, perhaps more so than we realize. Even where we thought we have produced good crops, trace element additions to the soil have raised yields, sometimes amazingly. If all our trace element needs were met, who knows what "super crops" and "super animals" we might raise? Some noted scientists go so far as to say that human life span might be greatly lengthened if our foods contained the proper amounts of these minerals.

Although trace elements may constitute less than one per cent of the total dry matter of a plant, they are often the factor that determines the health of the plant. Some soils are naturally deficient in trace minerals. Others have been made deficient by erosion, intensive cropping, loss of organic matter and chemicals.

TRACE MINERALS — Table

Trace Minerals	Where Deficient	Required By	Hunger Signs	Accumulator Plants and Other Sources
BORON	Widespread	Plants	Dwarfing of alfalfa, heart rot of beets, corking of apples, stem cracking in celery, discoloration of cauliflower	Vetch Sweet clover Muskmelon leaves Granite dust
COBALT	East and North Central States	Animals	Anemia, muscular atrophy, depraved appetite, poor growth	Vetch Most legumes Kentucky bluegrass Peach tree refuse Basic rocks
COPPER	Atlantic Coast States	Animals and Plants	Paralysis, anemia, falling in animals; poor growth, dwarfing of tomatoes, dieback of citrus trees in plants	Redtop Bromegrass Spinach Tobacco Dandelions Kentucky bluegrass Lignin (wood shavings, sawdust)
IRON	Southeast	Animals and Plants	Anemia, salt sickness in animals; chlorosis in plants	Many weeds
MANGANESE	Many varied soils	Animals and Plants	Poor milk production, deformity of hogs, poultry; poor growth, chlorosis of tomatoes, gray speck of oats and peas, poor leaf color in plants	Forest leaf mold (especially hickory, white oak) Alfalfa Carrot tops Redtop Bromegrass
MOLYBDENUM	Many varied soils	Plants	Necrosis of leaf edges	Vetch Alfalfa Rock phosphate
ZINC	West Coast and South	Animals and Plants	Hair loss, skin thickening in animals; poor fruiting, dieback in citrus, white bud in corn, top blight of some nut trees	Cornstalks Vetch Ragweed, Horsetail Poplar and hickory leaves Peach tree clippings

Much of the trouble caused by trace element deficiencies can be eliminated by making the best use of accumulator plants, some of which are listed in column at far right.

Quick-acting chemical fertilizers, through the medium of base exchange, release the trace elements locked up in the soil colloids very rapidly. Conversely, says the U.S.D.A. Bureau of Chemistry and Soils, the use of organic plant foods like animal and green manures, compost, wood ashes, tankage and the like tends to conserve them.

That's one reason why European farmers consistently get 75 bushels of wheat from soil tilled for hundreds of years, with never a worry about trace element lacks. Constant manuring always returned at least some of the elements removed by crops. Too, the high organic matter content thus maintained helped release all the trace minerals present.

Composts and sewage sludge are excellent for correcting natural and man-made deficiencies. Coming from all over the earth, garbage and sewage composts contain the wastes of New Jersey carrots, California oranges, Brazilian coffee—hundreds of organic materials sure to provide a wealth of varied trace elements. Seaweed and fish fertilizers are also high in them, especially in the iodine needed by animals and man.

Adding trace minerals in chemical form can be highly dangerous. As with most chemical fertilizers, it is all too often an art to apply them. Many are needed only in tiny amounts—more than one ounce of molybdenum per acre will make pasture plants so toxic they poison animals eating them. In some soils, only 20 pounds of chemical boron can ruin a potato crop. Each species of plant has its own requirements and tolerances. Too, a little too much of one element may make it "displace" another. Some need others to work—cobalt needs copper and iron present before it can cure certain cattle illnesses.

Trace element troubles are often due to imbalances rather than deficiencies. Using organic materials, such as rock dusts and the "accumulator" plants, will give your soil a balanced diet. (You can also use agricultural frit as a source of trace elements. Although marketed by duPont, it borders on being a natural trace element source—consisting of mineral-rich pulverized glass.)

Eliminate Deficiencies

For specific deficiencies, you can sheet-compost or apply as a mulch the accumulator plant richest in the needed element. Some can be grown as a green manure.

The table gives an indication of the plants to use. Apply them when needed or regularly to insure a balanced supply of trace elements. Don't overlook Nature's bounty—leaves, for instance, are often twice as rich in minerals as manure. Weeds, too, because they bring up trace elements from the subsoil, are rich sources. Corn grown uncultivated with ragweed yield up to 60 per cent higher, and is more disease-resistant.

Unlike chemicals, these materials also maintain both soil pH and structure, and increase its vital microorganisms. All these affect the availability of the trace elements.

Just how important these elements are to the farmer we have only begun to realize. The McCollum-Pratt Institute for the Investigation of Micronutrients recently found that variations in the trace mineral supply produce definite changes in the enzyme concentration of a plant, thus affecting its quality as well as yield. Even trace elements considered non-essential have been found to act this way. Thus we may some day discover that even the "rare earths"—yttrium, lanthanum, dysprosium and others present in the minutest quantities— are needed by plants, another reason for supplying a balanced organic diet.

COMPOST LITTER METHOD FOR POULTRY

A new thick litter method in poultry raising, which had been developed by Prof. Kennard from the older "built-up litter system," was introduced to the Dutch Division of the World's Poultry Science Association. Experiments both in America and the Netherlands brought results so favorable that the method has come into widespread use here and throughout Holland.

The following notes, taken from an Information Bulletin of the International Research Group on Refuse Disposal, outline this effective deep litter method, explaining how it benefits poultry and the poultry raiser, and provides a litter compost of high fertilizing value at the same time:

In the thick litter method, hens and chicks are left in pens on a 30-50 centimeter thick layer of organic matter such as straw, corncobs, wood shavings, horse manure, peat bedding, and, recently, refuse compost. The fowls spend their entire life on this bedding, never being let into the open. The bedding may be used for 3 to 4 years without renewal, assuming that an intensive bacterial flora with heat production therein is correctly maintained. It is necessary to control the temperature of the bedding layer. If necessary the bedding layer can be turned (aerated) or fresh organic matter may be mixed with it. The bedding must not be too damp (danger of rot) which can occur particularly in winter in poorly aerated pens. A strong ammonia odor is an indication that the aeration is insufficient. But the bedding layer must not become too dry or the microorganisms will cease their activity. In this case the bedding must be sprinkled with water and then stirred up.

With proper use the following advantages are provided by this method:

(1) Labor saving. The bedding no longer has to be changed every 7-14 days. A thick litter bedding may be used for at least 3 years.

(2) The fowls always have a warm bedding which is of greatest importance, especially in winter. Thus fewer diseases occur. On bedding that is too cold the chicks tend to huddle too closely together and many victims of asphyxiation are found.

(3) Mortality is lower because fewer infectious diseases occur. The greatest danger in chick-raising is caecal coccidiosis, and most losses are traced to it. With the use of the deep litter method, coccidiosis almost never has a fatal outcome and the use of drugs, such as sulfonamides, is unnecessary. Ammonia is formed with the decomposition of chicken manure in the deep litter bed and serves effectively in controlling the oocysts of coccidiosis. Although chicks become infected with coccidiosis, the disease takes a very mild course. The chicks form antibodies which prevent later infections. Perhaps antibiotics also play a role in this connection but nothing is definitely known yet.

(4) Cannibalism subsides markedly. It frequently appears in poultry raising and can cause much damage. Why cannibalism fails to appear or is significantly less among chickens raised on deep litters is not understood. Perhaps the fowls on deep litter are occupied the whole day with scratching and picking, especially if feed is strewn on top of the litter. Because of the scratching, the animals have more exercise which is beneficial to their health.

(5) Better growth of fowls on the deep litter. In all experiments the weight of fowls raised on deep litter was at least 10 per cent greater than that of fowls raised by the hygienic method. Ten-week old chicks raised on deep litter had the same weight as 12-week old chicks maintained on standard bedding in one experiment. Probably the animal proteins, also vitamin B-12, contained in deep litter play a significant role.

(6) Better results in brooders with eggs from fowls

raised on deep litter. This factor may also be ascribed to animal protein factors.

(7) Space savings. The opinion prevailed until recently that chickens needed to run in the open with provision of at least 15 square metres per fowl, preferably on a grassy plot. The new deep litter method has shown that such runway is not only unnecessary but even undesirable as the runway area is eventually always infested with intestinal parasites (among others, coccidiosis and worms). The danger of intestinal infections is therefore considerably increased. The deep litter method has shown more advantage in maintaining chickens permanently in pens. Space requirements are barely one square metre for 3 hens and loss from infectious diseases is very considerably diminished.

The deep litter method is now generally used in the Netherlands and many poultry raisers use urban refuse compost for this because it is cheap and easily worked. Other materials such as straw, wood shavings, etc., are also mixed with the compost. As refuse compost contains valuable mineral components (phosphoric acid, lime, trace elements), it is particularly well suited for this purpose. After use in chicken pens, the compost has acquired very high fertilizing value and can be used to considerable advantage in farm or garden soil improvement, or may be sold for this purpose. Experiments are in process in the Netherlands using raw refuse alone as a thick litter bedding. The material soon dries out because of the resultant high temperatures and must therefore be rewetted from time to time. Results to date are very promising.

—B. TEENSMA, Engineer Amsterdam

(Information Bulletin No. 4, International Research Group on Refuse Disposal.)

ANAEROBIC COMPOSTING FOR THE FARM

Up until quite recently, digesters were designed only for very large composting operations, viz., municipal projects. There has, however, been invented an anaerobic composter which is practical to build for farm use. Following is a report on the farm digester, written by Clarence G. Golueke, research biologist at the Sanitary Engineering Research Laboratory, University of California:

412

California researchers have found that anaerobic composting offers great promise for an inexpensive and sanitary method of disposing of manure. Waste materials are placed in airtight container where bacteria convert green matter to humus.

Reduction to a stable humus by anaerobic digestion seems to offer great promise for a relatively inexpensive and yet completely sanitary method of disposing of manure. Described most simply, the process consists of dumping or flushing all wastes into an airtight container in which bacteria can break down the organic matter to form humus and a combustible gas. The procedure provides sanitary treatment of organic wastes and results in a great reduction in flies. It also makes possible the efficient and economical recovery of some of the waste carbon as methane for fuel. It produces humus and nutrients for use on soils. Moreover, both liquid and solid wastes may be treated in one operation. Practicality of the process has been demonstrated by its successful use on European farms.

In practice about 50 per cent of the carbon available for

413

gas production is converted to gas. This may be used for heating, refrigeration, or any purpose applicable to natural gas. For example, a ton of waste will normally yield about 2,000 to 2,600 cubic feet of gas per digestion cycle, depending upon the proportion of organic matter and carbon content of the waste. Table 1 gives estimates for gas production per ton of manure for different digestion periods at different temperatures.

TABLE 1

Temperature °F.	Gas produced in cu. ft. per day	Production in months
60	5.3	12
68	10.5	3
73	21.2	3
83	35.3	2
93	70.6	1

The evolved gas is approximately two-thirds methane and one-third carbon dioxide. It contains 140-170 calories per cubic foot. Thirty-five cubic feet of the gas at a total of 6,000 calories compares to one quart of alcohol, 52.5 cubic feet of manufactured city gas, or 2.2 kilowatt hours of electrical energy. The humus remaining after digestion is comparable to that obtained from digesting sewage sludge. It has a nitrogen content varying from 1 to 2 per cent by dry weight.

Certain basic factors must be considered before deciding on a digester installation. Important among these are climate, number and size of digester tanks, gas requirements and storage, and material and labor costs.

Climate is the most important factor for a small installation. Digesters function most efficiently where freezing temperatures are infrequent and of short duration. Decomposition and gas production are negligible below 50 degrees F., satisfactory above 60 degrees or 70 degrees F., and most rapid at about 80 degrees F. Although a cold climate may be counteracted by heating the digester, most of the gas produced will be used for heating with little for other purposes.

Digester size and number will depend on the quantity of wastes available. For example, 1,400 pounds of cow manure

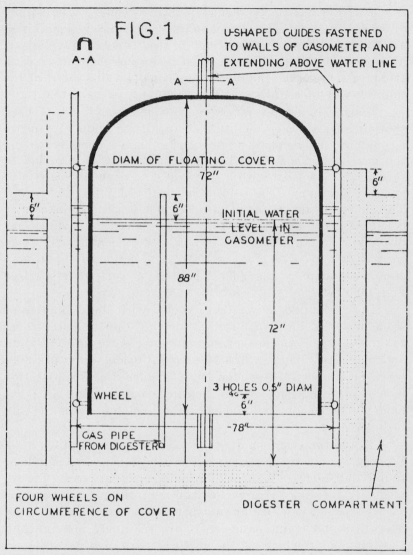

FIG.1

A-A

U-SHAPED GUIDES FASTENED TO WALLS OF GASOMETER AND EXTENDING ABOVE WATER LINE

A — A

DIAM. OF FLOATING COVER
72"

6"

6"

INITIAL WATER
LEVEL IN
GASOMETER

88"

72"

WHEEL

3 HOLES 0.5" DIAM

6"

-78"-

GAS PIPE
FROM DIGESTER

FOUR WHEELS ON
CIRCUMFERENCE OF COVER

DIGESTER COMPARTMENT

Chart shows section of gasometer for manure gas plants having a compartmental-ized digester. Bottom and walls are concrete; shape may be square or round.

without bedding and with normal moisture will require approximately one cubic yard of digester space. Space requirements for an equivalent manure naturally will increase according to the amount of bedding used. In estimating the volume of digester space required, it should be remembered that only a portion of the daily output of the cattle on a dairy farm will be available for the digesting plant. Some will be lost on the fields when the cattle are grazing.

The digester tanks should be located close to the supply of waste to avoid excessive hauling. In a dairy installation a setup consisting of a clamshell or other bucket traveling on an overhead rail could be used to transport manure directly from barn to tank. Liquid wastes could be flushed into the tank by way of a drainage system connecting barn and tank.

Inasmuch as gas is produced continually and is used sporadically, storage facilities should be provided to insure a constant and adequate supply of gas. This is done by storing the gas in a gasometer. The gasometer may be circular or square and provided with a water seal to prevent gas escape or air admittance. The bottom and walls may be of concrete. The cover should be metal in order not to produce excessive gas pressure since the weight of the cover determines gas pressure. Pressure may also be adjusted by center weights on the gas holder cover. Figure 1 shows a section of the gasometer for manure gas plant having a compartmentalized digester.

Digester tanks may be constructed with steel, concrete or stone masonry, lined with cement mortar. Concrete structures are preferable because they can be made water and gas-tight and may easily be reinforced to resist inside water pressure when built above the ground level. Figure 2 shows a section of a manure digester with a floating cover serving as a gas holder. Dimensions will depend on the volume of the manure to be treated.

The initial cost of a digester plant may seem rather high. When this cost is amortized over a period of years, it will be found that such a plant will provide a cheap and effective means of treating farm wastes and controlling fly production as well as serving as an inexpensive source of fuel. The operating and maintenance costs are relatively insignificant. Loading and removal of the material is a matter of labor, part of which would be expended in the normal hauling of manure from barns to stack. Moreover, the effort required would be less than that needed to transport the untreated manure from the vicinity of the barns to a suitable storage site. Maintenance of the equipment is limited to painting the metal parts to prevent corrosion. Such a plant should last more than 25 years if it is well built and corrosion of the gasometer is prevented. (*See also Anaerobic discussion in* MUNICIPAL AND COMMERCIAL COMPOSTING *chapter.*)

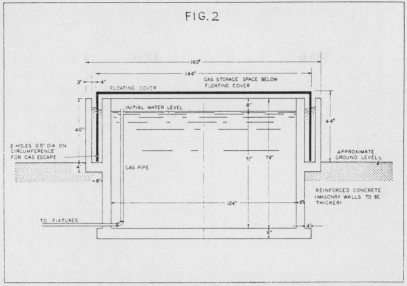

Sectional diagram of a manure digester tank with a floating cover serving as gas holder. Volume of manure to be treated determines dimensions for individual units.

Humus Development Studied

Of particular interest to organic farmers is a study made by U. Springer and A. Lehner of the Agricultural Institute for Plant Cultivation and Protection, Munich, Germany. The scientists made a special study of the aerobic and anaerobic decomposition and humus formation of important agricultural and forest organic materials.

The study was conducted over a period of 4 years by following the decomposition of various organic materials in flask experiments. Analyses were made at periodic intervals. The results of the analyses were calculated on a moisture-free basis for comparative purposes.

The results showed the scientists that under aerobic conditions green vegetation decomposes more readily than any of the other organic materials tested. Straw was next easiest to decompose. Leaves, pine needles, peat moss and high moor peat followed in that order, high moor peat being the hardest to decompose.

During the first month, it was observed that intense humus formation occurred. However, it was one to two years before the highest yield of humus possible was obtained. In the case of green vegetation, analyses showed that considerable quantities of base-bound humic substances occurred. The

417

other organic materials showed lesser quantities of these sub-stances.

In general, it was noted that decomposition was slower under anaerobic conditions than under aerobic. However, more humus was formed from the same amount of material under anaerobic conditions. Increased numbers of micro-organisms were observed under anaerobic conditions. The scientists said that their development appeared to follow a rhythmic course during the decomposition of the organic material.

The results of the 4-year experiment indicate that ana-erobic conditions are best for the organic farmer to follow. This is done by protecting composts of stable and green manure from the air as much as possible. The experimental results obtained by these and other scientists show that pro-tecting stable and green manure from the air during the decomposition stage, prevents much loss of valuable plant nutrients and aids in the development of humus.

THE BIO-DYNAMIC METHOD
FOR THE FARM

The bio-dynamic method of gardening and farming is closely aligned with the goals of the organic method in that both strive to improve the humus content of the soil. Whereas most organic gardeners don't differentiate between compost of varying materials, the bio-dynamic gardener mixes care-fully portioned amounts of certain raw materials to form com-post according to specified formuli. The bio-dynamicist is intent on producing compost in such a way as to lose as few nutritional elements as possible. Much research has been done at bio-dynamic experimental farms to show the effect of bacterial action on the decomposition of manure and compost. According to bio-dynamic adherents, this research has revealed what proper fermentation conditions should be and one of their major aims is to reproduce these favorable con-ditions so that compost and manure will not lose valuable elements.

Bio-dynamic preparations have been introduced to aid in the humus-forming process. Much of the original work in producing these preparations was done by the noted Austrian philosopher-scientist, Dr. Rudolf Steiner. Today the leader in this country is Dr. Ehrenfried Pfeiffer, once a student of

In applying the bio-dynamic concepts to farming, great care is taken to build compost of specifically portioned amounts of raw materials so as to aid bacteria and retain nutrients. While more involved, this system is close to organic method.

Dr. Steiner. Studies are now being conducted at the Biochemical Research Laboratory, Threefold Farm, Spring Valley, New York, under the auspices of the Bio-dynamic Farming and Gardening Association.

Following is one of the typical recommended bio-dynamic preparations:

Preparation No. 502: This preparation is made from the yarrow blossoms *(Achillea millefolium)*, fermented together with deer bladders over a period of 6 months in earth during the winter. The analysis of the available minerals shows a decrease of potassium from 1.05 per cent to 0.13 per cent, an increase of calcium from 0.05 per cent to 0.375 per cent, *i.e.*, of 75 times; a slight decrease of magnesium from 0.01 per cent to 0.005 per cent. Phosphate remains stable at about 0.06 per cent. The major increase is again observed in nitrate nitrogen from 0.07 per cent to 2.5 per cent or 35.8 times the original. Nitrogen fixing bacteria have migrated into the

419

preparation and lived and worked there. According to Dr. Steiner, the originator of these preparations, No. 502 has a stimulating effect on the use of sulphur and potassium by plants in their growth. This in turn effects the building up of protein and carbohydrates and their balance. This preparation, as well as the others, acts as a biocatalyst.

Here, in the words of Dr. Pfeiffer, is a brief explanation of the principles of bio-dynamics:

"Bio-dynamic farming and gardening looks upon the soil as upon a living organism and regards the maintenance and furtherance of soil life as fundamentally essential in order to preserve the soil's fertility for generations instead of obtaining a certain number of cash crops and then giving up work on the land because of its exhaustion. The maintenance of soil life is vital also in order to protect the soil from erosion and to create, improve and augment the humus content. This will result in a fine, crumbly structure and provide the necessary organic colloids. In addition it will grow a superior quality of products, which will mean better feeding for livestock and better food for human beings.

"The nearer a soil is to the neutral state the better possibility it has for humus production. Increasing acidity deteriorates the humus.

"The better a soil is protected against the bleaching and drying effects of the sun's rays, the better the humus is preserved.

"The better a soil is aerated, the more soil life is developed and the more humus produced.

"The more a soil is protected against dry and water-consuming winds, the better the humus production is maintained and hard-crust formation as well as loss of water avoided.

"Each kind of plant develops its own type of humus through its roots and leaves which fall and decompose around it. Crops either consume, maintain or produce humus.

"Mixed cultures are apt to preserve the fertility of the ground on account of certain beneficial effects from plant to plant, through mutual protection, through plant hormones and the kind of humus developed. The old-fashioned gardener obtains a black earth in his garden which a farmer never could produce in his fields.

"The loss of humus must be replaced by humus. Soil life must be stimulated by means of organic decomposed material in the striving towards the state of neutral colloidal humus.

420

Plastic coverings are another way to obtain anaerobic conditions during composting. This photograph, taken at the Ida Cason Callaway Gardens in Georgia, illustrates how large-scale composter makes use of combined windrow-airless principles.

"Soil improvement is obtained by proper humus management, *e.g.*, by the application of sufficient organic manure and compost in the best possible state of fermentation, also by proper crop rotation, by proper working of the soil, by protective measures such as wind protection, cover crops, green manure, diversified crops rather than mono-cultures, etc., and mixed cultures so that plants aid and support each other.

"Proper humus management is based on farm manure and compost as the most valuable fertilizers. They contain organic matter on which the soil bacteria and earthworms can feed and then revitalize the soil. They contain colloids which absorb moisture and mineral solutions in the ground, form a crumbly structure and eliminate the danger of erosion.

"Farmyard manure usually loses 50 per cent of its nitrogen content from the day it is produced until it is plowed under. The careful storage of manure in heaps covered with earth, as taught by the bio-dynamic method, avoids this loss almost entirely. Organic matter has not yet reached the state of neutral colloidal humus. Complicated fermentation processes must first take place in the manure heap. The final

421

result is either badly smelling decay with loss of nitrogen and breakdown to ammonia and carbonic acid or a transformation into neutral colloidal humus. The bio-dynamic method produces the right fermentation. Certain bio-dynamic preparations are inserted into the manure heaps in order to speed and direct fermentation and preserve the original manure values. This fermentation is usually completed in from 2 to 5 months.

"The same principles apply to compost materials. When collecting and piling up such materials one obtains an additional source of organic fertilizer. Everything which is apt to decompose can be used, as leaves, grass cuttings, weeds, old rotten hay, corn stalks, garbage, pond cleanings, road scrapings, slaughterhouse refuse, bone, hoof and horn meal, wool, etc. These materials are piled up in alternate layers, interlayered with earth and a thin coating of quick lime and treated with the bio-dynamic preparations. The bio-dynamic literature describes this process clearly. The fermented compost material is especially good for the improvement of lawns, pastures, flower beds, vegetable gardens, shrubbery, alfalfa, clover, etc. If properly done the fermentation of compost material into humus takes place in about 4 to 12 months, according to climatic conditions.

"Experience has shown that on a 100-acre farm with an annual manure production of 150-200 tons of manure about 100-120 tons of waste material in addition could be collected and composted.

"Proper crop rotation is essential in order to preserve the fertility of the soil. The general rule is that soil-exhausting crops such as corn, potatoes and mangels in the fields and cabbage, cauliflower, etc., in the garden alternate with soil-restoring crops such as all plants of the leguminous family— peas, beans, clover, alfalfa, etc. Furthermore, deep rooting crops have to alternate with shallow rooting ones, crops which require manure with those that do without it. A carefully thought out crop rotation is the opposite of monoculture which in the long run completely exhausts the soil. The crop rotation plan must be made in accordance with soil, climatic, and market conditions and has, therefore, to be worked out individually for each case including farms, flower and vegetable gardens.

"Proper working of the soil consists mainly of knowledge of the right time and right depth of plowing, of harrowing, disking, cultipacking, rolling, etc. Much skill and experience

As explained by bio-dynamicist Dr. Ehrenfried Pfeiffer, manure from a 100-acre farm will average 150-200 tons per year, and an additional 100 to 120 tons of waste material can easily be collected and composted by use of bio-dynamic formulas.

are needed. A cultipacker applied at the right time, at the beginning of dry weather, can preserve the moisture for a long period. Deep plowing of too wet a soil can ruin a field for many years. Only thoughtful experience combined with investigations, such as the taking of soil profiles, enable maximum efficiency in soil treatment."

—DR. EHRENFRIED PFEIFFER

ADVANTAGES OF COMPOST FARMING

To summarize, I am going to list 36 reasons why compost farming is superior to farming or gardening with artificial fertilizers. When anyone says that making compost heaps is too much work, he overlooks the fact that the work is not *extra;* that is, to be added to the sum total of the work on the farm. It is work that is taken from other operations on the farm, and with the lapse of a few years the total work on the organically operated farm will be much less than before.

1. *The general fertility level of the farm or garden is greatly improved by the organic method.*

2. *This method improves the soil's mechanical structure* which includes its granulation, tilth and increase of pore

423

spaces. It is a great improver of heavy clay soils. Sandy soils are made more cohesive, retain moisture better and do not dry out so rapidly.

3. *It makes for ease of cultivation.* Individual cases show that where it used to take 9 hours to hand-hoe an acre of potatoes, it now takes only 7. Another case shows that where it used to take 4 days to hoe beet fields, with the softer, looser organically treated soil it now takes only 2.9 days (Dr. Pfeiffer). On a 437-acre farm, operated by this method without any chemical fertilizers, a farmer was able to dispense with one team of horses, thus saving feed, stable space, grooming labor, etc. Does this not compensate for the labor of making compost heaps?

4. *It eliminates valuable waiting time.* The farmer can get back on the soil quicker after a rain. Because of the spongy, porous soil structure there is less mud and stickiness, or soil broken into clods. The soil is more mellow. Gardens that were formerly too sticky to work when wet, and which immediately baked hard as a brick, and formed large cracks in the surface when dried out, became easy to work after being handled in the organic manner. Hand cultivators push through such soil much more easily. Where land has been treated with artificials, and gets the benefit of only occasional, small amounts of organic matter it tends to become harder and harder.

5. *It increases the soil's water-holding capacity.* Estimates go all the way from a 20 per cent to 50 per cent increase in the soil's ability to absorb and hold rain water.

6. *It prevents soil erosion and reduces flood hazards.* I have seen the benefits on my own farm where the water, in heavy rains, does not come dashing along with anywhere near the volume or violence that it used to. A great deal of money could be saved in engineering devices such as the building of drains, contours, dams and terraces if farmers were to improve the structure of their soil by using more compost on their land. According to Howard, "this is the real way of stopping soil erosion."

7. *It prevents hardening of the surface soil by driving rains.* Where soil is hard and has poor mechanical structure, the impact of a hard rain will create a surface crust. On some farms you can actually pick up large hard crusts from

Among the most important benefits of compost farming—particularly for the Southwest—is the prevention of drought, wind or flood damage. Texas farmer Idus Gillett shows soil improvement brought by organic method over several years.

the soil surface. The porous, spongy structure of an organic soil prevents this.

8. *The earthworm multiplies greatly,* because organic matter is its natural food. Artificials kill or drive them away. The earthworm is one of the best friends of the farmer, aerating his soil and actually manufacturing topsoil. Earthworms have been known to add one-fifth of an inch of topsoil to the land in only one year.

9. *It multiplies the microbial population of the soil.* Bacteria and fungi increase tremendously when soil is enriched organically, aiding the growing processes enormously. Better aeration and more constant moisture greatly encourage their increase.

10. *Land can safely be plowed more deeply.* Where land is organically rich and has the proper mechanical structure, you can do almost anything with it. The topsoil layer becomes thicker and you can plow deeper.

11. *Hardpans will not form.* If there is a hardpan it will gradually disappear, especially with the aid of earthworms who will gradually crumble it up. When we first purchased our farm there was one depression where rain water accumulated and didn't seep into the ground for days because of such a hardpan. Now this never occurs at that spot.

12. *There is no danger of a plow-sole.* The same tendency of chemicalized soils which make them bake hard and form clods creates a plow-sole at the point where the plow shears the soil. This is a hardpan-like formation. This does not occur in an organic soil because of its softness and mechanical structure.

13. *Heavy machinery does not compact the soil as much.* An organic soil has a springiness which makes it rebound after the weight is removed. On soils that are hard-packed the weight of tractors, trucks and heavy combines only makes this condition worse.

14. *The soil has much better aeration.* This is quite obvious and is one of the most important requirements for optimum soil fertility. Aeration is made possible by the proper crumb structure of the soil as well as by the burrows of earthworms. The pore spaces permit a greater surface for the film of soil water to adhere to. In well-aerated soils ground air is kept in motion by the wind blowing on the surface. Such air movement helps check pathogenic (dangerous) bacteria. Good aeration is necessary for the proper development of roots. Some soils suffer from asphyxiation and the roots practically strangle. This has been proven to be a specific forerunner of plant disease.

15. *Soil made darker by humus absorbs heat more quickly and more effectively.* This is the principle of color in insulation. White keeps heat away and the darker the color becomes the more heat it absorbs. This enables the land to

warm up much earlier in the spring so that work can start and seeds begin to germinate. The bacteria start working as soon as the temperature goes up. The amount of moisture and air space in the soil also has an important bearing on soil temperature.

16. *Dry weather advantages.* Ordinarily, just as one doesn't plow when the soil is too wet, one cannot plow when it is too dry, or the soil will blow away. The organic system which stores up moisture doesn't have this disadvantage. In dry weather the land cools sooner in an organic soil, and more dew is precipitated. Under drought conditions an organic soil will fare better due to its stored up water.

17. *It may actually improve rain conditions.* Robert H. Elliot, who followed the organic system, with the addition of a method of growing deep-rooted crops such as chicory and orchard grass, says in *The Clifton Park System of Farming:* "It is important to note too that the air passing over a humus-fed soil would be cooler and more moist than air passing over a mineralized soil. The dew-fall therefore would be greater and when the land throughout the country becomes generally humus-fed, the rainfall would be more advantageously distributed and fall over a greater number of days in small showers instead of in heavy falls as in the case when land is clothed with forest."

18. *It transpires less water through the leaves.* In other words not only does it store more water, but it gives up less of it than a hard-packed soil. As a rule it requires several hundred pounds of water to be lost or transpired through the leaves of a plant for every pound of dry matter produced. In a research bulletin of the Nebraska Agricultural Experiment Station, it is shown that on good soil, well-manured, the loss of water is only about a half of what it is on an unmanured soil. This is a point of vast significance, especially in regions where the rainfall is deficient at some time during the growing season, and this condition applies to the major part of the great Mississippi Basin.

19. *The manure produced from cattle fed on an organically operated soil improves in quality from year to year.* It becomes progressively richer so that eventually less is required. In about 15 years a point is usually reached where the farm or garden can get along without any fertilizer help

whatever for a few years. Manure from a chemicalized farm has far less value.

20. *Making compost by the Howard process increases the available manure by 300 per cent.* This is obvious, since ordinarily only the available manure would be used, whereas by our process 6 inches of grass, leaves, weeds, etc., must be used for every two inches of stable manure.

21. *Compost heaps preserve all the food elements in the manure.* Due to the manner in which the green matter, manure, earth and ground limestone are interlayered in the compost heap, there is little loss whereas in the old-fashioned manure heap, sometimes more than half the values are leached out. There is a good deal of nitrogen fixation during the ripening process in a properly made compost heap. The Howard type compost heap is made in a manner that takes advantage of the natural action of soil bacteria, fungi and moulds. There are also no smells or flies as found in manure piles.

22. *Composts have a residual effect.* In experiments with ordinary manure 48 per cent was used up the first year, 24 per cent the second, 15 per cent in the third and 13 per cent in the fourth year. But in using composts some residual effects were felt as much as 15 years later. This builds up what farmers call "high condition."

23. *When following the organic system your grounds look neater.* Weeds are cut down periodically for use in the making of compost. When cut this way they do not go to seed and spread. Lawn cuttings, trimmings and other matter usually left around are carefully gathered.

24. *Weeds can be cultivated more easily out of an organic soil.* In the soft crumbly, organic soil, the hoe or cultivator pulls the weeds out more easily. You don't have to wait until after a rain to weed. In a chemicalized soil the weeds in dry weather seem to be embedded in cement.

25. *Compost is a "safer" material than just ordinary stable manure.* In growing tomatoes, for example, the use of raw manure in many cases results in maximum stalk and plant growth but minimum fruit. Compost is a finished material whereas raw manure has to be worked on by soil organisms to break it down with resultant bad effects on the crop. My impression is that the raw manure as it breaks down supplies an excess of nitrogen in the form of ammonia and the tomato plants respond by excessive vegetative growth and

a minimum of reproductive growth, *i.e.*, fruit. Raw manure can also burn plants if applied direct.

26. *Compost kills out weed seeds.* In applying raw manure to the land the farmer and gardener are actually, in many cases, planting a crop of weeds. In the compost heap, the fermenting action kills off most of the weed seeds.

27. *There is less risk of crop failure.* Due to the complications involved in the use of chemical fertilizers, plant diseases, acid conditions from overuse of chemicals, etc., there is an occasional crop failure. Wind storms blow down stalks of corn and cereal plants such as wheat, oats and barley. This practically never happens where the soil is rich in humus and where plants are accordingly strong and healthy enough to stand on their own legs due to the better root systems they develop.

28. *There is very little plant disease.* In chemical farming and gardening the plant is not nourished properly and thus its resistance is low. Crops raised with plenty of compost seem to be much more immune to disease. Waksman in his book *Humus* says, "Plant deficiency diseases are usually less severe in soils well supplied with organic matter, not only because of the increased vigor of the plants but also because of antagonistic effects of the various soil microorganisms which become more active in the presence of an abundance of organic matter."

29. *The insect menace is reduced to a minimum.* For some reason most insects do not seem to attack healthy plants. Insects are selective in their tastes and those which have not been imported seem to have been trained by Nature to prefer the sickly or imperfectly grown plants. It is Nature's method of doing away with the unfit. Plants grown with chemicals, not being 100 per cent healthy, seem to attract predatory insects.

30. *Few, if any, poison sprays are needed.* On farms and gardens where the organic method is practiced few poison sprays have to be used on vegetables and plants because insect and disease troubles are at a minimum. Large amounts of time and money are thus saved. In heavily infested areas, where compost farming by one or a few farmers only is but an "island" subject to insect invasion on a large scale, sprays may be needed for emergency use, but they can be kept to a minimum.

31. *No chemical treatments are needed for seeds.* Chemicalized farming seems to produce seeds which either harbor or fall easy victims to the organisms of various diseases so that modern agricultural practice demands that all seeds be given a poison bath to kill them off. This practice is not necessary on the organic farm or garden.

32. *It builds health.* In an English school where food was raised by the Howard method there was soon noted a great improvement in the health of the children. In Singapore a similar experiment conducted with a few hundred coolies produced like results. There are many other cases on record which would seem to indicate that the use of humus produces the old-fashioned food rich in vitamins and minerals. There would be a considerable saving in doctor's bills if all our food were raised by this method.

33. *Farm animals fed on organically produced feeds are healthier.* Sir Albert Howard fed cattle on feeds raised with humus. He allowed them to rub noses with a neighbor's cattle that had the highly contagious hoof-and-mouth disease. None of his animals caught the disease. There is much proof that the terrible prevalence of diseases of all kinds in farm animals is to a great extent due to their being fed with the devitalized feeds raised with chemical fertilizers. Animal disease is a sure sign of bad farming.

34. *Foods raised organically taste better.* Modern foods grown commercially are losing their old-time taste. Vegetables raised with chemicals are tougher and more fibrous and do not have the full-bodied taste that food has which is raised with compost. Wines in certain sections of France from grapes grown organically are famous for their wonderful taste. Recently in New Zealand, it was discovered that the native cheese tasted better. This was found to be due to the use of less chemical fertilizer under war-time difficulties and restrictions.

35. *The general quality of the crop is much higher.* In England a wealthy farmer who owned many thatched-roof cottages discovered that straw from organically grown crops lasted twice as long as a roof of ordinary straw. In France hay growing in certain sections where practically no chemical fertilizers are used commands a big premium and is shipped long distances for use by race horses. The keeping quality of foods grown organically is far superior. Nowadays when a

430

pumpkin is grown with chemical fertilizers it gets mouldy a few days after it is cut open.

36. *Humus seems to counteract the effects of poisons in the soil.* To quote Waksman's *Humus* again, "The toxicity of plant poisons becomes less severe in a soil high in humus than in a soil deficient in humus; high salt concentrations are less injurious; and aluminum solubility and its specific injurious action are markedly decreased."

There are many more reasons that could be mentioned, some of them quite technical, but those cited show how ridiculous it is for anyone to say that the organic method is impractical because it requires a little extra work to make the compost heaps. This statement is usually made by persons who do not realize all the other advantages and savings in the equation.

While a farmer is applying chemicals to wheat seeds, a thing which would be unnecessary if he were running an organic farm, he could be turning over a compost heap. While he is spraying his fruit orchard he could be making 5 or 10 heaps, depending on the size of the orchard. While he is sitting up with a sick cow he is losing valuable energy which could be used in the compost-making department. While he is fretting in the spring because his land is too wet and cold to start plowing he could be making compost heaps. And so the story goes all the way down the line. Compost farming does not mean more work. In reality it means far less work.

Chapter **12**

ANIMAL MANURES IN COMPOSTING

The use of chemical fertilizers dates back to the middle of the last century. Before that time farming was carried on almost exclusively with the aid of animal manures and other residues which originated on the farm, and in many cases with composts made of decaying animal and plant matter. In many European countries chemical fertilizers were practically unknown even until very recent times. Hitler's march into

Poland, for example, was followed soon after by very large shipments of chemicals, in order to increase food production. Many of the peasants had never before handled it in their lives.

In very early days man began to utilize various materials which he found on his farm or nearby, which seemed to give him better yields. The Romans used lime and when they overran England they introduced it there. England had tremendous deposits of chalk which, from then on, have consistently been used as a soil dressing.

Wood ashes also have been used as a fertilizer since long before Roman times. About 1650, saltpeter, a natural product obtained from manure, decaying organic matter and wood ashes, was discovered to have fertilizer value. Saltpeter (potassium nitrate) is used also for making gunpowder. Other materials dabbled in from time to time as fertilizers have been bones, coal ashes, charcoal, gunpowder, turpentine, tallow, oyster shells, flower of brimstone and citrated tartar, to mention a few.

In the main, however, the average farmer in olden days depended on animal manures, green-manure crops and other vegetable and animal residues. Where he followed established and well-tested cultural practice he obtained good results. Where he was lax and violated fundamental agricultural principles he was visited by crop failures. Whole countries in ancient days were turned into dust-bowls when the farmer sinned against the land.

Ferrero, one of the greatest of modern historians, has traced in *The Greatness and Decline of Rome* the decline of Roman agriculture through absentee ownership and one-crop specializing, and showed how it paralleled the economic trend of that great empire. Roman agriculture in the days when Rome was becoming great was a well-balanced, self-contained industry with sheep and oxen as the principal animals, and wheat, olives and grapes as the most important plants. The sheep furnished wool for the clothing, the oxen were the work animals and, with the sheep, provided the meat. The lower, level fields along the rivers and on the plains produced wheat and pasturage; the rougher land grew the olive for oil or the grape for wine. The labor was largely that of the owner, or was carried out under his direct supervision. Grain was sold to the cities for articles not produced on the farm.

As the empire grew, the culture of the olive and grape

Returning a farm's animal manure to its soil is as vital to the fertility of the land now as it was in centuries past. Dust bowls and deserts followed violation of this basic natural law in ancient lands, just as it has resulted in depleted soils today.

became more profitable than that of grain and the growing of wheat declined. Olive and grape growing represent much hand labor and the cheapest was that of slaves, and trained slaves could be bought very cheaply as a result of military conquests. The small farms were gradually given up and united as great estates where the work was done by slaves under a trained overseer who might also be only a slave, while the owner lived in luxury in the city of Rome. The country now was no longer independent. Grain had to be purchased abroad and the great capital was dependent on the arrival of grain ships from North Africa.

Ferrero used to visit America frequently. He said that he could best study in this country the subject nearest to his heart, the decline of a great republic. And agriculture was one of the most important factors in that decline.

The greatest virtue of the old-fashioned farms was that they were self-contained and had a balanced complement of both crops and livestock. Monoculture, the running of a one-crop farm with practically no animals, was rarely seen in America—except in the South where the worst cases of worn-out land are to be found today. It took scientific agriculture with its test tubes, chemicals and laboratories to encourage farmers generally to run a farm as a factory, in many cases on a 100 per cent chemical basis. What happens in such cases is land "mining." The soil soon loses its structure. Plant diseases break out. The crops become deficient in nourishing qualities and other troubles are encountered.

Luther Burbank, whose name is a symbol to horticulturists, built a basic foundation for his experimental work by loading his soil with a tremendous amount of animal manure. On his 4 famous acres at Santa Rosa, California, he spread 1,800 loads of barn manure before he started. This is an enormous amount of organic material for only 4 acres and demonstrates his leanings towards the old-fashioned way of preparing the soil as contrasted with his ideas in connection with producing new kinds of plants.

Burbank had been raised in New England where the soil is normally poor and from his early experience he had learned that in order to find out what a plant really can do, it must be given a full and rich diet and the best thing he knew for this purpose was the material with which the poor soil of his native state had been enriched—*i.e.*, with animal manure.

More than one billion tons of animal manure are produced in this country every year. It is estimated that this amount contains plant food values that are more than 6 times that of the artificial fertilizers used in the same period. By following the Howard method of composting, this billion tons of manure can be increased 300 per cent, and, at the same time, food values for growing plants can be improved. It also means that a given number of cattle can maintain the fertility of more than double the number of acres under methods commonly used now. This does not mean that we need fewer animals. The more we have, the greater use can be made of all their products.

Animal manure by itself is an unbalanced fertilizer—unbalanced chemically as well as biologically. There may be too much urine and too little cellulose, or vice versa, thus preventing the microbes from performing their work efficiently. By following the Howard method of making compost, not only will the proper biological processes proceed smoothly in the decomposition, but the materials—plant and animal—of the compost heap, provide every needed soil-food element.

Animal manure when used alone decomposes in the soil much more slowly than plant matter, although certain types of plant matter, such as pine needles, wood shavings and sawdust, are slow to decay. However, when manure is composted along with plant matter by the Howard process, decomposi-

Large-scale composting of this country's one billion tons of animal manure produced annually can increase this volume 300 per cent, and make available plant
food that has 6 times the fertilizer value of the artificial materials used in the same
period. This Wisconsin commercial plant uses dairy manure to prepare compost.

tion takes place much faster. The association and position of
the various materials, and the other factors, such as aeration
and heating, bring about a more accelerated break-down in
the animal matter than would occur if it were plowed under.

When manure is not composted, but is permitted to
weather under all kinds of unfavorable conditions, the "ban-
dits"—the anaerobic bacteria that can live and work without
oxygen—destroy much of its valuable nitrogen, which goes
up in thin air. One method of saving some of this nitrogen is
to use a large amount of bedding for cattle. Conversely,
where little bedding is used and manure is heaped in piles,
"fire-fanging" occurs—a form of very destructive fermentation. Such manure has very little value. But the chief reason
why sufficient bedding must be used is to absorb the urine.
Fifty per cent of the value of manure is contained in the urine.

Ordinary manure heaps smell, attract flies and sometimes
become so saturated with rain during heavy storms that much
of the valuable nutrients are washed away, sometimes as much
as one-half. Manure heaps are often carelessly piled where
surface drainage water washes into them. Some farmers
shovel manure through a window of the barn and let it

accumulate under the eaves where excessive rain water washes valuable elements away.

Bulletin 92, entitled *Farm Manures*, issued September, 1932 by Clemson Agricultural College of South Carolina, states:

"With the present lack of attention given to saving manure, the loss between animal and field is enormous. It is doubtful that 20 per cent of the manure produced in South Carolina is actually placed in the fields."

Farmers often carelessly destroy manure and then spend hard-earned money in purchasing artificial fertilizers, because it seems like less work. In the long run, they are making more work for themselves and their families. I know of cases where farmers did not avail themselves of opportunities to get free manure because it involved trucking a few miles. Many farmers actually sell manure. In most cases it will be found that they are tenant farmers. The land is not theirs. They do not have the incentive to invest in fertility, for next year they may have to move to another patch. Recently I stopped to check at two farms that had a sign out "Manure for Sale." Both of them were run by tenant farmers. Sometimes a very large dairy will sell manure because they do not grow much of their feed. Their cows are largely fed on concentrates. In China manure is valued so highly that every bit of it is scraped off the roads and used.

There are many reasons why raw manure except in emergencies should never be applied as a fertilizer unless it is done well before the crop is grown and given a chance to decompose. The *first* reason is the same as that which applies to the plowing under of a raw green-manure crop. The bacteria and fungi, in having to break down so much raw matter, must consume a great deal of the available nitrogen and other food elements in the soil to furnish energy, thus depleting it for use by the new crop. In many such cases very disappointing results are obtained and benefits are not observed until the year following, when the enriched dead bodies of these microbes become available.

Second: Weed seeds in the manure are not killed off, as in the compost heap. Thus many farmers by applying raw manure actually plant a crop of weeds as well as insect eggs and spores. Where fresh manure is obtained from outside sources new species of weeds may be introduced to the farm as well as certain disease organisms.

436

Third: Where a herd of cattle has Bangs or other diseases the organisms are planted in the soil. The high heat of the composting process kills off these dangerous organisms. The germ of Bangs disease causes undulant fever in man. Its organisms can live in the soil for many years. *U. S. Farmers' Bulletin No. 1568* recommends that all rabbit manure be burned to prevent re-infection. This is a tremendous waste; fortunately other Government bulletins recommend its use as a fertilizer. Careful composting of such manure would make it absolutely safe as a fertilizer. It is dangerous to use it raw.

Fourth: Plant and human health can suffer because of the absorption by the plant of half-rotted albumin and other dangerous substances from raw manure. Clubroot is a common plant disease aggravated by the use of raw manure.

Urine is an extremely important fertilizing substance, but it, too, should not be used raw. Where it is applied direct to the land it can have a caustic effect. Four-fifths of the potash in the manure is in the urine. It contains half the nitrogen but practically no phosphorus. Urine is rich in the most important substances needed to create a fertile soil. Many farmers shamefully waste animal urine, not realizing the value it has if properly employed.

There are growth-promoting substances in manure, called *auximones,* which are roughly comparable to vitamins and hormones in their effects. Very little is known about them, except that they are abundant in the growing tips of plants and it has been demonstrated that manure from animals feeding on fertile land is richer in them than that from animals grazing on poor land. The possibility exists, however, that these auximones are in reality none other than varieties of vitamins.

In the *Journal of Medical Research,* Volume 14 (1926), there is an account of an experiment at Madras, India, related by Sir Robert McCarrison, M.D., which proved that where animal manure was the fertilizer medium the crop of grains contained more vitamins than where commercial fertilizers were used. There are many other experiments which prove the same thing and authorities attribute these results unquestionably to growth factors in animal manure.

Professor W. H. Schopfer, Director of the Botanical Institute, University of Berne, Switzerland, one of the world's greatest authorities on the subject of plants and vitamins, says in his book, *Plants and Vitamins:* "The action of animal excreta cannot be overlooked. Because of their high vitamin content the feces of horses and other large animals serve as excellent media for the culture of numerous fungi . . . finally, manure applied to the soil represents another source of growth factors. Bonner and Greene (1938) found the following figures for a few manures: Arizona steer manure 0.13 mg., local steer manure 0.08 mg., dairy manure 0.13 mg., of thiamin per kilogram. The presence of growth factors in natural manures must contribute to their superiority as compared with artificial fertilizers. This superiority has been established for a long time."

As a farm continues to be operated in the organic manner and its soil grows more and more fertile, its manures likewise grow richer. Eventually much less manure is needed. Where 10 tons of compost per acre may be needed at the beginning of a program in 5 or 6 years of operating with compost only 5 tons per acre may be sufficient.

It stands to reason that manure from a sick animal is not up to the quality of that from a healthy one. In the same way manures from cattle that are fed high quality feed are much superior to that of cattle depending on an inferior food ration. It is this difference in quality of manure that affects in direct ratio the quality of food and its taste, when grown in soil with such manure. For the very same reasons weeds, leaves and other green matter originating on an organically-operated farm, are superior in soil nutriments to that from a farm where chemicals are relied upon.

The best manure, from the point of view of ease of fermentation or decomposition, comes from feeding cattle hay, grass, alfalfa, plus a reasonable amount of grain and a small quantity of a supplement like soy-bean meal. Where too much concentrate is fed, cottonseed and soy-bean meals, etc., the manure will be too sticky and more resistant to decay.

The analyses of various kinds of manure such as horse, cow, steer, pig, sheep, chicken, and others, show a great deal of variation as to nitrogen, phosphorus and potash content. Chicken manure is richest in all 3, for fowls do not excrete urine, and therefore might serve its purpose best by being mixed with other manures. Its habit of burning plants when used fresh shows the necessity for composting it before use.

Many poultrymen sell their manure and do not produce their own chicken feeds. With the aid of this rich organic material they could produce a far superior kind of feeding matter than they can purchase. They would thus have much better results with their chickens. The nutritive quality of the eggs and meat would be higher. I have even seen cases where poultrymen had difficulty in disposing of their accumulated chicken manure, having to accept a very low price for it.

Horse manure has the characteristic of easily "fire-fanging" if allowed to accumulate in heaps. To counteract this tendency it should be watered liberally. Horse manure has the good quality of preventing the harmful actions of denitrogenizing bacteria. That is why good results will be obtained if it is mixed with other manures, even when making compost heaps. Pig manure is highly concentrated and is best when mixed with the excretions of other animals.

There are a few cautions in connection with the use of animal manures if you insist upon applying them to the land without composting. Fresh manure is always acid. For the average vegetable and farm crop a too acid condition may interfere with plant growth. Where too much raw manure is used for tomatoes it will result in maximum stalk and plant growth and minimum fruit. This does not occur when well-finished compost is used. Be careful in purchasing horse manure that it isn't "spent" manure.

I have noticed for sale in some of the stores bags of cow manure, with a notation in very tiny letters near the bottom that superphosphate has been used as an absorbent. This is no doubt due to the fact that it is standard practice in dairy-barns to sprinkle superphosphate in the manure every day as a deodorizer and to lock in the nitrogen. I do not recommend it.

To sum up; if possible, never use raw animal manure. If you cannot compost it let it rot under conditions that will preserve most of its nutrients. But for superior crops make compost of it. Balfour in *The Living Soil* describes an interesting experiment: "A large scale test, involving 40 fields, was made on the late Sir Bernard Greenwell's estate of humus manufactured by the Indore process versus best quality farm-yard manure, that is to say, well-rotted manure that was practically pure dung. Load for load the compost showed in every case better results." This experiment was described in detail in the *Journal of the Farmers' Club of London* in 1939. I would rather use 5 tons of well-made compost than 15 tons of raw manure.

MANURE HANDLING

Dr. Clarence Poe, Senior Editor of *The Progressive Farmer*, reminisces in a February 1959 article about the "old days" on the farm, when "fertility for crops largely came from the barnyards." Then he recalls how Dean Vivian of Ohio Agricultural College burst forth into song:

> If I could grasp old Homer's lyre
> And sing with true poetic fire,
> To what great theme would I aspire?
> Stable manure!

It is even more important today to realize the value of manure, to understand how to handle it properly and to the greatest benefit—and to put this knowledge into practice.

The excreta of agricultural animals, along with stable litter, constitutes one of the oldest and most effective fertilizers known to man. The rise of chemical fertilizers in the 20th century has led to a decrease in the amount of manure utilized by world agriculturists. This wasteful misuse of natural fertilizer is often rationalized by farmers and agriculturists, who allege that the supply is not adequate for the need for fertilizers. This is faulty reasoning. In 1889 there were 13,663,000 horses in the United States and 50,331,000 head of cattle. Today there are fewer horses—about 3,000,000 total—but almost 100,000,000 head of cattle. There has also been a subsequent rise in the number of other livestock. The problem is not insufficient manure, but its misuse.

It has also been calculated that a farmer by wise management of his animal manures can return to the soil 70 per cent of the nitrogen, 75 per cent of the phosphorus, and 80 per cent of the potash which was taken out by the home-grown plants his animals eat. This is a considerable saving when it is realized that a dairy cow gives 27,000 pounds of manure annually and a horse, 18,000.

Actually only a small fraction of the potential crop producing and soil-conserving value of manure is used. Approximately half of the excrements from farm stock is dropped on pastures and uncultivated ground. Vast amounts of manure in stockyards, piggeries, poultry farms, and other animal industries are considered worthless wastes and are dumped on uncultivated lands. On most farms the manure is so badly handled that it suffers enormous losses of nitrogen

Mineral-rich manure from stable gutters is automatically conveyed by barn cleaner through opening directly into manure spreader at this up-state New York organic farm. An estimated 70 to 80 per cent of the nitrogen, phosphorus and potash in the feed of animals can be returned to the soil by careful use of their manure.

through improper fermentation and drying, and of nutrients due to the draining off of the urine and leaching of the solid portion of the manure by rain and surface water. Fermented manure loses ammonia if allowed to dry on the field before it is worked into the soil.

There is also a loss as a result of the inefficient use of manure as, for instance, when it is not applied at the season, in the manner, at the rate, or to the crop which would give the greatest return.

In view of these facts it is safe to assume that only from a third to a quarter of the potential value of the manure resource of the country is now realized. The present wasteful and inefficient methods of using manure seen in all sections of the country are sufficient evidence that many farmers do not understand the true nature of manure, the perishable character of its most valuable constituents, and the direct money loss incurred through its improper treatment. This situation is doubtless due in large part to the increased use of artificial chemical fertilizers during the past 25 or 50 years.

The two chief manure robbers are *leaching* and *evaporation.* Together these two forces steal much of the active nutrients in manure—one by washing them out, the other by drying them off into the air.

How can this tremendous loss be stopped? What is the best way to store manure? How should it be applied to the soil? For the complete answers, we contacted soil specialists all over the United States. They are all agreed on these main points:

1. Spread fresh manure daily and turn it under immediately or as soon after spreading as possible;

2. Store manure in an enclosure with a cement floor to prevent leaching;

3. Provide plenty of litter or bedding to absorb liquids.

Daily Spreading

Many authorities recommend getting the raw manure into the ground immediately, plowing it under before any nutrients escape. Speed is all-important; therefore the manure spreader should make its rounds every day.

Some agronomists argue that too much emphasis is placed on adding only rotted manure. In many cases, especially in the home garden, fresh manure is often too hot and quick-acting, so rotted manure is safer to use than equal amounts of fresh. But the reason it's safer is that the rotted manure has *lost* much of its quick-acting ammonia as well as so much organic matter that the phosphoric acid and potash remaining are *relatively* increased and the fertilizer action is in better balance. However, this result is obtained at heavy cost in losses of nitrogen and organic matter, and too often of potash also. So these agronomists point out that it would be more economical to use smaller amounts of fresh manure and supplement it with rock phosphate and potash, which would result in better use of available nitrogen.

442

Cement Floor Enclosure

As everyone knows, it isn't always possible to spread manure daily because of the weather, time of year or other work. In such cases manure must be stored. And when it comes to storing manure, a cement floor pays for itself in one year by just about ending leaching.

The pile should be about 4 feet high, steep-sided and flat-topped. No cover is needed, since the manure pile usually receives enough rain to prevent heating, but not enough to cause much leaching. All authorities agree that heating or fermentation are to be avoided in order to conserve nitrogen and other nutrients.

Importance of Litter

Storage in loose-run barns or sheds with concrete floors is also recommended—if plenty of bedding or litter is used. In this case, the manure is permitted to accumulate while the urine keeps it moist and the animals trample it compact.

Litter of bedding is valuable in conserving nitrogen and keeping the animals healthy and comfortable when it has the following characteristics:

1. highly absorbent, thus preventing loss of urine;

2. fixing capacity for ammonia and potash to prevent loss;

3. easily obtainable and cheap;

4. contains residual plant food of its own to add to the over-all nutritional value of the manure;

5. not be too coarse to prevent proper compaction or reduce animal comfort;

6. not be dusty or able to be kicked aside readily.

Opinions of Experts

From Indiana's G. P. Walker: Practical handling of manure for holding down nutrient losses and at the same time avoiding excessive labor requirements varies somewhat with the type of livestock. Most dairymen with cows housed in stanchion barns try to keep their manure hauled and spread as fast as it is made. Where cows are housed in tramp sheds with generous bedding, the manure is allowed to accumulate under tramping and hauled out and spread at less frequent intervals.

Beef cattle feeders allow the manure to accumulate with

considerable bedding either under cover or in open feed lots, usually until the particular lot of cattle has been fed out.

From Florida's G. C. Horn: The best method to store manure is to compost the manure to exclude as much air as possible. A pile with as small a base as possible is best. This type of pile need not be covered if it is properly compacted. It is absolutely necessary to use a good litter to catch the liquid portion of the animal excrement because this liquid portion contains a high percentage of nitrogen and potash. Peat moss is excellent, as are cereal straws for use as litter.

Worst Way

"The poorest way of managing manure, and unfortunately—an all too common one—is to pile it on the top of the ground outside of the barn. There it lays with rain waters washing through it which can flush out the nutrients and allow them to drain away." So comments Rutgers specialist Wallace Mitcheltree.

Spreading Manure

Manure left in the pen after the animals have been removed soon dries and loses much of its nitrogen. Fermented manure can lose as much as 45 per cent of its nitrogen value when left on the field to dry. It is obvious then that manure must be turned under as soon as possible if it is to be of most value as a crop and soil builder.

Spreading manure on a cloudy, humid day is also recommended because evaporation is slowed under these conditions. Correct amounts of manure to the acre per year depend on soil, crop and region. It is generally agreed that a small amount of manure, applied annually, gets better results than larger amounts applied in alternate years.

In Maryland, 6 tons per acre are recommended for hay and pasture crops containing less than 50 per cent legumes; 10 tons are advised for corn. Normally only one application is recommended annually for each crop, usually on fields to be planted to corn.

Pennsylvania agronomists recommend plowing manure under for row crops as well as to winter grain that will be overseeded to a grass-legume mixture. The grain should be top-dressed after the ground is frozen. For corn, potatoes, tobacco, and grass sods, 12 to 15 tons per acre are advised.

A dairy cow provides 27,000 pounds of manure every year. Misuse rather than insufficient quantities is the principal cause of valuable fertilizer loss. Manure should be spread on a humid, cloudy day so that evaporation of nutrients is minimized.

The average farmyard manure contains the major and trace elements in the following relative amounts:

Farmyard Manure Analysis	
nitrogen	1
phosphorus	0.29
potassium	1.13
calcium	0.94
magnesium	0.26
boron	0.00092
cobalt	0.0000055
copper	0.00053
molybdenum	0.0000034
zinc	0.0043

Problem Is Misuse

Proper handling of manure is more important today than ever before. While there are fewer horses now than at the beginning of the century, the number of cattle has almost doubled, from 50 to 100 million. There has also been a corresponding rise in the number of other livestock; so the problem is not so much *insufficient* manure as *misuse* of manure.

445

It has also been calculated that a farmer by wise management of his animal manures can return to the soil 70 per cent of the nitrogen, 75 per cent of the phosphorus, and 80 per cent of the potash which was taken out by the home-grown plants his animals eat. This is a considerable saving when it is realized that a dairy cow gives 27,000 pounds of manure annually.

Manure is still the most common organic fertilizer used by farmers. Anything done to stop the manure robbers will pay off well.

(*See also: Manure in chapter on* MATERIALS FOR COMPOSTING.)

Compost Straw Retains Nutrients

There is better retention of nutrient materials if more straw is added to cow manure each day before it is thrown on the compost pile, report scientists J. Köhnlein and H. Vetter, Hermann-Weigmann Strasse 3-11, Kiel, Germany. This was noted when tests were run by adding 4 to 12 pounds of straw per day for each cow to the dung, and composting for 2½ months. The larger weight of straw raised the retention of ammonia nitrogen from 0.23 to 0.29 per cent and total nitrogen from 1.94 to 2.33 per cent. Phosphate was increased from 1.21 to 1.25 per cent, potash from 1.98 to 2.76 per cent, and lime from 1.95 to 2.36 per cent. The carbon to nitrogen ratio remained unchanged.

For each cow organic farmers should add about 12 pounds of straw, or other fibrous organic material such as ground corncobs to the compost pile, before throwing on the manure. In this way a significantly higher amount of valuable nutrients will be retained. The increased organic matter will also help to condition and enrich the soil. It's not necessary to weigh every fork or shovelful of straw or cobs. A big fork of straw or a couple of scoops of cobs will be about right for each cow.

LIQUID MANURE

Liquid manure is often recommended for fertilizing house plants as well as outside plantings.

There are several ways of making liquid manure, but the following method is easy, economical and not a bit messy.

As soon as the weather is warm enough to keep water from freezing, get 3 large 100 pound sugar sacks and fill each one with a mixture of fresh cow, horse and chicken manure in equal parts. These are then suspended in 60-gallon steel drums, one to each drum and then the drums are filled full of warm water. Be sure the sacks of manure are under water. Some gardeners "bury" the drums in an inconspicuous place.

After you have made sure that the bags are under water, cover the drums and let the manure steep in the water for 30 to 45 days. At the end of this time, remove the manure sacks and add enough water to the liquid manure so that it is about the color of weak tea. By filling the drum to within one inch of the top, the strength of the solution is generally right for all general purposes. The main purpose of the liquid manure is to give plants a boost just before they start to bloom, so the liquid manure can be made up at any time in order to be ready in time for the flowers and shrubs as they come into bloom.

Liquid manure should be applied to the ground around the particular plants which are to receive it; then washed in with water. One can save a lot of steps and labor if he can apply the manure just before a good rain, but by all means, see that it is washed into the soil where it will do the good for which it was intended.

Many gardeners give plants 3 applications a year in the proportion of one gallon to 5 square feet of plant bed. For shrub groups use the same proportion.

—MYRON PARISH

HANDLING POULTRY MANURE

The average hen gives off about 140 pounds of manure a year, or every 100 birds produces about 7 tons of manure. It was estimated that a mixture of a winter's accumulation of dropping board and floor litter manure, without adding any other fertilizers, contained 2 per cent nitrogen, 2 per cent phosphoric acid and 1 per cent potash, the 3 essential elements needed for plant growth. This would mean that each ton of chicken manure would contain 40 pounds of nitrogen, 40 pounds of phosphoric acid and 20 pounds of potash.

Studies of poultry manure made at the Pennsylvania State Agricultural Experiment Station indicate that laying hens, on the average, produce 138 pounds of fresh manure annually having a moisture content of about 76 per cent. A turkey produces 339 pounds of fresh manure with a moisture

A striking example of large-scale manure composting is found at the plant of the Chicago Stockyards Compost Co. Square 20-ton capacity digesters have heated air injected into them to speed bacterial action. At present the plant composts about one-third of yearly 50,000 tons of manure produced at world's largest stockyards.

content of 74 per cent. The N-P-K-composition of fresh hen manure was found to be 1.48 per cent nitrogen, 0.96 per cent phosphoric acid, and 0.47 per cent potash. Fresh turkey manure contains 1.31 per cent nitrogen, 0.71 per cent phosphoric acid, and 0.49 per cent potash.

Both hen manure and turkey manure tend to lose nitrogen as they age. The loss of nitrogen may be reduced by drying or other methods, the simplest and most efficient of which is the dropping pit. The henhouse should contain a brick-sided compost pit large enough to accommodate the bird population. Over the pit are placed coarse wire screening and roosts. The hens loaf and sleep over the pit and the droppings fall into the pit and are immediately composted so that the nitrogen is fixed and unable to escape into the air. Such composted poultry manure can be applied to the soil immediately before seeding or transplanting vegetable crops. (*See* MATERIALS FOR COMPOSTING *and* HOW TO USE COMPOST *chapters; also* COMPOST LITTER FOR POULTRY IN COMPOSTING METHODS FOR THE FARMER *chapter*.)

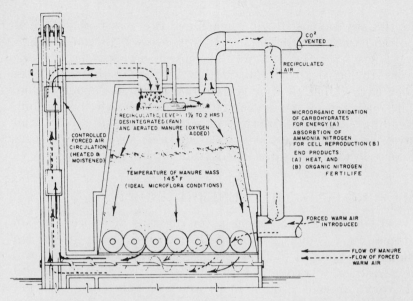

CO² VENTED

RECIRCULATED AIR

RECIRCULATED (EVERY 1½ TO 2 HRS)
DESINTEGRATED (FAN)
AND AERATED MANURE (OXYGEN ADDED)

MICROORGANIC OXIDATION
OF CARBOHYDRATES
FOR ENERGY (A)

ABSORBTION OF
AMMONIA NITROGEN
FOR CELL REPRODUCTION (B)

CONTROLLED
FORCED AIR
CIRCULATION
(HEATED &
MOISTENED)

END PRODUCTS
(A) HEAT, AND
(B) ORGANIC NITROGEN
FERTILIFE

TEMPERATURE OF MANURE MASS
145° F
(IDEAL MICROFLORA CONDITIONS)

FORCED WARM AIR
INTRODUCED

FLOW OF MANURE
FLOW OF FORCED
WARM AIR

Composting process (aerobic decomposition) by Union Stockyards method. These scientifically designed digesters are probably the most efficient now operating in this country. They dry the manure in addition to composting it.

COMPOSTING MANURE IN CHICAGO STOCKYARDS

Perhaps the most successful example of the use of digesters to compost industrial waste is the plant of the Chicago Stockyards Compost Co. The present plant is capable of composting approximately one-third of the 50,000 tons of manure produced annually by the stockyards.

"Don't let anyone tell you that manure is easy to compost," was the remark made by the plant manager. He claimed that because of the high percentage of straw their raw material offered a real challenge. Their digestors are square in shape and hold 20 tons of material at a time. Because heated air is injected into the digestors to speed bacterial activity, the manure is composted in 24 hours. The plant operates 24 hours a day. Compost from the stockyards is sold nationally through retail stores under the trade name Fertilife.

The Organic Compost Corporation at Germantown, Wisconsin with George Klein, as president, has been active in compost production for a number of years and his firm has continued to grow steadily since he formed it in 1950.

Klein and his plant manager have engineered and built a

continuous compost turning machine. It drives under its own power right through the compost windrows, thoroughly lifting and mixing the material. The cost of building the machine was $14,000, but Klein claims that because of the experience they have gained they could now duplicate it for about $8,000. The operator of the turner rides 12 feet above the ground. Bedding materials, ground corn cobs, chopped alfalfa and straw are composted along with cattle manure. (*See* MUNICIPAL AND COMMERCIAL COMPOSTING *chapter.*)

MANURE AND THE GENERAL PUBLIC

In my daily newspaper a few months ago I read of an attack on an old custom of French peasants—piling up manure in front of their houses. In the city of Douzy, France, it has actually precipitated a political crisis. The mayor and the town council wanted more tourists, but tourists do not want manure under their noses. So the mayor and the 6 town councilors, who were launching a "visit Douzy" campaign, decreed that the manure should be hauled away under penalty of severe fines.

The incensed peasants revolted and refused to pay the fines; the town fathers became angry and resigned. The result is that the piles of manure are still right on the town's main road, and no one is getting anywhere.

May we enter into this dispute as arbitrators? The peasants are only doing what their ancestors have done for centuries. They have learned that the soil thrives on this manure, and the French, being a thrifty race, also are aware of the financial savings in using manure as against chemical fertilizers. But here the issue is not a fight against manure *per se,* but the location in which that manure should be piled.

There must be a reason why the French peasants want the manure right in front of their houses. In fact I can see several reasons. First, there must be a saving of labor. The cows and pigs are housed close to the house. From that position the manure can be hauled to the rest of the farm with the least amount of labor. Secondly, it is important that the manure be stored in a spot where the rains will not run into it and dissipate much of its value. The house is usually built on such a spot—a place that is well-drained. The rains run in the fields and could make the position of a manure pile there very insecure. Thirdly, there actually may be a sense of pride in leaving the manure pile in front of the house. It is a sign to the neighbors of a well-managed farm. It gives the farmer himself a feeling of a job well done. All his life he has come to know this pile as a friend, as something which gives vigor and well-being to his crops. It gives him a pleasant feeling akin to having money in a bank. And now come these unfeeling councilmen and the mayor, who wish to have it stuck in some obscure corner of the farm where it would weather and be forgotten.

I should imagine that the peasant, standing next to this heap so often, radiates kind feelings into it, and perhaps the process is vice versa also. Experiments that have been made show that intense praying into them has made plants grow more vigorously. Don't laugh! There are electric radiations from the human body that can be measured, and that can affect other objects—animal, vegetable or mineral. Perhaps that is what actuates a green thumb. It's like the case of a farmer who once told me that he won't have a farm hand unless he talks to the chickens. The loving talk is accompanied by beneficial magnetic or electric emanations from the body which could even be of help to a chicken. But who knows? Perhaps in a distant, neglected corner of the farm, a pile of manure standing neglected and disregarded, without the daily company of the farmer, would not thrive as well, or conserve as much of its nutrients.

Eliminate Odors by Making Compost

Now, what is our suggestion? Actually, the tourist is not against manure, as such. He is against the smell. So, why not treat the manure in such a way that the smell is eliminated? This can easily be done by making compost out of it. Thus the farmer will be encouraged to gather or save all kinds of residual vegetable matter which he now discards or burns up. In making compost, according to the Sir Albert Howard method, 3 times as much vegetable matter is used as manure. Thus in the end his fertilizer will be 4 times as much as he had to begin with. And by the application of a little soil in the layers and on top of the heap the odor will be effaced. One can also cover the top of the heap with fragrant hay which also aids a great deal in conquering odors.

Wouldn't it be wonderful if the mayor and his 6 councilors would issue a decree that henceforth all manure originating on the farms of Douzy must be composted, using with it 3 times as much refuse plant matter such as leaves, weeds, grass clippings, table cuttings, etc.; that no farmer be permitted to sell manure, and furthermore that every farm in Douzy should have enough cattle and other animals to supply it with sufficient manure for the needs of the farm?

It would be possible, by doing this, to get so much publicity that people would come to Douzy in droves from all over France. In fact if this were done I am sure that I would go to Douzy to see an enterprising village and people who are not afraid to go into an adventurous project that means better health to its soil and people. It could then be an example to the rest of the small villages of France and to the rest of the world.

The trouble is that officials of cities govern in an impersonal way. They rarely go deeply into the social and scientific implications of the rules and regulations they decree. They rarely probe beneath the surface. They go by axioms that are fallacies, but have been believed in so long that they are hopelessly encrusted in the minds of people. Manure is something dirty and filthy in the public mind, so the councilors consider it dirty and filthy and to be gotten out of sight at any cost.

But they should know that manure is of the essence of life. It is a device of nature to continue life, and it is their duty and obligation as governors to teach that fact to their citizens as well as to the stranger who is in their gate. They should proclaim to all the world that in Douzy the people cherish manure and give it its true value, that they wish to keep it by their side, and care for it tenderly, for in its decay there is a birth of new healthy life.

Same Problem at Home

Back home we have the same problem in connection with compost heaps in built-up sections of cities. Neighbors complain to health officers who begin to shriek bloody murder, believing that the whole neighborhood will immediately become infected with the most deadly of diseases. But if they would only take the trouble of doing a little investigating as to what compost is and what it can do for the health of the people they are responsible for, they would encourage more of their neighbors to have compost heaps.

This reminds me of a time a few years ago, on a visit to San Salvador in Central America, when we inspected a large plant that made compost for sale on a production basis. The health department was concerned about the health of the employees of the plant and had a doctor check it over a period of several years. To their amazement they discovered that these people were healthier than the average of other workers in San Salvador. Evidently there are organisms in the compost which are beneficial types, such as antibiotics, and which prevent infections of various kinds from occurring. One should not jump to hasty, ill-conceived conclusions.

Last May my wife and I had to go from Freiburg, Germany, by car to get a plane in Zurich, Switzerland. Our route lay through the picturesque Black Forest. We were fascinated by the many quaint houses we saw with well-made manure piles right next to the kitchen door. This is not Hansel and Gretel stuff. And we saw this right up to the outskirts of the city of Zurich. The heaps had weathered, and there was no odor from them. And the people accept them as part of their lives, like eating or going to church. It is their salvation, and they know it.

—J. I. RODALE

Chapter 13

APPLYING COMPOST ON THE FARM

SPREADING COMPOST ON FIELDS

The finished compost may be applied to the fields with a manure-spreader, or forked out of a wagon as it moves very slowly over the field. Sometimes when it is time to plant a crop the compost is only half-completed. It may then be necessary to spread it anyway as the process of humification will continue in the soil.

To get good results with the average crop, it is advisable to use about 10 tons of compost to the acre. In later years, after a general improvement in soil fertility has occurred by enrichment with humus, 5 tons to the acre will be sufficient. Truck farmers sometimes apply 50 tons of manure to the acre.

Some farmers apply their manure or compost only when they plant corn in the rotation, figuring that it leaves a residual value sufficient for the 3 or 4 remaining years in the rotation. Experimental work done at the Ohio Agricultural Experiment Station seems to show that it is best not to use all of the manure with the corn. This work is described in the *Ohio Farmer* which states:

"L. E. Thatcher of the agronomy department of Wooster describes one set of tests in which the crop residues and manure are used in different ways in a 4-year rotation of corn, soybean hay, wheat, and mixed alfalfa-clover-timothy hay. The yield records for 15 years show an average of about 2 tons of mixed hay per acre when all the manure is plowed down for corn. Where the manure was one-half plowed down for corn and one-half disked into the seedbed for wheat, the mixed hay yields were 2.2 tons per acre, and when one-half the manure was used as a winter mulch on wheat the hay yields averaged almost 2.5 tons per acre.

"Results of this experiment as well as several others, show that dividing the manure between the corn and the wheat does not reduce the yield of the corn in the rotation. One reason for this is that the better hay crop means a better sod crop to plow under for corn. In the experiment cited above, yields of corn under the 3 methods were practically identical at a little over 70 bushels per acre."

If the farmer has compost ready in the summer he can apply it where a grain crop such as wheat or oats has just been taken off, although this may be complicated by a nurse crop such as clover coming up which was planted in the grain earlier in the spring. The farmer will not find it as easy as the gardener to use up his compost quickly. He may decide to use it in the fall when planting winter wheat and barley.

If compost has to be stored it is best to move it under cover. The simplest way is to use a very heavy straw mulch or one made from withered weeds, or simply canvas. As soon as the compost is completed, certain chemical changes take place which reduce its value. Anaerobic bacteria which act without oxygen begin to act and stored heaps should be turned from time to time and watered. Where many heaps are made they should be covered for winter protection with straw or hay or leaves. If compost is stored in a shed or an outhouse it may be placed on a concrete floor as it is desired to slow down decomposition. The heaps can be covered with wet burlapping.

Compost applied at an approximate rate of 10 tons to the acre brings good results with the average crop. This cabbage will yield up to 30 tons per acre on the muck soil in which it is planted if given adequate organic matter, such as compost.

Method of Applying

It is most advisable to spread compost on a cloudy day as the sun will dry it out and some of the valuable chemicals such as ammonia which are in solution in the water will escape into the air and be lost. The farmer should plow it under or disk it in as soon as possible after spreading. Dr. Ehrenfried Pfeiffer says "Controlled experiments in Holland have shown that if the yield of immediately-plowed-in-manure is reckoned at 100 per cent, then the yield from manure that has lain on the field 3 days is only 86 per cent, and the yield from manure that has lain on the ground for some weeks is correspondingly less." Dr. Pfeiffer feels that (rotted) manure should "be plowed under within 3 hours if it is to retain its full value."

In the *Pennsylvania Farmer* of January 9, 1943, J. B. R. Dickey gives further support to the same idea. He says:

"Old-timers used to tell us that the best plan was to spread manure and plow it down immediately, before it had a chance to dry out. Science now proves they had the right idea. In a Danish experiment, run on 4 different crops over a term

455

of years, if the increase in yield of the first crop due to the manure plowed down as spread were rated at 100, manure spread 6 hours before plowing, presumably in mild weather, gave an average increase of only 82; spread 24 hours before plowing averaged 72; and 4 days before plowing only 56. This is an almost unbelievable loss and it would seem very worth while for some American scientists either to verify or disprove it and to work out practical methods of reducing a national, annual fertility loss which make some others, now in the limelight, appear trifling."

If a large field is to be manured it would be advisable to do it in portions and as you place the compost in a small section, follow it up immediately by plowing. As much as half the nitrogen will be lost if the manure is allowed to lie too long.

Please note that the above experiments have been performed with manure and not compost. Manure and compost are very different things. I do not believe that the loss would be anywhere nearly as great if compost were allowed to lie instead of manure because it is not so rich in ammonia or nitrogenous compounds which might escape into the air. At any rate experimental work should be performed to test this point.

Weight of Compost

It is difficult to estimate exactly the weight of a compost heap as the materials and other conditions vary so greatly. As a very rough average, however, it may be stated that there are about two cubic yards to the ton. Weight will, of course, vary depending on the water-content of the compost. Suppose your heap is 10 feet by 20 feet by 3 feet high. Its total cubic footage then would be 600 before allowing for the slope of the sides. About 20 per cent should be deducted on account of such slope which then leaves 480 cubic feet. As there are 27 cubic feet in a cubic yard we divide 480 by 27 and get 17.7 cubic yards. Since there are two cubic yards to a ton, this particular heap would amount to approximately 9 tons.

Winter Conditions

The question as to when to spread compost ties in with seasonal conditions. In winter, in average medium cold to really cold climates, the biologic action in the compost heap stops, and for all practical purposes making compost in winter is not to be recommended. If one wants to have finished com-

Easily adapted to the equipment and practices with which farmers are familiar, the sheet-composting method enables even the largest of farming operations to enrich the soil naturally. Here an Iowa clover crop is being turned under by tractor.

post to apply in April or May, it will have to be started about August or at the latest September, except in more temperate regions. Compost heaps can be assembled during warm spells in winter time, but it will be necessary to have some way of keeping a supply of earth from freezing so that it may be sprinkled in the heaps.

In greenhouse gardening, it may be important to have a continuous supply of compost and insulated sheds may be constructed which will permit the process of composting to proceed even during really cold spells. In such cases, very little of such a shed should be above ground. It might consist of a roof set on the ground, the entire shed itself being underground, thus preventing the heat from escaping.

USING SHEET COMPOST ON THE FARM

The use of such equipment as the hydraulic manure loader, silage cutter and automatic elevator greatly reduce the labor involved. Sheet composting also lends itself well

457

to other farm equipment and practices with which every farmer is familiar.

After the organic matter is on the surface of the ground, either in the form of a cover crop or spread green matter, manure may be applied with a manure spreader or fork at the rate of from 2 to 10 tons per acre. Finely ground raw limestone may be applied with the manure or applied separately at the rate of from one to two tons per acre. Apply finely pulverized phosphate rock at the rate of one-half ton per acre.

After the manure, lime and phosphate rock have been spread over the green matter, all these materials must be incorporated into the surface layer of the soil. It does not matter what equipment is used to do this, so long as the organic matter is near enough to the surface of the soil where there is sufficient oxygen from the air to enable the aerobic organisms to break down the organic matter and convert it into humus. If the plow is used, do not plow deeper than 4 or 5 inches. Other suitable equipment include the disk, rotary tillers and other types of tillers.

Moisture and Temperature

The moisture necessary for the composting process is inherent in the green matter and the soil, and is renewed from time to time by rain. The moisture factor is important in the decomposition process of organic matter in the soil. Sheet composting should not be attempted in regions where sufficient water is not available in the form of rain or irrigation water. The rate of decomposition will vary also with the temperature and will proceed most rapidly when aeration, moisture and temperature all are optimum for the organisms of decomposition.

Decomposition

As soon as the organic materials have been worked into the soil and to the extent that environmental conditions are favorable, decomposition begins. The soil organisms secrete digestive enzymes which digest the carbohydrates, sugars, starches, celluloses and lignins; the proteins; and the fats in the soil. The composting process begins slowly but increases rapidly under favorable conditions.

During the time the soil organisms are consuming the organic matter in the soil, they require large amounts of nitrogen and other plant nutrients for their use. Those nutrients will be returned to the soil and be available to the plants as the soil organisms die and their highly nitrogenous bodies decompose. However, there is a temporary depletion of nitrogen from the soil which makes it inadvisable to grow plants while organic matter is decomposing in the soil. The condition of nitrogen depletion may be considerably reduced with the use of highly-nitrogenous organic matter. High-nitrogenous materials that may be advantageously used in this way are ground-up legumes and legume seeds, *i.e.*, soybean meal, or dried blood, paunch manure, cotton seed meal, castor pomace, many marine products and others.

The time required for the complete transformation of raw organic matter into humus depends upon the nature and fertility of the soil, the amount of organic matter involved and the conditions which favor the activity of the soil organisms. Any farmer can, by digging into the soil, determine how the decomposition is progressing, and when it is complete. This is no more difficult than checking a baking potato or a fowl in the oven by the housewife. Some kinds of plant material will break down more rapidly than others. Cellulose breaks down more rapidly than lignin. Leguminous plants break down much more rapidly than the straw of wheat and other grains. Accordingly leguminous cover crops lend themselves especially well to the sheet composting method of fertilization.

When Planting Is Safe

When the organic matter has been more or less completely converted into humus, the crop may be planted. With some crops, as corn, the seeds may be planted before the sheet composting process is entirely complete, because the corn kernel contains sufficient food to feed the corn seedling for two weeks or more. But humus formation in the soil should be completed by the time the fibrous roots develop from the base of the young plant and reach out for nutrients for the growing corn plants.

Sheet Composting vs. Turning Under Green Matter

There are one or two fundamental features of the plowing in of a green crop involving the balance in the soil, which appear to be very little understood. The microorganic balance is often thoroughly upset in old pastures which have not been plowed for many years and the soil in consequence is in a very unhealthy condition. If this is true, a crop grown on this soil will be similarly affected and will not in itself be complete in balance. If this crop is plowed back into the soil this lack of balance and any special deficiencies will be accentuated, for instead of introducing humus to the soil which is in perfect order, you are only increasing the ground's defaults and deficiencies. By using animal manure and natural rock materials such as raw limestone and phosphate rock in conjunction with the green crop, the product of decomposition is balanced in nutrient elements. Sheet composting thus provides a highly concentrated organic matter to the soil providing a balanced condition of plant nutrients for healthy, vigorous growth.

MANURES

Manures are a basic part of every farm composting program. The entire question of handling and applying manure is presented in the chapter on that subject.

BUILDING SOIL ON A 200-ACRE FARM

Operating a 200-acre farm organically is much easier now than 10 years ago. That's the opinion of Joseph Carsten of Deer Valley Farm in Guilford, New York. "We can do the organic soil-building job with less work and time," says Carsten as he ponts to the fields that he and his son, Ted, are proud to farm.

The basic step in the Deer Valley Farm's soil-building program is the proper handling of manure. Each year well over 400 tons of manure, mostly cattle with some pig and poultry manure included, are composted. Here is how they have worked out their mechanized program:

During winter, the barn is cleaned out twice daily before each milking. Rock phosphate, powdered kelp, and other mineral fertilizers are sprinkled right in the gutters—an operation that takes less than a minute. About 20 to 40 pounds of these mineral fertilizers along with some 50 to 100 pounds of dolomite are spread per load (about a ton). Lime is important since the sedimentary shale soil on the farm is very sour with a pH that had tested between 4 and 5. A great deal of straw is used as bedding for the animals and this is forked into the gutters also. Then the automatic barn cleaner is turned on and the mineral-enriched manure is conveyed directly into the manure spreader.

Winter weather permitting, the manure is hauled as close as possible to the field where it will be spread the following spring. During periods of heavy snow, the manure is hauled to a place convenient to the barn. In spring, the piles are turned several times; then the finished compost is spread prior to plantings of corn and spring wheat at the rate of about 10 tons to the acre. For certain fields they have been plowing 10 tons to the acre, quite often even 20 tons, in their effort to build up the soil there. (No manure is usually applied before seeding oats unless the field is exceptionally poor.)

Manure is also spread in fall for crops such as rye or winter wheat. In addition to the manure, Carsten gets about 50 tons of leaves that are brought in from the nearby town of Norwich. Other materials that go into the composting program are roadside trimmings of plant materials and sawdust. These are mixed in with the manure, often shredded by a hammermill first.

While Carsten admits that there is a certain amount of extra work involved in making use of these materials on the farm, he is positive that the benefits are a great deal more than a small amount of extra work. He also has found that this program has saved him quite a bit of money in chemical fertilizer costs as well as the cost of organic fertilizers if he didn't follow his composting program.

ROTARY TILLERS AND SHEET COMPOST

Rotary tillage methods have been developed because of a desire to simplify and speed up the process of preparing soil for planting. Ordinary tillage methods require the use of a plow, disk and a harrow before seed can be planted. Sometimes a field is also dragged to break up clods and firm the seedbed. Developers of rotary tillage equipment hoped to be able to build a machine that would do those 3 jobs in one operation. They have succeeded.

Rotary tillage has another advantage. It provides a better means of incorporating sheet compost, crop wastes and other organic matter into the soil than the plow-disk-harrow combination. Plowing tends to bury organic matter in a layer 4 to 6 inches deep, often too far below the surface to allow optimum decay and breakdown by microorganisms. Rotary tillage mixes such organic matter into the soil evenly through the full tillage depth.

Farm-scale rotary tillage is steadily growing in popularity, but it has so far failed to be adopted by the great majority of farmers.

COMPOST-IRRIGATION BUILDS SOILS

Thousands of acres, especially in the southwestern United States, which previously were low-yielding, can now be turned into high-producing land. Compost-irrigation, the latest development in organic farming techniques, is chiefly responsible for this amazing fertility build-up in the soil.

Clinton Ray, whose farm is located near Mesa, Arizona, is one of the many Southwestern farmers who has used compost-irrigation successfully. He is using a waste organic material that is readily available in his area—cotton gin trash; by irrigating through the cotton gin trash compost pits, and by sheet composting with the same organic material, he's been able to step up productivity rapidly.

Here is how the Arizona *Farmer-Ranchman* recently described Ray's technique:

"The method used by Ray in composting gin trash is to put a pit in the irrigation ditch. During irrigation, the water flows through the stack, carrying plant food and micro-organisms into the field. In addition, he side-dresses his crops with the compost, using a cattle feeder truck for the purpose."

Ray believes that the pit can be any size, but should not be made more than 6 feet deep. "When the trash settles," he says, "it resolves to about 4 feet, which is the ideal depth." He has 5 of these compost pits in his irrigation system, each containing 150 tons or more of gin trash.

All of the material is bought from 5 gins located near his farm. Since Ray treats the trash with a bacteria additive, he does not have to turn the compost at any time—the bacteria does the work for him.

Two years ago he was getting a short-staple cotton yield of $1\frac{3}{4}$ bales; last year his yield climbed to $2\frac{4}{5}$ bales. Long-staple yields increased from $1\frac{5}{16}$ of a bale to $1\frac{3}{4}$ bales.

Similar increases were made in vegetable production, particularly tomatoes. A few years ago Ray was producing about 300 flats to the acre, and they were poor keepers. Last year he produced 1,000 flats per acre on 7 acres. He says they were better keepers and brought him a premium of 25 cents a flat on the market.

At La Mesa, New Mexico, an ingenious method of compost-irrigation has proved exceptionally fruitful for farmer George Stoy. Small particles of compost are washed off a huge compost pile and carried to the soil to begin bacterial action.

Ray cleared land for this farm out of the desert about 15 years ago, building up a fruit and vegetable farm in addition to straight cropping. His 15 acres of robin and redwing peaches have been in for 10 years and are producing well. Three acres of late royal and early gold apricots yield well each year.

"I treated my peach orchard with organic material from the first," Ray points out, "and it has been improving every year. I can't say the same for my vegetables and field crops, which I fertilized the usual way. No matter how much I fertilized, yields kept dropping down. I recognized that the soil had a tremendous lack of organic material, so finally I turned to sheet composting with gin trash. This was an improvement, but I didn't get the marked improvement until I treated the trash with bacteria. It gave me improved soil structure. Land, for example, that took 12 hours to sub up during irrigation, now takes only 3."

About a year ago, Joe Ellsworth leased part of the Ray farm for a big dairy operation. The lease worked out this way: Ray is to provide feed for the cattle; in exchange, he gets the manure for fertilizer use. Gin trash was spread in

463

the pens and treated bacterially. As a result of their agreement, Ellsworth's cows are healthier, and the manure-trash combination is giving Ray a very rich fertilizer which he is using on his alfalfa.

Ray has found ladybugs effective in controlling the yellow clover aphid. It's over a year since he purchased any, and yet there are thousands of ladybugs in the fields at this time.

All Southwestern farmers should take note of how well a compost-irrigation system has worked for Clinton Ray. The system isn't difficult or expensive, yet the rewards are more fertile soils and greater crop yields.

COMPOSTING ON TEXAS FARM

The high fertility on the Idus Gillett farm in the El Paso Valley of Texas accounts for the increased acreage production Gillett has had without using any commercial fertilizer. (Previous annual cost for fertilizers and sprays ran about $30 per acre.)

The key to his farming success is compost, which he has applied at the rate of 300 tons yearly to his 105 acres, or about 3 tons to the acre. Gillett builds his compost heaps with manure he obtains from railroad livestock cars. He waters the "green" manure heaps down about every two weeks until they create humus by their natural actions. The steps are quickened at times by adding "seed" humus from a compost heap that already has passed through the internal process to rich humus.

This humus is then spread on the land either by dump spreader or through irrigated water. The "pure" humus is fed into the irrigation water and automatically reaches the land in proper proportion. Humus that includes sand, which is often desired, is broadcast by spreader.

The decomposed material is distributed in his irrigation water for two reasons. First, because sheet composting sometimes doesn't work in this semi-desert country; second, the water absorbs the salts of the compost, neutralizing much of the alkali present in the soil.

Compost is distributed at every irrigation—once before planting when Gillett readies his ground for seed, and again 90 days later, about July 1st, to mulch the ground around the young plants. A third irrigation is made in mid-August if water is available.

Key to a decade of organic-method success on the 105-acre Idus Gillett farm at El Paso, Texas, is his yearly use of 300 tons of compost. The finished material, along with rock phosphate and potash, is spread through irrigation water.

During the last 25 years, prior to 1950, Gillett had noticed a steady decline in his soil's fertility. "When I first started farming here, the land was virgin soil, abundant in soil organisms. But after a decade, it was evident that productivity was declining, wilt damage increased, and the soil was hardening to a cement-like degree, entirely devoid of organic matter."

The only way he could maintain reasonable production was by heavy application of commercial fertilizer for each crop. But Gillett's organic farming techniques have completely reversed the downward trend, until now he believes his land has reached its original state of virgin fertility.

Compost materials are readily available and cheap in the El Paso Valley, which is known as well for its milk production as it is for its cotton. Farmers can get manure from local dairies at rates of about $2 per ton, plus $1 for hauling, while local poultry producers will give them chicken droppings if they clean the barns.

ORGANIC IRRIGATION FOR COTTON

George Stoy, La Mesa, N. M., farmer, has turned to organic land treatment to up cotton production on his farm by a quarter of a bale per acre.

In doing so he has used one of the largest compost piles in the Southwest during the past 4 years.

465

Stoy is sold on the treatment method which has turned his 80 acres from hard, crusted soil to pliable, springy dirt.

Stoy's compost pile, which is 25 by 75 feet in size and from 5 to 8 feet in depth, is located within a few feet of his well.

For the past 4 years Stoy has hauled in 200 tons of burrs and other waste annually from cotton gins in the area. The job of constructing the pile begins each year in September and lasts through the ginning season, ending in December.

A large pit, or tank, several feet larger than the compost pile has been dug about 30 feet from Stoy's well. Each September the gin waste is piled in the center of the tank. At the end of the ginning season the waste pile is topped with a layer of manure about 12 or 14 inches thick.

When irrigation time comes Stoy simply starts pumping water from his well which has an output of 2,500 gallons per minute.

The water spills into the tank around the compost pile, washing tiny particles of the compost off the pile and carrying billions of them into the irrigation ditches and to Stoy's cotton fields.

Compost Spread

A water line from the well runs to a point above the center of the pile and spills a constant stream on the pile. This water soaks into the pile and seeps out of the sides.

A field laborer spends most of the time in the tank, using a shovel to skim the compost from the sides of the pile and agitate it thoroughly, breaking it into the smallest organic particles.

Stoy uses no other fertilizer or soil conditioner.

In addition to his production increase Stoy points to the fact that the number of earthworms, always a sign of healthy soil, has increased greatly on his land.

He uses water which has run through his compost tank to irrigate about 30 pecan trees on which the yield has increased.

A number of farmers in the El Paso Valley are treating their soil with compost, using the same method. Most of them use several small pits instead of one large one.

—Reprinted from the *El Paso Times*

"VERTICAL COMPOSTING"

The following report, reprinted from *The Farm Quarterly*, illustrates the effectiveness of "vertical composting"—A cross between sheet composting, deep tillage and mulching.

When Jim Spain sat down in the lecture hall at Purdue University to listen to still another paper on soils at the 1953 Winter Agriculture Conference, he hardly expected to be struck with an idea that may revolutionize our methods of subsoiling. Yet, before the hour was up, he had it—a plan combining two old practices, mulching and deep tillage, which in its first trials promises to conserve water, improve drainage, increase aeration, permit deep root penetration, and slow down erosion. Spain and his associates have been thinking, planning, and working for 4 years to bring this idea to practical fulfillment.

The lecture that triggered the idea was given by Dr. A. R. Bertrand who was speaking on the subsoil fertilization research that he and Dr. Helmut Kohnke had pioneered. By applying fertilizer deep, Bertrand pointed out, we encourage deep root penetration which opens small channels in the soil for water infiltration and aeration. By this method, Bertrand hoped to overcome one of the major disadvantages of deep tillage. Chiseling deeply into the soil opens a channel through the hard packed subsoil to permit water and air to enter, but with the first rains, the soil begins to reseal itself and reform the barrier. It was at this point that the thought flashed into Spain's mind, "Stabilize the channel! Stabilize the channel by filling it with crop trash."

Some of Spain's associates laughed at the idea, but he was encouraged when men like J. B. Peterson, head of the Agronomy Department at Purdue, and his office mates, Don McCune and Garry Williams, urged him to go ahead and develop it. Putting the idea into practice proved easier than Spain had thought possible.

"From the first," he said, "we had thought of a forage harvester as a way to pick up the mulch, chop it, and blow it down into the channel. But just how we were going to get the mulch to go into the channel worried us. McCune and I took our problem over to Ag Engineering and they told us it would be as easy as pie. Bruce Liljedahl over there, gave our problem to his class in machinery design and in the spring of '55 they came up with the basic plan which was a subsoiler with two wings welded on behind to hold the channel open for a few inches beyond the chisel. This gave us the opening down which we could blow the straw."

Disappearing Cobs

In the summer of 1955, Spain and his associates hooked this winged subsoiler behind a Caterpillar D2 tractor and pulled a forage harvester behind a second tractor to begin their first experiment. "We were working with rank, high clover," Spain recalls, "and decided to take one-half a swath. It simply disappeared down the hole. Then we took the full 5-foot cut, and it, too, was swallowed up. We also had a truck load of corn cobs with us and we tried them. Two husky boys shoveled them into the chopper as hard as they could and the cobs disappeared without a trace. That first trial gave us a surprising idea of how much the channel would hold."

Later they took their rig into wheat fields and blew the dry straw into the channel. They found that straw and other dry material tends to fluff out more in the channel, which holds the channel open better. They also found that the dry soil after wheat harvest was just right for deep tillage. Wet soil compacts the earth along the walls of the channel, smearing it over so that there is little penetration of water through the glazed surface. During the summer they used their vertical mulching on flat land and contoured the sides of hills as they tried to work out the best uses for the new technique. In 1956, they eliminated the second tractor by using a draw bar extension to pull the forage harvester behind the D2.

In the fall of 1955 they had their first chance to look over their work and see how it was holding up. Rain, at the rate of 5 inches in 3 days, gave them a chance to compare vertical mulching on part of a field with deep tillage without mulching on the rest. The dividing line was perfectly apparent on the surface of the field after two inches of rain had fallen—that part which had been chiseled to 20 inches without mulching was covered with standing water; on the other half of the field the mulching channels were drinking in all the water that came and there was none on the surface.

Eliminates Water Runoff

They then dug away the earth from a channel to show it in cross section. Free water was standing in the channel 12 inches below the surface. As the rain continued, the channels gradually filled, but none of the 5 inches of water escaped

This rough-surfaced field is examined by a Kansas farmer after tilling a green manure crop into the rows. Practices like this and deep fertilizer placement help maintain soil fertility, combat dry-weather-area cracking and erosion.

as surface runoff. The 20 inches along each side of the channel had provided 40 inches of surface for the water to penetrate and had created a passageway for the water to enter the soil and reach the more absorbent lower levels.

On a hot, muggy day in June, 1956, a one-inch shower fell on these plots. Then rain came so fast that only the top two inches of soil were wet before the water began to run off. But no water was lost from the vertically mulched plots. Again a cross section was cut to see what was happening. The surplus surface water, which had run off the other plots, had been funnelled deep into the subsoil on the mulched plots where it had spread out. There, 12 to 18 inches below the surface, this water was available for growing crops.

With this same cross-section technique, they were able to study the different mulching materials they had used. The fresh sweet clover, they found, had first compacted far more than the straw and other dry mulch and had then decomposed to the point where it had almost disappeared after only 4 months. From these observations they drew one of their first conclusions—this system was not well adapted for putting down green manure.

469

Worms Replace Mulch

The channels that had been mulched with straw, corn cobs and trash were, even after a year in the ground, all that Spain had dreamed of when the idea first struck him. Plenty of mulch still remained in the cut to hold it open for another year, perhaps 3 or 4; and a new development had taken place which excited him. With air penetration and plenty of mulch had come earthworms. They had honeycombed the sides of the channel leaving the soil loose and crumbly with their castings. After examining the results of a single year of this activity, Spain is convinced that even after the mulch is all decayed or consumed by the worms, the activity of the earthworms will have stabilized the channel area into a porous, absorbent strip through which the surface water can penetrate deeply.

Though Spain and his associates are very enthusiastic about the results of this first year's work, it is hard to get any scientist to make recommendations so early in the game. They have gone on in 1956 to put vertical mulching on slopes where they can measure every drop of runoff; they have put it on fields where they can compare it with deep tillage and with deep placement of fertilizer; they have tried combining vertical mulching with deep placement of fertilizer; and they have experimented with different spacings of the channels.

Though they may show what the layman considers a maddening restraint about making recommendations, the scientists are still quite human about guessing what the results of this work may be. They feel quite sure that vertical mulching will have its best results when the soil is dry and there is plenty of good mulching material as there is in late summer following small grains. They also feel that it may work very well after corn, particularly when the corn has been harvested early and the dry soil is right for deep tillage. Corn stalks, husks, and cobs, they have found, make excellent mulch.

Filling Soil Cracks

"Out in Oklahoma and Texas, where I spent most of my life," Spain said, "the dry weather cracks the soil almost every year and gives the farmers a version of deep tillage and out there we have found that subsoiling usually doesn't pay. With the first rain both the natural and man-made cracks seal up and we get water racing across the fields, we get sheet erosion, and to top it all off we lose the water that we need so desperately while the subsoil remains dry. I am convinced that vertical mulching will be of real value there. I also think it will do well on rolling grass farms where heavy soils and winter freezing prevent good water penetration."

On poorly drained land, Spain believes that vertical mulching can make it possible to increase the spacing between tile lines. Digging the mulched channels at right angles to the tile lines creates a drainage grid with the mulched channels providing a short-run drainage system and the tile carrying the water over the long run. Where the drainage problem is localized in potholes, vertical mulching should be able to do the job alone. On most parts of the fields the channels will improve the drainage and prevent the runoff onto the low potholes. And on the holes themselves, it will break through the hardpan and allow the water to escape.

This new technique also opens up exciting possibilities for farmers who have wanted to use sprinkler irrigation, but have held off because of poor drainage. There is little use in sprinkling on the water if you can't get penetration, but with vertical mulching, water can penetrate deep into the root zone.

Another irrigation practice—the heavy watering of soil to leach out the surface salts—may be improved by this new discovery. Western soils men who work with this leaching problem feel that vertical mulching will improve the chances of washing the harmful salts out of the root zone and down into a deeper horizon where they will do less harm.

How to Space Mulch

The problem of spacing between channels is difficult because here the scientists must deal with the slope of the land, and the nature of the soil, as well as the purpose of the treatment. In their own experiments, however, they are using a wide range of spacings. For runoff and erosion control on gently sloping land, they have spaced the channels 80 inches apart so that a pair of corn rows will fit between each pair of channels. In the future, they plan to try corn on steep land—even up to a 15 per cent grade—spacing the channels 120 inches apart.

In order to keep the mouth of the channel from silting over on this steeper land, they will allow a 20-inch strip of sod to grow on each side of the channel mouth. This will still leave them room for two rows of corn between each pair of channels. Both the channels and the corn will be worked on contour.

The next channels will be placed midway between the old water-absorbent channels which will add to root penetration as well as to the water-holding capacity of the soil around the roots. With the alternate wide middles, it will be possible to seed a winter cover in the late summer or early fall.

In their drainage experiments, they are using spacings from 5 to 30 feet, hoping to bracket the best spacing for the soils on which they are working. For supplemental drainage, the channels will not need to be completely filled, most of the water movement being in the bottom half of the channel. However, for runoff and erosion control, they feel that it is very important to fill the channel completely and protect the entire channel so that the surface does not become sealed over.

This brings up what is perhaps the most important practical factor in determining the spacing of the channels—the amount of material available on the field to fill them. If it takes a strip of stubble 10 feet wide to fill the channel, you can't very well space the channels any closer than 10 feet without hauling in extra material.

In practice, Spain and his fellow workers have found that two rows of corn stalks from a stand of corn that runs 85 to 90 bushels to the acre will do a good job of filling a channel. An 80-inch strip of heavy wheat or oat stubble is also about right. It takes a lot of material any way you look at it.

As yet, no vertical mulching machinery is available from manufacturers. The equipment used at Purdue was modified and assembled in their Ag Engineering shop. The major change involved is a modification on the subsoiler. It takes a lot of power and traction to pull such a tool through heavy soils. This means either a small crawler tractor or a large 4 or 5 plow wheel tractor. A self-powered forage harvester is necessary because of the power requirements and the problems involved in using the power take-off with the tool bar and draw bar mounted on the tractor. Since the changes are slight, and simple, it shouldn't be long before some company comes up with the tool to do the job.

FERTILIZING FARM PONDS

How you feed your pond will determine the quantity and quality of your fish harvest. One thousand pounds per

472

Manure or compost and finely ground rock phosphate are suitable fertilizer for the farm pond. Spread 1,000 pounds of compost and 500 of phosphate in equal portions from May to September to feed algae, on which the pond's fish subsist.

acre of manure is good. Compost may be substituted for the manure, and 500 pounds finely ground rock phosphate is another good feeder. These fertilizers may be spread in equal amounts once a month from May to September. They go to feed, not the fish, but the minute organisms called algae and plankton which the fish eat. This microscopic plant life is the green scum which forms on a pond in summer. If the water in your pond is clear for more than a foot down, there are not enough algae—fertilize quickly.

But don't overfertilize. Too much will reduce the oxygen content of the water and injure the fish. Excessive feeding that makes very dark, scummy water can be overcome by spreading lime. Never use copper sulphate, as recommended by some experts, to clear the water. In more than a very minute two parts per million, it will kill everything living in the pond.

AIR-SPREAD COMPOST

Perhaps the most novel and modern idea in farm-composting has recently come out of New Zealand. It has to do

473

with applying compost *by air*. Following is a report from a New Zealand newspaper:

"Compost was spread by aeroplane over farmland for the first time in New Zealand in the Maraetotara Valley. The experiment, which could lead to a greatly expanded demand for compost, was conducted on the estate of the late Mr. C. J. B. Beauchamp.

"The use of compost has a dual significance: it is a practical example of returning to the land town and domestic waste—from which the compost is manufactured—and it marks an almost revolutionary change in New Zealand techniques for pasture improvement.

"Other Hawke's Bay farmers have experimented with humic compost on farmland, but the application in the past has been by means of surface spreaders, and practically no attempt has been made till now to apply it to steep hill country.

"Mr. R. Tregerthan, the manager of the Beauchamp estate, said previous experience with compost on the property had shown its value in establishing clover. Compost had also proved itself in re-establishing growth on slipping faces.

"The pilot of the aeroplane, Mr. N. C. Down, was also interested in the experiment from an airman's point of view. There was an additional safety factor for the pilot, he said, as compost is light, much lighter than super."

Chapter 14

THE EARTHWORM'S ROLE IN COMPOSTING

THE EARTHWORM IS NATURE'S CHAMPION COMPOSTER

As earthworm breeder Dorothy Hewett expresses it, "To the animal we've been pleased to call 'lowly,' God apparently assigned the mightiest task in the world—the task of keeping the surface of the earth forever renewed; the task of forever

Nature's greatest composters, earthworms toil unceasingly to "digest" organic matter, returning raw wastes as fine humus. Domestic types are widely propagated for use in garden and farm soils, composting and (non-agriculturally) for fish bait.

converting back into topsoil—humus—every bit of waste matter left over by man and beast, as well as every bit of dead vegetation, so that the earth might forever stay pure—cleaned up—and able to support all the life that lives off it in a forever condition of health, wealth and perfect enjoyment.

"Now, of course, the earthworm was given helpers to carry out his vast job—helpers in the form of billions upon billions of tiny microorganic creatures who do miraculous preliminary work. But the earthworm seems to be the chief executive, the coordinator, the homogenizer, and the final deodorizer, purifier and vitalizer of the waste; because not until it has been swallowed, digested, and excreted by him in particles that break down to the size of finely-ground black pepper, has the waste matter actually become earth again.

"One of the greats of our own time and country, Dr. Thomas J. Barrett, who originated the idea of harnessing (domesticating) the earthworm—raising him intensively in boxes or pits full of compost—had this to say in his beautiful book, *Harnessing the Earthworm:*

" 'In contemplative mood, we hold a handful of rich, dark earth—humus. It is without form, yet within it all forms are potential. It is without structure, yet within it all the wonders of civilization sleep. It appears dead, yet within it all life resides . . .'

"This rich, dark earth—this humus he is referring to— is the product of the earthworm."

Another earthworm researcher, George Sheffield Oliver, echoes this: "Few creatures equal the burrowing earthworm a necessity to better health and greater growth to plant and vegetable life, and, therefore, indirectly is of the utmost importance to man.

"The burrowing earthworm is Nature's own plough, her chemist, her cultivator, her fertilizer, her distributor of plant food. In every way, the earthworm surpasses anything man has yet invented to plough, to cultivate or to fertilize the soil.

"While it is unquestionably true that plants and vegetables grow and reproduce their kind without the aid of the earthworm, most naturalists claim that all fertile areas have, at one time or another, passed through the bodies of earthworms.

"It is likewise unquestionably true that the finest plants and vegetables will become healthier and more productive through the activities of this lowly animal which the ordinary person considers useful only to break the early bird's fast or to impale on a fish hook."

Albert Howard's Studies

Sir Albert Howard also studied the value of earthworms and their activities. He says: "How can earthworms assist the gardener? In the first place they keep the soil fit for its population by providing a ventilating system in the shape of their tunnels. By this means the life of the soil obtains its supply oxygen from the atmosphere and also expels its used-up air. Moreover, these tunnels allow the surplus rainfall to drain away into the subsoil. In the second place the earthworms condition the food materials needed by the roots of plants. This is accomplished by means of their casts which in a garden soil in good condition may exceed 25 tons to the acre in a single year. The casts are manufactured in the alimentary canal of the earthworm from dead vegetable matter and particles of soil. In this passage the food of these creatures is neutralized by constant additions of carbonate of lime from the 3 pairs of calciferous glands near the gizzard, where it is finely ground prior to digestion. The casts which are left contain everything the crop needs—nitrates, phosphates and potash in abundance and also in just the condition in which the plant can make use of them. Recent investigations in the United States show that the fresh casts of earthworms are 5 times richer in available nitrogen, 7 times richer in available phosphates and 11 times richer in available potash than the upper 6 inches of soil. The earthworm is, therefore, the gardener's manure factory.

"The reaction of the roots of a crop like the potato to a fresh worm cast is illuminating. A few years ago in South Lincolnshire, while investigating the root development of this crop, I observed that the fine roots of the potato plant in passing downwards into the subsoil always made full use of the tunnels of the earthworm. In these galleries fresh worm casts are constantly being deposited. Whenever a fine root passed one of these deposits, it at once formed a weblike network of new roots which closely invested the cast and penetrated it in all directions. Then the root continued its downward passage into the subsoil. Obviously the potato was removing something from the casts, otherwise this network of new roots would not have been developed. The recent work in the United States explains what it was the roots were seeking.

"Feeding the crop is not the last service performed by earthworms. They are the ideal soil analysts and furnish the gardener with a report on the state of his land far more instructive than anything the soil scientist has so far provided. All that is necessary is for the gardener himself to make a rough count of the earthworms in the top spit of soil and to observe their color, general condition and above all their liveliness. If, in each spadeful during the autumn digging, one glistening, red, active lob-worm occurs, about the thickness of a man's little finger, then all is well with the soil and the quality of next season's crop is assured. There will be no need for plant nutrients of any kind: no anxiety need be felt about pests. But if the worms are few, coiled up in balls, or pale in colour and sluggish in their movements, then the next crop will be poor and trouble with pests will be inevitable. In this country our old and experienced gardeners pay great attention to the earthworms and often base their manuring largely on the indications they furnish. In the cases of the

Sahara the tribesmen also make great use of the earthworm as a soil analyst. They judge the value of land by the number of worm casts appearing on the surface.

"In return for what the earthworms do for the gardener, all that is needed is to supply these animals with the right kind of food and to avoid the use of unnatural nourishment. Earthworms thrive on farmyard manure, or better still on freshly made compost manufactured from vegetable and animal wastes." This last fact is, of course, the one in which composters are most interested, for they can utilize the earthworm's waste-eating abilities to make better, richer compost.

WHAT ARE EARTHWORMS?

What sort of creature is an earthworm? Pick up a garden worm and examine it closely. You will see that it consists of a closely-linked series of rings. There may be anywhere from 100 to 400 of these, according to the size and kind of the worm, and they form a muscular chain from the elongated head without eyes, nose or ears, to the tapering tail.

For its size one of the strongest creatures in all creation, the earthworm is tough, flexible, wiry and perfectly shaped for its burrowing existence underground. A specimen weighing less than one-thirtieth of an once can shift a comparative ton of stone weighing two ounces, over 60 times its own weight. By its very nature, it is little more than a digestive organism, everything being subserviated to the processes of the alimentary canal which runs the length of its elastic body. Blind and impetuous, the worm seeks and disposes of food without ceasing. It has no encumbrance unconnected with feeding and digestion, but sufficient instinctive intelligence to enable it to exist wherever it happens to find itself.

By means of tiny clusters of erectile bristles set at intervals along its length, and a self-secreted slimy, lubricating mucous, the worm is able to burrow through even the heaviest soil. The bristles grip at one end while the other is pulled along, and the whole movement is rippling rather than snake-like. If you run a finger along a worm backwards, these fine stiff bristles may be felt. Without them it would have difficulty in getting along. Cut a hapless worm in two with your spade, and the head end will usually grow a new tail, and live, but never vice versa. It can stretch or shrink its length at will, and can burrow to depths of 12 or 14 feet or more. Cold and wet weather send most worms down deeper than their normal feeding region of from 1 to 4 feet beneath the surface.

From the worm's own point of view its most important feature is its oval mouth which is protected by a long, overhanging lip. This helps to push aside most of the soil as it tunnels its way along while the rest is swallowed greedily passing straight into a bird-like crop in the neck, where minute fragments of grit grind down everything into a fine, moist paste. Leaves, grass, stems, rubbish—all are reduced to a smooth residue, which is then swiftly digested in the thread-like stomach, the creature extracting its own nourishment from the soil. Stones up to one-twentieth of an inch across are swallowed and incorporated in the gizzard, larger ones are eaten around and thus started on their slow sinking process which is finally completed by the deposit of layers of worm-casts on the surface.

Bracing its body for the effort, and anchoring itself by its tail in its burrow, a worm can grasp and pull down underground quite large fragments of rotting vegetation and animal matter—the dead or dying refuse that litters the earth. Tougher food is first coated with a kind of saliva to aid the digestive process. In this country it has been estimated that 3 inches of completely new topsoil from castings is deposited by worms every 15 years, and where the earthworm population can be increased, the rate of this vital work can be appreciably stepped up. Although blind, worms are sensitive to light, and feed mostly at night, rising to the surface after dusk and burying themselves again before daybreak.

Different Types

There are several different species of worms, from the common earthworm of our gardens and fields, to the brandling found in manure heaps and beloved of anglers, and the 9-feet monsters which gurgle their way into the squelchy mud of Australia. Worms are found all over the globe, except where it is too hot and dry for them to exist.

As these untold myriads never rest or hibernate, but dig and tunnel unceasingly for 15 years or more, constantly yielding this incredible fertile layer of cast soil, it is small wonder that the earth has been rich for some many thousands of years. The sweetness of the Nile Valley, for instance, for so long the home of a civilization, is owed to the hordes of hungry worms that wait each year for the huge flood of waste vegetable matter the river brings down at flood-time. The same is true of fertile areas all over the globe, and worms have been working in this way long before the advent of man.

All worms are hermaphrodite, producing both eggs and sperm. When two meet, they clasp together in a strange, slimy embrace, overlapping one another to about a third of their lengths, heads facing opposite ways, and locked together for all the world like a Turk's Head knot. Thus each fertilizes the other's eggs, which are then passed over the body in a tube which is cast off in the form of a yellow lemon-shaped cocoon. Each cocoon may contain up to 20-odd tiny eggs, which hatch out into minute, white, threadlike worms in about 10 days. But if these cocoons are dried out or kept in the refrigerator, they may be preserved for as long as 18 months. They may thus be sent all over the world. Once placed in the right conditions for hatching, the eggs then yield their young worms at once. As all worms are male and female in one body, only a single cocoon full of eggs suffices to start up a colony.

Work of Darwin

Ever since Aristotle there has been a good deal of lore about worms, but little real information. Naturalists and scientists of all ages have been curious about them, but few recognized their real importance in the scheme of things. Finally, Charles Darwin published his great book *The Formation of Vegetable Mould Through the Action of Earthworms, with Observations on Their Habits,* at the end of his life, in 1881.

Darwin had studied earthworms intensively since his college days, 45 years before, and he placed on record his conclusions about the power for good contained in the world's worm population. "Vegetable mould" was his name for fertile layers of topsoil, and he stated: "Worms have played a more important part in the history of the world than most persons would at first suppose." He found that "all the vegetable mould over the whole country has passed many times through, and will again pass many times through, the intestinal canals of worms." So when Aristotle spoke of worms as "the intestines of the earth," he was not far wrong.

Darwin's painstaking treatise ranked with his other great book, but lay on library shelves for over 60 years. Students of biology and agriculture read it as a matter of course, but everyone assumed that the great Victorian scientist had said all there was to say about the subject. Much more recently, however, other minds have been pondering the unseen life of earthworms, and new conclusions are emerging. Much of Darwin's book was found to be true and helpful, but he was factually wrong on a number of matters, notably the numbers of worms in the soil. He estimated that arable land carries an average of some 53,000 worms to the acre, but recent research at the Rothamstead Experimental Station have shown that even poor soil may support 250,000 worms to the acre, while rich fertile farmland may have up to 1,750,000. Fields recently put down to grass have most worms.

Sir E. J. Russell, late director of Rothamstead, found a direct relationship between the amount of earthworms present in the soil and the application of farmyard manure. In his book, *Soil Conditions and Plant Growth*, he states that in a soil where no manure was applied, only about 13,000 earthworms per acre were found, whereas where substantial amounts of dung were plowed under, over 1,000,000 were counted.

He also says, "Where earthworms are active in the soil, organic matter is distributed throughout the layer in which they operate, but where, in cool climates earthworms are few or absent, there is much less mixing; the dead vegetable matter accumulates on the surface, becoming a partly decomposed, acid, peaty mass, in which the normal soil decompositions are not completed. The surface vegetation becomes profoundly modified, only few plants being able to force their way through the mass of dead material. As they die their remains also lie on the surface, and may, if the rate of decomposition be sufficiently slow, accumulate to form a bed of peat."

Working to Make Humus

Dr. Ehrenfried Pfeiffer has discussed the earthworm's composting activities: "One animal is devoted exclusively to the humus production—the earthworm.

"The earthworm is a specialist, and as such needs proper attention. Of the different varieties and species, two groups are of particular interest to the gardener. Type number one is a long bluish, rather thin type, which transforms all organic matter in the soil into humus, and particularly so if the soil has already undergone certain changes. Type number two is rather short, thick, reddish and is the manure and compost worm. Its main duty is the transformation of fresh manure and compost and other matter that is just in the first state of rotting. Type number one would not touch, for instance, fresh manure, but makes the best possible use of decomposed manure and compost.

"How does it work out, this transformation of organic matter into neutral colloidal humus? The worm eats earth and small parts of leaves, straw and all kinds of organic particles in the soil. Both earth and organic matter are mixed in the mouth and intestines and digested with the help of an intestinal juice rich in hormones and digestive ferments. One peculiarity speeds up this process, namely, "saliva" glandular juice with an organic calcium compound. The final result of the rather complicated digestive system, full of wisdom, is the neutral colloidal humus. The earthworm excrements, the so-called castings, are the richest and purest humus matter in the world. Analyses have shown that they contain more than 10 times as much of valuable plant nutriments such as nitrogen, phosphates, calcium, etc., as the surrounding soil. A Polish scientist, Niklewski, has devoted much study to the humus contained in the earthworm castings and has stated their richness in humus colloids and their importance for the development of fine hair roots.

"Unfortunately, the life cycle of the earthworm is rather limited. The little fellow is highly specialized. A type number one worm will not propagate in a fresh manure heap; neither will it migrate and accustom itself to a clay soil from a sandy soil or vice versa. It is locally soilbound. The type number two, the manure earthworm, will not multiply in soil except if sufficient manure or compost is present. It is in our interest, therefore, to assist the worm's life. If well-rotted manure or compost is added to the soil, you will see the little fellows multiply as long as they find moisture and warmth. In the fall before the frost and during an extended drought, they migrate to deeper quarters and remain inert. But before that time, if well provided with rotten manure and compost, they will propagate and at least the egg capsules may remain for future activity.

"The manure-compost earthworm develops in the manure or compost if the heap is in direct touch with the soil and covered with earth, and in the case of compost heaps if earth is interlayed with the compost. As long as proper moisture and warmth conditions are maintained, this type worm will propagate and gradually transform all manure and compost material into humus. The limits of the worm's lives depend upon drought, low and high temperatures. Heaps which heat up too much, above 125 degrees F., are destructive to the worm, as well as frozen heaps and soil. While the Southern climate in general is less favorable to the "earth" type of worm because of its periods of drought and heat, it is very helpful to the compost type as long as there is enough moisture, and this can be maintained by watering the manure or compost heap.

Worm Capsules

"The earthworm population of a compost or manure pile can be increased by adding earthworm egg capsules. The late Doctor G. S. Oliver, of Los Angeles, California, and his successors have developed a process which is very successful for breeding worms. If proper conditions in a heap are maintained the worms will propagate by the thousands."

The question is often asked, do earthworms eat the roots of plants, especially the fine root hairs? So long as there is humus or organic matter present there will be no eating of roots. Where the farmer or gardener permits the soil to become so sterile that worms in desperation may turn to the organic matter present in living plants and their roots for sustenance, there will arise also other more evil consequences. On the other hand, where there is sufficient compost in the soil, by a combination of action between the earthworms and the compost, the root growth will become very vigorous and the number of fine hairs thereon will far outnumber those on plants growing in a soil that contains less organic matter.

Earthworms can work in any kind of soil, even clay, but in that case it will take longer for the worms to cultivate it thoroughly. Ordinary earthworms will thrive only in the kind of soil they are born in. In taking some of these creatures from a sandy soil and transplanting them to a very heavy clay loam, most of them will die off. Where earthworms are bred in boxes from a strain of worm that has long lived in captivity, it will be found that they will live in almost any kind of soil.

Dr. Thos. J. Barrett in his book called *The Earthmaster System* draws attention to the acceptance in conservative agricultural circles of the fact that the earthworms brought about tremendous increases in yields of crops. He says, "We quote from a book on 'Soils: Their formation, properties, composition and relations to climate and plant growth, in the humid and arid Regions,' by E. W. Hilgard, Ph.D., L.D., Professor of Agriculture in the University of California, and director of the California Experiment Station. Pages 158-159:

" 'Wolney has shown by direct experimental culture in boxes, with and without earthworms, surprising differences between the cultural results obtained, and this has been fully confirmed by the subsequent researches of Djemil. In Wolney's experiments, the ratio of higher production in the presence of worms varied all the way from 2.6 per cent in the case of oats, 63.9 per cent in that of rye, 135.9 per cent in that of potatoes, 140 per cent in vetch, and 300 per cent in that of the field pea, to 733 per cent in the case of rape.' "

Dr. Barrett mentions a letter he received from a practical earthworm culturist, a Georgia farmer, Mr. R. A. Caldwell, who says, "I have planted Moss Rose in experimental pots, same age and condition, one pot with worms, one without; invariably, the one with the worms will take on new zest and life, and I have had them make such wonderful growth as 16 to 1. Petunias in boxes, I have also grown in such size and profusion as to be unbelievable to one who never had a demonstration of the earthworm's fertilizing and cultivating ability. Petunias in soil of identical fertility with the aid of hundreds of worms burrowing about their roots, produced leaves 1½ to 1¾ inches wide by 3 inches long, while those in the boxes without the worms were yet ½ inch wide by 1 to 1¼ inches long; and the worm-fertilized plants were many times as long as the others."

Since earthworms are so valuable, it behooves the gardener and farmer to learn how to "harness" them so as to take advantage of their composting abilities.

EARTHWORMS IN FARM COMPOSTING

Most farmers do not make compost in heaps, due to the labor involved in piling up large amounts of organic material and delivering the compost to the fields. They rely instead on sheet composting, working the materials into the upper few inches of soil, or mulching, letting the materials compost on the soil surface. Both of these methods are excellent practical ways to increase earthworms and derive the benefits of their activities.

Two U. S. Department of Agriculture scientists, Drs.

Henry Hopp and Clarence Slater, made some notable experiments with earthworms under these conditions. They took extremely impoverished clay subsoil, containing no earthworms and virtually no organic matter. Lime, manure and fertilizers were added, and a moderate stand of barley, bluegrass and lespedeza was grown. On one plot they left this growth alone, on another they cut it and allowed it to lay on the surface and added some earthworms.

By the following June, the plot containing worms had grown 5 times as much vegetation as the plot with no worms. Furthermore, the worms' activities had stimulated the better types of vegetation so that they were covered with a rich growth of clover, lespedeza and grass, with almost no weeds. The plots with no worms grew nearly all weeds.

Drs. Hopp and Slater studied the soil in the worm plot, and found it to be greatly improved in structure. Water entered 4 times faster than it did in the non-worm plot, and aeration was also better. The soil in the worm plot had twice as many aggregates—individual "crumbs" of soil—and these aggregates were twice as durable as those in the soil containing no worms. This improved structure, coupled with the high fertilizer value of the worm casts, were the reasons for the fine growth of the crops on the worm plot.

Sheet composting and mulching, then, will cause the earthworms present in a soil to multiply and benefit that soil greatly. The organic materials serve as food, and in addition, as protection against summer heat and winter cold, so that the worms can keep on reproducing and working in the upper levels of the soil in all but the hottest or coldest weather. These worms are, of course, the "type number two" mentioned by Dr. Pfeiffer, the long bluish ones which occur naturally in soil.

Good rotations will help to increase earthworms. Experiments in Maryland showed that a row crop-small grain-hay rotation produced 5 times as many worms as continuous cropping. The larger amounts of crop residues left in and on the soil accounted for this, and increased yields of all the crops were the result.

Crop Residues

A report on how earthworm activity is influenced by the handling of crop residues comes from Drs. R. M. Smith and D. O. Thompson of the Temple, Texas, Agricultural Experiment Station. In the April-May, 1954, issue of *Crops and*

Soils, they state: "If you live where rainfall is higher than the 30- to 40-inch belt of Texas, you might have thought that earthworms were of no importance this close to the border of the sub-humid West. But when it rains in the Blackland and westward into the Grand Prairie, the earthworms are ready to work.

"Five to 8 tons of fresh worm casts per acre have been picked up from the soil surface after one good rain on the Texas station. And as much as 25 per cent of the plow layer of soil in good condition has been separated out by hand as recognizable worm casts. This amounts to half a million pounds per acre and is what the researchers call big workings in any part of the country.

"Heavy grazing puddles this clay soil when it is wet and destroys worms. Overgrazing at any moisture content damages soil structure and prevents worm benefits. A short rest from grazing often brings back the worms in large numbers.

"Where a two-foot layer of soil profile was taken off 20 years ago, and the soil seeded to native grass, the worms are busy building new soil. The greatest activity that we have seen is in ungrazed native grassland on the Temple Station. Conditions are evidently ideal for dense populations, and the heavy grass protects all the casts that are formed.

"Many worms coil up and rest in the subsoil. They start working when moisture and other conditions are right.

"In cotton land, we have found places where they have coiled and rested at depths of 4 to 5 feet. And the worms, themselves, go even deeper than that into the soft marl that lies under many Blackland soils.

"Where hard chalk or limestone is found at shallow depths in the Grand Prairie, they coil in the soil above this rock and seem to survive long periods of drought. They are ready to work fast when rains come.

"Wherever land is covered with dead crop residues, worm casts soon appear. A part of the reason is the protection that the mulch gives to fresh casts. They are not beaten to fine pieces by rains. The mulch also provides needed food and protects the worms from sun and from being squeezed to death by farm machinery or animal hoofs.

"Year after year, much of the Blackland grows row crops, one after another. This is hard on worms.

"One of the things that hurts them most is tractor wheels. They just can't stand the strain, especially when the soil is wet. Usually the only worms found in such land are small, like thread or wire. It's a case of the good dying young.

"But even so, a few small worms can be found. Short rests from the wheels of machinery let the young grow and reproduce.

"Where heavy machinery has never been used, in small runoff plots, the surface soil is riddled with holes and rich in casts, even where corn has been grown every season for 20 years. There is 10 per cent or more of quick-draining soil pore space in these plots. Worm action accounts for much of this space, which assures air for crop roots.

"Even so, there appear to be more worms where crop rotations include small grain or grass and sweet clover. Going into the second winter with biennial sweet clover on the ground, in 1952, 5 tons of casts per acre soon appeared. The heavy soil could thus take in lots of water that might have been wasted as runoff, if it had not been for worm openings into the storage rooms of the subsoil.

Size of Casts

"The size of worm casts varies, but not so much as the size of worms. Most casts are between $\frac{1}{25}$ and $\frac{1}{10}$ of an inch in diameter. When mixed with a small amount of finer particles, this size is excellent for seedbeds. It is also big enough to resist being washed away by sheet erosion.

"Pore spaces among aggregates of this size are about one-fourth as big as the unit soil particles. This is enough space for water intake at high rates of several inches per hour. We are not likely to get runoff because of dense soil surface until worm casts have been destroyed.

"Worm casts, as well as other soil aggregates, unfortunately, are often destroyed by rain, machinery, or trampling. Tests with Blackland soil have failed to show any greater water-stability for worm casts than for ordinary particles. The type of raw organic matter that the worms eat may influence the stability of the casts.

"In each of 6 comparisons, earthworm casts contained more organic matter than the whole surface soil in which they were found. The average difference was 37 per cent of that in the whole soil. The actual organic matter contents were 3.33 per cent for the worm casts and 2.43 per cent for the whole soil.

"Of course, earthworms can't create organic matter.

They concentrate it by eating and digesting various crop residues, and by inoculating it with microorganisms. The process is one that may well increase the availability of plant nutrients and favor productivity.

"When residues are left at surface by subtillage methods, earthworms appear to thrive. Tractor wheels do less damage when the load is spread by surface straw, stalks or stubble. These organic materials also feed the worms, and help protect their workings from sun and rain.

"We don't know how far trash mulch and worms can go in maintaining or improving the condition of our heavy clay soils, but present results look promising for the future.

"Earthworms are here. They penetrate tight soils. They make excellent aggregates. They digest and concentrate organic residues and plant foods. These are things that we are continually trying to do by other means.

"Is it possible that we are failing to use one of our best soil-building tools, simply because we are looking for something that has a new name or that comes from far away?"

Avoiding Artificial Fertilizers

One further point: the farmer who wishes his soil and crops to benefit from the work of nature's champion composter must avoid the use of all chemical fertilizers, sprays and dusts. These are fatal to worms. Nitrogenous fertilizers, for example, because they tend to create acid conditions, wipe out earthworms rapidly. Dead worms are found on the top of the soil in huge numbers whenever a chemical fertilizer is applied, and one garden magazine recently went so far as to suggest that frequent applications of a chemical fertilizer was the quickest and easiest way to get rid of worms. In Australia, the use of superphosphate on pastures almost totally wiped out even so hardy a specimen as the giant 9-foot-long Gippsland earthworm. DDT, toxaphene, lime sulphur, mercuric chloride, lead arsenate and a host of other chemicals have also been shown to be deadly to earthworms.

The consequences of destroying worms with chemicals can be disastrous, as witness the case of the golf course which set out deliberately to destroy these soil builders. A certain species of earthworm had become a particular nuisance, throwing up casts that destroyed a putter's accuracy. So greenskeepers attacked him with a variety of powerful chemicals. Result: with no earthworms to aerate it, the soil under the grass became compact, air and water could not get into it, and the grass died!

Occasionally a farmer will have a piece of ground that is so badly eroded and run down that it is practically impossible to find an earthworm in it. While there are probably a few undernourished, scrawny worms present somewhere in this soil, and these will multiply when organic materials are provided, the farmer can hasten the worms increase by adding special earthworms bred in boxes, pits or similar arrangements. These will be the red, manure or commercial worms, a breed which feeds on raw organic wastes. Provided the farmer supplies copious organic material when he puts these worms in the soil, the build-up of fertility and increase of naturally-occurring worms will be speeded up. The breeding of these worms is covered in the following section.

GARDEN COMPOSTING AND EARTHWORMS

The so-called breeder worm is the one in which the gardener will be most interested. These are sometimes called commercial or domesticated worms, and are actually the red or manure pile worm. They are sold under many trade names, such as Red Wigglers, Red Hybrids, California Reds and others.

By adding earthworms to a compost heap after the heat of fermentation has subsided, mechanical turning is not necessary. The earthworms grow and reproduce so rapidly that they soon occupy every part of the heap and greatly aid the composting process. About 3 weeks after building the heap, simply make holes in it here and there and put 50 to 100 worms in each. Or by grinding the plant materials into relatively small pieces and making the heap only a foot or so high, earthworms may be added immediately for carrying on the composting process from the very beginning, as occurs in nature.

Many gardeners increase their worms by growing them in special culture boxes. Any good-sized wooden box will work well. Fruit or vegetable lug boxes, approximately 17 by 14 by 6 inches, are fine and can usually be obtained from any food market. You can place the boxes in a corner of the basement, garage or shed, under the house or outside in a sheltered place.

This size box accommodates 500 full-grown breeders, or half a pound of pit-run (mixed sizes), which ordinarily amounts to 800 or so worms from babies to breeders. Since the usual earthworm order is for either 1,000 breeders or one pound of pit-run, you'll need two made-over boxes to start off with.

Basic Recipe for Culture Box Compost

Note: This recipe will make enough for just one box.

Spread a 12-quart pail of finely-screened topsoil out on a flat surface (floor or work-table) until it is leveled out to a layer 3 inches high; similarly spread over this a 12-quart pail of finely-ground peat moss that has been thoroughly soaked beforehand in water, for 24 hours, and then drained or squeezed free of dripping water; spread over this a 12-quart pail of crumbled horse, cow, sheep or rabbit manure; sprinkle whole surface of this layered pile with a mixture of food made by thoroughly mixing a cupful of dry cornmeal with one (or two, if you have it) pound canful of coffee grounds.

Now with a small trowel, start at one end of the pile and systematically toss, turn, mix and aerate this compost, until you get to the other end of the pile; then go back and forth again—tossing, mixing, fluffing—taking only a little at a time.

The ideal moisture-content is reached when you can squeeze a handful of compost in your fist and have it hold together in a wet but not dripping mold. Test your compost now. If it needs more moisture, sprinkle some water over it gently and evenly and let it penetrate through the loose pile. Repeat this whole tossing, mixing and moistening operation once a day for 5 days.

On the fifth day, before you toss it put your hand down into the heart of the pile to test it for heat. If it is cool to the touch, your work is done; if there is the slightest warmth, keep mixing and moistening once a day until it is thoroughly cooled. Earthworms will crawl out en masse if your compost is warm; if they can't escape, they burn up—actually melt and die.

Filling and Stocking the Culture Box

It usually takes the average earthworm hatchery from 1 to 3 weeks to fill and ship your order. Find out when you place your order and get your boxes and compost ready ahead of time. We are now going to assume that your worms have

490

The idea of "harnessing" earthworms—domesticating and raising them intensively in boxes or pits filled with compost—was originated by Dr. Thomas J. Barrett. A fruit or vegetable box about 17 x 15 x 6 inches will hold 500 to 800 worms.

arrived and are setting in their containers waiting to be planted in your culture boxes.

1. Toss and fluff up your compost again, just in case it got lumpy or packed while waiting for the worms to arrive. Also test it for moisture and re-moisten, if necessary.

2. Lay a piece of burlap, corrugated cardboard, or a few folded sheets of newspaper over the loose-lath false bottom of box.

3. Evenly spread about a half-inch layer of dried lawn clippings, withered small weeds, or crushed dried leaves. (*Note:* Use no grass that has had weed-killer or chemical fertilizer applied to it. Earthworms are very sensitive to chemicals and won't work in compost that is not to their taste, but will pile up in bunches along the walls of the box and eventually crawl out.)

4. Fill with compost to within 3 inches from the top of box.

5. Dump half of your breeders into each box (don't tire them out by trying to count out exactly half—just guess it). Or, if you've purchased pit-run, put half of those (by guess)

in each box. If you are stocking your box indoors, turn on a 100-watt light about a foot above the box to make the worms go down into the compost quickly.

If you're working outdoors, the sunlight will accomplish this. Worms don't like being exposed to strong light. If the weather is raw or dark, go inside with this operation. Cold worms scarcely move. Under right conditions, they'll burrow down in 5 to 30 minutes. Any that remain on top after that are usually either cripples or dead. Just ignore them. When you have covered them over with the compost you'll be adding, they'll decompose and disappear.

6. Now fill your box with compost up to within an inch from the top. This gives your worms a depth of 6 inches of compost to work in, which is their *minimum* requirement.

7. Mix a handful of very dry cornmeal with 3 handfuls of coffee grounds. (This will be enough to do two boxes.) Sprinkle two handfuls of this in two ridges on top of compost (in each box), keeping two inches away from both the sides and the ends of the box. These open spaces will give the worms a chance to escape from this feed in case it heats up temporarily.

8. Fill box to rim with dried lawn clippings or similar material. Press these into a mat by using a light board, being careful to tuck all the grass inside the walls of the box. Lay a piece of well-soaked burlap over the grass, or any kind of cloth the size of the box, being sure to tuck it in so none of it hangs over the rim. The burlap should be about half an inch from upper rim when pressed into place. Worms will crawl along overhanging burlap or grass and get out.

9. Improvise a sprinkler by punching small nail holes in the bottom of a 2-pound coffee can. Pour a quart of water into the can and sprinkle your box evenly through the burlap, covering the whole surface. Avoid wetting the outside surface of your box.

After your culture boxes multiply and you begin stacking them 4 or 5 high, you can make yourself a pipe and right-angle nozzle sprinkler, thus eliminating the need to lift your boxes around when all the attention they require is weekly watering. The reason we always water through the burlap and grass from now on is to distribute the water evenly and gently, thus causing a minimum of flooding of the channels that the worms have made for themselves down below.

492

Storing and Stacking

Except for watering your boxes once a week, and keeping an eye on those two ridges of cornmeal-coffee mix after about the third week, your first two culture boxes will need no more attention until it comes to subdivide them into 4.

The *temperature* of your storage place should get no lower than 50 degrees, nor higher than 75 degrees, for best results. Worms work best and breed best at 60 to 75 degrees. Below 60 they begin to get sluggish, and at 32 degrees and lower they are completely dormant—merely balling up somewhere to await better conditions.

While it is all right to keep your stack outdoors during the milder weather, where it is protected from excessive heat, wind and rain, you must bring it in for the winter if you live in a cold climate.

Here's a timetable for subdividing culture boxes:

boxes stocked with breeders—divide after 30 days;
boxes stocked with pit-run—divide after 40 days;
boxes stocked with eggs and spawn (babies)—divide after 90 days.

The week you are planning to divide, don't water the box. The mealier the material, the easier it is to handle the worms. The last operation after dividing will be the usual watering. A good tip when handling worms is to keep a can of dry soil at hand and keep rubbing your palms and fingers in it to keep them from getting gummy.

Dividing a culture box is about a 15-minute job. It should be done in strong sunlight or under a 100-watt light hung about a foot above the box. This encourages the worms to go down quickly into the compost, as they don't like being exposed to strong light.

Harvesting the Castings

Beginning about the fourth month after starting your original boxes, you will notice that the bottom 4 inches of material (the breeders' home) is getting blacker and blacker, and finely granulated. It will look as different from the original coarse compost as day is from night. These are the castings.

Again, you will have refrained from watering the culture box during the week you are planning to do this job. After going through the usual steps of scraping down to the breeders, as above instructed, turn the breeders' box upside down onto a cardboard under a strong light. Pile the castings up in a tall, tight cone, and give the worms time to get clear down to the bottom-center of the cone in a solid mass. This should not take more than 20 minutes. Then go back and start lopping off the top of the cone in double handfuls—collecting same in a pail.

Then start cutting in around the base of the cone. Keep these two maneuvers up until you see the boiling mass of worms at the bottom. Lift them up in both hands and immediately plant them in a newly prepared culture box as you did in the beginning, when they first were shipped to you.

In the castings there may still be eggs and white spawn. The eggs you can lift out with a spoon, as mentioned. The spawn will go down and roll up in balls and masses under the light, if given plenty of time, and may be planted in another box.

Branching into Outdoor Pits

After you've racked up 10 or 15 culture boxes full of worms, you are ready to introduce as many as you want to spare into outdoor pits. Just be sure to remember that the worm works best in the upper 6 to 10 inches. It's folly to throw a pile 3 to 5 feet high at him. Rather, make your pit long and shallow.

Plan to plant 500 breeders or 1,000 mixed sizes per cubic foot of compost and they will do their job quickly and well. Be sure to have a solid, or a ½-inch wire netting bottom on your pit to keep the moles from ravaging it. Planking, shiplap, or a thin layer (one inch) of concrete will do. The sides can be similar wood, 4-inch concrete walls, or concrete blocks. An over-all height of two feet provides room for 10 to 12 inches of compost on the bottom and protective layers of dry leaves, wilted grass, or hay, to shield the worms from the elements.

—DOROTHY HEWETT

Research in England

A noted English gardening authority, Philip Wells, tells of his work with earthworms: "My birthplace was in the County of Kent, England, always known, because of the fertile land, as 'The Garden of England.' This fertile soil which offered its super-abundance of luscious market-garden produce

A compost heap or pit is the ideal way to propagate earthworms. They can be fed to chickens, used for winter compost making in your basement, and put into garden soils where there is a large amount of unfinished compost or raw organic wastes.

to the nearby city of London, had its soil surface crowded with earthworm castings.

"The soil of the farm on which I was born, was always kept 'in good heart,' by the important and necessary activities of myriads of earthworms. In the same County of Kent, there once lived Charles Darwin, who through his writings became known as the greatest authority on earthworms. He stressed the great achievement of earthworms in the soil by their helping to create topsoil, or 'vegetable mold' as he termed it.

"But Darwin lived years ago—in the 19th century, to be exact. Research in the past decade, however, has made organic growers even more desirous of increasing the earthworm population.

"It would be well for us—and the earthworms—if we were to learn some of the startling and interesting facts about these helpful creatures.

"A very successful experiment was made by the writer using a special cabinet made with marine plywood and a small electric light to perform the task of helping to breed earthworms successfully in one place and at the same time direct the worms to place their castings in an entirely separate department. By doing this, the castings could easily be removed for growing better potted house plants or selling to regular customers. A friend recently termed these worms in the specially constructed cabinet, as 'the world's first, house-broken earthworms.'

"Even though there are several thousand earthworms in a wooden container and that container has holes in the bottom for drainage purposes, it has been found that the worms will not attempt to escape if an air space of about two inches is provided between the bottom of the container and the ground. So that we are careful where we apply pressure, it is well to remember that the great numbers of earthworms that are sometimes seen on the surface of the ground after a heavy rain have, no doubt, been forced to the surface by the closing of their burrows, due to swelling of earth because of the water.

"Commercial breeding on a large scale is accomplished by the use of large wooden boxes, two feet square and 8 to 9 feet long, which will properly hold up to 200,000 earthworms. A good, tested and proven breeding medium placed in these breeding boxes, is as follows: One part each of German peat (pH 6), cow or horse manure and a good dark brown humus. Place at the bottom, as the first layer, about two inches of sand or gravel, this for drainage. Place about 5 inches of the described mixture on top of the drainage materials, a double handful of cornmeal, which is particularly good worm food.

"You can now place approximately 5,000 worms—large and small, the run-of-the-mill—which have come to you with some of the culture in which they were living. Capsules should also be included in the shipment to you.

"Within a month you can add another 5 inches of materials, and if you wish more earthworms, do this until your box is filled to within 4 to 6 inches of the top. There will be a terrific increase of numbers of earthworms.

"It is most important to keep the box material damp, in fact, a little on the wet side. In about a month you should be able to remove and sell the earthworm castings from the top few inches. If you wish to sell some of your earthworm stock, you will find them all herded together about 5 inches down from the surface. Some breeders of earthworms sell the castings, large and small earthworms and capsules by the bushel measure. Potted house plants do especially well in castings which can be obtained from a special worm-breeding and feeding medium.

"Have you ever noticed the tree leaves, pieces of grass and weeds that have been drawn by the earthworm to his burrow entrance? This is nature's unmistakable sign of what earthworms eat and how they live—it is raw organic matter. Soil particles are also devoured which help in digestion and are passed into the body as a means of making burrows or tunnels in the soil. These are later excreted on top of the soil—a very unique method of constructing their own subway!

"By using the worms' natural instincts, you can solve your garbage problem, without fuss and definitely without odor.

"The plan is a very simple one; here it is: Collect tree leaves, flower stalks, weeds and lawn clippings, etc. Mix them together well and dampen the mass thoroughly. Select a convenient corner in the garden to erect an inexpensive bin of cedar wood. The one I have used is 40 inches square and 38 inches high, easily erected without tools, and it holds a ton. As you throw the organic materials into the bin, mix in a shovelful or so of earth.

"Wait a day or so to allow fermentation heat to pass off, and then make a hole in the materials and empty the vegetable garbage into the hole and cover up completely. Raw fat and meat may be included in small quantities.

"Place from 1 to 5 thousand earthworms in the breeding bin. The activity of aerobic bacteria in addition to the worms, will convert objectionable odors into pleasant aromas. Be sure to try this outdoor method of breeding.

"Some years ago I had a problem—a definite problem. It was during the time that I was building the first Earthworm-Culture-Castings Cabinet. To my utter dismay one morning, I discovered earthworms all over the cement floor—they were everywhere. It was not a case of juvenile delinquency, for these were fully grown adults.

"To prevent this happening to you, see to it that the following conditions exist: (1) Ample food. (2) Proper moisture. (3) Maintain a soil reaction of about pH 6.

"By the way, if you yearn for a really complete nutrient earthworm casting or manure, I suggest you add to the organic materials, as you mix and dampen them, about 5 pounds each of both pulverized potash rock or greensand and pulverized or colloidal phosphate rock."

EARTHWORM FARMS

As people have come to realize the earthworm's value as a super-composter, earthworm farms have sprung up all over the country. Such earthworm hatcheries range in size from a few breeding boxes in a basement to active, large-scale businesses.

"Worms are my only business, and I'm doing real well—better each year," says Harvey Lindsey, owner of the Alamance Worm Ranch in Haw River, North Carolina. In 6 years, he's built up a basement hobby into his now-thriving enterprise, which he believes is the largest one of its kind in the world.

Millions of worms are shipped each year from his 13 acres that include well over 50,000 square feet in worm beds. Often in a single day, 250,000 worms are shipped.

Lindsey has done a great deal of experimenting, and it has resulted in a highly systematic and efficient set-up.

Each earthworm bed is 7 feet wide by 20 feet long; a cement block runs through the center, dividing each bed into 3½ feet. Each row extends about 200 feet. Materials that are used in the bedding mixture include a compost of corn cobs, peat moss, manure, hay and straw. "The more variety, the better," says Lindsey, although he doesn't use any sawdust in the beds.

The beds are built up to about 22 inches deep in the center and curve to the sides. The ground slopes rather sharply, so that the water sprinkled from time to time on the worm beds can drain off.

A "roof" of wooden slats protects the worms from both the drying effect of a hot sun and from washing away in heavy rain. Lights are turned on in stormy weather to encourage the worms to stay in the beds. In winter, a 6-inch layer of straw is spread over all the beds as additional protection. The straw is removed in early spring and will be used in the next bedding preparation.

Lindsey changes the earthworm beds each fall. He moves the old mixture into another storage area, where the worms are salvaged for another two years. Some of this material is also added to the new beds as a starter. During the third year, the material is sold as castings which analyzes 2.5 nitrogen, 2.9 phosphorus and 1.4 potash.

Cardboard boxes with holes prepunched in them are used to ship the earthworms all over the country. Worms are first counted and graded, about 100 to 120 to a pint. They are shipped in clean peat moss, which has been soaked in water for 12 hours; later the water is squeezed out prior to the peat moss being placed in the carton.

Lindsey advises his organic gardening customers to keep the worms in a cool, shady place, such as a basement. The temperature should vary between 40 and 70 degrees. Worms should never be exposed to extreme heat or cold. A barrel cut in half makes a good container for keeping them. Make about 6 ⅛-inch holes in the bottom; covering the holes with screen wire, using roofing cement to secure edges. Then fill the barrel 6 to 8 inches with an equal mixture of well-rotted manure, rich topsoil and peat moss. Keep this moist (not soggy-wet) at all times.

Feed them at least once a week by sprinkling about two cups of laying mash or corn meal over the top—working in a little and then watering lightly to soften the food.

Lindsey's success and the quality of the earthworm castings have convinced 10 greenhouses in nearby Greensboro and Burlington to use only an organic mixture of half castings and half topsoil. They don't use any chemical fertilizers and find that now their plants develop 2½ times quicker than by any other method used previously.

Many booklets have been written to help man understand the value of earthworms and how to breed them. The latest edition of Earl Shields' "Raising Earthworms for Profit," provides much information on commerical earthworm breeding. It is priced at $2.00, and is available from Shields, Mountain Home, Arkansas.

The booklet discusses the whole range from getting started with breeders, building indoor and outdoor pits, "harvesting" the crop, to postal regulations for shipping, packaging and selling. Here are a few of the points he makes:

Domesticated Worms: refers to pit-bred worms; the red worm comprises 80 to 90 per cent of all commercially grown worms, since they are so much easier to raise than other types; red worms are basically the same, though they are sold under a variety of names, as Red Hybrids, Red Wigglers, Egyptian Reds, California Reds, Red Gold Hybrids, etc.

Multiplication Miracle: Based on the premise that each worm lays only two capsules per month and that each capsule hatches only two worms, if you start out with 1,000 breeders in January, by the end of the year, you'll have over a 1¼ million worms and egg capsules. By the end of the second year, the total will be over a billion!

Pioneer Researchers: Commercial earthworm growing owes its origin to the dedicated missionary work of pioneer scientists and researchers whose consuming interest was the value of earthworms in soil improvement . . . such men as Charles Darwin, Sir Albert Howard, George Sheffield Oliver, Dr. Thomas Barrett, J. I. Rodale and soil conservationist Henry Hopp of the U. S. Department of Agriculture.

Getting Started: You can start with mature banded breeders, which will get you off to a faster start, or you may order pit-run (mixed or all small worms) at lower cost. Pit-run, if it contains a considerable percentage of large worms, plus egg capsules, may in fact be an advantage because the young worms will adapt themselves more readily to their new environment. Pit-run will take a little longer, possibly 30 to 60 days, to reach the stage at which you would be starting with banded breeders.

Constructing Outdoor Pits: For commercial earthworm growing, Shields recommends using pits instead of boxes. Concrete, cement or cinder blocks, hollow tile, or treated timber are suitable materials for building outdoor pits. For convenience, rectangular pits should not be more than 3 or 4 feet wide; length can vary, but pits can be partitioned off every 10 feet or so. A pit 3 x 20 feet will maintain about 50,000 mature worms; with several turnovers a year, Shields estimates a 200,000 yield annually.

Usually breeders dig outdoor pits from 16 to 24 inches deep, depending upon the climate. In the milder sections of the country, pits are often built entirely above ground. A 3 to 5-inch layer of coarse sand, gravel or crushed limestone in the bottom of the pit helps take care of excess water. It's a good idea to place boards, spaced an inch apart over this layer so that you won't be digging it up when working the pit.

Stocking: Load the pit with about 12 inches of compost and plant it with about 50 to 100 mature breeders per square foot of pit surface, or 100 to 150 pit-run worms. When worms have burrowed inside the compost, make a trench along the sides or middle of the pit and spread ground corn meal, poultry mash, etc. Wet it down and cover pit surface with boards or burlap.

Many growers believe that bedding should be changed every 6 months or so, as its food value becomes exhausted. This can be done, without much loss of worms, by feeding heavily to bring them to the top, then recovering most of them from the top 2 or 3 inches of the bedding. A more convenient way, if your project is expanding, is to divide the old pit in the middle, fork half of the bedding, worms and all, into a new pit; spread out the old bedding in both the old and new pits, and add fresh bedding to both of them to bring the compost up to the proper level.

Converting Garbage to Humus

Using earthworms to dispose of garbage by turning it into fertilizer is an excellent idea. Dr. William H. Eyster says: "The disposal of garbage is a problem that must be dealt with by every American family. In the country and small town it is a problem that must be solved by each family. In the larger towns are private parties who collect the garbage for a fee and use it for feeding hogs. In many boroughs and in cities are tax-supported community garbage services which collect the garbage on specified days. The collection of garbage which usually is hauled to a dump and destroyed represents a tragic waste of highly valuable and essential organic materials which are so much needed by our garden and farm soils. It is easy to see that a gardener who sends his garbage away to the dump via a garbage collector is robbing his soil of its greatest need, i.e., its organic matter.

"A highly satisfactory family garbage composter can be made as follows: Dig a pit 4 feet square and 3 feet deep and fill it with a compost heap made according to the Indore method: In the bottom of the pit put a layer of plant materials 6 inches deep and wet it until it has the moisture content of a squeezed sponge. Over the plant material place a layer of manure two inches thick (one inch of poultry manure is sufficient), a 1/8-inch thick layer of soil, and a sprinkling of pulverized limestone. Repeat this layering until the pit is filled. After the heat of fermentation has subsided, add at least 1,500 earthworms. This may be done by opening the top at different places, introducing some of the worms, and again closing the top. Sixty days after the earthworms are introduced, the composter will be ready for operation.

"As garbage accumulates it is put into the composter by opening a hole large enough to receive it. After the garbage is placed in the hole, it should be covered by some of the material removed from the hole. The next accumulation of garbage should be put in a hole similarly, but in a different part of the heap. After a composter of this type is well established, it will take care of the garbage of a family of 6 persons. A charge of garbage will be converted into compost in about 3 days. After the pit has been used for a time and is rich in colloidal humus, half of it should be removed and used on the garden, flower beds, or lawn and refilled with plant and animal materials as originally. At intervals of 2 to 3 months the compost in the older half of the pit should be used and filled with fresh organic matter.

"The earthworm composter may be used also for disposing of the wastes from dressing poultry for the market or for the kitchen. Prepare a pit as described above and inoculate with earthworms. When the pit contains a large population of earthworms, remove one-half of the material in the pit as follows: Rake off the top of the pit, and remove one-half of the contents of the pit. Then put down a layer of weeds or other plant material 6 inches deep. On this layer of weeds place the feathers, heads and water used in removing the feathers. Cover these animal materials with another layer of weeds. Over this layer of weeds place a layer of clay soil. On the layer of soil put the entrails and other parts of the animals that are to be discarded. Then cover these animal materials with a layer of weeds 6 inches thick. Over the layer of weeds place a layer of soil. Then rake back over the pit the top cover to a thickness of 6 to 8 inches. Experience with this type of composter for disposing of the wastes from a poultry dressing plant has been that the heap sinks 12 to 15 inches in 3 days. An examination shows that in this time the waste materials except the feathers are almost completely decomposed by the earthworm.

Garbage Composting

An article in the *St. Paul Pioneer Press* tells of a gardener's experiences with garbage composting: "Millions of wriggling earthworms perform a daily miracle in Henry C. Schmidt's home—the conversion of garbage into rich, black soil. To Henry the lowly earthworm is the nostrum for St. Paul's garbage disposal headache.

"Twice a day, garbage pail in hand, Henry trots down

the narrow cellar stairs in his home at 427 Sherburne Ave. He walks over to a 50-gallon drum in one corner of the basement, scoops back an inch of soil and dumps in the mealtime refuse.

"That's all there is to Henry's garbage chores. Inside the drum is a fisherman's dream—millions of earthworms in all stages of growth from the white thread-like younguns to the reddish, corpulent elders.

"There's no offensive odor in the Schmidt basement, even if you sniff with your nose an inch away from the drum. It smells like a freshly-plowed field or a forest floor after a rain.

"Henry is a dry cleaner and spotter by trade, but he has been studying earthworms for 20 years. It has become more than a hobby with him. The slight, graying man now has embarked on a one man crusade to 'glorify the earthworm as a cheap, efficient garbage disposal plant.'

"So confident is he of the earthworm's chemical ability that he says, 'Give me 160 acres of the poorest soil in St. Paul and within 6 months I'll not only take care of all the city's garbage but be turning out a super-fertilizer that can be sold for gardens and farm use at a profit of half a million to a million dollars annually for St. Paul.'

" 'I poured castings in a soluble form over one bed of peonies and left another untreated,' he says. 'The treated plants had 189 blooms, the untreated plants only 79 and they were much smaller and lacked the glowing beauty of the treated blooms.'

"He also experimented on small grains. In every instance the yield was 25 to 50 per cent better. His findings are corroborated by soil experts the world over.

"If you're interested in making your own garbage disposal plant, Henry doesn't mind telling you how. He starts out each year with the 50-gallon drum partially full of earth, raked leaves, grass and mixtures of manure and chicken mash. A commercial preparation of soil microbes is then introduced, followed by the earthworm colony. A layer of damp soil follows.

"A hole is punched in the bottom of the drum through which earthworm castings in soluble form seep, to be collected in storage jars. This solution is used each spring in fertilizing the Schmidt garden. The earth from the drum also is put back into the garden and the drum is refilled as before."

ADDING EARTHWORM COMPOST

Your earthworm beds will in no time become the main source of fertility for your soil. You can remove up to two-thirds of the finished material, with the worms in it, and use it on your plants at any time, although fall is recommended so they can work through the winter (except in very cold sections) and get the soil ready for spring. Mix in more raw materials with the worm-soil left in the beds or pits, so they can get right to work again.

To treat a tree or shrub, dig 6-inch holes a foot deep and two feet apart out to the drip line of the branches. Fill these with water and let it soak in. Then put a couple of handfuls of the worm culture, including mature worms, young ones, eggs and humus, in each hole, fill it with the soil previously removed, and water well. A 2- or 3-inch mulch of grass clippings, leaves, hay or other organic material placed all around the plant will insure a plentiful supply of food so that the worms will continue to multiply and produce fertilizer. Also, it will keep the soil moist and protect them from summer sun and winter freezing.

To rejuvenate a lawn, remove the sod carefully in spots 3 to 4 feet apart and dig holes to implant the worms; then replace the sod. In building a new lawn, add the worms before the seed is sown.

Any part of your garden, from rose bushes to flower beds to vegetable plots, can be inoculated with earthworms. Dig the holes about a foot deep and several feet apart, and use 2 or 3 handfuls of culture to each hole. Replace the soil, but don't pack it tightly—let the water you apply immediately afterward settle the soil.

Small trenches can be dug between rows of plants and culture planted in these. Always be sure to include plenty of the culture soil, to aid the worms in acclimating themselves to their new home. Water well, and mulch whenever possible.

Castings are the finest top-dressing for any plant or lawn grass, and a mixture of one-quarter castings to three-quarters soil makes an excellent medium for young seedlings when transplanting. Castings are fine for house plants and window boxes too, or these may be inoculated with worms just like other garden plants.

Thousands of gardeners testify to the value of earthworm compost, Hollis D. Bremer of La Grange, Texas for example, states: "Where I am now living, everybody told me that it is almost impossible to raise anything in that soil, for they had already tried it and had no luck. Because I am an enthusiastic sticker to the organic method, I determined to raise roses as they had never been raised before. This particular locality is rather unfavorable for raising flowers, because it always gets too hot suddenly.

"In my rose bed I applied material from my worm beds. This material was placed on the bed at a thickness of 3 inches and then spaded under. My compost which I use in worm beds is made of an ordinary standard formula and after having had worms in it for 6 months, you can imagine the richness of the compost; it was practically 100 per cent castings.

"This worm bed material was applied in the early fall. After the roses were planted I immediately covered the bed with a leaf mulch to a thickness of 2 to 3 inches. This leaf mulch provides food for the soil and worms and at the same time keeps down grass and weeds and retains moisture.

"To my amazement the roses grew as I have never seen them grow before. I prune them down to about 10 inches twice a year and twice a year they grow to a height of 5 to 6 feet. They bloom profusely in a blaze of brilliant colors."

A Productive Garden

Roy L. Donahue, Chairman of the Department of Agronomy, University of New Hampshire, uses earthworms and mulch to build a wonderfully fertile, productive vegetable garden. He says: "Nearly 4 years ago I was spading under an old strawberry bed in preparation for planting a garden. But I never planted a garden there that year nor any year! Lazy? Maybe a little. No interest in gardening? No. Soil too wet or too dry? No, guess again.

"The answer was worms—fishworms, angleworms, or, as some of my ungrateful friends call them, mudworms. We found so many worms that I put up a sign, 'WORMS,' and all of the fishermen who passed along the state highway knew what I meant, and paid one cent each for them.

"It was a Sunday, and before supper I had sold 100 worms at a penny each. (Later I learned that the good wife, when she saw me put up the worms sign, said to our children, 'That man should have his head examined.' And she was right.) The next day the children took over the business and have been operating it with success for 3 seasons.

"But not without effort—organic effort, that is. Each year on a plot 20 by 40 feet we have added perhaps 50 bales of hay, and on occasion we bought and added poultry manure, dried molasses, and cornmeal. Always we kept the surface of the soil covered with hay or manure, since drying kills earthworm egg capsules. In dry weather we watered the earthworm bed, but it never got too wet, even in wet weather. With plenty of hay as a cover, the worms lived in the hay when the soil became too wet.

"The harvest? Approximately 50,000 worms from the 20 by 40 bed, and there are probably as many worms there now as when we started 4 years ago.

"Worms always get scarce in the driest part of the summer so, as a supplemental source of worms, we bought several loads of chicken manure and dumped it nearby. Worms were in the manure when the soil became too dry. In addition, our son started raising worms in fruit lugs in the basement. The easiest source of earthworms during either a wet or a dry period is our old hen manure pile in which we have always buried our garbage. Earthworms have kept down all odors and have reproduced faster there than in any other location.

"Earthworm food for future years we supplied last summer when our neighbor gave us 90 bales of hay, spoiled as cow feed by rains. He was so glad to get the hay hauled off the field that he loaned us his truck free of charge. We invested only about two hours of labor in food for thousands of earthworms for 2 or 3 years.

"Now about the vegetable garden. I always mulch between the rows with as much old hay as I can pile on. This year I laid 4-inch thick sections of baled hay side by side to serve as a mulch between the rows of vegetables.

"Weeds? Yes, we had some weeds. Once I moved the hay mulch from one row at a time, scratched the weeds out with a hand scratcher, and collected about 100 earthworms per square foot, which we sold at one cent each. One dollar per square foot is fairly good wages for weeding the garden. Three times more during the season I pulled the few weeds that had come up through the hay mulch. With such a mulch system, weeds pull up by the roots quite readily.

"What kind of a garden did we have? My sister-in-law from Kansas said, 'I've never seen such a beautiful garden.'

" 'The easiest gardening I've ever done,' I answered. 'Do you use mulch?'

"'I can't get any,' almost complaining when she made this remark. (In a few weeks I visited these relatives and instead of kewpie dolls or fattening candy, I gave them 10 bales of alfalfa hay to use as a mulch.)

"I have gardened in Texas, Mississippi, Kansas, Michigan, New York and New Hampshire. And always I have dusted or sprayed to control insects and diseases. Not so this year. For the first time in my 30 years of gardening, I have not used an insecticide or fungicide on the vegetable garden. There were a few insects on the beet leaves but they soon disappeared. (Secretly I had hoped that the insects would eat the beets because I don't like beets.)

"Vegetables produced by this no-insecticide system included 3 varieties of tomatoes, green beans, lettuce, beets, carrots, broccoli, cauliflower, Swiss chard and asparagus."

EARTHWORMS IN THE ORCHARD

An article some years ago in the *Valley News,* Montrose, California, told of an orchardist who achieved excellent results by putting earthworms to work on litter under his trees: "Near Redlands, California, is an orange grove that people come miles to observe. It demonstrates a unique natural method of orchard culture.

"This 40-year-old grove stands out among its neighbors in a way that even a layman can see. The foliage is thicker, a richer green, even at the top where others of its age show thin foliage and bare twigs. The trees are well filled with fruit and records show that they produce crops just as outstanding as their appearance. But the truly remarkable thing about this grove is the fact that these results are obtained with less labor, less water, and less fertilizer than is used by any of the neighbors.

"The present owner took possession 17 years ago. Since that date, no plow, harrow or cultivator of any kind has been allowed in the grove. Weeds have been eliminated by hand labor. At first this caused extra expense; but since no weed is allowed to go to seed, a few hours labor once a month is now all that is needed.

"The absence of mechanical cultivation is the first puzzle which this grove presents to horticulturists, for the necessity of soil conditioning has long been recognized. Actually this need has not been ignored here, but the owner depends, not on machinery, but on the 'world's first and most efficient plow,' the lowly earthworm. He has created conditions which are favorable to earthworms and in response they have multiplied until they are much more numerous than in other groves. Their network of burrows has aerated the soil far more effectively and much deeper than mere surface cultivation could hope to do. At the same time, the feeder rootlets, which in an orange tree are very near the surface, are left undamaged, and therefore ready to absorb a maximum of food.

"Even more puzzling to the orthodox grower is the fact that this grove thrives on less than 50 per cent of the water required by others. The answer once more is explained by the burrowing habits of the earthworms. They prefer the cooler soil under the trees and dig most of their burrows there with very few out in the sunny spots. During irrigation, a large proportion of the water enters the soil through these burrows, with the result that most of it goes under the trees where the roots can use it, while much less than usual is wasted out beyond the root zone.

"But the fact about the grove which seems hardest of all to comprehend is its fine health in spite of what seems to be a very inadequate fertilization plan:—a little synthetic nitrate occasionally, nothing else in 17 years. Once again the earthworms furnish the answer, this time by their digestive processes. Earthworms depend for food on dead organic matter, leaves, old roots, etc. After being digested and ejected, these substances are changed in character so that they are soluble and immediately available as plant food. A close examination of litter under the trees reveals thousands of leaves which have been completely consumed except for a delicate skeleton composed of their veins. The worms have put this material back into the soil, for re-use by the trees. Without them, it would be a very long time before the same material would become available for plant food.

"Earthworms also eat and pass through their bodies large amounts of earth. A small organ similar to a chicken's gizzard grinds up the soil particles to extreme fineness. New surfaces are thus exposed to the dissolving action of the irrigating water, and plant food elements are released which otherwise would remain locked up inside the grains of soil. Couple this with the fact that earthworms work to a depth of 6 or 8 feet, constantly bringing new dirt from these levels to the surface, and it can easily be understood how trees can thrive for a long period without the addition of new feed elements to the soil.

"Earthworms are nature's own means of soil building and conditioning. No orchard or garden can do its best without them. There are many kinds, some much more effective than others, and the study of their use and culture will repay anyone who grows fruit and flowers."

RABBIT BREEDERS

Earthworms fit into many specialized composting operations, too. In his book, *Raising Hybrid Earthworms for Profit*, Earl B. Shields tells the following story: "Rabbit breeders, within the last several years, have discovered a vein of gold beneath their hutches . . . where formerly they had only an unsightly and insanitary accumulation of rabbit droppings, fly breeding urine, unsavory odors, and a lot of hard work involved in an attempt to keep the area clean and inviting.

"Today, in hundreds of modern rabbitries, rabbit droppings are feeding millions of fat and sassy domesticated earthworms . . . the cleaning problem is all but forgotten . . . rabbitry bred flies and objectionable odors have disappeared . . . and best of all, the breeder has a priceless new source of cash income at practically no increase in operating expense.

"Rabbit manure, plus the wasted feed from the hutches, is one of the finest of all earthworm feeds. By building pits or bins beneath the hutches, and stocking them with earthworms, the earthworms consume the droppings as they fall, turning them into finely pulverized, odorless humus. This humus, in turn, absorbs the urine and deodorizes it; prevents moisture accumulations and discourages fly breeding.

"Bins of 2″ x 12″ lumber (or other suitable materials) with provision for drainage, are installed on or slightly above the floor level. They should be a few inches larger than the hutch area, to catch all droppings, urine and feed wastes. A few inches of compost in the bottom of each bin is sufficient for starting the worms. After that the rabbits will supply new food materials daily and the worms will make their own compost.

"The only work involved is watering to keep the pits moist (as in any other earthworm operation) and an occasional leveling off of accumulated droppings. The contents of each bin should be forked over every 2 or 3 weeks to keep it loose, and to pulverize any encrusted manure.

"If eventually the bins get too full, the operator can bag the casting-rich fertilizer removed and offer it for sale, direct or through seed and garden supply stores. No richer plant food, or potting soil, can be found anywhere."

Poultrymen similarly put earthworms in their compost litter in the poultry houses, where they help to break down the droppings and litter into humus, and also serve as food for the birds. Their work helps to make the birds healthier and the poultry house free of odors and disease.

Chapter 15

PERSONAL EXPERIENCES

A general summing-up of the results of using compost can best be accomplished by listening to the success stories of organic gardeners and farmers. The crops they have grown, the animals they have raised, and their own levels of health are living testimonials to the benefits of compost.

COMPOST AND YIELDS

Since the size of a crop is very often the most important "bragging point" to a gardener or farmer, let's look first at the yields achieved by some organiculturists.

A "Five-by-Five" Tomato

It was a very hot summer in 1957 in McKeesport, Pa. Most plants "dried up and withered." But "Mister Five-by-Five," the Marglobe tomato seedling which Art Ryden had planted in a backyard compost pile, just grew and grew and grew—tomatoes.

It grew 400 of them—big, fat, juicy fellows which totaled 100 pounds. The vine itself attained near-record dimensions of 5 feet in height, 7 feet in length and 5 feet in width—literally five-by-five.

While no mulch of any kind was used, the plant was

Extending his arms full width, gardener Art Ryden of McKeesport, Pa., tries to show surprising growth of his "five-by-five" tomato plant. He had started the Marglobe variety in a backyard compost heap, later harvested 400 big juicy tomatoes.

off to a good start late in April in the Ryden compost pile. The weather after planting was "warm and rainy but the nights were not frosty." The seedling was about 12 inches long and Art Ryden planted it horizontally 4 inches under the surface. "All the leaves were buried except the last two which were on the two inches above the ground."

Despite this somewhat unconventional technique, the plant prospered. The compost pile was made up of leaves, some grass, weeds and soil which "clung to the weeds"—not too impressive a mixture. But its nutrients went straight into the seedling and enabled it to weather one of the driest summers in the record books. It must be added here that it benefited from a heavy watering once each week—10 gallons.

By the end of September the entire plant was enclosed in plastic to protect it during the chilly nights. The tomatoes were no longer ripening with mid-summer speed and the plant was finally and completely stripped in mid-October. By then it had yielded over 400 tomatoes.

Giant Squash

R. B. Glines of Grants Pass, Oregon, tells this story:

"I have a compost heap of 2 or 3 tons which is built up about as fast as I use it. Alongside this compost pile, a banana squash seed came up volunteer. I could hardly believe a vine could grow as fast as it did. After the first squash was about 6 inches long, I measured it every day and I found that it grew in length one inch every 24 hours. At the end of about 40 days when it had turned pink, I picked it and had it weighed. It was 42 inches long, and weighed 83 pounds. There were 9 more squash on the vine ranging from 20 to 60 pounds, and I don't know how big they would have been if the frost had held off 2 or 3 weeks. The vine covered 300 square feet and the squash weighed approximately 350 pounds. I sold the large one to the local PTA for 6 cents per pound. At that rate the value of the 10 squash would have been $21. Not bad for one seed and some compost! That compost pile has only started to work. By the way, the compost was made up of leaves, grass clippings, weeds, vegetable tops, garbage and anything I could find that would compost, even refuse from dressed chickens, milk, wood ashes, etc."

Another gardener who has produced giant squash is Glen Ruchty of Olympia, Washington. Compost piles are the secret of Ruchty's success. In addition to lawn clippings and fruit tree branches, old clothes, newspapers, magazines and scraps from the dinner table go into the compost piles along with a generous supply of leaf mold from a nearby stand of trees. To hasten decomposition, Ruchty keeps the piles damp and stirs them periodically. To many organic farmers Ruchty's compost ingredients may seem a bit unorthodox and generally not recommended, but in his case the end justifies the means.

Glen's garden was once a gully and is now filled partially with trash. The uppermost layer of this fill is about 3 feet deep and is open on one end. Protruding from one end are sections of charred stumps, lengths of worm-eaten lumber, burned-out light bulbs and current literary material—including the heavy Sunday issues of newspapers, copies of leading magazines and a couple of books.

This season Mr. Ruchty produced a crop of squashes that grew to phenomenal proportions. The smallest was 68½ pounds and the largest tipped the scales at 129½ pounds. This, indeed, is an impressive record, and presents an interesting contrast with his vegetable garden which shows amazing results also. To a casual observer, the picture of Mr. Ruchty's garden may be a bit garish but the vegetables grown are as luscious as any produced on a typical well regulated organic farm or garden.

A Bushel of Sweet Potatoes

Vernon Ward is proud of his organic garden. "We have been digging our organic sweet potatoes, and some huge ones have turned up. One weighed 7 pounds, 15 ounces. Another, from the same hill, weighed 6 pounds, 5 ounces. Thus, the two largest potatoes in a single hill weighed 14¼ pounds! This one hill yielded a bushel of potatoes.

"I have no idea what the record size for sweet potatoes might be, but this is a sweet potato section, and nobody around these parts has ever seen one as large as our largest, which missed the 8 pound mark by one ounce. This potato is now on view in a nearby community store, and is a pound and a half larger than the 'record' potato on display in the office of the Washington (N. C.) *Daily News* in the county seat of Beaufort County. The manager of the sweet potato auction block in Bethel, one of the largest marketing centers of North Carolina's sweet potato industry, has never seen this potato's equal. Anyway, it's a pretty hefty potato, to say the least, and a bushel of potatoes from one plant is unusual, to say the least.

"Our family cooked and ate the number two potato from this hill weighing 6 pounds, 5 ounces. Of course, it served us for several meals. It was most delicious in flavor, very sweet and delicate, and was of the smoothest texture, very tender and juicy. We have never eaten a finer sweet potato.

"Our outstanding potatoes were grown in a section of the garden that has not been cultivated for at least 5 years. Last year, on the particular spot where our best potatoes grew, we had a small compost heap where we composted largely kitchen waste together with small quantities of seaweed, small fish and fish scrap, crab scrap, grass and weeds. Last fall over this spot and a considerable area we spread oak and other leaves and twigs, pine needles, and grass clippings which we raked from our grounds. This compost material was spread over an area of turf which was not previously plowed, disked, or cultivated in any way, and was piled to a depth of hardly more than 12 inches. My idea was to improve this particular area by sheet composting.

"By spring this material had rooted down to an average depth of approximately 6 inches. Digging into the bed at a few places, we found the soil underneath moist and friable; turf and weeds had been smothered out and were rotting. Earthworms from our small compost pile had scattered throughout this composted area.

"When planting our sweet potatoes, we had some plants left over and were looking around for somewhere to set them. Something might as well be growing in the compost bed, I thought, so we set plants roughly 6 feet apart each way throughout the leaf-covered section. We simply parted the leaves where we wanted to set the plants, set the roots into the earth by hand, and pulled the leaves back around the vines, using no tools at all. This was absolutely all we did to these particular potatoes until sweet potato digging time; they were just no trouble at all.

"The plants set in the compost bed paid no attention to the dry weather. They just grew and grew until soon we had a lush green growth over the entire area. The vines were as thrifty as could be all season and always dark green. Some of the neighbors predicted we would have 'all vines and no potatoes,' a prediction which aroused both my dander and my curiosity.

"So before it was proper time to dig potatoes, I dug in and found a potato that weighed over 4 pounds. This held the neighbors off fairly well until time to dig the potatoes, but, naturally, aroused my curiosity more than ever.

"The first hill we dug in the leaf bed yielded a half bushel of potatoes and set me digging for the bushel hill, which, the more we dug, the more firmly I expected to find. And, as I have told you, we found it."

Fifty-Seven Lilies to a Stalk

Mrs. R. B. Moore of Tennessee credits compost for the magnificent growth of her lilies. "Organic gardening does pay. I grew 57 Philippine lily blooms on one stalk and 35 on another. This is most unusual, 10 to 15 being the ordinary number, although sometimes as many as 30 develop.

"A friend gave me 5 Philippine lily bulbs, two large bulbs and 3 smaller ones, and since I had made my first compost pile I decided to see what this rich, black stuff could do for these choice bulbs. I saw! It was astonishing! Even the friend who gave me the bulbs had seen nothing like it.

"I planted the bulbs in half compost and half soil in November. Then as soon as rains had settled the ground, I spread several inches of straw over the row, for in this part of Tennessee we have some very cold spells in the winter.

"These sweet-scented, pure white lilies are a favorite of mine. In addition to being beautiful, they bloom late in September after other lilies have bloomed and gone. So, from the time they pushed through the ground in early spring to September when they were in full bloom, I watched these lilies carefully. It was when they were half grown that I noticed the stalks of two were particularly sturdy. Before long I had to stake them. Later, I had to put in much larger stakes. And when the buds started to appear, I realized there would be a large number in the top of the best stalk. When I thought the cluster was as large as it would get, I counted the ½-inch buds. There were 85 on this one stalk. Only 57, however, became full-sized blooms. The others blasted and dropped out.

"I give compost credit for this surprising cluster of lilies, for my friend, who sells Philippine lilies at so much a bloom, had no stalks in her large lily pot to compare with mine. Indeed, organic gardening does pay."

Avocados Deluxe

Down in the sunny subtropical avocado region of Southern California near Fallbrook is one of the leading advocates of more natural farming methods and conservation of the soil. He is old-timer A. H. Anthony who has already lived a full lifetime but who is still like a youngster in his everlasting enthusiasm about fertile soil, earthworms, and mulches.

He is one of those rare individuals who combines business ability with a genuine love for the soil and natural things. He believes that man is a steward of the good earth rather than a plunderer. A quarter of a century ago he made a fortune in the sheep business in Wyoming and lost it in oil in California. Starting anew in 1922 practically from scratch with only about $3,000 he made a down payment on 40 acres of land near Fallbrook and since then has built back and developed, according to official Calavo records, the highest yielding and highest paying avocado grove in California.

There are 60 acres in avocados of the Fuerte variety at the present, and this unusual grower has grossed as high as $3,000 per acre from part of the grove, half of which was net profit. He has an 8,000 pound per acre annual average production based on the past 11 years and has taken more than half a million dollars off his trees in the form of fruit during these 11 years. To give some idea of his production, in 1952 he got 1800 42-pound boxes of avocado fruit off one 5-acre section of his grove. But his record is from a Benick avocado tree which produced 36 42-pound boxes of fruit in 1946!

How does a man get such high production of high quality fruit year after year?

A walk out under the trees gives a clue to the answer. Once a year a liberal application of poultry manure is made around each tree and this covered with straw. This together with the pulverized prunings (from his Fitchburg chipper which reduces pruned limbs to chips) and other organic material which he adds whenever he finds an opportunity has resulted in a shallow, 2-layer compost heap around and under each tree. This has been done over the entire 60 acres of trees. They are spaced 40 feet apart and between them where there is no mulch is a thick grass sod. Many people advocate the opposite of this, or the clean culture system whereby the surface is kept free of all vegetation by regular cultivation, thus removing the competing vegetation, which compete with the trees for plant foods and water. When asked about this point Mr. Anthony replied, "Grass cover competes yes, to some extent, but it also controls erosion *which is more important.*" He does his cultivating with a mowing machine.

Under the trees where the mulch is thickest when the top inch or so of black humus is gently raked aside, thousands of tiny feeder roots can be seen honeycombing every inch of soil. These roots feed heavily from the very surface and must have aeration such as is given by a mulch. Here decomposition of the mulch is constantly releasing nutrients needed by the tree for growing and nitrogen fixation by Azotobacter and other bacteria. Sick avocado trees, as those with the dreaded avocado root rot, show no surface feeder roots such as these, so needless to say, he is one of the few growers who doesn't have to worry about this disease.

Another thing you notice under the mulch under each tree is the literally thousands of earthworms. They are there in all stages, big ones, little ones, and eggs, all mixed in among the numerous castings. The soil is literally perforated with burrows of these creatures which are seen to be large, plump, and exceedingly active. One of the secrets of this unusual orchard, then is the presence of *a compost heap under each tree.*

Health from Giant Crops

Plants reaching into the Oklahoma sunshine to a height of 21 feet are a bit rare to say the least. Tomatoes 17½ inches in circumference seem out of place in this section of the country. But there is at least one man that produces plants and flowers that far exceed the fondest dream of the seed catalog illustrator. The secret of this giant food? Why, it's organic gardening, and the man behind these deeds is Walter J. Madson, of Tulsa, Oklahoma.

Walter Madson is a robust man in his early 60's. His graying hair is a fitting crown to the 6-foot 2-inch frame of unbounded energy. And to complete the picture, we see a deep tan that comes only from working many hours with nature under its sunlamp. You soon realize that here is a man that has found some of the secrets of life that many thousands are missing.

"My life has not always been this way," Madson is quick to exclaim. "Until about 8 years ago, I was a walking drugstore, a pharmacist's delight. The druggist grabbed the money I managed to save from the doctor."

Mr. Madson decided to change his ways and try to lose his popularity at the drugstore. He heard about the health qualities in organic foods and—after careful research—decided to try the organic gardening method for himself.

The first step was the building of a compost heap. This seemed the simplest way to start the process.

He had read that the properly constructed compost pile would have no odor, no matter how ill smelling any one of the parts might be. Madson gave this theory a first class test. Going to the fish market, he obtained waste matter and trimmings from the proprietor. Much to his surprise, there was not a trace of odor, even in this outstanding—and perhaps "distinctive"—test.

Within 6 months after starting practicing organic eating habits, Madson noticed an improvement in his health. First he was able to work longer without growing tired. The visits to the doctor became less and less frequent and finally ceased.

"In time," he states, "I felt like a new man, and with an entirely new outlook on life. For the first time in more than a score of years, life had a full meaning again."

The Madson garden yields enough produce to fill the 12-foot freezer in his basement, as well as furnishing food for the table during the growing season. Many of his friends are amazed at the size and quality of the food grown, not to mention their amazement when told that 31 different varieties of plants are grown each year.

Walter Madson sums up the basic idea of organic gardening by saying, "From healthy soil stems healthy plants. And thus healthy food for our bodies. Follow this simple wisdom, by putting into the soil only what nature has planned for it. This means that we are working with nature—and not against her—and will enable us to become healthier and better fed all the while."

This has been a basic rule in his life. Last summer (which was unusually dry for Oklahoma), he produced record-breaking crops—lima beans that climbed to the top of a 26-foot trellis and back to the ground again, tomato plants 20 feet high and 17½ inches in circumference. And all this without the aid of artificial watering.

As a secondary line of adventure, Walter Madson turned his talents to the growing of flowers. Not to be outdone by his plants, the flowers also grow to giant size. A friend of his was lecturing to a local garden club and made the statement that a particular flower grew to the height of 18 inches. After the meeting, he invited the lecturer over to view his plants. They measured 46 inches in height.

In open flower beds, as well as in his greenhouse, the principles he lives by are put to good use. Roses have been a weakness of his. The cuttings are placed in organic soil between November 15 and December 15. By the end of the growing season next year, the roses look like 3-year-olds, while in reality they are not a year old at the time. Many rose fanciers (using conventional methods) judge them to be much older than they are. The one thing that fools them is that they bloom profusely the first year. One of them grew to the height of 6 feet in less than a year. All this from a cutting.

In a "postage-stamp" garden just 20 x 40 feet, Michael DeMeo of Port Washington, N. Y., raises flowers, fruits and vegetables. His astonishing variety of plants comes from many continents and thrives in his humus-rich soil.

A "Jungle" Gardener

The extremely limited space in a suburban lot doesn't faze Michael DeMeo, of Port Washington, N. Y. With only inches to work with, this organic gardener grows more plants of greater variety and beauty than you could find in many a greenhouse or botanical garden. "You name it, I have it," he says with pardonable pride, pointing to plants from Central America, Italy, the Orient. These, plus prize flowers, fruit and vegetables—on a 20-by-40 garden plot!

DeMeo violates practically every orthodox rule of gardening. Cacti won't grow in heavy shade? It does in this organic garden. Grow Japanese chrysanthemums outdoors? He has raised these normally hothouse plants in his garden and they are as lovely as any growing under the most rigid controls of heat and moisture.

He has even grown a banana tree in his backyard, and right now he has a marrow vine creeping through his dogwood tree and producing fruit nearly 5 feet long (young marrow, a member of the squash family, is edible, but if allowed to grow becomes a huge "caveman's club" hanging from its vine).

What's his secret? There is at least 8 inches of compost all over his garden, with a foot-and-a-half under his roses and melon vines.

DeMeo composts every natural waste he can get hold of. His neighbors bring their grass clippings, leaves and rubbish by the basketful to the heap behind his garage—and take away some of the finest plants they ever saw. The whole neighborhood is populated with DeMeo-compost grown flowers, trees and shrubs. His fellow office-workers—he is a telephone company district manager—have also been given hundreds of plants and cut flowers.

He adds chicken manure to his compost when he can get it, but he's not at all fussy about things like proportions or turning the heap. He believes the variety of wastes and long curing time make the compost both neutral and laden with ample minerals and available trace elements for every kind of plant.

If you have no room to make a compost heap on top of the ground, says DeMeo, put it below! He sometimes digs trenches 18 inches deep and buries organic wastes in them. Given time to cure, these materials become perfect black loam.

Gardening at different levels is another of DeMeo's "make-every-inch-count" secrets. He digs 18-inch-deep trenches in his matured-compost soil and plants lilies at one level, tulips at the next, Dutch iris at the third and crocuses at the top. "Then when the weather gets warm, I plant my annuals in between them. The compost is wonderful stuff. Things just have to grow."

Propagate roses outdoors in December? That's really flouting the rules. But DeMeo has had considerable success rooting clippings of many varieties in his compost soil. He does not put them under glass or give them any other protection. Mortality is surprisingly low. He has propagated dozens of his 70-odd kinds of plants with equal success.

When Mike wants another peach tree, all he does is throw a peach pit out his kitchen window. Two years later he has his tree. When he wants some pansies or columbine he just broadcasts the seeds around the ivy or under his raspberry bush. Presto, up they come. "It's the laziest garden anyone could want," he says.

Because the plants grow so close together, weeding is almost completely eliminated. But he does have to weed out the calla lilies, pansies and nasturtiums that spring up everywhere, thanks to the potency of his compost which causes practically everything to seed itself profusely. His lawn hasn't a sign of crabgrass, but it's all he can do to keep the roses, ivy and sweet peas from overrunning the place, they spread so fast.

The absence of disease and insect damage is remarkable. His plants are the cleanest you would want to see. Many normally loaded with bugs in his area have none at all. DeMeo's garden has never been injured by drought, although watering has often been severely restricted in his town. It is a neverending wonder to his neighbors how his peach tree bears luscious crops year after year—with never a spray, either—while theirs suffer badly from the heat.

"If I had more room," remarks DeMeo, "I'd have to give up my job to keep ahead of the plants. Don't ask me how I do it. I know plants, and I believe in Nature. I apply her time-tested soil-building methods to the things I grow, and they never fail me."

COMPOST AND SOIL PROBLEMS

Some gardeners face special, acute soil problems. Does compost help them?

Subsoil into Topsoil

Catharine W. Scudder tells this story:

"When I went to Wisconsin in 1944 I found my sister struggling with a suburban lot which had been filled in with subsoil. The garden was divided in 3 parts, a lawn bordered with flower beds, a vegetable garden with raspberries, grapes, and rhubarb, and an herb garden. Spading in any part of it revealed a sticky, yellow subsoil. I suggested that we try Organic Gardening and we spent the summer hoarding green material. We tried to include some of the plants mentioned in the manuals on compost heaps as beneficial to bacterial action, and used chamomile from the flower garden, chicory from nearby fields, yarrow from the herb garden and dandelions from the lawn. Together with kitchen waste, leaves, and weeds from both gardens, we had a sizable heap and started building two compost heaps each about 7 by 8 feet and 5 feet high, on September 1. We made layers of green material, then strawy manure from a nearby packing plant, and earth and lime according to the prescribed formula. One heap was turned once, then owing to the labor involved we decided to let Nature and the earthworms take over. Holes were made with a broom handle and these were filled with water occasionally and in dry weather the entire heap was given a thorough soaking. The Wisconsin winter put an end to our labors in December.

"The following April the heaps seemed to be pretty well broken down into fine black soil. A good share of it was spaded into the vegetable garden, leaving a 6-inch layer on top. The remainder was divided between the flower beds and the fruit garden of red raspberries, grapes, and rhubarb, with a portion reserved for potting and the cold frame. We planted carrots, beets, onions, turnips, kale, spinach, squash, bush and pole beans, cucumbers and green peppers, tomatoes, sweet basil, parsley, and lettuce in a muslin-covered frame.

"The cucumber patch 9 by 15 feet planted with hybrid and Minca varieties, yielded beyond our fondest expectations. The vines planted in May under hot Kaps remained green and healthy until frost. They made a dense growth on the ground, then wandered over to climb the grape arbor where long green cucumbers hung among the purple grapes. There were no pests and no diseases. In a year of tomato blight our plants had no blight and produced ample tomatoes for the table and to can. Our Simpson lettuce under its muslin cover was of fine flavor and crispness until August. The rhubarb, which had drooped the year before, produced mammoth stacks of wonderful flavor, entirely different from the acid product of the preceding year. All of the vegetables were of superior flavor and size.

"The flower garden was a thing of beauty all summer, with a marked change in the size of the flowers.

"Except for the initial spading of the garden and turning our compost heap we had no outside help. One noticeable effect is the diminution of weeds. The 6-inch layers of weed-free compost effectively smothered most of the weeds. It was late summer before the usual amount of weeds appeared. One does not need to dwell on the advantage of this in gardening."

Mulch-Surface Composting

Mrs. Lucille Shade, a "subsoil gardener" of Medina, Ohio, had a similar experience. Mrs. Shade let her subsoil plot lie idle for the first 6 years of her ownership. Then she read about the miracles of Ruth Stout's year-'round mulching system, which generated an idea. "It occurred to me," said Mrs. Shade, "that a year-'round mulch should stop the erosion on the slope and should allow topsoil to be slowly deposited as the mulch decomposed." Fortified with the memory of Miss Stout's success, Mrs. Shade proceeded that summer to (1) spread manure over the entire depleted area, (2) plow it under, and (3) make a trial planting, alternating rows of corn with hills of cucumbers. She then mulched the entire area with partly-rotted straw, which she covered with a layer of new straw.

To the amazement of the family, both corn and cucumbers yielded normally in their subsoil environment.

The year after the successful trial, Mrs. Shade decided to try growing tomatoes in the same area. Before setting each plant, she gave it a running start on the season by digging into the soil a generous handful of bone meal and a double handful of compost. Again, as the year before, results were gratifying. According to Mrs. Shade, "They grew rapidly and I picked the first ones on July 25, fairly early for northern Ohio. These tomatoes did not produce as much foliage as they would have on better soil, and they did not bear as heavily as usual. They seemed more prone to cracking and uneven ripening, but in spite of these faults I had many bushels of delicious, red, ripe tomatoes, free from pesticides." That September, Mrs. Shade carried home from the county fair a blue ribbon—*won by her subsoil-grown tomatoes!* Her experiment was a success.

Today, Mrs. Shade knows her job isn't finished, and she plans to continue to build up the subsoil area (which in a few years won't even be considered subsoil) by annual additions of manure, compost, other organic materials and, of course, the year-'round mulch. Eventually, she hopes to grow even root vegetables in this soil—a real test of soil friability and fertility.

Miniature Homestead

Frank Fiederlein of New Britain, Conn., also had a subsoil problem—but today he has a beautiful miniature homestead on his 50-by-140 lot.

"People just don't dream of the vast variety of vegetables and fruit they can grow organically on a small plot," says Frank. "They think they need loads of topsoil, bags of chemical fertilizers and all kinds of deadly sprays to grow anything at all.

"But we didn't need any of these things. In fact, we did not even have any topsoil to speak of on the part of our land that now raises our vegetables. But today we have a constant supply of fresh vegetables all through the growing season— plus all the fruit we can eat, a really lush lawn and a huge variety of flowers. And we never spent a cent on chemicals."

When Frank and Cecile Fiederlein moved into their new Cape Cod home 4 years ago, the grounds presented a real problem. The group of houses of which theirs is one is situated on a street cut along the side of a hill. In order to make the street and the rows of homes on each side of it level, the builders bulldozed a cut across the hillside. This meant a huge amount of soil was removed from the Fiederlein's place— to a depth of 10 feet in the rear. And what was left? "The worst collection of stones, sand and gravely subsoil you ever saw," says Frank.

But he had the answer. "First we took out all the rocks, stones and pebbles, saving them for rock mulching or building retaining walls. Then that autumn we started to build soil, using the trench method. We dug 2-feet-wide trenches, about 12 to 14 inches deep. Having no manure, we mixed in half-decayed leaves and pine needles, with a little lime and cottonseed meal added."

The following spring, Frank planted some tomato plants (mulched with leaves and pine needles), string beans, cucumbers and carrots. The results were surprisingly good. "The tomatoes were the envy of the neighborhood. Besides having enough for our family and friends, my wife put up 55 quarts for the winter."

In the fall of that year (1955), Frank again dug in semi-decayed oak, elm and maple leaves from the woods. He also occasionally buried small amounts of clean garbage—potato and carrot peels, lettuce and cabbage leaves and the like. Then during the winter he was able to get some fairly well-rotted turkey manure, which he spread after sieving. In the spring, small quantities of lime and potash and phosphate rock powders were incorporated into the soil.

"Without realizing it, I had prepared a welcome home for

untold numbers of earthworms. Today I can't turn a spade-ful of soil without finding as many as two dozen worms in it.

"And the crops—well, I was amazed. I had 20 tomato plants, grown from small packets of seed, that produced tremendous crops. Cecile put up 75 quarts from that 1956 garden. The peas were plentiful, my lettuce, radishes and spinach came in strong. Our supply of Tendergreen beans was constant. My Detroit Dark Red beets grew rapidly and were delicious. I had some wonderfully tasty long slim carrots, grown from seed requested from the Massachusetts Experiment Station. And the harvest of cucumbers from 4 hybrid vines was too much for the family.

"I knew my soil was really coming alive. It was starting to show a wonderful texture, open, well aerated and able to hold plenty of moisture. I could see it was becoming vital and healthy, not like the sad-looking dead stuff you so often see in gardens where chemicals are used."

That fall he put turkey manure on the vegetable plot, digging it in last spring. He also buries the turkey feathers—"they decay very quickly." Mulching materials are constantly applied throughout the growing season. Frank uses grass clippings, garden refuse, leaves and pine needles. A little lime is sprinkled on the pine needles to counteract their acidity. Virtually no weeding has to be done. The mulch is dug in in the fall.

He says there is still some slight unevenness in the texture of his soil, but this is gradually disappearing as more organic materials are incorporated. It is fast becoming a rich, dark loam, far from the dusty, light-colored sand it was originally. Soil tests show an abundance of nutrients.

"Here's a funny thing: the nurseryman told me my Korean cherries would not grow more than 5 to 6 feet high. Already they're over 9 feet tall!"

Another heavy producer is his blueberry bed. A little over 50 feet long, it contains 13 plants of 6 different varieties (to insure a long harvest).

"To make the blueberry bed, I dug out a trench 4 feet wide and about 18 inches deep. I filled it with the top 2 or 3 inches of soil from under some pine trees, plus pine needles, sawdust, semi-decayed leaves and sand. Around the roots I used a mixture of sand, loam and peat moss. Each year I add a 2-inch layer of pine needles. The yields are getting better all the time."

The rich lushness of his lawn, despite drought and a municipal ban on watering, is another accomplishment of which Frank is justly proud. He spreads compost on it in early fall, then lightly applies sieved turkey manure on top of the snow or just before a spring rain. The excess is later gathered. By mid-April he had cut the velvet carpet 4 times, which amazed his neighbors no end.

"Everything grows like magic with organics," Frank says. "Three years ago I bought some tiny cactus plants from the five-and-dime. Now one of them is over 4 feet tall."

Making Clay into Loam

Paula Seidel of Michigan had a garden which was "a mess of sticky red clay you could hardly step on without getting mired." But the liberal use of compost cured this condition. Here is her story:

In 1942, when Victory Gardens were called for, we decided to abandon the old, disease-ridden plot we had been using, for some good, fertile soil. The best bet seemed to be our clothesyard, which apparently had never been cultivated but which had been for some years a chicken and rabbit run. But the soil (largely red shale which, I understand, is only partly decomposed rock) was such a heavy, sticky clay that the children had once used it for modeling. The first time I dug into it, the only sign of life I discovered was a pathetic earthworm about as big as a pin.

"At that time all I knew about soil restoration was (1) the traditional use of barnyard manure—which was out because we didn't have any; (2) a magazine report by a columnist who had buried garbage in a poor spot in her garden and soon found it, instead, the most productive part; (3) an article by a farmer who built an inch of good topsoil by disking in all kinds of organic waste—old cornstalks and cobs, chopped up roadside brush and tree prunings, sawdust, straw, weeds, waste from local canneries and slaughter houses, etc. Stimulated by those experiences, I systematically dumped on the garden that winter all the waste materials I could find—wood ashes, garbage and vegetable trimmings, even the vacuum-cleaner dust. In the spring, after adding leaves raked from the lawn, we mixed and spread it all and plowed it under.

"That summer the garden was fairly successful, although the soil still couldn't be touched when wet; after a rain I wouldn't even walk on it to pick lettuce. But my efforts paid off, for the soil did not bake, as did all the other clay in the neighborhood. As lack of space was a problem, especially for our favorite crop, peas, I spaced all my rows 13 inches apart (just the width of my cultivator) and put a row of peas between each two rows of the longer-season things. As soon as a row of peas had borne, I would pull the vines and use them, with lawn clippings, as a mulch in the 26-inch space left between the remaining rows. This kept weeds down and also prevented the soil from drying out. A little soil scattered on the mulch started it decomposing, and as the earthworms worked on it, they added valuable humus to the soil. Thus (and by setting out tomato, cabbage, pepper, and broccoli plants after harvesting the first radishes, lettuce, etc.), I get two crops from practically all my garden. At the same time, by adding, year after year, all kinds of green waste in summer, kitchen waste in winter, and some 4 inches of leaves each spring, I have put back into the soil more minerals than I have taken out, even with my 2-crop system. And the garden has increased its production until in 1948 I broke all my records by loading our table with top-quality vegetables all summer, giving away sacks of them, canning 150 quarts, and filling a locker with frozen goods. The only manure I've had has come from the few broilers we raise each spring; it has been worked in around the choicest plants or put under the mulch.

"Last fall, when pulling some root crops, I shook rich black dirt from them. Not a vestige of that sticky red clay remains. I don't know how scientific my theories and methods are, but I have seen them work a miracle in my red shale garden."

Strip Compost System

Mrs. Lois Hebble of Decatur, Indiana, uses a strip compost system to grow fine crops from her yellow clay soil:

"I have worked out a way to make compost in strips that lets me make 2 to 4 inches of humus a year in my garden soil.

"Every year I choose a strip of garden from which I have harvested peas or early corn. After the crop is done I simply start piling manure, leaves, sawdust or anything I can accumulate on long strips right over the old vines or stalks. In other words, each row has become a long compost pile right where I want the compost to be—no hauling to be done.

"By the next spring, of course, these piles have sunk down

527

considerably. However, it is still not suitable for planting any of the small seeds that are sown in rows, so I plant melons or squash or cucumbers in this. For each hill I scoop out a small hole and fill this with a shovelful or two of garden soil, then plant the seeds in this.

"Later in the summer, just before the vines start spreading out too much, I cover the strip with a good weed-smothering layer of old hay. By the following spring the soil under this strip has become mellow and 'homogenized' enough to plant the smaller 'row seeds.' This method also keeps the garden crops in constant rotation.

"Far more satisfactory than the results from the strips of manure, etc., are the results obtained from strip composting leaves. This, I must tell you, is my 'baby,' my favorite. In the fall I choose a very wide strip of garden where I want my potato patch to be the next year. Leaves are piled all over this spot almost 3 feet deep.

"By spring they have packed down and already the earthworms are hungrily working up through them. When the time is right, I plant the potatoes by laying them in long rows right on top of the leaves. The potatoes are then covered with 12 or 14 inches of straw. Sometimes I have to put a little more on later on if I see any potato tubers sticking through.

"The first time I tried planting potatoes in leaves, I made the mistake of pulling the leaves back and sticking the potatoes down under them next to the soil. The spring rains were heavy and the leaves kept the potatoes too wet and some rotted. So that is why I now plant *on top* of the leaves and cover with a good heavy mulch at planting time.

"When it is time to dig the potatoes, I just pull the mulch aside and harvest. The potatoes are the best-tasting, smoothest and largest I have ever grown. I might add that so far I have never seen a *single* potato bug on the potatoes I grow this way.

"Now at last I feel I have found the *best* way to garden. Strip by strip my garden is turning from hard, yellow clay into the rich, black loam I have always wanted."

Best Program for Lilies

Experimenting with various mulches and top-dressings to find what organic materials were best for lilies, gave Henry Eckstein of Lilydale Gardens, Milwaukie, Oregon, some ideas for improving his vegetable garden soil.

The Giant Himalayan lily, which is the specialty of this gardener, grows in lush beds of woodsy soil, and towers 10 feet or more high, hung with long, white, trumpet-shaped bells. These beds are in the light, open shade given by a mixture of native evergreen and deciduous trees. In sunny fields beyond the trees, grow other lilies and gladioli; another section is used for small fruits and vegetables.

Everywhere the visitor notices heavy crops, large plants and fine mellow ground.

"It wasn't always that way," says Eckstein. "Sawdust, what I call barn sawdust, has made the difference. See those extra tall leeks just now in bloom, and the parsnips beyond them? That was the worst spot on the place, sticky and ill-drained; besides, it had been over-limed. It has taken 4 years of compost spreading to make the change you see."

By barn sawdust he means sawdust used on the floor of a cowbarn, which with the manure added to it, is piled up for about a month or more before being spread on garden ground. Similar sawdust litter from a poultry house, composted a short time, was spread on a plot of ground in early March, where an application of rock phosphate had been spread in fall. Leaving the sheet compost on the ground for 7 weeks to get the benefit of spring rains, Eckstein then turned it under and prepared the ground for tomatoes.

In July, plants on this ground were exceptionally large, healthy and showed a heavy set of green fruit. At the farther end, where a small portion had been left untreated purposely, the difference in the plants was easy to see. The control plants were under-sized and had little fruit set.

A plot of blueberries, intercropped with corn, produced fine fruit in July on young bushes, while the corn was just about to tassel out. Thick, healthy stalks and numerous ears to the stalk showed that the corn was going to produce heavily. Here the composting was barn sawdust, turned under in the corn rows, but used as a summer mulch along the rows of blueberries.

Eckstein has sawdust in various stages of composting, piled up where the Oregon weather can reach it. "It takes two years to make the sawdust, loose and dry, fresh from the mill, into this dark brown, moist-appearing, woodsy-smelling product. This is safe for lilies, for anything, as a mulch to hold in moisture and keep weeds down and to fertilize the soil. With manure added, the time is lessened."

Results in Connecticut

Edward P. Dorsey of Connecticut says, "We have been gardening in hard clay soil for more than 40 years. Dark red, yellow and the lighter, brown clays. At first, we found it difficult, tiring and discouraging. We have tried numerous soil-correcting experiments. Some were successful. Fine peonies, delphinium and other popular perennials, flowering shrubs, fruit trees, grape vines, tasty vegetables and a variety of flowering annuals were a comforting reward for our effort.

"In the earlier years, we used pick, grub-ax and a sturdy spade to break up the tough, layered clay. Now, an easy thrust of the spading fork loosens the fertile, friable and abundantly productive soil.

"We have at different times mixed in sand, traprock dust, peat moss, shredded redwood bark, leaves, woodchips, sawdust and even the highly advertised "miracle soil conditioners," artificial fertilizers and chemical stuff. But, happily, all of that is now changed. We have gone completely overboard for the easier and more satisfactory organic method. And we haven't used any kind of poisonous spray or plant dusting powder in years. We haven't found it necessary.

"We now use plenty of compost. And we keep a heavy mulch of straw on the garden all year round. We compost about everything that can be converted into soil-enriching humus. While we formerly mixed considerable compostable materials and all of the aged cow manure or chicken manure directly in with the clay, as a trenching or sheet compost, we have decided to compost all of this material, starting this year. We believe that pit or cabinet composting will destroy most of the weed seeds and insects or insect larvae among the leaves, stalks or litter. And, the finished compost will provide quicker assistance to the growing plants than just raw materials in trench or sheet composting.

"We have gardened in different areas over the years but have always found a clay conversion problem to contend with. After moving to our present location a few years ago, our friends assured us that we couldn't grow anything in that hopeless, brown clay. It was, in reality, just a subsoil. Before the builder started to develop the area, one of the former owners had sold the topsoil. The builder added a very thin layer of loam for lawn purposes. It produced the scrawniest lawn imaginable. We added more loam and then reseeded it. The hard, brown subsoil was the worst clay that we had ever encountered. The hoe barely chipped it. The rake just scratched it.

"We didn't know about rotary type garden tillers at that time. To dig up the garden area that we wanted would be quite a job. We didn't have the time for such an undertaking. So we hacked out shallow grooves or trenches, along the planting rows and filled these with compost and some of that hard clay. After firming each trench by walking on it, we added aged cow manure and more clay. A heavy straw mulch was added and the garden was forgotten until spring. Without removing the straw or digging, we set out our plants and seeds in spring, using a pronged, gardener's trowel. Our friends didn't laugh at the harvest. We had fine tomatoes, squash, cucumbers, beans and other very tasty vegetables. And plenty of them. Yet, we realized that we had only surmounted the first hurdle.

"More compost was needed to complete the surface soil improvement and to correct the deeper clay for better drainage. This job is progressing satisfactorily. Shrubs, small fruit trees and grape vines have been planted in wide, deep holes to allow ample root space. Plenty of compost was added and some of the partly improved topsoil. Some of them bore fruit this year. The shrubs added welcome color. A few trees, planted in small, shallow holes, died of root rot. That impervious clay retained water like a basin. Roots became waterlogged.

"A test sample of the improved clay garden soil submitted to the School of Horticulture last fall brought a report showing 5 per cent humus. We felt encouraged. Some day we may again relocate and find the fertile, friable, well-drained soil all gardeners dream about. But, for the present, we are 'stuck with clay.' And we know, from long experience, that we can lick any of its gardening problems by battling it the organic way."

Sandy Soil Profits from Compost

In a West Texas area beset by dust storms, soil erosion and dwindling farm yields, there is a small spot of land called Eason Acres that stands out like a beautiful landscape painting on a bare wall.

Eason Acres is not just a nursery, or orchard, or vegetable farm, but a combination of all 3. The highly productive part comprises only about 8 acres, but its owner, Jimmy Eason, sells more farm products from it than most neighboring farmers do from much larger acreage.

Eason does it by farming nature's way, that is depending upon organic fertilizers and legume crops to keep the soil fertile. He says the secret of growing big healthy plants is first having a healthy soil. And to keep soil in this condition, he practices a continuous enriching program, which includes a large compost pile, besides other green matter that is hauled in.

"You can grow anything if you have good soil and plenty of water," he said. "I have small irrigation wells, but find the mellow soil and vegetative cover keep the soil cool. As a result, I don't irrigate as often as many irrigation farmers in the area."

Eason was once considered a radical by his neighbors. He made a claim he could make more profit on a 20-acre farm than they could on 160 acres. Prove it, they said, so Eason proceeded to do just that.

"It was quite a struggle at first," he said. "I came right out of the barber shop in 1943, and bought 50 acres of this sand dune land. I couldn't buy less, so I rented out 30 acres. Later I decided to concentrate on 8 acres and farm the rest in feed crops.

"I had something in mind which has proved true since then. Why couldn't a man take a few acres, build up its fertility, then farm every square foot of it the way it should be done."

He first leveled the sand dunes, then planted legumes. He also built a large compost pit and started putting every bit of vegetative matter in it he could grow or find. As the orchard and garden took shape, so did the organic content of the soil grow. Before long the soil became dark and mellow, and plants grew almost twice as big as on the sterile soils around it.

Eason has never stopped his soil building. He even takes the bermuda grass clippings from his lawn and puts them in the compost pile. Also the tree leaves, even the tumble weeds that still bound across his place from neighboring farms.

Eason specializes on rose bushes which go to customers in a 50-mile radius. This amounts to several hundred dollars a year. There is also a good profit in the garden products, which include peas, beans, okra and other vegetables.

He has a greenhouse 20 by 60 feet where he grows nearly every kind of flower adapted to the southwest. Most of these are planted in small paper cups or clay pots, and sold when they reach a height of 3 to 6 inches.

In two large lath houses 50 by 75 feet and 80 by 200 feet, Eason grows bucket plants, which include all kinds of shrubbery and woody plants. In one he has several square yards of St. Augustine lawn grass which has been a big seller. Because the soil is so mellow and fertile, the grass grows rapidly and he sells several hundred square feet of it at about 25 cents per square foot.

On the rest of the place which he does not cultivate intensively, Eason has been planting clover, vetch and other legumes. Last year he had so much work at home that he decided to rent out this land. The tenant said at the end of the year he made as much maize on one acre of Eason land as he did on 10 acres elsewhere.

Sheet Composting for Sandy Soil

Keith D. Larson of South St. Paul, Minn., was faced with the same sandy soil problem. "In the spring of 1950 I purchased a new home and discovered that the contractor during the grading of the lot had removed all of the topsoil in the area of the yard that I intended to use for my garden. The remaining soil was only fine sand such as one might use in an hour glass. Therefore, it was apparent that I either had to haul away some 20 tons of sand and replace it with topsoil or 'doctor' up the sandy soil I had acquired. I chose the latter course and decided on sheet composting my sand pile.

"To start the garden developmental project I spread a little more than ½-inch of a commercially prepared compost (composed of ground meat scraps, bone meal, blood and vegetable matter) over the entire garden area. After this was leveled off I covered it with about ¼-inch of rich black soil. This good soil contained many earthworms and likewise must have contained billions of helpful bacteria for starting the composting process. To protect the worms and bacteria against being killed by drying and to hasten the composting process the entire mixture was thoroughly wetted down. This composting was started on April 22.

"By June 26, I was eating radishes from the garden, and from then on a profusion of fine specimen vegetables were available.

"Flowers, too, had greater color intensity than those of my neighbors who used highly concentrated fertilizers. I asked one of the University faculty about this difference and he stated it was undoubtedly due to the fact that the organic material I used furnished a better and more complete environment for the growth of the flowers, which resulted in deeper and more intense colors in the blossoms."

Worms, Manure and Compost vs. Sand

Thomas Caples tried compost and earthworms for a sandy soil. "Recent inspection of several plots in which organic methods of various kinds are used have convinced me that very few of my fellow enthusiasts have wholeheartedly attempted to exploit the possibilities of earthworms. Because I am extremely worm-conscious I have long pondered the best way in which to maintain a high worm population in my garden; I found that no matter how many I bred and introduced into my vegetable and flower beds they quickly dwindled to whatever number the organic matter present could maintain. Yet in my unfinished compost and manure heaps they positively thrived and multiplied prodigiously. What would happen, I wondered, if I put a heavy mulch of unripe compost and manure on my beds? Certainly the worms would flourish, but would the soil become sour and acid?

"There was only one way to find out; so I sowed a crop of garden peas and when they were tall enough mulched them with half-ripe compost and strawy manure straight from the stable. Worms and capsules at the rate of about 600 to the square yard were added from my breeder boxes. I deliberately chose a legume for the experiment; if there was any acidity accruing from the use of the partially decomposed matter, then an acid-hating crop such as peas would soon make it apparent.

"Those peas didn't turn a hair at any stage, and they finished up so well that one of our leading magazines used a photograph of them to illustrate a gardening article of mine. The bushes grew tall, strong and healthy, and they carried a tremendous crop of the most luscious peas I have ever tasted. And my 'soil' was virtually a pure, white sand.

"The experiment was obviously a success; so I began using the same kind of mulch on the whole of my flower and vegetable plots. Subsequent crops of other vegetables, and carnations, dahlias, pansies, zinnias, roses and many other flowers have turned out equally as well. There hasn't been a single failure. After 12 months of this mulch-and-worms tech-

534

nique I have seen enough to suggest that under garden conditions it is the most spectacular of all the organic methods."

Hard Adobe Yields to Compost

Mrs. Dorothy Bates of Riverside, California, conquered hard-packed adobe with liberal applications of compost. "In the spring of 1951," she says, "I purchased two acres with a house and a well equipped with an electric pump. This is a little foothill community of about 400 homes. We are not serviced by any irrigation system, so must depend on a limited water supply from our small wells.

"There was nothing growing on the land except a few desert sages and scattered annual grasses, which dried up in a few weeks. The soil was adobe, so hard and dry that the only way to get garden seeds to come up was to cover them with a straw mulch and water every day until the seedlings were established.

"Needless to say, the first year garden was not very successful. Most of the plants that did get through the hard ground in the spring were burned up later by the hot dry winds.

"In August of the same year I bought 500 earthworms and started a compost pile. In this I put weeds and straw, the 500 earthworms and manure from a couple of hogs and some chicken manure. By spring of 1952 I had about one ton of compost which I used in my garden. That year I had fair success, but it still needed frequent watering to keep things growing. One ton of compost on a garden plot about 50 by 100 yards was not enough to build up this hard adobe. However, I had gotten earthworms started in the soil and I mulched between the rows with straw and chicken manure. During the hot, dry weather the earthworms burrowed deep into the soil. I watered by sprinkler method and noticed when the soil was moist on top the worms came up and ate the mulch and dead leaves under the plants. They left a layer of fine black castings, which I believe is the best fertilizer in the world.

"In the fall of 1952 the soil was beginning to be spongy and water retentive. In this part of California we have mild winters and my fall and winter garden is now a great success. I have onions, radishes, parsnips, turnips, beets, carrots, spinach, cabbage, cauliflower, broccoli, lettuce, endive, chard, peas, parsley and other herbs for flavoring. Will soon have asparagus, artichokes, rhubarb, strawberries, boysenberries, peaches, plums, etc. Some of my cabbages weighed 10 pounds each this year.

"However size is not so important as flavor and nutritional qualities and these are without doubt found in organic vegetables and fruits. This I have proven to my own satisfaction in adobe soil that in 1951 was too hard to drive a pick into.

"Now, when visitors walk through my garden plot they marvel at the rich green color of the leaves and the flavor of the vegetables. And they say the soil feels like a soft carpet under their feet. I do not cultivate, but leave that chore to the earthworms. I have the only all-year garden in this community."

Adobe Problems in Arizona

Elizabeth Rigby also had adobe problems in her Arizona garden. She says, "Adobe is the Spanish word for sundried mud brick, while earth from which such bricks can be made is called adobe soil. Usually red or yellowish in color, adobe occurs in many parts of the American Southwest where, in conjunction with a dry climate and 'hard' water, it confronts the gardener with numerous special problems.

"A soil suitable for making brick is not likely to be the best garden material, but neither is it the worst, as we discovered when we moved to Arizona, bought an adobe house, and set out to make a garden in the same kind of soil as that from which our house had been built.

"Adobe soil is heavy clay, sometimes with an admixture of silt. It is likely to be rich in minerals, almost entirely deficient in humus. Of all soil types it is one of two (sand is the other) that will benefit most conspicuously from organic gardening methods.

"Being heavy, it requires aeration. In its natural state it will contain no earthworms (ants and tunnelling gophers aerate it for the native vegetation). It will be alkaline, with a pH of at least 7.5 and probably higher. Because of this, some essential nutrients, phosphorous and iron among them, will be unavailable. When you irrigate, as you will have to, the soil's alkalinity will increase and the 'dobe tendency to bake and puddle will become a gardening menace.

"Is it hopeless, then? Not at all.

"The first step will be to add humus. By this every one of the problems named above will be minimized, some entirely

536

Along with a parched climate and "hard" water, Arizona gardeners face the problem of that crusted adobe soil—from which mud bricks are made. Organic gardener Elizabeth Rigby overcame these handicaps with organic techniques.

eliminated. The soil will be lightened and given air. It will become easier to till. Moisture will seep down and be held instead of running off. In this converted 'dobe, earthworms may be planted and will flourish. Since humus is a neutralizer, the alkalinity will be brought down to a point suitable for many garden plants. (Cottonseed meal, applied 5 pounds per 100 square feet, is said to be excellent for lowering the pH.) Even the vital iron which has been there all the time (the red in our adobe is iron oxide) and the locked-up phosphates may be freed to some extent. You will still have to supplement them, however, by using ground phosphate rock, and, if iron-deficiency symptoms appear, by the application of acid organic materials such as peat moss, sawdust and oak leaves.

"Patience will be needed if you plan to start a garden in virgin adobe. Impatiently we waited a full year before planting a single seed. It took us that long, in this climate and without as yet knowing where to obtain enough makings, to create our first compost. It took us that long after the plots had first been broken (in some spots a pickaxe was required!) to get them into even a semblance of "condition." But today, after 5 years of adding compost and manures, of digging in mulches and garden wastes, our converted adobe will grow almost anything.

"That *almost* is important, though, for unless you have all the time in the world and enjoy conquering apparently insurmountable obstacles, you will not try to grow truly acid-loving plants in Southwestern adobe soils, since without intensive and specialized treatment such soils will always remain somewhat on the alkaline side—their basic original content and the need for continuous irrigation (which brings up the lime) will see to that."

Compost in the Desert

On three-quarters of an acre at Cottonwood, Arizona, Walter Whitehead is turning stony, adobe clay desert dirt into humus-rich soil. At the same time he is turning the skepticism of his neighbors into growing interest in his methods.

Whitehead was a newcomer to organic gardening in late 1952. He had already farmed his land one season with chemicals, while previous owners had poured chemicals on the place for years. In addition, acrid sulphur smoke from two nearby copper smelters had burned the land for some 35 years. The place was "farmed out" and burned almost to the point of barrenness. Only a tangle of weeds—and rather a sparse tangle at that—plus some 40 undernourished fruit trees were growing there.

His first step toward organic rehabilitation of the land was a mistake, he says. In a burst of enthusiasm he spread a large quantity of raw cow manure over all. It took a full year for the bacteria-poor soil to break it down and assimilate it. An avid student of the literature of organic methods, Whitehead quickly discovered his mistake. He proceeded to beg all the weeds, twigs, leaves, straw and other organic matter he could haul from his neighbors. He even cut and gathered the material himself.

A portion of this matter he spread on the land, working it lightly into the soil. Some he used as mulch. The largest part he composts in a bin 4 feet by 4 feet by 5 feet.

From a sawmill in Cottonwood, he obtains free all the sawdust he will haul. Afraid at first that the green sawdust from ponderosa pine would be too full of turpentine, he became convinced through his studies it would be valuable instead of harmful. He spread it cautiously at first, however, and was amazed at how quickly it worked into the soil. He has used dozens of full half-ton pickup loads since and finds it an invaluable humus builder and soil conditioner. There has been no evidence of harm from the turpentine content, especially in his desert soil.

Basically, Whitehead says, his Arizona soil is excellent. Of a combination volcanic and sedimentary origin, it is rich in calcium, phosphorus and potassium as well as in trace minerals. However, when Whitehead took over, it was virtually devoid of humus and thus of nitrogen, the adobe clay base baking hard in the Arizona sun and accepting water about as well as a duck's back.

In 1953, his first year of strict adherence to organic principles, he had a moderately successful garden, somewhat more productive than his previous year's chemical garden. But he was plagued with a heavy infestation of nematodes which ruined his beans, carrots, beets and cucumbers and seriously retarded almost every other crop.

In 1959, by the peak of the growing season and of mid-summer heat, Whitehead was convinced he had the nematodes on the run. He says not 25 per cent of the infestation remains. In the next few seasons he confidently expects to have the soil perfectly clean.

Whitehead is positive his initial success against this stubborn plague is the result of the cumulative effects of his overall organic gardening program. Specifically he attributes it to the fact that bacterial balance is beginning to be restored to the soil. The beneficial bacteria are being bred in his compost and are being given a congenial environment in the many organic materials he is working into the ground. He has not yet made nearly enough humus, he says, but feels confident that the nematodes will continue to disappear as humus, rich in beneficial bacteria, is built.

In Arizona irrigation is, of course, a necessity. Originally he had great trouble getting penetration of water. He had to build little dams in the furrows to puddle water and hold it long enough for it to soak. Now, after only two years of organic rehabilitation, the soil accepts water so much better it takes 3 to 4 times as long for the same head of water to flow from the top of the garden to the waste ditch at the bottom. By the time a small trickle (which used to be practically a flood) is running in the waste ditch, he knows his land is thoroughly wet, down deep into the subsoil. At first he had to irrigate at least once a week. Now, depending, of course, upon Arizona's infrequent rainfall and the intensity of wind and sun, the interval between irrigations runs from 2 to 3 weeks.

While weeds are controlled almost entirely by his organic mulches, Whitehead not only renovates yearly but also cultivates several times a year. In this way he stirs the bottom, partly decomposed layer of mulch into the soil. He finds one of the advantages of mixing sawdust generously with the other mulching material is that sawdust does not break down as fast as grass cuttings, hay, etc. Thus the sawdust helps keep the heavy soil open and loose even while helping to make humus. It also drops readily down into the deep cracks and crevices opened up by the renovator or cultivator.

In his garden space, Whitehead has and will continue to set aside a strip of ground 20 per cent of the width of the garden. In this he plants alfalfa, clover, guar and similar soil restorative crops. He moves the strip each year, thus constantly rotating crops and restoring the soil. The cuttings he uses for a mulch and compost. In the remaining 80 per cent of garden space, he never plants the same crop two years in a row.

There has been no need for him to use rock fertilizers. However, since the nutritive value of the soil has tended to be spotty during the first two years, he has had occasion to do some local fertilizing. In a 50-gallon metal drum, he keeps a burlap bag full of compost soaking in water. When an individual plant shows signs of hunger, he dips out some of the water from this drum around the plant. However, he warns that in the beginning he was too generous and "burned" a couple of plants badly; it's mighty potent fertilizer after it has been brewing a couple of weeks.

Whitehead expects to have two successful plantings a

year, one in early spring to yield during the summer, the other in early September to yield root vegetables into December or later—providing there is a typically mild Arizona fall and early winter. In addition to turnips, beets and carrots, his fall planting this year includes tomatoes, lettuce and peas as an experiment. If he is successful, it will mean a significant broadening of agricultural horizons for the entire Verde Valley, in which Cottonwood is located, for these crops have never been grown successfully there that late.

Sandy, Acid Soils Can Be Productive

Faced with a typical "light sandy" soil composed of approximately 70 per cent sand, 20 per cent silt and 10 per cent clay, these New England gardeners overcame the rapid drying and loss of nutrients that go along with it. Here's how Betty Brinhart of West Hatfield, Mass., describes the treatment given a soil type generally very difficult to correct—and the results they achieved from their compost-plus improvement program:

It is quite discouraging to decide to go into gardening, and suddenly find yourself up against a sandy, depleted soil that cannot even grow grass.

When we bought our country home several years ago, we had gardening in mind. The purchase was made in winter which prevented us from checking the land. But we felt certain it was fertile enough to grow a garden.

When the ground thawed in spring, we inspected the garden site. We couldn't have been more disappointed had we unknowingly purchased an acre of sand dunes on the shores of Lake Erie. The soil was a dirty yellow, and so sandy that the cracked surface glistened in the sun. Only a few dried grass stalks stood here and there like forgotten souls. From all appearances this soil couldn't even support weeds. How, then, could we possibly grow flowers and vegetables in it?

My husband kicked at the ground in rage. The fine sand whipped about us on the strong wind.

"Can't grow anything in this, that's for sure," he said, feeling cheated and angry. I felt the same, and, momentarily gave up all hopes of gardening.

But, there was no peace within me. This was *spring!* Time for tilling and planting. Why not sow some seeds? I chose radishes. The nobs never formed. The poor plants eventually bolted to seed, and dried up.

New England soil, as well as that of northern Michigan, northwestern Minnesota, northern Wisconsin, New York, New Jersey and Alaska, is naturally sandy, and of the Podzol type. It was formed by the accumulation of organic matter on the surface with a downward movement of clays in colloidal solution to create a lower, rubbery layer of heavy clay. The topsoil is a thin layer of acid humus sprinkled over an even more acid yellowish-brown subsoil.

The only advantages of such a soil are that it warms up quickly and drains well. The disadvantages are too numerous to mention. Two things, however, can be corrected easily. They, in turn, will remedy the other defects.

One is soil acidity. The application of agricultural lime will sweeten the soil and induce growth. The second is the complete lack of organic matter deep within, hence no earthworms. Organic and rock fertilizers, mulches, barnyard manure, compost, green manure and earthworms, can alter this.

When we learned how to bring fertility to our soil, we decided to make our garden productive no matter what. Lime was applied. And several large truck loads of aged manure were brought in. This was scattered and plowed under. For the rest of the summer, we mulched the land with grass clippings and hay. Large earthworms were dug up in a near-by bog and placed in the garden.

That fall, leaves were added to the mulch. Then the two were plowed under to hasten decay. The following year we repeated the process, adding limestone. The third spring we applied natural ground rock and balanced organic fertilizers. This we disked in, then planted the garden. The vegetables grew and produced, but showed signs of undernourishment.

All that summer we mulched between rows, and added leaves in the fall. Next spring this was plowed under and the garden again planted. This time the plants showed pep and vigor. The soil had lost its yellow hue, no longer caked in the heat, and retained moisture longer. The plants did well beneath the thick, damp mulch, and produced moderately. Our garden had, at last, reached productivity.

But we did not stop here. We felt production could still be increased. We have continued to feed and mulch our garden until today, it seems to be at its peak. The soil is now sweet and clean smelling, a dark brown in color, is loose enough to dig out a carrot with your fingers, retains moisture the

Excessive alkalinity is a soil condition that most Southwest gardeners and farmers must contend with and correct if they want productive gardens. Californian Regina H. Jones did it with compost, hay mulch and a sand-straw-manure mixture.

summer long, and yields as we never dreamed possible. Our tomatoes are almost too heavy for their vines; carrots reach 8 inches into the ground; our beets grow rapidly to a large size, yet remain sweet and tender; 5 of our cabbage heads can fill a bushel basket; and our potatoes are things to marvel at. All this from a hopeless, leached-out soil that couldn't support radishes. It took 5 years of determined work, but now we have a garden to be proud of.

Compost Revives an Alkali Bed

Excessive alkalinity is a condition in which the pH of the soil is abnormally high. Common throughout the Southwest, this imbalance actually makes the soil too "sweet," prevents it from maintaining needed microorganism life and from supporting any of the usual moderately acid-loving vegetables or flowers.

(A pH of 7.0 is neutral; readings below that figure are progressively more acid; above it, more alkaline. A simple soil test will readily indicate your soil's status.)

Regina Hughes Jones tells this story of her alkali soil:

"The first time I surveyed my garden plot on our new, 1-acre California ranch, 3 years ago, my heart plopped. *My* garden? It was owned by desert weeds and devil-grass!

"I slashed my hoe experimentally. It rang on the flinty ground and bounced out of my hand. I let it lie and marched off to hire a tractor.

"The plow turned up lumpy masses of dry, alkali-streaked soil. Powdery dust billowed everywhere. That night, we wet down every square inch; in the morning, we broke up the clods, pulling grass and weeds and raking thoroughly.

"Neighbors advised gypsum as a neutralizer, but we knew the superior values of organic matter, and in mid-April we used a load of half-rotted alfalfa hay to mulch.

"In the fall, we spread loads of sand, straw and steer manure over the ground and added a mulch of leaves, grass clippings and half-rotted vegetation.

"The improvement in the soil, when we ran a disk over it in the spring, made us chuckle with satisfaction and pride; we'd won Round One against 'Mr. Alkali.'

"The spot I selected for my flower garden was choked with puncture briers and weeds. Again my first move was to plow the strip; then I dug, pulled and raked the devil-grass roots clear. The soil under these areas began getting soft and pliable. I spread a load of sand and steer manure over it and wet it down.

"By morning, the clods were softer. I raked them till they pulverized. I planted roses, dahlias, mums and canna lilies. Each time I watered them, during the following weeks, I worked up the soil.

"In April, I planted zinnias, bachelor buttons and dwarf marigolds, wetting the soil enough for sprouting before I planted, since water applied afterwards increases the hardening tendency of alkali soil.

"When the plants were two inches high, I began mulching. Each week, I dug in the old mulch and applied fresh clippings. This year's abundance of blooms heralded another 'win' over alkali.

"This is what I've learned about alkali:

"Alfalfa hay and a sand-straw-steer-manure mixture are the best mulch and fertilizer. The month of October in California, just before the rains start, is the best time for an all-over spread of manures and various humus.

"Plants which grow readily in alkaline soil are those

which throw off a neutralizing acid, which frees the minerals in the soil around them. The tomato is one of the strongest alkali neutralizers. Cucumbers and cantaloupes also resist alkali, but grapes, strawberries, raspberries, rhubarb and peaches have little resistance to it.

"Nevertheless, during our first year, we set out a long row of grapes: concord, agawam and muscat. The first season was cruel. Some died from alkali chlorosis; all but one Eastern concord wore a sickly yellow look.

"I fed them all summer with steer manure and sand, mulched them thoroughly with grass clippings, leaves and alfalfa hay. The next year they showed light green instead of yellow, and by fall, they were throwing out new healthy shoots.

"This year, they boast dark green foliage. They have climbed 6 feet and are loaded with fruit—another row of soldiers who battled alkali and won!"

ORCHARDS, BIG AND SMALL

Perhaps no other part of agriculture has suffered so many troubles in recent years as fruit growing. Orchardists have been beset by disease problems and decreasing size and quality of fruit as never before. Stepping up their chemical fertilization and spray programs is the solution generally recommended, but the hard school of experience has shown that this only intensifies the problem. Compost, on the other hand, cures it, quickly and permanently, as the following examples will show.

Reviving Citrus Grove

Oliver R. Franklin of Fort Myers, Florida, revived a dying citrus grove by piling compost materials around the trees. As he tells it:

"Down here in southwest Florida we have so much rain all year long that the soluble plant food elements are often washed away before the crops can make use of them. Advice on composting and mulching has helped me to grow some very tasty vegetables and fruits.

"When I bought a small citrus grove here a few years ago, I found the oranges on many trees were quite small and bitter, lacking in fruit sugar. Some trees were slowly dying away—they call that 'spreading decline' disease down here because a program of heavy applications of chemical fertilizer had destroyed the soil bacteria that naturally prey on the ever-present nematode, thereby upsetting the normal ecological balance. I simply trimmed back the dead wood and mulched the ground under the trees in several inches of half-decayed wood shavings from an old sawmill site.

"Now, two years later, the fruit is large and sweet, the leaves are bright green and healthy, and new growth is replacing the vacant areas in the spread of the trees.

"They told me that bananas did poorly here in the low ground near the river, and from the looks of those growing in nearby yards it appears believable. However, I planted mine in the same kind of soil, but shocked the neighbors by capturing islands of water hyacinths floating by in the river, and pitching them ashore with a hay fork and mulching the bananas a foot deep with them. I figured that the rains had washed a lot of soluble minerals and trace elements into the river to be captured by the weeds, and I wanted some of it back.

"When the hyacinths decayed around the bananas, I mulched them deeply with the most aged shavings and saw-dust I could find. The plants responded by growing twice as tall as their parent stock, with none of the usual root rot and *no* insect pests."

Another Florida Experience

H. J. Kuppers tells this story of another grove:

"In years gone by it was the ambition of nearly every business and professional man in the citrus area of Florida to own a grove. True to this tradition, a former postmaster had acquired a grove of about 15 acres about 5 miles from New Smyrna Beach, Florida. He engaged the usual caretakers who follow the accepted methods from fertilization to spraying. Had this procedure been a success he should have had a comfortable income in his declining years. His health and income failed and for about 7 years the grove stood in complete lack of care and deteriorated.

"This grove came to the attention of Mr. and Mrs. George Brenzel of Milwaukee, who had been spending their winters in New Smyrna Beach. In the spring of 1948 they bought the grove. They disked the grove lightly and sowed a cover crop before going north for the summer. In the fall this cover crop was disked in lightly.

"In the spring of 1949 they applied an organic mixture (made of citrus pulp, tobacco stems, castor pumice and peat moss) around the trees at the rate of 6 tons for the grove. This application was repeated annually and has created a healthy, dark sandy loam around each tree. In 1952 they applied 10 tons colloidal phosphate and 10 tons pulverized granite. In 1953 they applied 30 tons pulverized granite. This caused cover crops to grow where none had grown before.

"In 1953 they found greensand available in Florida at lower prices and at that time they applied another 10 tons colloidal phosphate and 10 tons greensand. Mr. Brenzel reports that this treatment has brought the following results:

1. More juice and better colored fruit.
2. Fruit matures earlier.
3. Trees grow faster and look better.

"At the time of my visit, May 14, 1954, Mr. Brenzel was preparing to disk in lightly a mixture of weeds and leguminous plants with the intention of sowing Hairy Indigo (*Indigofera Hirsuta*) for the summer leguminous cover crop to be disked in lightly next fall. These cover crops now grow from 4 to 5 feet high where formerly none would grow. The soil directly under the trees is worked with hand hoes each year, so as not to injure the roots. The grove has not been sprayed since 1942. There is no sign of insects (pests) or of diseases. All trees have very dark green, glossy leaves indicating the highest degree of health and vitality.

"The fruit production of the grove has increased about 3 times the amount it produced in 1949. An analysis of a sample of oranges in December, 1953, showed the following values over the average of Florida oranges:

1. 14.8 per cent more minerals (food value).
2. 37 per cent more juice.
3. 67 per cent more sugar (flavor).

"Their method of marketing was never premeditated. In 1949 they started to ship to a few friends who are health minded. These people sent other customers. In 1952 they started running ads in *Organic Gardening, Prevention* and *Herald of Health* with excellent results.

"In 1952, 1953 and 1954 the entire crops were sold by mail, excepting 400 bushel in 1954, which became too ripe to ship and were sold to the juice plant.

"While the average citrus grower in Florida is worrying about meeting the cost of production most of the time, the Brenzels have their crops engaged ahead each year to customers who want shipments at regular intervals of from 1 to 4 weeks. One of their customers has this to say:

'Don't worry about the color of your oranges, for everyone here has enjoyed them and above all are thankful that they are not gassed or dyed, for after all that is the important thing. They are the most delicious oranges I have ever tasted. Kindly ship another 10 bushel at your earliest convenience.'

"The Brenzel fruit weighs well over the standard of 55 pounds per bushel, indicating solid, well-developed fruit."

Rescuing a Papaya Tree

Edwin H. Abrams saved an uprooted papaya tree with compost.

"As an experiment the writer tried using a large quantity of mulch on a papaya that had been uprooted by a heavy wind. It was at first decided to destroy the tree, as its roots were largely out of the ground. Instead of doing so, the tree was propped up at an angle of some 30 or 40 degrees, and many loads of compost and garden soil placed over the roots until it was well covered. When it was found that the tree was still alive, and even putting out new branches while bearing heavily, more and more mulch was added from time to time, and it made a surprising comeback.

"It not only matured the large crop of fruit that it carried when overthrown, but actually put out several sturdy limbs and grew a large crop of good sized fruit on these in addition."

California Award-Winner

The orchard-gardens of Dennis B. Seale are well known throughout the Santa Clara Valley where he has made his home the past 10 years, and he is an enthusiastic exponent of the organic method of growing fruits and vegetables. Although his orchard is made up of more than 30 prime fruit trees, many of them bearing up to 5 different fruits, and an abundance of nuts, berries and vegetables, it is planted on only 1½ small city lots in the middle of town.

Los Gatos, California, which has a mild climate conducive to gardening, is near Santa Rosa where Luther Burbank maintained his extensive experimental plants. But Mr. Seale places the credit for his numerous blue ribbons won each year at the Santa Clara County Fair squarely where credit belongs . . . to full-time, exclusive organic culture.

In 1953 he won 48 ribbons at the Fair for his fruit and vegetables. Twenty-four Firsts, 20 Seconds, and 7 Thirds. This year he did better than he has ever done, although 1955 was a difficult year produce-wise for California. Sixty-six awards came to this organiculturist, 35 Firsts, 21 Seconds, and 10 Thirds. These triumphs are an old story to Dennis Seale, however, for this vigorous and hearty, 75 year old ex-postman, has always been a dyed-in-the-wool believer in the extra-superiority of plants grown with organic methods only. His abounding good health attests, also, to the vitality of the vitamin-filled food he grows in his own yard.

Visitors to Mr. Seale's place are amazed at the rich, black fertile-looking soil under his fruit trees. They notice the cleanliness of his grounds without a trace of insects or pests, with no rotted fruit lying around (this is common in California gardens). They notice, too, how healthy and green his trees look the year round and how smooth and waxy their bark is to the touch, not rough or scarred.

When he first came to Los Gatos from Visalia, California, after retirement from the Post Office Department there, he bought his house and the lot next door with the thought in mind of establishing a fruit and vegetable produce interest which would bring him some extra money as well as provide food for his own family's table.

By carefully planning his orchard in order to utilize every inch of space available, Mr. Seale laid out the lot in this manner: first he set a row of fruit trees out, about 20 feet apart, then a row of grapes on a lattice, a row of berries (thornless blackberries, boysenberries, raspberries, and so on), then another row of trees, having the berry vines between the rows. As the trees grew larger, he planned to take out the vines should they become crowded. He put his vegetables in small plots wherever there was open ground enough to plant them, growing corn on the back of the lot where space permits, and low ground plants such as strawberries on the front of the lot where they will get the sun. He also plants radishes, onions, turnips, squash, beets, peas, beans, etc., at the front of the orchard.

Because of his lack of space he grafts his fruit trees

extensively, and gets as many as 5 different kinds of fruit from one tree. One of his best bearers produces two kinds of peaches, a plum, an apricot and a prune. He usually uses an apricot as his root stock, since that tree grows well in this area.

He uses a system of close crop rotation, planning his planting in such a way that when one crop of vegetables is maturing and being harvested, the next one is coming on. For example, he plants Irish potatoes with sweet potatoes in the same row. The Irish potatoes, maturing first, may be dug out, leaving room for the sweets to grow to maturity for later harvest. In this manner, by using all the tricks he can think of, he is able to realize the maximum return for his minimum of space.

Mr. Seale root-feeds his trees with compost twice yearly, pulling the dirt away from the roots for a depth of 6 or 8 inches and in an area of about 6 feet around the tree. He fills in this ring with finished compost and covers it over with the soil again, watering it down well.

Among his prize-bearing fruit trees are an Everbearing lemon which produces around 400 pounds of lemons per year, some of which measure 9 and 10 inches around with a tape measure. Also winners are an Elephant Heart plum, a Burbank HalBerta Giant peach and his Golden Delicious and Double-Red Delicious apples. These trees are mostly Stark Brothers fruit trees and as he sells the young trees, also, he is proud to show the results of good care of the full-grown ones to his prospective customers.

Mr. Seale, a busy man for one three-quarters of a century young, prepares and sells his prize-winning fruit and vegetables in a neighborhood grocery. His produce always commands good prices because it is cleaner, better looking, and usually appears at market earlier in the season than that brought in by larger produce growers of the area.

1300 Organic Apple Trees

Grow a really big apple orchard *organically?* Most people —including those who favor the organic way—insist that it's mighty tough. Raising field crops or even a few fruit trees by natural methods is one thing, they emphasize, but large-scale orcharding—especially apples—is quite another. Yet one stubborn Virginian has not only done it, against unusual

Orchardist A. P. Thomson rejuvenated a "mined-out" 45-acre farm in Front Royal, Virginia. Using a "fortress" rock fertilizing method, along with liberal compost application, he has developed the 1300-tree apple orchard into a productive one.

odds, he's done it extremely well! Today, his 1300-tree orchard, productive and even more promising, is one of the finest and most fertile to be found anywhere.

But let's look back at the start of this surprising project. In 1944, after a long period of service with the Navy as a diesel engineer, A. P. Thomson bought a 45-acre farm in the colorful Shenandoah Valley. The land had been literally "mined" for nearly 250 years. Once rich and high-yielding, its soil had lost practically every vestige of fertility through careless tillage. Still, Thomson thought of his being the fifth generation to farm this land bordered by the Blue Ridge and

Allegheny mountain ranges—and became downright determined that he would revive it.

How did he accomplish it? Actually, by concentrating on a fundamental truth Thomson himself has put it this way: "An apple cannot give you the living elements and delight that you need and want if it comes from a tree itself deficient because of the deficiencies of the soil."

And so, before a single apple tree was set out, a vigorous program of re-building the soil was begun. In the fall of 1945, Thomson turned under 5 years' accumulated growth of lespedeza, broom sage, foxtail, berry vines and assorted weeds. Over 15 tons of organic matter per acre were composted and incorporated in the soil. Several hundred tons of manure were applied. More than 100 tons of corn fodder were composted by the Indore method, developed by Sir Albert Howard, and also added to the soil. Now, even the tree prunings are shredded and allowed to lay as compost.

In addition, Thomson applied 500 pounds per acre of ground phosphate rock, then sowed a mixture of alfalfa, sweet clover, mammouth, alsike, some brome, rye grass and oats— all as a further soil-enriching cover crop. He soon found, though, that the heavy loam soil was too acid, and so in the fall of 1946 broadcast 315 tons of limestone rock. By the following spring, growth was luxuriant, much of it over lanky Thomson's head. It took hold on the farm's bare galls and it completely stopped erosion. In October, he disked under the heavy cover, planned to use brome, oats and alfalfa as a new cover for his orchard's middle rows, and was ready to plant apple trees by December.

When it came to choosing varieties, Thomson selected first the Golden Delicious, a variety especially suited to his locality. Among its advantages are that it is a very high quality apple when grown well; it's a heavy bearer and a good pollinator. Another feature is that it attains an appetizing golden yellow color as it ripens. On the other hand, it hasn't found much commercial orcharding popularity because it requires a long season to mature and is one of the most winter-tender varieties. Furthermore, it is particularly susceptible to injury from chemical sprays and from mice.

Just the same, Thomson wanted to grow this variety. He wasn't going to use any poison sprays—and he was certain that the organic methods he was following would overcome the other difficulties and provide him good yields of a high-quality fruit that should be popular. Choosing this apple suggested a good name, Golden Acres Orchard. It's a fitting designation and one that aptly describes the glowing farm today. In addition, he planted Red York Imperial, another variety well suited to the area. Both this and the Golden Delicious are superb for eating raw and cooking.

The trees at Golden Acres were spaced 38 feet by 40 feet apart, contrasting with the 15 feet to 22 feet spacing usual in commercial orchards. Thus, Thomson's trees are far enough apart to prevent touching at maturity, whereas the average grove becomes like a jungle. Although production per acre can't be as large, the whole orchard is benefited because the trees and fruit get better air circulation and more sunlight, and because room is provided for those enriching cover crops.

Thomson's orchard management includes another unusual feature that he calls the "fortress method." Around each tree, in a circle 5 or 6 feet in diameter and over 6 inches deep, he places approximately 500 pounds of half-inch dolomitic rock. What's this do? Thomson cites 4 major advantages:

1. It gives the trees greater anchorage against strong winds, a protection otherwise lacking where they are widely spaced.

2. It absorbs a large amount of heat from the spring sun, creating convection currents during frosty nights to provide some protection for bud and bloom.

3. It discourages mice from burrowing in around the trunks and damaging or killing the trees. (The area has an abundance of the pine and meadow mouse.)

4. As the rock "weathers," it becomes a source of calcium and magnesium for the trees' continuing requirements.

Sawdust mulching is also practiced. Thomson spreads a ton per acre each year between the rows. He uses aged Blue Ridge Mountain hardwood sawdust, selected because the rock and virgin soil of these mountains affords the trees many valuable trace elements. And, he notes, the sawdust takes up excess nitrogen produced by the legumes. In late fall, a winter hay mulch of 200 pounds per tree is applied—only to the drip line.

Currently, the entire orchard is sheet composted 4 or 5 times a year with the legumes and grasses grown between rows, not only to maintain but steadily increase the soil's fertility and structure. A rotary cutter is used to macerate this growth so that decomposition can take place quickly and a rich humus released for the trees to draw upon.

Then, too, earthworms aren't forgotten, nor their tremendous contribution to any soil-building program. Right from the start, Thomson began a sizable worm-breeding project, added them to all 45 acres and used them in compost and mulch piles. With some initial help from earthworm-specialist Dr. Thomas Barrett, the farm's earthworm population has grown to over 5 million per acre—all working constantly to enrich and aerate the soil.

A pointed sidelight on what these earthworms can do is found in one 60-year-old Pippin apple tree originally at Golden Acres. In 1950, Thomson discovered this tree was dying. He added a million earthworms to its soil. By last year it had not only regained health, but yielded 51 bushels of fine apples.

As for insect control, always a major problem in apple growing. Thomson relies on some very effective, natural measures, plus an army of natural allies. In February, he applies a miscible oil dormant spray which checks scale, mites and developing eggs of many orchard pests. For severe outbreaks of codling moth, an extract prepared from the root of a British West Indies tropical plant has been used experimentally and found helpful. Called Ryania, this spray is very mild and leaves no residue.

In additon, there's a host of predators on hand. Ladybugs and praying mantids do their share, and thousands of birds, encouraged by the multiflora rose hedges around Golden Acres, willingly pitch right in. Those hedges, by the way, also draw swarms of welcome bees who contribute to the pollinating job throughout the orchard. When some Japanese beetles showed up in 1954, Thomson put four teaspoonfuls of milky spore disease powder around each tree and hasn't had any difficulty with these troublemakers since.

Now, what about the harvest, the apples themselves? Without resorting to chemical fertilizers, hormones, defoliants, or poisonous sprays (most orchardists pour on DDT, arsenic, lead, copper, methoxyclor—to mention just a few), the Thomson orchard now yields from 30 to 40 bushels per tree of top-quality, really healthful apples. These crisp, good-looking fruits can be eaten—nutritionally rich skins and all—*without* the cumulative dangers of all those toxic and artificial concoc-

At height of picking season, Thomson sorts heavy harvest of his healthful Golden Delicious and Red Delicious variety fruit, which get no poison spraying or chemical fertilizing. Helping are his 84-year-old dad and two apple-munching youngsters.

tions, and *with* all the natural flavor and food value put into them by good soil.

In 1958, the returns from matured trees totaled some 4,000 bushels, which brought an over-all average of 3 dollars each. Most are sold via mail order to both retail consumers and wholesalers. 1957 was the first year the enterprise met expenses (Thomson has invested all available funds since 1939), but the future looks good. The orchard is a young one, all of the 1300 trees being 12-year-olds or under. Frenchie Tolliver, capable orchard manager for Golden Acres, believes the '59 yield will double last year as more of these trees approach maturity.

COMPOST ON A FARM SCALE

A growing number of organic farmers are proving that, despite the scoffing of the "experts," compost can be the basis of a profitable farm operation.

An Illinois Example

Since 1941, when the Ernest Halbleib family of McNabb, Illinois took over the old homestead, their foremost object was to increase their land's fertility.

The Halbleibs use no chemical sprays on their 300-tree apple and peach orchard. "Much of the damage of insects and fungous diseases," says Mr. Halbleib, "may be overcome by the organic soil itself. If this does not completely achieve the result desired, we use a spray of colloidal phosphate."

The farm has 20 colonies of bees, which produce honey of high quality from trees and plants growing in a humus-rich soil. It is sold in 3 forms—strained, raw unpasteurized and comb.

Since starting organic farming, the Halbleibs have raised the protein content of their wheat from 12 per cent to nearly 17 per cent and to a yield of 63 bushels per acre. Their open-pollinated corn has increased in yield until 90 bushels per acre is common.

Three small mills process part of the grains grown into whole wheat flour, whole rye flour, whole corn flour, whole corn meal, whole rolled oats, cracked wheat cereal, cracked rye cereal and oats groats. Practically everything produced is sold direct on the farm or shipped to consumers all over the country.

"Our system of farming," says Mr. Halbleib, "is not one of medicating the soil with chemicals, an indication it is sick, but with feeding it. In additon, the humus from our compost adds greatly to the texture and to the moisture-holding properties of the soil, and aids much in its retention against erosion."

The basis of their soil-building program on the 183-acre farm is 54 head of Holsteins, which furnish much manure. Plenty of straw is used for bedding, which absorbs the liquid part of the manure. The manure is never used raw on the open fields. Instead, it is hauled to a large compost pile, where a bacterial activator hastens its decomposition to a matter of days. All leaves, weeds, corn stalks, cobs and table garbage also go into the pile. It all combines to produce a compost of high quality.

When placed in the fields and plowed under, all its nutritive value is immediately available for plant growth. "When raw manure is plowed under," says Mr. Halbleib, "long periods of time elapse before the decomposition is completed and the nutritive value made available."

The crop rotation also helps to build the soil. This consists of one year corn, one year soybeans, one year small grain seeded to a grass-legume mixture, which is pastured for 2 or 3 years.

"All our efforts are toward quality rather than quantity. If any kind of business is good only for the immediate cash returns, we do not consider it of much value. We prefer health, which can come only from good foods—health for ourselves and for those who buy our products. Our aim is to give our customers and ourselves everything in our products that the Lord put into them."

Sixteen Acres in New Jersey

Carl Lanz is a soft-spoken, hard-working farmer. Just about alone, he manages an astonishing 16-acre strip of land in eastern New Jersey. His methods are simple, effective and natural. And his produce and returns are outstanding.

From the Lanz farm, located in the Montclair Heights section of Clifton, New Jersey, you can see the famous New York skyline. In fact, the trip into the center of busy Manhattan takes only about 20 minutes—a point which is undoubtedly connected with the recent building boom in this area.

Yet, the sector has been farming country for centuries. This particular farm is one of just a handful now remaining. It's been in the Lanz family for more than 60 years. Today, its rich black soil, bright and brimming vegetation, and extraordinary crops are as visible as that skyline on the clearest of days—and stand as sturdily in tribute to the value of the organic method and to the man who has so diligently put it into practice.

Key to the remarkable growth and maintenance of ideal soil at this farm is an abundance of leaf mold compost. Over the past 10 years, Lanz has had truckloads of autumn leaves willingly deposited by the neighborhood city of East Orange. These have aged and decomposed into the finest imaginable humus. From 6 to 8 sizable heaps of composting leaves are continually in preparation. With the aid of a manure-loader, they are periodically turned to help the breakdown into finished humus.

Lanz has found that this leaf mold, which he uses very liberally—but only when completely composted—provides a maximum of balanced fertilizing. Having such an abundant, constantly-renewed source of leaves, he is enabled to do without manure or ground rocks—and, of course, without chemicals. His compost, coupled with careful crop alternating, the action of millions of earthworms, and the return of legume-crop residues, delivers an optimum amount of all major and trace elements and every soil-requiring mineral. Lanz suggests that other farmers living near cities investigate the possibility of having these communities bring them their collected leaf loads, and starting a similar operation.

Early in the period of building his land to this level, Lanz cultivated and bred earthworms. Now they are very populous and very helpful, he doesn't need to supplement those that revel in the high organic matter content of his soil and constantly reproduce and increase their number.

For his vegetable and berry fields, Lanz applies from 100 to 200 tons of the leaf mold per acre. Throughout the year, a 6-inch or greater depth of rich, dark humus is maintained. He doesn't weed—and he's plowed only once in the past 9 years. A number of wild grasses and weeds, which thrive between the rows of his crop fields, are simply turned back into the soil, providing an additional source of green organic matter.

And speaking of green, just how lush and vigorously healthful this farm's vegetation really is can perhaps be seen from the objective of a recent visitor Lanz had. The caller was from a chlorophyll company—and was after sample cuttings of plant growth. Its deep green, persisting despite the driest stretches of weather, is one of the foremost points noted readily by anyone even glancing at these fields.

In fact, the way in which this soil and its produce overcomes drought and prolonged periods of unfavorable weather is just plain remarkable and about the strongest possible testimony to the effectiveness of the method employed. Lanz doesn't irrigate, nor cart water in any manner to his fields. Yet at the height of dry spells during the past few years the soil, just an inch below the surface, has remained constantly moist.

Two other results of this system are obvious and noteworthy. Lanz has no plant disease whatever, and insect damage is almost non-existent. In a prolonged tour of the farm, the only insects a visitor could notice were loads of bees, busily collecting nectar and pollinating plants and fruit trees, and some of the always helpful, aphis-destroying ladybugs.

Carl Lanz has worked 23 years at building his farm to the natural level of fertility and productiveness it now has. Almost 7 years ago, the Soil Conservation Service made a check and report on it. One of the most outstanding commentaries possible is found in the summary of this report: "Soil under this system of culture," stated the SCS, "is very friable and absorbent of moisture so that additional conservation practices ordinarily required are here unnecessary."

When the conservation survey was made, limestone had been recommended to help maintain a desirable pH. Lanz purchased a quantity of this, then found it wasn't needed! His fertilizing, mulching and cover crop program keep the soil at an ideal 6.5 to 7.0 (neutral) pH.

Then, too, at the time of that report there was an unplanted back hillside sector which showed up to 75 per cent topsoil erosion and, in some places, well below that into the subsoil. Lanz proceeded to remedy this. Today it is part of an expanding fruit tree development and is filled with a number of apple, pear and peach varieties. Incidentally, there's an attractive and very practical wildlife border of multiflora roses along the entire west boundary.

Lanz has a keen interest in his orcharding project. Not only is he growing a wide selection of strains among these fruits, but he's also trying some cross-breeding in order to develop new and stronger varieties. Most of his trees are 4- and 5-year-olds, although in growth and appearance they look far more advanced. From the blossoming and setting seen in May it was apparent that he'd have a good-sized, healthy crop this year.

Fertilizing these trees is another aspect in which Lanz is very interested. Around many of them he has placed 1 to 2 tons of the leaf compost. With a number of others, however, he is experimenting with a wood chip mulch. This seemed to be working very well; the chips break down from the underside in closest contact with the earth and provide a slow, continually-renewing source of organic matter and microorganism activity. At the same time, the 5- or 6-inch wood chip mulch helps conserve moisture and prevent sunbaking damage around the young trees.

Besides the fruit, the Lanz farm produces tomatoes (planted in 12-foot-wide rows because they grow and bear so prolifically), onions, beans, beets, carrots, cabbage, rhubarb and other crops. Visitors cannot resist commenting on how sturdy, bright-colored and appetizing his rhubarb looks, and how completely different it is from the ordinary rhubarb found at the grocer today. Berries grown include strawberries—which are about the size of silver dollars—and red raspberries.

An Oasis in Droughts

The Lempke organic farm in Washington County, Arkansas, has been a veritable oasis in the recent severe droughts in that area. When they bought the place in 1942, they had only 20 depleted, rock-strewn, eroded acres that scarcely produced a scraggy crop of ragweed. The Lempkes farmed by standard practices, using chemical fertilizers and sprays.

Four years passed. Much had been attained: fences, new barn, and chicken house built; fine young vineyard started; family gardens in production; meat and dairy animals for family use on the farm. But a heavy toll had been exacted. The first flush of enthusiasm and ambition had spent itself; the family health level was down to an annoying low. Fortunately about this time Mr. Lempke made a contact that convinced him that foods high in nutritional value—grown from soil rich in the elements needed to produce such foods and free from the residues of poisonous sprays and caustic fertilizers—would go far toward improving the family health pattern. However, in abandoning the standard fertilizing and spraying practices some efficient substitute must be forthcoming—and rapidly. Hence was born another compost-builder and follower of farming principles.

To an already busy schedule had to be added the task of collecting tons of raw materials that could be turned into compost. There was no scarcity of materials to be had—for the labor involved: brooderhouse litter, mowed weeds, loads of leaves, old hay and straw, barnyard manure and bedding all went into great heaps of compost. The compost went onto the gardens, the berry patches and the vineyard. In the spring, rye and vetch were planted in the vineyard but the vetch didn't come up that first year; the rye grew to be about 24 inches high; it was, however, plowed into the soil in time for peas to be planted in the fall. They were, in turn, also worked into the soil. This practice was followed 3 years, and the third year the rye grew so tall it stood above the posts that support the wires and plants. That fall the peas grew so tall and heavy Mr. Lempke was unable to work them into his topsoil with his one-horse equipment, but had to get a neighbor to come in with his heavy tractor and disk to do the job. That year about 800 dollars' worth of sawdust was hauled in to be used as mulch—mostly on the vineyard. Some rock phosphate, wood ashes, and limestone were used to help soil fertility but Mr. Lempke stresses the fact they were used very sparingly. He feels that heavy applications are not required nor desirable. Much mulching and some sheet composting is being done at the present time to conserve energy and time for some other urgent projects such as putting up the fine new building just erected by Mr. Lempke, with son Lawrence's help, to be used as workshop, garage, and small living apartment.

Heavy mulching in the berry beds has provided a fine-textured, moist soil that accounts for the growth and production of better-than-average berry crops. On a hot, dry day in early August, 1952, at the peak of a bad drought, Mr. Lempke dug down through the deep mulch of leaves and old straw on his fine raspberry bed and brought up a handful of earth so moist that when squeezed it formed a ball that held its shape until tossed onto the ground—this, when all about deep dust and parching vegetation were the common sights.

Their healthy young vineyard produced a crop of well-developed grapes that ripened several days ahead of the area average, and were marketed in small baskets rather than by the ton to the local grapejuice plant.

Since only comparative evaluation has meaning for most of us, let's consider the results of this 4-year period during which the organic method has been diligently applied on these 20 acres. Always there's cause and effect—the means to an *end*—so in this project there's cost. It can be summed up thusly: brains, brawn, time, and a modest outlay of capital. The reward? Immense benefits on an expanding horizon, according to the Lempkes. Of first consideration to most of us is that gnawing item of dollars and cents. So, current dividends are: practically all of the family's food supply plus some market surpluses. In 1952 they had wheat and rye for cereals and bread; the best of fresh vegetables such as asparagus, potatoes, onions, beets, squash, corn, tomatoes, okra, and yams for summer use and for winter storage. Berries and grapes were produced on a larger scale and considered cash crops, although both are used generously by the family, as are apples. Notwithstanding long hours of work and the necessary regularity of chores, the program also includes the important segments of eggs, meat, and dairy products for family use and market surpluses.

Benefit number two is that factor of family health. Actually, it's the key to the whole experiment. No absurd claims are being made in that field, but so appreciative are they for genuine measurable progress that it gets frequent discussion, and from various angles. To even a casual observer, the difference stands out in the smiling eyes, the unbounded vim and pent-up "steam" of the young ones. Gone from their daily lives are the gnawing constant nuisances of skin irritations, headaches, styes, poor appetites and indigestion. Gone also is that shrunken morale one feels in falling short of projected goals. In its place is discernible, earned dignity at having an honest conviction verified. So, while the great drought of 1952 wrought immeasurable hardships, it unquestionably afforded evidence to a group of interested individuals that the organic method is superior. The Lempkes have again proved the old adage: "It's an ill wind that blows nobody good!"

A Doctor on Soil Building

Dr. Howard G. Laskey of Rhode Island is halfway between the backyard gardener and full-time farmer classifications. He has some very definite ideas on soil building.

"Chemical fertilizers are wrong," Dr. Laskey says. "Nature never intended vegetables and grains to grow in ground strewn with powdered chemicals and then saturated with chemical sprays. Growing things demand natural fertilizer because they are growing in a living medium, the soil."

Dr. Laskey believes this so strongly that every winter he spend hours and hours on his half days off and on week ends piling tons and tons of material for his compost piles. Into these he puts anything that will decay into humus, dark earth rich in the organic matter that growing things need. In the list are kitchen garbage, hedge trimmings, ditch scrapings and seaweed. After 6 months in the winter and as little as 3 weeks in the summer these are converted into a rich loam.

In essence, the key to Dr. Laskey's farming methods is just this—to make the highest possible use of the natural fertilizers that abound on most diversified farms. "Soil is a living thing," Dr. Laskey says, "and when a natural fertilizing method is available, it is far better than chemicals. Within each cubic centimeter of the soil are growing plants, seeds, spores and enzyme producing bacteria. If the farmer introduces an artificial material into this community of living things he upsets a delicate balance. He may for a few years produce high crop yields, but in time he will destroy his soil."

Dr. Laskey points to dust storms as nature's warning signs that the top 4 inches of soil—the life giving belt in which growing things can take root—are gradually being destroyed by chemical fertilizers. And during the last 7 years he has gradually been engaged in a land reclaiming project on his farm, which generations of old style agriculture had reduced to 85 acres of acid, dry, sandy soil supporting as its main crops scrub pine, brush and weeds.

"Nature has been warning us for years," says Dr. Laskey, "but we have not heeded her warning signals. We say that things don't taste as good as they once did—that apples aren't as sweet, or that oranges don't have the same flavor. We say, when we can get it, that beefsteak isn't what it used to be. This isn't all nostalgia for something that once was. There is a very good reason for feeling so."

Dr. Laskey believes that chemical fertilizers leave their imprint upon the produce grown in fields where they are used. Analysis has shown, he says, that cereals grown in chemically, rather than naturally, fertilized soil, have a markedly higher starch content. This means that they aren't so firm, that they are softer and lack flavor.

He cites studies of the crystal structure of filtrates made from wheat and other crops harvested from artificially and naturally fertilized soil. "Even after one generation, there is a marked difference in crystal patterns, showing that a radical change has occurred," he says.

Crops of wheat from the same seed are grown in neighboring fields, one fertilized artificially, the other with natural materials. Under laboratory conditions, samples of the two harvests are processed with copper chloride. A few drops of the filtrate are placed upon glass plates and permitted to dry. As they dry, they form a crystalline pattern, something like frost on a window pane.

"There is a difference in crystal structure after only one generation," Dr. Laskey says. "This means that artificial fertilizers actually have changed the wheat, and it shows up in the harvest. But we don't have to confine ourselves to laboratory experiments. For years, the Department of Agriculture has been concerned over a steadily dropping fertility rate in strains of wheat. As modern strains lose their fertility, after a few generations of being grown under current methods, new strains are brought in to replace them. The interesting thing is that these new strains come from primitive areas in the world, where so-called modern methods of farming are unknown."

Partly as an experiment in New England farming and partly as a revolt against commercial flour "from which the goodness has been extracted by the miller," Dr. Laskey is growing his own wheat and making his own bread from his own grain. His is the only farm in Rhode Island producing wheat for bread flour.

"Like corn that goes from field to table within an hour, so wheat from home-grown grain is far superior to what can be purchased in the store," Dr. Laskey says. "It has a nutty, sweet flavor that only those of us who were brought up on a farm years ago can remember. Wheat grown on naturally fertilized soil produces better flour for two reasons. It is higher in gluten and lower in starch—it makes a firmer loaf of bread. And it is not ground into flour and then stored for weeks, or even months, while it loses its natural oils."

Dr. Laskey farms this way not merely for greater crop yields but better-tasting vegetables. He points to studies indicating that we are better off if we eat food grown in soil that is naturally fertilized and on which a minimum of weed- and pest-controlling chemical sprays have been used.

"Since I started farming this way 7 years ago and began eating the produce grown on my farm," Dr. Laskey says, "I've had fewer minor illnesses." Although he has maintained no clinical records on his family—his wife and two teenage daughters, Patricia and Stephanie—Dr. Laskey says that all have benefited.

Compost in the Nursery

Stanley Bulpitt, owner and operator of Brookside Nurseries, Darien, Connecticut, is probably the first nurseryman in the country to prove that compost can pay off in the nursery.

"Stan the organic man," as he is known to his neighbors and customers far and wide, runs a 10-acre nursery founded by his late father, Henry Bulpitt, some 29 years ago. For the past 10 years it has been operated on strictly organic lines. In 1944, Brookside converted to non-synthetic fertilizing, and now boasts a complete line of organic soil conditioners, plant foods, composting and mulching machinery and other products and services tailored to the needs of organic gardeners and farmers.

No chemicals in any form are ever used or sold by Brookside—a revolutionary concept in the nursery field.

Stanley Bulpitt is "all-out organic." He and his family eat only organic food—their third child, born last November, has never tasted anything but completely natural food.

Bulpitt has developed "compost soils," a fine product for the home garden. It is proving a good seller, particularly to people who do not have time or the room to make their own compost.

The Bulpitt compost soils are made this way:

Vegetable matter of all kinds is piled, using the Indore method, and left to stand for 3 months, but without any turning. At the end of this time, it is shredded thoroughly by machine and mixed and repiled. Bacterial cultures are then added to help break down the coarse particles and complete decay. The piles are kept covered with canvas to prevent leaching by rain and allowed to stand again for two months or until needed.

The final product is made up of one part this compost, one part composted cow manure (fresh cow manure allowed to decay 90 days with bacteria and rock phosphate added), and one part cover-cropped soil. If the resulting product is somewhat heavy, some sand is mixed in.

To each cubic yard of this mixture Bulpitt adds 57 pounds of minerals—granite and phosphate rocks and dolomitic limestone. This makes a balanced product, high in plant foods and close to neutral in reaction.

He also makes leaf mold compost the same way. The shredded oak leaves heat a fair amount even in winter, enough to sustain bacterial growth and produce a well decayed product by spring. This oak leaf mold is a fine acid compost with phosphate rock added but no lime. When it is to be used for strictly acid-loving plants, he adds dried fish to increase its mineral content.

Peanut shells are another material from which he produces excellent compost, and he has a "pilot plant" to make compost from garbage. An Agromat is used to shred and grind up even the toughest garbage; it converts even bones into compost material in 30 minutes. The ground-up wastes have no noticeable odor and rapidly become wonderful black compost. Bulpitt hopes someday to get his town to compost its collected garbage in a municipal composting plant.

An entire room in his office is devoted to trophies and ribbons he has won at flower shows all over the Northeast, and for several years he has consistently been a top winner at the International Flower Show in New York City, against stiff competition from many of the country's largest nurseries. Much of his landscaping work involves large estates, and his customers unfailingly rave about the quality of his compost-grown trees, shrubs and flowers.

Nursery for the World's Largest City

The 200-acre New York City Park Department Nursery on Riker's Island is also built on compost. Located in the heart of the city, it's a verdant spot of rich beauty, with sound effects provided by the drone of huge Constellations from LaGuardia Field, a stone's throw across the bay.

New York City long had a problem getting enough trees and shrubs for its 25,000 acres of public parks and countless miles of parkways. So back in 1940, Park Commissioner Robert Moses and Director of Horticulture David Schweizer decided to grow their own—on a mammoth garbage dump standing out in Hell Gate's treacherous narrows.

With 45 years of accumulated rubbish, the site was just one huge compost heap. Much of it is still "cooking." In some places, the heat of decomposition still makes "hot spots," where steam rises like miniature volcanoes.

But these spots are rare now. Some 125,000 trees and shrubs are thriving on the rich soil. It has an average of 20 to 25 per cent organic matter! Everything rots, even the auto tires and old beer cans, reports Mr. Schweizer. Only the bigger pieces of scrap metal were dredged out of the surface soil.

Mr. Schweizer is a fair, slightly-built man with the organic gardener's vivid enthusiasm for making soil from practically anything. All the abundant weeds, for instance, are either cut when 2 to 3 feet high and allowed to lay as a mulch, harrowed in, or put on the compost heaps that dot the nursery. "Every weed makes soil," says Schweizer. "And so does any plant or animal matter, even if it's pretty far removed from its original form." As proof of this he offers "button compost." It's made from chips and shavings from a factory in the Bronx where buttons are made from casein, a component of milk. Mr. Schweizer and his foreman, Patrick Smith, mixed 100 cubic yards of this waste material with ashes, garbage and the like. The finished product, after a few months of decomposition, is the finest black compost, crawling with earthworms, ever to feed a plant. At last analysis, it contained 12 per cent nitrogen.

Schweizer has an 18-inch tree hole digger which he uses to make holes in the compost. This lets in rain to aid the rotting process.

There is a prison on the island, and much of the work in the nursery is done by the inmates. Warden Edward Dros believes the healthful work in the soil contributes greatly to the lack of disciplinary problems. And even the prison refuse becomes nursery soil. The chicken houses are a source of poultry manure, which is mixed with peat moss for fertilizer.

The rich black soil never has a wet spot. It soaks up water like a sponge, no matter how heavy the rain. Windbreaks are planted on the hills, between the beds and all around the edges of the island. Salt water spray never seems to harm the trees, thanks to the buffering effect of all that humus in the soil.

Although there was much decayed organic matter when the Park Department took over the island, Schweizer planted cover crops of rye, millet, soybeans and alfalfa (alfalfa is still grown, and used as feed for the animals in the city zoos). These green manure crops were plowed in to improve the texture of the soil. No chemical fertilizers are ever used. Insecticides are also unneeded—the nursery is also a bird sanctuary, and the lively pheasants, plovers, mourning doves, catbirds and blackbirds consume the bugs.

Dig up any plant in the nursery, and you'll find it has a dense, tight clump of roots. The tilth of the soil is excellent, probably way down to the 80-foot depth it reaches on the big hill of 115 acres where the most garbage has been piled.

A two-inch straw mulch is used on the propagating beds and around the young trees. Sawdust is applied liberally, too, and a mulch of salt hay covers beds seeded to *Viburnum dentatum* and *Cornus mas*. Yew cuttings are grown for a year in a greenhouse before being planted outdoors. Some of the privet cuttings grow 4½ feet tall in two years. Mountain laurel flowers beautifully in the nursery's experimental beds, and various kinds of shrubs are interplanted between the trees out in the rows.

Sweet gum, dogwood, hawthorne, tulip, Washington thorn and ginkgo trees are some of the many kinds grown from seed. They grow fast: alders reach 12 feet in 5 years, sycamores are 15 feet high by their sixth birthday. Peach trees can be found volunteering in several spots, from pits brought in with the garbage.

One of the high spots of a visit to the Riker's Island Nursery is a look at the Chinese chestnut trees. Mr. Schweizer grows his in button compost, and the richness of this "made" soil can be seen both in the fine growth of the trees and in the thick weeds growing around their bases.

Here's a partial list of the other trees and shrubs the nursery produces: black walnuts, flowering crabapples, roses in abundance, Japanese holly, birches, American elms, locusts and Japanese lilacs. Every plant is an eloquent testimony to the quality of the garbage-dump soil and the work of the organically-minded men who till it.

Experiences in Other Lands

Here is a letter received recently from Captain C. E. Misener, of Wainfleet, Ontario, Canada:

"Another spring is in the offing and it looks like a very busy one for me. My success in growing tomatoes for the canneries has brought many orders from additional canneries. The Grand Valley Canners of Dunnville, Ontario, for whom I grew last year, have shoved aside many orthodox growers and asked me to boost my acreage 10 times. The demand for my Organic Pure Foods is forcing me to grow 25 acres of vegetables. I have increased my raspberries to 32 acres and my strawberries to 7 acres. But now I have to put in 20 more acres of raspberries, 10 more of strawberries, 5 acres of black currants, and 5 acres of black raspberries.

"My original worm population of 1200 Red Wigglers imported from Hughes Worm Ranch, Savannah, Tenn., has increased to 100,000,000. I have two Selvi Digesters that are busy with fresh manures which I leave in the digesters for a month and then shred them and mix with farm wastes, sawdust, grain dust, and corncobs. This I spike with rock phosphate and use all my wood ashes for potash. I add a little agricultural lime rock and then put the mass in big beds about 3 by 3 by 75 feet. The Red Wigglers take over from here and they really do a job. The labor cost is negligible when one considers the great benefits. My yields have been tripling and the products are of such high grade they command as much as double the market prices. And the demand is growing alarmingly.

"I put tomatoes in a field infested with cutworms last spring. Of course they were all planted in earthworm compost. I did not lose a plant of the 6800 I planted. Last fall I watched closely while disking this land and couldn't find a single cutworm. I had no blights, no cats-eyes, no splits—only wonderful flavors, excellent textures, and high-keeping qualities which graded from 94 per cent to 100 per cent under government inspection. This grade was after taking out the exceptionally fine fruit for basket trade. My yield was about 20 tons to the acre. *Not an ounce of poison sprays or chemical fertilizers were used.* The credit must go to earthworm compost. I used nothing else.

"I managed to compost-feed only half my raspberries but the yield of the whole patch was boosted 3-fold and the fruit was very superior. American tourists who are organically conscious bought the berries and sat down right here and ate them. They had no fear of poison. Neither, for that matter, did the birds and bees. The bees came in clouds from all over and really did a magnificent job of pollination.

"It is my intention to sheet compost and boost this with the regular compost. When the nutritive values of organic matter can be raised with earthworms to such a high level it is an economic measure to expand earthworm composting considerably.

"Originally our only sure crop was a big and unhealthy deficit. In two short years the picture has changed and I intend throwing away the red ink permanently."

Problems in Ecuador

From Ecuador comes this story from Oliver S. Mabee of the United Andean Indian Mission: "Our two primary agricultural problems are lack of water and lack of organic matter in the soil. The correction of the latter will improve the former by increasing the water-holding capacity of the soil. Compost has been our biggest aid in building organic matter supplies, but green manuring has also been used.

"One example of the potentiality of organic matter: Our first compost pile, a very small one, was thinly spread on a piece of arid soil which had just grown a sparse crop of corn less than knee-high. After the first dressing—a very light one

—vegetables were sown. The crop was poor by our North American standards, but was more than fair when compared with crops around us. We noted that some moisture remained in the soil of the plot during the dry summer, even though untreated soil alongside was quite dry.

"At the end of the first year a second and heavier dressing of compost was applied and the land sown to vegetables. An entirely satisfactory crop was produced. Then an oat experiment was sown on the same ground and with it a forage plot. The oats grew higher than my head (whereas the same varieties grown under field conditions were about knee-high) and the best varieties yielded at the rate of 77 bushels to the acre! Hubam clover, the following forage crop, was almost 3 feet high at the oat harvest and no record was kept of the amount of clover cut off with the oats. But it continued growing during the driest part of the year and 4 months later yielded the immense crop of 28 tons per acre green weight!"

Chapter 16

INFLUENCE OF COMPOST ON INSECTS AND PLANT DISEASE

Insects annually nullify the labor of over one million men in the United States today. Americans pay an insect feeding bill of well over a billion dollars a year due to crop damage. In addition to this, a great deal of money is spent for insecticides, and more for spraying and dusting equipment and the labor of applying bug-killers.

However, a new approach to the insect problem has very recently come into being, stimulated by the compost school of gardening and farming. This approach is based on growing evidence that it is the health of the soil that is responsible for plant health, for resistance to insects and disease.

Sir Albert Howard called the insect pest, not an enemy, but *Nature's censor*, an agency to remove the anemic and sickly from agriculture, and at the same time perform the

Plants that are prone to disease and to insect attack are sick—and sick plants are indications of sick, imbalanced soils. An obvious corollary follows: soils kept well-supplied with natural, balanced fertilizers reflect this in producing healthy plants and will be more resistant to infection or pests—like these tomatoes, for example.

office of "signalman" to warn us of lowered fertility, to admonish us to quickly correct the soil deficiencies which its presence reveals.

According to modern scientific research, sick soils mean sick plants—and sick plants like sick people are wide open to attack from a multitude of foes. On the other hand, a healthy plant, grown on a balanced, fertile soil, can and will resist most insect pests.

Evidence of this is piling up. The Iowa Agricultural Experiment Station reports that pea aphis feed far more often on plants weakened by mineral deficiencies of the soil. Plants in good soil were found to have greater resistance to the pests.

Dr. William Albrecht of the University of Missouri showed in a series of carefully controlled tests that spinach grown on fertile soil resisted the attack of thrips, while that grown on poor soil was destroyed by these enemies.

An article in the U. S. Department of Agriculture magazine *Agricultural Research* tells how workers at the Beltsville, Md., Research Center found that mites on well-nourished bean plants were easier to kill with insecticides than mites on poorly nourished plants. Plants grown in soil that had the proper balance of all nutrients had the easiest-to-kill mites.

A Science Service bulletin released May 29, 1952, said: "Some insects and snails prefer diseased plants as food and this food preference seems to benefit them nutritionally. Dr. C. E. Yarwood, plant pathologist at the University of California's College of Agriculture, has found that pests, in many cases, prefer diseased leaves to healthy ones.

It is only in the last decade or so that we have come to realize the complex nature of insect food selection. Previously, scientists were content to say that an insect liked a certain food, and that was that. The potato beetle likes potatoes, the corn borer favors corn. They thrive on these, just as man thrives on certain favored foods.

A Matter of Diet

But now we have learned that the nutritional needs of insects are very different from those of man and animals. Where man thrives best on a high protein diet, insects go for carbohydrate. They need it more in their system of operation. An insect can jump the equivalent of the Empire State Building in one jump, comparatively speaking, and it needs a lot of carbohydrate for that energy. So when one plant has more carbohydrate than another, an insect will seek it out and prefer it. As research at the Missouri Agricultural Experiment Station has shown, plants which get no organic matter produce an unbalanced amount of carbohydrates at the expense of protein and trace minerals. Insects, it seems, prefer these "sweet" plants and are able to attack them more easily.

How can insects sense a plant that has this imbalance? Preliminary work shows that an imbalanced or biologically weakened plant emits an odor that attracts bugs. The Bartlett tree research laboratories report weakened trees give off an odor that lures bark beetles and borers. Healthy trees, con-

Vigorous, bug-free leaf growth, as exemplified by this compost-grown comfrey on the farm of Wilbert Walker in Hagersville, Pa., illustrates the statement of a leading agricultural scientist, Professor Leonard Haseman, that "insect pests choose and breed more abundantly on weak, undernourished plants or crops and livestock."

versely, either give off no odor of this kind at all, or emit one that repels the bugs.

Professor Leonard Haseman of the University of Missouri has studied the influence of soil minerals on insects and his findings were summarized in the *Journal of Economic Entomology* for February, 1946. He states that better feeding of plants will reduce the insect pests while the latter will attack sickly, undernourished plants. He found that the greenhouse white fly attacked tomatoes only where there was a phosphorus or magnesium deficiency in the soil. The chinch bug thrives and multiplies where corn is grown under conditions of nitrogen deficiency and is known to thrive, says Dr. Haseman, on eroded and poor hillsides. Fertile bottom lands are much less infected. Haseman comes to the conclusion that the indications are "that insects require less of minerals and that they may actually thrive best on shortages of certain minerals."

He expanded on this subject as follows: "In nature there

are abundant illustrations of insect pests choosing and breeding more abundantly on weak and undernourished plants or crops and livestock. Take for instance lice on calves. It is the weak, underfed, and undernourished, rough-coated, weaned calves and not those suckling, fat, smooth-coated ones which are often eaten up with lice. Also, a weak, sickly hen in the flock will always carry most of the lice.

"Chinch bugs tend to collect and breed more heavily on corn or wheat up on the eroded slopes than down at the foot of the slope where the eroded soil minerals and organic matter pile up. In this case it is the high level of nitrogen in the vigorous crop at the foot of the slope that the bug is unable to take. As is well known, the chinch bug never attacks the legumes, and soybeans planted with corn may even help to protect the corn crop from attack by that pest. To prove that high levels of nitrogen in the soil and taken up by the plant will protect corn from chinch bugs, we here at the Missouri Agricultural Experiment Station have reared the pest on seedling corn plants grown on low and high levels of nitrogen and have found that they thrive, breed better and live longer on a diet low in nitrogen. What then is more simple in dealing with this pest than to keep soil fertility high with plenty of nitrogen supplied with legume green manures supplemented in other ways.

"We here, have also found that the small greenhouse thrips likewise seek a diet low in nitrogen. Luxuriant New Zealand spinach plants grown on high levels of nitrogen and calcium were untouched by the thrips while the small weak plants grown alongside on low levels of these two soil minerals were practically eaten up by the pest. Here clearly this insect pest prefers and thrives better on its chosen crop grown on deficient soil at least so far as lime and nitrogen are concerned.

"In these experiments, however, we are finding that some insects prefer plants as food when they are grown on soil rich in nitrogen and lime. Take, for instance, common plant lice. They seem to need a rich proteinaceous diet, and are usually found feeding on the tender tip growth where plant physiologists tell us the sap is always richest in nitrogen. They seem to call for less carbohydrates in their diet and actually throw off in their liquid excrement great quantities of sugar as so-called honey dew. Also, the European corn borer seems to thrive best on land which grows the best corn. In cases of those insects which demand more nitrogen and

A side-by-side comparison resulted when California writer Warner G. Tilsher planted a weak, stunted kale plant next to a strong one. Sickly plant at right drew a heavy infestation of aphids while healthy kale at left remained free of pests.

richer diets we have reasons to hope we may be able to reach them by still keeping up the soil fertility where it should be but possibly by varying some of the minor elements, or possibly by stepping up still further potash and other carbohydrate-producing soil elements. We may in this way make our bountiful crops untasty for insects but increasingly nutritious for man and beast.

"In fighting our insects through the soil, we are trying to make the crop either less acceptable to them or less satisfactory to them as a normal diet. The insects' ability to produce abundant offspring is known to be closely linked with the chemistry of the food they eat. For instance, the queen honey bee, the only individual female in the hive which ever normally reproduces, is from infancy fed on highly nutritious, predigested royal jelly diet. All the worker bees are likewise females, but they are fed on a thinner diet and as a result their ovaries remain undeveloped. If through the soil we can reach our insect pests with diets that tend to slow down their power of reproduction we will have won the major battle with our insect foes."

In the *Hutchinson News Herald* (Kansas), April 28, 1950,

this item appeared: "James Turner, 5 miles south of Sharon, has made an interesting observation during the current green-bug infestation.

"He has a 60-acre field of wheat, part of which has been in sweet clover. On that part the bugs have done no damage but on the 30 acres which have not been clovered, there is plenty of evidence that the pests have been working.

"It may be that the wheat on the clover ground is larger and more vigorous and therefore able to stand the continual sucking of the insect but Turner says there just aren't as many on it. Maybe the greenbug just doesn't thrive on wheat growing on soil which has plenty of nitrogen in it. It seems to be that way with chinch bugs. They first attack corn or sorghum growing on soil with a low level of fertility. The big, rank crop down in the bottom is shunned."

Biological Life

The teeming biological life of a soil is another vital consideration in bug control. The mycorrhizal fungi, for example, abundant in soils where there is ample organic matter, actually feed plants substances that give them resistance to aphids and other insects. These fungi, which are not found where chemical fertilizers are used, live on the roots of many plants and feed them plant foods from the soil humus, plus their own digestive products (mainly valuable protein). Healthier plants are always found where mycorrhiza abound. The Iowa Experiment Station proved they unlock food elements from the soil; pine seedlings with mycorrhizal fungi had 4 times as much phosphorus as those lacking the fungi. Bacteria and molds of many kinds also impart varying degrees of insect resistance to plants.

Compost vs. Plant Disease

In his book, *Humus*, Dr. Selman A. Waksman, discoverer of streptomycin, states: "Plant deficiency diseases are usually less severe in soils well supplied with organic matter not only because of the increased vigor of the plants but also because of antagonistic effects of the various soil microorganisms which become more active in the presence of an abundance of organic matter." At the Connecticut Agricultural Experiment Station this was confirmed in experiments with fusarium rot of squash seeds (Bulletin 500, Nov. 1946, Physiology of Fusarium Root Rot of Squash).

576

Research testing at the Connecticut Agricultural Experiment Station showed that fusarium rot of squash "did not persist as long in the humus-amended soil as it did in ordinary field soil . . ." Vegetable crops, like those seen growing above, stand a far better chance of avoiding any plant infection when grown in enriched soil.

Quoting from this bulletin: "It is especially interesting to note that the fungus did not persist as long in the humus-amended soil as it did in ordinary field soil or sand-amended field soil. Either of two theories might explain this behavior. First, the increased microbiological activity of saprophytic organisms might usurp the nitrogen supply and effectively starve the pathogene for this essential element. This is known to occur in the case of certain other soil-borne parasites. Soil analyses run on the various samples, however, refute this theory since they showed a higher available nitrogen content in the humus-amended soil than in either of the other two.

"The remaining theory advanced here to explain the relatively short existence of the root rot Fusarium in the soil with a high organic matter content is that of antibiosis. Waksman and Horning (1943) and other authors have pointed out the omnipresence of soil organisms which produce antibiotic substances. It is quite probable that in the organic-amended soils, such organisms thrived and produced substances toxic to *Fusarium solani f. cucurbitae*. In the field soil and sand-amended soil, the biological activity of such organisms must necessarily have been lower because of the limited nutritive conditions prevailing there.

"The results of this experiment coincide with several observations made on the survival of the root rot fungus in soil and in organic compost. In one case, year-old compost originally containing diseased squash fruit and vines failed to serve as inoculum when transferred to the greenhouse for experimental purposes. This observation lends support to the antibiosis theory since this compost had been prepared after established commercial procedures and thus always should have contained a sufficient supply of available nitrogen."

Antibiotic Substances

That soils produce a great number and variety of antibiotic substances is well known today. B. P. Tokine, writing in *Science et Vie,* says: "Ten years ago one might have doubted whether antibiotics were widely diffused in nature. Today it can be affirmed with certainty that all plant organisms— whether bacteria, birch, mushroom, mold or pine tree—emit antibiotics which are diffused in the air, in soil and in waters.

"The quantity of antibiotics released varies according to the plant, season, climate, time of day and nature of soil.

"It appears that antibiotics are necessary for plants in order to protect them from bacteria, molds, insects and other enemies; this is confirmed by a multitude of facts. Antibiotics insure some kind of immunity for plants.

"In horticulture the Russian biologist, T. A. Tovstoles, shows that certain antibiotics kill the hemiptera which produces a sort of spiders' web and is a parasite which attacks more than 100 different plants, industrial and decorative."

Further confirmation is found in an article in *The Country Gentleman* of February, 1944, by Sidney J. Gates:

"Little has been said about this new cure for root rot. Perhaps this is because this remedy, in its outward aspects, is so very simple. The cure for root rot of cotton consists in nothing more than turning under leguminous organic matter

With plant deficiency diseases and troublesome insect pests kept under control naturally, the organic gardener multiplies the advantages of his gardening by this method. There's more healthful fun, less cost and bother, and better returns.

in the fall or spring before the cotton crop is planted. A heavy dose of stable manure will affect the same end, though the latter is seldom available in sufficient volume to be a large factor under most root rot infested cotton-farm conditions. But this leguminous-organic-matter treatment of cotton soils has long been known to be highly profitable, even when no root rot is present.

"It is not through the chemical action of this rotting material that the cure is brought about. The answer lies in the fact that teeming bacteria in the soil, these bacteria no doubt embracing thousands of strains, take on renewed life under the stimulation of this, their seemingly pet food supply. Some of these stimulated bacteria strains are dread enemies of the root rot fungus. The bacteria not only destroy the fungus on contact, presumably as certain bacteria destroy our own body tissue, but the antipathy between these two organisms goes much further. In artificial-media cultures the root rot fungus dies even on the approach of the enemy bacteria growth.

"The discovery leading to its control comes from C. J. King, Superintendent of the U. S. Department of Agriculture field station at Sacaton, Arizona. King observed one summer in a section where alfalfa had been added, that there was little or no root rot damage while alongside, to the very sharp margin of where these treatments had been given, the cotton crop was almost devastated by root rot.

"But this new and successful root rot control method—that of altering the soil microbiology by feeding it with decaying leguminous material—is far bigger than the mere announcing of the abatement of a curse to Southwest cotton, devastating as the curse has been. *Fertility* is a chemist-proffered term. The word 'productivity' gives the realistic picture to the practical farmer. For years we have been twiddling over the proper proportion of N, P and K and more recently over so-called trace elements, while the understanding of the broad phases of the soil-productivity mystery is not only confused, and unknown, but grossly neglected."

Plant-Protecting Organisms

Further thoughts on plant-protecting organisms in the soil come from William H. Eyster, Ph.D.: "It is a common observation in pot experiments that certain diseases, such as the root rots of cereals, are more destructive in sterilized soil than in comparable non-sterilized soil, both being equally inoculated with pathogenes. If bits of the original soil are introduced into the sterilized soil, however, the micro-flora are quickly reestablished, the pathogene checked, and the disease reduced. This would seem to indicate that the micro-organisms in the soil protect plants against certain soil-borne pathogenes or limit their damage. Soil treatments which

Peppers are among the plants most susceptible to nematode infestation and damage, according to reports from the Florida Agricultural Experiment Station. Their tests, as those of many other stations and researchers, showed mulch and organic matter application of greatest benefit in curtailing the widespread root-knot injury.

favor the growth of these soil organisms enhance the natural biological control of cotton root rot and of cereal root rots by introducing organic manures, of potato scab by green manuring, and of Rhizoctonia damping-off by acidifying the soil surface layer.

"It has been found that a heavy mulch reduces root-knot injury to plants by nematodes. According to Thorne, when a crop of sweet clover is plowed under the heat and gas from the decaying materials kill large numbers of nematodes, including cysts. Linford reported that the decomposition of organic matter in Hawaiian soils was associated with a reduction of galls on roots of cowpeas. The decomposition of organic matter results in an increase of nema-trapping fungi, fungus parasites, predaceous nematodes and predaceous mites. It seems possible that the beneficial effect of the mulch in reducing root-knot injury results from some metabolic by-product in the decomposition of the organic matter, to the stimulation of some organisms antagonistic to the parasitic

581

nematode, or to an improved fertility condition which permits growth of the plant in spite of the parasitic nematode."

Research on Nematodes

Concerning nematodes, here's a report from the University of Florida's Agricultural Experiment Station:

"Among the plants which are susceptible to nematode injury and consequently may be greatly benefited by mulching, are . . . okra, tomatoes, peppers, eggplant, squash, cantaloupes, watermelons, beans, celery, and lettuce.

"Like practically all forms of animal life, nematodes have their enemies. Among the most common and efficient of these enemies are certain kinds of fungi which live in decaying vegetable matter. This doubtless accounts for much of the importance and advantages of a mulch.

"Rotting vegetable matter piled around the plants has a very marked effect in checking the development of root-knot and in enabling the plants to withstand the disease. In practice, one piles around the plants to the depth of many inches or even a foot any available vegetable matter that will decay. Dead grasses, weeds and leaves are excellent. Persons living near a stream or lake with water hyacinths will find these plants particularly suitable for a mulch, since they hold water for a long time. Fungi developing in this rotting vegetable matter have been seen by a number of investigators to trap nematodes and to enter their body."

The fungi do their work of destruction in a number of ways. In some cases, the fine threads of the fungus have branches which form loops, and these loops in turn form 3-dimensional networks something like crumpled wire netting.

The networks secrete a sticky fluid when they come into contact with the nematode, and the nematodes are caught as effectively as a fly by flypaper. After the fungus catches the nematode, it then sends branches into its body, or grows into it itself; and simply absorbs its tissue.

Another way in which fungus traps nematodes is by sticky branches which reproduce rapidly and form little circular loops in which the worm is trapped.

A third mechanism consists of sticky knots at the end of stalks. These knots hold the nematode and form a structure inside which spreads out, and thus destroys the worm.

Still another way in which nematodes are trapped is by the formation of a constricting ring to 3 cells on a stalk. The nematode puts its "nose" into the ring accidentally; the cells swell, and the ring closes.

Dr. C. L. Duddington of Regent Street Polytechnic, London, says: "These fungi exist in the soil in their own right; and the farmer anywhere faced with the nematode problem can hardly do better than to give his land as many organic treatments as he can in the form of manure, compost, and other natural materials. These not only encourage the operations of predaceous fungus; but are, in themselves, rich sources of it."

Farmers' Bulletin 2048, *Controlling Nematodes in the Home Garden,* has this to say: "Unless acquired while the plants are small, a moderately severe infestation may not seriously retard growth or reduce yields under good growing conditions, including ample fertility and moisture. By incorporating into the soil large quantities of organic matter, the severity of the infestation may be reduced, and growing conditions will be provided in which the plants are better able to grow despite the disease."

Cotton Wastes Made Disease-Free

Composting of cotton plant residues following ginning operations destroys the Verticillium wilt organism and eliminates it as a possible source of added infection in next year's crop, according to E. E. Staffeldt, assistant professor of biology at New Mexico State University.

The continued addition of non-treated, infested gin trash to productive land could lead to greater spread of wilt in New Mexico, the biologist said.

Staffeldt's composting experiment is described in the November 1959 issue of the *Plant Disease Reporter,* a U. S. Department of Agriculture publication. It was run in cooperation with the U. S. Cotton Ginning Research Laboratory, Mesilla Park.

The experiment indicated that temperatures developing in the 4 trench-type compost piles killed the Verticillium wilt organisms.

The gin trash was put through a hammermill, watered before being put in the test piles and watered again as it was placed in the enclosures, which were 6-by-8-by-2-foot pits. Wilt-infected stalks were planted in each pile. Treatments of the 4 piles included soil biotics, Fertosan, fungi, and a non-amended check. Temperatures were recorded for 36 days, and the highest was 68.3 degrees centigrade in the check pile.

Regular addition of organic matter to southern New Mexico soils is desirable because of their low inherent organic content, Staffeldt said. Gin trash is one source of organic matter, and much of this plant material from the cotton-growing areas of New Mexico harbors Verticillium wilt organisms. An increasing amount of this material has been returned to the soil without prior treatment during the past few years.

The biologist said that some farmers began adding cotton gin trash to their fields as soon as it was available, others waited until after frost, and still others used it for cattle bedding before applying it to the fields. Regardless of these methods of applying gin trash to fields, Verticillium wilt organisms remained alive.

The Chamberino Gin in Dona Ana County has been composting its plant material wastes for several years, Staffeldt said. The gin composts all its waste in one large pile.

Potato Scab

Concerning potato scab, organic gardener Hugh H. Ward, has this to say:

"For those who are not familiar with potato culture, it should be pointed out that soils only slightly acid or mildly alkaline favor the growth of pathogenic organism, *Actinomyces scabies*, which causes a scab on the potato skin. Although this injury does not make the potatoes inedible, it ruins their marketability.

"To avoid such injury to the crop, potato farmers try to keep their soil quite acid, that is, in a pH range of 4.8 to 5.2. I was told by the soil scientist at the nearby government agricultural station that it is becoming necessary as time goes on to keep the potato soils at lower and lower pH reactions in order to control scab.

"In Suffolk County, Long Island, where my experiments were carried out, it is generally considered impossible to grow scab free potatoes in a 'sweet' soil. The conventional method of fertilization is a green manure crop of rye seeded in the fall and plowed under in the spring just before planting, combined with the application of 5-10-5 commercial fertilizer at the rate of ½ to 1 ton per acre. Lime is used sparingly or avoided entirely. The only organic matter is the small amount supplied by the decomposition of the rye.

"Realizing the importance of organic matter in supplying adequate and properly balanced microbial life in the soil, but at the same time knowing high acidity creates an unfavorable environment for the development of many beneficial microorganisms, I decided to test the theory that properly made compost applied in adequate amounts, under mildly acid or slightly alkaline soil conditions, will supply the microbial life necessary to check the injurious scab organism. It is nature's way to protect the health of the soil through the constant fight between beneficial (saprophytic) organisms, living on dead or decaying matter, and injurious (pathogenic) microorganisms, parasites of growing plants. According to Dr. Waksman, Organic manures stimulate the development of saprophytic organisms in the soil, and are thus able to check the activity of the pathogens, which are destroyed by the saprophytes.' In order that nature may carry out its appointed role, the soil must be in proper balance as to energy building material (compost) for microbial life and favorable environment in which the latter can develop.

"My test plots consist of light sandy loam one foot deep over yellow sand. In 1946 when I started the experiment, soil tests showed a reaction of pH 5.6 and, as noted by the Agricultural Extension Service, favorable to the development of the potato scab organism. I marked off two plots, separated by a 3-foot path, one designated the control and the other the test plot. The conventional treatment for potato culture was used on the control, that is, rye was seeded in the autumn and turned under in April 1947 just previous to planting Irish Cobblers and Green Mountains with 5-10-5 commercial fertilizer applied under and to the side of the hills. On the test plot, at the same time that rye was planted on the control, I applied Indore compost at the rate of 10 tons per acre and turned it under immediately. Incidentally, a rototiller was used in turning the soil of both plots at all times. Again in the spring at planting time a similar application of Indore compost was made and rototilled in. Both plots were cultivated twice during the first 6 weeks of growth and no spray or dust was used to control insects or disease. Certified seed of the early and late varieties, Irish Cobblers and Green Mountains, respectively, was planted in both plots.

"When the early potatoes were dug in the last week of

July, the control showed 90 per cent of the tubers heavily infected with scab, while the test plot yielded beautiful clean skin potatoes with scarcely a trace of scab."

The following year he repeated the experiment, but noted that the test plot now had a pH of 7.2. "The higher alkalinity of the test plot as against the control was undoubtedly due to the compost which received some lime and bone in its preparation. However, I was pleased that my soil had become more alkaline, as the experiment, if successful, would have more significance. Reference is made by Dr. James Small in his book *pH and Plants* to findings that the optimum pH range for the development of *actinomycetes scabies* is 7.2–7.5.

"At harvesting time for the early potatoes, Irish cobblers, the control again showed the heavy scab infection on practically all the tubers. In complete contrast, the test plot crop was comprised of excellent clean skin potatoes with a yield of 50 pounds per 20-foot row or a rate of 725 bushels per acre. This compares with an average yield in Suffolk County of around 300 bushels.

"The two major conclusions to be drawn from my experiments are, (1) the compost (humus) increased the potato yield by supplying the source of energy for the soil microorganisms, which in turn liberated and circulated the plant nutrients. To quote again from Dr. Waksman's *Humus,* 'Most of the microorganisms inhabiting the soil depend upon the plant and animal residues and upon humus for their nutrients. As a result of their activities, the elements which are most important for the growth of plants, especially carbon and nitrogen, are kept in constant circulation.' (2) Microbial antagonism stimulated by the composted organic matter checked the development of the injurious scab organism."

Soil Condition and Insects

The physical properties of the soil can also affect insect incidence. In an item in the February 17, 1951 *Science Newsletter*, it is stated that a pest that causes extensive damage to germinating bean, corn, pea and other seeds is the seedcorn maggot. The article says that this maggot is associated with low soil temperatures and high soil moisture.

When compost is used, the physical condition of the soil is changed in such a way as to depress the activities of this pest. In the first place, when organic matter is continually applied, the soil gradually darkens, and it is a known fact

The physical condition of soil has a lot to do with insect incidence. Here John Neff of Landisville, Pa., stretches son Gary's hand to measure height of their wheat, grown on composted land and untroubled by bugs, as are all crops they raise.

that the darker the soil becomes the more heat it will absorb. A white sandy soil may be 10 degrees less in Fahrenheit than a dark muck soil. With regard to high soil moisture, a soil full of organic matter can take in more rain but it holds it without as much waterlogging as a soil which has lost its tilth or structure through reliance on chemical fertilizers rather than compost additions. In the latter, in heavy rains the water is likely to be trapped by a hardpan 6 to 12 inches down and build up heavily from there, until it creates a wet condition suitable for the seed-corn maggot. With plenty of organic matter in the soil, both the temperature and the moisture

587

condition are more apt to be unsuitable to the breeding of this pest.

One further point: earthworms are another agent for the destruction of bacteria. Scientist Gordon M. Day discovered that a bacteria called *Serratia marcescens* is destroyed in the digestive tract of earthworms. Although *Serratia marcescens* is not a disease bacteria, there are deadly forms in the same family that in all probability are also killed.

Compost Against Insects

Some organic gardeners have had interesting experiences with curing plant disease and insects with compost. Leonard Wickenden, for example, tells how he used compost, sifted and dusted over the leaves of eggplants that were yellowing, and cleared up the yellowing. He reasoned that the antibiotic content of the compost reacted on the fungus disease which was probably causing the yellowing.

Here's one from Mrs. W. A. Cornog of Portland, Ore.: Before she used compost, her berry plants were diseased. "They were covered with worts, lumps and tumors over the lower stocks and roots of the canes. We were told it was caused by virus and is a form of plant cancer. Well, we grubbed them out and planted some next to the patch, but they were sick and puny. I analyzed the soil and found we had practically no phosphorus or potash in the soil. So just for an experiment, I applied the lacking elements and added compost and we had boysenberries 2 and 3 inches long. Last week I read an article that doctors have discovered cancer patients lack salts of potash in the blood stream. No wonder my berry plants had cancer. The new plants and ones planted on the old patch since we added the needed elements and compost show no sign of disease."

Regina Hughes Jones of Visalia, Calif., had an apricot tree infected with gummosis, a gummy exudation on the trunks and branches caused by disease. She applied compost in a deep layer all around the tree, but by that autumn the trunk and the main limb were all that were left. The next spring she decided she might as well replace the tree, but when she went out to dig it up, she saw the one brown limb shooting forth green branches in every direction. "That was more than two years ago," she says, "and the tree has attained more than its former size, and is entirely free of the gum."

This apricot tree was near death from gummosis, a dreaded trunk disease of fruits in particular, when California gardener Regina Hughes Jones started a sustained compost-treatment program. Within a year the tree had recovered completely, showed no signs of the brown rot infection, and began to be productive.

(For a more complete description of this, see the chapter on How to Use Compost.)

Harry P. Burgart of the Michigan Nut Nursery, Union City, Michigan, tells of this experience with witches-broom:

Not too much is known about witches-broom, the walnut disease that is worrying growers throughout the East and being quarantined against on the West Coast. Witches-broom has been recognized by growers for the past 15 years. I have been growing nut trees for 21 years and have seen the disease kill trees that apparently were growing too fast or those that were undernourished. In the past, when I saw a tree developing the fine, stringy, growth of witches-broom I would just cut it down because they invariably would winter-kill during the following winter.

It seems that all trees of the genus Juglans such as the black walnut, the English walnut, the Japanese walnut and the butternut are subject to witches-broom when growing conditions are not properly balanced. Also I have seen the disease attack trees that were not grafted on congenial root-stocks, such as when the butternut was grafted on Japanese walnut root or vice versa. This goes to show that it does not pay to use just "any old rootstock" for a tree.

Usually my losses in nut trees were limited to smaller trees in the nursery, here and there. About 4 years ago I decided to work over a young black walnut tree near my garage to English walnut by grafting onto the limbs. Conditions were favorable and the grafts took well. Being very much enthused with my work, I had my soil tested and found it needed phosphate. Superphosphate was available so I scattered it around my tree to encourage growth from the grafts. It did; the grafts I had set during May made a growth of over 3 feet that summer.

My topworked English walnut tree started out nicely the next spring. Growth continued normal until about midsummer. Then it happened! My tree started developing the fine, stringy, growth of witches-broom. That really made me feel "weak-in-the-knees" to see my favorite tree doomed to die! About that time two State Foresters stopped in and when I showed them the tree they shook their heads feeling sorry for me.

In desperation I thought of trying out some "Organic Methods" as a last resort to save my tree. I got busy right away and dug up the sod around the tree and carried it away. Then I decided to get a few wheelbarrow loads of the earthworm-infested compost that was left behind my packing house. This was spread several inches deep where I had removed the sod. Over the compost I wanted to place stones but was unable to find any around. Back of my garage I found a pile of bricks from an old chimney. Why not use them in place of the stones. First I brushed off as much dirt and soot as came off easily, then I painted them with white wash to make them look presentable.

By fall my English walnut tree did not look any worse nor did it look much better. My hopes were low when I took the bricks aside so I could put down a 5-inch layer of oak and maple leaves, neighbors had been glad to get rid of. After the leaves were laid down I replaced the bricks on them to hold them from blowing away. Confidentially—I figured the tree as good as dead anyway, so never thought to take a picture of the witches-broom growth.

During the long Michigan winter that followed I would sit inside where it was warm and look out at my "sick" English walnut tree, figuring how I would go about cutting it down when spring arrived.

Spring finally did come around again and with it lots of work, so I only gave the tree a casual glance as I passed it. April was almost gone and my "sick" tree had not started growth yet. After a warm rain I went outside one morning to let my eyes rove over the buds of my tree and saw they were swelling and turning red. It was still alive! I rushed into the house to spread the good news.

That tree put out a vigorous but normal growth throughout the entire summer. The Organic System had saved my tree! Incredible! I could not help but talk "organics" to everyone who came that summer. Even now, 3 years later finds my English walnut tree thriving, without a trace of "witches-broom" in its top. This last spring it set 6 fine nuts—its first crop—and at this writing the nuts are as large as small apples.

Even after all this had taken place I was still a little skeptical as to the value of the "Organic System" in curing witches-broom. My next opportunity for a test came after the English walnut had made full recovery. That spring I had grafted several rows of butternut trees in my nursery. All grew quite well until mid-July and then I noticed that one little graft was suddenly developing witches-broom. As a further check I decided to give it the same treatment "in a smaller way" as the English walnut tree had received earlier.

Magic again! That little butternut came through the winter with flying colors. Yes, it came out with a perfectly normal growth that spring and I decided to keep it for observation. It reached a height of 4 feet by fall and the following summer it bore 3 fine butternuts, while this summer that little butternut is going to mature 16 healthy butternuts.

Infested Orange Grove

Dr. Charles Northern of Florida tells of a friend who found compost a cure-all for several plant ills. "For instance, in an orange grove infested with scale, when he restored optimal fertility to the soil, the trees growing in that part became clean, while the rest remained diseased. By the same means he had grown healthy rosebushes between rows that were riddled with insects. He had grown tomato and cucumber plants, both healthy and diseased, where the vines had intertwined. The bugs ate up the diseased and refused to touch the healthy plants."

Dr. Norman W. Walker of Anaheim, Calif., who holds a Doctor of Science as well as medical degree, has an interesting theory on why pests attack a sickly, undernourished plant. With the lowering of basic health, he says, comes a lowering of the vibrations in molecules of the cell. The cell structure becomes unsound and unbalanced—diseases multiply, and the "scavenger" promptly appears to finish up the job, and the "victim" is removed from the land of the living.

"On the other hand, the higher the state of health, the higher the vibrations, and the 'pest' whose vibrations are on a lower level receives a distinct shock when he comes in contact with the healthy plant." Just as the light shock of an electric fence will keep a cow in the pasture where she belongs, so will well nourished, vibrant plants repel a pest. "Of course, this line of agricultural research is only 200 years ahead of our time," he says. But soil scientist Arnold P. Yerkes of International Harvester's Farm Practice Research program has stated that the newest phase of agricultural research is the field of electricity and its workings in and on plants.

Chapter 17

COMPOST AND THE HEALTH OF ANIMALS AND MAN

Compost, we have shown, produces plants resistant to disease. But do these plants confer better health and well-being on the animals and people eating them?

The answer is an unqualified "Yes!" Compost-grown

Are foods grown in compost-enriched soil better for the people and animals who eat them? Mounting and consistent evidence says they emphatically are. Not only are they free of toxic chemical residues, they have higher nutritional values as well.

plants are definitely superior in nutritional values, and organic food is the cornerstone of good health.

That this is vitally important to every man, woman and child living today—and to future generations as well—is becoming increasingly apparent to those concerned with the falling level of health in our nation. And this level is falling alarmingly.

Last year cancer was more prevalent than ever before. We had more heart disease. It is the leading cause of death, killing young people before the age of 40 all over the land. We had more ulcers, more rheumatism, more high blood pressure, more diabetes, and more mental disease. Fifty per cent of the hospital beds in America are filled with mental patients. The incidence of degenerative diseases is rising steadily.

What's responsible for this nationwide unhealthiness?

The one biggest cause is malnutrition. Our foods do no contain the proper amounts and balance of elements that build healthy bodies.

SOIL RELATION TO HUMAN HEALTH

At the very foundation of good nutrition is the soil— soil that is fertile and alive, that is kept in shape to grow plants as nature meant them to be grown. The life and balance in this soil is maintained by returning to it those materials which hold and extend life in a natural cycle, and aid in replenishing the nutrients needed to produce healthy, life-supporting crops. Soils that lack vital plant nutrients cannot possibly give these food values to what is grown in them.

Soil and Food Value

Comparatively few people appreciate the extent to which the condition and treatment of the soil govern the food value of what is taken from it. To most, a fruit or vegetable or grain is just that, and while there may be outward variations in appearance and quality, and perhaps some differences in taste appeal as well as in the price per pound or dozen, that's about all that is realized. But that is definitely *not* all. Nutritionally there are other, much more important differences. The mineral and organic content of a soil, its acid-alkaline status, and consequently the culture it receives determine the amount of every food element, major and trace minerals, vitamins, carbohydrates, etc., in the produce taken from that soil.

In a review entitled, *The Mineral Composition of Crops with Particular Reference to Soils in Which They Were Grown,* Kenneth C. Beeson of the Bureau of Plant Industry, U. S. Department of Agriculture, has stressed this fact, stating in part: "The inability of some soils to supply in proper amounts and proportions those elements essential to the well-being of man and animals has been known for more than a century. Investigations of certain nutritional diseases during the last 25 years have emphasized the importance of soils, for, throughout the world, the occurrence of bone diseases, nutritional anemias, or of the effect on animals of excessive quantities of some inorganic elements has been characterized by the interspersion of normal and abnormal areas . . . It is believed . . . that many nutritional diseases are

Peppers grown at the Organic Experimental Farm by both the organic and chemical methods were tested by an independent laboratory for nutritive qualities. Those raised in soil fertilized with compost were higher, especially in vitamin C.

caused by deficiencies or excesses of particular minerals in food plants grown in different soils, in different localities, and with different cultural practices."

Do the amounts of essential minerals really differ much in foods grown on various soils and by different methods? Indeed they do. Noted soil scientist Firman E. Bear of Rutgers University recently prepared a report which includes the Variation in Mineral Content in Vegetables. His accompanying chart of major and trace mineral differences in 5 tested vegetables showed an astounding range of variation in these elements.

For example, tomatoes varied more than double the amount of phosphorus in the highest to lowest content comparison. The same vegetable showed differences of nearly 3 times the content of potassium, 5 times that of calcium, more than 6 times that of sodium, boron and cobalt, 12 times more magnesium, 53 times more copper, 68 of manganese, and 1938 times more iron in the highest to lowest samples!

This has been confirmed by research conducted by the experiment stations of 6 southern states. In spinach, for example, they found a 4-fold variation in phosphorus, a 32-fold variation in iron content. Another important conclusion

595

was that high phosphorus in the soil meant high phosphorus in turnip greens. And *high organic matter in the soil meant high phosphorus, calcium and iron in turnip greens.*

The *"Medical Testament"*

One of the most important and challenging documents on this subject was issued some years ago by a group of 600 English physicians. They called it their *Medical Testament,* and we here reproduce it in full:

After more than a quarter of a century of Medical Benefit under the National Health Insurance Act, we the Local Medical and Panel Committee of Cheshire, feel that we are in a position to review our experience of the system.

Constituted by the statute to represent the panel of an area, such a committee is in touch with all the family doctors —in the case of Cheshire some 600—within and on its borders.

How far has the Act fulfilled the object announced in its title—"The Prevention and Cure of Sickness?" Of the second item we can speak with confidence. If "postponement of the event of Death" be evidence of cure, that object has been achieved: the greater expectation of life which is shown by the figures of the Registrar General is attributable to several factors; but certainly not least to the services of the panel. The fall in fatality is all the more notable in view of the rise in sickness. Year by year doctors have been consulted by their patients more and more often, and the claims on the benefit funds of Societies have tended to rise.

Of the first item, "The Prevention . . . of Sickness" it is not possible to say that the promise of the Bill has been fulfilled.

Though to the sick man the doctor may point out the causes of his sickness, his present necessity is paramount and the moment is seldom opportune, even if not altogether too late for any essay in preventive medicine. On that first major count the Act has done nothing. We feel that the fact should be faced.

Our daily work brings us repeatedly to the same point: "This illness results from a life-time of wrong nutrition!"

The wrong nutrition begins before life begins. "Unfit to be a mother"—from under-nutrition or nutritional anemia— is an occasional verdict upon maternal death. For one such fatal case there are hundreds of less severity where the frail mothers and sickly infants survive. The reproach of the bad

596

teeth of English children is an old story. In 1936 out of 3,463,948 school children examined 2,425,299 needed dental treatment. Seeing that the permanent teeth develop from the 17th week of pregnancy and that certain foods, accurately known since 1918, are the condition of the proper growth, that is a reproach which should be removed. With it would go the varied host of maladies that spring from diseased teeth. That its removal is practicable is shown by Tristan da Cunha. Most of the population of the little island, people of our race, living on the products of sea and soil, have perfect teeth which last them their lives.

Rickets, for which England was a byword when Glisson described it in 1650, is still with us. Gross deformities are rarer, but the big heads, tumid abdomens, flaccid skins, bulged joints and pinched chests are a commonplace of infancy; and even at school age 3,457 cases of rickets with 6,415 others of spinal curvature were found in 1936 by the School Medical Officers in 1,727,031 inspections.

Yet its prevention by right feeding is so easy that every dog breeder knows the means for swift correction.

Rickets is a heavy contributor to the C_3 population. The maternal Mortality Committee found that there is much less in Holland where butter, milk, and cheese are plentiful and the women by virtue of their generally healthy skeletal development are protected against the risks that are commonly faced by women in the industrial areas of England.

Nutritional anemia is of two kinds, one subtle and apt to happen during pregnancy, the other simple and due to too little iron in the food. It is known that anemia especially of the latter kind is common, especially among children, and women, who need much more iron in their food than men. An inquiry into the food of 1,152 families showed that 10 per cent spent 4^s a week per head on food, 10 per cent over 14^s whilst 4 more groups, of 20 per cent each, spent 6^s, 8^s, 10^s, and 12^s respectively. The food of the 3 lower groups was definitely deficient in iron. It is certain from this that nutritional anemia amongst the poorer classes is far commoner than is recognized. Here is an example: The blood color was tested in two groups of school children, one a "routine sample" of children, the other specially selected on account of poverty. Only half the poor children had a blood color of 70 per cent of normal. The final item of our indictment is constipation. Advertised aperients are a measure of its prevalence and the host of digestive disorders which result from it are a substantial proportion of the conditions for which our aid, as doctors, is sought. Yet the cause in every case—apart from rare abnormalities—is the ill choice or ill preparation of food. It is true that we are consulted on these conditions when they are established and have to deal with the effects—gallstones, appendicitis, gastric ulcer, duodenal ulcer, colitis and diverticulitis—of years in which the body has been denied its due of this constituent of food or burdened with an excess of that. Other means of cure than proper feeding are called for at this late stage; but the primary cause nonetheless was wrong nutrition.

Those 4 items, bad teeth, rickets, anemia, and constipation will serve as the heads of our indictment; but in truth they are only a fragment of the whole body of knowledge on food deficiencies which different investigators from Lind and Captain Cook to Hopkins and the Mellanbys have unlocked.

But it seems to us that the master key which admits to the practical application of this knowledge as a whole has been supplied by Sir Robert McCarrison. His experiments afford convincing proof of the effects of food and guidance in the application of the knowledge acquired.

In describing his experiments, which were made in India, he mentions first the many different races of which the population, 380 million, is composed.

"Each race has its own national diet. Now the most striking thing about these races is the way in which their physique differs. Some are of splendid physique, some are of poor physique, and some are of middling physique. Why is there this difference between them? There are, of course, a number of possible causes: heredity, climate, peculiar religious and other customs and endemic diseases. But in studying the matter it became evident that these were not principal causes. The principal cause appeared to be food. For instance, there were races of which different sections came under all these influences but whose food differed. Their physique differed and the only thing that could have caused it to differ appeared to be food. The question then was how to prove that the difference in physique of different Indian races was due to food. In order to answer it I carried out an experiment on white rats to see what effect the diets of these different races would have upon them when all other things necessary for their proper nutrition were provided. The reasons for using rats in experiments of this kind are that they eat anything a man eats, they are easy to keep clean, they can be used in large numbers, their cages can be put out in the sun, the round of chemical changes on which their nutrition depends is similar to that in man, and, a year in the life of a rat is equivalent to about 25 years in the life of a human being. So that by using rats one gets results in a few months which it would take years to get in man. What I found in this experiment was that when young, growing rats of healthy stock were fed on diets similar to those of people whose physique was good, the physique and health of the rats were good; when they were fed on the diet similar to those of people whose physique was bad, the physique and health of the rats were bad; and when they were fed on diets similar to those of people whose physique was middling, the physique and health of the rats were middling. . . .

"Good or bad physique as the case might be was, therefore, due to good or bad diet, all other things being equal. Further, the best diet was one used by certain hardy, agile, vigorous, and healthy races of Northern India (Note: the Hunza, Sikh and Pathan). It was composed of freshly ground whole wheat flour made into cakes of unleavened bread, milk, and the products of milk (butter, curds, buttermilk), pulses (peas, beans, lentils), fresh green leaf vegetables, root vegetables (potatoes, carrots), and fruit, with meat occasionally. Now in my laboratory I kept a stock of several hundred rats for breeding purposes. They lived under perfect conditions; cleanliness, roomy cages, good bedding, abundant fresh water, fresh air and sunlight—all these things they had; and they were fed on a diet similar to that of a race whose physique was very good. They were kept in stock from birth up to the age of two years—a period equivalent to the first 50 years in the life of human beings. During this period no case of illness occurred amongst them, no death from natural causes, no maternal mortality, no infantile mortality except for an occasional accidental death. In this sheltered stock good health was secured and disease prevented by the combination of 6 things: fresh air, pure water, cleanliness, sunlight, comfort, and good food. Human beings cannot, of course, be so sheltered as these rats were, but the experiment shows how important these things are in maintaining health.

"The next step was to find out how much of this remarkably good health, and freedom from disease, was due to the good food: food consisting of whole wheat flour cakes, butter, milk, fresh green vegetables, sprouted pulses, carrots and occasionally meat with bone to keep the teeth in order. So I cut out the milk and milk products from their diet or reduced them to a minimum, as well as reducing the consumption of fresh vegetable foods while leaving all other conditions the same. What was the result? Lung diseases, stomach diseases, bowel diseases, kidney and bladder diseases made their appearance. It was apparent, therefore, that the good health depended on the good diet more than on anything else and that the diet was only health-promoting so long as it was consumed in its entirety, so long, in fact, as it contained enough milk, butter and fresh vegetables.

"Many more experiments were done which showed that when rats or other animals were fed on improperly constituted diets, such as are habitually used by some human beings, they developed many of the diseases from which these human beings tend to suffer: Diseases of the bony framework of the body, of the skin covering it and of the membranes lining its cavities and passages; diseases of the glands whose products control its growth, regulate its processes and enable it to reproduce itself; diseases of those highly specialized mechanisms—the gastro-intestinal tract and lungs—designed for its nourishment; diseases of the nerves. All these were produced in animals under experimental conditions by feeding them on faulty human diets. Here is an example of such an experiment: Two groups of young rats, of the same age, were confined in two large cages of the same size. Everything was the same for each group except food. One group was fed on a good diet, similar to that of a Northern Indian race whose physique and health were good, and of which the composition is given above. The other was fed on a diet in common use by many people in this country; a diet consisting of white bread and margarine, tinned meat, vegetables boiled with soda, cheap tinned jam, tea, sugar and a little milk: a diet which does not contain enough milk, milk products, green leaf vegetables and whole-meal bread for proper nutrition. This is what happened. The rats fed on the good diet grew well, there was little disease amongst them and they lived happily together. Those fed on the bad diet did not grow well, many became ill and they lived unhappily together; so much so that by the sixteenth day of the experiment the stronger ones amongst them began to kill and eat the weaker, so that I had to separate them. The diseases from which they suffered were of 3 chief kinds: diseases of the lungs, diseases of the stomach and intestines, and diseases of the nerves; diseases from which one in every 3 sick persons, among the insured classes, in England and Wales, suffer."

These researches were minutely made on a large scale and, but for the food, the conditions of each group were identical and ideal. Their results to our minds carry complete conviction—especially as those of us who have been able to profit by their lesson have been amazed at the benefit conferred upon patients who have adopted the revised dietary to which that lesson points. It is far from the purpose of this statement to advocate a particular diet. The Eskimos, on flesh, liver, blubber and fish; the Hunza or Sikh, on wheaten chappattis, fruit, milk, sprouted legumes and a little meat; the islander of Tristan on his potatoes, seabirds' eggs, fish and cabbage, are equally healthy and free from disease.

But there is some principle or quality in these diets which is absent from, or deficient in, the food of our people today. Our purpose is to point to this fact and to suggest the necessity of remedying the defect. To descry some factors common to all these diets is difficult and an attempt to do so may be misleading since knowledge of what those factors are is still far from complete; but this at least may be said, that the food is, for the most part, fresh from its source, little altered by preparation and complete; and that, in the case of those based on agriculture, the natural cycle

Animal and Vegetable →

Soil → Plant → Food → Animal → Man → Waste
is complete.

No chemical or substitution stage intervenes.

Sir Albert Howard's work on the nutrition of plants, initiated at Indore and carried from India to many parts of the world, seems to constitute a natural link in this cycle.

He has shown that the ancient Chinese method of returning to the soil, after treatment, the whole of the animal and vegetable refuse which is produced in the activities of a community results in the health and productivity of crops and of the animals and men who feed thereon. . . .

Though we bear no direct responsibility for such problems, yet the better manuring of the home land so as to bring an ample succession of fresh food crops to the tables of our people, the arrest of the present exhaustion of the soil and the

Soil fertility has an important effect on the appearance, taste and nutritional worth of all foods. What this difference in quality (and yields) can mean is readily seen in these pictures of California farmer Louis Badders, as he packs king-sized carrots for health-minded customers and examines lettuce in the field (*opposite page*).

restoration and permanent maintenance of its fertility concern us very closely. For nutrition and the quality of food are the paramount factors in fitness. No health campaign can succeed unless the materials of which the bodies are built are sound. At present they are not.

Probably half our work is wasted, since our patients are so fed from the cradle, indeed before the cradle, that they are certain contributions to a C_3 nation. Even our country people share the white bread, tinned salmon, dried milk regime. Against this the efforts of the doctor resemble those of Sisyphus.

This is our medical testament, given to all whom it may concern—and whom does it not concern?

We are not specialists, nor scientists, nor agriculturists. We represent the family doctors of a great county, the county, said Michael Drayton, of which "such as soundly feed": a county which gives its name to a cheese than which there is none better, though to most Englishmen, alas only a name;

a county where the best farming is still possible, which should minister to the needs of its own industrial areas and of a far wider circle. We cannot do more than point to the means of health. Their production and supply is not our function. We are called upon to cure sickness. We conceive it to be our duty in the present state of knowledge to point out that much, perhaps most of this sickness is preventable and would be prevented by the right feeding of our people. We consider this opinion so important that this document is drawn up in an endeavor to express it and to make it public.

(Signed by the Members of the Local Medical and Panel Committees.)

Influence on Quality

In *An Agricultural Testament*, Sir Albert Howard states, "The influence of humus on the plant is not confined to the outward appearance of the various organs. The quality of the produce is also affected. Seeds are better developed, and so yield better crops and also provide livestock with a satisfaction not conferred by the produce of worn-out land. The animals need less food if it comes from fertile soil. Vegetables and fruit grown on land rich in humus are always superior in quality, taste, and keeping power to those raised by other means. The quality of wines, other things being equal, follows the same rule. Almost every villager in countries like France appreciates these points.

"The effect of soil fertility on livestock can be observed in the field. As animals live on crops we should naturally expect the character of the plant as regards nutrition to be passed on to stock. This is so. The effect of a fertile soil can at once be seen in the condition of the animals. This is perhaps most easily observed in bullocks fattened on some of the notable pastures in Great Britain. The animals show a well-developed bloom, the coat and skin look and feel right, the eyes are clear, bright, and lively."

Numerous examples can be found citing the great improvement in human health when growers begin raising their crops with compost. *The Lancet,* British medical journal, reported a case in New Zealand: "In 1936, Dr. G. B. Chapman of the Physical and Mental Welfare Society of New Zealand, persuaded the authorities of a boys' school hostel to grow their fruit and vegetables on soils treated with humus. This has since been done, and a striking improvement is reported in general health and physique, particularly as regards freedom from infections, alimentary upsets and dental caries."

The New York Times on June 30, 1940, also discussed this case, identifying it as the Mount Albert Grammar School. According to the *Times:* "Dr. Chapman advised that a change should be made from vegetables and fruit grown in soils fertilized by chemicals, to produce raised on soil treated only with humus. The results were startling. Catarrh, colds, and influenza were greatly reduced and in the 1938 epidemic of measles, the boys had only mild attacks whereas new admissions succumbed readily."

Tooth Decay

Here is an interesting item from the *Dental Record* of February, 1950, by Dr. Arthur A. Blake, concerning the incidence of tooth decay in an English school:

"Figures from the Royal Commercial Traveler's Schools show that in 1939: 50 per cent of the children had 0–2 cavities; 32 per cent had 3–5 cavities; and 18 per cent had 6 or more cavities. In 1941: 56 per cent of the children had 0–2 cavities; 27 per cent had 3–5 cavities; and 17 per cent had 6 or more cavities.

"A new head gardener arrived in 1941 and the school became self-supporting, growing its own food and using only organic methods. Pigs and chickens supplied animal waste. Even clippings from the playing fields supplied some of the green stuff.

"We now have the figures for 1949. In fact, the figures from 1945 to 1949 are amazingly consistent. Among the boys, 99.19 had 0–2 cavities, among the girls it was 97.5 per cent with 0–2 cavities; 0.81 per cent of the boys and 2.5 per cent of the girls had 3–5 cavities, and not one child had 6 or more cavities.

"No change has taken place other than that in the school gardens."

Here is another item, a letter that appeared in *The Field Magazine*, January 6, 1945: "I was interested in your letter from 'Dental Surgeon' because my 7-year-old son and I have only just paid a routine visit to the dentist. He seemed unusually impressed by the excellence of my son's teeth and asked me if he had had any special diet. I told him: No. That he had eaten no meat (including eggs) up to the age of 3 years, but since then had eaten meat and exactly what he liked. I added, however, that we grew as much of our food as possible on composted soil and that for more than his lifetime we have never used an ounce of artificial fertilizer.

" 'You have given me the answer,' said the dentist. 'Now I understand why he has teeth like that.'

"In my own case, my teeth used to collect huge quantities of tartar. Every year it had to be scraped off. We began using compost instead of artificials towards the end of 1936. When I went to my dentist in 1942, after a lapse of 2½ years, I expected a terrific scraping to occur. There was no tartar to remove. Another two years elapsed before I went again, this last time. There was very little tartar behind two teeth, and that was all.

"We have used compost for just about 8 years, and for the last 5 of those years my teeth have lost their unpleasant habit of collecting tartar. Is this a coincidence? It might be. But I was telling this story to someone else, and she has had exactly the same experience. Incidentally, I asked the dentist if war-time diet could have anything to do with it. He did not think it had, because he finds now just as much tartar collecting on his other patients' teeth as before the war."

—L. F. EASTERBROOK
Phyllis Mead, Treyford,
Midhurst, West Sussex.

Additional evidence is found in an item in *The New York Times* on May 29, 1947, with the heading, "Traces Bad Teeth to Soil:"

"Schenectady, N. Y.—Tooth decay as well as serious illnesses might be traced to our eating vegetables and other foods that were grown on soil deficient in calcium and other minerals, Dr. George D. Scarseth of Lafayette, Ind., director of research of the American Farm Research Association, declared in a General Electric Farm Forum address here.

" 'It is not difficult to see how a deficiency of essential vitamins and minerals may cause weakened teeth with subsequent decay and abscesses,' Dr. Scarseth pointed out. 'Neither is it difficult to suspect that prolonged abscesses, pouring toxins into the blood stream, might well show up eventually in kidney disturbances, high blood pressure, or heart disease.'

"Dr. Scarseth said that data collected by physicians, biochemists, agronomists and engineers working on the problem of soil deficiencies 'indicate there must be a close relationship between the fertility of the land and the health and well-being of the animals that consume the crops.' "

Comparative Tests

As far back as 1926, Dr. Robert McCarrison performed some experiments with grains at Madras, India. He found that compost-grown grains contained more vitamins. This discovery is summarized in the *Journal of Indian Medical Research* (14:351, 1926).

In the summer of 1948, two batches of oranges were sent to the Pease Laboratories in New York City. One batch was raised organically by Mr. John E. Volkert of Orlando, Fla., the other was the same variety grown by a neighbor of his with chemical fertilizers. Mr. Volkert's oranges had 30 per cent more vitamin C than the chemical ones. Two batches of wheat were also sent to the Pease Laboratories—one from the Organic Experimental Farm, the other from a neighboring farm that uses chemical fertilizers. The organic wheat had 40 per cent more thiamine (vitamin B-1).

The report of the work of the Biochemical Research Laboratory, Threefold Farm, Spring Valley, N. Y., for the year 1949, had this to say regarding the nutritional content of vegetables raised there without chemical fertilizers: "Vitamin testing was begun during the last year. So far, we have made tests for vitamin A, B complex, thiamine and riboflavin. It has been shown that vegetables grown on biodynamic soils have 50 to 80 per cent more vitamin A than vegetables grown on soil treated with mineral fertilizer."

In tests on the Organic Experimental Farm in 1951, oats and wheat were analyzed for protein, vitamin and mineral content. The organic oats were 28 per cent higher and the organic wheat 16 per cent higher in protein than the chemically-fertilized crops. In vitamin B, the organic plots averaged 111 per cent higher than the chemical plots, and calcium averaged seven per cent higher.

Here is the report of Dr. Howard E. Worne, Philadelphia biochemist who made the vitamin determinations:

Oats			
	per 100 grams		Differ-
	Organic	Chemical	ence
Thiamine Portion of Vitamin B (B1)	610 Micrograms	317 Mcg.	92%
Riboflavin Portion of Vitamin B (B2)	152 Micrograms	56 Mcg.	171%
Nicotinic Acid Portion of Vitamin B	19 Milligrams	9.5 Mill.	100%
Protein	16.4 Grams	12.8 Grams	28%
Calcium	58.3 Milligrams	46.7 Mill.	25%
Phosphorus	362.5 Milligrams	373.4 Mill.	3%

Wheat			
Thiamine Portion of Vitamin B	941 Micrograms	451.7 Mcg.	108%
Riboflavin Portion of Vitamin B	278.2 Micrograms	120 Mcg.	131%
Nicotinic Acid Portion of Vitamin B	89.6 Milligrams	54.8 Mill.	63%
Protein	12.8 Grams	11 Grams	16%
Calcium	40.7 Milligrams	33.4 Mill.	29%
Phosphorus	374 Milligrams	377.7 Mill.	−1%

607

Yields were also consistently higher:

Oats (Variety Clinton)		
Compost	2 lbs.	4 oz.
Chemical Fertilizer	2 lbs.	2 oz.
Chemical Fertilizer and Manure	2 lbs.	7 oz.
Sheet Composting	2 lbs.	9 oz.

Wheat (Variety Thorne)		
Compost	2 lbs.	9 oz.
Chemical Fertilizer	2 lbs.	8 oz.
Chemical Fertilizer and Manure	2 lbs.	1 oz.
Sheet Composting	2 lbs.	9 oz.

A similar test in 1954 showed that peppers grown with compost had approximately 15 per cent greater vitamin C content than did commercially-fertilized ones.

Experiments of this kind are being conducted today with increasing frequency all over the world. In India, A. S. Varma and N. B. Das of the Indian Agricultural Research Institute, found that the application of organic manures to the soil on which corn is grown apparently causes the resulting seed to have more valuable protein and oil and less indigestible material than does the application of chemical fertilizers. The tests were made with corn grown with 12 different combinations of organic manures and chemical fertilizers.

Protein Content

Particular attention is being paid to the protein content of compost-grown crops. Protein is one of the most vital substances needed by the human body. It is used to build new tissues and repair old ones. As far as maintaining life is concerned, not even the vitamins outrank it in importance.

A physician, Dr. William Coda Martin, recently wrote: "There is much evidence to show that deficient soils upset the process of building proteins in the plant; whereas in organic soil the proteins are properly synthesized. The proteins are not only increased in amount but contain a more complete supply of amino acids, especially tryptophane and lycine. Analysis reveals that wheat is producing less protein and more starch each year. A recent report shows that our hybrid corn contains about 6 to 7 per cent protein while corn grown organically contains 11 to 12 per cent protein. It is believed that the low grade protein is imperfectly formed and thus will reflect in the health of the animal and humans."

Dr. Joe D. Nichols, M.D., says, "Poor land grows food that is poor in vitamins, poor in enzymes and poor in its protein quality. All this means sick people. The most common disease in America today is hypoproteinosis, that is, not enough protein, or protein of poor quality. . . . There is one way and only one way to make land rich, and that is just exactly like the good Lord does on the floor of the forest. He puts back into the land 3 parts of dead plant matter and 1 part of dead animal matter. That is what leaf mold contains. This puts everything back into the soil, the major elements plus the trace elements, plus dead and decaying organic matter—and all in the proper proportions. And when we say dead and decaying matter, that presupposes that at one time the material had life.

"This is of tremendous importance. You must have death and decay, if you expect to have life and growth. This is a natural cycle that no chemist can get around, no matter how many degrees he may have behind his name. The end result of the decaying process is amino acids and carbonic acids. The amino acids are the little building blocks that the plant uses to make proteins of high quality. How can a plant produce proteins of high quality when it had no amino acids present in the beginning? The answer is that it cannot. This is the fundamental reason why the proteins produced on the farms of America are of poor quality."

More Starch, Less Food Value

In an article in *The Land* magazine, Dr. William A. Albrecht, Chairman of the Department of Soils of the University of Missouri, states: "While our crops have been yielding bushels per acre bountifully, those bushels have consisted mainly of the photosynthetic product, starch. At the same time those crops have been synthesizing for us less and less of their biosynthetic food products, particularly proteins. The soil that has been eroding more and more because of its declining fertility is the same soil which, for the same reason, has been giving us less and less protein, the food constituent so basic to reproduction and growth of all forms of life.

Implied, then, in our conservation of the soil, is our struggle for food protein in order that we may survive.

"One needs only to look at the soil map of the world to see the rather limited areas where the fertility is sufficient to produce hard wheat or to grow protein. These areas are in Central United States, in Soviet Russia and in most of the British possessions. There are none mapped as such in Germany and Italy. When foods of more than mere caloric values are required to win a war, there are suggestions that it was reasons residing in the soils of the different countries that classified them as the victors or the vanquished. It is no great stretch of the imagination to see who the present great powers are in terms of soils that produce protein-rich foods. Can it be beyond the elastic limit of the imagination to see the world problem as mainly a food problem when once the soil fertility pattern is understood and when we remember that more than only calories and bulk are required of the foods that really dispel hunger? If we are to carry the major part in providing proteins for war-torn peoples whose older soils have dwindled in their capacity to grow such quality foods or even to provide oils and fats, shall we not approach that responsibility cautiously and raise the question whether we do not need conservation of our own soils in a degree never yet contemplated?"

In another article in *The Mennonite Community*, Dr. Albrecht cites a study of the condition of the teeth of nearly 70,000 inductees into the Navy in 1942: "When arranged by longitudinal belts two states wide and considering these in going both westward and eastward from the Mississippi River, this map of dental health of our young men reflects the soil fertility pattern clearly.

"For the area two states wide adjoining the Mississippi River on the West, each Navy inductee had, as an average, 8.38 cavities, 3.70 fillings, or a total of 12.08 caries in his mouth. Farther west by two states, each mouth reported 8.80 cavities, 4.30 fillings, and 13.10 caries. For the west coastal states the corresponding figures were 9.10, 6.40 and 15.50 respectively. Thus, in going from the midcontinent westward the numbers of cavities and fillings of the teeth per inductee mounted by more than 25 per cent as poorer health.

"Much more serious are the implications concerning the health of the teeth, according to these data, in going from the midcontinent eastward. For the belt of two states wide

610

just east of the Mississippi River there were 10.06 cavities, 4.89 fillings, or 14.95 total caries. Much worse are the conditions for the Atlantic belt of states where the records give 11.45 cavities, 6.10 fillings, and 17.55 total caries.

"While we have none too good a health condition of our teeth even in the midcontinent with its soils of maximum protein-producing power in the better fertility supply, the teeth are poorer as one goes westward to the less developed soils, and much poorer in going eastward to those excessively developed and less fertile. Only the soils more fertile in terms of making more protein in plants give better health of the teeth.

"When we make more health maps of our country in terms of other body parts and functions, very probably we shall find the same suggested relations between their health and the soil as is indicated for our teeth. Since the teeth are an exposed part of the skeleton, shall we not expect a map of our 'creaking bones' to point back to a map of the soil's contents of lime and phosphate of which bones consist almost completely? Since we can build no better bodies than is permitted by the quality of the foods we eat; and since the agricultural business of food creation can scarcely put the quality of its products higher than is allowed by the fertility of the handful of dust into which the warm moist breath of air, rainfall and sunshine is blown; is it a fantastic stretch of the imagination of anyone who tills the soil to believe in the close relation between our soils, our foods, and ourselves? The growing science of the soil is reminding us more and more that already 2000 years ago they were emphasizing the importance of a handful of dust in the creation of man."

This much is evident: the protein drop in our crops has paralleled the organic matter drop in our soils. Fertility mined out of the soil means lowered protein content. More specifically, protein is made largely from nitrogenous compounds, hence a shortage of nitrogen causes a definite lowering of protein in the plant.

In 1896, the University of Illinois started a series of corn experiments. Using open-pollinated Burr White, they planted the highest protein yielders each year. Today they have the highest protein corn in the world, containing as much as 22 per cent protein. Average yields, however, have been less than 50 bushels per acre.

To raise yields, they combined some of this corn, giving

611

14 to 16 per cent protein, with selected inbred lines of good yellow corn. Farmers planting this hybrid, however, reported getting only 11 per cent protein—*which experts attributed to a nitrogen lack in the soil.*

This is a significant point in the protein problem: hybrids have increased corn yields. But bigger yields mean the available nitrogen in the soil must be spread over many more corn plants—each plant thus gets less. Only by practicing the return of all wastes to the soil can the protein problem be solved.

Trace Elements

A great deal of attention is also being given to trace elements and their place in the nutrition of plants, animals and humans. Dr. William D. McElroy of Johns Hopkins University has studied the effects of trace elements and other nutrients on the enzyme systems of plants. From his work he has concluded that unbalanced plant foods can mix up a plant's enzyme system and actually make it inferior in quality long before it appears stunted or shows the discolorations which we call hunger signs. Iron and copper deficiency reduced enzyme activity in tomatoes by over 80 per cent.

Another investigator along these lines is Dr. Ira Allison of Springfield, Missouri. Over the years he became more and more convinced that a good many diseases of modern man are based, primarily, on malnutrition. And a great deal of that malnutrition, he was certain, was peculiarly enough a "starvation-on-a-full-stomach" type. In other words, he believed that a man might literally be starving even while eating an ample supply of what he might term the "proper foods"—starving because those "proper foods" were being grown on land lacking in the basic elements needed in the human system.

Dr. Allison has worked mostly with Ozark cattle suffering with Bang's disease. He took blood samples and had them analyzed with a spectograph. In each sick cow there was a deficiency in the trace elements, but those same elements were present in the blood of healthy cows. Milk analysis revealed corresponding deficiencies and so did soil analysis. Another thing which his experiments revealed was that cows fed salts of the trace elements were immune to the disease even though in constant proximity with the diseased animals.

Dr. Allison knew he had something now. He began to experiment with sick animals with trace element salts and

Research specialists have discovered a direct relationship between the quantity of trace minerals in the soil and the vitamin content of foods raised on such soil. As supplied through compost application, these minor elements are of vital importance to health, make produce like the strawberries above richer in food value.

kept a number of "control" animals to validify his findings. The results were highly gratifying. The sick animals began to respond. Within a few months their blood tests showed a complete negative check for Bang's disease. They were cured.

He then extended his experiments into the realm of human life, with similar amazing results. The same minerals that cure cattle of Bang's disease also rid the human body of undulant fever and other diseases amounting to a list possibly as large as 200.

In the meantime, Dr. Francis Pottenger, Jr., of Monrovia, California, was working along the same lines in cooperation with Dr. Allison with the trace elements as a nutritional factor in the treatment of tuberculosis which has won him wide acclaim.

In *The Merck Report* for July, 1949, appears an article written by Drs. Albrecht, Allison and Pottenger telling the story of their investigations. On the basis of a study involving the feeding of 1,800 patients with supplementary diets containing an abundance of trace minerals, including manganese, copper, cobalt, magnesium and zinc, the results obtained were so spectacular that the researchers came to the conclusion that deficiency of these trace minerals may be the cause of multiple diseases now considered of bacterial origin, including undulant and Malta fevers, to which the report was especially devoted. The following are among the symptoms which they found to be due to lack of trace minerals, since diets containing such minerals were found to relieve them: fevers, constipations, enlarged spleen, mental depressions, arthritis and backaches.

Summing up, the authors conclude that "varied nutritional deficiencies, including trace minerals, may be the common cause of multiple symptoms, including the presence of these particular microbes (which, in this case, cause brucellosis)." This was shown by the fact that the ingestion of foods containing trace minerals led to a prompt recovery. Their studies indicate that trace minerals, and not bacterial agents, are the determining factors in the causation of a large number of diseases whose cause is obscure. Harmful bacteria commence to thrive, and corresponding disease symptoms start to appear, only when there is a marked deficiency of trace minerals, which deficiency provides the underlying cause of many diseases—in animals and human beings as well as in plants. It may be assumed that either trace minerals act as toxins to harmful microbes or that friendly, protective ones require trace minerals for their propagation and effectiveness, which seems more probable. When the minerals of life exist in a proper balance, the organism is healthy and resistant to disease germs, whereas when mineral metabolism is disorganized, diseases manifest themselves.

Both Dr. Albrecht and Dr. Charles Northern, an Alabama physician who turned to the study of soil chemistry, found that there is a direct relation between the quantity of trace minerals in the soil and the vitamin content of foods raised on such soil. In fact, one might be led to ask whether many of the so-called vitamins were not really the result of the assimilation of specific trace minerals by plants. By addition of a small amount of manganese to a field growing tomatoes, a certain food processor increased the vitamin C content of the tomatoes threefold. A similar increase of the vitamin A content of apples was brought about by application of boron around the apple trees, in this case the increase being 100 per cent.

Livestock that is provided a steady diet of naturally grown feed and given sound, sensible care invariably proves resistant to the diseases that plague most domestic animals. They are healthier, more productive, and do not require the incessant use of antibiotics, hormones, special additives, and other artificial treatment.

Trace elements, it is thus evident, as supplied through liberal compost additions to the soil, are of vital importance in health building and the prevention of disease.

FARM ANIMALS

An English farmer, F. Newman Turner, reports some very conclusive work in the nutritional cure of disease with his own farm animals. This is an excerpt from his book, *Herdsmanship:*

"I left the university with the deep bewilderment about animal diseases, which I imagine is common to all agricultural and veterinary students. The only certain thing about animal diseases seemed to be man's inability to prevent or cure most of them. It was not until I had experienced these diseases in my own herd and started at the beginning in my attempt to eliminate and prevent them, instead of accepting the diseases and treating them as inevitable, that I discovered the root cause of most of them. Until in fact I discovered that there is only one disease of animals and its name is man!

615

"The solution was then simple. If I could get the animals back to a life as nearly as economically practicable to what it was before man perverted them to his own use, and provide them as fully as possible with all the requirements of health available under natural conditions, it was reasonable to assume that health would be restored and maintained.

"That in fact has been my experience, and in this section of the book I publish the treatments evolved from this assumption, which have been proved effective when used by farmers themselves on their own cattle in all parts of the world.

"But first let me give you some of my experiences which led to the discovery of the simple natural cures for diseases which have hitherto seemed incurable by the involved methods of orthodox veterinary science. I have previously written about the diseases which drained my resources and nearly ruined two herds of cattle; how artificial manures were dispensed with entirely and how manuring entirely by natural means and feeding my cattle mainly on organically grown food and herbs, I restored my herd and my farm to health and abundance from the stage when 75 per cent of my animals were suffering from contagious abortion, sterility, tuberculosis and mastitis.

"I spent large sums of money on vaccination and the orthodox veterinary treatment of sterility, and the only result was increasing disease. Some cows aborted their calves as often as 3 times after being vaccinated, and one after another the cows were declared by the veterinary surgeon to be useless and incapable of further breeding after he had applied a succession of orthodox treatments and failed. He told me that I should never be safe from these diseases until I adopted a system of regular vaccination of all my cattle as they reached the age of 6 months; I must also fatten and sell the sterile animals and tuberculosis reactors. In spite of pressure, I resisted all this advice, largely because I had not the capital to replace the 'useless' animals which I was advised to dispose of, and partly because I was in any case becoming convinced that we had been tackling disease from the wrong end.

"When 25 per cent of my cattle continued normal and healthy lives in the midst of millions of bacteria of all kinds, I became convinced that the much maligned bacteria were not the primary factor in the cause of disease. After many years' working on that assumption, with the gradual elimination of so-called contagious diseases from my farm, although I am

616

regularly taking diseased animals in for treatment, I have reached the conclusion that bacteria are not only *not* the main cause of disease, or abnormality in the body, but Nature's chief means of combating it. What we choose to call harmful bacteria are ineffective or inactive except where the abnormal conditions exist to make their work necessary. If we allow them their natural function, to clear up a diseased condition, and do not continue the malpractices which gave rise to the abnormality, leaving the body entirely free of external sustenance until the cleansing work of the bacteria is done, correcting deficiencies only with natural herbs, and then only introducing the patient to natural food grown with organic manuring, good health is the natural outcome.

"In experimenting with that disease of the cow's udder, mastitis, I have taken the discharges of cows suffering from it and applied the virulent bacteria to the udders of healthy cows, with no ill effect whatever to the healthy cow. This is a disease which is said to be spread from one cow to another by invasion of the udder with bacilli. Strict germicidal measures are claimed to be the most effective form of prevention and treatment, yet mastitis is costing the farmer more and more every year.

"My own cows suffered most severely with this disease when everything to do with them was almost continuously submerged in disinfectant and when I was using all the orthodox treatments. Every farmer knows that his cows *will* get mastitis under orthodox methods of management and would continue to do so even were they kept under glass cases. The fact is that this disease is merely a catarrhal condition of the udder, brought about by feeding cows for high yields on foods in which the natural elements, vitamins and plant hormones, essential to proper endocrine functioning, either never existed because the food was grown from a soil dying of chemical poisoning or in other ways deficient, or were removed in the process of manufacture.

"For many years now my farm has been manured exclusively by natural means, and the animals fed almost exclusively on naturally grown crops.

"Kept under this régime, the sterile animals I was advised to have slaughtered have come back to breeding again and formerly useless cattle have been turned into a valuable pedigree herd, the only cost being hard work and a respect for

Nature. Had I taken the veterinary surgeon's advice I should have been ruined.

"Encouraged by success with my own animals I advertised for other farmers' rejects, particularly those that had been declared incapable of breeding by veterinary surgeons. Regularly, now, I am curing these cows with which orthodox treatment has failed, and only in cases where physiological defects prevent breeding has cure been impossible.

"Similarly with tuberculosis I have reclaimed reactors which would otherwise have been useless. All my work indicates that tuberculosis can permanently be prevented and, in its early stages, cured on food grown in properly managed soil, provided an adequate diet of mineral-rich herbs is given.

"Magnesium deficiency, which is a disease arising from the destruction by potassic manures of a trace element in the soil, has been cured at Goosegreen Farm. One animal suffering from this deficiency lay stretched out as though dead for 10 days. By a course of warm water enemas, plain water drinks and no foods until the animal was so emaciated that some sustenance was indicated, then introducing diluted molasses and fresh mineral-rich green food, I got the animal back to health. She has since given me several strong calves, 900 gallons of milk in each of two lactations, in spite of her 10-day coma."

Sir Albert's Experience

In this connection we can also mention Sir Albert Howard's experience with 6 pairs of oxen on his experimental farm in India. They were fed with green fodder, silage and grain, all produced by the organic method. Quoting from his *Agricultural Testament* (Oxford Press), Sir Albert said, "I was naturally intensely interested in watching the reaction of these well-chosen and well-fed oxen to diseases like rinderpest, septicaemia, and foot-and-mouth disease which frequently devastated the countryside. None of my animals were segregated; none were inoculated; they frequently came in contact with diseased stock. As my small farmyard at Pusa was only separated by a low hedge from one of the large cattlesheds on the Pusa estate, in which outbreaks of foot-and-mouth disease often occurred, I have several times seen my oxen rubbing noses with foot-and-mouth cases. Nothing happened. The healthy well-fed animals reacted to this disease exactly as suitable varieties of crops, when properly grown, did to insect and fungous pests—no infection took place."

618

Better-Fed Livestock

Following is part of a speech given by the Earl of Portsmouth before the House of Lords:

" 'When I started to farm some 20 years ago I was thoroughly up to date with modern ideas, but gradually by trial and error—far more often, I may say, by error than by success—I revised all my previous notions. I found again and again that, despite what analysis proved, the quality of bought food was very low compared with the very genuine food value in my own home-grown foodstuffs. For instance, in a comparison between protein in beans and in oil-cakes, my beans won every time. The same thing was used in home-grown oats. The old analysis showed their food value to be very low, yet practical experience in feeding home-grown oats to my own cattle showed the value of the oats to be much higher than anything that could be bought, except the most expensive foods. I found that my animals had a bloom. That experience brought me back to the necessity for consulting nature instead of trying to beat her. I have come, therefore, through the very hard force of circumstance and by practical trial on my own land, to believe that there is more in the way we treat the soil than there is in any methods of trying to get the maximum out of the soil by artificial means.' "

On the same page is given Lady Balfour's experience with young pigs. She says, "These animals if kept shut up in sties or houses, which is the only way that they can be kept by allotment holders, are very subject to white scour which attacks them when they are about a month old. I have proved to my satisfaction that if these young pigs are kept supplied with fresh soil from fertile land, that is, rich in humus and where no chemicals have been used, they do not suffer from this trouble. The soil should first be given when the pigs are about a week old, and should be continued up to the sixth week. You would be surprised at the large quantities that these baby pigs consume. Now here is the interesting thing. If the soil be taken from land that has received the usual dressing of chemical manure, and no compost, it is quite ineffective either as a preventive or cure for this complaint."

Fundamental Rules

Melvin Scholl, Iowa livestock expert and agricultural writer, has this to say: "Too often we forget one of the fundamental rules of agriculture: that the livestock farmer makes his money not in the barn or feed lot but in the fields. The animals, whether they be beef or dairy, are merely the machines which process the raw materials that come from the soil. We are coming more and more to realize that many of our diseases have been proved to arise not from infections but from deficiencies. One of the best dairy feed salesmen in the country has stated publicly many times that 95 per cent of the problems dairymen have with their cows can absolutely be prevented with proper feeding and management.

"It would seem wiser, then, to remedy these faults in the meticulous care of the soil itself, rather than to correct such things afterwards in the feed lot by the simple but illogical expediency of adding antibiotics to an inadequate ration.

"We err, too, when we dismiss the probability that Nature herself provides the answer to many of our problems and ills of nutrition, of disease, etc. She has, it would seem, a definite code of laws that points away from the total domination of curative medicines, disinfectants, and antibiotics in the direction of a philosophy based upon natural law.

"By a process known as mycorrhizal action, the bacteria, moulds, and fungi actually feed the plants by translating mineral fertility into a highly available form and passing it on to them. Not all the virtues of organic materials are connected with fertility alone. It is now well-known that all the miraculous antibiotics such as penicillin and streptomycin are the products originally of molds and fungi, and it is well-known that all antibiotics discovered up to date, save penicillin, come directly from the fungi and molds of soils high in organic content and preferably soils fertilized heavily with barnyard manure. Such soils, it seems highly likely, would be much less likely than poor soils, low and deficient in organics, to carry the malignant germs of disease against which the antibiotics and their sources, the fungi and molds, are such bitter foes and destroyers.

"There is already evidence to show that on farms the record of diseases ranging from foot rot to mastitis has declined steadily to a virtual zero as the organic content and consequently the fertility and the high quality of mineral nutrition has improved. It is likely that the increased quality of mineral nutrition not only has checked diseases arising from deficiencies but that the number of harmful bacteria within the soils has greatly diminished as fungi, molds and beneficial bacteria increased.

620

A significant recent find in poultry husbandry is the discovery that the compost litter system is highly beneficial. In this method, the poultry litter is allowed to become "built-up." It has cut chick mortality, raised flock health and production.

"There is no substitute for good management and no better way of raising dairy heifers than nature's way—that of limited amounts of milk, and liberal quantities of high-quality hay from soils rich in minerals and organic content.

"There is proof that nutrition does play a very important role in bacterial infection. Certain B vitamins play a signficant role in antibody synthesis and antibody production is diminished in severe protein deficiency. Experiments with rats showed that corynebacterium, isolated from lesions of young pantothenic-deficient rats, produced a similar disease when inoculated into other pantothenic-deficient rats, but rats on complete diets were resistant. The susceptibility to infection increased steadily from the tenth to fortieth day on the pantothenic acid-deficient diet.

"Animals, as well as humans, show a much greater resistance to disease when fed on well-balanced diets, from foods grown on mineral-rich and organic soils. Also, the need for antibiotics is practically nil."

Built-up Litter

One of the most interesting of recent discoveries is that the eating of compost is extremely beneficial to poultry. This is the basis of the "built-up" or "compost litter" system now gaining wide popularity. Instead of cleaning out their poultry houses regularly, poultrymen simply add more litter material —straw, shavings, sawdust and the like—and let it build up. The birds' dropping continually fall on this, and the result is a compost heap on the floor of the poultry house.

This new-fangled wonder-worker was discovered more by accident than through planning or experimentation. Poultrymen used to buy expensive litter material. When it got dirty, they cleaned it out and put in fresh. But lack of time and wartime labor shortages made it impossible to clean regularly. When the house got dirty and smelly, the poultryman just threw in some more litter, and prayed that nothing disastrous would happen.

On the contrary, something pretty remarkable occurred. The more litter he put in the house, the more his chickens thrived! They ate their own dropping and grew healthy on them. Disease practically disappeared. The birds grew bigger faster, layers increased their production, and feed costs went way down.

Some work at the Ohio Experiment Station soon provided the answer to this seeming miracle. During the war, Mr. D. C. Kennard of the Poultry Science Department decided to find out how little of the scarce, high-priced animal feedstuffs like fish meal, meat scrap and milk by-products you could give chickens and still get eggs of good hatchability (animal protein is vital for hatchability). He soon found you could eliminate all expensive animal protein in the diet of chickens on compost litter without lowering the hatchability of their eggs. He also noted that compost litter-raised chickens were healthier and more productive.

Built-up litter, he proved, is an excellent source of A.P.F. (the animal protein factor), of which vitamin B-12 is the principal element. B-12 is important to the growth, health and reproductive capacity of all animals and people.

Why does built-up litter produce this element so well? Because the same thing happens in it as in a compost heap. Soil bacteria, fungi and molds form which change the manure and litter particles into humus. In doing so, they produce huge quantities of high-protein feed, rich in vitamin B-12 and other minerals and vitamins. The chicken manure and waste vegetable matter of the litter are transformed into food, just as compost bacteria make rich plant food of composted organic wastes.

And as in compost, disease germs die under bacterial attack. Antibiotics are constantly being produced. Contagious diseases like Newcastle disappear, and parasites such as large round worms and cecal worms are greatly reduced. Eggs show a much higher percentage of fertility, evidence of increased vitality. Sick birds recover, and poor layers begin to exceed the production of their normal sisters.

Further proof that the chicken is what it eats comes from Rutgers University. Since so much recent research has shown that saturated fats in the diet are a cause of hardening of the arteries (arteriosclerosis), they are producing eggs with unsaturated fat by altering the formulas fed to laying hens. Quoting the *Seattle Times*, May 26, 1957:

"By changing the formula it is possible to produce an egg which contains what the scientists describe as an unsaturated fatty acid. This fatty acid is similar to vegetable oils rather than 'saturated or animal fats.'

"Since the feeding formulas need only be changed by substituting vegetable oils for animal fats, Dr. Fisher expects that it may not be too long before farmers are producing the new egg. It has been found that vegetable oils which contain unsaturated fatty acids help prevent hardening of the arteries.

"In the research the scientists found that by addition of 10 per cent linseed oil to the feed, the fatty acid in eggs has been changed so that it is comparable to corn oil. The linseed-oil-reinforced rations add calcium silicate for the purpose of soaking up the oil.

"The egg resulting from this ration is described by Dr. Fisher as having a light yolk. He reports that no off-flavor or undesirable effects have resulted.

"At the present time the Rutgers-produced eggs are being tested at the Rockefeller Institute to determine if they have the same effect as oils in treating arteriosclerosis patients.

"Similar tests have been conducted with corn oil, soybean oil and other vegetable oils. Trials also will be conducted with fish oils, but these present the problem of fish flavor carrying over into the eggs."

A few more items from recent medical and agricultural

literature will serve to reinforce our argument that compost-grown food is the basis of good health:

Dr. James Asa Shields, Assistant Professor of Neuropsychiatry at the Medical College of Virginia, has this to say about multiple sclerosis: "We have a story of depleted soil, soil that man in the western world has attempted to correct by the use of a few chemicals. These chemicals are inadequate to meet the full needs of plants and animals as they represent only a few of the protoplasm's mineral needs. These chemicals have the capacity to disturb the mineral balance and the natural fauna and flora of the soil. People whose food comes from soil fertilized with chemicals appear to have more degenerative diseases, more vascular diseases. Multiple sclerosis is a degenerative disease. Its clinical characteristic of acute or subacute onset, with symptoms that improve or disappear, points to involvement of the circulation.

"People who are fed on food produced by incomplete, inorganic fertilizers appear to be more liable to circulatory disease, more liable to central nervous system circulatory disease, more liable to vascular constrictions and dilatations, more liable to perivascular infiltration and to edema in their nervous systems and local glial proliferation due to disturbed mineral balance in their bodies and their blood streams. Therefore, when greater demands (the precipitating factors of multiple sclerosis) are put on their vulnerable bodies, these people develop the syndrome of multiple sclerosis.

"The conclusion, thus, is indicated that the incomplete fertilization program carried on in Germany, England, Europe, and the United States is contributing largely to the inadequacy of the quality of the diet, with deficiency of trace elements and unknown factors, contributing to and being largely responsible for the presence of multiple sclerosis in what appears to be ever-increasing incidence in the occidental world. It is also indicated that the use of complete and natural manures in the oriental world may be the factor in producing a more adequate diet, thus explaining the Orient's freedom from multiple sclerosis and some of the other degenerative diseases."

MENTAL HEALTH

Can the good soil-good food relationship affect mental health and disposition? It seems it can. Not only do travelers report that the Hunza people are so pleasant of disposition

624

There is an inevitable correlation between an increase in mental illness and the abuse of our topsoil. Where man has foolishly upset nature's routine of returning all available organic matter to the soil, there has erosion and sterility and desolation resulted—and there has sickness, both physical and mental, followed.

compared to neighboring peoples who do not follow their farming methods, but also, in the words of the Mir (ruler) of Hunza state, "The bulls in Hunza are not ferocious and no danger to people. They are harmless and very gentle."

Carrying this farther, it is even possible that our rising crime rate may be due, in part, to poor soil management. This item appeared in the *Chicago Daily News* of December 5, 1949:

"South Bend, Ind.—The ground you walk on can lead you into crime—or keep you honest.

"The Rev. Marionous Van Rooy, O.F.M., of Utrecht, Holland, who is visiting the University of Notre Dame this week during an American tour, can back up that statement with figures.

"Poor soil, which means poor crops, increases the number of crimes against property, Father Van Rooy, professor of criminology at the University of Utrecht, has discovered."

Dr. Francis Pottenger, previously mentioned, has also said, "Some phases of juvenile delinquency can be traced to

The role of compost in our nation's more-than-urgent soil conservation program is often overlooked or forgotten. Whether by individual effort or by large-scale municipal action, composting projects can defeat land destruction such as this.

vitamin deficiency. It is time for us to start corrective measures to maintain health through proper nutrition."

In New Knoxville, Ohio, the Brookside Farms Laboratory Association is conducting a broad program of research to prove that healthy soils produce healthy plants and animals. Edward R. Kuck, founder of Brookside, describes its work thusly: "A coordinated study of the soil, plants and animals on each farm has developed information which has never before been available. Here is developed the statistical proof of cause and effect of the nutritional unbalances and deficiencies that may exist in the soil. Here is brought to light the effect of the unbalanced and deficient soils, not only with regard to the productive capacity and quality of the plants grown, but also how these deficiencies affect the livestock which subsists on these plants and plant products."

Here are some excerpts from a paper Mr. Kuck has written, entitled "Organic Matter—The Wealth of Nations":

"Of all the wealth in this world—jewels, precious metals and all that man considers valuable—none is so priceless and

Contrast the sheet erosion and depleted appearance of the field seen on the preceding page with the lush growth of avocadoes in the California groves of Phil Arena, well-known organic farmer, who has adhered to organic methods for many years.

so vitally important as the 'Organic Matter Complex' of our soil.

"Since the third day of creation, when the Lord created the grass, shrubs and trees, Mother Nature has sown, harvested and stored the bounty of her crops in the granary of the soil. Here, through alternate processes of decomposition and mineralization, the accumulation of life-giving substances has been constantly increased and developed into virgin soil.

". . . By upsetting nature's routine of returning to the soil all that it formerly produced, man—through cropping and grazing the soils—began to take away from this treasury of the soil some of the life-sustaining substances to the degree that today many soils have become severely depleted of much of their life-giving properties and the accompanying vitality which these soils formerly possessed.

". . . Is it possible that in our own America we similarly notice a slow physical and mental decline of our people, almost consistent with the wasting away of our precious treasure,

627

the 'Organic Matter Complex' of our soils? Unlike the robust physique and the purposeful individuality of our pioneers, we see our population today gradually reducing in health and tending toward mass psychology in their human relationships. ". . . Unlike fertilizer materials, organic matter is not bought—but is acquired only by proper management on the part of the farmer who realizes its true worth. Wise is the farmer who will recognize the fact that the 'Organic Matter Complex' in his soil is his true bank account and that constant withdrawals without adequate deposits must lead to eventual bankruptcy. Let us stop 'mining' the soil of its true life and health-sustaining treasure—its 'Organic Matter Complex'—and instead learn to 'manage' our soil so that we may increase its bank balance and thereby provide a prosperity of greater wealth and optimum health."

SOIL CONSERVATION AND COMPOST

There is no doubt that compost is decidedly valuable in gardening and farming for top results, produce quality, and lasting soil fertility. Yet, the full extent of its significance in national soil conservation is frequently overlooked or forgotten.

The problem of soil conservation is today a tremendously important one—one that goes well beyond strictly agricultural concern. It is the fundamental means of reducing the overwhelming damage caused annually by drought, by erosion, and by floods. It has a direct, primary influence on our whole economy, on the standard of our living, on just about every aspect of our production and labor, and on the freedom and well-being of every generation we'd like to think our country will have in the future. Indeed, it affects those who could not distinguish a dandelion from an orchid as much as it does those who earn their livelihood from the earth.

Soil erosion destroys the productivity and value of over half a million acres of land a year in the United States. Conservation and organic measures are the principal, urgent ways of halting this tremendous loss, and starting the methods to overcome the damage and bring better land use.

Soil conservation implies much more than the average person considers. It includes re-forestation, grassed waterways and watersheds (which are much more effective than symptom-rather-than-cause-treating dams), contour tillage,

628

strip cropping, terracing, diversion ditches, mulches and windbreaks.

The basis of all conservation and of erosion, flood, and plant disease or insect control is, of course, stronger soil— soil made fertile and resistant and capable of supporting essential plant life. And organic matter, compost, and natural mineral fertilizing is what makes this possible.

Chapter 18

SIR ALBERT HOWARD
AND THE INDORE METHOD

Sir Albert Howard's life is inextricably woven around the soil and the improvement of the soil and, as you know, his work gave birth to the organic movement. Thus, Howard, the soil and the organic movement are so closely entwined that one cannot be fully understood without at least a surface view of the other two.

Sir Albert was fortunate in being born and raised in an English country home. No amount of book or laboratory training could have taken the place of boyhood years spent among the problems and uncertainties of a family whose livelihood depended on the soil. Those years gave him a practical touch with agriculture that he never lost.

Education

His education at London and Cambridge Universities does not seem to have made a deep impression upon him and still, someone in those impressionable years must have drawn his attention and stirred his enthusiasm for plants and plant diseases. That teacher seems to have been Marshall Ward, a professor at Cambridge University. Ward had one of those uncompartmented minds that could roam over the whole field of plant life and touch every branch of it from the bacteria and fungi to the higher plants with the fingers of genius. Ward had been the student of some of the great botanists of his day and had served as an assistant to the zoologist, Huxley,

Sir Albert Howard, foremost pioneer of organic methods and inventor of the Indore composting system, devoted a lifetime of remote travel and hard work to establishing the scientific principles that support natural agriculture.

the most noted biological teacher of his generation. In contact with such a mind as that of Marshall Ward, Sir Albert must have taken on some of those habits of thought and methods of approach to scientific problems, that made specialized technicians who knew only one small segment of their subject, almost as undesirable as investigators as those who were entirely ignorant of the subject. That Sir Albert Howard must have profited by Marshall Ward's influence is shown by the fact that he won honors in botany and plant diseases and after his graduation was appointed as a lecturer in botany and especially in plant diseases to the West Indies. He was stationed at the agricultural college on Barbados. This was in 1899 when he was 25 years old. Again he was fortunate. Barbados is the oldest, most civilized and cultured of all the many British colonies; it is like a little bit of England transplanted to a tropical island setting.

Early Work in Biology

Howard's work here was to investigate the diseases of the cultivated tropical plants and to lecture to teachers on school gardens and to planters on plant diseases. He was not entirely happy in his work for as he later wrote, he was only a "laboratory hermit" without contacts with the large planters and without any opportunities for experimentation or for testing the treatments he might devise. In spite of this lack, however, he wrote some excellent scientific papers even if later he came to speak of them slightingly as "learned reports fortified by a judicious mixture of scientific jargon."

Return to England

His 3 years here were all a part of his training, especially in the background it gave him of tropical plant diseases. His return to England in 1902 as botanist to the agricultural college at Wye in Kent in the great hop-growing region of southern England gave him an entirely different training. He continued the breeding work on hops that had been started by the former head of the school, Mr. A. D. Hall, who is better known as the famous Director of the Rothamsted Experiment Station.

The two sexes in the hop are borne in flowers of separate plants. The male plants have no value except for their pollen; commercial hops all come from the female plants. But, unless at least 4 male plants per acre are always scattered among the female flower-producing plants, the hop yield was cut down and the plants were susceptible to disease. Sir Albert was particularly proud of the fact that he was able to point out this necessity for male plants. It was a good practical contribution to the knowledge of hop growing and he was primarily and always a practical investigator. During his stay at Wye he had learned much about plant breeding, a still further piece of good fortune.

Transfer to India

His 3 years at Wye were followed by an appointment in 1905 as Economic Botanist to the Agricultural Research Institute at Pusa near Calcutta in Bengal in northeast India. Here followed another period of learning. The crops were new to him and the methods of growing them had to be mastered, a task which he reckoned at 5 years (1905–1910). His teachers were the natives whom he watched growing their crops of wheat, tobacco, chick peas and linseed with no artificial fertilizers or sprayings. From these observations he arrived at an important conclusion: "The birthright of every crop is health."

The motive power for all farm operations in India is the ox. On his experimental fields, all his oxen remained healthy and none of them contracted the common contagious diseases such as rinder pest or foot and mouth disease although they had frequent chances of infection from animals on adjoining farms.

Soil-Health Conviction

From these observations on both plants and animals, Sir Albert was led to the conclusion that the secret of health and disease lay in the soil. The soil must be fertile to produce healthy plants and fertility meant a high percentage of humus. Humus was the key to the whole problem, not only of yields but of health and disease. From healthy plants grown on humus-rich soil, animals would feed and be healthy. To produce this humus and soil fertility, the Indian cultivator had to depend on the manure of his cows and bullocks.

Shortage of fuel in India has forced the poorer classes to use dried dung as fuel for cooking, in this way decreasing severely the manure returned yearly to the soil. To replace a part of the manure lost in this way as fuel, the Indore method of making humus from any plant remains was devised.

In this method only a part of the humus is manure, the larger part may be any plant remains available. Howard credits the Chinese with the basic ideas on which he built his humus piles. The Chinese had kept their soil in a high state of fertility and supported an enormous population by carefully utilizing every bit of organic remains, even human excreta, and returning it to the land in the form of humus.

Transfer to Indore

The land for experimentation at the Pusa Station was limited and the division of the work into air-tight compartments such as plant breeding, mycology, bacteriology, agricultural chemistry, etc., prevented any one man from attacking any problem except that of his narrow specialty. A transfer in 1924 to the Indore Institute of Plant Industry gave Sir Albert a free hand to experiment in any or all biological and agricultural fields. The opportunity was what he had been looking for. He could work on a large scale on this farm of 300 acres and, while the experimentation was supposed to be on cotton raising, he could spread out into the general problem of soil fertility which he felt was the real basis of everything agricultural. It was here that he developed his compost-making technique and here the work was done for which all the other positions had been only a training.

Publication of Book

Sir Albert Howard published his humus methods and results in collaboration with a chemist, Mr. Y. D. Yad, in 1931 in the book *The Utilization of Agricultural Wastes*. Into this book went more than 30 years of experience and observation in the laboratory and fields on soil in England, the West Indies, and India. It marked his crowning achievement as a scientist.

With the publication of this book and his retirement from active scientific duties in 1931, Sir Albert regarded his career ended. But, as a matter of fact, it was only a change of base, from India to England, and the beginning of a 16 year campaign to impress on England and the world the importance of humus in the soil. His later books have all been written with this end in mind. While without any means to continue personal investigations on humus, humus making and the use of humus in agriculture, he was still able from his years of experience and his wide correspondence with all parts of the

633

world to interpret work being done in many lands as a result of the stimulus that he had given in showing the essential position which humus must hold in any permanent agriculture that was to grow healthy plants and animals. He remained to the end, receptive of new ideas and approaches to the humus problem and never developed that closed mind which is too frequently the accompaniment of advancing years; the fixed conclusion that all had been done that was of any importance and that the last word had been written and was in the text books.

The Liebig Era

The 90 years from 1840 to 1930 might well be called the era of Liebig and chemical farming. Liebig's work seemed to be so absolutely unassailable from any possible attack that it was rapidly accepted not only in Germany but throughout the world. Liebig's laboratory at Giessen became the focal point for students who wished to specialize in agriculture or biological chemistry and from that laboratory they carried back with them his methods and theories. They translated his books into their own languages. The principle upon which his plant nutrition theory was based was so simple that any farmer untrained in chemistry could grasp it and understand the immense practical conclusions to be drawn from it.

Liebig's approach to the problem of plant nutrition was purely chemical and disregarded any biological elements. It was not only purely chemical; it was inorganically chemical since organic chemistry (the composition of the carbon compounds) was still in its infancy.

His technique was to analyze chemically the ash of the dried remains of any plant for its inorganic substances: nitrogen, phosphorus, potassium, calcium, sodium, sulphur, iron, etc. This analysis was the answer to the question, What materials does the plant take up from the soil? The carbon compounds came from the air as carbon dioxide (carbonic acid gas) and the nitrogen salts were derived from the soil so they were always included in such an analysis.

To grow a plant such as a sunflower successfully with chemicals, all that was necessary to know was the composition of the ash. If the inorganic materials were supplied as chemicals soluble in water and in about the proportions that they occur in soil water, a plant could be grown to full size and maturity in water cultures. Hydroponics is the modern version of the Liebig ideas. Boiled down to its essentials, it may be

634

stated still more briefly as: the inorganic chemicals which once made a plant, if they are applied to another small plant should make another one just like it.

In compounding such chemical solutions, it was soon found that 3 elements: nitrogen, phosphorus and potassium occurred in all plants and were withdrawn in quantity from any culture solution. These 3 were the basic elements but they had to be supplemented by smaller quantities of calcium, magnesium, iron, sulphur, etc. Crops removed large quantities of nitrogen, phosphorus and potassium from the solution or the soil and these chemicals had to be replaced if crops were to be grown successfully on the same land year after year.

Liebig's theories and laboratory experiments were now transplanted to the garden and field. With nitrogen, phosphorus and potassium compounds needed for crop production, the problem was up to the chemists to supply these chemicals as cheaply and as readily available to the plant as possible. The N-P-K mark on every fertilizer bag sold today, was the answer of the chemists and the chemical manufacturers.

Establishment of Rothamsted Station

The original Liebig work and theory was of the academic type—what would be referred to as "the ivory tower" variety of investigations. But as soon as the practical and highly profitable financial returns from the exploitation of the "ivory tower" theory became evident, an entirely new set of faces appeared and an abundance of money was available to finance further experimentation and to exploit this new, rich chemical field. The famous Rothamsted Agricultural Station was established in England by Lawes, the inventor of superphosphate, who contributed both scientifically and financially to its support. From this station and from government stations in the United States and other countries, Liebig's theories were elaborated.

Between the years 1840 and 1914, these chemical fertilizers were used to supplement the huge quantities of stable manure still available from the work animals, horses, mules and oxen, the motive power of the farms. The introduction of gasoline-propelled trucks and tractors made many of these animals unnecessary; manure became scarcer and the shift to chemical fertilizers increased every year. Shortage of farm labor over the entire world during the war still further increased our dependence on tractors and chemicals.

Need for Howard's Leadership

A bold, courageous scientist with a broad training in all the newer biology: plant breeding, plant diseases, and fertilizers as well as with a practical agricultural field experience was needed to throw down the gauntlet to interests as firmly entrenched as the Liebig theories and the chemical fertilizer industry. The century-old Rothamsted Station with its brilliant array of scientific Directors and soil chemists had spread its influence over the government-subsidized experimental work in England and the United States as well as in Germany. The theoretical work based on that of Liebig seemed unassailable. The purely chemical plant nutrition theory held all the key positions in experimental work and was backed by the almost unlimited financial resources of the gigantic chemical fertilizer companies which were in many cases interlocking throughout the world.

In the United States, with a few notable exceptions, the soil experimenters were chemists with the chemical viewpoint and with little training or interest in the biological and living parts of the soil. Humus was recognized as an important factor in soil fertility but always in a secondary position to the inorganic chemicals. The physical properties of humus, such as its capacity to hold water and soluble chemicals, or to prevent heavy clay soils from caking when dried out were emphasized rather than the possibility that the humus might itself furnish chemicals that were essential for normal, healthy plant growth. Plant nutrition involved only quite simple chemical compounds, or even the ions into which these compounds might be split when in the soil water.

Basis of Howard Theory

The essential feature of the Howard theory of humus and plant nutrition is that the organic remains which constituted the humus, supplied in some way, chemicals which plants found necessary for their growth and health. As a corollary to this absorption by plants of these complicated compounds, growth substances, or whatever they were, Sir Albert added his suggestion, derived from his observations that animals or humans that feed on plants grown on chemically fertilized soil will also be lacking in some of those qualities which give health and vigor.

The use of humus in successful, permanent agriculture was not new to Sir Albert Howard and he would have disclaimed any pretensions to being its discoverer. He insisted that the 100 years in which Liebig's theories have been tested had shown that mankind had gone downhill in general health although the life-span had been lengthened and that our cultivated plants had become an easy prey to the attacks of fungi and insects, especially the so-called degeneration and virus diseases. We had fed more people but we had fed them poorly although their stomachs had been filled. He was simply insisting on a return to the old farming methods of the pre-Liebig era when manure was the standard farm fertilizer. He wished to supplement the manure by the use of any plant or animal remains available.

While the length of life in man has doubled during the last century, many diseases have much more than doubled in the number of deaths they cause. Mankind has learned through medical research to control the diseases of the early days, diphtheria, scarlet fever, and intestinal disorders, as well as the infective diseases of the middle period of life such as typhoid, tuberculosis, and venereal diseases but has not been as successful with the diseases of the later years. These diseases seem to have obscure or undetermined causes: poor teeth, pernicious anemia, arthritis, and that bane of the later years, cancer. In livestock, the foot and mouth disease is threatening cattle raising. In plants, a group of so-called "degenerative" diseases due to ultramiscopic viruses require constant vigilance on the part of plant breeders and plant pathologists to keep them in check as do new and unexplained outbreaks of fungus troubles such as the recent disastrous epidemic of the late blight of the tomato in this country.

Tribute to Accomplishment

England has bred in the past 3 centuries some great innovators and leaders in agriculture and in the sciences upon which successful agriculture is based. Land drainage, liming soil, rotation of crops, the introduction of clovers and the turnip into the crop rotation, and the work and importance of the earthworm have all been the work of some man who was willing to try something new and tell his friends and neighboring farmers about his success. It is too early after Sir Albert Howard's death to say just how high his name will stand on this great honor roll but it will be there and undoubtedly well up toward the top. No man can say at this time just how much influence this great English scientist's work and writings will have on the trend of agricultural practices. The pressure of a dense population on an insufficient food supply in the British Islands which has to be supplemented from abroad, will make the people much more willing to listen to any proposal that promises even a measure of relief.

Here in the United States, agronomists in our agricultural experiment stations will tell you that they are constantly bombarded by letters containing queries on the humus methods with suggestions that their experimentors get busy on humus problems. The pendulum of pure chemistry as a basis for plant nutrition seems to have begun to swing back from the extreme position it had attained at the beginning of the century and much of the credit for this change must be given to Sir Albert Howard.

Chapter 19

MUNICIPAL AND COMMERCIAL COMPOSTING

INTRODUCTION

Population growth and the general shift from rural communities to cities and suburban areas continue to intensify the problem of municipal waste disposal. The best solution is one that will satisfy all sanitary requirements, do the job economically, and provide a useful end product.

The 3 current methods of garbage disposal are incineration, landfill and dumping. The sanitary landfill has its disadvantages. These include: long distance haul to suitable sites are often necessary; scarcity of suitable sites in heavily populated areas; winter conditions, as ice and snow, can make operating almost impossible; future use of fill sites is limited; and lack of available cover material may prohibit use of method. Dumping has the obvious disadvantages of health and fire hazards. Disadvantages of the incineration method are air pollution, difficulties in salvaging useful material, waste of potential organic matter, high capital cost, high operation and maintenance costs, high skills required for successful operation.

Composting has clear advantages over all 3, which can be summed up as follows:

1. Conversion to a highly usable end product;

2. Compared with the sanitary landfill method, a centrally-located compost plant would reduce hauling costs which often approximate 1 to 3 dollars per ton. Getting rid of the non-compostable residue from the composting operation is less costly then by landfill;

3. Salvaging metals, rags, etc., is more economical in a composting operation because of the plant's design;

4. A well-designed compost plant can handle dewatered sewage solids, especially if mixed with ground refuse; (Cost of treating sewage solids by composting is about half the cost of conventional disposal methods in a modern sewage plant.)

5. Composting principles used for garbage and trash disposal also apply to any industrial wastes, so that a municipal plant could be used for the combined disposal of these wastes. (See the chapter on Composting Industrial Wastes.)

Of course, another basic advantage to composting is the fact that use of compost by gardeners and farmers would be increased tremendously, thereby aiding in the conservation of our nation's soil.

Disadvantages to the municipal composting idea have been described as follows:

1. Disregarding the sale of the end product, the capital and operating costs for a plant are high. Estimates are that the costs would be approximately comparable to incineration. Land requirement is also comparable to incineration;

2. Difficulties in marketing the end product;

3. Need for properly trained personnel;

4. Relatively small experience in modern plant operations.

Following are some questions and answers concerning composting, which have been prepared by Dr. John Snell of the consulting engineering firm of Michigan Associates in Lansing:

How can composting benefit a city?

Sanitary landfills have been the most popular method of garbage disposal, but the high cost or unavailability of suitable land is causing a major problem for this type of disposal. Composting can be performed in a central location and in a small compact area, thus, avoiding long haul distances and the constant search for new land.

Many sewage plants have become overloaded, and disposal of sewage sludge has become a real problem. Composting can convert sewage sludge into a safe, valuable product and completely eliminate large anaerobic digesters, sludge drying beds, and dried sludge landfill areas. Composting can solve these and other problems while saving a community money.

How much is finished compost worth?

Compost produced from normal domestic garbage will have about 3 per cent nitrogen, 2 per cent phosphorus and 1 per cent potash. Considering the current market value of straight chemical fertilizers, the NPK components of compost is worth about $17 per ton. Because of its soil conditioning qualities, compost has sold for as high as $40 per ton. It would be safe to say that finished compost of good quality should sell for $10 to $20 per ton. Increased crop yields give a value of between $20 and $40 per ton. (Whenever possible, a municipality should arrange for a commercial fertilizer company to market the end product.)

Is there a market for finished compost?

The people of the United States buy over 20,000,000 tons of commercial fertilizer every year. Two general markets for compost exist. One moderate size market is for sacked refined material for gardens, nurseries, lawns, flowers and shrubs. The second, and inexhaustible market, is for crude bulk compost for the farm. Retail price for the first may be $40–$80 per ton or more, while it might be only $5–$20 per ton in bulk. The true value to a farmer as fertilizer and humus is about $20–$25 per ton.

What size city could consider composting for sale purposes?

There is an economic breaking point in regard to selling finished compost. Cities under 20,000 in population could prob-

The conversion of garbage into a highly usable end product is one of the advantages offered by municipal composting. Many engineers believe that a well-designed compost plant can treat dewatered sewage solids as well as industrial wastes.

ably not expect to make a net profit on overall disposal costs. Smaller cities would still realize a savings over other methods of disposal, but the smaller quantities of compost produced would limit market profits.

Is scientific composting a reliable proven process?

Yes. In competent engineering hands, there should be no hesitancy to employing the composting process should it be shown to be the best economic solution for the particular problem of waste treatment and disposal.

Critical Stage

In many areas, perhaps your own, the garbage disposal problem has reached the critical stage. Most municipalities have zoned incinerators or sanitary landfills out of their own borders—requiring that it be hauled to outlying districts or into neighboring counties. The trouble arises from the fact that none of the communities want to handle garbage in their own confines—they would rather dump it in some other location. But it costs a lot of money to haul garbage over long distances for disposal, and, with the mass movement to the suburbs, there just aren't that many locations available.

WHAT IS GARBAGE?

Basically, garbage is composed of putrescible organic matter, mainly wastes from the preparation, cooking and consumption of food; waste from handling; storage and sale of produce. On the other hand, refuse is a mixture of garbage and trash. The trash refers to non-combustible household refuse as metals, tin cans, glass containers, rags, sweepings, leaves, hedge trimmings, etc. However, the terms *garbage, refuse* and *trash* are often used interchangeably. Thus you can see that in any discussion of refuse collection, it is important that the terms be clearly defined, since its meaning varies from town to town.

Garbage does not generally include food-processing wastes from canneries, slaughterhouses, packing plants, etc. As defined previously, garbage originates primarily in kitchens, stores, markets and restaurants, and other places where food is consumed, stored or cooked. In many communities, garbage represents 20 to 30 per cent by volume of the total refuse collected.

Dr. M. S. Anderson of the United States Department of Agriculture's Soil and Water Conservation Research Branch has written as follows on "Compost As A Means of Garbage Disposal":

"Garbage is an important waste product of every home and of other institutions where food is prepared for human consumption. It consists of a variety of organic materials, including fruit and vegetable trimmings from many kinds of plants, fragments of lean and fat meat, and substantial quantities of bones and other animal parts. The various materials present in garbage consist essentially of the major food classes known as carbohydrates, proteins, fats and minerals; fibers also are present. The water content is usually high—70 to 80 per cent. Such material undergoes spoilage rather rapidly under favorable temperature conditions. Garbage is usually of unpleasant odor, particularly when animal products are included.

". . . Garbage contains material of possible value for agriculture and, to a limited extent, for industry because of its crude-fat content and methane-gas potential. Since garbage must be disposed of in some manner, a challenge is offered to soil and plant scientists and to municipal officials to find economic methods of disposal. Conversion into composts and subsequent utilization for soil improvement is one of the procedures considered."

"Composting in the 1950's," observed expert John Snell, former head of Michigan State's Department of Civil Engineering, "has progressed about as far as automobiles had in 1900." But it is a fair prediction that "during the next 50 years, composting will in its own way be of *greater total benefit to mankind than has the automobile*." For example, tests at Michigan State showed that in 2 to 3 days, high-rate composting can convert raw organic wastes, as garbage or sewage solids, into a stable organic fertilizer, containing about 3 per cent nitrogen, 2 per cent phosphorus and one per cent potash.

Figures prove that, for all but small plants, finished compost can be produced at about $4–$10 per ton (20 per cent moisture) or $2–$5 per ton on the basis of the wet, raw garbage (50–70 per cent moisture). According to Dr. Snell, even if the organic fertilizer (3-2-1) were thrown away, the composting process would still be less expensive than incineration with average costs of about $3–$6 per ton.

High-rate composting can be completely enclosed; flies and rodents are not attracted to the dry end product; although desirable to remove bottles and cans, this is not essential to the process; as compared to incineration, composting is also free of any ash or residue problem. There are, of course, certain items in municipal refuse which cannot be composted. These are either not brought to the plant or are separated out on a sorting belt. This material includes tires, rocks, etc.

NATIONAL ECONOMIC VALUE

Here are some more appraisals made by Dr. Snell: In order to estimate the national economic value of composting, it will be necessary to start with a few facts, make certain assumptions and then make a few simple calculations. Overlooking all communities in the United States under 500 persons, there remains about 12,500 municipalities with an average population of 8,000 or a combined total population of about 100 million persons.

Taking garbage, sewage solids and industrial wastes at two pounds wet weight per person each day, this gives 36 million wet tons or 9 million dry tons of organic waste per year. Assuming an average waste content of 3-2-1 and the fertilizer market value for nitrogen, phosphorus and potash per ton as $400, $200 and $100, the following is a summary of the annual value of all the potential compost:

270,000 tons of nitrogen	$108,000,000
180,000 tons of phosphorus	36,000,000
90,000 tons of potash	9,000,000
460,000 tons of organic materials ...	169,200,000
Total estimated annual value	$322,200,000

BASIC PRINCIPLES

Prof. Robert F. McCauley of Michigan State University's Department of Civil Engineering has written a clear and concise description of municipal composting principles. Here is a summary of Prof. McCauley's opinions:

Modern large-scale composting is an aerobic process in which waste organic materials are ground or shredded and then decomposed to humus in windrow piles or in mechanical digesters, drums or similar enclosures. In this aerobic process, the breakdown is carried on by bacteria which require a continuous supply of oxygen for life. It is necessary, therefore, for oxygen to reach each small particle of decomposing material. So long as the oxygen supply continues, the material decomposes rapidly; temperatures generated by the bacterial activity are high and no foul odors are produced.

However, if the oxygen supply is greatly restricted, a mixture of aerobic and anaerobic decomposition takes place and anaerobic bacteria, which live in the absence of oxygen, establish themselves. The result is an extremely offensive stench. For this reason, an adequate supply of oxygen is essential to all properly conducted composting operations.

Three Necessities

In both digester and windrow composting, according to Prof. McCauley, oxygen from the air diffuses through spaces in the damp, shredded, waste material and dissolves in the moisture film which surrounds each waste particle. From this moist film, aerobic bacteria obtain the oxygen needed for their growth, permitting them to multiply by utilizing the waste for food.

The initial depth of oxygen penetration into these small particles of waste is not great and decomposition proceeds from the outside of each particle toward the center. Therefore, almost any solid organic waste can be composted if an adequate oxygen supply is maintained and if environmental conditions are proper for growth of aerobic bacteria. From this it follows that *grinding, adequate oxygen supply* and *proper moisture level* are the primary considerations in successful composting.

For refuse, garbage and similar wastes, it has been found that a moisture content of about 50 to 60 per cent by weight is ideal. This moisture level is near the range often encountered in garbage from municipal collection. When garbage has a moisture content in that range, is shredded into fine particles, and built into 3 feet high windrow piles, there will be a rapid temperature rise. After a single day, the temperature reaches 100 degrees; after 4 days, it's up to 160 degrees or higher, especially if the pile is turned.

By the end of the first day, the heap has developed a strong acid odor; bacteria which can utilize this acid for food then multiply and in a few days, the acid odor disappears and a pungent, sweetish smell replaces it. Finally, with repeated turnings, the temperature drops rapidly to that of the surrounding atmosphere, and soon the material resembles rich black earth.

Research workers in government and industry have made a great deal of progress in working out new equipment and processes for improved composting methods. Many highly regarded workers in the field believe that the time is here to set up more pilot plants which will lead directly to full-scale operations.

Thus we believe that the time has finally arrived when enough information about garbage and refuse composting has been accumulated to enable cities and private industry to go into the business of converting refuse to fertilizer. In fact, this conclusion was expressed in the bulletin, *Reclamation of Municipal Refuse by Composting,* published in 1953 by the Sanitary Engineering Project of the University of California at Berkeley. They based their conclusion on the quite impressive amount of research they have done on the composting of garbage in heaps or windrows.

Here are some of the fundamental principles offered as a result of the California Sanitary Engineering Project:

Carbon-Nitrogen Ratio

The carbon-nitrogen ratio must be close to proper balance for composting to take place rapidly.

For composting operations, a ratio of available carbon to nitrogen should be about 30:1 for optimum results. (The carbon in lignin is not readily available.) Higher ratios indicate a nitrogen deficiency, and lower ratios a nitrogen excess. Successful operations can be carried out with materials having higher ratios, but a longer time is required. Under such conditions, sewage sludge can be added to the refuse to lower the C/N ratio. At lower ratios composting is rapid and complete, but nitrogen may be lost in the form of ammonia. Since nitrogen is an important nutrient in cell growth, this loss should be avoided so the finished compost will be a more valuable soil conditioner.

The C/N ratio has a direct effect on the conservation of nitrogen during the composting process. In his book, *Composting*, Dr. Harold B. Gotaas points out that of the major nutrients—nitrogen, phosphorus, and potash—nitrogen conservation is the most important in most areas of the world, because so often the shortage of nitrogen limits the amount of food that is produced. Nitrogen is also more difficult to conserve than phosphorus, potash, and the micro-nutrients which, owing to the chemical condition in which they are present, are lost only by leaching. Nitrogen may be lost by leaching, but the major loss comes from the escape of ammonia or other volatile nitrogenous gases from the compost material to the atmosphere.

Nitrogen loss as ammonia in aerobic composting is affected by the C/N ratio, the pH, the moisture content, aeration, temperature, form of nitrogen compounds at the start of composting, and the adsorptive, or nitrogen-holding, capacity of the composting materials.

Since organisms utilize about 30 parts of carbon for each part of nitrogen, a C/N ratio in the raw compostable material of around 30, which has been found most satisfactory for good composting, would also seem satisfactory for tying up or binding the nitrogen in biological cell material and thus preventing its escape. Various research workers have reported optimum ratios of C/N to avoid nitrogen loss under different conditions of from 26 to as high as 38.

A ratio of available carbon to available nitrogen of about 30 or more permits minimum loss of nitrogen, but it should be pointed out that the ratio of carbon to nitrogen measured chemically is often not the ratio of available carbon to available nitrogen. Since most refuse contains considerable amounts of cellulose and lignins, which are resistant to biological decomposition, and since most of the nitrogen is usually in a readily available form, an actual C/N ratio of considerably over 30 may be necessary to provide maximum conservation of nitrogen.

Basically there should be little drop in nitrogen conservation below the maximum when the initial C/N ratio is above the ratio utilized by the organisms. When carbon is in excess of the ideal C/N ratio, the organisms will require all the nitrogen for decomposition of the carbonaceous materials. Investigators in New Zealand found that the most rapid composting was achieved with a C/N ratio of about 26. However, their nitrogen losses when composting materials with initial C/N ratios of 22 to 29 were around 50 per cent. Scott reports nitrogen losses of up to 60 per cent in some of his experiments, but these occurred when the C/N ratio was low. Nitrogen losses of around 50 per cent were observed in the University of California studies when the C/N ratio was in the range 20 to 25, but from about 30 upwards the nitrogen loss was very small.

Nitrogen Conservation in Relation to C/N Ratio			
Experimental Test	Initial C/N Ratio	Final Percentage of Nitrogen (dry basis)	Nitrogen Conservation (per cent)
1	20	1.44	61.2
2	20.5	1.04	51.9
3	22	1.63	85.2
4	30	1.21	99.5
5	35	1.32	99.5
6	76	0.86	108

Waksman found that in manure composts, nitrogen was conserved only when the C/N ratio was adequate and when immediate decomposition set in, resulting in the transformation of soluble forms of nitrogen into insoluble forms. Whenever decomposition was delayed, owing to too low or too high a temperature, losses of volatile forms of nitrogen occurred. From 85 to 90, and possibly 95 per cent, of the nitrogen in the raw materials can be conserved if the C/N ratio is high and other avenues for nitrogen loss are controlled.

According to Gotaas, there are 3 phases in the relation of nitrogen supply and conservation to available carbon in biological decomposition: (a) when the amount of carbon is low with respect to nitrogen, i.e., when more nitrogen is available than is necessary for the organisms to utilize the carbon (low C/N ratio), very considerable quantities of ammonia and volatile forms of nitrogen will be given off and lost; (b) when the requisite amount of nitrogen to carbon for bacterial utilization is present, decomposition proceeds without appreciable loss of nitrogen; (c) when nitrogen is low in relation to carbon, some of the organisms will die and their nitrogen will be re-cycled as previously described under aerobic composting. Small additional amounts of nitrogen may be picked up by nitrogen fixation when conditions are satisfactory. Hence, in all 3 phases there is a tendency to reach the same final amount of nitrogen—that which can be held by the bacteria when the compost is in a stabilized condition. In the first phase nitrogen is lost, in the second it is stabilized and conserved, and in the third it is re-cycled, conserved, and sometimes accumulated. This illustrates that composting operations can be conducted to conserve most of the nitrogen in wastes.

Grinding Material

"*Grinding or shredding of raw refuse* produces a number of beneficial results which hasten decomposition," the California report states. The California Sanitary Engineering Project used a hammermill, which worked satisfactorily, and Michigan State University used a Ray-Mo Grinder to shred garbage before it entered their digester.

The importance of grinding, oxygen supply and moisture are apparent from the decomposition chart in which 4 idealized conditions are shown.

On the chart, prepared by Prof. McCauley, (a) represents the volumetric relationship of a garbage pile before grinding.

Composting Periods Reported From Different Operations

System	Materials	Reported By	Time	Conditions
Aerated digester	Selected garbage plus sewage sludge	Frazer, N. Y.	7 days	Field production
Aerated digester	Garbage	Michigan State College	3–5 days	Pilot plant
Aerated digester	Mixed refuse	Dano Corporation	3–5 days	Pilot plant
Pile turned	Garbage and straw	University of California	5–9 days	Experimental
Piles turned	Mixed municipal refuse containing garbage	University of California	10–21 days	Field production
Piles turned	Mixed municipal refuse containing garbage plus sewage sludge	University of California	10–16 days	Field production
Piles turned	Cow and pig manure and straw	University of California	10–16 days	Field production
Pits turned	Air-dried refuse and night-soil	Ficksburg, South Africa	30 days in pit; 4–6 weeks "ripening"	Field production
Pits turned	Air-dried refuse and night-soil	Calcutta, India	20 days	Field production
Piles turned infrequently	Mixed municipal refuse	Dannevirke, New Zealand	20–30 weeks	Field production
Pits aerated	Selected refuse and sewage sludge	Dumfriesshire, Scotland	6 weeks' composting; 6 weeks' maturation	Field production
Piles turned	Mixed municipal refuse	Compost Corporation of America	20–30 days	Field production
Piles turned	Municipal refuse containing no garbage	VAM at Schiedam, Netherlands	3–6 weeks	Field production
Piles not turned	Municipal refuse containing no garbage	VAM at Wijster, Netherlands	4–6 months	Field production
Pits not turned	Refuse containing no garbage, night-soil, ash, etc.	India	4–6 months	Field production
Piles	Refuse, vegetation, and night-soil	Malaya Kenya	2 months 2 months	Field production
Pits turned	Refuse containing no garbage, night-soil, manures, straw, and soil	North China	2–8 months	Pilot plant and field production

—*Composting*, Dr. H. B. Gotaas
World Health Organization

In this figure it can be seen that moisture is adequate and that the large volume of voids permits an easy flow of air to all parts of the garbage pile. However, the small surface area of the waste material in this pile permits only limited digestion to take place and a long period of time, perhaps several years, will be required to decompose the garbage to humus.

In (b), this same pile has been ground in such a way as to form the material into a porous heap made up of small garbage particles, water and a large volume of voids. Even when a part of the void space is filled with moisture, enough "free air space" remains to permit a continuous supply of oxygen to reach the composting particles of garbage.

In (c), moisture content has been increased to about 70 per cent and the voids have been largely filled with water so free air space is no longer adequate for proper oxygen supply. This pile will become anaerobic and foul odors will be generated.

In (d), anaerobic conditions will also develop due to inadequate free air space, but in this case the loss of free air space is due to settling of the compost heap and not because of excess moisture content.

Temperature

Energy in the form of heat is produced during aerobic biological metabolism, and this heat will destroy pathogenic microorganisms. Doctor T. Gibson, Head of the Department of Agricultural Biology at the Edinburgh and East of Scotland College of Agriculture, says:

"All the evidence shows that a few hours at 120 degrees Fahrenheit (49 degrees centigrade) would eliminate them completely. There should be a wide margin of safety if that temperature were maintained for 24 hours."

During aerobic composting there is a rapid rise in temperature to 55 to 70 degrees centigrade in the first 3 days, followed by a steady decline as organic matter is stabilized. Opinions differ regarding the optimum composting temperature. Many operators favor 60 to 70 degrees centigrade.

Aeration

As cited by Prof. McCauley, aeration is necessary for aerobic composting in order to obtain the rapid, nuisance-free decomposition which is characteristic of the process. Without sufficient air (oxygen), the process goes anaerobic and con-

650

tinues, but with the production of objectionable odors. Aeration is also useful in reducing a high initial moisture content in composting materials. Inadequate aeration will lengthen the time required for composting.

Time Required for Composting

The time required for satisfactory stabilization of organic refuse depends upon (a) the particle size (b) the initial C/N ratio (c) the moisture content and (d) the maintenance of aerobic conditions. In present composting operations, times will vary from about 48 hours to several months, depending upon the method used and the degree of proper application of the science of composting.

When to Turn Large Heaps

Following is the general turning formula for composting set up by the California composting project:

If the moisture content is 40–60 per cent, turn at 3-day intervals. About 4 turns required.

If the moisture content is 60–70 per cent, turn at 3-day intervals. About 5 turns required.

You can see that by turning at more frequent intervals, the composting process can be completed in about 12–18 days. These figures are particularly applicable to garbage composting, but would also apply to other material provided it is not too strawy or woody. Turning of the heap is always done mechanically in large composting projects.

One fact pointed out was that turning will not reduce the heat generated by a heap. There was a slight heat loss of 5 to 10 degrees after turning, but the temperature rose to its original level 2 to 3 hours later.

Compost made from garbage is considered finished when it can be stored in large piles indefinitely without heating. At that stage it is still slowly active, however, and will decompose all but plastic-lined bags. Finished compost is usually grey-black in color, although you can't aways tell when it is finished by looking at its color. Garbage assumes the color of rich soil long before it is finished composting.

Bacterial Inoculants

Bacterial inoculants were tested quite thoroughly by the California researchers. The results were completely negative. In other words, the investigators found that plain city refuse with nothing else added composted just as fast as when bacteria were added. A more complete discussion of this subject is given elsewhere in this book.

Dr. Harold B. Gotaas in his excellent book, *Composting,* cites many references to experiments which prove that the number of bacteria is seldom a limiting factor in composting; if the environment is right, the indigenous bacteria, which are much better adapted than forms attenuated under laboratory conditions, will multiply rapidly. The experiments show that nothing is gained by the addition of special inocula to the compost pile. This evidence is supported by the fact that most of the successful European composting operations do not use special inocula.

According to Dr. Snell, "experiences at Michigan State, Japan, Formosa and elsewhere, indicate the importance of mass seeding of composting materials at the beginning of each stage of digestion. Composting time can be reduced to a minimum by re-cycling about 2 to 5 per cent of the material toward the end of each stage of digestion back to the beginning, and thoroughly mixing it with the raw material. This operation reduces the lag time for the growth of the microorganisms required to rapidly carry on the digestion of the compounds decomposed during each digestion stage."

Moisture

Moisture content of the refuse can significantly influence the time needed for composting. "Under normal conditions, the moisture content of municipal refuse will generally fall between the 40–60 per cent range most suitable for composting," mentions the California report. Excess moisture can seal off the flow of air through the heap and prevent the functioning of air-loving bacteria. Too little moisture can prevent the growth of the organisms also, by depriving them of the water they need for growth (metabolism).

Windrows

Garbage can be placed in an open pile or windrow— actually the most widely used composting method. Windrows may be any convenient length, but the depth is somewhat critical. A maximum of 5 or 6 feet and a minimum of 4 feet is recommended.

The following discussion on windrows and piles appears

Windrow composting, where the treated refuse is placed in open piles as pictured above, is a widely used method. Material should be loosely stacked, about 5 to 6 feet high and ordinarily 8 to 12 feet wide. Compost is turned at regular intervals.

in the book, *Composting*, by Dr. Gotaas (published by the World Health Organization of the United Nations).

"The material in aerobic compost piles should be loosely stacked to allow as much space for air in the interstices as possible. The windrows or piles may be of any convenient length, but the height of the pile is somewhat critical. If piled too high the material will be compressed by its own weight, thus reducing pore space and resulting in increased turning costs or in an extended period of composting if anaerobic conditions develop. In some instances the maximum practical height may be governed by the equipment used for stacking the refuse, or by the tendency of the pile to become excessively hot. Large piles in warm weather may reach temperatures excessively high for bacterial life.

"Piles that are too low lose heat rapidly, and optimum temperatures for destruction of pathogenic organisms and decomposition by thermophiles are not obtained. Also, if the piles are too small, the loss of moisture may be excessive, especially near the edges, and decomposition will be retarded.

"Experience will quickly demonstrate the most suitable height of pile for any particular refuse. Five to 6 feet is about

653

the maximum height for any refuse, and 3½–4 feet is the minimum for most shredded fresh municipal refuse. The height can be greater in cold weather than in warm weather.

"The initial width of a windrow should usually be about 8–12 feet at the bottom for convenience in turning and heat insulation. However, other dimensions and arrangements have been used, including the placing of stacks against each other. In dry weather the cross-section is usually made trapezoidal, with the top width governed by the width of the base and the angle of repose of the material, which is about 30 degrees from the vertical. Vertical sides on stacks are satisfactory if the material is not shredded and can be so stacked without too much additional cost. In rainy weather the cross-section of the pile should be more semi-circular or rounded like a haystack so that the water can run off, in which case the height may be increased slightly and will be partially governed by the maximum width.

"When using long windrows for large-scale municipal composting, any convenient length is satisfactory. A windrow may be lengthened by adding the material for one day where the previous day's operation ended. After material has composted for a few days it may be combined into one pile if desired. The windrow layout should be planned for the most efficient materials-handling and the most satisfactory utilization of the area.

"The volume of composting refuse will decrease to between 20 per cent and 60 per cent of the original volume, according to the character of the materials and the amount of compaction. The weight of matured compost is usually 50–80 per cent of the original weight of the refuse after removal of scrap salvage and non-compostables, the actual figure depending upon the character of the materials and the moisture loss. If the raw material contains large quantities of organic matter, the weight loss will be much greater than when the mineral or ash content of the initial material is high."

Forced Air

Experiments at Michigan State have indicated the importance and efficiency of Forced-Air being used in conjunction with windrows. In many instances, natural ventilation does not give adequate oxygen and control and therefore requires considerably longer to obtain the same degree of composting.

Organisms in Composting

Dr. Gotaas makes these observations about the types of organisms that influence the composting process:

Compostable waste materials (garbage, refuse, night-soil, manure, sewage sludge, and miscellaneous vegetable matter) normally contain a large number of many different types of bacteria, fungi, molds, and other living organisms. Only very limited data are available regarding the variety of different organisms and their specific functions. Waksman and others, in extensive studies of the microbiology of aerobic composting of manure and other organic matter, have shown that a variety of microorganisms have a variety of specific functions, and that no single organism, no matter how active, can compare with a mixed population in producing rapid and satisfactory decomposition. It appears that more species of bacteria are involved in aerobic decomposition than in anaerobic putrefaction. There is little information on the bacterial species active in anaerobic composting, but several investigations concerning the bacteria which are important in anaerobic digestion of sewage sludge have been made. Many of the same organisms are no doubt as active in anaerobic composting as in sludge digestion. However, since the environment of anaerobic compost stacks, particularly as to moisture and nutritional materials, differs greatly from that of sludge digestion tanks, the biological population would also be expected to differ.

Although many types of organisms are required for decomposition of the different materials, the necessary variety is usually present and the organisms thrive when environmental conditions are satisfactory. During decomposition marked changes take place in the nature and abundance of the biological population. Some of the many species will multiply rapidly at first, but will dwindle as the environment changes and other organisms are able to thrive. Temperature and changes in the available food-supply probably exert the greatest influence in determining the species of organisms comprising the population at any one time. Aerobic composting is a dynamic process in which the work is done by the combined activities of a wide succession of mixed bacterial, actinomycetic, (listed separately from other bacteria because of their distinct role in composting) fungal, and other biological populations, each suited to a particular environment of relatively limited duration and each being most active in the decomposition of some particular type of organic matter, the activities of one group complementing those of another. The mixed populations parallel the complex environments afforded by the heterogeneous nature of the compostable material. The succession of populations reflects environments constantly changing because the temperature and substrate are in a state of continual flux. The substrate changes because of a steady breakdown of complex foodstuffs to simpler compounds. Except for short periods during turning, the temperature increases steadily in proportion to the amount of biological activity, until equilibrium with heat losses is reached or the material becomes well stabilized.

In aerobic composting the facultative and obligate aerobic representatives of bacteria, actinomycetes, and fungi are the most active. Mesophilic bacteria are characteristically predominant at the start of the process, soon giving way to thermophilic bacteria which inhabit all parts of the stack where the temperature is satisfactory; this is, eventually, most of the stack. Thermophilic fungi usually appear after 5–10 days, and actinomycetes become conspicuous in the final stages, when short duration, rapid composting is practiced. Except in the final stages of the composting period, when the temperature drops, actinomycetes and fungi are confined to a sharply defined outer zone of the stack, 2–6 inches in thickness, beginning just under the outer surface. Some molds also grow in this outer zone. Unless very frequent turning is practiced, so that there is not adequate time or conditions for growth, the populations of fungi and actinomycetes is often great enough to impact a distinctly greyish-white appearance to this outer zone. The sharply defined inner and outer limits of the shell, in which actinomycetes and fungi grow during the high-temperature active-composting period, are due to the inability of these organisms to grow at the higher temperatures of the interior of the stack. The thermophilic actinomycetes and fungi have been found to grow in the temperature range between about 45 degrees and 60 degrees centigrade. In the University of California studies, the temperature of the outer shell in which these organisms predominated varied from 48 degrees centigrade at the outside boundary to 58 degrees centigrade at the inside boundary. Frequent turning—such as is sometimes necessary for fly control—inhibits their growth,

656

since the cooler outer shell is turned into the interior before they can develop in large numbers.

No attempt will be made here to show the detailed role of groups of organisms or specific organisms in decomposing different materials. Various investigations have shown that many different types of thermophilic bacteria apparently play a major role in decomposing protein and other readily broken down organic matter. They appear to be solely responsible for the intense activity characteristic of the first few days, when the temperature has reached 60–70 degrees centigrade and major changes in the nature of the compost stack are taking place, i.e., when the stack is drastically shrinking and the appearance of the material is undergoing rapid change. They continue to predominate throughout the process in the interior of the piles, where temperatures are inhibitory to actinomycetes and fungi. Carlyle and Norman noted that bacteria constituted the active flora in all of their mixed flora experiments on thermogenesis in plant decomposition.

In spite of being confined primarily to the outer layers and becoming active only during the latter part of the composting period, fungi and actinomycetes play an important role in the decomposition of cellulose, lignins, and other more resistant materials, which are attacked after the more readily decomposed materials have been utilized. There are many bacteria which attack cellulose; however, in the parts of compost stacks populated chiefly by bacteria, paper exhibits very little evidence of breakdown, whereas in the layers or areas inhabited by actinomycetes and fungi, it becomes almost unrecognizable. Considerable cellulose and lignin decomposition by the actinomycetes and fungi can occur near the end of the composting period, when the temperatures have begun to drop and the environment in a larger part of the pile is satisfactory for their growth. Hence, in the interests of their activity, turning should not be more frequent than is necessary for providing aerobic conditions and controlling flies. Among the actinomycetes, *Streptomyces* and *Micromonospora* are common in composts, *Micromonospora* being the most prevalent. The fungi in composts include *Thermonmyces* sp., *Penicillium dupontii*, and *Aspergillus fumigatus*.

It should be noted that since the necessary organisms for composting are usually present, and will carry on the process when the environment is suitable, an extensive knowledge of the characteristics of the various organisms is not necessary for operating a compost plant. A more detailed knowledge of the organisms, however, may lead to further improvements and economies in the process.

pH Reaction

According to Dr. Gotaas, the initial pH of garbage, refuse, manure, and other compostable material is usually between 5.0 and 7.0 unless the waste contains ash or other highly alkaline materials. If the material has undergone putrefaction before being received for composting the pH will be near the lower value. When the initial pH is between 6.0 and 7.0, the pH of the composting material will usually drop a little during the first 2 or 3 days of aerobic composting, owing to the formation of some acid. If the pH is 5.0 or 5.5 there will be little change during this period. After 2 to 4 days the pH usually begins to rise and will level off at between 8.0 and 9.0 towards the end of the process. The control of the pH in composting is seldom a problem requiring attention if the material is kept aerobic, but large amounts of organic acids are often produced during anaerobic decomposition on a batch basis. Ash, carbonates, lime, or other alkaline substances will act as a buffer and keep the pH from becoming too low; however, the addition of alkaline material is rarely necessary in aerobic decomposition and, in fact, may do more harm than good because the loss of nitrogen by the evolution of ammonia as a gas will be greater at the higher pH. Since the optimum pH for most organisms is around 6.5 to 7.5, it would probably be beneficial if the pH could be maintained in that range. However, since composting is necessarily more or less of a batch-process operation, minor changes in the pH must be expected.

Apparently, initial pH values of 5.0 to 6.0 do not seriously retard the initial biological activity since active decomposition and high temperatures develop rapidly after the material is placed in the stack, but the temperature does appear to increase a little more rapidly when the pH is in the range around 7.0 and above. The usual waste materials available for composting present no problem of pH control.

DEVELOPMENT OF COMMERCIAL COMPOSTING PROCESSES

The technical bulletins issued by the Sanitary Engineering Research Project at the University of California in Berkeley have done much to advance commercial composting knowledge. Much of the following summary of composting processes that have been used in this country originally appeared in a bulletin issued by that group. Though some of these processes are no longer considered practical in view of recent technological advances, we describe them here because of their historical significance.

The Indore (Traditional) Process

As explained in a previous section, Sir Albert Howard developed a method of composting in trenches or in heaps, employing either sewage sludge, night soil, or manure as a seeding material to provide necessary microflora. The method was developed in India during the period 1920–30, and is an adaptation and systematization of practices which have been observed in China and India for centuries, i.e., the traditional process. Refuse material, such as straw, garbage, tree clippings, etc., is alternated in layers with night soil and sewage sludge. The material is placed in piles not to exceed 5 feet in height and extending in area as much as is practicable. The foundation layer generally comprises small branches or similar materials, which permits air to circulate through the heap. The first layer above the foundation is about 6 inches thick and consists of plant residues such as grass or leaves. The second layer consists of animal manure, garbage, fish trimmings, etc., and is about 2 inches thick. The third layer, about $\frac{1}{8}$-inch thick, should be of earth mixed with a small quantity of lime or wood ashes (about one per cent). This layering should be repeated until a height of 5 feet is reached, and then the entire pile covered with a layer of earth about $\frac{1}{4}$-inch thick. If the pile is very large in extent, it is recommended that vertical funnels or chimneys be formed by rotating a rod or crowbar which has been pushed into the pile. The chimneys should be about 3 to 4 feet on centers. This method will give satisfactory results if the moisture content is maintained at the proper level, estimated at approximately 30 per cent. The fermentation period is about 90 days, during which the materials are turned twice by manual methods. The liquors draining from the fermenting materials should be collected in sumps and re-circulated through the mass.

Jackson and Wad, who worked with Howard, improved the original Indore process by using half-digested sewage sludge as seed material, a procedure which reduces the fermentation period to approximately 15 days. This modification therefore greatly increases the practicability of the Indore method for large-scale installations.

The Indore process is primarily adapted to hand labor and is consequently chiefly useful where labor as well as land is cheap and abundant. It should, however, be possible to mechanize the process by arranging trenches in such a way that the material can be dumped directly into them from the collecting trucks. The material in the trenches could be turned as required (approximately every 5 days) by use of power shovels; or trenches could be built with ramps and scoop or bucket-equipped tractors employed. On completion of the fermentation, the material could be mechanically removed, sorted, ground, dehydrated, and transferred to storage or directly to point of use.

The material resulting from this process is gray to dark brown in color, of inoffensive odor, resembles freshly turned earth, and should contain somewhat less than 30 per cent moisture at the end of the fermentation period. Compost of this moisture content is handled with some difficulty; hence it may be desirable to decrease the moisture content further by either air-drying or heat-drying prior to use. It is estimated that man-hour requirements for the production of a ton of finished compost should be of the magnitude of 8 hours by hand labor, and proportionately less as mechanization of the installation increases.

The chief disadvantages of this method are the following:

1. The labor requirements are relatively high.

2. There is lack of protection from rain, wind, snow, etc., and consequent difficulty in accurately controlling the environment.

3. Although it is said that this process will not cause any appreciable odors, it is believed to be almost impossible to decompose heterogeneous material of this nature with a total absence of generation of sulfides, ammonia, indole, skatole, mercaptans, and similar substances associated with anaerobic processes.

4. Strict pest and vector control measures would have to be employed to eliminate nuisance and to protect the public health.

The Indian Council of Agricultural Research has modified the Indore Method, and it is still used widely there under the name, *Bangalore* process.

The Beccari Process

The Beccari process was developed by Dr. Giovanni Beccari of Florence, Italy, while doing research on the problems of storing manure. The problem was to conserve manure during the months when it could not be used on the soil in such a manner that a minimum of nitrogen would be lost through the action of denitryifying organisms. In the course of these researches, Dr. Beccari developed an insulated cell of approximately 20 cubic yards capacity, into which the material would be placed for storage. It was soon noted that the material removed from these cells bore a striking resemblance to the humus obtained from compost heaps. A logical outcome of this observation was the attempt to use this Beccari cell for the composting of organic wastes, street sweepings, etc.

As originally designed, the Beccari cell consists of a simple cuboidal structure, with a loading hatch on the top and an unloading door on the front. Vents are incorporated into the structure; these are provided with valves or other closures which serve to exclude the air during the first stage of the process which, by design, is anaerobic.

After the maximum temperature of approximately 150 degrees Fahrenheit has been reached, the vents are opened and air allowed to circulate through the cell. The attainment of the maximum temperature takes approximately 18 days, during which time the volume of the mass has shrunk considerably, allowing for considerable circulation of air when the vents are open. The opening of the vents presumably serves to change the process to an aerobic one; owing to the nature of the compacted mass in these cells, very little oxygen probably will be able to diffuse to the center of the agglomerate, and the process could best be described as operating under only partially aerobic conditions. The opening of the vents and the consequent circulation of air serve to dry out the mass, since the heat generated in the process causes considerable evaporation. For this process, it is also claimed that there is no production of ammonia, hydrogen sulfide, or other obnoxious gases, and that all the gas produced will comprise odorless water vapor and carbon dioxide. The required total retention period is from 35 to 40 days.

The Beccari process is operating successfully in Italy and France, where there are reported approximately 50 municipal installations. One interesting project is that constructed at St. Georges, France, where the process was improved by adding air to the cells during the fermentation period. The project comprises 40 cells each with 700 cubic feet capacity, elevated 10 feet above the ground to facilitate removal of the contents. The cells are filled with settled sewage solids together with decanted garbage, and the digestion period lasts 20 days. After fermentation, the composted materials are sorted and the humus sold to farmers. Another plant is that at Geneva, which employs the Boggiano-Pico modifications of the Beccari method. Instead of cells, this plant has a hermetically sealed tower having a capacity approaching 56,500 cubic feet, which is filled from above and emptied from below. Air is introduced from below at a pressure of 7 atmospheres. The fermentation period is 35 days.

Another interesting application of the Beccari method was made by Jean Bordas in 1931, who used a fermentation silo designed for continuous operation. Air is introduced upwards, along the walls and through a central pipe, and water is also added to increase moisture content. The silo is divided by means of a grate into upper and lower sections, the upper section containing a platform, feed inlet, and a small tower for absorption of ammonia gas by superphosphate, and the lower section containing openings for the discharge of liquid drainage and of solid material. The raw garbage is charged in loads of 700 cubic feet, together with some 20 pounds of urine or steep liquor plus a small amount of horse manure, the latter materials being interspersed between layers of wastes. After loading, the wastes are moistened with about 50 gallons of slightly warmed water or manure liquor. After 12 to 15 days the grate is opened, permitting the charge to fall to the lower chamber where it now occupies considerably less volume (420 cubic feet), and on top of this partially composted mass is added another 700 cubic feet of the raw materials. The grate is then closed and another 700 cubic feet of raw materials placed in the upper chamber, thus establishing the loading cycle. Practically all of the volume of the silo is continuously utilized, and at equilibrium only 20 days are required to complete the composting. The final product is enriched through addition of superphosphate from the absorption tower.

In the United States attempts to employ the Beccari process were made by 5 municipalities located in Florida and New York (Scarsdale) in the period 1920-30. These installations have since been discontinued.

C. G. Hyde of the University of California, made a report to the City and County of San Francisco in which he describes the operation of the 5 American plants and the Florence installation in considerable detail. Professor Hyde estimates that approximately 5 man-hours were required to load and unload a Beccari cell; since each cell should produce approximately 5 tons of compost, the man-hour requirement per ton of compost would be approximately one hour. The main difficulty with the Beccari cells as constructed in the United States was the fact that the loading hatches and unloading doors were constructed of wood which warped under the influence of moisture and heat, and prevented the establishment of a tight seal. Thus, some of the drainage found its way around the cracks and became an attractive nesting ground for roaches and other vermin. This difficulty could be avoided by constructing these cells of non-warping materials, and furnishing the unloading door with an inflatable rubber gasket to insure tight sealing. The drainage could be collected in sanitary sewers and either disposed of through the municipal sewerage system or recirculated through the fermenting mass.

The Verdier Process

The Beccari process has attracted many inventors who have modified it in one way or another to obviate one or more of these difficulties. The most notably successful among these modifications is the Verdier process, which is employed successfully in the French city of Cannes, among others.

The process is essentially the Beccari process with the modification of recirculation of the drainage liquor. While details of this plant have unfortunately not become available, it appears that the plant operates about as follows: The material is dumped into a receiving pit, ground, and placed into the Beccari cells while spraying it with the drainage liquor. The vents of these cells are so arranged that the shrinkage of the mass acts as an automatic valve to admit air into the chambers. The material is unloaded from the cells onto an unloading ramp, whence it is transferred to a screen; the tailings are returned to the compost and the screenings are packed and distributed as fertilizer. These modifications made by Verdier seem to have been very successful, resulting in reduction of the retention time to approximately 20 days.

VAM Process

Following is a description of Holland's VAM system, given by Prof. Harold B. Gotaas in his book, *Composting:*

The VAM processing procedure—utilized in the Netherlands since 1932 by N. V. Vuilafvoer Maatschappij (VAM), a non-profit utility company formed by the government for the disposal of city refuse—is essentially an adaptation of the Indore process for composting large quantities of municipal refuse, which contains little garbage or readily putrescible food materials. In the original process, unground refuse was placed in long high piles which, during composting, were sprinkled periodically with recirculated drainage liquor; the decomposed material was then shredded by a hammer-mill and sold as a soil humus. In new installations, however, the refuse is first shredded in a special grinder developed by Weststrate, the director of VAM. This grinder resembles a rimless wheel with U-section spokes pin-hinged at the hub, and rotating above a horizontal base with a diameter of about 15 feet or more and with alternate rough rasp plates and sieve plates. The shredding is accomplished by the revolving hinged spokes rasping over the roughened plates. Salvagable materials are segregated and picked out before the shredding is begun; non-shreddable materials are removed twice a day from the shredder. The shredded refuse, as it falls through the sieve plates, is picked up on a moving belt and conveyed to a place where it can be readily sprinkled to control the moisture, and turned from time to time to provide aeration, during the composting period.

The content in VAM compost of trace minerals has been analyzed as follows:

Element	Per Cent (dry weight)
Copper	0.01 –0.06
Manganese	0.002–0.03
Zinc	0.007–0.023

Element	Per Cent (dry weight)
Boron	0.005–0.007
Molybdenum	±0.001
Magnesium (as MgO)	0.11–0.34

The Frazer Process

Valuable work in the field of composting was done by Mr. E. Eweson, biochemist of Long Island, whose patents were assigned to the Frazer Compost Corporation of Chicago. The salient feature of this system is the use of forced aeration with "soil air," i.e., the atmosphere obtained from the digestion cell itself, possibly modified the retaining of carbon dioxide produced during the process.

It was partially mechanized, and included bars used to move the material through the coarse screens separating the 4 decks. The retention time employed was from 5 to 7 days on each deck, and it is claimed that complete stabilization occurred in about 20–28 days. The refuse to be composted was shredded and placed into the uppermost deck, through which the soil air was blown under controlled conditions. After 5 to 7 days the partially finished material was shaken down to the next deck and so on over 5–7 days until the product passes out at the bottom, through a 4–6 mesh screen, leaving about 10 per cent tailings which are used to start the process over again. The product emerges sufficiently dry for bagging. Neutrality was maintained by adding ground limestone rock, and ground phosphate rock had been used to enrich the finished compost. No additions other than limestone were made to the refuse as loaded. The digester had about 3,000 cubic feet capacity and thus could treat about 50 tons of garbage and refuse at one loading. A demonstration unit was set up at the Chicago Union Stock Yards and another at Bay View, Long Island.

The Earp-Thomas Process

This process was developed by G. H. Earp-Thomas of High Bridge, New Jersey, a pioneer of municipal composting in the United States. Many years ago, he developed his principle of the "continuous-flow digester," a vertical cylinder divided into eight sections or floors and fitted internally with rotating booms and plows. The organic waste, after having been ground to a pulp-like consistency, is introduced to the top section of the digester where it is inoculated with bacteria.

The waste "works" its way down, floor by floor, heating up as it descends. After 24–48 hours, it has reached the bottom layer and the composting process is considered by the inventors to be complete.

Earp-Thomas digesters are used in several countries,

including France (Paris) and Korea (Seoul). A pilot plant was recently set up outside Reading, Pennsylvania.

Here is a more complete description of the continuous-flow digester, as described by the Earp-Thomas firm:

1. Pulverized or ground organic waste is conveyor-fed into the top deck of the digester. Input waste has been mechanically sorted to remove glass, metal, plastics, rubber, and other non-digestible substances.

2. Specially cultured depurating aerobic bacteria are added to input waste through an automatic hopper feeder.

3. First stage of digestion begins. Bacteria synthesize sugars and multiply rapidly, producing starch-digesting enzymes. Rate of growth of anaerobic bacteria is immediately inhibited. Temperature: 80–100 degrees Fahrenheit.

4. Proteolytic bacteria produce enzymes to break down proteins into amino acids. Sulphates of ammonia, nitrites, and nitrates are produced, which are then utilized by cellulose organisms in the next stage. Temperature: 100–110 degrees Fahrenheit.

5. In the third deck, the rate of bacterial oxidation rises. Temperature increases to the optimum range for cellulose bacteria, which multiply and start break-down of hemi-celluloses, alpha celluloses, and lignin. Temperature: 110-130 degrees Fahrenheit.

6. In decks 4 through 8, thermic aerobes heat and further tenderize resistant tissues, and hydrolize and dehydrate descending bacterial bodies and organic matter. Resistant anerobes and spores are, in most cases, either split, with their interiors steamed and hydrolized, or attacked in their tenderized condition, so that the starch, protein, or mineral content of each organism is digested by enzymes which could not penetrate cell membranes before "cooking." Aeration and digestion combine to eliminate anerobic growth and prevent the precondition for reheating. Final drying is accelerated by suction blower, drawing controlled air flow through lower deck filtering screens. Temperature: 130–180 degrees Fahrenheit.

Each deck of the digester is fitted with 16 or more slowly rotating plows, driven from a vertical central shaft. Material is pushed outward on one deck, inward on the next, toward openings through which it falls to the next stage.

This process has been criticized by many engineers because of its apparent mechanical weaknesses which have caused many operating difficulties. The requirement for a royalty payment and purchasing inoculating bacteria has also brought criticism to the process.

The Dano Process

The Dano Process has been developed in Denmark, since about 1933, and is currently used in over 50 composting plants.

Under the Dano method, crude refuse is delivered to a refuse hopper whence it is conveyed by a moving floor to an elevating belt conveyor. The refuse is passing a magnetic separator in the upper pulley of the belt conveyor for the extraction of tins and the like and is then delivered to the Dano-Bio-Stabilizer.

The Bio-Stabilizer is a rotating cylinder which contains up to 5 days' supply of refuse, depending on the degree of treatment required. As the dry wastes are delivered to the cylinder they are moistened by the addition of sewage sludge and/or water.

The cylinder rotates slowly and as the wastes move in a screw path towards the outlet, they are thoroughly mixed and granulated by abrasion. Air is added at low pressure in controlled amounts through ducts fitted with valves ranged throughout the cylinder.

An environment is thus created within the cylinder where the action of aerobic microorganisms is stimulated thereby ensuring a rapid decomposition of the wastes under inoffensive conditions.

Temperatures up to 140 degrees Fahrenheit are spontaneously developed within the mass of wastes being treated, thereby ensuring the destruction of pathogenic organisms.

The processed wastes discharged from the Bio-Stabilizer are delivered by a conveyor belt to a specially designed screen where the compost is separated from durable matter and delivered by a conveyor belt to a storage bay.

From 100 tons of crude refuse between 65 and 75 tons of

compost can be produced. Generally final "curing" is done in windrows.

Anaerobic Processes

All of the composting methods previously described have employed aerobic stabilization as the principal mechanism in the process, although, as noted, some of the action is anaerobic.

In the United States, certain communities are disposing of garbage by grinding and discharge into the sewers. At these places, the ground garbage is largely recovered in the sewage sludge, and undergoes anaerobic digestion with it, and hence is recovered as fuel gas and humus. As compared with aerobic-anaerobic composting, disposal of organic refuse by anaerobic digestion with sewage sludge has the distinct advantage of making efficient use of existing sewer and sewage treatment facilities. Use of the sewers for transporting the ground garbage may decrease or even eliminate separate collection in some areas, and existing sewage treatment plant digestion facilities need simply be expanded as required to care for the extra load.

Home Garbage Grinders

Many homes are installing garbage grinders today. This trend could be perfectly taken care of by compost plants devised to dispose of refuse and sewage solids together. The garbage would merely be transported by the sewers rather than the garbage trucks. Comments Dr. Snell on this development:

"It should be kept in mind that garbage by weight is only about 1/6th of the total weight of household refuse. Therefore there would not be too much savings in the use of household grinders. Also, the addition of all of the garbage of a community by grinding in the kitchens, would have the following effect on a sewage treatment plant:

"1. Double the total solids reaching the plant, and double the sludge produced;

"2. Not affect the hydraulics of the plant noticeably;

"3. Increase the size of the sludge digestion tanks by 100 per cent. It would increase the secondary treatment facilities, such as aeration tanks, by 35 per cent."

EFFECT OF HIGH TEMPERATURES ON DISEASED ORGANISMS

Thermal Death Points of Some Common Pathogens and Parasites

ORGANISM

Salmonella typhosa: No growth beyond 46°C; death within 30 minutes at 55° to 60°C.

Salmonella spp: Death within one hour at 55°C; death within 15 to 20 minutes at 60°C.

Shigella spp: Death within one hour at 55°C.

Escherichia coli: Most die within one hour at 55°C and within 15 to 20 minutes at 60°C.

Endamoeba histolytica cysts: Thermal death point is 68°C.

Taenia saginata: Death within 5 minutes at 71°C.

Trichinella spiralis larvae: Infectivity reduced as a result of one hour exposure at 50°C; thermal death point is 62°C–72°C.

Necator Americanus: Death within minutes at 45°C.

Brucella abortus or suis: Death within 3 minutes at 61°C.

Micrococcus pyogenes var. aureus: Death within 10 minutes at 50°C.

Streptococcus pyogenes: Death within 10 minutes at 54°C.

Mycobacterium tuberculosis var. hominis: Death within 15 to 20 minutes at 66°C; or momentarily heated at 67°C.

Corynebacterium diphtheriae: Death within 45 minutes at 55°C.

—Prepared by the Sanitary Engineering Research Project, University of California

COMPOSITION OF GARBAGE AND GARBAGE COMPOSTS

In his report, "Compost As A Means of Garbage Disposal," Dr. M. S. Anderson has written that:

"The composting process brings about drastic decrease in the carbohydrate content of garbage and accomplishes varying degrees of decomposition of other organic constituents, with the evolution of carbon dioxide and some loss of nitrogen. Large quantities of nitrogen are transformed into the cells of bacteria. Such organisms have been shown to contain about 7 to 11 per cent of nitrogen on a dry basis. The tissues of fungi

669

may contain about 4 to 6 per cent of nitrogen. Such microbial cells often constitute a substantial part of the mass of a matured compost. Some workers have estimated that as much as 30 per cent of the nitrogen may be present in these forms.

"The chemical composition of garbage and of composts derived in considerable part from garbage, varies widely. The table shows the nitrogen contents of garbage from several cities. Some of these values are for single samples and some are based on averages for an indefinite number of samplings.

Average Nitrogen Contents of Raw Garbage from Several Cities, Dry Basis

Location	Nitrogen (per cent)
Washington, D. C.	2.70
Hastings, New York	2.20
Yonkers, New York	2.50
Chicago, Illinois	1.24
Savannah, Georgia	1.22
Canton, Ohio	2.08

—Dr. M. S. Anderson

"Since garbage consists essentially of plant and animal products, it is well to take a look at a summary of the chemical compositions of such materials. Professor E. Truog and associates of the University of Wisconsin have compiled the percentage contents of the various elements normally found in whole plants. The values stated below are the percentages, dry basis, of usual occurrence, but are not necessarily average or limiting values.

Element	Amount Present, Dry Basis (per cent)
Carbon	45
Oxygen	43
Hydrogen	6
Nitrogen	1–3
Phosphorus	0.05–1.5
Sulphur	0.05–1.5
Potassium	0.3 –6.0
Calcium	0.0 –3.5
Magnesium	0.05–0.7

"Minor elements are designated below as parts per million (p.pm.).

Iron	10–1500
Manganese	5–1500
Zinc	3–150
Copper	2–75
Boron	2–75
Molybdenum	only a trace

"Somewhat less complete data covering the composition of meat products are available through the American Meat Institute. The approximate percentages of several elements in meat are as follows:

Element	Content in Whole Plant (per cent)
Nitrogen	6.8
Phosphorus	.5
Potassium	.8
Calcium	.03
Iron	.01

"Bones are of much higher phosphorus and calcium content than meat, about 10 per cent phosphorus and 23 per cent calcium. The nitrogen content is about 4 per cent.

"Chemical composition of garbage varies widely because of the constituent materials, their quantity and composition. On a dry basis, raw garbage contains about two per cent nitrogen, two per cent phosphoric oxide (P_2O_5), and one per cent potash (K_2O). The national annual plant nutrient supply in urban garbage is probably about 50,000 tons each of nitrogen and phosphoric oxide and about 25,000 tons of potash. These are sizeable tonnages but represent only small percentages of the total plant nutrients consumed as fertilizers in the United States. They correspond to about 2.5 per cent of the national consumption of fertilizer nitrogen, 2.2 per cent of the available phosphoric oxide and 1.3 per cent of the potash.

"The compositions of various composts derived from garbage and from garbage mixed with other waste organic materials have been reported. The wide differences shown in composition are probably due in part to variations inherent in the garbage used, in part to composting method and duration of decomposition, and in part to conditions of storage after preparation.

"Garbage composts usually contain 1 to 2 per cent of nitrogen. It is possible, however, to reach somewhat higher nitrogen levels. Unpublished data from varied sources covering 98 samples of experimental and commercial composts showed nitrogen contents grouped as follows:

Less than 1 per cent .... 36 samples
1 to 2 per cent .... 38 samples
2 to 3 per cent .... 20 samples
More than 3 per cent .... 4 samples

"The inadequacy of the present knowledge of the composition and behavior of garbage composts made it desirable to collect for study some composts prepared by various methods in different parts of the United States.

"The ranges of values for constituents are wide: nitrogen varies from 0.44 to 4.11 per cent, phosphoric oxide 0.42 to 2.98, potassium oxide 0.22 to 2.50 and ash 13.0 to 80.6 per cent. The pH range is 6.3 to 8.1.

"The ash contents of 8 of the 13 samples studied exceeded 65 per cent; two samples had ash value as low as about 13 per cent. It is apparent that a little soil or other mineral matter added to improve aeration or for other reasons, greatly increases the ash in the final product after much of the organic material has been decomposed. Material with an ash content as high as 65 per cent will be difficult to market as a commercial product; the organic fraction is too small.

"The secondary elements, calcium, magnesium and sulphur, and the minor elements, boron, copper, zinc, manganese and molybdenum, are not considered specifically in this study. It is recognized, however, that such materials are normally present in naturally-occurring organic materials. It may safely be assumed that minor elements are present in composts in variable quantities and that these constituents may be of some value when added to soils that are deficient. The order of magnitude of occurrence of these elements may be assumed to be a little greater than the values shown for whole plants. Oxidation of a part of the carbon compounds originally present would tend to increase the percentage of the remaining constituents."

Chemical Composition of Certain Composts Prepared Wholly or in Part from Garbage: Analyses Reported on Moisture-Free Basis

Sample No.	Location	Total Nitrogen (N)	Phosphoric Oxide (P_2O_5)	Potassium Oxide (K_2O)	Ash	pH
		per cent	per cent	per cent	per cent	
1	California	0.44	0.42	0.38	79.2	7.5
2	New York	1.47	2.25	1.63	72.0	7.6
3	Arizona	.83	.88	.76	73.0	7.2
4	Maryland	4.11	2.98	.69	31.5	6.8
5	Georgia	1.54	.70	.80	13.7	7.8
6	Pennsylvania	.63	1.10	.22	80.6	7.4
7	Oklahoma	.92	.60	.55	68.0	8.0
8	District of Columbia .	.98	.68	.82	75.8	7.2
9	New York	1.68	.87	.45	66.5	7.4
10	New York	.91	1.98	.65	78.0	6.3
11	East Lansing, Mich. .	3.33	2.31	1.56	34.6	6.8
12	Lansing, Mich.	2.64	2.22	2.50	26.5	8.1
13	Lansing, Mich.	2.23	.77	.70	13.0	7.3

Nitrification Characteristics of Certain Garbage Composts Incubated at 30°C. for 4 Periods

Sample No.	Location	Total Nitrogen (N)	Portion of Total Nitrogen Converted to Nitrate in—			
			3 Weeks	6 Weeks	8 Weeks	10 Weeks
		per cent	per cent	per cent	per cent	per cent
2	New York	1.47	0.16	0.22	0.24	0.25
3	Arizona	.83	.26	.41	2.00	4.02
4	Maryland	4.11	3.42	4.12	5.08	6.20
5	Georgia	1.54	.16	1.98	3.22	3.82
7	Oklahoma	.92	1.63	2.54	2.65	3.06
8	District of Columbia	.98	1.79	3.14	4.12	4.41
9	New York	1.68	2.59	3.24	3.82	4.12
10	New York	.91	3.90	5.03	6.15	7.18
11	Michigan	3.33	.55	1.17	1.19	1.22
12	Michigan	2.64	.17	.47	.61	.73
13	Michigan	2.23	1.68	3.62	5.17	6.08

—*Prepared by* M. S. ANDERSON,
Agricultural Research Service

DESCRIPTION OF SOME
U. S. COMPOSTING PLANTS

Arizona

Chimney Effect Composting

For 5 years, the U. S. Public Health Service operated a 12-ton-per-day composting plant at Chandler, Arizona.

The Arizona researchers found that decomposition in a heap was most active in an area 2 to 4 inches below the surface of the composting wastes and extending down 10 to 14 inches. Little decomposition took place toward the bottom center of the heap, since the temperature was low and the oxygen content was near zero.

Turning and mixing the material in the windrow did not solve the problem, according to the men in charge of the compost study, engineers Paul Maier, Edward Williams and George Mallison. The solution they did work out could be called "chimney effect" composting, since the gases within the compost pile, being warm—are lighter, and would tend to rise through the pile.

In order to get enough oxygen throughout the heap, materials to be composted were placed on elevated wire mesh racks instead of on the ground. As a result, air entered the heaps from below and created a natural upward draft. Careful inspection showed that the material in the heaps underwent a complete cycle of heating and cooling without turning, only an occasional sprinkling being required.

Results of Original Tests

During the preliminary experiments at Phoenix, more than 70,000 pounds of municipal refuse and other organic wastes were converted into a high grade compost. These tests indicated the following:

1. Compost could be produced consistently from municipal waste materials in 6 weeks by grinding, adjusting moisture and carbon-nitrogen ratio, placing the material in aerated bins and regrinding. (A wooden bin, 2½ feet wide, 6 feet long, and 4 feet deep, lined with hardware cloth, was most effective. A bin of similar dimensions but with *nonporous* sides *failed* to provide sufficient aeration.)

2. Raw sewage sludge can be used successfully as nitrogen supplement to help break down organic waste

Pictured above is the receiving apron, primary conveyor, grinder and electromagnetic metals separation unit of the plant built and operated by the U. S. Public Health Service at Chandler, Ariz. Research showed importance of "chimney effect."

materials; that is, the sludge was used to vary the carbon-nitrogen ratio. For example, raw garbage has 25 times as much carbon as it has nitrogen, or a carbon to nitrogen ratio of 25. However, most city garbage has a high content of paper and similar materials and therefore a correspondingly higher percentage of carbon to nitrogen. If these materials are to be broken down quickly, the nitrogen level must be increased, and the Arizona studies show that sludge can effectively do this. As mentioned before in this chapter, carbon to nitrogen ratio of 30 is about the most effective for optimum compost activity.

3. There were no objectionable odors at any time after grinding, and flies were not attracted to the end product.

Compost Plant Built

The success of the small-scale pilot experiments resulted in the building of a demonstration compost plant in Chandler, Arizona. Designed to handle about 70 tons of wastes per week, the Chandler plant was as satisfactory as the previous trials indicated.

At Purdue University's Twelfth Industrial Waste Conference, the heads of the Arizona compost project reported that the initial grinding of the garbage and other refuse produced materials of reasonably uniform size up to 3 or 4 inches. Glass is pulverized to a coarse, sand-like material, while cans and other ferrous metal are separated from the ground material by an electro-magnetic separator. A second grinding reduces the material to a finely ground, fluffy texture with almost all particles under one-half inch.

Data for processing of refuse showed a cost of $5.60 per ton for processing with a return of $2.30 per ton from salvage. Grinding processes which were developed seem to be satisfactory for aerobic composting. Operating costs for a larger 70-ton-per-day plant were estimated to be $1.75 per ton.

An experimental machine used for the project included a conveyor belt, a first-stage grinder which shreds tin cans, an electromagnet to remove the shredded tin cans and other metal, and a second-stage grinder which completes the process and drops the material into a truck. The material then was hauled to 15 aeration bins for decomposition. The compost was used experimentally at Arizona State University for fertilizer.

This Arizona plant was an experimental one, and is no longer being operated.

Dano Plant in California

A garbage composting plant has been operating in Sacramento, California under the direction of Dr. Ralph Scovel, president of Dano of America, Inc., 2206 K. Street, Sacramento. The plant has been successfully processing about 30 tons of mixed refuse per day collected in the Sacramento area since October, 1956.

At the Sacramento plant, garbage trucks dump refuse directly onto a conveyor system, where a salvage operation is performed. The remaining refuse, frequently containing as high as 60 per cent paper, is mechanically conveyed to a large (about 80 feet long, 10½ feet diameter), slowly rotating drum called a bio-stabilizer.

As the drum rotates, water and air are introduced. This action thoroughly mixes the refuse and keeps it aerated; grinding also takes place; temperatures up to 140 degrees are rapidly reached. After 24 hours in the bio-stabilizer, the "green compost" is loaded directly into large trailer trucks equipped with manure spreaders. This compost is then spread on low-

Here is the main unit of the garbage composting plant in Sacramento, California, which uses the Dano method. Garbage trucks dump refuse onto a conveyor which takes the material into a large, slowly rotating drum where it stays for 24 hours.

quality soil where the final stages of decomposition take place.

Reports Dr. Scovel: "Full scale experiments have also been conducted using hundreds of tons of digested sewage sludge, animal manures, grass, garden trimmings and cannery wastes, in each case mixed with refuse from residential areas. The results show that any and all organic wastes can be successfully composted, which agrees with the findings of other investigators."

Following is an analysis of the DANO compost made by a San Francisco Laboratory:

Analysis of the Glass-Free Sample on a 15 Per Cent Moisture Basis

Total nitrogen (N), per cent	1.31
Total phosphoric acid (P_2O_5), per cent	1.73
Insoluble phosphoric acid (P_2O_5), per cent	0.15
Available phosphoric acid (P_2O_5), per cent	1.58
Total potash (K_2O), per cent	0.58
Water soluble potash (K_2O), per cent	0.53
pH value (1:9 solution)	6.4
Organic matter, per cent	59.0
Carbon/Nitrogen ratio	26

Minerals on Glass- and Silica-Free Sample

Matter insoluble in acid, per cent 10.1
Calcium (Ca), per cent 2.53
Alumina (A1203), per cent 4.60
Iron oxide (Fe203), per cent 1.31
Sulfates (SO4), per cent 0.41
Chlorides (C1), per cent 0.48
Iodide (I), p.p.m. 2.5

Additional Metals Found by Qualitative Spectographic Analysis

Listed in Approximate Order of Magnitude			
0.05 to 0.5 per cent	*0.005 to 0.05 per cent*	*Less than 0.005 per cent*	
Magnesium	Titanium	Copper	Strontium
Sodium	Manganese	Cobalt	Vanadium
	Molybdenum	Zinc	Chromium
	Lead	Tin	Bismuth
		Boron	Nickel

Compost Corporation of America

In the early 1950's, the Compost Corporation of America developed a 5-stage operation for large scale municipal and industrial composting.

As originally designed, refuse was to flow mechanically from unloading stage throughout other steps. After sorting, the garbage was blended with other available organic materials. The material was then formed into windrowed piles upon the ground in the open where it remains for fermentation and stabilization.

This phase of the operation was specifically designed to utilize other municipal and industrial organic waste, such as waste from food processing, meat packing, breweries, and other industries. By combining these other organic materials with the garbage, the problem of their sanitary disposal would also be solved. It was possible as well to utilize sewage solids in either a digested or an undigested state.

Fermentation by the COM-CO Process was partially aerobic. It took place in the long windrowed piles that are out in the open, upon unimproved land. Fermentation period was between 18 to 24 days. During this time, organic matter

This is part of the composting units at Williamston, Michigan, where sewage and garbage have been converted to a soil conditioner. Each of the two composting units has 8 chambers, with a capacity of 6 cubic yards each (or about 4½ tons).

is completely stabilized with temperatures as high as 80 degrees Centigrade. This long period of fermentation at high temperatures purifies the materials, preventing the passing of diseased organisms.

According to COM-CO estimates, each installation required approximately 1.5 acres of land per 100 tons per day of incoming refuse plus two acres for plant and buildings.

The mixed garbage was dumped on the concrete floor, where it was shoved on the elevating conveyor, passed the magnet and blower to the sorting area. Here bottles and other noncompostables were removed.

On an open air dirt platform, soil and manure were added to the garbage. Percentages varied from 5 to 10 per cent for soil added and from 10 to 25 per cent of manure added.

Then the mix went to a grinder where it was chopped into pieces averaging about one inch in size. Just before entering the grinder, it was sprayed with a bacterial spray in concentrations of one ounce of spray per ton of mix. The spray, prepared by Dr. E. E. Pfeiffer of Spring Valley, N. Y., was said to contain 32 kinds of bacteria particularly adaptable to garbage decomposition.

The chopped and sprayed mix was spread in rows. Under normal weather conditions, it thoroughly composts in 3 weeks with one turning. During the process it reaches a temperature of 160 degrees Fahrenheit.

Final step in the process was to dehydrate the compost, pelletize it and package it for sale. Another screening took out glass and metal bits not removed in the original sorting process. This plant is no longer in operation.

Michigan

Under the direction of the Sanitary Disposal Corporation of Lansing, Michigan, a plant to convert garbage and sewage sludge into compost was built in 1956 in Willamston, Michigan.

The compost is made from garbage, including a considerable amount of corn cobs derived from a local grain elevator, combined with undigested sewage solids from settlement tanks dewatered to a cake of about 65 per cent moisture. The contents are ground, then conveyed by tube to the top of 4 double sets of steel chambers (8 in all), each holding 5 tons. The temperature attained is 125 degrees Fahrenheit. The composting period is 21 days, and the material is re-ground on leaving the chambers.

Oklahoma

The Naturizer Company of Norman, Oklahoma, under the direction of Norman Pierson and Howard Furlong, has set up a composting plant which produces 10 tons daily. Source of supply is the refuse hauled to the plant site by the city of Norman Sanitation Trucks.

As the plant originally was set up, the city trash trucks dump the refuse in long windrows, 4 or 5 feet high. A culture of bacteria is sprayed upon the windrow, and the mound is then wet down. The outside is kept damp during the processing. Within 36 hours the bacteria have gone to work and the temperature of the pile has risen to about 160 degrees. The piles are turned every 4 or 5 days, bulldozers shoving the material and churning it up thoroughly. The outside must be kept damp; still there must not be enough water to make the mound soggy.

The windrow system did not prove to be efficient enough to meet the needs of a city for disposal. The composting time was long (3 weeks or more), which made it unfeasible in terms of space requirements for a city of any size. The turning necessary for aeration was expensive and the exposed windrows were much influenced by weather conditions. Since grinding and salvage were not used, the amount of undecomposable material (glass, plastics, metal, rubber, etc.), ran as high as 60 per cent. There was also concern on the part of the Health Department as to whether or not all of the material was subjected to the heat necessary to kill pathogens.

In order to offset these disadvantages, a completely enclosed, continuous flow, mechanical system incorporating a digester was developed and tested. Individual units of machinery have been in operation for 2½ years at the plant in Norman and a pilot plant using the complete process has been in operation since November of 1955.

The flow of refuse through the plant goes through 4 phases. The first is Receiving and Salvage. The trucks dump unsegregated refuse into a hopper at ground level. The material goes by conveyor into an enclosed storage bin, large enough to handle a day's intake if necessary. This hopper is equipped with automatic fire controls as well as drainage to facilitate cleaning. From this bin, the material is fed onto a picking belt where salvageable items (corrugated cardboard, metal, rags, etc.), are removed. Large undecomposable items, such as tree stumps, refrigerators, tires, etc., are also taken out at this point. There is space provided for processing the salvage and for automatic loading facilities. The corrugated cardboard is automatically shredded and baled with a unit designed by the Company.

The next phase is Grinding and Mixing. The grinding machinery was developed through Company research.

At this point in the process, raw sewage solids, digested sewage sludge, and/or wet garbage may be used as a moistening agent for the dry refuse. Although not essential, since water may be used instead, these wastes increase the speed of composting and improve the quality of the end product.

From the grinder the refuse goes by bucket conveyor into the top row of cells in the digester for the decomposition phase of the process. This machinery was also developed by the company. It is in these cells that the actual bacteriological reduction takes place. For maximum bacterial action they are designed to give control over moisture and temperature and provide daily aeration—automatically.

The composting material stays in the digester 6 days, for 4 of which the temperature in the cells is higher than necessary for the sterilization of plant and animal pathogens. This temperature assures the absence of larvae and weed seeds in the finished product.

Aeration of the composting material is assured by dropping the material daily from one cell to the next, immediately below it. At the end of 3 days, the material is fed through a grinder similar in design to the primary grinder. This second grinding further reduces the aggregate size and opens up new surfaces for bacterial action.

At the end of an additional 3 days of composting the material has lost its original identity and is similar in appearance to well-rotted cow manure. It is conveyed from the last row of digesters through a final grinder. This final grinding allows almost all of the composted material to pass through screens. With this process less than 10 per cent of the incoming refuse is unsalable either as salvage or product.

The final phase is similar to the system worked out by the Company in its production of Naturizer during the last 3 years. This phase of the process covers Screening, Bagging, and Storage. Finished compost has unique characteristics which require special consideration for screening and bagging. The sales of the finished product are seasonal. The material stores very well in the open and since drying facilities are provided, it may be stored until needed for bagging during peak seasons.

It was estimated that for a plant with a capacity of 150 tons per day (incoming refuse), the cost would be approximately $2,500.00 per ton of rated capacity. This includes all of the necessary machinery and equipment as well as an attractive building and office. The land requirements, not included in this cost, are approximately 4 acres, which includes the office and plant site as well as storage area.

The cost per ton to produce a salable compost was estimated at $3.04. This included labor, fuel, building and machinery repair, state and city taxes, and certain miscellaneous items. It also included the labor and maintenance costs of the salvage operation.

682

Depending upon the market in a given location, the salvage operation alone is expected to return more than $3.00 per ton of incoming refuse. The return from the sale of the finished product could be used to amortize the initial cost of the building and machinery and to pay a return to the city or private group operating such a plant.

The retail price on the Naturizer produced is $70.00 per ton, bagged, and $27.50 per ton, bulk, f.o.b. the plant. At these prices it has not been economically feasible to use this product for field application, but has been used extensively by greenhouses and nurseries, and by homeowners for lawns and flowers.

Pennsylvania

In the mid-1950's, the Organic Corporation of America set up a composting plant in McKeesport, Pennsylvania, which was only in operation for a short time.

Here is how the McKeesport plant operated:

Garbage and rubbish, all picked up in one operation, were hauled to the plant and dumped through a chute onto an oscillating steel conveyor. Fifteen feet long and 4 feet wide, this conveyor was made by the Link Belt Company. This distributes the material evenly and passed under large magnets which extracted heavy scrap metals for salvage.

The garbage, still containing bottles, tin cans, paper, and other trash, then passed into a primary grinder and then a secondary grinder. (Both the grinders were built by the Gruendler Crusher and Pulverizer Company of St. Louis.)

The McKeesport plant was said to be capable of handling 150 tons of garbage during an 8-hour shift.

However, management difficulties appeared to be as much of a handicap as engineering troubles in the closing down of the plant.

STUDY AT BATON ROUGE

The following report is a summary of a detailed engineering study of refuse disposal for the city of Baton Rouge, Louisiana. The study was conducted by Michigan Associates of Lansing.

"*Baton Rouge's* 3 incinerators, totaling 60 tons per day capacity, were so overloaded that in 1946, they were abandoned in favor of the sanitary landfill method of disposal. It is estimated that the existing 4 disposal areas will soon be full, or otherwise unavailable, necessitating new means of refuse disposal.

"The purpose of this report is to study possible methods of disposal with special emphasis on 3; namely, sanitary land-fill, incineration and composting. Collection costs for each method of disposal are also studied so that both collection and disposal costs are taken into consideration. Recommendations are made for new refuse collection and disposal methods that may be adopted for the city of Baton Rouge.

Solution in Composting

". . . For 1960, it is considered that one 400 tons per day plant be located at Valley Park. This plant would be expected to receive 295 tons per day of raw material and would cost $1,511,640. In 1980, it is considered that a 240 tons per day plant be located at the corner of Airline Highway and Green-well Street, and which would receive 240 tons per day. The remainder of the material, or approximately 342 tons per day would, in 1980, be handled at the 400 tons per day plant at the Valley Park location. The total cost of the two plants would be $2,425,165. Amortization costs are assumed at 4 per cent over 20 years for the building, over 12 years for the fixed machinery, over 8 years for the mobile machinery, and over 6 years for the trucks. It is also estimated that about 30 per cent shrinkage in weight takes place between the Baton Rouge raw material and the finished compost during the composting process.

"The actual value of compost as a fertilizer and soil conditioner is estimated between $20.00 and $40.00 per ton, but has been assumed at a conservative value of $5.00 per ton for purposes of this study. The Louisiana Farm Cooperatives, Inc. have expressed interest in the total plant output at a unit price approximating $5.00 per ton.

"A study of the economics of salvage indicates that the salvaging of cotton and wool rags, plus ferrous and non-ferrous metals is profitable, and that the salvaging of tin cans is questionable under present market conditions.

"The summary of costs, revenues, and net profits expected for the composting process is given as follows:

684

Condition	1 Plant Handling 295 Tons Per Day For 1960 Conditions		1 Plant Handling 400 Tons Per Day For 1967 Conditions		2 Plants Handling 582 Tons Per Day For 1980 Conditions	
	Yearly Costs	Costs Per Ton	Yearly Costs	Costs Per Ton	Yearly Costs	Costs Per Ton
Amortization ..	$148,870.	$1.619	$153,495.	$1.230	$206,810.	$1.137
Operation and Maintenance .	99,660.	1.084	151,210.	1.212	240,797.	1.324
Revenue from Compost	321,748.+	3.500	436,800.+	3.500+	636,311.+	3.500+
Revenue from Salvage	11,717.+	.127+	15,907.+	.127+	23,172.+	.127+
Revenue from Private Dumping	7,578.+	.082+	10,288.+	.082+	14,980.+	.082+
Profit Expected .	$ 92,513.+	$1.006+	$158,290.+	$1.267+	$226,856.+	$1.248+

Note: "+" indicates profit.

"On the basis of disposal costs alone, it may be concluded that composting is far superior to either landfill or incineration. Final conclusions, however, must be based on the overall collection plus disposal costs rather than disposal costs alone.

"Comparisons of the costs of the 3 methods of disposal, including the costs of pickup and haul, are summarized for the 1960 conditions as follows:

Method	Sanitary Landfill		Incineration		Composting	
	Yearly Costs	Costs Per Ton	Yearly Costs	Costs Per Ton	Yearly Costs	Costs Per Ton
Pickup Costs	$ 500,872.	$ 5.487	$500,872.	$5.487	$500,872.	$5.487
Haul Costs	506,874.	5.553	200,561.	2.197	216,373.	2.370
All Disposal Costs ...	135,278.	1.027	234,058.	1.777	40,669.+	0.307+
Total Costs	1,143,024.	12.067	935,491.	9.461	676,576.	7.550

"Similar comparative costs exist for the 1980 conditions.

"The conclusions drawn from a study of the tabulated comparative costs is that composting is the most economical method which can be adopted by the city of Baton Rouge. Composting will save approximately $258,915. per year, as compared to incineration, and $466,448. per year, as compared with sanitary landfill for the 1960 conditions. The savings would about double by 1980.

"Composting is recommended as the method which should be adopted by the city of Baton Rouge as the means of disposal of the municipal garbage and trash. A 400 ton plant at Valley Park should be constructed immediately while a second 240 ton plant is estimated as being required about 1967."

Number on Drawing Board

While the number of existing composting plants are limited, it is encouraging to note that there are a fairly large number of modern municipal composting plants being planned currently. Thus more information should be available soon.

CALIFORNIA SANITARY ENGINEERING PROJECT

As a part of an overall study of municipal refuse collection and disposal in California, the Sanitary Engineering Projects of the University of California conducted a search of literature and series of laboratory and field scale investigations of the composting of municipal refuse and other wastes. The principal findings and conclusions obtained from these studies and from an analysis of the data obtained are summarized as follows:

1. Throughout the world there exists a great interest in composting; and within the United States there is an increasing awareness of the need for reclaiming instead of destroying organic matter.

2. Intensive farming exhausts the organic constituents of the soil unless humus is added. Humus such as might be obtained from the composting of municipal refuse benefits the soil by:

(a) Improving soil structure

(b) Increasing moisture holding capacity

(c) Preventing leaching of soluble inorganic nitrogen

(d) Making phosphorus more readily available to growing plants

(e) Increasing buffer capacity of the soil

(f) Adding nutrients, especially nitrogen, phosphorus, and potassium, as well as essential trace elements.

3. Reclamation of municipal refuse by composting might offer a logical solution to some of California's problems by:

(a) Providing humus needed by heavy or formerly arid soils, the large scale farming of which is fundamental to the State's prosperity.

(b) Offering a new method of refuse disposal where population growth has taxed the capacity of existing landfill disposal sites; smog has caused a re-examination of the practice of incineration; or increasing standards of sanitation and public health make present practices unsatisfactory.

4. Historically, composting has been motivated by man's search for food rather than by his need for getting rid of his refuse. In America the latter problem has been of more immediate concern. This explains why composting of municipal refuse has been practiced in Europe for some time without spreading to the United States as did water and sewage treatment.

5. Successful European methods are not directly applicable to the United States because of:

(a) Dissimilarity in the nature of refuse to be composted.

(b) Difference in psychology of the public with respect to space, time, mechanization, and need and use of the product.

6. Traditional methods of composting involve a combination anaerobic-aerobic process which requires long periods for decomposition, often accompanied by aesthetic nuisances. Modern methods made use of the rapid, nuisance free decomposition of organic matter thermophilic, facultatively aerobic microorganisms.

7. The practice of composting throughout the world has been largely an art rather than a science. In the United States fundamental studies of the decomposition of organic matter had been made but their engineering applications to the composting of municipal refuse were unexplored.

8. Promotion of municipal composting in the United States has been generally directed toward the sale of patented cells, digesters, and secret processes rather than to the production and sale of compost.

9. Factors held by various proponents of composting to be essential to the process include inoculation with special organisms, seeding with manure or partially decomposed organic matter, recirculation of liquids and gases, forced aeration, and addition of enzymes and hormones.

10. The factors fundamental to composting are those fundamental to any aerobic biological process: initial population of microorganisms; available nutrients, temperature, hydrogen ion concentration, moisture, and aeration.

11. Microorganisms are indigenous to municipal refuse in such great numbers as to make inoculation entirely superfluous.

12. Seeding of municipal refuse with horse manure in amounts up to 30 per cent of the total weight produce no beneficial effect on the rate of decomposition.

13. Recycling of partially composted material has no measurable effect on the composting process.

14. The addition of soil for the purpose of inoculating a compost of municipal refuse is of no demonstrable value.

15. Neither of two commercially produced inoculums tried improved the process in any respect.

16. Facultative and obligate bacteria, actinomycetes, and fungi are most active in the composting process. Apparently thermophilic bacteria play a major role in decomposing protein and other readily broken down organic material; actinomycetes in decomposing cellulose and lignin compounds; and fungi, being limited by temperature, play a lesser role.

17. Shredding accomplishes mixing and aeration and facilitates bacterial invasion of refuse by breaking down natural barriers, and exposing greater surface to attack.

18. Normal city refuse contains nutrients sufficient for rapid aerobic composting.

19. The rate of decomposition is a function of the carbon-nitrogen ratio of a refuse. The higher the C/N ratio the greater the length of time required for composting.

20. In a typical compost of municipal refuse the temperature rises to 50 degrees centigrade within one day and to more than 60 degrees centigrade in 2 to 3 days. In small piles the rise is somewhat slower, often discontinuous during the transition from mesophilic to thermophilic populations.

21. A maximum temperature of 73 degrees to 75 degrees centigrade is attained during the composting process—sufficient to kill pathogens, and flies in all stages of development.

22. Heat lost in the process of turning a compost is regained in 2 to 12 hours, depending upon the size of pile and the stage of decomposition at time of turning.

23. Hydrogen ion concentration is not limiting in the composting of combined municipal refuse.

24. In materials having a pH of 5.5 or less, which is below that of typical city refuse, calcium carbonate will raise the pH slightly during the initial stages of decomposition. Any

beneficial effect on degree of decomposition which may result from adding calcium carbonate is out-weighed by a serious loss of valuable nitrogen.

25. The organisms involved in aerobic composting require relatively small amounts of oxygen, although more than can be supplied by simple diffusion into the pile. Turning appears to be the best practical method, as forced aeration drys the material excessively, short circuits, and involves excessive costs.

26. The fundamental steps of a rapid, aesthetically acceptable, reliable, and economical method of composting include segregating, grinding, stacking, turning, and regrinding. The course of the process and the time required are determined by moisture content, aeration and the C/N ratio. Controls include moisture adjustment and frequency of turning and require a knowledge of how to judge the condition of compost by temperature, odor, color, physical appearance, and laboratory tests.

27. Some degree of segregation is prerequisite to the grinding of municipal refuse. Tin cans, miscellaneous metals, glass and ceramics, rocks, etc., should be removed either at the household or at the disposal site.

28. The compostable fraction of municipal refuse, as observed at Berkeley is 66 per cent. This is in general agreement with analyses previously made in other California cities.

29. Grinding of refuse is necessary for rapid aerobic composting. It renders the material susceptible to bacterial invasion, makes it homogeneous and provides a beneficial initial aeration. It may be that a mixing device might be developed which would adequately break up certain types of refuse at less cost than an initial grinding.

30. The aim of grinding is to chop refuse into small pieces. There are no special size requirements, but the material must not be pulped lest it become too soggy to compost. If a hammermill is used, a 1½-inch screen opening should be about the minimum.

31. Municipal refuse is extremely abrasive, and equipment specially to grinding it has not been developed in the United States.

32. Ground refuse may be composted in windrows. The maximum height of pile should probably not exceed 5 or 6

feet to avoid compaction. The minimum height of pile to maintain good insulating properties is about 4 feet. The maximum width of pile should be about 10 feet although it is not critical and may depend upon the method of turning used.

33. Composting of municipal refuse may be done in the open in dry climates. Investigations are needed to determine the best procedure under rainy conditions.

34. Ambient temperatures common in California have no apparent effect in reducing the temperatures within a compost pile. Berkeley studies showed that wind, likewise, had little effect.

35. Turning a compost accomplishes aeration, insures uniform decomposition, and exposes all pathogens and insect larvae to lethal temperatures inside the pile.

36. Turning should be done on about the third day after grinding and repeated at intervals thereafter, depending on the moisture content and structure of material.

37. If a compost becomes anaerobic, it should be turned daily until aerobic conditions are restored.

38. Equipment especially adopted to turning compost has not been developed. Such equipment should be self-propelled and designed to turn the outer shell of the pile into the interior.

39. The moisture content for good composting depends upon the nature of the material. For municipal refuse it lies between 40 and 65 per cent. The moisture content of mixed Berkeley refuse after grinding averaged 49 per cent.

40. Excessive moisture content may be reduced by daily turning or by the addition of straw, soil, paper, etc. Turning seems the most practical method, as additives are expensive to apply, lower the quality of the product by dilution or by raising the C/N ratio, and are less effective than turning.

41. For rapid composting without loss of nitrogen a C/N ratio of 30–35 is needed. A C/N ratio above 50 slows the process and lowers the quality of the finished compost. At C/N ratios below 30 nitrogen is lost. The C/N ratio of mixed Berkeley refuse averaged 33.

42. The C/N ratio of refuse may be decreased by removing paper or adding soil, or increased by adding paper or straw.

43. The course of a normal compost is characterized by
(a) A rapid rise in temperature, followed by a leveling off and

690

slow decline without appreciable fluctuations; (b) no putrefactive odors; (c) a progressively darkening color.

44. The onset of anaerobiosis may be recognized by (a) a sudden drop in temperature; (b) putrefactive odors; (c) a pale green color in the interior of the pile.

45. Anaerobic conditions can not be prevented by normal turning schedules when moisture content is excessive. Reducing the moisture content by daily turning will, however, overcome anaerobic conditions.

46. A compost is nearing completion when its temperature begins a steady decline. Finished compost is characterized by:

(a) Dark gray or dark brown color,

(b) Neutral, slightly musty, or earthy odor,

(c) A C/N ratio of 20 or less—or more if carbon is in a difficultly available form.

47. The time required for composting varied from about 12 days, for a C/N ratio of 20, to about 21 days for a C/N ratio of 78.

48. Regrinding of finished compost makes it more uniform in texture, improves its appearance, and increases the ease of applying it to the soil.

49. Municipal refuse composts readily with either raw or digested sewage sludge, the permissible amount of sludge depending upon the moisture content of both sludge and refuse. The effect is to increase the nitrogen in the final product.

50. Composting of cannery wastes with municipal refuse seems to offer a promising solution to the problem of disposal.

51. Composting of municipal refuse in the open will not create a fly nuisance.

52. Composting of municipal refuse has not been put on a commercial basis in the United States. Until more is learned from practical operations all estimates of the economic feasibility of composting are of quite limited accuracy.

53. Any appreciable production of compost in California would presumably have to be marketed to large scale agriculturists and there is little evidence by which to estimate their reaction to the product.

54. Market development beyond specialty gardeners and nurserymen can not be expected to precede the availability

of a firm supply of compost. Hence the first cities going into composting on a municipal basis may have to take certain market risks.

55. Agricultural acceptance of compost will depend upon the economy with which it can be purchased and applied to the soil. The development of special agricultural machinery for spreading compost will await its availability in quantity.

56. There would seem to be a good possibility for risk capital in the composting business, provided private enterprise can secure proper rights to public-owned refuse.

57. Composted municipal refuse will probably have to sell on its considerable merits as a soil conditioner rather than as a commercial fertilizer after being fertilized.

58. With the development of equipment especially suited to the handling of municipal refuse, and further studies of the economics involved, composting represents a very hopeful method for reclaiming municipal refuse while producing a product immensely valuable to agriculture.

ENGINEERING ASPECTS OF HIGH-RATE COMPOSTING

The following report, prepared by Dr. Snell, is designed to summarize information on high-rate composting which may be of interest to engineers. It is a portion of a paper presented by Dr. Snell before a meeting of the American Society of Civil Engineers:

In order that the engineer might have a basis for comparison with methods and processes familiar to him, high-rate composting might be compared to anaerobic sludge digestion and to the activated sludge process. The comparison with conventional methods may seem unfair because composting takes place with organic matter in a much more concentrated form than does conventional sewage sludge; however, it does give some basis for evaluating the composting process.

Anaerobic Sludge Digestion versus Composting

For digestion at 90 degrees Fahrenheit (25 days detention) mixed primary and activated sludge require a minimum of 1.0 cubic feet of digester capacity per capita or 100,000 cubic feet for that same population. The per capita sludge gas production is about 1.25 cubic feet per day and about 0.50

cubic feet of this would be required to heat the digestion tanks themselves. Estimating 650 BTU's per cubic feet for sludge gas—the value of the 0.75 cubic feet of excess gas per capita per day is 0.049 cents (based on an average commercial rate for natural gas with 1,000 BTU's cubic feet and costing 10 cents per 100 cubic feet). For 100,000 people the excess gas is worth about $50 per day or $18,000 per year.

For high-rate composting the same quantity of sludge dewatered to 55–60 per cent solids in a highly porous condition would weigh about 30–35 pounds per cubic feet and would occupy only about 0.015 cubic feet per capita or 1,500 cubic feet per 100,000 population. For a 4 day composting digestion cycle 6,000 cubic feet or only 6 per cent of the storage volume required for anaerobic digestion is required.

The value of the end product (at $20 per ton with 20 per cent moisture) is

$$\frac{1,500 \times 32.5 \times 42.5}{2,000 \times 80.0} \times \$20 = \$260$$

for the 13 tons produced per day or $95,000 per year. These figures are given only to show that the loss of gas production in switching from anaerobic digestion to composting is compensated for several times over by sale of the end product. The relative cost of operation should be comparable and capital cost of the plants should be considerably less for the high-rate composting.

Activated Sludge Process versus Composting

Although the conventional high-rate composting process is adaptable only to porous solid wastes a comparison to the activated sludge process will be valuable to the engineers, especially those who would advocate "burning up" of most of the organic matter in the aeration tank and omitting the final sedimentation tank.

Since the rate of flow of air greatly affects any activated sludge figures, 3 rates 6, 12, and 18 cubic feet per minute per 1,000 cubic feet of volume have been selected. Figures are calculated from Mr. H. R. King's article (23) and are for a 10 per cent air diffuser plate area and a 15 foot depth. Power figures are based on a 65 per cent compressor efficiency and 1.25 pound line loss.

For the high-rate compost process, calculations are based on a 4 foot depth of material with forced air (3 inch water head loss). Optimum moisture content of 55 per cent is used with an O_2 utilization rate of 0.0244 grams O_2 per 100 grams dry weight per minute or 366 pounds oxygen per hour per 1,000 cubic feet (at 25 pounds compost cubic foot). The calculation also assumes 50 per cent oxygen utilization from the air.

From a study of Table 1, it is evident that the power requirements of composting are 1.0–1.5 per cent of that for activated sludge and that the rate of oxygen utilization on a volume or ppm basis is 100 to 300 times as great. Oxygen utilization on a dry solids weight basis is very comparable however.

These comparison values are given only to stimulate interest in the possibilities of the high-rate composting and are not given as design criteria.

Table 1.

Comparison of Activated Sludge Process with High-Rate Composting

	Air Flow Rate CFM/ 1000 cu. ft.	Activated Sludge Process	High Rate Composting	Comp. Ratio: Act. S.
Watt Hours Power per pound O_2 Absorbed (22)	6	140	Without Stirring	.009
	12	160	1.2	
	18	170	With Stirring 2.5	.015
Oxygen Absorbed ppm/hour	6	23		290
	12	40	6,600	165
	18	55		120
Oxygen Absorbed lbs./hr./1000 cu. ft.	6	1.4		260
	12	2.5	366	150
	18	3.5		105
Oxygen Absorbed lbs. O_2/100 lbs./hr.	3000 ppm (at 12 CFM)	.004	(55% Moist) .66	165
	Dry wt. (at 12 CFM)	1.33	Dry wt. 1.46	1.1
	% of dry wt./day (at 12 CFM)	32%	% of dry wt./day 35	1.1

Description of M.S.U. Experimental Facilities

The various phases of the Michigan State University composting research, although closely correlated and inter-related, were separated into 3 general areas.

1. Basic laboratory research.
2. Experimental continuous flow pilot plant.
3. Experimental windrow composting.

Briefly, the pilot plant consisted of a large grinder, a storage tank and an 8 level, 10 foot diameter vertical type digester modified, for research purposes, from the basic Earp-Thomas type design. The plant started by using the storage hopper as a crude dewatering tank for the raw garbage and ended by employing a continuous flow dewatering press. The rather unsatisfactory bucket conveyor was replaced with a screw and a tubular conveyor. The plant, under satisfactory operating conditions, handled 3 to 5 tons of ground separated domestic garbage daily. A proto-type Crane digester of about one-half ton per day capacity was tested and improved over a 9 month period. Except for mechanical breakdowns and mechanical changes the pilot plant ran from July 1953 until September 1955 and during these periods the 3 to 5 tons per day of separated domestic garbage from East Lansing was handled at the plant.

The windrow operation included 3 main areas of interest; (a) composting of ground garbage in air-tight insulated 50-gallon drums in which the material was removed and shredded periodically, and in which air flow was recorded, and oxygen utilization and carbon dioxide production and other measurements and tests were conducted, (b) small outdoor windrow piles of about 1 to 4 cubic yards, (c) composting in windrows of about 300 tons of garbage using a front-end loader and a large shredder. Oxygen and carbon dioxide studies were made with probes and control tests run on both these series of experiments.

The basic laboratory studies were designed after some understanding of composting was gained from preliminary windrow and pilot plant studies. The resulting laboratory unit was designed to give constant stirring (1/5 r.p.m.) under constant and controlled conditions. Twenty-two of these one pound plastic digesters were constructed in early 1954 and have been used in many series of experiments. In addition to oxygen utilization and carbon dioxide production measurements, many other chemical and bacteriological tests were run to determine the rate and degree of aerobic decomposition at various temperatures and moisture conditions.

The laboratory studies also included studies on permeability and the rate of diffusion of oxygen into ground garbage under various conditions. Also included was a special emphasis on determination of suitable yardsticks and basic bacteriological studies.

Essential Criteria to Obtain Maximum High-Rate Composting

In order that an organic waste material may be stabilized rapidly (2 to 4 days) the following criteria are considered, by the author, to be essential:

(a) Material should have a C/N ratio of 50:1 or less and have no serious deficiency of essential foods and be within normal pH range (5.5–8.0).

(b) Material should be finely ground.

(c) Moisture should be controlled to 50 to 60 per cent throughout the process.

(d) Recycling of seed compost (2 to 10 per cent of very active partially composted material).

(e) Constant slow stirring or intermediate stirring every 5 to 10 minutes.

(f) Air should reach all parts of the composting material with at least 50 per cent of the oxygen remaining.

(g) Temperature should be controlled throughout the process.

(h) The pH should be prevented from going too high to prevent nitrogen loss.

(i) The process should be continuous flow in 3 or 4 stages including recycling of seed and thorough mixing for each stage. The last stage may combine slower digestion with natural drying from the produced heat.

It should be understood that complete breakdown does not occur during this period of 2 to 4 days. The putrescible protein and the sugars and a considerable proportion of the starches will break down leaving, almost untouched, the cellulose, woodfiber, lignin and other resistant materials. There may, however, be no need for further breakdown. Further decomposition can, in most instances, be accomplished more advantageously in the soil where plant growth will be benefited by the presence of soil organisms and by the end products of their metabolism.

Variables Studied and Those Requiring Further Study

Those who have had some experience with composting research will appreciate the difficulties in studying a dozen or more variables when the essentials of the overall process are not fully understood. It may be 10 to 20 years before there has been enough work to thoroughly understand the many variables and their relationship with one another. The difficulty of research becomes more obvious when it is stated that as far as is known all of the major essentials of high-rate composting have yet to be reproduced in a laboratory scale experiment.

The reason for this is the difficulty in handling, feeding, removing and measuring small quantities of ground, moist, solid organic material on a continuous flow or even an intermittent flow basis. Thus the M.S.U. laboratory digesters were of batch type. The only true high-rate experiments were conducted in the pilot plant when it was operated under controlled conditions and fully backed by the whole laboratory research personnel. The laboratory work was not true high-rate composting because batch runs have all the lag periods for bacterial population buildup for each stage. Even with this serious limitation the lab experiments were the most important phase of our research.

Of the 12 variables listed for study only two have been pursued intensively. These are: (1) *effect of per cent moisture* and (2) *effect of temperature* on the rate of composting. These will be discussed in some detail in succeeding paragraphs. Other variables, yet to be as scientifically explored, are discussed briefly as follows:

(3) pH: Normally, raw garbage is rather acid, pH 5.0–6.0. Although aerobic digestion proceeds reasonably well at this pH, adjustment to a slightly high pH gives evidence of speeding the process. As garbage digests the pH slowly rises until at the end of the process it reaches pH 8 or even 9. High pH

conditions and high nitrogen content will generally result in a substantial nitrogen loss. It is believed this loss can be prevented by controlling the pH and insuring an ample oxygen supply.

(4) *Oxygen Supply:* It is rather well accepted that only part of the oxygen required for digestion comes from the atmosphere and the remainder is obtained from the breakdown of organic compounds themselves. It can be readily demonstrated, however, that the process is greatly retarded by lack of the presence of some gaseous oxygen at all times. Without almost continuous movement of the digesting mass or forced air or both movement and forced air, it is practically impossible to fulfill this condition.

(5) *Carbon Dioxide Build-Up:* The importance of a high percentage of CO_2 in contact with the digesting mass has been pointed out by Eric Eweson but has not, as yet, been substantiated by others' work.

(6) *Ratio of Carbon to Nitrogen:* The importance of the ratio of carbon to nitrogen has long been understood and was recently substantiated by the University of California experiments. The importance is seen when it is understood that the microorganisms need the nitrogen to build up their population and that they need the carbon for energy. Waksman points out that a ratio of carbon to nitrogen of 30:1 is ideal for most microorganisms. As digestion proceeds carbon is converted into carbon dioxide and liberated, whereas nitrogen is stored in the protoplasm of the bodies of living organisms. If the conditions are not ideal and too much nitrogen is present some of it may be lost as nitrogen gas or as ammonia. When soil is mixed with completed compost with a carbon nitrogen ratio of 20 or less the compost should not temporarily rob the soil of its natural nitrogen. Generally richer wastes with lower carbon nitrogen ratios, say 50 or less, compost more rapidly than those with a higher ratio, say 50 or greater. The effective ratio of carbon to nitrogen controlling the rate of composting does not necessarily represent a carbon nitration ratio for the mixture as a whole but is more likely to represent the ratio in the material more readily digested.

(7, 8, 9) *Deficiencies in essential foods, fineness of grind and uniformity mixing* are all obviously important points to those understanding biological decomposition and will not be further commented on at this time. It will be some time yet before these finer points can be thoroughly investigated and evaluated. The effect of fine grinding is to speed up the process in that such grinding gives the microorganisms more surface area on which to grow. However, as will be seen later, fine grinding cuts down the porosity and thus the supply of oxygen through the material.

(10, 11, 12) *Seeding and Reseeding; Batch or continuous flow; and Stirring or Stationary:* With the limited data yet available these 3 subjects might best be lumped together for a brief general discussion. Although it has been demonstrated by both the University of California and Michigan State University that composting can be very satisfactorily accomplished without employing any special seeding cultures, it has not, however, been completely established whether these cultures do or do not have some merit. There is evidence to show that there is tremendous value in the inoculation of the raw garbage with substantial quantities of partially processed material in which the desired organisms are already predominant. Likewise, the marked rapidity of a continuous flow process as compared with the batch process has been demonstrated. Again, continuous or frequent intermittent stirring or mixing has an accelerating effect on the process. It is believed these phenomena can best be explained by the following hypothesis: The seeding and reseeding and the stirring which occurs in a continuous flow multistage process largely eliminates the lag periods required for the various biological populations to build up in the batch type of process. In each stage of digestion the physical and biochemical environment may be kept at an optimum and large masses of the most desirable microorganisms are present and continuously brought into contact with a supply of fresh food from the preceding stage of digestion. Thus the same work accomplished in a 2 to 3 week batch process can be effected in a 2 to 4 day continuous flow multistage stirring process if the proper environment is maintained and seeding and reseeding are practiced.

Yardsticks to Measure Degree and Rate of Composting

One of the present handicaps to the compost researcher today is the lack of an adequate yardstick for digestion. Men, long associated with the art of composting, have depended upon appearance, odor and feel of the end product to determine whether or not it has been properly composted. More scientific yardsticks are essential. It is not desirable to carry the digestion process too far because less organic material will then be available for enrichment of the soil. However, it is desired that the material be stabilized to the extent that upon being remoistened and piled (1) it will not over-heat (2) lose appreciable nitrogen (3) become offensive. The exact point during the digestion process at which all of these criteria are fulfilled is difficult to determine for routine work. It becomes highly desirable that a test be developed which can readily show exactly how far the digestion process has proceeded. Because of the wide variation in the nature of materials to be composted it is possible that no single criteria or yardstick can be used for all organic wastes.

For example, the change of pH during the normal course of digestion of garbage or animal manure from about pH 5–6 to 8–9 has proven to be a very useful yardstick. Other wastes with a high initial pH of about 8 have almost no change so under these conditions pH is useless as a yardstick.

Oxygen consumed and ash are considered the best primary practical yardsticks for degree of digestion, although pH and transmittance are good quick indirect methods when used as a routine control where their relationship with other yardsticks have been previously established. BOD is a useful yardstick but is more time consuming and offers certain laboratory problems.

Table 2.

Summary of Yardsticks to Determine Degree of Composting as Applied to Ground, Separated Garbage

Test	Used	Raw	Finished	Reliability
1	pH	5.0–6.0	8.0–9.0	Only indirectly related and not reliable
2	Chemical Oxygen Demand	—	—	85% reduction
3	Oxygen Consumed	—	—	25% reduction
4	Ash	10%	20%	Difficulty in obtaining representative samples
5	% Transmittance (6a)	70%	10%	Only indirectly related. Not reliable

The following 4 tests were tried by Mr. W. G. Turney but developed technical difficulties not readily overcome and until further work is done are not dependable yardsticks: (a) relative stability (b) BOD (c) chlorine demand (d) iodine demand.

Other less scientific but commonly used tests are (a) appearance (b) odor and (c) generation of heat.

During the composting process the material changes from a brown to a black and from a fibrous to a friable appearance. The odor of raw garbage may vary from rancid to putrid while that of well composted material has a slightly earthy or sometimes musty odor. Generation of heat as a yardstick is unreliable and depends on the degree of oxygen available, insulation, seeding, per cent moisture, pH, time, surrounding temperature, etc. It is possible that these variables may be studied and a reliable controlled test result but no definite conclusions should be drawn from this test at present. All but very old compost material will reheat. To carry the digestion process to the point where reheating will not occur may be impractical and perhaps undesirable. Development of a reheating test may also prove to give a quantitative answer on the momentary rate of digestion.

Yardsticks for rate of digestion which have proven useful are (1) oxygen utilization and (2) carbon dioxide production. For these yardsticks to be used on pilot scale of plant work may require the removal of a representative sample to a laboratory size digester where standard temperature can be maintained and adequate, continuous stirring provided. These two yardsticks have been the main method of measurement employed in most of the M.S.U. research. Carbon dioxide produced in these experiments was absorbed by bubbling through caustic before the oxygen utilization was measured directly by reduction in volume. The oxygen measurements are rather easy to make at frequent intervals whereas the carbon dioxide production requires titration of the caustin solution and replenishment each time. Unless this is done with utmost care, inaccurate results may be obtained.

On plant scale experiments oxygen uptake and carbon dioxide production can be reasonably well estimated by making air flow measurements and also frequent analysis of the exhaust gases. Such a procedure, when practical, is strongly recommended as a control in the operation of full scale plants.

Effect of Moisture

When the M.S.U. experimental work began it was known from the work of others that moisture was an important factor; yet little was it realized how critical a factor moisture was and how narrow the moisture range was for peak digestion rates. If the material is too dry—insufficient moisture exists for the metabolism of the microorganisms and if the material is too moist—the pore spaces are filled, the surface area reduced and the material becomes anaerobic because oxygen cannot penetrate as rapidly as it is required.

Ten M.S.U. experiments on composting ground garbage at moisture contents varying from 25 per cent to 68 per cent were set up in the one pound laboratory digesters and run for 140 hours. These tests showed that for this particular type of material that is ground, separated, domestic garbage at 40 degrees centigrade batch digestion, the optimum per cent moisture lies in a narrow range of *52 to 58 per cent*. This work explained many early difficulties at M.S.U. in attempting to digest garbage at 70 to 80 per cent moisture.

Effect of Temperature

Laboratory digestion experiments during 1955 at Michigan State University included a series of 10 studies designed to measure the effect of temperature on the rate and degree of digestion. The limitations of these experiments include (1) the batch composting process was employed, (2) temperature was kept constant during all stages of digestion, (3) at higher temperature (65 and 70 degrees centigrade) it was impossible to maintain a percentage of moisture satisfactory to good digestion, (4) there was no seeding and reseeding procedure followed so as to develop optimum organisms for any temperature level. Despite these limitations it was felt that results obtained may be of value to the engineer and future researcher.

Ten different temperatures ranging from 25 degrees to 70 degrees centigrade were investigated. In so far as possible the moisture content of these units was held at 56 plus or minus two per cent. It was found impossible to maintain the proper moisture content at the 65 and 70 degree temperature experiments. A study of these two figures indicates that comparatively good digestion can be obtained at temperatures ranging from 35 degrees through 60 degrees centigrade. Temperatures ranging from 40 through 55 appear to be considerably better, however, and the optimum temperature, at least, as indicated by these experiments, appears to be at about 45 degrees centigrade. It should be noted that during the early stages of digestion a higher rate of oxygen uptake was obtained at 35

702

degrees indicating that the initial or acid stage of digestion has a lower optimum temperature. The initial pH of the material at all temperatures was 5.6. The experiments held at 25, 30 and 35 degrees centigrade had a high initial drop to pH 4.4 and then a slow rise but they never reached what is considered a satisfactory pH level.

When these batch type experiments at a constant temperature are compared with the pilot scale experiments employing continuous flow, multistage type operation, it is evident that a single level of temperature does not represent optimum condition for high-rate composting. Digesting material in the pilot plant experiments showed temperatures on the first two decks of 30 to 35 degrees centigrade and rising slowly on the lower deck to temperatures of 60 to 65 and appear to have produced much higher rates of digestion. Other factors such as seeding and reseeding may overshadow the effect of the temperature changes; however, a great deal more experimentation is necessary before one can say with any degree of surety what the optimum temperature may be for the various stages research is required to conclusively determine and understand of digestion.

Nitrogen Changes During Composting

Nitrogen studies at M.S.U. included over 750 qualitative tests for the presence of nitrates and nitrites and over 300 quantitative tests for ammonia and total nitrogen. These were run on the raw material and in various stages of digestion in all 3 types of composting: laboratory, pilot plant and windrow. Some very interesting results have been obtained yet more research is required to conclusively determine and understand the phenomenon of the partial loss of nitrogen during the process and also to determine how this loss can be prevented.

Table 3 shows where nitrates or nitrites were or were not found. Nitrates and nitrites were *present* in all samples of fresh garbage tested. Likewise they were *present* in 100 per cent of the samples from upper decks 1 and 2 of the 8 decks in the pilot plant and were present during the first 48 hours in the laboratory digesters. Nitrites and nitrates were *absent* 100 per cent of the time in all samples taken on the lower decks 5 to 8 inclusive and after 70 hours in the laboratory digesters. On intermediate decks 3 and 4 and between 48 and 70 hours nitrites and nitrates were absent part of the time and present part of the time. In the windrow piles they were absent in the

Table 3. *The Presence or Absence of Nitrates or Nitrites During the Composting Process*

Sample Type and Location	Number of Tests	Nitrates or Nitrites Present or Absent
Raw garbage	60	Present
Drain fluid from raw garbage	55	Present
Garbage at top of dewatering tank	50	Present
Garbage at bottom of dewatering tank	50	Present
Drain fluid from dewatering tank	50	Present
Digester—Deck 1	30	Present
Digester—Deck 2	30	Present
Digester—Deck 3	30	Absent 5 times Present 25 times
Digester—Deck 4	30	Present 11 times Absent 19 times
Digester—Deck 5	30	Absent
Digester—Deck 6	30	Absent
Digester—Deck 7	30	Absent
Digester—Deck 8	30	Absent
Windrow compost—layer above actinomycetes layer	20	Present
Windrow compost—layer containing actinomycetes	20	Absent
Windrow compost—layer below actinomycetes layer	20	Present
Laboratory digester—start	10	Present
Laboratory digester— 6 hrs. after start	10	Present
Laboratory digester— 18 hrs. after start	10	Present
Laboratory digester— 30 hrs. after start	10	Present
Laboratory digester— 47 hrs. after start	13	Present 10 times Absent 3 times
Laboratory digester— 59 hrs. after start	13	Present 1 time Absent 12 times
Laboratory digester— 71 hrs. after start	10	Absent
Laboratory digester— 122 hrs. after start	10	Absent
Laboratory digester— 207 hrs. after start	10	Absent
Laboratory digester— 336 hrs. after start	10	Absent

actinomycetes layer (layer between 2 and 4 inches) and present above and below this layer.

This seems to indicate that nitrates and nitrites are either utilized biologically at a higher rate than produced or that the composting material, although aerobic and an active oxidizer, does not have a sufficiently high oxidizing potential for nitrifying reduced nitrogen compounds. Certainly these composting materials do not hold the existing nitrates or nitrites in their oxidized state. The raw garbage used in the M.S.U. experiments was unusually high in total nitrogen because it was a separated wrapped garbage from an above-the-average income residential community and also often contained quite a number of dead chickens from the Agricultural Experiment Station. Total nitrogen tests on the raw material varied from a low of 3.0 per cent to a high of 8.0 per cent with an average of 6.3 per cent (on basis of total dry solids). Ammonia nitrogen of the raw material varied from .25 to .40 per cent.

It is quite likely that with inadequate aeration the total nitrogen content, during composting, cannot be held above 1.0 to 1.5 per cent.

The relatively low values of ammonia nitrogen observed in the M.S.U. experiments (0.25 to 0.5 per cent) probably represent only a transition stage, and if ammonia concentrations become larger it is lost to the atmosphere. Although by no means conclusive, it would appear that total nitrogen above about 3. per cent will be lost during composting unless the pH can be held below about 5.0–6.0. This can perhaps be accomplished by adding sulphur dust at the right stages or by the addition of trash to lower the per cent of total nitrogen. It may also be practical to collect the lost nitrogen by passing the exhaust gases through an acid filter or scrubber. Carbon determinations as such were not run as controls on M.S.U. experimental work. For those accustomed to thinking in these terms, a rough approximation can be had by use of the following formula:

$$C = \frac{100 - \% \text{ ash}}{1.8}$$

Thus during composting the average raw material with 10 per cent ash, 6.3 per cent nitrogen calculate to have a C/N value of 8.0 while the final product with 20 per cent ash and 3.0 per cent nitrogen calculates to have a C/N value of 15.

The C/N ratio required so as not to temporarily rob nitrogen from the soil and thus reduce crop yields is estimated to be about 20:1.

Preliminary Carbohydrate Studies

Carbohydrate breakdown during the composting process has been studied at M.S.U. on a qualitative basis only. Tests have been made to determine the presence or the absence of cellulose, hemicellulose, starch, disaccharides and monosaccharides. The results of this study are given, along with the nitrogen values, in Table 4.

It appears that the high-rate composting process does not cause much breakdown of the cellulose but most of the disaccharides and monosaccharides (soluble sugars) disappear quickly and are probably the chief cause for the initial lowering of the pH. Although the qualitative chemical test indicates that starch disappears rather quickly, a microscopic examination indicates that some starch grains remain to the end of the digestion period.

Preliminary Phosphorus Studies

One of the advantages claimed for the presence of organic matter in the soil is that leaching of plant nutrients is greatly reduced. This may be accomplished in part by holding the moisture like a sponge and in part by absorption. Also in the case of phosphorus and to a degree with nitrogen, leaching may be prevented by the actual changing of the elements themselves from soluble ionized salts to insoluble organic compounds or they may actually become a part of living micro-organisms.

Studies were made at M.S.U. by composting ground garbage with P32 labelled triple super phosphate (48% P_2O5) at the rate of 150 pounds of 20 per cent super phosphate per ton of dry raw garbage. (This was equal to 30 pounds of P_2O5 per 600 pounds of dry organic matter, assuming 70 per cent moisture.)

Since the nitrogen level might effect the phosphorus change, 3 levels of 0, 100 and 200 pounds added ammonium nitrate per ton of raw garbage were tried. By taking counts of the radio-activity of the P32 left in the washings of the material the amount made insoluble in body protoplasm was obtained for each level of nitrogen. Results indicated that at the end of 336 hours of composting at 40 degrees centigrade

Table 4. *A Summary of Carbohydrate Studies on High-Rate Composting*

Sample Type and Location	Cellulose and Hemi-cellulose	Starch	Disac-charides	Monosac-charides
Raw garbage	Present	Present	Present	Present
Dewatering tank	Present	Present	Present	Present
Drain fluid from dewatering tank	Absent	Absent	Present	Present
Digester—Deck 1	Present	Present	Present	Present
Digester—Deck 2	Present	Present and Absent	Absent	Absent
Digester—Deck 3	Present	Absent	Absent	Absent
Digester—Deck 4	Present	Absent	Absent	Absent
Digester—Deck 5	Present	Absent	Absent	Absent
Digester—Deck 6	Present	Absent	Absent	Absent
Digester—Deck 7	Present	Absent	Absent	Absent
Digester—Deck 8	Present	Absent	Absent	Absent
Windrow compost— layer above actinomycetes layer	Present	Present	Present	Absent
Windrow compost— layer below actinomycetes layer	Present	Present	Absent	Absent
Windrow compost— layer containing actinomycetes layer	Present	Absent	Absent	Absent
Laboratory digester at start	Present	Present	Present	Present
Laboratory digester 6 hrs. after start	Present	Present	Present	Present
Laboratory digester 18 hrs. after start	Present	Present	Present	Present
Laboratory digester 30 hrs. after start	Present	Present	Absent	Absent
Laboratory digester 47 hrs. after start	Present	Present Absent	Absent	Absent
Laboratory digester 59 hrs. after start	Present	Present and Absent	Absent	Absent
Laboratory digester 71 hrs. after start	Present	Absent	Absent	Absent
Laboratory digester 122 hrs. after start	Present	Absent	Absent	Absent
Laboratory digester 207 hrs. after start	Present	Absent	Absent	Absent
Laboratory digester 336 hrs. after start	Present	Absent	Absent	Absent

in the batch continual stirring lab digesters, 96 per cent of the phosphorus had been converted from the soluble leachable state into the insoluble organic state. No difference between the samples containing different amounts of nitrogen could be determined.

Preliminary Volatile Acid Studies

In the composting process, as in the anaerobic digestion process, the excess concentration of volatile acids can be a serious problem causing severe inhibition or perhaps causing a complete breakdown of the process. In the anaerobic digestion of sewage sludge a slowdown occurs at about 2,000 ppm (0.2 per cent) volatile acids and a complete stoppage occurs before a concentration of 5,000 ppm (0.5 per cent) is reached. Fortunately the composting process appears to be much less sensitive to volatile acids and concentrations of 10,000 ppm (or 1.0 per cent) do not seem to cause any serious inhibition.

Mention should be made that the volatile acid test at M.S.U. had to be accomplished with particular care including titration under an atmosphere of nitrogen to obtain reproducible results. Results are calculated from the following formula:

$$\% \text{ Acid} = \frac{\text{Vol. NaOH} \times \text{Normality of NaOH} \times 8.58}{\text{Dry wt. of sample in grams}}$$

The test measures the sum of the volatile acids and the volatile salts. The detention time for the 8 decks in the pilot plant can be assumed to be about 4 days. If the rise and succeeding fall of a high concentration of volatile acids is an indication of passage of two stages of composting, it should be noted that the rate of digestion in the pilot plant is about 5 times that in the laboratory digester, that is, 4 days as compared to 20 days.

It might also be assumed that composting is probably incomplete as long as volatile acid concentration of 4,000–5,000 ppm persists.

Bacteria Population Studies

Although considerable work has been done at Michigan State University on the number and type of organism found under various conditions only a summary of these data will be presented here. Table 5 shows the predominating types of organisms found in laboratory batch experiments and various temperatures during the course of digestion.

There appears to be a fair correlation between bacterial count and oxygen uptake.

Oxygen Transfer

There are two ways gaseous oxygen can be supplied through the pore spaces into the mass of composting material: (1) by diffusion (2) by mass movement of the gas through the pores.

Mechanical stirring alone merely accelerates the above methods and should not be considered a separate method in itself. The concept of mass flow of a gas through a porous space will be dealt with in the following section. The relative importance of these two methods of gaseous transfer will also be discussed.

The modern theory of diffusion of gases in soils has been dealt with by a number of authors. The special application of diffusion to composting was the subject of a doctorate thesis in December 1955 in the Civil Engineering Department at Michigan State University by B. J. Shell. The basic research undertaken by Dr. Shell, under the direction of the author, represents, as far as is known, the only experimental work of its kind. Only a summary of the findings and the engineering applications can be presented in this paper.

In order to better understand the concepts of diffusion, let us discuss a specific example. Let us assume a 24-inch diameter by 12-inch high insulated drum filled with gently packed seeded ground garbage with a moisture content of say, 58 per cent. The drum is open to the atmosphere on the top but otherwise tightly sealed. If the material is actively digesting, the oxygen contained in the pore space is used up rather quickly. Carbon dioxide and moisture are produced. Heat produced during this biological oxidation raises the temperature of the material.

If it were not for the phenomenon of diffusion the 21 per cent oxygen originally present in the pore space would be quickly replaced with carbon dioxide and composting, which is an aerobic biological process, would soon stop.

Diffusion may be described as a process of intermolecular bombardment and thus a continued intermixing of all gases present in a given space. Thus it appears that all gas molecules have a tendency to move in all directions and distribute themselves evenly in all spaces open to them. In our example, oxygen from the atmosphere diffuses into the lower pore spaces where it is converted biochemically into carbon dioxide. The carbon dioxide produced, on the other hand, diffuses from the lower pore spaces up to the surface and is dispersed into the atmosphere. The rate of total movement of a gas by diffusion is related as follows:

1. Directly to the partial pressure of the gas itself.
2. Directly to the interconnected free air space available.
3. Directly to the gradient.
4. Inversely to the length of travel.
5. Inversely as the square root of the molecular weights.

It is interesting to note that the free air space volume in our example was measured to be 33 per cent and the relative rate of diffusion expected as compared to no restriction would be 0.25. The rate of diffusion through the full 12-inch thickness was measured to be 1.1×10^5 grams of O_2 per minute per square centimeter of surface. On the basis of the maximum oxygen demand measured at Michigan State University of .0244 gram O_2/minute/100 grams dry weight of material only .0005 gram can be supplied by diffusion. Thus diffusion supplies only 0.7 per cent of the maximum oxygen required in this 12-inch depth of material. For only a 4-inch or a 2-inch depth of this same material the percentage is increased to 2.6 per cent and 5.0 per cent respectively. It is seen that although diffusion alone supplies only a small percentage of the maximum O_2 needs during composting, it is also noted that layers of compost 2 to 4 inches in thickness are much more readily supplied with oxygen than are thicker ones.

Table 6 taken from the experimental work of Dr. Shell gives the engineer a good idea of the amount of O_2 which can be supplied composting material by diffusion alone under varying conditions of depth and per cent moisture.

The material employed in all of these experiments was finely ground, separated, domestic garbage. Table 6 also gives some of the other physical relationships important to diffusion.

Table 5.

Summary of the Predominating Types of Organisms Found During Laboratory Experiments

Temp. °C.	2 Days	4 Days	6 Days	8 Days	10 Days	12 Days
25	Pseudomonas	Pseudomonas 1/3 Flavobacterium	Flavobacterium	Flavobacterium	Flavobacterium	Mixed
30	Pseudomonas	Pseudomonas 1/3 Flavobacterium	Flavobacterium	Flavobacterium	Bacterium	Mixed
35	Flavobacterium	1/2 Bacilli 1/2 Actinomycetes	Molds (mixed)	Mixed	Mixed	Bacilli
40	1/2 Bacilli 1/2 Molds	1/2 Bacilli 1/2 Molds	Bacilli-Molds	Bacilli-Molds	Bacilli	Bacilli
45	1/2 Bacilli 1/2 Molds	Bacilli-Molds Actinomycetes	Bacilli	Bacilli	Bacilli	Bacilli
50	Bacilli	Bacilli	Bacilli	Bacilli	Bacilli	—
55	Bacilli	Bacilli	Bacilli	Bacilli	Bacilli Actinomycetes	—
65	Bacilli Actinomycetes	Bacilli Actinomycetes	Bacilli Actinomycetes	Bacilli Actinomycetes	Actinomycetes	—
70	10% Bacilli 90% Actinomycetes	10% Bacilli 90% Actinomycetes	10% Bacilli 90% Actinomycetes	Actinomycetes	—	—

Table 6.

Physical Relationships of Ground Domestic Garbage and Relative Diffusion Rates

% Moisture	Bulk Density	% Free Air Space	% Porosity	Relative Diffusion Rate For Various Depths of Material Compared with Free Air Space			
				2"	4"	8"	12"
41	.2830	44.5	75.5	.623	.567	.510	.397
50	.2540	39.0	78.0	.510	.442	.397	.318
58	.2443	33.0	78.9	.482	.414	.314	.250
64	.2557	28.0	77.9	.335	.272	.250	.227
70	.3070	22.0	73.4	.278	.193	.182	.056
Blank	—	—	—	1.00	—	—	—

Many of the terms used in the table are those which have been adopted in the studies on diffusion of air in soils. They may be defined as follows:

$$\% \text{ Moisture} = \frac{\text{Dry Weight of Material} - \text{Wet Weight of Material}}{\text{Wet Weight of Material}}$$

$$\text{Bulk Density} = \frac{\text{Dry Weight of Material}}{\text{Volume of Material Wet (Before Drying)}}$$

$$\text{Porosity} = 1 - \frac{\text{Bulk Density}}{\text{Particle Density}}$$

$$\text{Particle Density} = \text{Specific gravity of particles} - (1.154 \text{ for dewatered garbage})$$

$$\text{Free Air Space} = \text{Porosity} (1 - \% \text{ Moisture})$$

$$\text{Relative Diffusion Rate} = \frac{\text{Diffusion rate for condition described}}{\text{Diffusion rate for open container of same shape and size}}$$

If it is desired to obtain the actual rate of oxygen diffusion the relative rates given in Table 6 need only be multiplied by the constant of 4.5×10^{-5}. The diffusion rate is then given in grams of oxygen per minute per square centimeter.

Porosity, as used here, means the free space occupied by both the water and the air. The free air space is the significant figure because it alone permits diffusion.

Oxygen Supply by Forced Air

Since diffusion alone supplies only 0.5 to 5 per cent of the maximum oxygen requirements the engineer should look to forced air as a method of supply.

Laboratory experiments were conducted by the author to determine the resistance to mass movement of air through the pore spaces of ground garbage containing 58 per cent moisture. The results show the lower 7-inch layer measured was compacted considerably more than the upper 7-inch layer. These experiments showed that for this particular material, air flows below about 15 cubic feet per minute per square foot were laminar while above 15 cubic feet per minute per square foot they were turbulent.

The maximum rate of oxygen utilization measured at Michigan State University during composting operations was .0244 grams O_2/min./100 grams of dry weight of material.

Average ground garbage with a bulk density of 0.25 had a dry weight per cubic foot of $.25 \times 62.5 = 15.6$ pounds.

$$1 \text{ gram of oxygen} = \frac{22.4}{32.0} \times \frac{1}{28.3}$$
$$= .047 \text{ cubic foot under standard conditions.}$$

The air pressure and volume required for various depths of material composting at the peak rate of digestion are given in Table 7.

These calculations would indicate that forced air under low heads is a very practical method of supplying oxygen to composting material.

It is of interest to explore the chimney effect of the pore gas in a mass of hot composting material where cold air is free to enter the bottom and see how much air would be drawn through by this temperature differential. Assume outside temperature at 70 degrees Fahrenheit and compost temperature at 170 degrees Fahrenheit. Air density is .0764 pound per cubic foot at 60 degrees Fahrenheit and 760 mm of Hg.

From Charles' Law the increase in volume of a cubic foot of gas on being heated from 70 to 170 degrees Fahrenheit is

$$\frac{476 + 170}{476 + 70} - 1 = 1.18 - 1.00 = 0.18 \text{ cubic foot}$$

The lift over a square foot of area is then —

$$0.18 \times .0764 \times \frac{12}{62.5} = .00264 \text{ inches water head.}$$

713

Table 7.

Air Pressure and Volume Required for Various Depths of Compost at Peak Rate of Digestion

Total Depth of Material	Cubic Foot Air Required per minute leaving 50% residential O_2 per sq. ft. of area	Head Loss Inches Water
1 foot	.77	.023– .036
2 foot	1.54	.092– .144
3 foot	2.31	.207– .324
4 foot	3.08	.368– .577
8 foot	6.16	1.47 –2.31
16 foot	12.32	5.9 –9.2

This lift will produce a flow of .056 to .09 cubic foot air per minute which is at 7 to 12 per cent of the maximum required when the material is 12 inches deep. It is interesting to note that for this 12-inch depth the oxygen supplied by the natural chimney effect in hot compost is 15 to 25 times that supplied by simple diffusion from the top only, or 5 to 9 times that supplied from both top and bottom.

Summary of Suggested Design, Criteria and Needed Applied Research

Some of the design criteria suggested in this section are based on various experimental pilot plant data or laboratory results while others are based on observations resulting from experience, or in some instances only on the author's judgment. Certainly any composting plant designed today should be as flexible as possible and should be operated with the view toward gathering further accurate data useful to design rather than just as a plant for processing organic wastes. It is unlikely that initial plants will have their various stages in ideal balance but this does not mean they cannot be successfully and economically constructed and operated.

Following is a list of references used by Dr. Snell in his "High-Rate Composting" report:

P. H. McGauhey and Harold B. Gotaas, "Stabilization of Municipal Refuse by Composting," Vol. 79, Separate 302, Proceedings ASCE.

"Reclamation of Municipal Refuse by Composting," Tech. Bulletin No. 9, June 1953, University of California.

Goluecke, Card and McGauhey, "A Critical Evaluation of Inoculations in Composting," Applied Microbiology, Vol. 2, No. 1, 1954.

"Second Interim Report of the Inter-Departmental Committee on Utilization of Organic Wastes," New Zealand Engineer, Vol. 6, No. 11-12 (Nov.-Dec. 1951).

John S. Wiley and George W. Pearce, "A Preliminary Study of High-Rate Composting," Proceedings ASCE, Vol. 81, Separate No. 846, April 1956.

Gordon W. Ludwig, "The Effect of Various Temperatures upon the Aerobic Digestion of Garbage," Master's Thesis, May 1954, Georgia Institute of Technology, Atlanta, Georgia.

"Preliminary Report on a Study of the Composting of Garbage and Other Solid Organic Wastes," July 1955, Civil and Sanitary Engineering Department, Michigan State University.

William J. Turney, "A Study Concerning the Establishment of a Yardstick for Garbage Digestion by High-Rate Composting," June 1954, Civil and Sanitary Engineering Department, Master's Thesis, Michigan State University.

Reginald F. Batzer, "Permeability and Fineness Modules of Compost," Master's Thesis, June 1954, Michigan State University.

Shi-Who, Kao, "A Study of Windrow Composting with a Soil Shredder," Master's Thesis, June 1954, Michigan State University.

B. J. Shell, "The Mechanism of Oxygen Transfer Through A Compost Material," Ph.D. Thesis, Civil and Sanitary Engineering Department, 1955, Michigan State University.

A. J. Gabbaccia, Lederle Lab. Div., American Cyanamid Corporation, Pearl River, New York, Confidential Reports on Batch Type Compost.

Darrel Doolan, "Union Stock Yards," 999 Exchange Avenue, Chicago, Illinois. Confidential Reports on Batch Type Composting.

T. A. Crane, Riverview Farm, R.R. #3, Malton, Ontario, Canada. Confidential Reports on Continuous Flow Digesters Using Garbage, Sludge and Leaves.

Yonosuke Kaibuchi, City Engineer, City Hall, Kobe, Japan. Preliminary Reports on Kobe City High-Rate Pilot Compost Plant.

Literature Survey, "The Effect of Organic Matter on the Soil," Z. Stelmach, Civil Engineering and Soil Science Departments, Michigan State University, Mimeograph 1956.

Hal Guthredge, "Refuse-Sewage Composting-Engineering Aspects," The Soc. of Engr., Journal and Transactions, Vol. XLIII, Page 135, Oct.-Dec. 1952.

J. C. Wylie, "Composting," Public Cleaning and Salvage, No. 495, Vol. XLI, November 1951.

J. C. Wylie, "Composting," Public Cleaning and Salvage, No. 492, Vol. XLI, 397-415, August 1952.

J. C. Wylie, "Interim Report on Composting," Dumfried County Council, Scotland, 1950.

N. V. Vuilafvoer Maatschappij, V.A.M., 67 Jacob Obrechstraat, Amsterdam, Z. Holland, 1953. "The Processing of City Refuse into Compost."

New Zealand, "The Utilization of Organic Wastes in New Zealand," New Zealand Engineer, Vol. 3, June 1948.

"Pilot Plant Composting of Municipal Garbage in San Diego, California," The Sanitary Engineer Research Committee, Rubbish and Garbage Section, Proceedings ASCE, Vol. 82, February 1956, Page 887, SAI.

H. R. King, "Mechanics of Oxygen Absorption in Spiral Flow Aeration Tanks," Part III, Page 1123, Sewage and Industrial Wastes, October 1955, Vol. 27, No. 10.

L. G. Romell, "Soil Aeration," Int. Review of the Science and Practice of Agriculture NSI, 1932, 205-33.

E. Buckingham, "Contribution to our Knowledge of the Aeration of Soils," USDA Bureau of Soils, Bulletin 25.

M. M. McCool and G. J. Bouyoucas, "The Aeration of Soil as Influenced by Air Barometric Pressure Changes," Soil Science 18, 1924, 52-63.

M. P. Deherian and M. E. Demoussy, "Sur L' Oxydation de la Mattere Organique du Sol," Ann. Agren 22, 1947, 305-337.

716

E. Wollny, "Unters Chungen Uber den Kchlena Awiegeholt der Bodenluft," Landw Versachs, Stat 25, 1880.

S. A. Taylor, "Soil Air-Plant Growth Relationships with Emphasis on Means of Characterizing Soil Aeration," Ph.D. Thesis, Cornell University, 1949.

J. W. Leather, "Soil Gases," Memoirs Department Agriculture India (chem. series), 1915, 85-134.

H. L. Penman, "Gas and Vapor Movement in the Soil; I. The Diffusion of Vapours Through Porous Solids," Journal Agriculture Science, 30, 1940, 570-581.

E. R. Lemon, "Soil Aeration and Its Characterization," Ph.D. Dissertation, Michigan State University, 1952.

D. Kirkham, "Field Method of Determination of Air Permeability of Soil in Its Undisturbed State," Proc. Soil Science Soc. Am., II, 1946, 93.

W. A. Raney, "Oxygen Diffusion As a Method of Characterizing Soil Aeration," Ph.D. Dissertation, Cornell University, 1950.

John R. Snell, "High-Rate Composting of Organic Wastes," Consulting Engineer, July 1954.

Robert Braithwaite, "A Study of Garbage Composting in Controlled Insulated Barrels," Master's Thesis, June 1956, Civil and Sanitary Engineering Department, Michigan State University.

RATING A COMPOST PLANT DESIGN

Dr. Gotaas offers this 12-point check when evaluating the design of any compost plant:

1. Are provisions made for the collection vehicles to handle the desired quantities of materials, including surges and peak deliveries to the plant, without undue delay?

2. Are provisions made for maintaining the flow of materials at a more or less uniform rate throughout the entire processing, so that individual units do not become a bottle-neck in the operation?

3. Are facilities provided to permit maximum economic recovery of salvable inorganic materials that are

non-compostable, and of organic materials which have a greater economic value when salvaged than when composted?

4. Are facilities provided for handling non-compostable materials which cannot be further processed for resale and must be disposed of as landfill or by other methods?

5. Are the facilities designed specifically to operate on the particular type of refuse in the area? Since the characteristics of refuse may vary widely from one area to another, it is necessary that the equipment be specifically designed for the particular conditions.

6. Is sufficient flexibility provided in the plant to cope with changes in the quantity and quality of the refuse without unnecessarily costly alterations?

7. Are provisions made so that the plant can be readily adapted to handle other organic wastes, such as sewage sludge and food-processing wastes, if there is a good possibility that it will be necessary and advantageous to do so?

8. Are provisions made for the control of decomposition to ensure a safe and satisfactory compost, free from pathogenic and parasitic organisms, and weed seeds?

9. Are the facilities designed to control fly-breeding and odors?

10. Are the market-preparation facilities adequate to produce the variety of compost products necessary to reach the greatest economic market potential?

11. Are provisions made for adequate market-preparation capacity and storage? Since the product must be sold in a highly seasonal market and long storage of the product in marketable form is usually not economical, such provisions are necessary.

12. Are facilities provided for simple economical loading and shipment of the final product?

Flow Diagram for a City Composting Operation

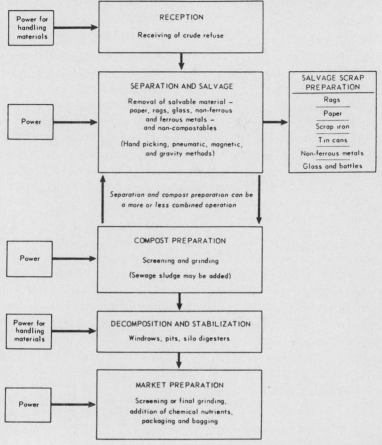

—*Composting,* DR. HAROLD B. GOTAAS
World Health Organization

THREE PROCESSES

According to Dr. Snell the 3 composting processes most fully employing the scientific principles learned to date, and still combining economy and efficiency, are believed to be the following:

1. *The T. A. Crane high-rate digester,* with a holding capacity of about 36 tons, or based on a 48 hour digestion period, about 20 tons of raw wet refuse per day. This is a 3 deck horizontal unit with two rows of slowly moving paddles on each deck. The only plant built to date is a 30 ton per day imitation of it constructed in late 1956 by Kobe, Japan. Results

of this plant follow. Construction costs of the Kobe plant are estimated to be $40,000, with operating costs of $2.20 per dry ton of compost end product or about half this price per ton of raw wet refuse. Material is sold to farmers at cost.

2. *The American Dross Disposal Corporation automatic turner and shredder.* When used in conjunction with forced-air windrowing. One was used at the Omaha stockyards where it was proposed to compost 140,000 tons of manure per year in the very small space of less than one acre for operating, and less than one-third of an acre for storage. A 14-day cycle was proposed. Material may be sold in bulk or dried and bagged. The cost of this plan is estimated to be $125,000, not including land. The operating, maintenance and amortization cost is estimated to be about $1.00 per ton of wet manure, or $2.50 per ton of dry compost (10 per cent H_2O).

3. *Bin Composting with forced-air* is being successfully employed as a second stage to high-rate composting in the Kobe, Japan plant. Results have not been received from Kobe for bins being employed as primary digestion units, but 30-gallon drum experiments conducted at Michigan State University and also at Kobe indicate real promise of rapid, efficient and economical composting. About 15 to 20 days are required, depending on conditions and raw materials. Costs should be comparable to the other two methods, yet there is less machinery to go wrong.

Dr. Snell further categorizes the different general approaches to compost as follows:

1. Mechanical Digestion—batch digesters as used at the Chicago stockyards and at Williamston, and continuous-flow digesters as Earp-Thomas, Dano, T. A. Crane and the Naturizer Company in Norman, Oklahoma;

2. Area Composting—composting ground, seeded material in bins 4 to 5 feet deep often using controlled amounts of forced air from a porous floor; and

3. Modified Windrows—piling material in long windrows. Pre-grinding is essential; forced air, pre-seeding, periodic turning and shredding make method more efficient. Windrows can be 4 to 6 feet high, 8 to 12 feet wide.

MAJOR FEATURES OF A PROPOSED PLANT

In 1957, Dr. Snell presented a paper on "Composting of Municipal Refuse" before the Canadian Institute on Sewage and Sanitation in Toronto. The following portions of his discussion are presented below, since we feel that his comments are just as applicable today as they were then:

1. *Choice of City for a Suggested Proto-type Plant*— Almost any location within the United States or Canada would be satisfactory. For maximum benefit, the city should be 100,000 or over, and should be one which disposes of its refuse by the combined pick-up method. Preferably, it should have a sewerage treatment plant of such design that the raw dewatered solid wastes of this plant can be diverted in whole or in part to the compost plant. It would also be desirable to have available separated household garbage so that it may be composted for short runs on a test basis. These runs would give reliable data for cities with separate collection systems.

2. *Location of the Compost Plant within the City*—The main criteria is that it should be central to the collection trucks, and have room for landscaping and expansion. If a sewerage treatment plant exists, the compost plant should be located near it so as to facilitate the hauling of dewatered sludge for composting.

If possible, it should be near railroad facilities. It should be on relatively inexpensive land. Isolation is not considered too important, for a correctly designed and operated compost plant.

3. *Nature of Materials to be handled*—For this first prototype plant, it is important that mixed refuse be the main organic waste handled by the plant. Arrangements, however, should be available for handling various mixtures of sewage sludge, and separated household garbage along with, as well as without, municipal refuse. Material not to be handled by the plant would include dirt, stones and materials from building demolition, tree trimmings (unless they had passed a wood chipper), non-organic industrial wastes, etc. These would be taken elsewhere to dump or burn. A reasonable percentage of coal ash should do no harm to the composting process.

4. *Methods of Pre-handling and Salvage* — Flexibility should be provided so as to take advantage of salvagable items when they are worth removing, such as bottles, tin cans, rags and miscellaneous metals. It is also necessary to remove large

objects for disposal elsewhere, such as automobile tires and tail pipes, refrigerators and large stones. It is proposed that this removal be done on a picking belt in combination with magnetic separaters.

5. *Pre-grinding of Materials*—An adequate design must include rugged grinders in duplicate so as to avoid the shut downs due to repair or maintenance. At present, large horizontal swing hammer Gruendler grinders would appear to be the first choice. Experience in the use of these grinders point to the possible need of two stages. A coarse grind would be followed by a fine grind. They would be located in series immediately following the picking belt. If either grinder failed, it could be temporarily by-passed during repair. It is concurred by manufacturers however, that an appreciably greater efficiency might result from a two-stage vertical grinder with a considerable reduction in over-all cost. When such a grinder becomes available, two grinders in parallel should be provided.

6. *Composting Processes Recommended for Proto-Type Plant*—It is proposed that one commercial unit of each of 3 methods be installed. It is possible that a fourth should be added. Many others are available, but the author's study indicates that the future possibilities and economics of these do not compare with those recommended. Those recommended are as follows:

(a) High-rate mechanical digester — the latest T. A. Crane digester is recommended as the best, plus the possibility of adding a Dano digester if sufficient funds are available.

(b) Modified windrow, employing forced-air and an American Dross Disposal automatic turning machine.

(c) Bin digester without turning, but employing forced-air.

7. *General Discussion and Diagrammatic Sketch*—A city should have no hesitancy in constructing a compost plant employing any one or any combination of the 3 recommended methods. Since any one of these recommended plants has yet to be constructed in the United States or Canada, it is suggested that the first plant be a proto-type, employing all 3 of these recommended methods. The receiving, salvage, picking and grinding operations would be common to all 3 of the

methods. After this pre-treatment, the material would be divided roughly into thirds and be treated by each of the 3 recommended methods. A plant capable of handling approximately a total daily intake of about 100 wet tons is suggested as being large enough to thoroughly test the economics as well as the scientific principles of each method. A rough figure for costs of 100 ton a day plant of this type should be $2,000 per ton, or $200,000. It would be difficult to attempt to design such a plant until the nature and variations of the materials are known and a site is selected.

The suggested plant would employ dual grinders, but no storage hopper. In addition to a high-rate digester and secondary curing bins, it would use additional bins (with forced-air) for composting of raw materials. It would also include windrow areas equipped with an inexpensive non-clogging method of blowing air through these windrows, and would use an automatic American Dross Disposal machine to turn and shred the windrows every few days.

Another approach to good testing of these 3 composting methods would be to construct 3 plants in 3 different locations. It is suggested however, that the cost of the preliminary handling and grinding of the material would be appreciably higher and each plant would be operating on different raw materials, making fine comparisons of less scientific value. The construction of many additional plants using each of these methods should follow. These plants constructed later would then be better adapted to all the particular conditions of the municipalities building them.

Suggested Methods of Financing

The ultra conservativeness of municipalities in adopting new methods even though they have been proven by local pilot studies and overseas proto-type plants is not easy to comprehend. Especially is this true when wasteful and costly disposal methods have been outmoded by less expensive treatment methods with full conservation of these solid organic materials. None-the-less, this conservativeness must be faced as a fact when discussing financing of a new type of plant. The following financing methods with comments on each is suggested:

1. By a grant from a foundation, or philanthropic individual. This is possible, but not likely, and would take a great deal of time and effort to sell.

2. By a grant from the federal governments of either Canada or the United States. (Same comment as for 1.)

3. By a single municipality which may decide it would like to try composting. (Example: Kobe, Japan. They were given only a 25 per cent subsidy and a great deal of encouragement from their federal government.) Japan is now planning 38 new plants on a 25 per cent federal subsidy basis. The main psychological drawback to this financing method is that one city is taking, or thinks it is taking, all the risk for other cities.

4. By the manufacturers of the composting equipment. Composting equipment as such represents a relatively small part of the cost of the whole plant, and the underwriting of a whole plant would greatly overburden even a well established manufacturer, to say nothing of one just becoming established.

5. By a joint venture of one or more municipalities and a privately formed company, interested in producing and selling compost.
   A workable suggested formula would be for the municipality or municipalities to share two-thirds, and the private compost company to share one-third, of the capital cost. The city would then deliver all the refuse free to the plant and the private compost company would operate it for 5 years, or until its capital had been regained with an agreed-upon profit. All salvage and compost would be disposed of by the private company.

6. Another feasible plan would be to form a cooperative venture of 5 to 10 interested municipalities. A next step might be to broaden the base further and call a meeting of those interested in such a cooperative venture. The leadership of a municipality in this effort would be most welcome.

Value to Municipalities of a Full-Scale Three-Way Proto-Type Compost Plant

When such a plant is constructed and operated, it is urged that as much be learned from it as possible. In addition to the normal operating crew, there should be at least two chemists and one bacteriologist employed to follow the operation, and thus, point the way to improvements. Furthermore, detailed cost data should be kept on each method and translated into maintenance and operating costs for a plant of each type alone. Many more chemical and bacteriological tests than those required for routine operation should be made and analyzed. It is believed that a National Institute of Health or Foundation grant could be obtained to defray the extra costs for research and economic studies of a proto-type plant of this kind.

Dr. Snell concluded his talk as follows:

"In closing, it should be stated that the cost of satisfactory present day refuse disposal methods vary from $1.00 to $6.00 per wet ton. Today a city employing a scientifically designed and operated composting process without considering the salvage or sale of the compost can at least match these costs and can in many cases appreciably lower them. If the sale of compost and the average salvage sale conditions are considered, then the treatment of organic municipal wastes by composting offers most cities over 100,000 population an actual and sometimes substantial source of revenue. Furthermore, it is firmly believed that conservation of these wastes should become part of our way of life, or eventually our nations will suffer."

Chapter 20

COMPOSTING OVERSEAS

In countries other than the United States, composting of municipal refuse is being practiced on a larger scale. Because disposal of town wastes by incineration and landfill is becoming an increasingly complex problem, authorities are closely examining the possibilities of composting. The need to conserve all natural resources is a basic reason for this increased emphasis on composting.

Since so much of the basic research on municipal composting originated in other countries, we now list descriptions of some methods and plants that have been in operation throughout the world. We have not tried so much to mention *all* of the composting plants, but instead to describe the different techniques employed under different situations.

AFRICA

In 1946, Sir Albert Howard wrote:

"South Africa has led the British Empire and indeed the world in recognizing the place of compost making in any well founded and progressive system of agriculture. The work of the compost-minded pioneers among South African farmers has spread like fire over the whole Union with the inevitable result that research work of real value and importance is now in progress."

Here is an example of why he held that belief.

In Kano, Northern Nigeria, composting was begun to deal with the disposal of domestic refuse, street sweepings, animal and human excreta. Since the early 1940's, adopting in principle the Indore process, experiments in Kano have resulted in the satisfactory and economic conversion of waste matter into humus of manurial value. Human and animal excreta, town and domestic refuse, have been composted into humus with remarkable success.

Previously, house and town refuse, stable manure, and market sweepings were dealt with by burning in incinerators of various designs, and in areas where a bucket system of conservancy was in operation night soil was disposed into Otway pits or by shallow trenching. Their combined values as fertilizer was thus lost to the heavily farmed area around Kano and the Province in general, but the farmers nevertheless conserved all available market and domestic sweepings including cattle, donkey, horse, sheep and goat manure to be used as fertilizer on their farms. These collections of market sweepings and manure deposited in heaps in and around rural villages and market places, where they undergo a natural process of putrefaction without any special treatment, unfortunately give rise to nuisance, such as offensive odors and fly breeding.

Conversion of existing pit latrines to the dry earth or bucket system added further to the problem for lack of available land for disposal of night soil within easy reach of the Township, but composting has made practicable the return of these waste products to the land as fertilizer that is eagerly

Overseas composting methods vary from small-scale heaps, such as the one shown on this Italian farm, to large, fully-mechanized plants capable of converting many tons of garbage and sewage sludge into a valuable soil conditioner in a short time.

sought by farmers near and far, bringing in even a small revenue.

Method—The Kano method of composting consists in the thorough and complete mixing of night soil with domestic wastes, loading the mixture into chambers or pits, and turning the mixed mass on 3 successive occasions. On the thirtieth day when the chambers are emptied, the resulting product is a dark, blackish brown material resembling soil, which is quite inoffensive and does not attract flies.

The process has also proved efficiently workable with slaughterhouses, wastes, and animal dung.

Experience has shown that failure to get composting working satisfactorily may be largely due to:—

(a) Not keeping the mass damp.

(b) Using fresh green leaves or freshly mown grass (tall grass should be broken up) without withering for a day or two.

(c) Failure to use a small proportion of domestic ashes in the mixing.

(d) Improper and haphazard mixing.

(e) Loading the pits too tightly.

(f) Exposure to heavy and continuous rains.

(g) Bad location of chambers which become water-logged during the rain.

(h) Filling chambers too high (over 3 feet 6 inches interferes with air supply).

The following observations are an indication that the process is progressing satisfactorily:—

(a) Steam rising from the mass from the second day; the whole mass hot; warmth can be felt by holding the hand over it.

(b) The mass begins to sink on the fourth day.

(c) Absence of smell, and no flies attracted to the mass.

(d) Presence of greyish white fungi just beneath the surface clearly visible as the mass begins to darken.

The advantages of the composting method as developed in Kano, Nigeria, and described, are:—

(1) A small disposal area is all that is needed; if the site is thoughtfully selected it is permanent.

(2) The process is applicable to communities of any size.

(3) The method can be applied not only to night soil but equally effectively for the disposal of abattoir wastes as well as animal manure.

(4) No offensive odors should arise if the process is carried out properly, particular attention being paid to thorough mixing, and charging of the chambers lightly and evenly.

(5) The process needs no very skilled supervision but must nevertheless be supervised.

(6) Fly breeding is prevented by the rapid rise in temperature of the mixed mass which remains in above 55 degrees C. up to the time of the third turning and removal from the chamber. Although a fair number of eggs hatch out within the first few days, a large number of the larvae do not survive the temperature in the center of the mass; others are destroyed in the process of turning; thus the nuisance is overcome.

(7) While the initial outlay may appear high, it is much cheaper in the long run than costs incurred in the provision of Otway pits, building of incinerators and their maintenance. Operating costs are also no greater than for incinerator and Otway pit labor.

(8) A small return is derived from the sale of compost; in Kano a donkey load of the compost is sold for only a penny.

(9) What is most important is that this method of disposal of both animal and vegetable refuse does not destroy valuable material, but rather converts it without serious nuisance or offence into a plant food or fertilizer that is the essential ingredient of fertile soil.

(10) Trenching or dumping of night soil into Otway pits, and incinerating or dumping into depressions and covering with earth the vegetable and other refuse yield no returns, while composting not only yields to the producer some small financial return, but benefits the agricultural community incalculably. Already marked results in enrichment of the soil of a heavily farmed area that needs fertilizer badly (the land is kept in almost constant cultivation without much attention to rotation of crops) has been observed, and its value is fully recognized and appreciated by the farmer. There has been no difficulty in persuading farmers to use the compost made from human excreta. Practical demonstrations have overcome all prejudices. We are in fact unable to supply all the demands for this fertilizer, although an average of 1,080 cubic yards of humus is produced monthly in the 6 sets of composting chambers. From 1941 to 1946, compost productions in Kano totalled 43,800 tons.

—Eric C. Gilles
Medical Officer of Health, Nigeria

CENTRAL AMERICA

San Salvador, capital of the Republic El Salvador, Central America, with its 200,000 inhabitants produces 80 to 100 tons of garbage daily. Of this, 25-30 tons consists of bottles, cans, rags, baskets and other rubbish not suited to compost making.

The first selection is done immediately at the place of discharge, where large non-compostable objects are ejected by hand. From this point, garbage is thrown on a plane with an inclination of 45 degrees and 12 feet wide. There it is spread evenly and, before getting to the hammer mill, it is selected once more from both sides of the conveyor belt. This work is done by 12 women. A magnetic pulley in the head of the mill selects metal objects which were missed in the hand process. Generally only small pieces are selected magnetically

1.

2.

3.

Composting at a Sugar Plantation on Formosa 4.

(1) Blocks of bagasse, the fibrous residue of the sugar cane (after the sweet juice has been extracted) is carried by women to compost heaps at the Taiwan Sugar Corporation. (2) The bagasse blocks are broken up and are soaked with a water suspension of hog manure distributed by a centrifugal pump and an 8-inch pipe system set up by the company. (3) Compost piles are approximately 50 feet wide by 100 feet long. Materials are built up layer on layer until about 4 or 5 feet high. This is a view of composting grounds. (4) After material is composted, it is loaded into baskets. Women are shown carrying baskets to rail cars which carry the compost to various Formosa fields for distribution.

—bottle caps, razor blades, pins, small cans, etc. A large piece of iron can do a lot of damage in the hammer mill. Precautions are taken to see that none enter.

The capacity of the mill is about 8 tons of selected garbage an hour. If the garbage contains more than 25 per cent green material, there is no need to add water for starting the process.

Passing the mill, the garbage is carried by conveyor belt to large tanks where garbage is piled up to a height of 10 feet. The heaps are turned every 10 to 12 days, so that enough aeration takes place.

The very moment the garbage leaves the hammer mill, manure is added by pails. Based on his experience, plant operator Erwin Carranza has found that there is no better starter than fresh manure especially from ruminants. Carranza believes that more than 10 per cent of manure should never be used or the compost will be overheated. At the present time, the manure content is only about 3 per cent, but this much is enough for a good starter.

After the second turning, lower heaps are preferred so that the material does not undergo high temperatures.

As it is desirable to turn the heaps every 12 days, the plant finishes compost in from 70 to 75 days. At the end of the sixth turnover, composting material converts to a loose mulch, ready to be used in fields and plantations. It is then brought to the storehouse, where it is piled no higher than 10 feet if possible. During harvesting time, higher piling is sometimes unavoidable.

The mineral content of the compost produced at the plant amounts to more than one per cent each in N, P, and K. The pH is a favorable 7 to 8.

CHINA

Composting of Refuse and Night Soil

The World Health Organization (WHO) reports: One point in the public health program of WHO is the improvement of refuse disposal techniques, or the collection, treatment and disposal of wastes from cities and villages. As a step in this direction, the Chinese government with WHO help has constructed in the City of Ping-Tung (Taiwan) an experimental refuse composting plant in which various methods can be tested and compared with one another. At the WHO public health seminar held in Taiwan, a proposal was made to enlarge the Ping-Tung experimental plant so that the large amount of night soil from dry privies could be incorporated with it. These studies will include the collection, treatment, and disposal of night soil for agricultural purposes, as well as its storage with regard to sanitary importance.

It has been shown that insanitary treatment and disposal of night soil can lead to spread of disease. But to date in China, no method of disposing of such matter in a sanitary manner has yet been found. Only partially dry material is suitable for composting. If it is too wet, anaerobic processes of decomposition predominate and no temperature rises result. Yet these rises are important for elimination of pathogenic microorganisms. The obvious solution lies in the mixing of the wet fecal matter with dry refuse and composting them. But in Taiwan, Japan, and other countries, the quantity of night soil collected far exceeds that of the dry refuse so that a surplus of wet wastes exists which must be treated otherwise. Thus experiments have been proposed by WHO, such as the pasteurization of the wastes with subsequent utilization or centrifuging the materials with final composting of the concentrated night soil.

—Information Bulletin No. 4
International Research Group
on Refuse Disposal

COLOMBIA

A preliminary engineering study for Bogota, Colombia, was completed by Michigan Associates in late October, 1958. This report recommended composting as a method of disposal for the 700 tons of municipal refuse produced by this city each day. The present method of disposal is by sanitary landfill.

The composting process, as proposed, consists of a complete method of treatment accomplished in the following manner. Municipal garbage and trash is delivered to the plant site by city collection vehicles. After passing over a weighing scale, trucks dump the refuse into long storage hoppers. Conveyors feed refuse from these hoppers onto picking belts where salvageable materials are removed. Picked refuse then proceeds by conveyor through primary and secondary grinders, which shred the refuse to a sawdust-like consistency. About 5 per cent of the ground material is sent to mechanical digesters. Exact control of moisture, temperature and degree of decomposition is possible in these units, and the partially digested refuse emerging, after 24 to 48 hours, is used to seed the remaining 95 per cent of the ground refuse. This seeded refuse is piled in long windrows and provided with the amount of fresh air required for efficient composting. Air is provided during this 10-14 day process by air ducts under the piles, and is further aided by a special truck-mounted turner and shredder. The process is simple, inexpensive and scientifically designed. It is odorless, and naturally produced temperatures of 70 degrees C. are attained, which kill all pathogenic bacteria. On the basis of 700 tons per day input, this plant would produce 355 tons of saleable compost per day.

The entire composting area is enclosed in a building 330 feet by 600 feet, and is complete with laboratory and office facilities, acoustical enclosure for grinders and motors, and building utilities. The plant is architecturally attractive and can be located in any area of the city without causing nuisance.

Construction costs for the entire plant are estimated as follows:

Building cost (based on Colombian
unit costs) = $ 610,670.00

Machinery, installed (based on
duty-free import) = 1,212,000.00

TOTAL COST OF PROJECT = $1,822,670.00

Estimated yearly costs for the Bogota plant are shown below:

Operating costs (including 29 man
crew, power & maintenance of
all fixed & mobile machinery) = $ 75,800.00/yr.

Amortization (Building at 5 per cent
interest, over 30 yrs. machinery
at 5 per cent interest over
15 years) = 167,500.00/yr.

TOTAL DISPOSAL COSTS = $ 243,300.00/yr.

The unit cost of composting is then $1.16 per ton

Income from sale of compost at
$5.00 per ton = $ 503,000.00/yr.

THE TOTAL NET PROFIT THEN = $ 259,700.00/yr.

On a raw refuse wet weight, this gives a profit of $1.24 per ton.

According to Michigan Associates, this means that at a profit of $259,700 per year, the composting plant for Bogota will pay for itself within a matter of 7 years, and will then be available as a source of income for the city.

DENMARK

The Copenhagen firm of Dano began to study the municipal composting problem in 1933 and, after some years of experimenting and research, succeeded in devising a method of converting urban refuse, by mechanical methods and under sanitary conditions, into a high-grade compost-fertilizer.

As described in the previous chapter, the refuse is conveyed to the plant in refuse vans of various types, or in bins. The machinery employed in medium and large towns consists of a rotary equalizer silo for hygienic storage and pre-treatment, plus a machine for grinding and homogenizing the refuse to form the compost. In smaller towns the latter machine, called an "egsetor," is sufficient. Usually, the refuse is dumped

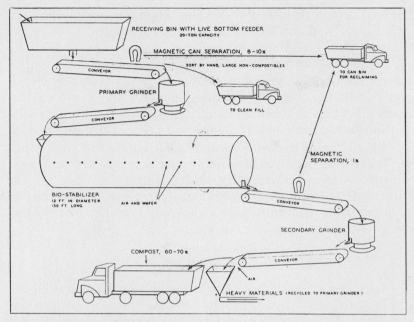

Schematic flow sheet for 150-ton per day Dano compost plant.

into a concrete pit, and an apron feeder at the bottom of the pit feeds it to a rubber belt conveyor, which feeds it in turn to the rotary silo. The rotary silo, by slow rotation, keeps the refuse in contact with the air, thereby preventing putrefaction, premixes the various ingredients, promotes distribution of moisture so as to bind dust, and starts the process of breaking the material down into small particles.

The pre-treatment refuse is then, by laminated plate conveyor, conveyed to the egsetor, where the grinding and simultaneous homogenization of a large volume of refuse is completed by rapid rotation. The compost leaves the machines on a belt conveyor as a pleasant, soil-like, and uniform powder. Dano plants are in use throughout the world, including Denmark, Sweden, Norway, Finland and the United States.

ENGLAND

The formation in England of the Joint Working Party on Municipal Composting indicates the strong interest there. This group is made up of representatives of The Association of Public Health Inspectors, The Institute of Public Cleansing,

The Institute of Sewage Purification, The Soil Association and an observer appointed by The Society of Medical Officers of Health. This group was formed because of "the difficulties which face local authorities today in the disposal of community wastes, both human and household . . . to bring together useful available information and to publish reports which will enable local authorities to examine municipal composting as a serious solution to the problems of sludge and refuse disposal."

The Interim Report issued in 1959 points out that composting can be constructed upon any scale which is found convenient. A local municipality that is interested may find it convenient to initiate an experiment which can be made with little capital expenditure yet which would provide material for use on that community's parks, etc.

Special Problems

In a report, "Compost Engineering," by Harvey Cole in *The New Scientist*, it was brought out that there are a number of special difficulties involved in composting British household waste. First, the proportion of compostable matter is low. "Some 60 per cent of the waste consists of dust, ashes and clinkers, and only about three-quarters of the remainder is suitable for making compost. Thus the compost heap can only dispose of the waste collected by the dust carts. And to take advantage of it, the non-compostable matter must be carefully separated at extra expense.

"By contrast, many towns abroad where solid fuel is not burned in domestic grates produce refuse which requires almost no sorting before composting.

"Secondly, the British farmer relies on mineral fertilizers, largely imported from overseas at considerable cost, and is not familiar with the use of compost. In order to break down this resistance the price of the compost would have to be kept low, which means that the cost of transporting it must be small. But it has not proved easy to find sites for composting plants both close to large towns and convenient for distributing it to farmers.

"The uncertainty of the market has produced a situation in which authorities are unwilling to set up composting plants for fear of being left with large quantities of unsold material. Yet they are unable to build up a flourishing market until the plant is in operation and they have compost to offer for sale.

Here is a view of the composting tower on the British Isle of Jersey. The tower has six floors, each self-emptying. The fermentation takes a week in the tower, the mass being dropped one floor each day. Sixty tons of compost are produced daily.

Compost Plant in Jersey

"The speed with which compost can be developed in suitable circumstances has been shown in Jersey. A plant has been operating there since 1957, producing 60 tons a day. The growth of the island's popularity as a tourist center rapidly increased its refuse problem. At the same time, the other main activities on the island—the growing of tomatoes, flowers and potatoes—called for a steady supply of compost. It was in

737

fact found that the compost had the effect of checking stemrot in tomato plants, an additional and uncovenanted benefit."

John B. Nesbitt of Penn State University's Civil Engineering Department has given a description of the composting operations at the Jersey plant based on his visit there in the summer of 1957. Here is Prof. Nesbitt's report, which appears in Penn State's Engineering Research Bulletin B-72, *Composting of Municipal Refuse and Some European Composting Operations:*

A densely populated British resort island famous for its bathing beaches, Jersey could not dispose of its refuse or sewage sludge by dumping on land or at sea. Its answer to this problem was a composting plant for the disposal of both wastes. After elaborate separation and preparation of the refuse, it was mixed with thickened digested sewage sludge and composted both by mechanical aeration in a vertical silo and by storage in windrows.

Refuse, exclusive of cardboard cartons from stores and shops, was dumped into a receiving hopper, where a conveyor belt lifted and transported it to a dual rotating-drum screen. Openings ⅜ inch in diameter in the first half of the screen separated dust and fine organic material from the refuse, and one inch openings in the second half of the screen separated cinders. As dust concentration was not uniform in the refuse throughout the year (ash from coal furnaces caused an excess in the winter), all dust was transported by a second conveyor belt to a storage bin, from which it was withdrawn at a uniform rate and added to the refuse again just before the composting step. The cinders and other material passing the one-inch screen fell on a short endless belt moving on about a 45-degree slope. The cinders bounced off the belt and were collected and dumped. The organic material stayed on the belt and was returned to the refuse.

A third conveyor belt then transported the refuse to a building where salvable materials were removed. Rags and nonferrous metals were hand picked, and cans and ferrous metals were separated magnetically. (Baled cans, scrap metal, and rags were sold as salvage in England.) The conveyor belt then delivered the refuse to a hammer mill grinder that completed the preparation of the refuse for composting.

At this point a parallel hammer mill shredded the cardboard boxes from stores and shops, after which they were added to the shredded refuse and carried by a fourth conveyor

The Earp-Thomas Digester in Paris converted raw garbage into finished compost in only 24 hours. The garbage goes in by conveyor at the top and gradually works its way down. Much of the composted material was shipped by rail for use by farmers.

belt to a rotary drum mixer. Also feeding the mixer were a fifth conveyor belt carrying dust from the dust storage bin, and a pipe carrying digested sludge from an adjacent sewage treatment plant. The contents of each of the last two conveyor belts were automatically weighed and the sludge flow measured. Automatic controls adjusted the speed of the belts and the flow of sludge to obtain a predetermined mixture.

After thorough mixing, the refuse, dust, and sludge were dumped into a bin where a clamshell bucket lifted and deposited it on the top floor of a 6-floor silo. Each floor in the silo was a series of half-cylinders, open side up, with a walkway in the middle. These half-cylinders could be rotated so that their open side was down, thus depositing the compost on the floor below and turning it in the process. The material remained on each floor one day, and at the end of the sixth day was stacked for 6 weeks in sheltered windrows 6 feet deep. During the 6 days in the silo, biological stabilization began and the temperature rose sufficiently to kill all pathogenic bacteria plus tomato and weed seeds. By the end of the sixth day, stabilization was sufficiently advanced that turning of the windrows was not required although it was done occasionally.

The compost was sold to the farmers on the island, who came to the plant and purchased it in bulk and used it as an organic fertilizer and soil conditioner. Most of the compost was used in its coarse state, but a small portion was more finely ground for those farmers who required it that way.

FRANCE

Garbage Digester in Paris

A large garbage digester has been operated by the City of Paris in the Villa Roma section. It was built under license from Dr. Earp-Thomas of High Bridge, New Jersey, through a French syndicate headed by A. G. Daudier. The syndicate operates under the name of *Fertilisants Agricoles Techniques*.

The garbage is brought in, and by a rather elaborate setup of equipment is processed so as to segregate the finer part of the garbage which goes by freight to farmers who let it ferment in piles for a year.

The digester is in 10 storys (small ones) of a total of 10 meters high, which is about 30 feet, and about 15 to 18 feet wide. The garbage goes in by conveyor at the top, and gradually works its way down from story to story. It takes 24 hours from raw garbage to finished compost.

Big trucks come in loaded with garbage which by means of a large grab is dumped on a moving conveyor where it is segregated. Men stand on each side and remove large pieces of wood, bottles, crates, big chunks of paper and any other large impedimenta that might cause trouble. The finer stuff moves over revolving drums with holes, and only the smaller pieces that fall through these holes are used for the digester.

The finer material then goes through magnetized rolls which remove all iron and steel parts, which are sold as scrap. Much of the paper is separated and sold in baled form. The material then goes through a grinding process where any bits of glass, porcelain, etc., are pulverized into powder form. Then there is a first treatment with Dr. Earp-Thomas' bacteria cultures, along with a quantity of residues from wine-making.

Seven to eight tons of compost were turned out every day. The cost of production several years ago was about $8.40 a ton and the selling price was about $24.00.

GERMANY

Compost Plant at Duisburg-Huckingen

The Duisburg-Huckingen compost plant was officially placed in operation December 16, 1957 after a long trial period.

Dumping refuse in canals, depressions, and the like has been forbidden for some time for the protection of two water works south of Duisburg. Composting was chosen as another means of disposing of refuse. As against incineration, this process has the advantage of lower construction and operating costs. In selection of the composting process, preference was given to the biostabilizer system developed by the Dano Company at Copenhagen because this process permits addition of large amounts of sewage sludge and requires only a short period of operation.

Laden refuse trucks dump into receiving bunkers. Raw refuse is transported on apron and belt conveyors to the composting plant. Scrap iron is sorted out by magnetic pulleys, conveyed to a press, and baled. In the winter, screens separate out the unwanted ashes. On the final sorting conveyors, valuable and brittle materials are picked out by hand. The refuse is then conveyed to rotating drums (biostabilizers) and mixed with sludge. Biological decomposition starts with forced aeration and continuous rotation of the drums, converting the refuse-sludge mixture to raw compost in 4-5 days. After leaving the drums, the compost is freed of glass splinters, stones, rags, and otherwise useless substances by screening. The compost is then immediately given up to agriculture or is piled temporarily in heaps. Screen residues are taken to the nearest dump.

Technical Data

Collection area: About 140,000 population = ⅓ the City of Duisburg.

Capacity: Refuse about 200 cubic meters = 80 tons per workday; Sludge about 10-20 cubic meters per day; Scrap iron about 2 tons per workday; Compost about 50-60 tons per workday.

Building size: About 21 x 35 x 9 meters = about 7000 cubic meters of enclosed space.

Size of the two biostabilizers: Length about 25 meters; diameter 3.5 meters; capacity about 250 cubic meters.

Installed motor power: About 200 kilowatts.

Construction costs: About 1.5 million German marks (about $357,000).

When a compost pile is undisturbed or not turned, it gives off hardly any perceptible odor. Odors given off when the pile is disturbed are mild, moldy, not unpleasant odors in the outer layers, a sour unpleasant odor at greater depths, and an extraordinarily penetrating putrid odor in the center. This anaerobic odor, originating from oxygen-poor and oxygen-free regions of the compost pile, then vanishes astonishingly quickly as soon as oxygen is again accessible to it. The opinion of experts up to now has been that a completely aerobic process throughout its course was practically odor-free.

It was therefore an unpleasant surprise to all when the new Duisburg-Huckingen refuse-sludge compost works developed a quite penetrating odor despite the undoubtedly aerobic decomposition process. Atmospheric conditions in the area are certainly unfavorable (misty weather) and the nearest blocks of houses are scarcely 50 meters from the plant which handles about 100 tons of refuse; nevertheless, the odor produced proved stronger than was expected. The odor could not be eliminated with either ozone or simple aeration, but disappeared completely with electrolytic combustion. The latter process, however, entails considerable operating costs for fuel so that another way had to be found.

Engineer Stahlschmidt of the Dano Company in Copenhagen, after thorough experiments at Coire, Switzerland, developed a process of air circulation combined with a two-stage cooler and water scrubber and installed it in the plant at Duisburg. The plant was again in operation in the beginning of November, 1957 and subsequently operates practically without odor. An official investigating commission, consisting of representatives of the neighborhood, press, health officials, and officials of the City of Duisburg, confirmed this. As an interesting attendant phenomenon, it should be mentioned that the decomposition process in the drums is apparently accelerated by the new air circulation procedure.

Analyses of the compost showed good results.

—Information Bulletin No. 4
*International Research Group
on Refuse Disposal*

Heidelberg

At Heidelberg the garbage trucks dump their contents into a moving mechanism which vibrates, thus moving it along. On the way a magnetized roller picks out iron objects. Hand-pickers pick out leather, plastic objects and utensils, bits of glass, wood, bones and all such inorganic objects. The metal is baled and sold. So are the bones. But the rest, comprising about 15 per cent of the total, is dumped into a large hole. Good bottles are also salvaged, for in Germany the wine, whiskey and soft drink companies have a planned campaign of re-using bottles.

The concession for salvaging is sold to a company whose employees are the ones who pick out salvageable materials.

The materials now move upward about the equivalent of one story and go into a large rotating device which turns slowly. The finer materials fall through holes into a lower chamber. The bigger stuff which does not fall through comprises about 10 per cent of the total. This goes through a device where the soft particles can go through. The hard parts are thrown to one side and carted to the dump. The material is then piled in circular heaps about 10 feet high.

In 9 days the heaps are turned . . . then again in 3 weeks. When turning there is a moisture control. If water is needed,

743

it is provided at this time. If the heap is too moist it is turned more often. If too dry water is given. The moisture is determined by an infrared lamp device combined with a scale of figures. About 10 grams of compost are placed into it, and when the infrared light goes on, it causes a dial to move on a graduated scale. Sometimes when a heap gets too dry it will catch on fire, so it is important that there be a close water control.

It takes from 3 to 4 months to compost in the piles depending on the season. In the winter it takes longer. It is turned 3 or 4 times or more before the extent of decomposition is considered sufficient.

The finished compost is sold at a price of 8½ marks per cubic meter. This amount weighs about 1,600 pounds. This is about $2.15, or about $3.00 a ton.

For making the turns a machine similar to the American Barber-Green is used. It has little buckets which pick up the stuff, carry it to the rear and dump it there. To make a finer product the stuff goes through a vibrator. This product is used on lawns and costs 16 marks for a cubic meter. The vibrator has 6-millimeter screens, the equivalent of about ¼ inch mesh. The rough offal that does not go through goes back into the regular compost.

This plant is large enough to take the garbage of 80,000 of the 120,000 population of Heidelberg. It handles 200 cubic meters of raw material a day. Of this amount 17 per cent becomes compost in summer . . . 27 per cent in winter, because of the coal ashes in the garbage.

HOLLAND

The Stichsting Compost group of Holland has published an excellent booklet, called "The Manufacture and Use of Urban Domestic Waste Compost in the Netherlands." The following excerpts from this booklet were given at a meeting of the International Research Group on Refuse Disposal:

"The Director-General of the Ministry of Agriculture of the Netherlands emphasizes that the maintenance and development of soil fertility is one of the most important problems of our time. From a study of the problems the following conclusions can be drawn: soil destined for cultivation should be enriched with humus; this in turn has resulted in an increasing interest in urban refuse as a possible source of organic fertilizer. The Dutch government made available a considerable sum from Marshall Funds for study of the problem besides creating a group—'Compost'—charged with developing methods for composting urban wastes and studying possible uses for the compost. This publication gives a succinct survey of the activities of the study group and of the Netherlands efforts in the field of composting and the use of composts.

"... Our arable soil is the keystone to our existence. This chapter concerns the important role of agriculture in the productive economy of the Netherlands. Agricultural products make up a considerable portion of goods exported and are also the raw materials on which a great part of Dutch industry is dependent. Agricultural production costs are rising and competition with other countries grows sharper. The only possibility of lowering production costs is to increase land productivity. Fertility of soil must be given full consideration and all possibilities for improvement given play.

"... Diminution of soil fertility is marked by reduced yield. Exhausted soils are unstable and easily eroded. Agricultural practices which result in erosion and soil exhaustion will, in time, transform the region into uninhabitable desert. Erosion is a serious problem in the United States, Central and South America, India, Africa, and other lands. Erosion has had a greater influence on the fate of mankind than wars. Maintenance of soil fertility is a problem of great importance to all humanity.

"... Holland is densely populated; only 0.6 acre of arable land is available per capita. Holland must produce as much as possible with this limited amount of land and increase production to meet population increase. There is a remarkable intensification of agriculture. Stable manure and compost were the only fertilizers formerly available and the fertility of the land was maintained at a high level with these. Supply became insufficient and in 1900 commercial fertilizers became available. Yields increased and almost all 'Oedland' (chemically poor soil) was rendered cultivable. Farmers lost interest in organic manures. Refuse compost became almost unsalable and the advantages of good preparation of stable manure have been forgotten.

"It was recently realized that, although chemical fertility of the soil was markedly increased by chemical fertilizers, the physical fertility has been declining. This discrepancy is particularly noticeable in the light soils of Holland. Harvests can no longer be increased in Holland by artificial fertilizers alone,

745

but they can be by increasing physical fertility through use of organic fertilizers.

"These symptoms show the decline in physical fertility of soil: (1) Increasing wind erosion; (2) Decreasing efficiency of synthetic fertilizers; (3) Increase of deficiency diseases in crops, particularly those due to lack of trace elements; (4) Increased susceptibility of crops to dryness; (5) Increased mechanical force required to work the soil; (6) Increased susceptibility of crops to parasitic root diseases; (7) Diminished certainty of crop returns and greater dependence on favorable weather. It is now recognized that more organic fertilizers should be used in Holland and the interest in refuse composting is increasing."

VAM History

The Refuse Disposal Company, Ltd., (V.A.M.) was formed by the Dutch government in 1932. This company founded a business for conversion of town wastes into compost at Wyster in the Province of Drenthe.

The late Mr. van Maanen put into practice the system of composting now used by the V.A.M. Mr. van Maanen was of the opinion that moisture, rather than air, was the basic factor needed to compost Dutch town refuse. Owing to the large number of empty tins, bottles, boxes, etc., the refuse is sufficiently aerated. By moistening the refuse, considerably quicker and better fermentation is obtained and the result is a better decomposed, more homogenous product. The watering installation in the works at Wyster must be looked upon as an essential part of the system applied by the V.A.M. Part of the watering is done with percolated and bacteria-rich water. Twenty-four hours after the sprinkling the temperature has risen to 140 or 158 degrees. These high temperatures have the advantage of killing germs, nematodes and the seeds of most weeds.

After having arrived at Wyster, town wastes are handled as follows: a train with town refuse runs on one of four viaducts 6.6 yards high and 520 yards long. When the train stops the side valves of the vans are opened automatically from the engine and the refuse drops on both sides of the vans, as these vans have a saddle-shaped bottom. The refuse is mechanically levelled and sprinkled. The next day another trainload is tipped, etc., until the refuse is a little more than 6 yards high and the viaduct is filled up. The process is repeated at the next viaduct.

This train, loaded with town refuse, is shown in the process of unloading at the Holland (V.A.M.) plant at Wyster. When train stops, side valves of vans are opened from the engine and refuse drops from both sides of the saddle-shaped vans.

When the refuse has been decomposing for 4 to 8 months (winter refuse 4 months, summer refuse 8 months) it is ripe. It is turned as much as possible and is finally dug out by a traveling grabcrane.

The grabcrane tips the refuse into a bunker and the latter automatically unloads its contents into trucks which are attached to an endless cable. These trucks take the refuse to the factory where it is unloaded by mechanical means.

In the factory the refuse is first put into vibrating screens where the heavy parts are screened out (bottles, tires, coconut mats, pails and pans, etc.). The refuse which passes through the meshes falls onto a conveyor belt. Any article made of iron is drawn out magnetically and then the remainder is pulverized in two large hammer mills. The pulverized product is called "V.A.M. Composts." The appearance is earthy and it is almost odorless. Glass splinters practically do not occur in the compost. The capacity of the factory is 80 tons an hour.

Second Compost Plant With Railroad Delivery

In the years 1950 and 1951 refuse was added from Groningen (145,000 pop.) and Zandvoort (15,000 pop.), and

Ameresoort (60,000 pop.) completed a 30-year contract with the Waste Disposal Company V.A.M. last year.

The refuse quantity from these cities gradually became too much for the compost plant at Wyster so that a second plant had to be built. This was put into operation in 1955 at Mierlo near Eindhoven (South Holland) in a region with sandy soil upon which compost acts very favorably. At first the refuse from Eindhoven and a few neighboring communities (total pop. 175,000) was handled but now the plant, second largest in Holland, has been provided with railroad delivery so that part of the refuse from the Hague can also be sent there. On August 2, 1957 the first refuse train was emptied from the new viaduct.

Plant capacity has been increased to 70,000 metric tons of refuse per year making about 50,000 tons of compost. Formerly the available refuse was insufficient for full capacity. Refuse is now transported to the plants at Wyster and Mierlo according to the need.

The composting plant at Mierlo uses the van Maanen system which has been improved by experience in operation of the plant at Wyster. Advantages of this system are the relatively low investment (somewhat more than two million Gulden) (about $550,000) and the low operating costs. Production can be regulated to the market so that compost need not be stored for a long time. The plant produces standard compost for agricultural use, garden compost, and material for hotbeds (hot manure).

—Information Bulletin No. 4
*International Research Group
on Refuse Disposal*

Almelo

The compost works at Almelo began operations in October, 1956. The plant operates according to the grinding (Raspel) system that is already in use in the Dutch composting plants at Vlissingen, Schiedam, Sneek, and Delft. The Almelo works is also equipped to mix activated sludge with refuse.

The following is an extract from the speech made at the dedication of the plant by Director General A. W. van der Plassche, Netherlands Ministry of Agriculture:

The Ministry of Agriculture of the Netherlands has long shown great interest in refuse compost production because

Pictured above is the V.A.M. composting plant at Mierlo, in southern Holland, which was built in 1955 when the refuse quantity from Dutch cities became too much for the Wyster plant to handle. Capacity is about 50,000 tons annually.

it is necessary to consider all possibilities assuring an appropriate livelihood for the farmers and horticulturists. The development of productivity by use of remedial measures is an important role in a positive agrarian policy. Great possibilities still exist in Holland in soil improvement and greater productivity by farmers and gardeners. The Netherlands government, therefore, encourages the use of composts of refuse and other materials valuable for improving the soil.

The Ministry of Agriculture not only promotes this principle but has made extensive financial contributions in the past 25 years for the conduct of research and practical studies in the field of the preparation of compost. The Government has used 10 million Gulden of Marshall Funds for the promotion of this work.

Large quantities of compost have been made available to agriculture and horticulture because of this support. It has also been possible to compare different composting processes from the technical, organizational, and economic viewpoints.

Thus, a plant operating according to the "van Maanen" system was installed at Mierlo, similar to the first plant using this process at Wyster, but in modern form. In Schiedam, an experimental plant has been using the "Raspel" (grinding) system. *The installation of a whole series of new composting*

749

plants has been made possible due to the fact that communities receive government credit without paying any interest when they submit completed plans for compost plant construction.

The Schiedam experimental station started operating in October, 1951, following a similar station at Vlissingen in 1950. Plants using the Raspel method were opened at Sneek (1954) and Delft (June, 1955). The Mierlo plant began producing compost for the eastern portion of the province of North Brabant in the fall of 1955. In May, 1956, the first Dano plant was opened at Venlo, and two similar plants were built at Enschede and Baarn.

Construction of these plants represents the end of the first stage, since the credit of 10 million Gulden has now been exhausted. Nevertheless, two other communities, Arnheim and Hengelo, have decided to build Raspel composting plants with self-financing. Thus it can be seen that various composting methods have been tested and compost production has been distributed to a certain extent throughout the country. This is important because, in shipping and distribution, decentralization keeps transportation costs down. We can assert that both horticulturists and farmers are showing increased interest in compost as is demonstrated by increased demand and sale of compost.

—From a Report Given at the
*International Research Group
on Refuse Disposal*

HUNGARY

Preparation and Utilization of Municipal Wastes

In Hungary, which lost a large part of its cattle herds after World War II and which had a sharp decline in fertility of the land due to intensive cultivation during the wartime economy, a strong interest soon appeared for the preparation and utilization of community wastes by composting. In contrast to most western countries, this interest arose from agricultural needs and, therefore, contributes to the fact that no special difficulties exist for the sale of compost in Hungary.

The need for sanitary collection, treatment, and appropriate utilization of municipal wastes urged public works and community management officials to find a satisfactory solution. Only isolated developments occurred up to 1949 in this respect. In a few cities private projects existed for collection and treat-

Holland composting plants make use of the "rasp"—a grinding device—such as the one shown here at Schiedam. Many new plants are planned, since Dutch government gives credit (at no interest charge) to cities which are building plants.

ment of city wastes (usually only night soil, market- and slaughterhouse-refuse). They operated with primitive hand implements and could comply with only a few sanitary requirements.

After the general taking over of private enterprise by the State in 1949, appropriate officials saw the need of finding a comprehensive solution in the field of urban waste disposal. Refuse collection and sewage disposal have since been the duty of the appropriate municipal department, consequently causing no immediate problem. Collection of night soil in towns partially or not served by sewers and of industrial wastes, as well as suitable treatment and utilization of all municipal refuse, however, still await solutions.

On the urgent recommendations of agriculturalists, city administrators, and public health officials, the government decided to establish a national organization for management of all organic wastes, apart from agricultural wastes. This organization was instructed to deal with all town wastes and municipal refuse such as sewage sludge, night soil and pig manure from the large feeding pens (all mixed with peat), as well as refuse from open markets, stores, slaughter- and cattle-houses, and industrial organic wastes. The treatment and utilization of these wastes also fall within the scope of the assignment. The organization, led by a central administrative board in Budapest, was quickly established country-wide. Plants were established in 1949 for the first time in the suburbs of the nation's capital and in larger cities of the provinces. Plants were systematically established in all urban areas during the next few years and in 1957 about a million tons of valuable organic fertilizer for agriculture were produced by 50 plants. Peak production has not been reached yet by far. In order to supply the plants with the necessary amount of peat, a national peat production association was formed which took over peat mining enterprises at the same time.

As part of the program, all sale of commercial fertilizer was placed under a joint authority, partly to eliminate possible undesirable competition from the commercial fertilizer industry and partly to synchronize production requirements of the various areas. Later, an Organic Fertilizer Division was formed, whose major duties consisted of:

(1) Testing of composting processes by chemical, microbiological, and plant physiological means in their individual phases. This should particularly answer the following questions:

   (a) Relationship between differences in aeration, temperature and microbial numbers and activity on one hand, and the losses in total solids, organic matter and nitrogen, as well as increase in humus content, on the other hand.

   (b) The influence of varying aeration and temperature on the survival of pathogens, intestinal parasites, and weed seeds.

(2) The mixing of sewage sludge and other organic wastes with urban refuse.

(3) Composting night soil with frozen peat refuse in winter.

(4) Composting wastes difficult to decompose, such as rice hulls, reed (thatch) wastes, hemp and flax wastes, etc.

(5) Effect of seeding with finished compost or microbial cultures.

The composting plants are located throughout the country on sites fixed by the public health officials beyond the limits of city dwellings and with direct access by road or barge. Their size varies with the quantity of refuse to be processed. They are only slightly mechanized (conveyors, motors and pumps);

still frequently use horse-drawn vehicles and hand labor. The plants themselves have charge of collecting night soil and sewage sludge; all other community and industrial wastes must be transported by those responsible for the waste at their expense to the nearest compost works, in compliance with a government regulation.

The night soil is mixed with peat wastes and composted at least 21 days in low windrows. In this time—established by regulation—the pathogenic microorganisms and parasites are claimed to be destroyed. As the windrows (piles) may not be disturbed for the 3 weeks, they are covered with a thin layer (about 10 cm.) of finely sifted aged refuse for protection against fly infestation and for better decomposition of the outer layers.

After the 21 days, the night soil-peat is sold or generally mixed with other wastes and further composted. The proportions of individual components of the mixture are specified by the research Institute according to prior analyses. Analyses considered are quantitative yield, C/N ratio, density, water and ash contents, microbial activity, etc. General guidelines: As far as possible in mixtures of plant and animal wastes, nitrogen-rich materials should be mixed with cellulose-rich materials, coarse with fine, wet with dry, and microbe-rich with microbe-poor refuse. If necessary, the materials are inoculated with liquid manure during preparation. A C/N of 30-35, water content of 45-55 per cent, and ash content far below 50 per cent are sought. The compost-mixture is piled into long windrows, generally with a bottom width of 3 to 5 meters and a height of 1.5 to 2.5 meters without pre-treatment. Aeration occurs through vertical, also frequently horizontal, air channels. The larger windrows are turned if the high temperature begins to drop. The decomposition time is 5-9 months, according to the nature of the materials and size of windrows.

The refuse of large cities is a special problem as its heterogeneous composition obviates the need for mixing other waste matter (such as sludge) and the daily mixture is so great that it often must be segregated. Before composting city refuse, the discards (metals, glass, bones, etc.) are sorted out, otherwise treatment proceeds like that for mixed composts. Screening also is provided before disposal. Winter refuse is not composted because of its high ash and cinder content.

There are no particular selling difficulties for disposal of compost fertilizers in Hungary. This is primarily due to the fact that farmers need organic fertilizers and do not take a stand against the use of compost fertilizers. Secondly, in the nationally controlled planned economy, production and demand are largely synchronized to each other, no competition existing between the commercial fertilizer and the organic fertilizer industries, especially now because insufficient chemical fertilizer can be produced. Selling price of compost fertilizer is set so low (4.10 Forints/100 kilogram = the cost of 1.25 kilogram of bread = about $0.35), that its purchase is made profitable to all farmers. This low sale price is far below present manufacturing costs which are somewhat more than double that amount. The difference is compensated for by a state subsidy to the production plant.

—Dr. G. Farkasdi
Giessen, Hungary
(Information Bulletin No. 4
*International Research Group
on Refuse Disposal*)

INDIA

As everywhere in the world, so in India: The present disposal system aims at fulfilling sanitary requirements rather than at systematic utilization of the manurial value of the refuse. The author estimates that at present less than 10 per cent of the city refuse is returned to the soil as food for future crops. This is doubly serious in India, because under its tropical conditions the organic matter in the soil is rapidly destroyed. "A sufficient supply of organic matter is necessary in soils in order to keep the soil in good physical and biological condition, and thus to ensure healthy crop growth."

Since in India cattle dung is widely used as fuel, and since, as most everywhere, liquid manure is not carefully preserved at the source the supply of farmyard manure for fertilizing purposes is insufficient to meet agricultural requirements. In view of this deficiency, the new source derived from city wastes becomes doubly significant. As a result, several methods of sewage and refuse disposal were instituted. The old-fashioned system which France first developed of letting human wastes dry out in trenches produces an unsatisfactory product, poudrette, which is low in organic matter and smelly; besides it is alkaline in reaction and colloidal in nature, quick acting and highly unbalanced. As it is rich in nitrogen, it produces leafy growth, burns crops, and may lead to severe crop failures. The rawness of the malodorous material makes it disagreeable to handle, especially in India where purity laws and social systems are closely tied up with one another. As a result, members of a special class have to be hired to handle this substance. This in itself limits its usefulness.

As a result, the system of compost making came into existence. It is handicapped by two factors, especially the sanitation aspect, but also the municipalities' relative disregard for agricultural necessities. Just the same, it is gaining ground. The rules set forth for composting centers were quite simple. They should be located on the side where the winds can carry the odors off, in India usually the east side, since west winds are the prevailing ones. Half a mile's distance is recommended since greater remoteness increases the cost of transporting the night soil. Trenches and tracks are laid out and dimensions for the number of population computed. Then a layer of *katchra*, road sweepings and garbage, is alternated with a quantity of night soil at the ratio 3 to 1. It can easily be seen that this corresponds with Sir Albert Howard's method of making Indore Compost—6 inches of green matter and two inches of manure. The final layer is *katchra*, 9 inches deep. "If the proper proportion is maintained, a man's legs should not sink in when walking over the compost mass at the end of the day."

The details, while applicable to similar structures elsewhere, need not be related here. Naturally, besides the trench system, an above-ground method of composting is possible. Testing for temperature, prevention of fly-breeding, and marketing the finished product were further points to be considered. Under tropical conditions with rainy seasons certain problems may arise which would not occur elsewhere. But, the heat in the compost heap and the sealing action of the outside or top layer is so that all fly eggs and larvae are destroyed, if the heap is correctly made or the trench properly covered.

How far has this method of balanced sewage disposal taken hold since it was first introduced? In 1946, there were over 400 municipalities which have trained workers, and over 300 have gone into actual compost production. Considering the number of townships that *might* take up composting, these figures are not so greatly impressive, but when you analyze the amount of compost produced, the ledger shows up quite well. 270,000 tons of compost were prepared, of which 4 provinces account for over 60 per cent. In order to secure good distribution, the government of India offered a subsidy based on the farmer's actual use of the material. This compares with similar subsidies granted to farmers in the United States toward the application of lime or phosphatic fertilizers.

—DR. C. N. ACHARYA, F.I.C.
Nagpur, India

JAPAN

In 1956, a mechanized composting system was set up in Kobe, with the help of the World Health Organization under the direction of Dr. John R. Snell. The composting method, which makes use of a grinder, digester, storage bin and mixer, converts garbage into fertilizer in 48 hours. Kobe produces daily more than 350 tons of refuse and garbage in addition to 240,000 gallons of night soil. The city office is spending annually some 400 million yen for their disposal inclusive of the payroll.

The new facility, when fully operated in November, will be able to convert 30 tons of garbage into 20 tons of fertilizer in 48 hours. The high-rate composting process is totally enclosed.

Test runs on the T. A. Crane type digester indicated rapid digestion at high temperatures with production of a high quality compost. Calculations indicate costs for interest, amortization, operation and maintenance will come to about $2.20 per ton of refuse; the end product is conservatively calculated to be worth $7.50 per ton to the farmer.

Japan is budgeting funds for a program of 38 High-Rate compost plants of a capacity of 50 tons per day or greater, each, during the next 5 years.

SCOTLAND

Like any other city, Edinburgh also has its problem of refuse disposal. Intensive growth of the city and suburbs has sharply increased the volume of refuse so that the existing plants are unable to handle the material. Refuse dumping sites are scarcely available now and covering soil is difficult to procure. Edinburgh's problem was to find the best and most economical method of refuse disposal and utilization.

The usual methods have been used to date in the 3 city refuse plants: mechanical screening-out of dust and ashes (which make up the greater percentage of our refuse), mag-

A common sight along Japanese roads is the compost heaps pictured above. Besides individual piles such as these, Japan is budgeting funds for large-scale composting plants like the one built at Kobe with help of the World Health Organization.

netic separation of iron components, hand sorting of discard materials. The rest was burned. The chief problem was now to find a substitute for the incinerators for which construction and operation costs are very high. Besides it was idealogically desirable to return the organic refuse to the soil.

Before World War II, thorough studies in Edinburgh showed that composting of sorted refuse was feasible and that there was a demand for compost. The methods used then still offered a few difficulties and requirements of area and time were quite high. These difficulties can be eliminated by the Dano biostabilizer method developed a short time later. In July, 1955 at the city Seafield depot, an experimental biostabilizer of 190 cubic yards capacity was built which has since handled the rejected material from an existing city refuse plant. The plant operates 8 hours per day and 5½ days per week. The raw refuse handled amounts to an average of 70-75 tons per week with a compost yield of 35 tons and a like quantity of noncompostable refuse. To each ton of material fed to the biostabilizer are added 270-360 liters of liquid, either sew-

Garbage disposal was a major problem in Edinburgh, Scotland, until plant shown above was built at Craigmillar. The plant manager reports that 35 tons of compost are produced daily, "the whole output taken by a local agricultural contractor."

age sludge or 2 per cent ammonia water from the gas works. Maximum temperatures in the biostabilizer reached 60 degrees C. Following is an analysis of the refuse compost made by the "Edinburgh and East of Scotland College of Agriculture":

Moisture 44.9%
In the dry matter:
Organic matter 48.8%
Ash 51.2%
Nitrogen 1.1%
Nitrogen in organic matter 2.3%
pH-value 7.0
C/N ratio 25/1

Demand for the refuse compost is large, particularly in agriculture, truck gardening, and by private garden owners. The selling price is 35 shillings ($4.90) per ton. Bagging and delivery are additional. A special sales organization has not been needed to date.

It was recently planned to build another refuse compost-

ing plant to handle 140 tons of raw refuse per day. Encouraged by good results in the experimental plant, we decided to equip the new plant with two biostabilizers, each with an operating capacity of 290 cubic yards. Financial savings from such a plant, considering yearly loan and interest charges as well as reduction in payroll, reveal a considerable economic advantage compared to the usual incinerator, even if the compost has to be distributed free of cost. However, a considerable income is expected from the annual sale of 3,500 tons of compost. The plant is expected to start operation in the middle of this summer.

Another biostabilizer plant will be built at Powderhall (works) and will replace the old incinerator which is in very bad condition. The experimental plant at Edinburgh has awakened the interest of the most distant experts; visitors from more than 40 different nations have inspected it.

—N. G. WILSON
Lighting and Cleansing Dept.
Edinburgh, Scotland
(Information Bulletin No. 4
International Research Group
on Refuse Disposal)

SWITZERLAND

After many years of searching for a suitable mechanical method for preparation of refuse, the Bühler Brothers Company, a machine factory in Uzwil, has built a refuse composting plant in Lower Uzwil.

Incoming refuse is dumped from collection vehicles into a bin that has a storage capacity of about 23 cubic meters. No pre-sorting occurs and even bulky garden wastes can be processed with the refuse. The contents of the bin are fed past a steel weighing belt to the first mill for coarse grinding. Here all the material is broken up into pieces of about fist size, including tin cans, glass, cardboard, paper, wood, textiles, etc. The heterogeneous material is now capable of being transported and separated. Ferrous metals are extracted in two stages and placed in containers for delivery to scrap iron dealers. Because of the preliminary grinding the tins are so reduced in volume that customary baling of scrap iron is unnecessary. The ground material, free of iron, is transported vertically upward through closed tubes by means of a Bühler chain carrier to a vibrating screen of coarse mesh which separates the refuse into two fractions.

The screened material consists of heavy components which are pulverized between the two large rollers of a rolling mill. This portion contains practically all of the glass and ceramics which, because of their brittleness, have already been broken into small pieces by the primary grinder. The sieve residue (tailings) is comprised of all lighter material and fibrous components, chiefly paper, rags, wood fibers, leather, plastics, and rubber. Further grinding of this fraction is not absolutely necessary because these items do not hinder the composting; on the contrary, they improve the porosity of the compost heaps. But since the larger pieces, particularly of textiles and plastics, are not decomposed in the usual composting time of 3-4 months, they are undesirable in compost for purely esthetic reasons. The process therefore provides further reduction of the tailings in a fine grinder which also accomplishes good mixing. The milled and ground materials are brought together on the last chain conveyor and are discharged into a storage bin outside the plant.

The 12 electric motors operating the various machines and conveyors are controlled from a central panel located in the office room. A single manipulation on the control board suffices for complete automatic, step-by-step, operation of all motors beginning at the primary conveyor ahead of the weighing belt and primary grinder. If a stoppage occurs at any place in the plant, the safety switch of the motor involved shuts it off and with it all of the motors preceding it in the circuit. All conveyors preceding the blockage are stopped immediately while those following it work on in order to clear the system. The break is indicated by signal lamps and the entire plant is shut down after about two minutes. Servicing the plant is therefore foolproof and (automatic control) enables the operator to perform his duties in the composting area during the grinding operation.

Indicating and recording instruments are installed in the sub-station for control of motors for the main machines. The feed of the heterogeneous raw materials requires special control measures. Thus, the belt drive from the receiving bin is coupled with the primary grinder over an electronically-controlled maximal flow pilot relay. If the integration of flow and time exceeds a certain value, then the feed into the primary grinder is interrupted for 5-6 seconds. In this way the feeding points of the grinding process are instantly balanced and overloadings are avoided.

The sorted and ground refuse, now only about a fourth of its original volume, is conveyed by simple means to the nearby composting slabs and is piled in windrows about 1.5-1.8 meters high. Experience has shown that 2 to 3 turnings are needed with a decomposition period of 3-4 months. After this period the decomposition process is practically completed and the finished compost may be piled into larger piles or released to consumers. The repeated temperature rises which the compost undergoes after initial placement and after turning serve as a guarantee that the end product is hygienically unobjectionable. Experiments were made with adding sewage sludge (digested and fresh) to the refuse being composted which further increased the value of the compost. Some of the analyses of refuse compost with stable manure for comparison are shown in the following table.

	Refuse Compost	Stable Manure
Moisture content (%)	41.0	77.5
Volatile solids (combustible matter) (%)	20.4	17.4
Humus carbon (inert carbon) (%)	5.8	5.2
Active organic matter (%)	14.7	12.3
Alkali-soluble humus (%)	4.8	5.0
Total nitrogen (%)	0.6	0.4
Phosphorous as P_2O_5 (%)	0.36	0.21
Potassium as K_2O (%)	0.43	0.43
Calcium as CaO (%)	5.3	0.9
Magnesium as MgO (%)	0.65	0.23
pH value	7.6	7.3

The analyses are based on the fresh material (wet weight).

—H. HURTER
Municipal Magistrate
Uzwil, Switzerland

THAILAND

A large mechanized composting plant is being built (1959) in Bangkok, the capital of Thailand, in southeast Asia. Instead of dumping the garbage collected from its population of 1,000,000 on the outskirts of the city, the refuse will be composted and sold. It is claimed that sale of the material will more than cover the approximately 3 million dollar cost of the plant and its operation.

The composting system is modeled after the plant in Jersey. Bangkok city officials contracted with two English firms, John Thompson Industrial Constructions, Ltd. and Composting Engineers, Ltd., who specialize in the design of composting processes. A pilot plant, which had been set up several years ago by the Thailand Department of Agriculture, has shown that the project's disposal method can produce high-quality compost.

The process is described as follows: Collected refuse is brought to the site and unloaded directly into two hoppers; all unsuitable material is removed by magnetic and manual sorting; salvageable material is separated for sale; the remaining compostable garbage will be shredded mechanically and refined in ballistic separators which remove fragments of non-ferrous metal and ceramics before sewage sludge is mixed with the garbage to form raw compost. This will then be conveyed and distributed mechanically into special chambers under conditions lethal to harmful organisms.

The composting process can be operated with or without sewage sludge. The garbage will be mixed with water if sludge is not added. With a suitable sewage system available, the conveying of sludge could be completely mechanized with both sewage wastes and refuse being disposed of in a combined composting plant.

The composting house is a 6-floored building, so designed that the composting material, delivered to the top floor level and mechanically spread over a series of troughs which form the floor, can be passed down from floor to floor by inverting the troughs. In passing from floor to floor, the material is automatically turned and aerated.

The plant, located in a suburb of Bangkok, is scheduled to start operation this year. Production capacity is about 90,000 tons annually.

INTERNATIONAL RESEARCH GROUP ON REFUSE DISPOSAL

A great deal of valuable information on European composting methods has been issued by the International Research Group on Refuse Disposal. Much of this information has been made available in this country through a series of Information Bulletins edited by John Wiley of the Technical Development Laboratories, Public Health Service in Savannah, Georgia.

The first objective of this international study group was "the establishment of criteria and the introduction of test methods for the evaluation of the quality of compost." A review of these reports reveals that this group is succeeding in its goal; the following excerpts on various composting phases show why this is true:

Mixing Digested Sludge With Refuse

The question of the mixture of digested sludge with municipal refuse is of great importance in many countries. We have undertaken some planned experiments concerning this and have drawn from them the following conclusions: without any difficulty, 30 per cent of digested sludge may be

DESCRIPTIONS AND DATA FROM SOME EUROPEAN COMPOSTING OPERATIONS

	Location of Plant					
Item	Edinburgh, Scotland Dano	Gladsaxe, Denmark Dano	Sollerod, Denmark Dano	Delft, Holland VAM	Schiedam, Holland VAM	Jersey, Great Britain
I. Raw Material						
A. Population served	500,000 Not all composted	54,000	25,000 Designed for 50,000	70,000	80,000	57,000 winter 95,000 summer
B. Quantity, tons/day	22	40	19 (designed for 38)	44 to 55	38	56-67 maximum 123
C. Composition	% by Weight	Tons/Day	Same proportions as Gladsaxe.	% by Weight Moisture: 36% winter 56% summer C/N about 50:1	% by Weight Moisture: 36% winter 56% summer C/N about 50:1	% by Weight Moisture: 20-30% C/N about 30:1

Composition (Edinburgh, % by Weight):

Fraction	%
Fine dust, 5/16"	21-42
Small cinders, 5/16"-3/4"	9-18
Large cinders 3/4"	5-15
Total ash	35-75

Composition (Gladsaxe, Tons/Day):

Fraction	Tons/Day
Compostable	32.43
Rejects	6.06
Salvage	1.51
Bones	0.08
Bottles	0.02
Bread	0.09
Metal	1.11
Rags	0.15
Glass	0.02
Bones	0.02
Other	0.04

Composition (% by Weight):

Fraction	Edinburgh	Delft	Schiedam	Jersey
Vegetable and putrescible	3-16	25-50	30-55	10-40
Paper	8-25	10-30 (plants, etc.)	8-20 (plants, etc.)	—
Metal	4-8	15-21	15-21	—
Rags	1-2	1-3	1-3	—
Glass	4-9	1-3.5 (460 tons/yr.)	1-3.5	—
Bones	0.3	0.4	2	—
Other	3-4	0.5-1.3	0.5-1.3	—
		0.6	0.6	—

D. Collection

Item	Edinburgh	Gladsaxe	Sollerod	Delft	Schiedam	Jersey
Times/week	2 at curb	—	—	2	City pays VAM 27¢/person/yr. Revenue $21,000/yr.	—
Trucks	60	—	5	6 (3.9 tons)	6	60
Men	180	—	15	18	18	—
Segregation	None. 1/5 garbage and paper collected separately, not composted. 280 tons/mo.	None	None	None. Most garbage collected separately and sold to farmers.	None. Most garbage collected separately and sold to farmers.	None. Special collection of cardboard cartons from stores and shops.

II. Preparation for Composting						
A. Separation	Magnetic for cans and ferrous metals. 4" screen before Bio-stabilizer. 7/16" screen after Bio-stabilizer.	Magnetic for cans and hand picking of above listed salvage.	Magnetic for cans. 5/8" screen after Bio-stabilizer.	Large wood boxes collected separately and burned. Bones, rags, glass, metals hand picked (1 man); magnetic for cans.	Same as Delft.	3/8" dust screen, extra winter dust stored and added in summer; 1" cinder screen; magnetic for cans; handpick rags, nonferrous metal.
B. Grinding	In Bio-stabilizer	In Rotor-Silo	In Bio-stabilizer	Rough grind by rasping machine (Dorr-Oliver). 3/4" holes. Roll crush and hammer mill to 1 mm. Hammer mill centrifugally separates rejects.	Same as Delft.	Hammer mill for cartons. Hammer mill for refuse minus screenings, cans and salvage.
C. Other equipment used	Receiving hopper, conveyor belts, dust extractors.	Receiving hopper, conveyor belts.	Receiving hopper, conveyor belts.	Receiving hopper, conveyor belts, worm conveyor, storage silo, water spray.	Same as Delft.	Receiving hopper, conveyor belts with scale and automatic speed control. Mixing cylinder for refuse, dust and sludge.
III. Composting						
A. Process used	Dano Bio-stabilizer, 5-day detention.	Dano Rotor-Silo 1-day detention followed by windrow.	Dano Bio-stabilizer, 5-day detention.	6 1/2' high windrows with 8-12 week detention. Turned once at 4-6 weeks.	Same as Delft.	6-floor silo. 1-day detention each floor. 6 weeks in 6' high covered windrows. Turning not needed but done occasionally.
B. Sewage or sludge	Sewage screenings added for disposal and moisture control. Ammoniacal liquor added for nitrogen.	Digested sludge from adjacent sewage plant added for moisture control and sludge disposal.	Sewage sludge or water can be added for moisture control if necessary.	No sludge. In winter water added at rasp and before windrow; in summer, only before windrow.	Same as Delft.	Sludge added to raise raw refuse to 65% moisture. All sludge from adjacent sewage plant to be composted.

DESCRIPTIONS AND DATA FROM SOME EUROPEAN COMPOSTING OPERATIONS—Cont.

Item	Edinburgh, Scotland Dano	Gladsaxe, Denmark Dano	Sollerod, Denmark Dano	Delft, Holland VAM	Schiedam, Holland VAM	Jersey, Great Britain
IV. Finished Product						
A. Quantity, tons/day	19.0	42.0	16.0	40-50	35	—
Compost "	10.4	34.4	11.5	34-42	30	25-30
Rejects "	6.3	6.1	4.0	6-7.5	5	—
Salvage "	2.3	1.5	0.5	Included in rejects.	Included in rejects.	—
B. Analysis, per cent						
Moisture	43	32	—	40 maximum	40 maximum	—
Solids	57	68	—	60 minimum	60 minimum	—
Organic	47	25	—	—	—	—
Ash	53	75	—	—	—	—
Nitrogen	1.1	—	—	—	—	—
Nitrogen in organic	2.4	—	—	—	—	—
pH	7.6	—	—	—	—	7.4
C/N	24.1	—	—	20:1	20:1	12:1
C. Bulk storage	Windrows up to 3 months with occasional turning.	Windrows from 2 weeks to 4 months.	Windrows	Windrows for 5 months maximum. Concrete block floor sloped and drained to sewer.	Same as Delft.	Windrows for 5 months maximum.
V. Disposal						
A. Compost	Sold as soil conditioner in bulk or returnable bags. Sold at plant or delivered within 5 miles of city line.	Sold as soil conditioner within 20 miles of plant, delivered in 5-ton trucks. 42¢/ton, revenue $4,500/yr.	Sold as soil conditioner, no delivery. 90¢/ton, revenue $3,800/yr., estimated.	Fresh-ground refuse sold as heating manure, $3.20/ton. Must add 9 lb. of sulfur/ton to control pH. Compost sold as soil conditioner, $2.60/ton. No delivery.	Same as Delft. Total income $25,000/yr. No delivery.	Sold as soil conditioner, about $7.00/ton. Total income about $70,000/yr. No delivery.

	Col 1	Col 2	Col 3	Col 4	Col 5	Col 6
B. Rejects	Material not passing screens taken to city dumps.	Dumped and used to cover industrial waste.	Used as land fill.	Incinerated or dumped by men renting salvage rights.	Same as Delft.	Combustibles burned, noncombustibles dumped.
C. Salvage	Garbage sold as hog food, $13.10/ton. Paper, cans, bones, rags, metal are sold. $280,000/yr. total.	Salvage listed above sold, $4,350/yr.	Cans baled and sold, $4.50/ton. Income $810/yr.	Rights rented to scavenger, $2,200/yr. He receives salvage proceeds and disposes of rejects.	Same as Delft, but rights rented for $6,250/yr.	Sold in England. Baled cans and scrap metal, $3.60/ton; rags, $6.25/ton.
VI. Operation and Cost						
A. Equipment	$100,000 in 1955	$100,000 in 1950 without buildings.	$110,000 in 1956 without buildings.	$156,000 in 1955, complete plant. Estimated $200,000 in 1957	$182,000 in 1951, complete plant.	$600,000 in 1956.
B. Electrical power	14-18 kwh/ton refuse	13 kwh/ton refuse	20-25 kwh/ton refuse.	9 kwh/ton refuse	9 kwh/ton refuse	6-8 kwh/ton refuse
C. Operators	2 full, 1 part time	3 1/2	2	1 foreman, 4 unskilled	Like Delft + 1 sales	1 foreman, 11 unskilled
D. Trucks and loaders	1 each	1 each	1 loader	1 loader	1 loader	1 cab with 2 trailers and 1 loader
E. Land area	1 acre	3.3 acres	2 acres	4 acres	2.5 acres	3 acres
F. Maintenance	After two years liner plates are being installed in Bio-stabilizer.	57¢/ton refuse/yr. for screen plates, conveyors, feed screw, tractor, grounds and buildings in '55-'56. 7 yr. average 15¢/ton/yr.	38¢/ton refuse/yr. for hammer mill rails twice per week; rasp plate holes, 1-2/yr; rasp plate pins, every 2 years.		Same as Delft.	Not available. Total operating cost $65,000/yr. excluding amortization. Repair hammers every 5 days.

—Prepared by JOHN NESBITT, Assistant Professor of Civil Engineering, Penn State University

767

added to the dry refuse. Fermentation runs a normal course, and neither in the chemical analysis nor in the bacteriological tests could we detect any considerable differences. The nitrogen content rose from 0.41 to 0.49 per cent which corresponds to an increase of only 0.08 per cent.

In one such trial, 4 tons of fresh refuse was mixed with 1, 2, 4 and 8 tons of digested sludge, with a water content of 95 per cent, and then composted. The composts thus obtained were compared by my colleague Kortleven with a compost from the same source, but to which was added only one ton of water. He made the comparisons at a pilot plant where 34 tons of compost were added per hectare (2.49 acres) of soil, for each trial.

It was shown that, in all experiments with composts of mixed refuse and sludge, an increase of about 5 per cent resulted in the harvests.

Besides, the fresh wastes may be utilized as a filtering medium for the undried sludge. In this way at least 200 per cent of sludge can be mixed in with the domestic wastes. It appears that the sludge is absorbed by the wastes after the manner of a colloid, while most of the water drains off at the base of the waste. It would be of value to repeat such experiments on a large scale, because they might make an important contribution to the solution of the problems of the sludges coming from sewage treatment plants.

—Dr. F. C. Gerretsen
Agricultural Experiment Station, Holland

Refuse-Sludge Compost

In trials conducted in parallel on tracts of very different kinds of soils, the 7-year experiments at Puch, Bavaria, showed that the refuse-sludge compost, consisting of two parts summer domestic refuse and one part of dried sludge (mixed and composted together) furnished an efficacious product for soil improvement and a good fertilizer.

... Refuse-sludge compost, made in a form suitable for use by farmers and gardeners and sold at a reasonable price, can serve perfectly to fill the gap in the humus supply.

—E. Stiegerwald
Bavaria

Results with Sludge-Refuse Mixture

Dr. Rohde has composted considerable amounts of partially dried sludge alone from the Berlin sewage treatment plant (70 per cent moisture). The material was turned many times until the moisture dropped to 60 per cent and then composted it in piles into which aeration tunnels were dug. However, sludge is mostly composted with refuse. To compost all sludge and refuse from any one region requires drying the sludge to about 70-75 per cent moisture. Dr. Braun reported better results using sludge concentrated in a vibrating thickener rather than on open sludge drying beds and believes this due to physical changes in structure due to the vibrator. Dr. Pöpel thought it was due to the water bound by the cells in sludge from drying beds. Results of research by the town of Gladsakse were similar to those by Braun and Allenspach in Switzerland.

Dr. Kick (Bonn) mentioned good results with sludge-refuse mixtures at Baden-Baden, attributing them to good mixing of the wastes. The raw refuse contains more potassium while the sludge, of course, contains more nitrogen and phosphorus. Poorer results were achieved with plain refuse composting.

> *—Summary of Discussions of Dusseldorf Compost Group*

Raw Materials for Composting

As summer urban refuse is low in ashes and rich in organic substances, it is particularly well suited to composting. Yet the organic content is still not high enough to make a high quality compost. Therefore, the addition of organic material such as activated sludge is to be recommended, preferably dried sludge. It has been observed at Weinsberg that, if liquid sludge is mixed with refuse, aeration of the compost heaps is insufficient and, as a result, an insufficient transformation of organic matter to humus results.

Costs of Composting Urban Refuse

Composting installations must be so planned that the compost, according to its value, finds buyers without excessive transportation costs. Production costs at Weinsberg are now about 6 German marks per cubic meter of refuse compost. Breakdown of cost figures are:

Transportation—8 per cent; composting—44 per cent;

screening the compost—32 per cent; removal of debris—6 per cent; machinery costs—7 per cent; interest on capital—3 per cent.

The production costs could be reduced by further mechanization of composting and screening operations. At such a price the product is far cheaper than any other purchasable organic fertilizer and concomitantly the valuable materials are returned to the soil.

—ERNST KLENK, *Director*
State Educational and Experimental Station
for Viniculture and Horticulture,
Weinsberg bei Heilbronn, Germany

Maturity of Compost

While it is difficult to define the concept of maturation of a compost, the amount of CO_2 production or appearance of nitrates may measure the end-point. Manure composts are considered stable with C/N of under 20, a degree of decomposition of 30-35 per cent (amount of the organic substance soluble in acetylbromide), and a ratio: nutritive humus/permanent humus of two. Well-decomposed compost shows a degree of decomposition of 40 per cent. Still more mature humus exists in brown and black earths, consisting of about 80 per cent permanent humus and the remainder chiefly uronic acid complexes which are biologically resistant. Soil conditions will determine whether a compost or stable manure of greater or lesser maturity should be used. Sandy soils poor in humus require a product rich in permanent humus, heavy soils require more nutrient humus.

—DR. U. SPRINGER, *Subdirector*
Federal Institute for Plant Culture and
Plant Protection, Munich

NEED FOR RESEARCH

The following points made by the International Research Group on Refuse Disposal stress the need for further research on municipal composting problems:

In the analysis of compost, it is essential to establish standardized methods of chemical and bacteriological testing. While sufficiently exact chemical methods are known for the determination of amounts of ash, total nitrogen, and total carbon, this is not the case for the determination of the amounts of combustible carbon, of the easily decomposable organic substances, and the assimilable nitrogen. Precise methods for bacteriological investigation are also lacking. It would be very desirable if at least one institute in each country were to occupy itself with the principles of analysis applicable to compost and the development of recommended methods, and that these institutes keep constantly in touch with each other.

Insofar as the composting itself is concerned, many problems exist that should be solved, such as that of the duration of composting in relation to the desired content of readily decomposable organic matter. Furthermore, the question of aeration of the compost should be thoroughly studied by the analysis of the gases of decomposition. Also the inmixing of sludge is a pertinent study question, particularly as regards its influence on the course of the composting. It is clear that the product should be analyzed frequently, both before and after the composting, and that the course of the temperature should be recorded.

Satisfactory investigations concerning the use of compost in horticulture and in agriculture can be conducted only by competent experimental stations. Such trials should be conducted with all the strictness required, and in an objective manner, in order to protect the farmers from economically or idealistic-sentimentally colored propaganda.

For the conduct of field or laboratory trials, the State experimental stations deserve primary consideration. While small, planned experiments undertaken by the composting plants themselves are important, positive results so obtained should be verified by official agricultural experimental stations, before the results are released to the public and allowed to be publicized. In this respect, too, particularly concerning the establishment of a more or less standard technique of analysis, international collaboration would be very useful and desirable.

A scientific basis of solid facts which would allow the explanation of the favorable or injurious action of compost under various circumstances, is still often missing and, when this has been the case for a long time, imaginations have been given free play. Such investigations can be conducted only by specialists, and oftentimes a costly, well-equipped laboratory is indispensable. Besides, these studies must often be conducted over a long period of time as, for example, the investigations concerning the formation of humus and its accumulation.

Chapter 21

THE USE OF SEWAGE SLUDGE
AS COMPOST

How good is sludge as a fertilizer and soil conditioner? Is it practical to use? What is its nitrogen, phosphorus and potash content? How safe is it? Is there an objectionable odor? What are the experiences of cities that have been marketing sludge? How much does it cost? Are users satisfied? How can more cities profitably offer their sludge as a fertilizer to local gardeners and farmers and thereby help defray the costs of operating sewage disposal plants?

Practically every city and town with a population above 2,500 owns and operates a sewage disposal plant. A substantial part of the municipal budget is concerned with the operation and maintenance of these disposal systems.

According to a Statistical Summary of Sewage Works in the United States, in 1957, 11,131 communities in the United States had sewer systems serving 98.4 million persons. This was slightly more than 57 per cent of the total estimated population of the country in that year. These sewer systems served communities having a census population of 102 million, of whom 96.4 per cent were connected to the sewer systems.

Of the 98.4 million population sewered, 22.3 per cent discharged raw sewage and 77.7 per cent treated sewage. If minor treatment—less than sedimentation—is not considered as treatment, sewage from 75.8 per cent of the population connected to sewers is treated.

The 76.4 million persons served by treatment resided in 8,066 separate communities and were served by 7,518 treatment plants. The majority, 61.8 per cent, of these plants furnished secondary treatment, and served 56.7 per cent of the population served by treatment. Secondary treatment plants served 44 per cent of the total population connected to sewers.

Present disposal techniques have come in for criticism recently, as public sentiment has come out more and more for cleaner streams. "It is thus essential that more of the organic constituents present in raw sewage be removed in processing plants serving our centers of population," Dr. Myron Anderson of the U. S. Agricultural Research Service points out. "A few of the disposal systems in operation recover a large part of the plant nutrients, except potassium, present in raw sewage. Sludges of high quality recovered after heating often are used directly as fertilizers. The sludge output of a large number of disposal plants is of low grade as fertilizer but has some value when applied to land in the manner that farm manure is used. The better grades of sludge are often sold to defray a part of the expenses of operating a plant."

You can see then that there are 3 good reasons to develop garden and farm usage of sewage sludge:

1. help solve the problem of stream pollution;

2. supply a tremendous source of organic soil conditioning material; and

3. defray some of the operating costs for disposal plants, thereby saving some money for the city.

One very important point to keep in mind is that the production of high-grade sludge is the result of the need to discharge good-quality water into our nation's waterways. Actually it is a by-product—which makes it economically realistic.

Increased Sale of Sludge

Sales of sewage sludge to gardeners and farmers throughout the United States have been upward in recent years. In cities such as Boise, Chicago, Wichita, Grand Rapids, Duluth, Omaha, Santa Fe, Schenectady, Houston, Roanoke and Milwaukee, superintendents of sewage treatment plants report that demand for sludge has been increasing.

F. C. Funnell, Jr., head of the Roanoke, Virginia sewage plant reports that his "customers use ground sludge at $2.00 per cubic yard on lawns. Unground sludge, at $1.50 per cubic yard, is used mostly in the gardens. Sales run about two-thirds of ground sludge to one-third of the unground. This is all in bulk sales since we do no bagging. Our experience with the material shows spectacular results on both lawns and gardens over and above the results expected from the nitrogen-phosphorus-potash analysis of the sludge."

Some of the larger cities market their sludge through fertilizer distributors. Others (most well known is Milwaukee) have set up their own marketing and advertising departments.

SLUDGE FOR FERTILIZING

Following is a report from *Agricultural and Food Chemistry* about the use of sludge as fertilizer: Activated sludge entered the agricultural scene as a fertilizer during the 1920's. Annual consumption rose; USDA figures show that about 100,000 tons of activated sludge were used last year for direct application. Based on the output of cities that make activated sludge, another 100,000 tons a year is used in mixed fertilizers. Other types of sludge with lower nutrient values account for another 35,000 tons.

The Sanitary District of Greater Chicago is the largest producer, with a daily output of 450 to 500 tons. In 1958 this added up to 131,000 tons, which brought the district some $2 million in revenue. The Milwaukee Sewerage Commission can make 180 to 240 tons per day, and about 70,000 tons is sold annually. Third big producer is Houston which turns out about 16,000 tons per year under the name of Hou-Actinite. Besides these cities which distribute beyond their own areas, many others sell or give away low-grade sludge locally.

At present, H. J. Baker Brothers is exclusive distributor of Chicago sludge. Houston sells in bulk to formulators who package the sludge and sell it as is, or use it as an ingredient in mixed goods. Demand for activated sludge is quite good, and prices are firm. From June through September, Houston quotes a price of $2.75 per unit of nitrogen per ton, plus 50 cents a unit of available phosphoric acid. For October to May the nitrogen price goes up to $3.00 a unit. The Chicago material is listed in the same price range. For average analysis sludge, these figures mean that cities receive from $15 to $18 per ton. The exception is Milwaukee, which prices its product higher to pay for packaging and distribution. In 1957 Milwaukee got an average of $35.81 for each ton of Milorganite sold.

Dr. Anderson reports that Washington, D. C. produces about 120 tons of damp, digested sludge daily. On a dry weight basis, this is equal to about 40 tons. Flash-drying equipment is available but not used, because of inability of the city to market the sludge at a price that covers cost of heat-treatment and drying. At present, damp sludge is available to anyone who will haul it away. Much of the product is taken by the National Capitol Park Service and by adjoining County governments responsible for upkeep of public grounds.

Baltimore, Maryland has a sewage disposal system that combines primary treatment with activation of part of the material, then subsequent digestion of all solids. The heat-treated material has a nitrogen content of about 3.0 per cent and is sold to a jobber for delivery to different fertilizer companies. The price at the sewage works is about 5 to 7½ dollars per ton.

Spraying Groves

Florida Sanitary Engineer, Ralph Baker, Jr., describes how "several of our cities, namely Orlando, contract with local fruit growers for the use of liquid digested sludge which is pumped into tank trucks and then is sprayed upon the local citrus groves. Contract prices are usually in the range of $3.30 per thousand gallons."

The great majority of cities do not sell their sludge, but make it available to local gardeners and farmers free at the plant site. In Illinois, for example, according to Sanitary Engineer Carl Gross, "virtually every city and sanitary district which operates a sewage treatment works makes the digested and air-dried sludge available at the treatment works to anyone. In a few instances, there is a nominal charge but in general, the sludge is available at no cost."

Since 1948, Richmond, Indiana has been hauling liquid sludge for the benefit of neighboring farms. William Ross, superintendent of the plant, estimates that over 4 million gallons were hauled last year alone. A similar practice is carried on at Marion, Indiana where usage has tripled since 1952.

For Beautiful Parks

"The City of Las Vegas has never placed on market the sludge from its sewage disposal plant. It has been the policy of the City to use the sludge for development of parks, recreational areas and cemetery facilities over the last few years," according to V. B. Uehling, Public Works Engineer. "The demand for sludge for these purposes by the Park Department has exceeded the actual supply. We've found that the sludge has been a very useful product in adding humus to the desert soils found in this area and in building the turfs within the park developments."

In Stratford, Connecticut the sludge is shredded for park use and is also spread and mixed with sand for a fill over the refuse dump. "When mixed with sand, it makes a good binder holding the sand from blowing away and helps support the growth of rye used for a cover until the ground will support a good grass," explains the Stratford plant superintendent.

In Oshkosh, Wisconsin sludge helped out the city's children. "We had a stock pile of sludge one year," R. Frazier, superintendent of the plant reports, "and the park superintendent wanted to recondition his soft ball diamonds. In working out a plan, the sludge was ground and mixed with sand and clay and placed on the diamond. The results were surprisingly good. The diamond was more easily maintained, more life to the ground, dried out easier after the rains, etc."

Report From Nebraska

Scientist William Rapp, Jr. of the Nebraska Sewage Treating Plant Section comments: "We have at the present time 171 sewage treatment plants in the State of Nebraska. Of this number I would say at least 125 to 135 are using their sludge for some kind of soil conditioning work. Many of our smaller plants do not have any organized program for the disposal of their sludge and if someone asks them for it they readily give it away. If not they simply pile it up until somebody wants it or if too large a pile accumulates they get rid of it by any method that suits them. The following plants have a definite program for the disposal of sludge:

Omaha—Sells their sludge to anyone wanting it; they grind it, sack it or will sell it ground in bulk.

Lincoln—Sells all of its sludge to a private company which manufactures an organic fertilizer from it.

Grand Island—Takes its sludge from the digester in a liquid form and sells it to farmers for a nominal fee by the tank truck load. They also distribute it onto the farm wherever it is requested.

"Other towns in Nebraska that we know are carrying on a uniform program of disposing of their sludge are Sidney and Imperial. The majority of sewage treatment plants do not produce enough sludge to make the selling of sludge profitable; therefore they distribute or use it on city parks or other city lawns as they see fit.

"I have long been interested in the utilization of sewage sludge as a soil conditioner and have had the State Department of Agriculture Laboratory run a large number of nitrogen determinations on Nebraska sludge. To date I have had about 40 samples analyzed for their nitrogen content, and I find they average 1.8 nitrogen, dry basis."

The Right Approach

LeRoy Van Kleeck, Principal Sanitary Engineer of Connecticut's Department of Health, has done much research

776

Pictured above are the settling tanks at the sewage treatment plant at Schenectady, N. Y. According to careful records kept by the plant superintendent, Cliff Irving, "there is a $60.00 saving to the city every day" because of the marketing of sludge.

regarding the use of sludge as a soil conditioner and "has advocated the use of sludge for the above purpose for some years. His excellent report, "Digested Sewage Sludge as a Soil Conditioner and Fertilizer," contains illustrations of his property where sludge was used for a number of years with very gratifying results. Engineer Van Kleeck estimates that at least 50 per cent of the sludge output from some 55 municipal sewage treatment plants in Connecticut is finding its way back to the soil.

"The use of sewage sludge we have found in Connecticut to be largely dependent upon a proper interest and approach on the part of the sewage plant superintendent. If he promotes its use and explains to people its limitations, it is favorably received by the public. In a few towns where no publicity is given to the material it is simply used as fill."

Schenectady Case History

Experiences at Schenectady, New York point up the validity of Mr. Van Kleeck's observation. "We have no special way of promoting our sludge soil conditioner, other than taking

777

advantage of every opportunity to tell the public about its organic content and its ability to improve most every soil. It is my firm belief that we who are in charge of a sewage treatment plant are in duty bound to see that these organics are returned to the soil." Those are the words of Clifford E. Irving, superintendent of the Schenectady plant. Following is a history of his plant's experiences in marketing sludge:

"It was not until about 1924 when the first successful attempt was made to sell air dried sludge to the public. At that time, Morris M. Cohn (now editor of *Wastes Engineering Magazine*), then superintendent of the Schenectady plant, offered this material for sale at the astounding price of 10 cents per load. This followed an unsuccessful attempt to give it away. By establishing a price for this product, the public was made to realize that it had some value. The farmers came with their trucks and loaded them until the springs were overtaxed. The customer wanted his money's worth and indeed he got it.

"Through the years, the price advanced to 25 cents per cubic yard. Some attempt was made to grind the sludge and offer it for sale at 25 cents per bag, the customer bringing his own container. With all of this promotion, a warning had to be issued with each sale, of the possibility of some pathogenic bacteria being carried over in the sludge. This naturally limited its use to those crops which went to the table cooked.

"By 1948 when plans and specifications were being drawn for the modernization of the Schenectady plant, we realized that we had a good market for organic soil conditioner and that we should do everything possible to take advantage of it. We, therefore, had designed into our specifications the now existing facilities, namely vacuum filters, flash drying, incineration, fly ash and odor control, and sludge bagging.

"The new plant was started in January of 1953, but it was not until January, 1954 that there was sufficient sludge available to start processing. During this time we were actively engaged in a sales promotion campaign. We talked Orgro (the trade name which we adopted for our organic soil conditioner) to everyone with whom we had contact. We took advantage of all free newspaper, magazine, radio or television advertising we could get. We spoke to farm groups, garden clubs, parent-teacher groups, etc. We never allowed an opportunity to pass without plugging our product. We ran experiments to prove Orgro's value to our own employees for they are our best salesmen. Next we packaged Orgro in neat, easy-to-handle 65-pound three-ply paper bags.

"When we opened the door for sales in April of 1954, the entire inventory was completely sold in two days. We then limited customers to two bags per sale until September when we were able to meet the demand. Since that time our sales and production have increased each year.

"The following chart will present a cost picture of a typical day's operation at Schenectady.

	Dry	Burn
Labor	$24.50	$15.75
Fuel	31.38	13.44
Power	10.44	10.88
Bags	12.00	0.00
Ash Removal	0.00	To be Determined
Total costs	$78.32	$40.07
Revenue	100.00	0.00
	+$21.68	—$40.07

"It is obvious from this chart that there is over a $60.00 saving to the city every day we operate."

The Schenectady sludge has an NPK analysis of 2-2½; annual output is 250 tons with less than 5 per cent moisture content, and is priced at $1.00 for a 65-pound bag.

Largest Commercial Setup

Milwaukee and adjoining suburbs have an up-to-date sewage purification plant—the first one to use the activated sludge method on a large scale and to produce a high-grade fertilizer as a by-product. Its activated sewage treatment method removes 98 per cent of the bacteria and 95 per cent of the solids in sewage. The sludge product, Milorganite, is guaranteed to contain 6 per cent nitrogen and 3 per cent phosphoric acid plus many trace elements needed for plant growth. Almost a million tons have been produced and sold since production started in 1926. According to the Milwaukee Sewage Commission, the annual revenue from the sale of Milorganite exceeds $1,350,000 and covers about half the cost of operation.

Topsoil Building in New York City

For several years, New York City has been spreading sludge over some of its municipal park areas as part of a "topsoil building" project. Mr. Edward Brady, Director of Special Projects of the New York City Park Department, developed an entirely new method of applying the sludge. Here's how it is done:

Tankers carrying the sludge deliver it at a pumping station on the bay (Jamaica Bay), where it is pumped through two 12-inch cast iron pipes to the park site. After the land is graded with earth-moving machines, a network of 6-inch aluminum piping, purchased from an irrigation equipment company, is laid all over the area to be treated.

At regular intervals along this piping, portable fire engine deckpipe nozzles mounted on dollies are set into the pipes. Thus the liquid sludge, relayed by gasoline centrifugal pumps, can be evenly distributed over large areas at a time, each nozzle sweeping back and forth under the control of a single man.

About a gallon of the sludge per square foot is applied at each spraying. It is allowed to dry about 3 days, depending on the weather, then disked in. Every section of ground is sprayed and disked 16 times, until approximately 4 inches of sludge have been applied. The diskings mix this in 7 to 9 inches. The result has been a rich, dark topsoil perfect for park lawns, golf course and other recreational facilities.

Cost-wise, Mr. Brady analyzes it this way: "It costs the Department of Public Works approximately $560 a tanker load (250,000 gallons) to transport and dump sludge at sea. Three loads a week used to be carried away from the treatment plant that now supplies the topsoil project. So the city is saving over $1,600 a week—and at the same time producing the most vital substance on earth from a material formerly a complete loss."

Sewage Irrigation in Texas

About one billion gallons of water are released daily from city sewage treatment plants in Texas alone. Several times that much are released in other water-scarce states.

Just imagine how many critical farm problems would be solved if some use could be made of this water. Some years ago, the citizens of Kerrville, Texas imagined just that and did something about it. They solved one of their city's biggest problems—sewage disposal—so that the system pays part of its own costs. As a result of their efforts, they are now using this water for crop irrigation.

New York City has been building topsoil in its parks by spreading sludge. Tankers carry sludge to pumping station where it is piped to the park site. Sludge is pumped over land; about a gallon of sludge per square foot is applied each time.

It all began about 25 years ago when Kerrville built its first sewage treatment plant and bought a 320 acre farm about two miles from town. The city began turning the treated sewage effluent out upon the land to prevent pollution of the beautiful Guadalupe River which meanders through the scenic Hill Country of Texas.

In 1949, reports *Soil and Water* magazine, the city installed a sewage-collection system and built a new treatment plant on the city farm. In 1952, the city fathers decided to make the sewage disposal system more effective and at the same time make the farm pay.

Their first step was to call on the Kerr County Soil Conservation District for help in developing a plan. Soil Conservation Service men tested soils, made a water analysis, and made a topographic map of the fields with soil good enough for profitable irrigation.

SCS engineers designed and staked out a dam for a 5-acre reservoir for holding the treated effluent which came from the plant. The city put equipment to work on the dam and laid a 16-inch pipe from the plant to the pond. Diversion terraces were constructed to divert hill water from the 90

781

acres to be irrigated, so that the structures wouldn't be broken by runoff water. Ditches were cut to carry the sewage effluent from the pond across the fields, and concrete drop-structures were installed to prevent erosion in the ditch.

Dirt "borders" about one-foot high were constructed on the contour across the fields at right angles to the ditch. These borders were actually little terraces about 30 feet apart, and the land between them was leveled with a maintainer. In this way the leveling was done with a minimum of dirt moving, each border "check" became a level field in itself and water could be turned onto it from the ditch.

The fields were fenced off from the surrounding pasture and seeded to a mixture of alfalfa, perennial rye, fescue, and Harding grass. They watered it with "effluent," piped in fresh water for livestock, and waited for the pasture to get good.

Below is their cost of installing the system on the 90 acres:

Earthen reservoir	$1,673
Diversion terraces	1,587
Irrigation ditches	4,539
Borders and leveling	4,396
Pump	500
Fencing and seeding	900
16-inch pipe	6,400
Livestock water pipe	375
Total cost	$20,370

Beef cattle, sheep, and goats now graze the irrigated pasture, the City of Kerrville makes a profit from the farm while operating a model sewage disposal system.

State health authorities are generally opposed to the use of treated sewage effluent for irrigation of fruits and vegetables because of the difficulty of enforcing regulations to avoid contamination. Growing animal feed or fiber crops is approved. Grazing of dairy animals on sewage-irrigated land is opposed because of the possibility of contamination by contact of the animals with the sewage effluent.

Soil Conservation Service engineers discussed the special problems of irrigating with sewage. Industrial wastes sometimes contain materials toxic to plants and detrimental to soils, they said. Sewage irrigation differs from conventional irrigation mainly in that a system must be used which can take

782

care of a continuous flow of water instead of having a water supply which is turned on and off as needed. Facilities must be had for storing the effluent during rainy weather when it cannot be applied to the crops.

The Kerrville disposal plant serves a population of about 9,000 with a daily volume of about 750,000 gallons. The 5-acre reservoir has a capacity of 30 acre-feet and can store a two-weeks flow from the plant.

Kerrville dilutes the wet digested sewage sludge with the treated sewage effluent and discharges it onto the land in the irrigation process. Thereby they eliminate the need for sludge drying beds and the tedious labor involved in removing and disposing of the sludge.

Some 100 Texas farmers and cities are using sewage effluent for irrigation.

Effluent on Crops

Tests on an 80-acre Stoughton, Wisconsin farm showed that sewage effluent could save crops from drought, increase yield up to 100 bushels an acre for corn and 4 tons per acre for alfalfa.

A report in the *Milwaukee Journal* gave the following information:

The Madison, Wisconsin metropolitan sewage district treats about 19 million gallons of combined sanitary and industrial wastes a day. No matter how good a job the engineers do in removing objectionable matter, there is always a percentage of soluble chemicals left in the effluent flowing from the plant. This cannot be removed without distillation, presently prohibitive in cost.

Careful tests made by the University of Wisconsin show that after treatment there are 24.8 parts per million of nitrogen, 25.7 of phosphorus and 13.1 of potash in this effluent released from the Madison plant.

In the case of the sewage plant effluent, these fertilizing chemicals are in a soluble form, ready to be utilized by the plants coming in contact with this sewage plant "waste."

Sewage Farm

Bakersfield, California has constructed a sewage treatment plant to augment the capacity of its original primary works—and to provide effluent which irrigates the city's 2,500-acre "Sewer Farm" which has been rented to a large farming organization. According to a report in *Wastes Engineering* magazine by T. M. Scott, superintendent of the Bakersfield plant, the use of 8,480 acre-feet of this primary effluent for crops not intended for human consumption has reclaimed marginal alkali land of low value into a fertile farm. This use of plant effluent eliminates the problem of disposal of primary-treated liquids into a stream that runs almost dry during arid periods, and produces water that is valued at between $4 and $8 per acre-foot in the San Joaquin Valley.

The city is located in a semi-arid portion of the valley. Farming operations are conducted mainly by irrigation, with little or no dependence on rainfall. The only watercourse in the vicinity is the Kern River which does not flow to the ocean but terminates in a lake on the west side of the valley. This river does not flow at a constant rate but varies from almost no flow to a flood stage, depending on the season of the year. The flood stage occurs in the early spring and is caused by snow melting in the mountains. The low flow occurs during the late summer and early fall.

For reasons of low flow and terrain, it is not feasible to dispose of sewage in the Kern River. There is also the cost factor of providing secondary treatment, which would be required due to the low dilution available in this receiving stream. The City of Bakersfield disposes of its sewage on a "Sewer Farm." All treated effluents from the two treatment plants are used to irrigate crops grown on this farm. The farm is leased to a large farming organization which pays a nominal rental. The company is required to furnish the labor for handling the effluent after it leaves the treatment plants.

The farm, up to 3 years ago, was mostly marginal alkali land of low value. However, the farming company has, since that time, developed the land by leveling and leaching out the alkali. At the present time it is a profitable venture for them and for the city. While the rent received by the city is very nominal, it has received the benefit of a great increase in value of the property.

At the present time the farming company is growing cotton, feed corn, milo maize, sugar beets, barley, and permanent pasture for cattle.

Activated or Digested?

The fertilizer value of the sludge produced depends largely on which processing method is used.

784

Seven-thousand-gallon tank trucks spread liquid sludge from San Diego sewage treatment plant on city-owned land. Sludge is 7 per cent dry solids. Experiments have been made with "sewer farms" where effluent is used for irrigation.

1. Activated sludge: This kind is produced when the sewage is agitated by air rapidly bubbling through it. Certain types of very active bacteria coagulate the organic matter, which settles out, leaving a clear liquid that can be discharged into streams and rivers with a minimum amount of pollution.

Generally, activated sludge is heat-treated before being made available to gardeners and farmers; its nitrogen content is between 5 and 6 per cent, phosphorus from 3 to 6 per cent. Its plant food value is similar to cottonseed meal—a highly recommended organic fertilizer.

2. Digested sludge: This type of residue is formed when the sewage is allowed to settle (and liquid to drain off) by gravity without being agitated by air. The conventional anaerobic digestion system takes about 10 to 14 days from the time the sewage reaches the sedimentation tank until the digested solids are pumped into filter beds, often sand and gravel, for drying. The final step is removal of the dry material, either to be incinerated or used for soil improvement.

A few medium-sized cities located in agricultural areas dispose of a part of their short-time activated and subsequently digested sludge in liquid form. This is delivered to farmers within a radius of about 10 miles and is used for direct application to land.

Digested sludge has about the same fertilizer value as barnyard manure. Nitrogen varies from 2 to 3 per cent, phosphorus averaging about 2 per cent. It often has an offensive odor that persists for some time after application to a soil surface during cool weather. "This odor differs greatly in character, however, from that of raw sludge," Dr. Anderson states, "since drastic changes have taken place during digestion. The odor from digested sludges may be eliminated by storage in a heap during warm weather."

SOLVING PROBLEMS

In order to come up with some suggestions for solving the marketing problems, let's examine some successful municipal operations where sales are increasing. You've already read the story about Schenectady, New York. Boise, Idaho is another good area where "excellent acceptance of the product has been promoted," according to plant superintendent A. J. Wahl. Following are our questions, Mr. Wahl's answers:

1. Do you have any research reports or general experiences of gardeners and farmers who have used the sludge (B I Organic—3½ per cent nitrogen)?

Farmers are the largest consumers. One purchased 100 tons, ground to his specifications. Last year the normal silage (corn) per acre was 18 tons. The average where B I Organic was used in the seeding operation of corn planting was 27 tons of silage. Other uses by local gardeners include landscaping, lawn and shrubbery planting.

The Department of Agriculture has made analyses of the dry marketable sludge. All their analyses as to nitrogen content show that material contains ½ to 1 per cent above guaranteed figure on bag.

2. What kind of sales promotion efforts do you make?

We have not prepared any promotional literature or done any local newspaper advertising. Practically all retail outlets handle B I Organic locally and sell the same as a soil conditioner.

3. Do you have any suggestions based on your own experience on how the marketing of sludge could be improved and made more profitable to cities?

Here are some suggestions:

(a) interest local farmers to use on such crops as hay, grain and corn;

(b) interest local gardeners and greenhouse operators to use in putting in new lawns and transplanting trees and shrubbery for local trade;

(c) all sludge to be sold in small amounts, as per sack. Sell through local distribution agencies;

(d) sell direct to all users in ton or more lots—ground and in bulk to lower the unit price;

(e) interest home builders and landscape architects in putting in new lawns and shrubbery;

(f) interest the general public to apply product on existing lawns in the months of December and January. During this time, the winter snow and moisture will carry the nitrogen value to the root growth—eliminate any perceptive odor and exhilarate lawn growth in the spring.

Importance of Merchandising

The Soil Booster Corporation has been marketing sludge in the Oklahoma City area using the trade names, Soil Booster and Start-Rite. Sales Manager Ray E. Penn makes the following observations about marketing conditions:

"The marketing of sludge-type products hinges on selection of certain types of individuals as dealers. Of course the first consideration is knowledge of the dealer regarding plants and their requirements. Second consideration—good merchandisers. And last but not least, continuous striving on the part of the company for more and better information to be supplied to the dealer.

"Unfortunately, efforts in the past have been based upon products which do not meet the demand of the public. The first factor is that of reduction of odor, which can be controlled only by proper digestion and processing. The second requirement is that the customer wants faster growth than can be stimulated by sludge alone. Therefore, it is necessary to fortify many sludges in order to get the results they demand, and much educational work must be done in order to overcome the prejudices of the people regarding this material because of its source.

"Another factor, in some cases at least, is the opposition of the public officials themselves. Another factor to be considered is the misinformation regarding the nutrition of plants and the so-called necessity of balanced fertilizer. Under this category we would also include the lack of knowledge and information regarding the soil, the function of the mineral elements, the function of enzymes, organic acids, antibiotics and other compounds necessary to plant growth. And might I say in this connection, that it is necessary to lead people into the purchase of organic fertilizers by gradual methods, even though we know it is best."

How Much to Charge?

The retail price depends, of course, on the nutrient content of sludge produced, costs of producing it, and demand. Costs range from 25 cents per 100 pounds, not bagged (N— 2.5 per cent, P—1.5 per cent) for Roanoke sludge to $3.15 retail price for an 80 pound bag of Boise sludge.

In Boise, the sludge is contracted to a local company. The sale price to the city is 40 cents per cubic yard as taken dry from the sand drying sludge beds.

The chart which follows lists prices charged by various municipal plants:

City	Brand Name if any	Annual Output	Nitrogen	Phosphorus	Sales Trend	Price
Birmingham, Ala.	—	48,000 cu. yds.	2.25	3.0	No change	$1.50 per cu. yd. rough grade, $3.50 per cu. yd. ground
Phoenix, Ariz.	Air Dried, Digested	About 5,000 tons	(no recent analysis)		No change	$3.12 per ton air dried
San Diego, Calif.	Nitro Gano	3,500 tons	2.75	4.54	Down	$6.00 per ton contract price, —$2.80 per 100 lbs., bagged
Bristol, Conn.	Sludge Soil Conditioner	600 cu. yds.	2.69	2.52	Up	$.25 per bushel, pulverized; $1.60 per yd., sludge cake
Boise, Idaho	B.I. Organic	200-350 tons	3.59	—	Up	$3.15 per 80 lbs., retail bagged
Chicago, Ill.	Dried activated sludge	125,618 tons	—	—	No change	All sludge shipped in bulk—no bagging
Fort Wayne, Ind.	—	3,000 tons	2.5	2.5	Upward	—
Indianapolis, Ind.	Indus	50 Ton per day	5	2.7	—	$22 per ton
Richmond, Ind.	—	1,184 = 4,060,000 Gal. of Liquid Sl.	(No analysis made)		Up	—
Mishawaka, Ind.	Digested sludge from Lagoon	152	2.66	1.12	Up	—
Jasper, Ind.	—	50 tons	5.89	3.49	Up	—
Marion, Ind.	—	921 tons	1.49	1.45	Up	—
Wichita, Kansas	Wichita Soil Conditioner	5,000 cu. yds.	2.1	.2	Up	$2.00 per cu. yd., loaded at plant, $3.00 per cu. yd. delivered in city, $4.00 per cu. yd. delivered 10 mi. beyond
Battle Creek, Mich.	Battle Creek Plant Food	200 tons	2.8	2.6	No change	$2.00 per 100 lbs., bagged
Grand Rapids, Mich.	Rapidgro	600 tons	2	2	Up	$1.00 per 80 lbs., bagged $40.00 per ton. F.O.B. the plant, one potting soil processor buys compost in bulk, blends with peat moss, sells 3 qt. polyethylene bags.
Williamston, Mich.	—	—	2.1	2.1		—

City	Brand Name if any	Annual Output	Nitrogen	Phosphorus	Sales Trend	Price
Duluth, Minn.	Soil Conditioner Sewage sludge fertilizer	44 tons	1.0	1.5	Up	$1.00 per 100 lbs., bagged
Grand Island, Nebr.	—	about 1½ ton per day	4.2	—	—	—
Omaha, Nebr.	—	500-600 tons	2.5	1.5	Up	$1.00 per 100 lbs., bagged $1.10. $15.00 ton delivered in bulk, grounded form
Flemington, N. J.	—	80 tons	—	—	No change	—
New Brunswick, N. J.	—	2,100 tons	1.77	2.18	Downward	—
Pennsauken, N. J.	—	200 tons	—	—	Upward	—
Santa Fe, N. Mex.	—	500 tons	—	—	Upward	$2.50 per 100 lbs., bagged ground
Schenectady, N. Y.	Orgro	250 tons	2	2	Upward	$1.00 per 65 lbs., bagged
Fargo, N. D.	—	12,000 tons	—	—	No change	$.50 per 1,000 lbs.
Oklahoma City, Okla.	Soil Booster Organic Fert.		6 (fortified)	2	Upward	$3.60 per 100 lbs.
Houston, Texas	Hou-Actinite	12,000 to 14,000 tons	5	3	Upward	Sold only in bulk $3.00 per unit of nitrogen, $.50 per unit of phosphorus
Roanoke, Va.	—	1,688 tons	2.5	1.5	Upward	$.25 per 100 lbs.
Fond du Lac, Wisc.	Fond du Green	2,000 tons	2	2	Upward	$2.00 per 80 lbs. bag, $18.75 per ton
Milwaukee, Wisc.	Milorganite	70,000 tons	5.5	4	Upward	Sold in bulk 2 bu.—$.25, cu. yd.—$2.00, Ground $3.00 cu. yd. No deliveries, sludge sold locally from plant
Oshkosh, Wisc.	Oshkonite	600 tons	2.09	2.65	No change	
Sheboygan, Wisc.	—	1,000 tons	1.96	1.65	Upward	$.50 per 80 lbs. bagged. (retail local) Carload shipments price $5.75 per ton. (Sold to broker)

Chemical composition of certain sewage and industrial sludges, analyses on moisture-free basis

Kind of sludge and location of plant	Primary fertilizing constituents			Acid-soluble secondary constituents				Ash	Reaction (pH)
	Nitrogen (N) total	Phosphoric oxide (P_2O_5) total	Potassium oxide (K_2O) acid soluble	Calcium oxide (CaO)	Magnesium oxide (MgO)	Sulfur (S)	Iron oxide (Fe_2O_3)		
	Percent	Percent	Percent	Percent	Percent	Percent	Percent	Percent	
Activated sludges:									
Chicago, Ill	4.81	6.86	0.30	1.63	0.82	0.76	13.87	39.22	4.6
Chicago, Ill	5.60	6.97	.56	2.22	1.03	1.14	7.41	37.39	5.3
Houston, Tex	5.77	3.08	.30	1.26	.50	1.06	4.36	30.18	4.5
McKeesport, Pa	5.68	7.38	.61	2.52	1.43	.98	7.09	37.93	5.5
Milwaukee, Wis	5.96	3.96	.41	1.64	.93	.95	7.13	27.73	5.0
Short period, or fully activated sludges, subsequently digested:									
Des Moines, Iowa	1.81	3.31	.40	7.37	1.05	1.10	3.42	61.44	7.0
Hagerstown, Md	3.13	2.81	.10	4.68	.86	.96	2.34	47.06	5.9
Hagerstown, Md	4.71	4.96	.74	5.07	1.45	1.00	1.75	33.34	6.5
Los Angeles, Calif	2.49	4.07	.21	3.92	.78	1.00	6.04	49.11	6.1
Digested sludges, primary treatment:									
Beltsville, Md	1.89	1.64	.19	2.22	1.01	1.17	3.37	56.22	5.6
Greenbelt, Md	3.12	.91	.24	1.91	.28	.61	1.53	38.22	5.5
Washington, D. C	2.06	1.44	.14	2.38	.60	.89	4.44	52.83	6.0
Imhoff tank sludges:									
Beltsville, Md	.97	.56	.18	.69	.44	.33	2.18	74.28	6.0
Rochester, N. Y	2.54	1.16	.29	2.14	.87	.91	3.15	42.79	5.4
Lagoon sludge:									
Indianapolis, Ind	1.71	4.32	.28	15.69	1.66	1.50	4.62	58.56	7.2
Industrial plant sludges:									
Luray, Va	1.22	.42	.09	37.98	1.57	.79	.40	51.27	11.6
Mercersburg, Pa	2.64	.87	.17	12.96	1.24	.93	1.33	38.87	7.2
Williamsport, Md	1.45	.50	.18	18.87	.68	.58	2.13	55.69	7.6

Minor element contents of sewage sludges calculated as parts per million and as pounds per ton of suitable compounds in dry sludge

Kind of sludge and location of plant	Copper (Cu)	Equivalent copper sulfate (CuSO₄.5H₂O) per ton	Zinc (Zn)	Equivalent zinc sulfate (ZnSO₄) per ton	Boron (B)	Equivalent borax (Na₂B₄O₇.10H₂O) per ton	Manganese (Mn)	Equivalent manganese sulfate (MnSO₄.4H₂O) per ton	Molybdenum (Mo)	Equivalent sodium molybdate (Na₂MoO₄.2H₂O) per ton
	P.p.m.	Lb.	P.p.m.	Lb.	P.p.m.	Lb.	P.p.m.	Lb.	P.p.m.	Lb.
Activated sludges:										
Chicago, Ill	385	3.0	3,300	16.3	6	0.10	190	1.54	45.4	0.23
Chicago, Ill	1,225	9.6	3,050	15.1	67	1.18	135	1.10	6.5	.03
Houston, Tex	1,035	8.1	950	4.7	8	.14	65	.53	6.7	.03
McKeesport, Pa	1,500	11.8	3,650	18.0	74	1.30	150	1.22	6.0	.03
Milwaukee, Wis	435	3.4	1,550	7.7	8	.14	130	1.06	13.5	.07
Short period, or fully activated sludges, subsequently digested:										
Des Moines, Iowa	315	2.5	1,350	6.7	7	.12	420	3.41	4.9	.02
Hagerstown, Md	490	3.9	3,050	15.1	7	.12	70	.57	3.7	.02
Hagerstown, Md	435	3.4	3,100	15.3	12	.21	60	.49	4.2	.02
Los Angeles, Calif	1,440	11.3	3,700	18.3	15	.26	265	2.15	12.0	.06
Digested sludges, primary treatment:										
Beltsville, Md	480	3.8	2,050	10.3	4	.07	790	6.41	6.8	.03
Greenbelt, Md	360	2.8	1,450	7.2	8	.14	120	.97	2.1	.01
Washington, D. C.	435	3.4	2,200	10.9	8	.14	140	1.14	5.4	.03
Imhoff tank sludges:										
Beltsville, Md	100	.8	610	3.0	3	.05	130	1.06	118.0	.60
Rochester, N. Y.	1,980	15.6	3,400	16.8	12	.21	60	.49	5.1	.03
Lagoon sludge:										
Indianapolis, Ind	755	5.9	2,750	13.6	7	.12	440	3.57	9.6	.05
Industrial plant sludges:										
Luray, Va	90	.7	75	.4	74	1.30	145	1.18	.4	.002
Mercersburg, Pa	200	1.6	220	1.1	271	4.78	260	2.11	23.6	.12
Williamsport, Md	130	1.0	260	1.3	100	1.76	760	6.17	7.2	.04

Prepared by Dr. Myron S. Anderson, Agricultural Research Service, USDA

Principal Characteristics of Sewage Sludges from Six Connecticut Sources

Source of sludge	New Haven	Stamford	Torrington	Wallingford	Waterbury	West Haven
			Type of sludge			
Physical and Chemical characteristics	Digested; FeCl₃ and lime; vacuum filtered	Digested; FeCl₃, lime; vacuum filtered; flash dried-	Digested; air dried on sand beds	Digested (Imhoff tanks) dried on sand beds	Raw, primary; FeCl₃ and lime; flash dried	Elutriated; digested FeCl₃; vacuum filtered
Moisture content (moist basis, per cent)	72	6	69	66	8	71
as sampled (oven dry basis, per cent)	257	6	223	191	9	245
pH as used	7.5	4.9	5.6	6.7	7.9	6.01[1]
Loss-on-ignition, per cent oven dry	42	54	43[2]	41	71	56
Total nitrogen, per cent air dry	1.5	1.8	2.3	1.3	1.6	2.5
Organic Carbon, per cent air dry	29	....	28	25	50	36
Total phosphorus, per cent air dry	0.67	0.27	0.58	0.31	0.50	0.60
Total potassium	VL[3]	VL[3]	VL[3]	VL[3]	VL[3]	VL[3]
Total calcium, per cent air dry	4.3	1.1	1.1	1.5	3.6	1.9
Total magnesium, per cent air dry	0.26	0.32	0.18	0.22	0.17	0.14
Cation exchange capacity air dry me./100 g.	25		27	18	23	32
Weight per cu. yd. as delivered, lbs.	1085	500[4]	1450	1378	428	1210[4]
Weight per cu. yd. water free, lbs.	300	477[4]	627	472	404	350[4]
Industrial waste	Some textile dyes	No appreciable amount	Wool scouring and metal-plating wastes	No appreciable amount	Large amounts of metal-plating wastes	No appreciable amount

[1] Subsequent samples tested 5.2 and 4.5.

[2] Average of six samples which ranged from 29 to 51%.

[3] VL—very low.

[4] Estimated.

—Prepared by Prof. Herbert H. Lunt, Dept. of Soils, Connecticut Experiment Station

Comparative Composition of Undigested and Activated Sludges

Fractions	Undigested Sludge New Brunswick per cent	Activated Sludge Milwaukee per cent
Carbon	25.0	36.1
Nitrogen	1.8	5.7
Ether-solubles	6.5	4.5
Alcohol-solubles	1.2	1.3
Cold-water-solubles	0.9	1.7
Hot-water-solubles	1.0	2.7
Hemicelluloses	0.0	2.5
Celluloses	0.0	0.0
Lignins	8.2	6.6
Crude proteins	11.4	35.4
Ash	55.4	27.7
Moisture	5.4	4.2
Alkaline permanganate value	51.1	63.4
Neutral permanganate value	65.4	75.2
Nitrogen nitrified in 40 days	16.0	53.0

—Firman E. Bear and Arthur L. Prince
New Jersey Agricultural Experiment Station

State Reports—General Practice of Sludge Disposal

State	Market	Token Fee	Free	City Use	Not used as Soil Conditioner
1 Ala.	X-L	X	X	X-E	
2 Ariz.		X-L			X
3 Ark.		X-L	X-L	X-E	
4 Colo.				X-L	X
5 Conn.		X-L	X	X	
6 Del.					X
7 Fla.		X-L		X	
8 Idaho	X-L				
9 Ill.		X-L	X-E		
10 Ind.			X		
11 Kan.	X-L		X		
12 Ky.					X
13 Me.					X
14 Mass.			X-L		X
15 Minn.	X-L		X		
16 Mo.		X-L	X		
17 Mont.			X-L	X-L	
18 N. H.					X
19 N. J.			X		
20 N. Mex.	X-L			X-E	
21 Nev.				X-L	X
22 N. Car.			X-E		X
23 N. Dak.					X
24 Ohio	X-L				
25 Okla.	X-L				
26 Penn.		X-L	X		
27 R. I.			X		
28 S. Car.				X-L	X
29 S. Dak.			X		
30 Tenn.	X-L		X		
31 Texas	X-L		X		
32 Utah					X
33 Va.	X-L		X		
34 W. Va.			X-L	X	
35 Wis.	X-L		X-L	X	
36 Wyo.			X-L	X	

Legend: X, General Practice; X-L, Limited Practice; X-E, Extensive Practice.

—Water and Sewage Works

NEW PROCESS AND STEAKS

The following two reports, showing new developments in sludge research, appeared in *American City Magazine:*

"The Baltimore sewage treatment plant recently started a preliminary pilot-plant operation to improve the physical characteristics of heat-dried sewage sludge. The material is sold as a base for fertilizer.

"An Allis-Chalmers compacting mill, installed at the plant, compacts the dusty and finely-sized material from flash drying equipment between two rolls into a solid sheet and prepares it for subsequent granulation. The granulated sludge is of uniform size and density, flows freely, and contains little dust.

"The pilot-plant will be used to investigate variations in feed characteristics to the Allis-Chalmers compacting mill before going into full scale production. To operate the commercial size Compactor mill on a pilot-plant scale, a Shaftex speed reducer slows the machine sufficiently to process test quantities of several hundred pounds per hour. After being changed to full scale production, the plant will turn out about 50 tons of dried sludge per day, the physical characteristics of which will be greatly improved by the compacting and granulating processes. The end product contains valuable nitrogen and phosphorous bearing compounds."

The second report follows:

Beef cattle may be fattened on plant life grown in sewage purification lagoons if present research proves successful. Scientists at Northwestern University have undertaken a study of the processes by which nutrients in municipal and industrial waste waters may be reclaimed as animal food.

Purpose of the study is to learn more about the organic compounds which have specific effects upon the one-celled green algae found in sewage stabilization ponds. Growth of algae in waste waters is essential in the reclamation process. The researchers will attempt to learn which organic compounds are present in fresh sewage and in sewage which has already undergone aerobic treatment.

The two-year project supported by a $19,144 grant from the National Institute of Health of the U. S. Department of Health, Education, and Welfare, is under the direction of Dean Harold B. Gotaas of the University's technological institute,

Marion, Indiana, is one of the many cities in the United States which makes its sludge available to local gardeners and farmers. To explain the use of sludge as a soil conditioner, the city issued a pamphlet detailing its advantages.

and Assistant Professor Wesley O. Pipes, department of civic engineering.

Dean Gotaas and William Oswald, while affiliated with the University of California, developed a process of producing animal fodder from municipal wastes. Although the process has been patented, it is not commercially practical at the present time.

AMOUNTS TO USE

The city of Marion, Indiana has printed an excellent little pamphlet which includes the following suggestions for using sludge as a fertilizer and soil builder:

"(1) For starting new lawns—prepare the seedbed by mixing the sludge with the soil. A maximum dosage of one part sludge to two parts soil may be used if the soil is of a heavy clay texture. Spade the ground to a depth of at least 6 inches making sure the sludge is thoroughly intermixed with the soil. Never have layers of sludge and layers of soil in the seedbed.

"(2) For feeding well established lawns—the sludge should be applied in the winter and early spring months when the ground is frozen. The lawn may be covered with a layer of sludge one-half inch deep during the cold months of December, January, and February. This cover will provide an insulation to protect the grass roots from the harmful effects of freezing and thawing during this time of the year. In addition, ample plant food will be made available for a luxuriant growth of grass in the spring.

"(3) For reconditioning old lawns—on yards or portions of yards where the soil has been too poor to support an average growth of grass, it is recommended that the procedure under (1) above be followed. It should be remembered that grass roots grow into the soil to a depth of 6 or 7 inches only when the ground is of such a composition that will permit this growth. To top-dress and seed a section of ground that has not been properly prepared is a waste of time and money.

"(4) For gardens and farm land—sewage sludge provides an economical means of replenishing farm and garden land with nitrogen, phosphorus, and humus material. It should be put on the land just previous to the fall or spring plowing and cultivated in to the soil. The sludge cake may be applied as a manure to farm land at the rate of 10 to 15 tons to the acre. The weight of the sludge is approximately one ton to the cubic yard. It will be sold at a price far below that of any commercial fertilizer now on the market.

"Your county agricultural agent will be glad to give advice as to the proper method of applying the sludge to give the best results for your particular use. Additional information may also be had by calling the Marion Sewage Treatment Plant."

CONNECTICUT STUDIES

Ten years ago, Prof. Lunt started experiments at the Connecticut Agricultural Experiment Station to "explore further the suitability of digested sewage for soil improvement and as a fertilizer. The work was done in greenhouse pots, outdoor soil frames, and field plots."

The general procedure was to apply the sludge once, usually at several different rates, and grow successive crops on the same soil without further sludge treatment. Lime and fertilizer were applied as needed. The results are summarized as follows:

1. The rate of application of digested sewage sludges

should be governed more by their nitrogen content than by the amount of organic matter they contain. High applications may supply too much nitrogen.

2. Sludge improves the physical condition of the soil, particularly its aggregation of particles greater than 1 mm. The improvement is readily observable in practice as well as measurable by laboratory techniques.

3. Sludges differ rather widely in their properties, depending upon the character of the sewage and the kind of processing used in the treatment plant. Most sludges are acid but some are highly alkaline. The organic matter content ranges from 25 or 30 to over 60 per cent. Some come from sewage containing industrial wastes.

4. All of the sludges tested contain relatively large amounts of zinc and considerable copper and boron in comparison with other common types of organic matter. Industrial wastes increase the concentration of these metals.

5. In acid soils, sludge is frequently toxic to plants, the degree of toxicity varying with the type of sludge, the rate of application, the soil, and the kind of plant. The toxic effects can usually be prevented by raising the soil pH to 6 or higher.

6. Of the several kinds of plants grown spinach was most susceptible to injury, seldom showing any favorable effects from sludge treatment. Grasses and grains suffered the least from trace elements, and they usually responded to fairly heavy applications of sludge even on acid soils.

7. In a greenhouse experiment, where Torrington and West Haven sludges were applied at 65, 130, and 260 cubic yards per acre, maximum growth of oats, beans, and spinach occurred at the medium rate. Beets and turnips on the other hand, showed maximum growth at the 260 yard rate. West Haven sludge, being lower in trace elements, produced the largest plants; but it also caused bean and spinach plants to have $1\frac{1}{2}$ to 16 times as much manganese as was found in Torrington sludge-treated plants.

8. In general, sewage sludge treatments delayed seed germination, particularly lettuce and radishes, although under some conditions Torrington sludge favored germination. It appears that the effect of sludge on germination is associated with the increase in total soluble-salt content, hence a similar result can come from fertilizers or manure.

9. In some situations the inclusion of a moderate amount

of woodchips or sawdust (25 to 30 per cent by volume) favors seed germination and plant growth as compared with sludge alone.

10. Heat-dried sludges, whether raw or digested, are slow to nitrify, hence may cause temporary nitrogen deficiency similar to straw or sawdust. None of the sludges nitrify as rapidly as does commercial dried manure with which they were compared.

It is concluded, on the basis of the results obtained in these experiments, that digested sewage sludge as produced in Connecticut treatment plants improves the physical condition of the soil and has a more lasting effect than does manure.

It also supplies nitrogen and some phosphorus and trace elements. When used under proper conditions sludge improves current crop yields. High applications may delay seed germination, but they seldom lessen the final germination count.

Because the various sludges differ in reaction and in composition, it is important to know the nature of the sludge to be used. The acid sludges, especially those from sewage containing industrial wastes, may have severe adverse effects on plants. Usually such toxicity, which is due to copper or zinc, or both, and probably to iron deficiency induced by these metals, can be avoided by liming the soil to pH 6.0 or higher. Applications of sludge as high as 150 to 250 cubic yards per acre can be used under some conditions, especially for such crops as grains and grasses even on acid soils. However, 50 cubic yards is a safer rate.

Where the crop requires a medium to strongly acid soil, the application of sludges for soil improvement must be made with caution, if at all. This is particularly true where the response of the crop to relatively high concentrations of copper and zinc is unknown. Light applications, i.e., 15 or 20 cubic yards per acre, may be permissible.

The Connecticut State Department of Health does not advocate the use of fresh digested sludge on crops that are to be eaten raw. If the sludge is applied and worked into the soil 6 months or so prior to seeding such a crop, no health hazard is involved.

HOW TO USE SLUDGE

In his report, "Digested Sewage Sludge as a Soil Conditioner and Fertilizer," Mr. Van Kleeck writes the following on how to use sludge:

800

"Sludge may be applied as a top-dressing in the case of trees or lawns; in the hill in the case of melons, squash, or other vine crops; or spread, then plowed or spaded into the soil. When used as a top-dressing, it should not be applied too thickly, especially on lawns, or it may choke the growing vegetation. Sludge may be applied when the ground is frozen or covered with snow. In such cases it is raked and pulverized into the soil in the spring.

"The pH of heat-dried activated sludge is low, generally averaging 5.0 to 6.0. Air-dried digested sludge after a short period of storage will normally show a drop in pH to about 6.0. Digested sludge cake conditioned with lime for vacuum filtration has initial pH values ranging from about 10.2 to 11.2, but this drops rapidly when it is mixed with soil or more slowly on storage, as a result of loss of ammonia. Tests show that pH of lime-conditioned sludges drops to about 7.5 in 2 or 3 days so that the danger of too alkaline a soil should not occur from the use of such sludge. Furthermore, experience shows that the continued use of any type of sludge unless previously conditioned with lime requires the periodic addition of lime to the soil to prevent harmful acidity.

HOW SAFE IS SLUDGE?

". . . A special committee of the Federation of Sewage and Industrial Wastes Associations reporting on the 'Utilization of Sludge as a Fertilizer' states: 'The committee knows of no case of sickness traceable to the use of digested sludge or activated sludge.' "

(In the U. S. Dept. of Agriculture report by Dr. Anderson on sludge he writes: "Activated sludges need heat-treatment before use as fertilizer. Such treatment is normally provided for material to be marketed. The heat used for drying normally accomplishes the destruction of dangerous organisms. This means that properly heat-dried activated sludges may be used with confidence regarding their safety from a sanitary standpoint . . .

"It seems that States have generally accepted the conclusions of the Committee on Sewage Disposal of the American Public Health Association that heat-dried activated sludges are satisfactory from a sanitary standpoint, and that digested sludges are satisfactory except where vegetables are grown to be eaten raw. All danger is thought to be removed by action in the soil after a period of about 3 months during a growing season.")

WHAT ABOUT RESULTS?

Here's what Mr. Van Kleeck says about the results of adding sludge to the soil: ". . . Sludge is particularly adapted to lawns. Sludge deepens the green color of grass and stimulates a luxurious growth. Its benefits seem noticeable for several years. It should be applied late in March and again if desired early in September.

"The homeowner may well use it for the flower garden. Here it provides a much needed humus for the hot summer months as well as a moderate but long yielding amount of nitrogen.

"Its use is also indicated for trees and shrubs. Trees fertilized with sludge frequently have a healthier foliage, both in amount and color, and retain their leaves for a longer time in the fall than nearby unfertilized trees."

PRECAUTIONS IN SLUDGE HANDLING

". . . Several years ago, the Connecticut state department of health forwarded to sewage works supervisors the following release on sludge use which outlines the precautions which should be taken:

"1. The spreading of raw (undigested) sludge in any form, unless heat-dried to a temperature of at least 1,000 degrees F. for 10 seconds, should not be carried out. Septic tank sludge should be considered as raw sludge.

"2. The discharge of liquid digested sludge on any land, other than the immediate grounds of a sewage treatment plant, is prohibited unless the method employed and the discharge location are previously approved by the state department of health and the local director of health.

"3. Air dried, or vacuum filter dried, digested sludge, preferably stored for a period of several months, may be used on lawns, and the soil surrounding trees, shrubs and flowers. It may also be used on land utilized for vegetable growing, provided the edible portions of the crops grow above the ground or the crops are such that they are cooked before eating.

"4. In the case of vegetables growing in contact with the soil and eaten raw, dried digested sludge should always be applied to the soil the previous fall and plowed under either immediately or the following spring before the crop is planted. No additional applications of sludge should be made during the growing season.

"5. Heat dried sludge is safe for use under all conditions because of the destructive action of heat upon the bacteria.

"6. The general public should be warned to avoid handling sludge with the bare hands and urged to wash carefully with soap and hot water after sludge handling operations."

Mr. Van Kleeck sums up:

"Soils repeatedly planted to growing crops are greatly benefited by the organic humus supplied by manures, peat moss, green cover crops or sludges. The value of sludge should not be judged solely by comparison of chemical analyses with artificial fertilizers, *but by the results it produces in plant growth.* Dependence exclusively upon commercial fertilizers without consideration for the maintenance of humus content and good soil structure is an unsound practice. . . ."

SURVEY RESULTS

In the spring of 1959, the editors of *Organic Gardening and Farming* magazine mailed 500 questionnaires on the use of sludge to a sampling of the magazine's readers. The response showed that about 15 per cent were using sludge in their gardens or farms and recommend its use to other gardeners and farmers.

A Chapel Hill resident with a half-acre garden who has been using about 3 tons per year said: "It's the only material I have found that will grow green grass in the shade. It keeps vegetables green all summer. I hope I can always get sludge."

A Houston man with a small backyard garden had this to say: "Everyone that I know who has used sludge from the municipal plant is pleased with results. The reason I quit using it was because my wife thought that all the bacteria from contagious diseases were not dead. This thought was raised by the polio incidence."

This comment points up the need to educate the general public on the safety of sludge . . . that is, the conclusions of the Committee on Sewage Disposal of the American Public Health Association mentioned previously should be given much publicity.

Another common worry about potential users of sludge is the resulting objectionable odor. One-third of the gardeners and farmers who answered our questionnaire said they had some complaints about objectionable odors.

A Santa Fe gardener has been getting sludge from the Los Alamos plant since 1950, using enough to cover his lawn, vegetables and flower garden on his city lot an inch or more deep. According to him, his results are excellent. "I don't seem to be able to grow dwarf flowers. There is an odor, but not objectionable, right after the first watering of the lawn. But none when dug into the soil. I use sludge along with vegetable garbage, from the kitchen. The sludge seems to aid in the decomposing of the vegetable matter; it's much faster than when sludge is not used."

Sewage Sludge and Garbage Disposal

In Europe much experimenting has been done combining sludge with garbage. At the 1957 meeting of the International Research Group on Refuse Disposal, it was reported that Berlin sludge is mostly composted with refuse. To compost all sludge and refuse from any one region requires drying the sludge to about 70-75 per cent moisture. Dr. Braun reported better results using sludge concentrated in a vibrating thickener rather than on open sludge drying beds and believes this due to physical changes in structure caused by the vibrator.

Jersey, the densely populated British resort island famous for its bathing beaches, could not dispose of its refuse or sewage sludge by dumping on land or at sea. Its answer to this problem was a composting plant for the disposal of both wastes. After elaborate separation and preparation of the refuse, it was mixed with thickened digested sewage sludge and composted both by mechanical aeration in a vertical silo and by storage in windrows.

The compost was sold to the farmers on the island, who came to the plant and purchased it in bulk and used it as an organic fertilizer and soil conditioner. A more detailed description of the Jersey plant and others is given in the chapter on Composting Overseas.

Chapter 22

COMPOSTING INDUSTRIAL WASTES

The purpose of this chapter is to impress executives with the over-all need and value—as well as profit potential—in making industrial waste products available for return to the soil. Because this need is a very real one, we are firmly convinced that the necessary processing, merchandising and distribution can be worked out. The result, of course, will mean increased profits, a solution to what may now be a waste "headache," and the return of essential organic and mineral matter to the soil.

In his book, *Commercial Fertilizers*, Gilbeart H. Collings, Professor of Soils and Head of Department of Agronomy, Clemson Agricultural College, S. C. has written:

"Although modern fertilizers are of little or no value as sources of soil organic matter, it is not at all improbable that the fertilizer industry will, at some future date, attempt to supply the farmer with cheap sources of organic matter."

INDUSTRIAL WASTES: VALUABLE AND IN DEMAND

A number of companies producing organic wastes have long catered to the garden and farm market. Buckwheat hulls, cocoa bean wastes, peanut shells and sugar cane wastes have been available to gardeners for many years, and reports have come to our office that within recent years supplies of this kind of material have not been sufficient to meet demand.

Wastes Make Good Mulch

The practice of mulching in the garden (covering the soil with a layer of organic material) has become quite popular as a means to keep down weeds, retain soil moisture and supply the soil's constant need for organic raw materials. Newspapers, garden radio programs and magazines have been publicizing mulching and its labor-saving advantages. As a result, gardeners are now using more mulch and more kinds of mulch than ever before.

Mulch should offer an interesting market for industrial organic wastes, because it is not judged for its fertilizer value. Any organic material of suitable particle size that is non-toxic to soil and plants can be used as a mulch. This takes in an extremely broad category of materials. For many categories, all the processing that is necessary is to adjust the moisture content and bale or package the material in units easy to merchandise.

Some organic wastes have in the past been scorned and held valueless for use even as mulch, but education by conservationists is removing old prejudices. Sawdust is an excellent example of the new value that organic materials have taken on in the eyes of farmers and gardeners.

Because sawdust is relatively slow to decay above ground, many people have assumed that it will not decay in the soil either. Several years ago, experiment stations began encouraging farmers and gardeners to return sawdust to the soil that created it. As the result of this advice, a great deal of sawdust has found its way back to the soil.

Many tough organic wastes are rich in lignin, the bond that holds fibers together. It has recently been discovered that lignin is one of the most powerful chelators, that is, lignin helps make minerals available to plants.

Chelators continually liberate the food elements in the soil that plants need to live. Because we have learned what chelators are and what they do, we now know that sawdust can make positive contributions to soil fertility and management. It is true that experimental work is needed to pinpoint the exact chelating ability of a variety of organic materials, but it would be a mistake to overlook this factor when considering the value of many organic industrial wastes to the soil.

Research Reveals Value of Wastes

Research is turning up more and more products that have properties of value to the soil. For example, tests at Rutgers University show that waste cellophane flakes stop evaporation, protect soil loss and control weeds. When mixed with limestone and fertilizer, cellophane can be composted to produce a product with the qualities of commercially available peat.

Reports issued by agricultural experiment stations in Florida and California show that "frit"—basically a glass compound—supplies trace elements to the soil needed for plant growth. In a report entitled, "Frits Give Plants a Helping Hand," prepared by the University of Florida, researchers H. W. Winsor and J. Fiskel write:

"Most glasses contain a considerable amount of lime, and lesser amounts of sodium, potassium, iron and sometimes boron. All these are plant nutrients. Thus, if they were present in sufficient quantity, and if the glass could be made more soluble, these and similar nutrients could serve as fertilizers. Agriculture is indebted to industry for the pioneering research in producing nutrient glasses."

The Ferro Corporation of Cleveland and the Glostex Chemical Company in Los Angeles are currently marketing these glass compounds for use by gardeners and farmers to supply trace elements to soils.

Other Industrial Wastes May Contain Needed Trace Elements

The term trace element, or micronutrient, is applied to elements which are needed in plant growth in minute quantities while the major elements, or micronutrients as nitrogen (N), phosphorus (P), and potash (K), are needed in larger amounts. Although trace elements are needed by plants in very small quantities in comparison to major elements, they are nevertheless just as essential to plant growth and reproduction. Trace elements commonly found to be deficient in many soils include iron, manganese, boron, zinc, cobalt, copper, molybdenum and iodine.

Many organic fertilizers contain a wide range of trace elements, and we feel there is a definite likelihood that many industrial waste materials may also contain amounts of these important minor elements.

Steel By-product

The waste material of steel manufacture—ferrensul— shows some promises as a source of trace minerals for growing crops on soils where such elements are needed. In tests at the University of Wisconsin, scientists grew plants in a greenhouse using the material as the source of calcium, sulphur, magnesium, iron and manganese.

Whey as Fertilizer

A report in the *Wisconsin Farmers Union* describes the possibilities of using excess whey as a soil builder:

"Three tons of cheese whey contain about as much plant food as a ton of manure, according to latest University of Wisconsin research.

"Soil scientists studying the fertilizing value of whey believe this cheese industry by-product has promise as a fertilizer in areas near cheese plants.

"Four years of study indicate that whey applications of 20 to 50 tons per acre stimulate grass growth. Applications as high as 200 tons per acre didn't harm the crop or the soil.

"Analysis of the whey shows that a ton contains around 3 pounds of nitrogen, three-quarter pound of phosphorus, and $3\frac{1}{2}$ pounds of potassium.

"Wisconsin's cheese industry produces some 5 billion pounds (2,500,000 tons) of whey each year, the research men say. While some of this is used for processing and some is given to farmers for feed, large amounts are wasted.

"The wasted whey causes disposal headaches because it increases the pollution problems of streams and municipal sewage systems.

"This research shows that whey can be put to good use on Wisconsin fields if a farmer or cheese factory has or can obtain equipment to haul and spread the material."

Fish Meal Fertilizer Wastes

According to a report in *Industrial Wastes*, "the clean-up of waste liquors produced in fish reduction processes began as a good-will pollution control measure, but it has since become, because of the value of the solubles reclaimed in the process, a very profitable operation." The report written by Fred S. Gallagher of H. W. Smith, Inc. goes on: "In fact, in the Menhaden by-product industry, reclaimed fish solubles, once just thrown away, now account for 20 to 25 per cent of the total production value. In a recent poor fishing year, they actually were the difference between profit and loss."

Menhaden fish solubles are rich in protein, vitamin B_{12} as well as other growth factors, and the fertilizer is commonly used in the tobacco growing industry.

A Mistake on Mesquite

Here's an example of how a lowly-regarded waste can be converted to a worthwhile material. A front page article in an issue of *The Wall Street Journal* headlined: "Mesquite,

Long-Time Range Menace, Finds Use as Cattle Feed" and began:

"The friendless mesquite tree, bane of Southwestern ranchers and farmers for years, has found a champion. On his sprawling Rio Vista ranch near Bigwells, Texas, businessman C. E. Doolin is feeding his drought-stricken cattle herd a mixture containing ground-up mesquite wood as its base. He's installed machinery for shredding and grinding top branches of the hardy tree, and blending it into a murky mixture of grain, molasses and cottonseed meal."

According to Mr. Doolin, mesquite makes inexpensive, nutritious feed that goes over big with the livestock.

Mesquite is a dwarfed, thorn-studded tree averaging about 12 feet high that grows abundantly on Southwestern prairie lands. Ranchers have always considered it a menace, and as a result, reports the Journal, "have burned it, stomped on it, soaked it with chemicals from airplanes and doused it with burned crankcase oil. All this is a mistake, according to mesquite-connoisseur, Doolin."

Mr. Doolin began his project of feeding mesquite wood to his cattle about 4 years ago after native rangeland forage became scarce because of the drought. The idea first took root when he discovered the *protein and mineral content of ground-up mesquite he had prepared as compost for flower beds.*

Mr. Doolin is looking for mesquite to turn into an "income crop," even after the current drought is ended. *He feels certain it has a future as a garden compost.*

"I can make money on mesquite," he believes, "selling it at $10 a ton." Peat moss sells for an average of $85 to $95 a ton retail in Texas, a good deal of it shipped in from Canada.

Although mesquite can by no stretch of the imagination be classified as an industrial waste, we do believe that it does point up the fact that wastes have a very real future in the farm and garden picture.

Ohio Canneries Pump Wastes Back on Land

Some time ago, Ohio State University issued a bulletin that "vegetable canners in Ohio are turning to a farming technique to solve their problems of waste disposal. They are pumping the waste products back on the land through sprinkler irrigation systems."

The spray irrigation process reduces cannery wastes so they will pass through a spray nozzle. Wastes are then sprayed on farm crop fields. "Cannery wastes handled this way add to the organic matter of the soil, increase crop yields, and are free of undesirable odors," reported Reese B. Davis, Ohio State University extension horticulturist.

Thus cannery wastes have already been established as a valuable material for plant growth.

Spray Irrigation of Mill Wastes

In the late 1950's, it became necessary for the Auglaize Division, Weston Paper and Manufacturing Company of St. Mary's, Ohio to look for a better solution for the disposal of its mill wastewaters. Until that time, the wastes went into the St. Mary's River, which has a relatively small flow at this point. In the dry summer and early fall months, the river has been unable to assimilate the waste it received.

According to a report by Harold C. Koch and D. E. Bloodgood in *Sewage and Industrial Wastes,* a careful investigation indicated that spray irrigation disposal offered better possibilities of solving the problem than other methods. Spray irrigation has been used successfully for the disposal of a variety of industrial wastes such as those from canning and milk plants.

The portion of land selected for the experiments covered about 14 acres on which alfalfa seeded the year before was growing. Ten spray locations were provided; these were spaced about 210 and 240 feet apart, except for 3, one of which was spaced at a lesser interval and two of which were spaced farther apart to better suit the contour of the land. Sprinklers rotated a full circle distributing water over a radius of 100 or more feet. Each thus applied water to a minimum of seven-tenths of an acre.

Here are the observations of Engineers Koch and Bloodgood:

"Records were kept of the amount of natural rainfall as well as of the amount of wastewater applied by spraying. On May 31, 1958, the minimum cumulative quantity of wastewater which had been sprayed on any one sprinkler area was 36.0 inches, and the greatest was 51.6 inches. Converting these data to average application rates sprayed per calendar day during any one uninterrupted period shows a range from 0.13 inch for the lowest to 0.48 inch for the highest. Adding the average rainfall of 0.08 inch per day which fell during the uninterrupted spraying periods, the average total daily quantity of wastewater received by the land ranged from 0.21 to 0.56 inch. Using an average of all precipitation figures for the entire experimental period reveals an application rate of 0.28 inch per day of wastewater, plus rainfall. Observations made during approximately 9 months of experimentation indicate that this rate of application can be increased, although the degree of increase must await further experimental work.

"Most of the area of land sprayed was covered with alfalfa which had been planted the year before the experiments were started. During the summer and fall months of the experimental period, the alfalfa was cut and harvested 3 times at what was considered to be very good yields. It was concluded that the alfalfa was in no way harmed but was actually benefited. This same planting of alfalfa returned nicely the following spring and showed no damage from the wastewater applications during the winter. A smaller portion of the land sprayed was planted in field corn which had appeared to thrive on the wastewater. Since these observations on the section of the crops and of the yields were made by persons experienced in raising in this area, it is felt that the water application rates have been well within the range in which these plants will thrive.

"Since the applied wastewater carries suspended paper fibers, a common question was whether the crops and the soil would not eventually be covered with a layer of paper. Actually, at no time has it been possible to find more than a few fibers adhering to the leaves of the plants. This has been true even directly after a spraying period. Except at a few small isolated areas where the lines were regularly drained, no fibers have been found lying on the surface of the ground. The isolated concentrations at some of the drains have quickly disappeared.

"The desirability of determining the effects on the chemical constituents of the soil has been recognized and analyses of soil samples have been made and others will be made periodically as the experiments are continued. Although the experimental data presently at hand in this respect are not complete enough to indicate any trends, no serious problems are anticipated."

SPRAY IRRIGATION OF DAIRY WASTES

Experiences with spray irrigation installations going back to 1947 (cannery wastes in Pennsylvania) have shown that this method is practical. Recently a group of engineers and soil scientists began a study to determine the effectiveness of spray irrigation as a method for the disposal of dairy plant wastes. This group included Gerald W. Lawton, George Breska, L. E. Engelbert, G. A. Rohlich, and Nandor Porges.

Here are the conclusions they made from their study:

1. Spray irrigation appears to be a practical, economical and satisfactory method of disposal of dairy wastes where the irrigated area is properly selected and reasonable care is exercised in the operation of the system.

2. The volumetric loading and the cation loading appear to be the principal design factors when considering spray irrigation. The BOD loading is much less significant than it is in the design of biological treatment systems.

3. Reasonable predictions of loading or irrigation rates of a given site may be made when soil conditions, type of cover crop, depth of water table, etc., are known. However, final design application rates can best be determined by observance of the crop under irrigation.

4. The waste-holding tank, during summer operation, should be small (perhaps 2 to 3 hours maximum detention time), should be emptied completely during each pumping period, and should be flushed frequently to remove accumulations of solids which will otherwise cause objectionable odors.

5. From a mechanical standpoint, winter operation of spray irrigation systems is possible in areas comparable to the latitude of central Wisconsin, but it must be assumed that a complete kill of the cover crop will occur. However, the irrigation operation may be reasonably carried out by having alternate plots available in order that reseeding may be accomplished readily.

6. An evaluation of the effect of run-off from the ice cover during winter and from the spring thawing of the ice cover itself should be made at each site, based on the dilution available by the stream and on other factors peculiar to the site.

7. Hot wastes that are damaging to the cover crop may be successfully irrigated by elevating the spray nozzles, thus allowing the waste to cool as it falls.

8. In some irrigated areas having poor absorption characteristics, the use of tile systems several feet below the surface

812

have greatly increased the flow of waste through the soil. The effluent from the tile systems has been found to be low in BOD and relatively stable. There are some soils, however, that are difficult to drain. Therefore, a thorough analysis thould be made before drainage is undertaken.

9. In cold areas, serious consideration should be given to alternate methods of disposal during the winter period.

AGRICULTURAL USE OF WASTE WATER

The California Report on "Waste Water Reclamation and Utilization" contains this information on agricultural use of waste water:

The A. Perelli-Minetti Winery, near Delano, California, utilizes its industrial waste effluents by irrigating the agricultural land surrounding the winery. The winery wastes consist of stillage and pomace, as well as wash water and waste cooling water. The stillage from the wine-making process is discharged from the winery at a temperature of 160 degrees Fahrenheit. This stillage is mixed with irrigation well water in a diluting ratio of 10 parts well water to one part waste. The diluted effluent is then discharged through irrigation canals supplying 610 acres of land. The pomace, consisting of the dewatered pulp from the crushed grapes, is also disposed of into this irrigation water. Thompson grapes are largely employed to produce sweet wines, and the waste from the manufacturing process amounts to about 375 pounds dry weight per ton of grapes. About 36,000 tons of grapes are processed each year, producing 3.5 milligrams of wine each year. The winery pomace is reported to contain on a dry basis: 1 to 20 per cent nitrogen as N, 1.5 per cent phosphorus as P_2O_5, 0.5 to 1.0 per cent potash as K_2O, and the remaining 80 per cent is organic. The diluted industrial waste water is applied to the land at a rate of less than 5 tons dry waste per acre per year. The pH of the diluted effluent varies from 6 to 8.2 depending on the tartaric acid present in the waste. It has been possible to use this water to reclaim alkaline land adjacent to the winery. After being reclaimed, the land is planted to cotton or is used to grow grapes. Minor odors are associated with this irrigation. The stillage is pasteurized because it is maintained at high temperatures and hence is not odoriferous. The suspended solids present in the irrigation water dry out and form a flaky crust. No significant fly, mosquito, odor or other nuisance conditions have been associated with this operation. The crops that are grown utilizing this irrigation water are reported to be satisfactory. This operation eliminates the necessity for expensive treatment of the winery waste while at the same time supplies needed fertilizer and organic matter to the soil. No trouble with plant diseases has been reported.

The Seabrook Farms Company of New Jersey has made use of cannery waste effluent for several years.

An open ditch is used to convey the waste from the head works to the pumps which send it to the spray nozzles.

There have been occasional flies and mosquitoes in the irrigated area, and some difficulty with odors has been experienced. There have been no health problems associated with the operation and no special requirements or restrictions have been placed on the irrigation system by the state and local health departments. The application of the industrial waste to the forest and farm soils has resulted in an improvement in the absorption of water by the soils. The effect on crop fertility has not been studied; however, it is known that no deleterious effect has resulted. The irrigation of vegetables has proven to be satisfactory in all respects. The Seabrook Farms operation appears to be a very economical and satisfactory method of disposing of this type of industrial waste, not only at an initial low cost but also at minimum operating expense.

At Visalia, California, a domestic type sewage containing some industrial waste from peach canning and milk processing plants has been utilized for irrigation for more than 30 years. The original water source for Visalia is a system of wells. The sewage treatment is varied because of the combination of new and old units at the sewage treatment plant. Screening, sedimentation, aeration, trickling filtration, and oxidation ponds are used. The daily flow varies from 6 to 9 mgd with an average 7 mgd, and all of the total flow is employed for irrigation of agricultural land. Approximately 25 per cent is used by adjacent farmers on their own lands, whereas the remaining 75 per cent of the flow is employed on municipally owned property. There are 26 acres of storage lagoons located on the 160-acre farm at the treatment plant. At a distance of about 4 miles, at the municipal airport, there are 10 acres of storage lagoons used to supply irrigation water for an additional 580 acres. All lagoons are 8 feet deep. The soil in the Visalia area contains silt sand, clay and loam. The depth to the ground water varies between 24 and 65 feet. There are 26 acres of walnut trees which last year produced 27 tons of walnuts. There are 106 acres of cotton land which are leased to private farmers by the city for $65 per acre per year, including the supply of effluent. Barley, millet, grain, sorghum, field corn, alfalfa, milo maize and nectarines are also irrigated with effluent.

COMPOSTING PHARMACEUTICAL WASTES

The following report from Sewage and Industrial Wastes was prepared by A. J. Gabaccia, Head of the Industrial Waste Department of Lederle Laboratories in Pearl River, New York:

"At the Pearl River plant of Lederle Laboratories from 6 to 10 tons per day of organic sludges are accumulated for disposal. This comes from fermentation of antibiotics, extraction of pharmaceuticals from animal livers, stabling of animals, and the sanitary sewage from 4,000 employees. Composting was included with other disposal methods in a study program for determination of a practical solution to this problem.

"The immediate scope of this investigation consisted of answering two questions:

"1. Can this industrial sludge be composted?

"2. If so, can a routine composting procedure be established?

". . . It was noted that the outstanding difference between the Lederle industrial sludge and the garbage type of waste was that the composition of pharmaceutical sludge remained fairly constant on an annual basis whereas garbage wastes have seasonal variations. The carbon to nitrogen ratio of Lederle sludge remained about 15:1 while garbage waste is reported to range from 10:1 to 80:1. Also, the operational control of the treatment plant provided the advantage that the industrial sludge containing domestic and animal solids would be free of such foreign matter as cardboard, tin cans, polyethylene wrappings, and glass.

". . . The pilot-plant investigations began at Pearl River in the summer of 1953. . . . By trial and error, a suitable moisture content of the initial material for satisfactory physical handling was established. The sludge was diluted with barn manures containing straw bedding and wood sawdust.

The ideal blend which gave the good composting results and was suitable for physical handling was:

Material	Per Cent by Weight
Treatment plant sludge	65
Stable manures	25
Sawdust	10

"In addition, one-half pound of finely divided phosphate rock was added for each 100 pounds of mixture. This blend, with a resultant moisture content of between 50 and 60 per cent, became the influent material for the first stage of composting.

"Before being added to the compost, the treatment plant sludge is dewatered on vacuum filters, using chemical coagulants to aid in the dewatering process. At one time these were ferric chloride and lime, but the iron in the finished compost was found to be harmful to lawns on which the compost was applied. For this reason the use of iron coagulant was discontinued and the dewatering was accomplished with lime. The resultant sludge cake varies from 65 to 85 per cent water and is of the approximate composition shown in Table 1. This table also shows the composition of the remaining raw materials for the compost.

Table 1.

Approximate Composition of Wastes from Lederle Laboratories Pearl River Plant

Item	Stable Manure (per cent)	Waste Treatment Plant Sludge (per cent)	Compost (per cent)
Moisture content	70	65–85	35
Organic content	—	70	80
Nitrogen	1.5	2–3	2.0
Phosphorus	0.1	0.1–0.3	0.8
Potassium	0.3	0.7	0.8

"The second variable believed critical for material in the early stages is pH. The treatment plant sludge with chemical additives has a pH of about 7.5 to 8. The pH of animal wastes also is alkaline. The sawdust has an initial pH of 3.0 to 4.0 But the mixed ingredients, after about one day, have a pH of 6.5 to 7.5, which is satisfactory for composting of the wastes.

"The box system permitted testing by trial and error some of the other important variables in composting, such as temperature, aeration, blending, reseeding, compactness, and reduction of particle size.

"An important factor in composting is to achieve proper temperature in the process. Fortunately composting masses have good insulation properties and retain the heat from the reactions, thereby maintaining elevated temperatures. High temperatures are required for the destruction of undesirable weeds and of pathogenic organisms.

". . . By using a gas analysis instrument, the compost material was probed to determine CO_2 and O_2 contents. It was noted that frequent shredding of material with an age of over two days definitely shortened the total composting time. From the results of many trials a routine procedure was established so as to produce satisfactory decomposition of these wastes in 6 to 8 days. The pertinent points in this procedure are:

"1. The sludge was diluted with animal manures and sawdust to give a moisture content between 50 and 60 per cent. This represented a mixture of about 65 per cent sludge and 10 per cent sawdust. Phosphate rock was added representing about 0.5 per cent of the batch weight.

"2. This mixture was seeded with about 10 per cent of material with an age of one stage or in this case one day.

"3. After thorough mixing the total blend was shredded and stored for 24 hours.

"4. The material in the other stages also was shredded daily, reseeding with 10 per cent of material one stage older.

". . . Since there is a seasonal market in the sale of compost and since there is a substantial amount of inexpensive land available, the short 6-day process was not a prime requirement. Therefore, the pilot-plant short-term process was modified to a full-scale shredding and windrow process covering a period of about 150 days. A 10-acre plot was converted for this use in 1955 and large-scale equipment installed. This consisted of a 30 cubic yards per hour shredder and a one cubic yard capacity front-end loader.

"An economic evaluation of the selected procedure indicated that the multi-stage method was practical and economical if a sufficient market could be found for the finished product to defray a part of the operating costs and to keep the compost from accumulating on the premises.

"The sludge dewatered at the treatment plant on the afternoon and midnight shifts is trucked to the composting site and dumped on a prepared bed of sawdust and animal manures. The total sawdust and other wastes are proportioned to the sludge to give the desired blend. Seeding from the previous day's batch is done by moving some of the one-day old material to the fresh batch with the tractor. After the sludge has been discharged, the mixing and blending of all the ingredients are done with the tractor by picking up material from the outer edges and making a new cone-shape pile next to it, similar to the procedure used for mixing sand, gravel, and cement. About one part finely ground rock phosphate is added for each 200 parts of the fresh mixture.

"To complete the blending, the mass of material is then bucketed through the shredder and piled in a long windrow next to the previous day's batch. The windrows are about 25 feet wide and as much as 15 feet in height, running a distance of about 300 feet.

"Periodically the masses are sampled for pH, moisture content, temperature, and BOD. The windrows are allowed to compost for a period of about 5 months, after which the entire windrow is turned over and moved by truck to a different location. This material is called "crude compost," since it has gone through the high temperature range and has dried out into large hard lumps. Small cone-shape piles of crude compost are made to permit additional drying. During dry weather this material is trucked inside a high roof building which holds about 1,000 tons of compost, representing about one-half year's production. Here the crude material is reshredded to a fine particle size, and to a moisture content of about 40 per cent. In final form it is a granular, free-flowing, dark brown material, with a slight humus odor. The finished compost is used on Lederle's grounds, by the nearby communities, and it is sold through a local dealer mainly for lawn treatment and soil conditioning."

Concludes Mr. Gabaccia: "Composting has been the best

and most practical method of treatment, disposal, and utilization of these wastes."

USE OF WOOD WASTES

Lignin has been classed as the largest waste in industry, pulp and paper mills alone discharging 2,000,000 tons of it annually. Sawmills and other wood working plants scattered throughout the nation can make readily available another 10,000,000 tons of wood waste, while forest and agricultural wastes have many times that amount potentially available. The use of lignin for fertilizers may rank among the most valuable outlet, on account of the large tonnages involved. Lignin is of special importance to soils, as a supplier of humus and organic matter.

The Key Question: Can lignin be used successfully for a fertilizer?

The Answer: A definite YES from Robert S. Aries, research associate at Yale University and field director for the Northeastern Wood Utilization Council. Here's his report:

"This use of lignin, long classed as 'the largest waste in industry,' is an 'extremely important discovery, because of the tonnages involved.'

"As a result of present day experiments, lignin may assume an important part in this nation's soil building and conservation program. It will be a 'wealth from waste' movement, since lignin at present pollutes the nation's rivers; as fertilizer, it will definitely aid in providing higher land values and richer soils.

"At the present time, we are taking more from our land than we are putting back. We cannot continue drawing upon our reserves indefinitely. By using lignin with fertilizers, however, the supplementary nourishment can be made to balance properly the offerings by the soil and at the proper time and in proper position within the soil.

"The depletion of soil minerals or added fertilizers through leaching and cropping can also be minimized if adequate amounts of lignin or other organic ingredients are present. In a forest, leaves drop annually and decay in order to pass their nutrient elements through the cycle of growth. This is almost a requisite for tree maintenance.

"Through the use of lignin in agriculture, similar results can be accomplished and the less fertile Eastern soils can approach the efficiency of the 'humid' soils of the Middle West. . . . If lignin is used on presently-fertilized soils which need humus and organic matter, it is estimated that the efficiency of these soils would be raised about 20 per cent."

Wood Wastes and Soils

The following report was originally published in *Crops and Soils Magazine* by H. W. Reuszer (Purdue University), R. L. Cook (Michigan State University) and E. R. Graham (University of Missouri).

Wood waste represents a large source of organic matter, which could and probably should be returned to the soil. But, for the most part, it is still unused.

The first questions a farmer normally asks before deciding to use wood waste are: Will it poison the soil? Will it make the soil more acid?

Research has shown that sawdust, when incorporated in the soil, does not increase the acidity. On the contrary the soil acidity quite often decreases slightly following decomposition of the wood.

Wastes from cedar and walnut trees have been reported as toxic to plants. However, there is little evidence that other common woods have any poisonous effects, as far as crops are concerned.

During their breakdown in the soil, wood residues interfere with the use of nitrogen by plants. As early as 1924, scientists learned that the addition of sawdust to soil produced a temporary shortage of available nitrogen. The deficiency shows up in yellowed, stunted plant growth. It is less pronounced if a legume crop is grown and can be overcome for other crops if available nitrogen is added.

Most experimenters have recognized the need for added nitrogen with wood residues, but they have not gathered enough information about the amount needed in wood decomposition. This is reflected in the wide range of recommendations on how much nitrogen to use.

Under laboratory conditions at the Pennsylvania Experiment Station, they found that the addition of 1½ per cent nitrogen to oak sawdust or one per cent to white pine sawdust prevented nitrogen deficiency in soils to which 6 tons of sawdust per acre have been added. Other studies on this point are underway at Iowa State College and by USDA scientists at Beltsville, Md.

Of course, nitrogen is not the only plant nutrient affected by sawdust. There is some evidence that sawdust or other wood residues also interfere with the availability of phosphorus and potassium in the soil. These questions are now under study in California, Oregon and Virginia.

One good quality of wood residue is its ability to improve soil physical properties. It aids in loosening the soil, which makes it easier for air and water to move into and through the soil. Tests have shown that wood residues usually give only small improvements in soil structure. At least 8 state experiment stations are now studying the question.

Wood residues have considerable value when used as bedding for livestock. For some years, sawdust and wood-chips have been the most widely used form of bedding in the Northeastern States.

Apparently, the resulting manure has given satisfactory results in crop production. In an 18-year experiment at the Rhode Island Agricultural Experiment Station and in a shorter test at the Pennsylvania Station, sawdust manure gave results similar to those obtained from straw manure. But little is known about the chemical make-up of wood-waste manure.

How much woody material should be added to the soil? In experiments, rates comparable to those of ordinary crop residues added to the soil have been used. More commonly, rates of 10 to 20 tons per acre and ranging up to 200 tons per acre have been used.

Year in and year out, it is quite clear that applications at a 200-ton rate cannot be kept up on a large acreage. But such a high rate might be justified with high-value crops under special soil conditions. With an application of this size, it is important to know the rate of breakdown for these wood residues and the role of nitrogen and other plant nutrients in decomposition and crop production. There is still much to learn here.

Wood residues are believed to have some influence on the population of small organisms in the soil. The rotting of wood under the natural conditions is brought about largely by Basidiomycetes or high fungi. The microorganisms that decompose fragmented wood particles at the surface of the soil may be entirely different from those organisms that break down ordinary crop residues. The difference may account for some of the prolonged or delayed nitrogen deficiencies which sometimes follow the application of wood residues to soils.

Satisfactory composts from wood residues would probably have many uses. One method for composting sawdust has been patented. A number of other methods are known, but most of them are similar to practices found satisfactory in composting other organic residues.

Other unanswered questions concerning the use of wood residues are:

1. What is the proper place in a rotation to use wood residues?

2. Do larger sizes of wood chips give results different from those obtained with sawdust? (Larger amounts of wood chips are becoming available from improvement cutting in forested land and from limb and slab wastes in lumbering operations.)

3. Do they have much value for field crops? (Wood residue mulches are most widely used on horticultural crops.)

4. Can wood residues, most abundant in rolling or hilly areas, be used as mulches for erosion control and for establishing of grass seedings on sloping land?

Experimental work throughout the United States is tackling many such problems in the use of wood wastes. But much of the work is piecemeal, so there is a real need for more study and research before farmers can take full advantage of this useful but neglected organic matter resource.

Research Shows Bark Builds Soils

The following report was issued several years ago by the Illinois Institute of Technology:

"A soil builder has been developed that opens up a vast potential market for bark—the normal waste material of the lumber, pulp, and paper industries.

"Scientists at Armour Research Foundation of Illinois Institute of Technology report that they have developed a method to convert bark into an inexpensive and unusually effective soil builder.

"In tests conducted with greenhouse plants and field crops, the product was found to be more effective in promoting growth and improving the soil than either peat moss or a commercial soil conditioner.

"Dr. C. Roland McCully, scientific adviser in the Foundation's chemistry and chemical engineering research department, said the bark soil builder, in conjunction with fertilizer, turns clay and sand into rich loamy soil in which plants grow at a surprising rate.

"McCully said the soil builder accomplishes these three things:

1. Loosens the soil and improves its moisture holding capacity.
2. Serves as a base for fertilizer.
3. Controls the rate at which the plants obtain their food from the soil."

Wood Chips Improve Condition of Soil

Wood chips can be a big help in soil management. They improve tilth, help resist compaction and erosion, increase pore space, promote earthworm activity, and strengthen the soil aggregates, or "crumbs," against breakdown by water.

George R. Free of the U.S.D.A. and Cornell University bases these talking points on the results he observed when wood chips were either top-dressed or plowed under at 7 tons per acre. He worked on a 5-year rotation of sweet corn, dry beans, tomatoes, cabbage, and canning peas seeded down with a legume.

From 3 to 10 times as much undecomposed organic matter in the soil was found under the chip treatments than under the no-chip plots at the end of 4 years. This shows how chips resist rapid breakdown in the soil and last longer than many crop residues.

Free's chip treatments showed less compaction and better tilth. And they showed a much higher percentage of "water stable aggregates" than in the no-chip treatments, indicating that the chips helped strengthen the soil's resistance to erosion.

Two or 3 times as many earthworms were found in chip treatments than under the no-chip plots. Free found also that top-dressing the chips reduced crusting and sealing of the soil surface, and in some cases gave higher yields than when plowed under.

Crops of Wisconsin Farmers Aided by Mill "Sludge"

The Wausau, Wisconsin Journal has reported that across upper Wisconsin in the paper mill belt, there are mounds of greenish, ill-smelling sludge piled in the fields. Farmers are just waiting for time and weather to spread this lime. At the mills, there are often a hundred or more farm trucks and wagons lined up for loads of the same material, scooped and shoveled from a giant hill poured out from the chemical vats.

Spurred by the Soil Conservation program, Marathon County in the last 10 years has used 247,000 tons of ground limestone, 16,900 cubic yards of this paper mill lime sludge and 36,000 cubic yards of marl from its lake bottoms.

The paper mill sludge, a residue, was put to practical application on farms by W. J. Rogan, a veteran county agent, who recommended its use to area farmers who faced the problem of finding a low-cost lime that would sweeten acid soils.

At that time, the sludge was a problem to the paper mills. The mill operators piled it mountain-high in their yards, poured it into streams, polluting waters and arousing the ire of fishermen. (See also the reports on previous pages of this chapter on spray irrigation of mill wastes.)

Lignin Helps Potatoes

Potato plants growing in soil treated with lignin showed a deeper green color and much more abundant foliage. Experiments conducted at the New Hampshire experiment station proved that there was a marked stimulus to growth, particularly in the early stages as a result of lignin applications.

Not only were the potatoes, grown in the soil mixed with lignin, heavier, but also the potatoes themselves were larger and there were fewer culls than on the control plants.

The New Hampshire report continues: "Lignin has a high absorptive power and acts as a sort of sponge. This means that it will hold moisture better, even when there has been no rain for a long period.

"Lignin is a porous material. When it is plowed under, it gives plants a better chance to develop by providing interstices for the roots to spread into. A better root system makes a better plant.

"First experiments with potatoes showed that they grow faster in a soil mixed with lignin. If these results are confirmed in field tests, it may mean that the potato belt can be extended to regions where the growing season is shorter.

"If the cost of transporting lignin from factory to field is not prohibitive, the farmer, through the use of what once was a worthless substance, will be able to grow a heavier yield of potatoes almost twice as high in starch and at least 15 per cent lower in moisture content. Effects on other vegetables will be just as marked."

Making Use of Vermont Bark

The Vermont Bureau of Industrial Wastes, under the direction of John Sayward, has been studying the potential uses for waste bark. Here are some of the points that their research has shown:

For dairy bedding, about *a bushel per day per cow* is required. It protects the cows, aids cleanliness, promotes milk quality and flavor, increases total production through cow comfort, and helps return valuable plant food to the soil. Adding labor and trucking to the 2 to 3 cents per bushel paid for sawdust at the mill, it *costs 8 to 10 cents per bushel* at the farm. With 286,000 cows in Vermont, the cost and volume of bedding needed are important. With some farmers traveling 100 miles at times to fetch bedding, *bark may well fill in* the short supply at favorable cost.

Tests so far indicate that *bark can indeed be ground* satisfactorily and produce a product of particle *size and moisture absorption* properties and bulk density suitable for *bedding*. It is expected that, as the bark project continues and more samples become available, more reliable information will be accumulated as to the behavior of various species and the effect of moisture content and season of the year.

Agriculture generally must see a *short range economic* return for its expenditures. With low nutrient content, bark is thus not a substitute for concentrated, convenient, low cost chemical fertilizers. However, its nutrients are above wood, and its *lime* content is far above even alfalfa. Nutrient contents as such are estimated to be worth only $1.30 a ton for sawdust, $2.00 for bark. But farmers already pay some *$6* a ton for sawdust for bedding, and there are other *overall values* to the farm.

Long-range and cumulative benefits may indeed be expected from use of *bark* on the soil, through slow release of nutrients by bacterial action but especially in *improved soil* characteristics. In contrast to common belief, woody materials are *not in general toxic;* plant growth may be retarded temporarily by nitrogen demands of bacteria decomposing it, but adding nitrogen easily corrects this. *Acidity* from woody materials is *only temporary* and may be counteracted by wise use of lime (or, in bark by its own high lime content).

In farming, *bark* is of interest *for biological values* as a factor in growth and nutritional quality of farm products. Bark is considered promising for *bedding,* particularly in *pen stables,* where bedding is thick and is kept long enough for *natural heating,* with occasional turning, to dry out barn liquids and keep cows more comfortable and warm; and a valuable soil amendment results. For this purpose, grinding bark from the debarker seems desirable.

Advantages are seen in bark as *mulch,* with benefits in weed-freeness, soil characteristics, and crop produced. Earthworms appear in numbers where bark is decomposing, a sign of *healthy soil.* Fungi and bacteria, which are plentiful in bark, benefit the *crumb structure* of soil.

Bark and woody materials may help *dispose* of farm and household or even cannery or municipal *wastes by composting,* not only returning organic matter to the soil but likely involving lower cost than usual disposal plants.

Bark is being studied and used elsewhere. Included are composting on the west coast; western softwood and eastern yellow birch for *orchid culture;* insulations; old bark from dumps for "tanbark" at racetracks and for *mulch;* bark for *poultry litter,* and bark for *fuel* (a destructive use, but preferable to mere dumping). Possible other uses include diluent for fertilizers and insecticides, insulation, filler for plastics, etc., source of chemicals and charcoal. Tests made by various manufacturers indicate that various types and makes of grinding equipment should be suitable for bark.

RESEARCH WITH WOOD WASTE IN WASHINGTON

Dr. Stanley P. Gessel, Associate Professor of Forest Soils, University of Washington has issued a most informative report, "Composts and Mulches from Wood Wastes." This report was issued as part of a program of the Institute of Forest Products to "encourage more complete utilization of the timber grown in Washington." Following are portions of that report:

The main detrimental factor associated with the use of wood products as soil conditioners lies in its temporary tie-up of nitrogen from the soil. For this reason the factors influencing this removal will be considered in some detail, as follows:

826

1. *Inherent resistance of wood products to decomposition.*

Plant growth responses to treatments involving sawdust or other wood-derived materials is influenced by resistance of the material to decomposition. Relatively inert or stable material, upon being added to the soil, resists decomposition, thereby disallowing a large build-up of microbial populations. Since it is the presence of microorganisms which cause the decomposition, the material which favors the greatest decomposition rate will also be the material causing the greatest initial nitrogen drain from the soil. Bollen and Lu classified a number of organic materials as to their decomposition rates. They found, after 50 days, the following apparent decomposition levels:

(a) Dextrose 60 per cent

(b) Wheat straw 48 per cent

(c) Red alder 40 per cent

(d) Ponderosa pine sawdust 33 per cent

(e) Western red cedar sawdust 33 per cent

(f) Douglas fir sawdust 30 per cent

(g) Pitch 30 per cent

(h) Western hemlock sawdust 27 per cent

(i) Bark 26 per cent

(j) Lignin 6 per cent

From the above table it can be seen that alder can be expected to cause a greater initial drain of nitrogen than Douglas fir or Western hemlock.

Also influencing the rate of decomposition is the size of the organic particle. This is due to the fact that rate is related to the exposed surface area of the organic substance. A large wood chip will decompose at a slower rate than a finer wood fragment. Wood chips can be expected, therefore, to support a smaller microbial population than that found in the finer fractions, such as sawdust. Consequently a smaller nitrogen drain will develop in a soil treated with chips. Woody material incorporated into the soil will also decompose more rapidly than will the same material on the surface, or poorly mixed with the soil.

2. *Soil type and soil aeration.*

The soil type can be expected to play a role in the decomposition of the organic additive through its influence on soil aeration. Coarse-textured soils, being permeable, have good infiltration rates and provide optimum aeration conditions. On these areas decomposition is accelerated, which results in a greater amount of nitrogen being utilized by the microorganisms. On heavy textured soils, or where soil drainage is impeded, microorganic activity will be correspondingly less and therefore the nitrogen drain will also decrease.

3. *Addition of fertilizers containing nitrogen.*

Any induced deficiency of nitrogen caused by microorganismal decomposition can be offset by an appropriate addition of fertilizer. The exact amount of fertilizer needed is dependent upon the rate at which the decomposition is occurring. This is a function, as explained above, of the resistance and size of the organic material and the aeration of the soil to which it is being added. It has been noted by several investigators that, in general, induced nitrogen deficiencies can be avoided with the addition of 10 to 20 pounds of elemental nitrogen per ton of sawdust during the first year. About one-half of this amount should subsequently be added during the second and third years.

4. *Prior decomposition of the organic material.*

With the use of a compost, it is not necessary to correct for nitrogen removal by microorganisms through the use of fertilizers. In theory, the organic material will have undergone an initial decomposition before it was added to the soil. During this period the microorganisms will have reduced the total amount of carbon present in comparison to the nitrogen. This is accomplished by the conversion of carbon compounds to carbon dioxide, which passes into the atmosphere. Under the influence of this lower carbon-nitrogen ratio, the microorganisms no longer rely upon the soil for supplementary nitrogen. In this case the organisms have increased to the limit of their food supply. In the composting of wood materials, the carbon-nitrogen ratio is reduced to a limited extent. However, the readily available forms of carbon are utilized, leaving the more resistant forms unchanged. Under these conditions, nitrogen is not depleted when the material is added to the soil, yet soil will still gain the many advantages of organic matter addition.

The principal benefits from using wood materials in soil are due to the physical changes which they bring about. Because sawdust and similar materials contain at the most only 3 pounds of nitrogen (N), two pounds of phosphate

(P_2O_5), and two pounds of potash (K_2O) per ton of dry material, they have little value as a source of these nutrient elements. When these materials are composted with organic products, the composition of nutrients is raised and a response in growth may be observed from the nutrients present in the compost. However, as with woody materials in general, the primary value of the compost is its influence upon the physical properties of the soil.

The Composting of Woody Materials

Of the types of materials suitable for composting, waste organic products are most often used and make the most economical compost. However, not all waste materials will compost satisfactorily, as the organisms which bring about decomposition require certain elements which are not present in sufficient amounts in some materials. The main deficiency in this respect is nitrogen. Nitrogen in the form of protein or organic compounds is generally readily available to composting organisms. In addition, other limiting elements, such as calcium and phosphorus, can be supplied in protein material. Therefore, in order to compost certain products, it is necessary to add an organic material with a higher nitrogen content. This nitrogen is available to the organisms and allows them to carry out decomposition. Woody products are low in nitrogen and therefore must have an additive which has a higher nitrogen content in order to obtain successful composting. It often is necessary, in the case of resistant woody material, to add a ready-energy source in order to initiate decomposition. Many organic wastes can supply this in the form of soluble sugars.

The amount of organic material which should be added to wood is variable and depends largely upon its nitrogen content and upon the length of composting period. Nitrogen fertilizers can be used to fortify the compost mixture, but by themselves are not entirely satisfactory for initiation of decomposition processes. When using low nitrogen organic additives, however, it may be desirable to add nitrogen fertilizer to increase the nitrogen in the compost. In commercial composting of woody materials, cost of the additives will have an influence upon proportions.

Woody Materials Available

The woody materials which are most commonly available in the State of Washington are sawdust, shavings, and chips.

Availability of bark will increase with the installation of more log debarkers. Sawdust and shavings are often available from commercial supplies in urban areas and from mills in outlying areas. Chips, from portable chippers used for disposing of brush and tree prunings, are sometimes available. In the future, these chippers will probably become more important as a source of wood chips, due to pruning of forest stands which are brought under scientific management.

Bark and pole peelings are sometimes available and are suitable for composting if they are ground or otherwise broken down. The resulting product is very satisfactory for compost purposes. Pole peelings from a mechanical peeler can also be handled in this manner with good results.

The size of the particle is an important consideration in composting. Coarse chips are not too well suited because they take longer to decompose. Very fine sawdust, such as produced by sanding processes, tends to pack and exclude air, thus retarding decomposition of the pile. Shavings decompose readily and are desirable, although ordinary sawmill sawdust is entirely satisfactory for composting.

The species of food material to use in soil is not as important a factor as is commonly thought. Hardwood sawdust, especially alder, is often considered superior to that of coniferous or softwood species, due to the fact that hardwood sawdust has a higher composition of plant nutrients. As this amounts to only 3.4 pounds more of total nitrogen (N), phosphorus (P) and potassium (K) per ton of sawdust, the paying of a considerable premium on hardwood sawdust for composting is hardly justified.

Another consideration that must be made when comparing species is the response when the material is added to the soil. Unaltered coniferous sawdust is more resistant to decomposition, and will therefore remain longer in the soil. This is especially important when one is concerned with altering the physical nature of the soil. Also, induced nitrogen deficiencies will be less probable with softwood sawdust, as compared with hardwood sawdust, when both are unaltered. In properly composted wood material, there should be no induced nitrogen deficiencies in any wood species.

The conclusion regarding species of wood is that the material should be chosen on the basis of low cost, availability, and form of material for complete composting, with species a relatively minor consideration.

Organic Materials

The primary requirement of an organic material used for inducing decomposition in woody composts is that it contain sufficient nitrogen and other elements. For practical reasons, the material should contain two per cent nitrogen or more. The mix ratio for a material with a two per cent nitrogen content probably should not exceed one part of sawdust to one part of organic material, by volume. Greater sawdust percentages than this would require fortification with a nitrogen fertilizer. On the other hand, a high-protein material such as fish meal can be added to sawdust in a ratio as low as 1 to 10 and satisfactory results will be obtained. Cheap, or waste, organic materials which are available for composting in Washington State, include animal and chicken manures; waste from fruit, vegetable and fish canneries; spent hops from breweries; sewage sludge and pea vines.

The physical nature of the organic material should be considered. Thorough mixing of the organic and sawdust causes the most rapid decomposition of the compost pile. Because most composts are made on a small scale, hand methods must be relied upon for mixing. A loose, dry material is much easier to handle and allows for a more complete mixing. It is very difficult to obtain a proper mix with wet or lumpy materials unless a compost mixing machine is used. These machines are available commercially and allow the use of materials which would otherwise be difficult to handle.

Chemical Composition of Woody Materials

Woody Material	Approximate lbs. Dry Wgt. per Unit (200 cu. ft.)	%N	%P P_2O_5	%K K_2O	Approximate total lbs. Nitrogen, Phosphorus, Potassium per ton dry wgt.
Douglas-fir Sawdust	2000	0.05	0.04	0.04	2.6
Douglas-fir Shavings	1500	0.05	0.04	0.04	2.6
Cedar Shavings	1400	0.04	0.04	0.03	2.2
Hemlock Sawdust	1900	0.05	0.04	0.05	2.8
Ponderosa Pine Shavings	1400	0.04	0.04	0.03	2.2
Alder Sawdust	2000	0.15	0.09	0.06	6.0
Alder Shavings	1500	0.15	0.09	0.06	6.0
Douglas-fir Bark (Ground)	2200	0.20	0.09	0.10	7.8
Larch Bark (Ground)	2000	0.20	0.23	0.13	11.2

Weight: The average weight of uncompacted (gravity-settled) green sawdust is 17.5 lbs. to 18.5 lbs. per cubic foot, or 470 to 500 lbs. per cubic yard, or 3,500 to 3,700 lbs. per "unit" of 200 cubic foot. Composted sawdust, which has a higher moisture content, will weigh between 600 and 700 lbs. per cubic yard, or 4,400 to 5,100 lbs. per "unit."

Ground Coverage of Sawdust Mulch or Compost:

	Depth of Application					
	1"	*2"*	*3"*	*4"*	*5"*	*6"*
1 cu. yard covers	324	162	108	81	65	54 Sq. Ft.
1 200 cu. ft. "unit" covers	2400	1200	800	600	480	400 Sq. Ft.

COMPOSTING SAWDUST WITH SEWAGE SLUDGE

Prof. James B. Reeves of Texas Western College of the University of Texas in El Paso has reported on sawdust-sewage sludge composting experiments in *Sewage and Industrial Wastes.* According to Prof. Reeves, composting sludge with sawdust produces a product which resembles leaf mold in texture, appearance, and odor. The compost is quite acceptable and offers a relatively simple way for the sewage plant operator to dispose of an otherwise troublesome waste. It is also beneficial to the land and adds moisture to the soil. Ullrich and Smith using digested sludge mixed with hardwood sawdust found that a completed compost could be obtained in approximately 11 weeks.

The composting operation was carried on as follows:

Air-dried sludge was placed in windrows approximately 300 feet in length. The sludge was combined primary and secondary which had been digested for a period of 45 to 90 days, followed by 4 to 6 months on drying beds. The proximity of residential areas is noted in the background. The compost site is approximately 500 yards from the drying beds.

The sludge windrows were approximately 6 feet wide at the bottom, 4 feet wide at the top, and 4 feet high. Windrows of hardwood sawdust were placed alongside. Mixing was accomplished by repeated folding over with a road grader. The combination was wetted with city water at 2- to 3-week intervals and turned with the grader. After 2 to 3 months of composting, the material was ground twice with a Royer Shredder, mixed, wetted, and placed in piles approximately 12 feet wide, 16 feet long, and 6 feet high.

The compost was composed of small particles, grayish in color, with a humus-like odor, and with good moisture retaining properties.

COMPOSTING SLUDGE WITH WOOD SHAVINGS

The city of Santa Rosa, California found an answer for its sludge drying and disposal problem by composting with wood shavings and street sweepings. A report in *Wastes Engineering* Magazine by Murray McKinnie, Sewage Works Superintendent in Santa Rosa, tells how this method overcame difficulties caused by inadequate sludge drying bed area, excessive rainfall, high cost of removing sludge cake from the drainage units, and the shock effect of supernatant disposal into the regular plant treatment units.

Much of the problem is caused by the fact that Santa Rosa is pelted annually with 30 inches of rainfall, the greatest portion falling from November to as late as May. The city engineers decided to try a proposed solution they first heard about being used in the San Francisco area—one at Redwood City and another in San Carlos.

In starting this method, the first step was to harrow all 8 sludge beds which were filled with partially dried sludge. Sufficient shavings—30 cubic yards—were purchased to use on one sludge bed. This material was spread over the dried harrowed sludge. This bed contained 41,300 gallons, or 21,800 pounds of sludge, by dry weight. On May 11, the first liquid sludge was spread on this bed.

During monthly intervals the sludge-shavings mixture was harrowed and one week after harrowing, the area was again filled with liquid sludge. The last, or fifth, filling was applied on November 5. During the May 11 to November 5 period, 100,500 gallons, or 65,200 pounds of sludge, by dry weight, were applied to this bed. This had all been applied on a sludge bed 50 by 100 feet in size. Not including the original dry sludge cake, over twice what could formerly be applied had been added to this bed without use of any labor to clean the area.

At the present time, the only positive result achieved by the composting process is that one sludge drying bed handled over twice the normal amount of sludge and that a poor supernatant has been removed from the plant at times of low flow. Both these results indicate that the city's money has been well spent.

Connecticut Tests

Experiments at the Connecticut Station, directed by soil scientist Herbert Lunt, have shown conclusively that digested sewage sludge from typical treatment plants in Connecticut has a very favorable effect on the properties of the soil. This was shown by increases (3 to 25 per cent) in field moisture capacity, and non-capillary porosity; in organic matter content up to 35 or 40 per cent; in total nitrogen up to 70 per cent, and in soil aggregation ranging from 25 to nearly 600 per cent.

Since chips and sawdust are deficient in nitrogen, and large applications of sludge may result in an excess of that element, the logical solution is to use a mixture of chips and sludge, advises Dr. Lunt. Experiments indicate that this combination is a very effective one, and is especially good where soils are urgently in need of increased organic matter content. The proportions to use vary with the nitrogen and carbon composition of the materials, but the total amount of carbon in the mixture should not be more than about 30 times the total amount of nitrogen.

Composition of Various Organic Wastes*

Material	Moisture %	Ash %	N %	P_2O_5 %	K_2O %
Antibiotic wastes					
Penicillin	75.3	29.5	3.85	4.13	1.08
Streptomycin	62.6	71.9	2.20	0.52	0.06
Apple pomace	—	—	1.70	—	—
Botanical drug wastes					
Cascara bark	75.8	9.7	0.54	0.03	0.00
Licorice roots	—	—	2.20	0.11	1.12
Pyrethrum flowers	25.0	12.1	2.07	0.58	2.58
Scammony roots	36.4	13.9	1.12	0.47	2.22
Soap bark	66.5	8.4	0.85	0.07	0.72
Cannery wastes					
Asparagus	93.8	12.5	3.96	0.91	3.54
Beet	94.2	7.0	2.57	0.52	1.92
Spinach	85.7	58.4	3.21	1.14	1.07
Sweet potatoes	90.0	10.2	1.84	0.46	0.72
Coffee wastes					
Chaff	3.0	5.5	2.58	0.19	2.10
Grounds, fresh	62.9	0.5	1.84	0.03	0.12
Grounds, composted pile	58.0	—	1.65	0.22	3.00

Material	Moisture %	Ash %	N %	P_2O_5 %	K_2O %
Cocoa shells	—	—	2.71	1.17	3.06
Cow manure	—	—	2.50	0.50	1.40
Duck manure	—	—	3.55	—	—
Garbage	49.3	28.5	1.07	1.16	0.83
Horse manure	—	—	2.85	—	—
Poultry manure	22.6	25.6	3.58	3.02	1.62
Sawdust					
Oak	45.6	2.1	0.12	0.002	0.12
Poplar	43.3	2.5	0.13	0.001	0.15
Seaweed	—	—	3.17	—	—
Sewage sludge	65.0	40.0	2.25	1.50	1.70
Snuff wastes					
Stem sand	7.5	38.8	2.81	0.77	4.54
Leaf sand	3.5	74.4	0.94	0.21	1.62
Sweepings	16.9	25.1	2.91	0.49	6.90
Soybean mash	84.0	15.1	4.81	1.49	0.78
Spent hops	79.1	4.4	2.13	0.66	0.42
Spent mushroom soil					
Horse manure base	37.0	75.1	1.36	0.32	1.32
Synthetic	29.7	76.2	0.80	0.21	1.32
Spent spice marc					
Carolina chili	16.2	8.3	3.41	1.03	3.84
Ginger	11.8	5.5	1.74	0.35	1.80
Nutmeg	37.3	4.3	1.25	0.40	1.26
Patchouli leaves	11.0	19.5	3.34	0.60	3.96
Spent tea leaves	86.0	3.2	4.41	0.29	0.24
Tobacco stems	20.0	21.5	1.96	0.63	10.80
Wool wastes	—	—	5.70	1.40	0.80

* Oven-dried basis. This list was included in a report, prepared by Drs. S. J. Toth and W. H. Kelly of Rutgers University, which appeared in the July-August, 1956 issue of *New Jersey Agriculture*.

Analysis of Waste Materials

Apple Pomace—Apple pomace decays readily if mixed with material that provides for proper aeration. Its value in the wet state is not high, since the nitrogen content is only one-fifth of one per cent. But when analyzing the ash content of apple skins, they had over 3 per cent phosphoric acid. The potash content is, of course, much higher, amounting to about 12 per cent of the ash, which corresponds to three-quarters of one per cent of the pomace.

Banana Residues — Analyses have shown that banana skins and stalks are extremely rich in both phosphoric acid and potash, rating from 2.3 to 3.3 in phosphoric acid and from 41 to 50 per cent in potash, on an ash basis. The nitrogen content is believed to be high, because these residues decompose very rapidly and must therefore offer an almost complete diet for bacteria.

Basic Slag—Basic slag is a by-product of the melting operations in steel manufacturing. It contains phosphorus and calcium. Basic slag breaks down rather slowly and does not release phosphoric acid quickly, though with sufficient speed if organic material is present in the soil. As a result of many experiments, it is safe to say that basic slag can be used if finely ground and employed in conjunction with manure or compost. In soils that are highly alkaline, greater amounts of organic matter should be incorporated anyhow to balance the alkalinity; if this is done, basic slag will show adequate results there too.

Beet Wastes—Numerous analyses of beet roots showed that their potash content varied from .7 to 4.1 per cent; the variation in nitrogen is less pronounced, and an average might be .4 per cent, while phosphorus ranges from .1 to .6 per cent. The leaves are not very different in their make-up, although their content in calcium and magnesium far exceeds that of the roots.

Brewery Wastes—Spent hops is the residue after hops have been extracted with water in the brewery. In their wet state, they have about 75 per cent water, 0.6 per cent nitrogen, 0.2 per cent P205. Moisture content varies considerably, and the analysis expressed on the dry matter is the most satisfactory figure. On this basis the nitrogen ranges from 2.5 to 3.5 per cent and the phosphoric acid about one per cent. Spent hops in their natural condition are to be regarded mainly as a source of nitrogen. In many areas, gardeners and farmers have been successfully using the hops in their natural condition, spreading it in the same way as farmyard manure. Many other growers have been composting the hops before applying to the soil.

Another brewery waste available is the material left over from the mashing process, composed of grain parts. This wet brewer's grain, which decays readily, has been found to contain almost one per cent of nitrogen.

Castor Pomace—After the oil has been extracted from

A fine mineral source, cotton gin wastes will decompose in a few months when piled in the open. They make a rich, valuable compost. Cotton gin wastes pictured above will be plowed into this sandy soil—sheet composted to improve structure.

the castor bean, a residue is left that is widely used as an organic fertilizer in place of cotton seed meal, because the latter is valuable also as feed. The nitrogen analysis of castor bean pomace is the decisive factor. It varies from 4.0 to 6.6 per cent, while phosphoric acid and potash analyze from 1 to 2 per cent, with greater variation occurring in the phosphorus content.

Citrus Wastes—Citrus wastes are most easily composted, nor is there any danger to the soil in their oils and resins, because these disintegrate in the composting process. Orange skins and citrus skins of all kinds are richer in nitrogen if the skins are thick; their phosphoric acid content is extremely high, and an ash analysis shows about 3.0 per cent of this valuable element in orange skins, while the potash content of the ash is 50 per cent. Lemons, as a rule, have a higher phosphorus content than oranges; grapefruit seem to hold the middle between the extremes: 3.6 per cent phosphoric acid and 30 per cent potash. Whole fruits, so called, culls are also useful, though their fertilizer value is necessarily lower than that of the skins, because they contain great amounts of water.

Coffee Wastes—Coffee chaff seems to be an excellent material for use in home gardens as well as farms. Over two per cent in both nitrogen and potash, chaff also appears very suitable for use as a mulch material. Its dark color is also an asset. Coffee manufacturers should make an effort to get local growers to use the chaff, also contact local fertilizer dealers for marketing. Material may lend itself to low cost baling rather than bagging.

Cotton Gin Waste—The cotton seed burrs are a source of potash. The fine waste and the more voluminous amounts of wastes containing cotton fiber are, as a rule, rich in nitrogen, because seed parts and lint are contained in them. When piled up in the open, this material will decay in a few months under Southern conditions into a rich and valuable compost without further additions.

Cotton Seed Products—Cottonseed meal is made from the cotton seed which has been freed from lints and hulls and deprived of its oil. Since cottonseed cake is one of the richest protein foods for animal feeding, little finds its way into the fertilizer business, so that nowadays the grower has to rely more and more on castor pomace. It is likely that meal can be imported from Brazil, but at present there is not much likelihood for great amounts becoming available to the fertilizer dealers. The special value of cottonseed meal lies in its acid reaction which makes it a valuable fertilizer for acid-loving specialty crops. The meal is used mainly as a source of nitrogen, of which it contains varying amounts, usually around 7 per cent. The phosphoric acid content is between 2.0 and 3.0 per cent, while potash is usually represented to the amount of 1.5 per cent.

One of the major fertilizers nowadays are cotton seed hulls and cottonseed hull ashes, especially the latter, which are used as a source of quickly available potash, of which there is from 15 to 23 per cent in the commercial product. But the phosphoric acid content is also considerable and usually above that of other plant products, namely from 7 to 9.5 per cent.

Feathers—Feathers are similar to silk and wool in that they contain considerable amounts of nitrogen. An analysis revealed that they contained over 15 per cent. Feathers will decompose readily, if kept very moist.

Fish Products—Fish scrap is very high in nitrogen and phosphorus, generally over 7 per cent for each. Dried ground fish, mainly used for feed mixtures, analyzes around 8 per cent nitrogen and 7 per cent phosphoric acid.

Pictured above is one of the conveyor units taking waste fish products for conversion into fish oils and other concentrates. One-third of a fish used for canning is recoverable waste, with the fish meal making excellent plant and animal food.

Felt Wastes—Analyze as high as 14 per cent nitrogen.

Grape Pomace—The left-overs from wineries, consisting of the pressed parts of the grape, contain beside a varied bacterial flora, especially yeasts, a certain amount of nitrogen, usually about one per cent, and smaller amounts of phosphorus and potash. This material is easily adapted to fast composting.

Leather Dust—Leather dust makes an excellent fertilizer material, high in nitrogen. The nitrogen content varies from 5.5 to 12 per cent, and it also contains considerable amounts of phosphorus.

Nut Shells—The composition of nut shells varies according to the nuts. Almond shells and pecans decay readily, black walnut shells which contain greater amounts of lignin, take longer; filberts and English walnuts decompose without trouble; while Brazil nuts and coconuts could be used only in ground-up form, in the same manner in which cocoa shell meal is utilized. The only analyses available refer to the latter product, which is given as 2.5 per cent nitrogen, one per cent phosphoric acid and 2.5 per cent potash.

Olive Residues—The analysis of olive pomace is given as

839

1.15 nitrogen, 0.78 phosphoric acid and 1.26 potash, while some olive refuse showed 1.22 nitrogen, 0.18 phosphoric acid and 0.32 potash. It is not known how olive pits would show up from a fertilizer standpoint, but there is little doubt that they too should be used for adding fertility to the soil, since they not only contain phosphorus and nitrogen in higher amounts than mere refuse, but also lignin.

Peanut Hulls—Peanut hulls are rich in nitrogen. Here is an analysis:

	Nitrogen	Phosphoric Acid	Potash
Peanut shells	3.6	.70	.45
Peanut shell ashes	.8	.15	.50

Pea Wastes—Pea pod ash contains almost 3 per cent phosphoric acid and 27 per cent potash. They can be composted with great ease since their nitrogen content, which is highest in green pods and vines, tends to produce a quick breakdown.

Potato Wastes—The potash content of tubers is usually around 2.5 per cent. Dry potato vines contain approximately 1.6 per cent potash, 4.0 per cent calcium, 1.1 per cent magnesium, and considerable amounts of sulphur and other minerals.

Rice Hulls—Rice hulls have been found to be very rich in potash and decompose readily when worked into the soil, thereby increasing humus content.

Seaweed—The value of seaweed has already received much publicity, and many firms have been marketing it successfully as a fertilizer.

Silk Mill Wastes—The main value of these substances is their nitrogen and phosphorus content. Silkworm cocoons contain about 10 per cent nitrogen, 1.8 per cent phosphoric acid and over one per cent potassium. By-products from silk mills vary in their composition, but are frequently among the most useful wastes obtainable. The nitrogen content of one sample was 8.37 per cent and the phosphoric acid value 1.14 per cent.

Tea Grounds—One analysis of tea leaves showed the relatively high content of 4.15 per cent nitrogen, which seems to be exceptional. Both phosphorus and potash were present in amounts below one per cent.

Tobacco Stems—The nutrients contained in 100 pounds of tobacco stems are 2.5 to 3.7 pounds of nitrogen, almost a pound of phosphoric acid and from 4.5 to 7.0 pounds of potassium. Thus tobacco stems make a good potash fertilizer in organic form.

Sugar Wastes—A waste product of sugar factories, filter cake makes a useful soil builder. Especially recommended for cane fields near factories. Usually applied at rate of 5 to 15 tons per acre. Addition of press cake to cane soils has helped to reduce greatly nematode infestation and damage.

Tung Oil Pomace—A by-product of the tung oil industry in the gulf states, comparable to castor pomace, the nitrogen content of tung oil pomace is about 6 per cent.

Wool Wastes (or Shoddy) have been used by British farmers living in the vicinity of wool textile mills since the industrial revolution in the early 19th century. Its fertilizing value lies entirely in its organic and nitrogen content. The wool fiber decomposes when in contact with moisture in the soil, and in the process, produces available nitrogen for plant growth. Generally, the moisture content of the wool wastes is between 15 and 20 per cent. It analyzes from 3.5 to 6.0 per cent nitrogen, 2.0 to 4.0 per cent phosphoric acid, and 1.0 to 3.5 per cent potash. (Also check the chapter on Materials for Composting.)

List of Research Reports and Reference Data for Further Information of Industrial Waste Materials for Garden and Farm Use

Industrial Wastes Treatment—By Hayse H. Black, Chief, Industrial Wastes Section, U. S. Public Health Service, Cincinnati, Ohio—Sewage and Industrial Wastes, Vol. 26.

Studies of High-Rate Composting of Garbage and Refuse— John S. Wiley, Senior Sanitary Engineer, U. S. Dept. of Health, Education and Welfare, Savannah, Georgia.

Fertilizer or Organic Material for Soil Improvement—By M. S. Anderson, Senior Chemist, Soil and Water Conservation Research Branch, U. S. Dept. of Agriculture, Beltsville, Maryland.

Disposal of Cannery Waste in Ohio—By. Prof. H. D. Brown, Ohio State University, Columbus, Ohio.

Photosynthesis Reclamation of Organic Wastes—By Harold B. Gotaas, William J. Oswald, Harvey F. Ludwig, The Scientific Monthly, December, 1954.

Fishery Feed Products—By Ralph C. Holder, National Fisheries Institute, 1614 Twentieth St., N. W., Washington 9, D. C.

The Use of Mulches—William A. Albrecht, Ph.D., Dept. of Soils, University of Missouri, Columbia.

Soil Fertility and Biotic Geography — William A. Albrecht, Ph.D., Dept. of Soils, University of Missouri, Columbia. Reprinted from The Geographical Review, No. 1, 1957, American Geographical Society, Broadway at 156th St., New York.

Utilization and Disposal of Poultry By-Products and Wastes— Marketing Research Report No. 143, U. S. Dept. of Agriculture, Washington, D. C.

Potassium Frit as a Special Purpose Fertilizer—University of California, Los Angeles.

Complete Study of Farm Uses for Organic Wastes—S. J. Toth and W. H. Kelly, July-August, 1956 issue of New Jersey Agriculture, Agricultural Exp. Station, New Brunswick.

Commercial Fertilizers: Their Sources and Use—By Gilbeart H. Collings, Ph.D., McGraw-Hill Book Company, New York.

Reference Material on Wood Wastes

The Use of Wood Chips in Agriculture — Bulletin No. 41, Northeastern Wood Utilization Council, Inc., P.O. Box 1577, New Haven 6, Conn., $2.00.

The Use of Wood Chips and Other Wood Fragments as Soil Amendments—Bulletin 593, The Connecticut Agricultural Experiment Station, New Haven.

The Use of Sawdust for Mulches and Soil Improvement—Circular 891, U. S. Dept. of Agriculture, Washington, D. C.

Marketing Sawdust and Chipped Wood—Bulletin 38, Northeastern Wood Utilization Council, Inc., P.O. Box 1577, New Haven 6, Conn., Price 50 cents.

Sawdust Composts in Soil Improvement — New Hampshire Agricultural Experiment Station, Durham, N. H.

General Recommendations Regarding Methods for Wood Waste Utilization—By Forest Products Laboratory, Forest Service, U. S. Dept. of Agriculture, Madison, Wisconsin.

An Inventory of Sawmill Waste in Oregon—By Glenn Voorhies, Bulletin No. 17, Oregon State Engineering Experiment Station, Corvallis, Oregon.

Uses for Sawdust and Shavings—By Forest Products Laboratory, USDA, Madison, Wisconsin.

The Influence of Waste Bark on Plant Growth—By Stuart Dunn, University of New Hampshire, Agricultural Experiment Station, Durham.

Field Plot Studies with Sawdust for Soil Improvement—University of New Hampshire, Agricultural Experiment Station, Durham.

Wood Flour: A Study in Wood Waste Utilization—By Edward D. Gruen, Monthly Review, Federal Reserve Bank of Boston, Boston, Mass.

Wood Wastes and Soil—Crops and Soils Magazine, 2702 Monroe Street, Madison 5, Wisconsin, January, 1957.

Influence of Lignin and Other Waste Materials on Plant Growth—By Stuart Dunn, N. H. Agriculture Experiment Station, Durham.

Uses for Forest Residues—By L. H. Reineke, Forest Products Laboratory, USDA, Madison, Wisconsin.

A Discussion of Waste Utilization—Timber Engineering Company, 1319 Eighteenth St., N. W., Washington, D. C.

Wood Chips for the Land—Leaflet No. 323, Soil Conservation Service, USDA, Washington, D. C.

Composts and Mulches from Wood Waste—By Stanley P. Gessel, Associate Professor of Forest Soils, University of Washington.

HOW TO DETERMINE THE VALUE OF YOUR OWN WASTE PRODUCTS TO THE GARDENER AND FARMER

A Typical Problem:

Company ABC wants to find out whether its waste product is useful as a fertilizer, soil conditioner and/ or mulch. What steps should the company take to learn the answer?

The first step is to find out the composition of the waste materials. Generally, a description of the materials composing the waste products is already in company files or can be obtained with minimum effort. Is there any substance that would prove toxic to plant life in the soil? This question can be answered by checking with your State Agricultural College or Experiment Station. Many of these stations will also test your material for its nitrogen, phosphorus, and potash content for $15 to $25. The College can most likely supply you with the name and address of a commercial laboratory in the state who can make a more complete analysis of your waste material, in case they are unable to test it themselves.

Here are the addresses of -state colleges and experiment stations:

Alabama Agricultural Experiment Station, Auburn, Ala.
Alaska Agricultural Experiment Station, College, Alaska.
Arizona Agricultural Experiment Station, Tucson, Ariz.
Arkansas Agricultural Experiment Station, Fayetteville, Ark.
California Agricultural Experiment Station, Berkeley 4, Calif.
California Agricultural Experiment Station, Davis, Calif.
Colorado Agricultural Experiment Station, Fort Collins, Colo.
Connecticut Agricultural Experiment Station, New Haven 4, Conn.
Connecticut Agricultural Experiment Station, Storrs, Conn.
Delaware Agricultural Experiment Station, Newark, Del.
Florida Agricultural Experiment Station, Gainesville, Fla.
Georgia Agricultural Experiment Station, Experiment, Ga.
Hawaii Agricultural Experiment Station, Honolulu 14, Hawaii.
Idaho Agricultural Experiment Station, Moscow, Idaho.
Illinois Agricultural Experiment Station, Urbana, Ill.
Indiana Agricultural Experiment Station, Lafayette, Ind.
Iowa Agricultural Experiment Station, Ames, Iowa.
Kansas Agricultural Experiment Station, Manhattan, Kans.
Kentucky Agricultural Experiment Station, Lexington 29, Ky.
Louisiana Agricultural Experiment Station, University Station, Baton Rouge 3, La.
Maine Agricultural Experiment Station, Orono, Maine.
Maryland Agricultural Experiment Station, College Park, Md.
Massachusetts Agricultural Experiment Station, Amherst, Mass.
Michigan Agricultural Experiment Station, East Lansing, Mich.
Minnesota Agricultural Experiment Station, University Farm, St. Paul 1, Minn.
Mississippi Agricultural Experiment Station, State College, Miss.
Missouri Agricultural Experiment Station, Columbia, Mo.
Montana Agricultural Experiment Station, Bozeman, Mont.
Nebraska Agricultural Experiment Station, Lincoln 3, Nebr.
Nevada Agricultural Experiment Station, Reno, Nev.
New Hampshire Agricultural Experiment Station, Durham, N. H.
New Jersey Agricultural Experiment Station, New Brunswick, N. J.
New Mexico Agricultural Experiment Station, State College, N. Mex.
New York (Cornell) Agricultural Experiment Station, Ithaca, N. Y.
New York State Agricultural Experiment Station, Geneva, N. Y.
North Carolina Agricultural Experiment Station, State College Station, Raleigh, N. C.
North Dakota Agricultural Experiment Station, State College Station, Fargo, N. D.
Ohio Agricultural Experiment Station, Wooster, Ohio.
Ohio Agricultural Experiment Station, Columbus, Ohio.

Oklahoma Agricultural Experiment Station, Stillwater, Okla.
Oregon Agricultural Experiment Station, Corvallis, Ore.
Pennsylvania Agricultural Experiment Station, University Park, Pa.
Puerto Rico Agricultural Experiment Station, Rio Piedras, Puerto Rico.
Rhode Island Agricultural Experiment Station, Kingston, R. I.
South Carolina Agricultural Experiment Station, Clemson, S. C.
South Dakota Agricultural Experiment Station, State College Station, S. D.
Tennessee Agricultural Experiment Station, Knoxville 16, Tenn.
Texas Agricultural Experiment Station, College Station, Texas.
Utah Agricultural Experiment Station, Logan, Utah.
Vermont Agricultural Experiment Station, Burlington, Vt.
Virginia Agricultural Experiment Station, Blacksburg, Va.
Virginia Truck Experiment Station, Norfolk 1, Va.
Washington Agricultural Experiment Station, Pullman, Wash.
Washington Agricultural Experiment Station, Puyallup, Wash.
West Virginia Agricultural Experiment Station, Morgantown, W. Va.
Wisconsin Agricultural Experiment Station, Madison 6, Wisc.
Wyoming Agricultural Experiment Station, Laramie, Wyo.

Have Your Product Used

It's most worthwhile to arrange to have local nurseries, gardeners and farmers conduct tests of your waste products. For nominal sums (and in many cases, without charge), many such growers will set aside small areas and run comparative tests with and without your waste materials.

To get a rough idea, perhaps employees in your own company could use the materials in their gardens. Another way to interest growers to try the materials would be to notify the editor of your local newspaper that you are making your wastes available to gardeners and farmers.

Your state agricultural college has facilities to conduct thorough tests of your material and will issue a confidential report to you of the results. Although this procedure can be quite expensive, there undoubtedly are many companies whose profit from waste products—if found to be valuable to the soil—would pay for these costs many times over.

Compare Your Product with Material Analyses

Analyses of a great many waste products have already been made and are available. For example, if your company has many tons of sawdust, wood chips, etc., there seems to be little need for you to go to further expense to have an analysis made. By merely checking the analyses given previously, you'll get a satisfactory knowledge of its composition. So be sure to check carefully all of the tables and material descriptions given in preceding pages.

What Kind of Processing is Needed Before Waste Products Can Be Marketed?

The kind and amount of processing required depends, of course, on the chemical as well as physical composition of the waste product. Several, such as buckwheat hulls, oat hulls, rice hulls, cocoa bean shells, and leather dust, are excellent for use in the soil in its waste form. Very often, sawdust, wood chips and coffee chaff can be distributed at least locally without further processing.

However, the great amount of wastes need some amount of processing if they are to be marketed for use by gardeners and farmers. In many cases, there is too much moisture; in others, the materials may be lacking in nitrogen or other minerals. The processing method which is most practical is composting.

Benefits of Composting

Technological improvements in grinding, shredding and digesting equipment have made composting the most encouraging entrant to the industrial waste picture in many years. In a short time, wood wastes, cannery residues, cellophane, food wastes of all kinds, paper mill sludge—all can not only be changed by composting into a salable material, but all can be increased in value to make a better fertilizer, soil conditioner or mulch.

The market for compost fertilizer has shown definite improvement since 1950. U. S. Department of Agriculture figures show that the consumption of compost (principally by gardeners) has increased from 416 tons in 1952 to 12,095 tons in 1955, an increase of about 3000 per cent. The consumption of natural organic fertilizers of all types has increased from 293,183 tons in 1950 to 461,100 tons in 1955.

With consumption of compost increasing as rapidly as it is, it is quite likely that market surveys would show that compost of average nutritional content could be sold in bulk to contract purchasers for from $15 to $20 a ton.

Equipment

The Thomas Registry, available in many public libraries, contains the names of manufacturers of equipment that is

846

necessary for composting. Manufacturers of grinders, shredders, materials handling and similar equipment are all listed there. These firms include Dorr-Oliver, Stamford, Connecticut; Sprout, Waldron & Company, Muncy, Pennsylvania; Food Machinery and Chemical Corporation, San Jose, California; Enterprise Engineering and Machinery Corp, San Francisco; Gruendler Crusher and Pulverizer Company, St. Louis, Missouri; W-W Grinder Corp., Wichita, Kansas; Combustion Engineering, Inc., Chicago, Illinois.

Trade Journals in the wastes field, as *Wastes Engineering, Industrial Wastes, Public Works, Journal of Water Pollution Control Federation, Compost Science, The American City,* and *Water and Sewage Works* carry the advertisements of many of these firms. Engineering consultant firms, as Michigan Associates in Lansing, headed by John Snell, offer invaluable aid to industrial firms seeking information about composting waste materials.

Chapter 23

THE VALUE OF COMPOST

The benefits of compost are many, encompassing wide-ranging effects on the soil, the growth of plants, and the health and well-being of animals and people consuming the plants.

Compost is organic matter, and organic matter is vital to life. As Roy L. Donahue, Chairman of the Department of Agronomy, University of New Hampshire, has said, "Organic matter is stored sunshine; destroy it and darkness will fall upon the face of the earth.

"At one time there was no organic matter on earth or in the sky. That was back in the beginning of the earth. Probably the first organic matter was made by certain specialized bacteria capable of using minerals such as sulphur and obtaining their carbon from carbon dioxide in the air. Their bodies contained carbon from the air and hydrogen and oxygen from both air and water.

"After these specialized bacteria fixed some organic matter other general-purpose bacteria then could get their energy from this source.

"Plants of low forms then came upon the earth. Plants which were green were able to use energy from the sun, carbon from the air, and oxygen and hydrogen from air and water to make organic matter. It is the green plant today on which we depend for the manufacture of organic matter. Animals must depend upon the green plant to furnish organic matter for their energy. Animals are not capable of making organic matter; neither is man. Both man and the animals must have green plants capturing and storing for their use sunshine, air, and water in the form of organic matter. Man and animals could not live a year if plants stopped growing.

"Most forms of bacteria in the soil, as well as fungi, earthworms and other soil flora and fauna are as much dependent upon organic matter for energy as are man and animals. And without this life in the soil, the soil itself would be lifeless and sterile.

"Nothing would grow well in a soil without organic matter. What is there about organic matter in the soil which makes it so valuable?

"In the first place, organic matter promotes a granular structure which permits a soil to hold more of both water and air. In other words, organic matter increases tremendously the amount of active surface in each square inch of soil. All chemical and physical activity takes place on the surface of each soil particle. This change brought about by more organic matter added to the soil means:

1. A more extensive plant root system.
2. More water entering the soil faster.
3. Less water flowing from the land and thus less erosion.
4. Greater aeration.
5. Less blowing of the soil due to a more moist surface.
6. A greater amount of water stored in the soil for use by plants.
7. Less soil baking and less crust formation.

"In the second place, an increase in soil organic matter keeps the soil at a more uniform temperature. In winter, soils with an organic mulch are warmer and in summer they are cooler than soils with no such organic blanket.

Compost is organic matter in its most valuable form for the earth that feeds, clothes and houses us. Organic matter is essential to life; without its return to the soil, an inspiring pastoral scene such as this would be impossible, as would be farming itself.

"Thirdly, soils high in organic matter, especially when used as a surface mulch, lose less water by evaporation into the atmosphere.

"In the fourth place, soluble plant nutrients which may otherwise leach out of reach of plant roots, are held in place by partly decomposed organic matter (humus). Plant nutrients so held by humus are readily available to growing plants.

"Decomposing organic matter is to growing plants what self-feeders are to livestock. This function may be labeled the fifth function of organic matter in soils. Growing plants need a continuous supply of readily available nutrients throughout the growing season. Not only must plants have

849

all 15 essential elements available, but these elements must be in the proper proportion to each other. In addition, sunshine, water, and air must be available in the right amounts at all times. Organic matter aids in directly promoting the proper amounts of all of these factors of plant growth except sunshine. And even more sunshine is captured when organic matter is adequate in the soil. Increased plant growth means that more of the energy from the sun has been trapped in the form of plant material. This too, is organic matter. Thus soil organic matter, when properly used, aids in the rapid regeneration of new supplies of organic matter. In other words, life generates life.

"The sixth function of organic matter in the soil consists of furnishing to growing plants, certain growth-promoting substances. These substances may be vitamins or minerals whose functions are not well understood by soil scientists. Certain germ killers (antibiotics) such as streptomycin, penicillin, and aureomycin, are derived from productive soils. These antibiotics are produced by certain soil organisms which in turn obtain their energy from soil organic matter. Soils high in organic matter thus appear to be healthier for plants and animals as well as for man."

PHYSICAL PROPERTIES

Nutrients, moisture, air, soil temperature and productivity, then, are some of the things influenced by additions of compost to a soil. Let us consider first the physical properties of the soil.

Remember how easily a handful of sand flows through one's fingers? Each individual sand grain moves freely of the other particles because the sand has no structure. You also know how plastic molding clay is and how much it resembles dough. Both of these materials lack internal structure and so they flow easily in whichever direction we push.

Now consider a moist lump of mellow loam. Pick it up and notice how well it retains its structure. Of course, if you exert enough pressure, you can crush it, but usually it will break up into smaller pieces which also exhibit the same kind of structure. The loam behaves this way because its sand, silt, and clay particles are aggregated or bound together in a definite pattern which gives the soil its structure.

The difference between soils which have and lack structure

is similar to the difference between a disorderly pile of bricks and a brick house where each brick is cemented in its own particular place. One has structure, the other does not.

Structure is important since it allows a soil to breathe and facilitates circulation. A heavy or clayey soil which has poor structure tends to become waterlogged or to slick over on the surface, preventing water and air penetration. Adding compost helps to loosen up this packed soil. It does this by opening up pore spaces which carry air and water down into the soil like so many little tunnels. A "crumb" structure is built, and a thin film of moisture is held on each crumb of soil where plant roots can utilize it as needed.

Sandy soils, which tend to let water drain away too rapidly, are also rebuilt into crumbs by organic matter additions. The fine particles are united into larger ones that can hold greater quantities of water in films on their surfaces.

The higher the humus content, the more moisture a soil can absorb and retain. Soil with ample organic matter lets raindrops seep gently into it, instead of splattering and churning up soil particles. In the latter case of a packed, crusted soil, a muddy drop of water is formed which will run over the soil surface as the first stage of erosion. A heavy rainstorm results in considerable runoff which carries away soil and fertility. And finally, disastrous floods occur—which we try to prevent by building huge dams, when the best preventive would be to make a "crumb" structure in the soil which results in myriad tiny runoff-stopping dams on its surface.

PROTECTION AGAINST DROUGHT

The permeability of soils amply supplied with organic matter is also a potent weapon against drought damage. Water is soaked up like a sponge and stored on the soil crumbs (100 pounds of humus holds 195 pounds of water). When the tiny root hairs can absorb all the water the plant needs from the films on these crumbs, they do not suffer from long rainless periods.

Another point should be mentioned here. In an old book, *The Clifton Park System of Farming,* we find: "It is important to note too that the air passing over a humus-fed soil would be cooler and moister than air passing over a mineralized (chemically fertilized) soil. The dewfall therefore would be greater, and when the land throughout the country becomes generally humus-fed, the rainfall would be more advantageously distributed, and fall over a greater number of days in small showers instead of heavy falls of rain, as in the case when land is clothed with forest." A darker soil, it has been found, causes more deposition of dew than a light-colored one. Humus-rich soils are darker and thus precipitate more dew.

That compost makes a soil light and fluffy, full of pore spaces, has been demonstrated on the Morrow Plots, in operation since 1876, on the campus of the University of Illinois. Professor H. J. Snider reports:

"Soil on the organically-treated land was found to be less compact and more easily handled in plowing and other cultural operations. A cubic foot of organically-treated soil weighed 75 pounds compared to 85 pounds for a cubic foot of untreated soil. This shows the untreated soil to be more dense and compact and consequently heavier. The organically-treated soil was fluffy and therefore lighter in total weight.

"A desirable soil has a physical make-up which is granular and will readily break up into small crumbs or clusters of soil particles. Soil scientists refer to these as soil aggregates. On the Morrow Plots the organically-treated soil was made up of 47 per cent of these crumbs or clusters compared to only 32 per cent of the soil where no effort was made to add organic matter and to keep the soil in a desirable physical condition.

"One of the highly important characteristics of a soil is its ability to hold water. On the Morrow Plots careful testing revealed that the organically-treated soil held 76 per cent of its weight in water, while the untreated land held only 56 per cent of its weight in water. Both soils were fully saturated and these percentages represent the relative capacity for holding valuable soil water. On the acre basis, these figures appear even more startling. When fully saturated, the organic soil held 1,520,000 pounds and the untreated soil held 1,120,000 pounds of water an acre. This was a difference of 400,000 pounds in favor of the organic system of soil building.

"These figures indicate that the soil organic matter, which is said to act as a sponge, helped retain many barrels of water with which to supply crops during those disastrous short drought periods so frequent in the Midwest.

"All of these soil conditions brought about by the organic system—such as a crumbly soil, a light fluffy condition, and an enlarged water-holding capacity—are mighty important to

In research conducted at the University of Illinois, a cubic foot of organically-treated soil weighed 75 pounds compared to 85 pounds for a cubic foot of untreated soil. The added density and weight make the non-enriched soil much more likely to become compacted, less capable of holding needed moisture and air.

whatever use the land is put; gardening, pasturing, growing farm crops, growing various trees, etc."

RATE OF EROSION

In an article in the Medical Journal of Australia, Dr. E. P. Dark says, "Speaking of the present rate of erosion in America, Jacks and White estimate that, if it continues, America, within a century, could become a Sahara; they believe that between 1914 and 1939 the world probably lost more soil than in all previous history.

"Werthen estimates that the U. S. A. loses by erosion 3,000,000,000 tons of soil annually, the Mississippi alone carrying 700,000,000 tons into the Gulf of Mexico.

"Mile high, those gloomy curtains of dust are the proper back-drop for the tragedy that is on the boards. The lustful march of the white race across the virgin continent strewn with ruined forests, polluted streams, gullied fields, stained by the breaking of treaties and titanic greed, can no longer be disguised behind the camouflage which we call civilization.

"There is no doubt that rapid erosion is going on in every continent; if it is not yet as disastrous as in America, that is probably because American agriculture is more 'advanced' than that of any other country, using more tractors, more bulldozers and more chemical manures in a desperate hurry to produce more crops than Nature intended should be forced from the soil. If in Australia erosion has not been so spectacular, it has caused, and is still causing, severe damage.

"Of course, every acre of eroded soil means less food production in a world where increasing population calls for more food; and less food must mean more malnutrition and more disease, which is certainly the concern of the medical profession. It is a fair assumption, then, that bad methods of soil management may contribute to the increase of disease, and we should be aware of that possibility.

"But nearly all erosion is only the end result of a progressive loss of fertility; really fertile soil is very resistant to erosion, particularly wind erosion, being firmly bound together by its organic content into what is known as the crumb structure. That is soil as Nature intended it to be, and can be seen at its best in any untouched rain forest. Such soil can be intensively farmed without destroying it as the Chinese have demonstrated during the past 4000 years. In their farming all the wastes, from crops, animals and humans, are returned to the soil as compost, which is as near as we can get to Nature's method of growing grass on the prairies and trees in the forest."

AIR IN THE SOIL

Aeration is also extremely important to the soil. One way in which air helps soil has been found by the scientists of the Ministry of Local Industries, Budapest, Hungary. Studies conducted by these scientists on the influence of various manures on soil, under various conditions, including the exclusion of air, show that air plays a vital role in the maintenance of soil productivity. Without air, soils tend to become alkaline. organic matter content decreases, active humus becomes deactivated, total and active humus content decreases, nitrogen content is reduced, and the carbon-to-nitrogen ratio is lowered. The study emphasizes the need for the continued addition of

Oxygen is essential to nitrate formation in soils, and an adequate supply of air is necessary for minerals to be transformed into forms plants can use. Farmland like this, which has a program of liberal compost application, benefits directly from the soil nutrients present in it and from the aeration and good tilth provided.

organic matter to form stable aggregates and maintain soil structure.

The presence of sufficient air in the soil is necessary for the transformation of minerals to forms useable by plants. In an experiment it was found that forced aeration increased the amount of potassium taken in by plants. All textbooks state that nitrate formation in soils can take place only in the presence of a liberal supply of oxygen. Many of the processes in the soil are oxidatious—sulphur transformed to sulphur dioxide, carbon to carbon dioxide, ammonia to nitrate. Oxygen is essential in these processes. Air is an urgent need of the many beneficial soil organisms that aid in these transformations. The oxygen gives the bacteria part of their energy. In addition, aeration helps the formation of mycorrhiza on the roots of many plants. The mycorrhiza is a fungus organism that acts in partnership with the roots of a plant to feed it valuable nutrients.

Liberal additions of compost materials also aid in solving the problem of hardpans. These are impervious horizontal layers in the soil anywhere from 6 inches to about two feet below the surface. A true hardpan is formed by the compacting together of the soil grains into a hard, stone-like mass which is impervious to water. Chemical fertilizers and compaction by heavy machinery are two of the causes.

When hardpans exist, the surface soil is completely cut off from the subsoil; plant roots, often unable to penetrate these layers, usually grow down to them, then extend horizontally over the hard top. This results in shallow-rooted plants that suffer from lack of nutrient elements otherwise available in the subsoil and from unavailable deep water supplies during dry periods.

Dr. William A. Albrecht tells us that normally deep-rooted crops like alfalfa simply will not grow deep in a shallow soil that overlies a hardpan or infertile subsoil. Conversely, shallow-rooted crops, given a deep, fertile soil, will go way down deep for minerals and water, and produce higher yields of better quality. Breaking up these pans with organic matter is the answer.

IMPROVING STRUCTURE

Exactly how does added organic matter bring about a favorable crumb structure in the soil? The mystery of aggregate formation has been solved in part by scientists Iimura and Egawa, National Institute of Agricultural Science, Tokyo. In tests made on the decomposition of organic matter and aggregate formation, it was learned that various soil fungi grow on the organic matter. Soil bacteria then come along to turn the fungal products into cementing materials. These cementing materials glue the tiny particles of soil together into coarse grains or "crumbs."

Soil microbiologist Dr. R. J. Swaby has done extensive research on the mechanism of aggregation. The following are excerpts from an article on his work which appeared in the *G. & N. Co-operator,* July 9, 1953.

Just how and why did soil particles form into aggregates and what were the roles of bacteria, plant roots and soil organic matter in this important phenomenon? One by one, the answers to these questions were unfolded in a series of copybook experiments at Rothamsted research station, England. They contributed much to the world's knowledge of soil biology, and gained Dr. Swaby a Ph.D. from London University.

At the beginning, Dr. Swaby reasoned that improved structure must be due to one or all of several things—the roots themselves, microorganisms associated with the roots, or to gums and resins produced by these organisms. So his experiments began.

First, he grew grasses in a sterilized soil and measured the structural changes. There were scarcely any. The grass roots were incapable of doing the job without the associated microorganisms which live and feed on them. These microorganisms were apparently the real soil binders, the grass roots acting merely as food.

Question number two—was it the microorganisms themselves or their gummy by-products which bound the soil into desirable water-stable aggregates? Microorganisms known to be gum and resin producers were isolated from soil and grown in laboratory cultures. Their gummy products were added to unstructured soil. There was little improvement in granulation. Apparently the gummy substances were not important.

One by one, the important groups of soil organisms were added to poorly structured sterilized soil at this stage and allowed to grow and increase. The effect on structure was carefully measured. There was a remarkable improvement when some were added. The soil became granulated and permeable to water.

Easily the most effective organisms were the fungi or molds. Plants grown in poorly structured soil increased dramatically in size when these were added to the pots. Soil aeration was improved and water permeability increased. Microscopic bacteria had no such beneficial effects. The threadlike mycelium of the fungi apparently wound itself around soil particles and held them together.

Using common fungi in the laboratory, it was possible to get a much greater soil aggregation than occurred in practice. Why was this so?

Dr. Swaby found the answer when he tried various mixtures of fungi and bacteria together. Some were incompatible. Soil aggregating fungi were attacked and killed by certain marauding bacteria, and this is apparently what happens in the field.

It seemed that there was constant war among the teeming millions of microorganisms in the soil. Some microbes devoured plant roots and organic matter and were themselves devoured by others.

Test plots at the Organic Experimental Farm show the effects of contrasted methods of fertilization on both soil structure and plant growth. Plot above has been chemically fertilized; its soil is hard and caked. Composted plot on opposite page had same plants and watering, yet shows much better structure and growth.

Microbial populations reach astronomical proportions. Dr. Swaby calculated that a gram of fertile soil could contain up to one-half mile of fungal mycelium. (A gram of soil will fit comfortably on a sixpence.) It might also contain about 10 million bacteria.

When fungi were added to a soil for testing they were supplied with a suitable food such as straw or molasses. On good food numbers built up quickly and soil structure was improved rapidly. Many things were tried simply by mixing them with the soil.

The more readily decomposable matter was best for improving soil structure. Young plant growth was superior to old lignified mature growth and straw.

There were still many puzzling features. The total aggregation which took place in the field could still not be explained solely by fungal activity. Also, the aggregates formed in the laboratory were much less water-stable than those formed under natural conditions.

When laboratory-made aggregates were exposed in the

paddock they were readily decomposed by bacteria and mites which ate the mycelium, or were easily broken by cultivation.

Aggregates formed under actual field conditions, however, were much more stable, particularly on some soils.

Walking on Harpenden common, at Rothamsted, one late winter's morning, Dr. Swaby noticed that some earthworm casts on permanent grassland were more resistant to the disintegration action of thawing snow than were similar casts on nearby wheatland. So, the role of earthworms was investigated. Worm casts from various types of soils were collected and tested in the laboratory. They were subjected to the same sieving technique used to test the permanence of aggregation.

Results showed that earthworms improved the permanence of aggregation of all soils they devoured. Their casts on grassland soil were particularly stable. Evidently, binding substances were derived from grass roots present in the soil during its passage through the worm. Elaborate experiments were made to explain this, and finally it boiled down to organic matter.

The extra organic matter in the grassland soil, with its greater number of roots, encouraged a vigorous microbial population in worms' intestines. These glued the soil into very stable aggregates. Earthworms accounted for another small portion of the field aggregation, but there was still some to be explained. Also, there was still the mystery of the very permanent aggregates found in the field. These were more stable even than worm casts.

Now thinking in terms of humus, Dr. Swaby began to treat soil crumbs with certain extracts of this. Humus is plant organic matter which has been partly decomposed in the presence of certain minerals. One extract known as humic acid gave remarkable results. It not only improved aggregation but increased the permanence of the crumbs already formed.

Humic acid is a complicated product formed during the breakdown of organic matter in the soil. It has so far resisted all attempts to unravel its involved chemical formula. In the presence of some minerals such as calcium and iron, a salt such as calcium humate was formed. This substance often proved more potent than humic acid as a means of increasing the permanence of aggregation, and explained the extreme stability of the crumb structure of some heavy red and black soils.

With X-ray analysis, chains of humic acid molecules could be detected inside actual clay particles, where they were held electrostatically. The presence of positively charged metals in solution increased the strength of the electrostatic bond and made the aggregate more permanent.

The picture was clearer now. Fungi which fed on plant roots bound soil particles into aggregates. These and others which it formed were made stable by mobile humic acid compounds formed during the active breakdown of organic matter. Organic matter improved the quantity and quality of aggregation.

But even the strong, humus-bound crumbs are broken down by bacteria. When some of them help in breaking down the organic matter to produce the humus extracts which aid aggregation, certain bacteria destroy these and other aggregates bound together by fungal mycelia.

And what does this mean agriculturally?

It means that provision must be made in crop rotations to feed organic matter constantly back into the soil to replace that which is broken down by bacteria. If this is not done, structure will suffer.

URONIC COMPOUNDS

The Delaware Agricultural Experiment Station has isolated some of the cementing compounds produced by soil organisms. Decomposing plant matter, they found, is converted into materials which can be combined to form uronic compounds. These uronides are forms of hermicellulose and serve as adhesives, uniting soil particles into loose, porous aggregates.

A great many varied kinds of organisms take part in the decomposition of organic material. The slimemolds or myxomycetes, for example, are active agents in this work. They also are antagonistic to many other soil microbes, and thus help to maintain the balance of nature among these lowest forms of life in the soil. Tiny one-celled algae perform the same functions, except that they use the carbon dioxide produced by other soil organisms to manufacture organic matter. In addition, some algae are nitrogen-fixers, making their cell protein from nitrogen in the air and enriching the soil with this element.

The Azotobacter bacteria also break down organic matter and turn atmospheric nitrogen into plant food. Scientists of the University of Sydney, Australia, have shown that even in the very dry soils of the Australian deserts, Azotobacter and algae are taking nitrogen from the air. They contribute up to 3 pounds of nitrogen per acre per year. With more organic matter and moisture than is present in a desert soil, of course, they contribute more. These organisms also break down rocks into soil.

One of the most widely distributed of all soil bacteria are the actinomycetes, a mold-like kind of fungi which makes up 20 per cent or more of the microbial life in an average soil. Although the largest proportion of them will be found in the top foot or so of soil, actinomycetes often extend to greater depths than the other soil organisms; they frequently work many feet below the surface at their job of breaking down dead plant matter, making food for the deeper-reaching roots of plants. Here they rapidly convert this material into a dark brown mass very much like peat. They secrete digestive enzymes that decompose the 3 most complex and abundant organic compounds in vegetable matter: protein, starch and cellulose. The actinomycetes do not fix nitrogen from the air, but they do liberate ammonia from complex proteins, and reduce nitrates to nitrites. They steal very little nitrogen from soil reserves, needing only one part of nitrogen for every 50 parts of cellulose they break down. And the humic material they produce, being very fine, has the ability to absorb nitrogenous materials and chemical compounds, residues of soil fertility which plants can then draw upon from the humus as needed.

Amount of Actinomycetes

The more fertile a soil, the higher its organic matter content, the more actinomycetes it will contain. And by rapidly decomposing plant wastes, they prevent these materials from overstimulating multiplication of other soil bacteria which need nitrogen and thus would use up nitrogen reserves.

One variety of actinomycetes is known to produce the growth vitamin, B-12. Some also make vitamin-like substances vital to the growth of other beneficial organisms living with them. And virtually all species of actinomycetes produce antibiotics.

A soil rich in all these varied kinds of organisms, then, is a highly efficient digestion system, converting raw materials into plant food and providing an ideal environment for plant roots. The larger the microbial population of your soil, the better this system works. This principle is illustrated by an experiment by Lady Eve Balfour; two different soils were used—one from a field where chemical fertilizers were used, the other from a soil enriched with compost and therefore having a much higher bacterial count. In each batch of soil a piece of cottonwool was dug in. After 4 months the cottonwool in the first soil had decayed about 10 per cent, but that in the organic matter-rich soil was 91 per cent consumed. Thus it is easy to see that additions of raw compost materials or half-finished compost break down very rapidly in such a soil. Subsequent additions are handled even faster, as the compost increases the digestion efficiency of the soil.

ROLE OF CHELATION

Compost has a powerful effect on nutrient availability, too. As it becomes humus it makes minerals available by 3 methods: chelation, solvation, and storage.

Chelation is the word scientists use to describe the claw-like action of the organic compounds in humus. Some of these compounds stretch out like an earthworm. As they swim around in the soil water they come into contact with minerals in rocks. When they do, both ends swing close together and grab hold of the mineral. The claw that is formed is so strong that it can yank an atom of mineral right out of a piece of rock. This gets the mineral out in the open where plants can use it for food. Soil scientists in the Agronomy Department, University of Illinois, Urbana, say, "The availability of plant nutrients may be greatly affected by the chelating ability of organic matter."

Another trick humus has for making soil minerals available to plants is called solvation. The University of Illinois soil scientists explain how humus solvates or dissolves minerals. "During the decomposition of plant residues," they say, "certain acids, particularly carbonic acid, are formed that dissolve soil minerals and make the nutrients more available to the plant."

Probably one of the most important properties of humus is its ability to store mineral nutrients. United States Department of Agriculture soil scientists Woods, Copeland and Ostrom say, "Humus is like a sponge in absorbing water and helps hold mineral elements in the upper soil layers. It is the seat of the greatest microbiological activity and acts as a nutrient reservoir." Agricultural experiments show that humus supplies plants with 95 per cent of the nitrogen they need, up to 60 per cent of the phosphorus, up to 80 per cent of the sulphur, and similar amounts of other minerals. These minerals are supplied to the plant as the plant needs them for food.

Incidentally, one of the reasons why plants growing in compost-enriched soils have better access to nutrients is because humus helps hold moisture in the soil (through its aggregating effect), and plant roots can get their food best when it is in liquid form. This helps to conserve soil fertility. Experiments by R. Chaminade of the National Horticultural School, France, show that humus in the soil stimulates plants to obtain their mineral nutrients at the expense of the more dilute nutrient solutions.

SOURCE OF NUTRIENTS

Compost itself is a rich source of nutrients. The greater the variety of materials used in making it, the greater the variety of nutrients contained in it. This includes not only the major elements, nitrogen, phosphorus and potassium, but also the minor elements (often called trace elements).

Although trace elements are needed by plants in very small amounts in comparison to major elements, they are nevertheless just as essential to plant growth and reproduction. Trace elements commonly found to be deficient in many soils include iron, cobalt, manganese, boron, zinc, copper, molybdenum and iodine. As little as 25 parts per million of nickel will reduce the growth of an orange seedling, for example.

Dr. Matthew Drosdoff states in the U. S. Department of Agriculture Yearbook, 1943-47, "The trend away from organic fertilizers and manures and toward the use of more concentrated materials has accentuated the need for supplemental elements. Manure and compost usually contain a balanced amount of minor elements and farmers who still use large amounts of these materials are less likely to encounter deficiencies of minor elements."

K. J. McNaught in a technical report appearing in the *New Zealand Journal of Agriculture* says that a general survey of trace-element deficiencies in market garden crops definitely shows that organic materials produce better vegetables for market. They have more of the vital minerals in them.

McNaught points out that the survey showed that crops not fertilized, and those fertilized with chemicals did not show the content of trace-elements that the organic fertilized vegetables did. McNaught says that this is definitely an effect of the use of organic materials in gardening. Pastures and field crops, he states, are more often deficient in trace-elements than garden crops for the same reason. Farmers don't add as much organic material to their farm lands as they do to their gardens.

R. E. Stephenson, writing in the *California Cultivator* of March 6, 1943, says: "No soil deficiency has yet been found but that it has been at least partially corrected by some kind of organic matter. Use of compost has reduced the need for additional minor elements, particularly boron, a lack of which has been entirely corrected when large amounts of compost were added. Organic materials contain some of all elements necessary for plant growth and in a relatively readily available form."

Colloids and Minerals

The medium by which organic matter transfers nutrients to plant roots is called base exchange. Colloidal (very tiny)

864

humus particles are negatively charged and attract the positive elements such as potassium, sodium, calcium, magnesium, iron, copper and the rest. Colloidal clay particles have this same ability, but not to as great an extent as humus. When a tiny rootlet moves into contact with some humus, it exchanges hydrogen ions for equivalent quantities of the mineral element, which is taken up into the plant.

The mineral-holding capacity of colloidal particles is very important to maintenance of fertility. Lack of soil colloids means that minerals are easily leached out by rain. As Dr. Ehrenfried Pfeiffer points out: "One can wash out a soil by frequent percolation until the filtrate no longer contains any minerals in solution. In many cases, the analysis of the soil before and after the washings does not correspond with the amount of minerals washed out. The holding capacity is quite different in soils with a high organic matter content from that of soils with low organic matter. In fact, a soil with high organic matter loses very little through washing out. In the same procedure, a soil plus soluble mineral fertilizer loses not only the added minerals, but quite a bit of its own hidden reserves, too.

"One can pour 7 times their weight in water through soils with high organic matter, in 12 washings, and not lose any appreciable amount of minerals."

Dr. Pfeiffer explains that this is why crops on low-humus soils exhibit fast growth after a rain—they are absorbing the minerals in solution—but "when drought sets in these crops come to a standstill, and start to head out much too early. Organic soils result in a slower growth during the same period, but the plants continue to grow on into the dry season, head out later, and thus accumulate more weight." They are drawing on the minerals held on the colloids, plentiful in a humus-rich soil.

TOXICITY PREVENTION

Another interesting point is that organic matter prevents toxicity from an excess of an element in the soil. Many authorities state, for example, that more than a small amount of aluminum in the soil solution is highly toxic to plants, and that excess aluminum prevents them from taking up phosphorus. In the *Massachusetts Experiment Station Bulletin Annual Report, 1948-49*, appears the following: "Actively decomposing organic matter results in more effective use of applied phosphorus in soils by the production of organic acids, some of which form stable complexes with iron and aluminum." The aluminum thus is "locked up" in a stable complex.

Selman Waksman in his book, *Humus,* says, "The toxicity of plant poisons becomes less severe in a soil high in humus than in a soil deficient in humus; high salt concentrations are less injurious; and aluminum solubility and its specific injurious action are markedly decreased."

Humus thus acts as a buffer in the soil. Garden and crop plants are far less dependent upon a specific pH in the soil when there is an abundant supply of humus. For instance, potatoes require a distinctly acid soil when the humus content is low. In less acid soils low in humus, potatoes are highly susceptible to potato scab. Add humus, and they suffer no potato scab even when the pH approaches the alkaline side of the scale.

In the periodical *Uebersicht* (Survey) of June 22nd, 1952, is the following interesting review: "Acid Plant Growth on Sour Soils."

Under this headline the "Umschau in Wissenschaft Und Technik" No. 4 reports about experiments with divergent acid-opposing species of certain plants to grow on acid soil had, until now, been explained by stating that these plants could not endure the high degree of acidity. The experiments cited in *Nature* (1951) showed, however, that growth of such soils was entirely normal when compost was added to that soil, in spite of the fact that the pH of the soil had only been slightly changed by this compost. The result of these experiments lead to the conclusion that the impeding factor for plant growth within acid soil cannot be the pH, but that there must be still other—up 'til now unknown factors."

On a biological-dynamic farm in Westfalen an excellent yellow clover grew on a soil that had a pH of 5.04. A well-known professor of soil science, when inspecting the farm, remarked dryly "Here, this clover shouldn't grow at all! These results get us again one step forward in the realization of how important it is to bring life into our soil by organic fertilizing."

A good way to cure excess alkali in soils and at the same time build up nitrogen has been discovered by S. P. Mitra and Hari Shanker, University of Allahabad, India. The scientists have been experimenting with different mixtures of organic materials and alkaline soil. They find that molasses and straw

Evidence that compost produces growth stimulators has been reported from the Agricultural Institute in Kherson, U.S.S.R. The experiments showed that humic acids in compost stimulate plant growth, and can spur both root and crop size.

are very good for curing excess alkali, and building up nitrogen. Next best is weeds. Neem cake (from Hindustan margosa or neem tree) is also good. The scientists explain that these materials are high in carbohydrates. Carbohydrates oxidize easily to form organic acids when exposed to air and sunlight. The organic acids then counteract the excess alkali in the soil. This lowers the pH of the soil and enables it to hold nitrogen. Nitrogen is built up in the soil while the organic material is oxidizing.

GROWTH STIMULATORS

Compost also produces growth stimulators. Evidence of this comes from L. A. Khristeva of the Agricultural Institute, Kherson. Experiments which he has been running on wheat, barley, potatoes, grapes, tomatoes, beets and other crops, show that even in very low concentrations, humic acids act to stimulate plant growth. At concentrations as low as 0.1 to 0.01 per cent increased growth was observed. Root systems in particular respond rapidly to the stimulating action of humic acids.

Tests to determine just how humic acids work, brought out the fact that they are in an ionically dispersed state. In this form they are readily assimilated by the plants as a nutrient. And this nutrition is over and above any normal mineral nutrition that plants get.

Another action of the humic acids is to stimulate the phenolase oxidative action and improve oxygen assimilation. This is particularly noticeable in the early stages of plant growth.

It was also noted during the tests on humic acids, that plants are able to assimilate other physiologically active substances. These include bitumens, vitamins, and vitamin-analogs. All of these substances, including the humic acids, are supplied in fresh organic matter or derived from it during the decay process.

So good were the results of the experiments, that scientist Khristeva suggests that soluble humates be used for fertilizing crops. He states definitely that they improve crops of various agricultural plants more effectively than do mineral fertilizers.

Another valuable compound produced during the decomposition of organic matter is carbon dioxide. This has two functions: it combines with soil moisture to make a weak carbonic acid solution which helps dissolve minerals, making them available for plant use. And some carbon dioxide returns to the atmosphere above ground, where it is utilized by the plant to make starch, sugars and other foods. It is known that plants can use much more carbon dioxide than is normally present in the air. In Germany recently tests were conducted to add carbon dioxide to the air of greenhouses in order to make plants grow better. Additions of compost to the soil accomplish the same purpose.

Colors of Flowers

Even the colors of plants are affected by compost feeding. The pigments that make up the green chlorophyll of leaves, as well as all the colors of flowers, fruits and crops, are manufactured from substances in soil and air. Carbon dioxide, nitrogen, magnesium are some of the elements that must be present in sufficient quantities to bring out the best colors. Compost-grown plants, because they get all they need of these elements, are more richly colored than plants that are grown without compost.

There is another reward of compost that is very important

to the gardener and farmer. Compost darkens soils and can raise the soil temperature as much as nine degrees. This allows earlier spring planting and extends the growing season beyond the normal time.

Also, there is evidence that because compost adds trace elements, it increases the cold hardiness of plants. Experiments at the Academy of Science, Leningrad, showed that the addition of trace nutrients helps corn plants resist the harmful effect of cold spells. The trace elements most effective in increasing cold resistance are copper, zinc, aluminum and molybdenum, and possibly others.

Weeds Halted

One final report: Dr. William A. Albrecht of the University of Missouri has proven that rebuilding the soil organically is an excellent way to stop the spread of many weeds. Here is his report:

It is becoming a more common complaint that "Broom sedge and Tickle grass are taking our pastures." Others say, "Those weeds have moved in from the South." All this has happened in spite of statutes against the spread of noxious weed seeds.

Broom sedge has come into prominence, especially as a left-over for winter notice, because the cows refuse to eat it. Tickle grass comes under the same category. That refusal has been the cow's way of telling us that such plant growth does not deliver enough feed value for her trouble of eating it.

Sanborn Field, at the Missouri Experiment Station, is giving its wise answer to the question of how to get rid of these noxious plants. It tells us clearly that Broom sedge and Tickle grass have come in because the higher level of soil fertility required for more nutritious feed plants has gone out. Rebuilding the soil is the answer.

Farm Pastures

Pasture farming with continuous grass must already have been in the mind of Professor J. W. Sanborn when, in planning this now historic field, he included two plots of continuous timothy. One has been given 6 tons of barnyard manure annually, the other no treatment, ever since the field was started. The manured plot has always been a fine timothy sward with early spring and late fall growths, and a quality hay crop of 2½ tons every summer. The one with no treatment has been getting so foul with growths other than timothy as to require plowing and reseeding about every 5 to 6 years. This called for the same treatment, for uniformity's sake, of the companion plot, even though weed-free. Broom sedge soon takes over the no-treatment plot as the major trouble maker.

These plots tells us that the trouble is not in the particular "invading power" of the Broom sedge, even if its fluffy, wind-borne seeds travel profusely and go everywhere. Both plots are equally invaded by the seed of this pest. However, Broom sedge appears on only the untreated plot, cropped to poor hay now much of the time. It grows right up to the soil line dividing these two plots. It does not cross that border. None has grown on the manured plot, always covered with a dense growth of good timothy. Other plots equally as low in soil fertility on this field are gradually being taken over by Broom sedge. Those with higher levels of productivity are free of it.

Prof. Sanborn says: "Fertilize the soil so it will grow grasses that make nutritious feed and these troublesome plants of no feed value stay out." "Poverty bluestem," as Broom sedge is sometimes called, is a mark of the kind of farming that fails to consider the fertility of the soil as the foundation of it. This pest has been coming more and more into what has been "pasture farming" because past cropping to grass, like to any other crop, without soil treatments, has brought the fertility down to where crops of feed value are failing and only those woody growths like this poor bluestem the cows reject are all that can be produced.

Tickle grass is also invading Sanborn Field. It has been taking over the last half of the 6 year rotation of corn, oats, wheat, clover, timothy and timothy where no soil treatments are used. The plots alongside given manure, phosphate, and limestone are free of it right to the straight line separating the plots and treatments. This poverty grass means poverty of soil fertility and thereby poverty in crop output of yields and of nutritional values. No other crop can grow luxuriantly enough on such low fertility to drive this pest out.

This weed has come in when the rotation was as long as 6 years. This is one claimed by some to be helpful for better yields and crops. It certainly has not been such. It has simply rotated the fertility of the soil out so much faster, that Tickle grass now comes in as major cover during those 3 years when there ought to be clover and timothy. Crops requiring no plowing have been rotated out and Tickle grass has been rotated in.

870

Chemical analyses of these pest crops confirm the suggestions by the cow and Sanborn Field. As pounds per ton, Broom sedge contained 2.14 of calcium, 2.18 of phosphorus and 88 of crude protein. For Tickle grass the corresponding figures were 3.04; 1.9; and 69. In marked contrast for a mixture of clover and grass from fertile soil and at similar growth stage the corresponding values per ton were 26, 4, and 181 pounds.

Nature's pattern of different crops growing on different places is the pattern of different levels of soil fertility nourishing them and correspondingly a pattern of different feed values in them. Declining soil fertility is pushing some crops out and letting others come in. According to these simple soil differences, then, we can drive out Broom sedge and Tickle grass by lime, manure and other soil treatments offering better nourishment for better crops that will keep these pest crops out. That Broom sedge and Tickle grass should go out when you put soil fertility in is merely the converse of the fact that they come in when the fertility goes out.

A TRUE TEST OF ORGANIC FARMING

Much useful and exciting information is contained in the 1957 report on the Haughley Experiment made by The Soil Association in England.

Few people in this country know about the Haughley Experiment, which is surprising since it is the most elaborate and significant experiment in organic methods being carried on anywhere in the world. If the agriculture colleges the world over will ever be convinced of the merits of organic methods, the Haughley Experiment will deserve much of the credit.

The Haughley Experiment is not a series of test tubes or flower pots or even test plots. It is *3 full-sized farms*, each operated completely independent under different methods of soil treatment. Here is the way it is divided:

1. A 32-acre farm operated without any livestock but with the use of chemical fertilizers and green manures.

2. A 75-acre farm operated by organic methods. Livestock is kept on the farm, all manure is composted, deep-rooted soil-building plants are used in the pastures and *no fertilizers or compost-making materials are brought onto the farm from outside.*

3. A 75-acre farm operated by chemical methods. The same type and numbers of livestock are kept as on the organic farm, but only regular pasture plants are used, not the deep-rooted kind. Artificial fertilizers are brought in from outside and all manure and crop wastes produced on the farm are returned to the soil, but are not composted.

The 3 farms that make up the Haughley experiment have been operated under those conditions for 16 years — even through World War II—and the point has now been reached where the data being collected have meaning and importance.

It is not too surprising that the stockless chemical farm has lost humus in its soil and the organic farm has gained humus. The chemical farm with livestock has maintained its humus content approximately the same. Most important, here is a demonstration that organic farming can increase humus content of the soil without bringing in fertilizers or organic materials from off the farm.

Crop yields on the organic farm have been up to or greater than yields on the chemical-livestock farm. And soil tests show that even though the yields on the organic farm are greater, the fertility of the soil is actually increasing, while on the chemical-livestock farm it is decreasing.

Also, ash determinations of silage and hay crops show that most often the organic samples have the greatest ash analysis, which indicates that a superior fodder is being produced on the organic farm.

Vitamin analyses made of the various crops produced have not shown signficant variations, but it does appear that the animals on the organic farm are reacting better to their diet than are the animals on the chemical-livestock farm. Not only are the organic cows producing more milk, but their milk has a higher protein content. Protein production per year of the organic cows averages 254 pounds, while that of the chemical cows is only 228 pounds.

Seasonal Variations In Soil Analyses

One of the most intriguing discoveries made at Haughley, however, concerns the seasonal variation in the plant food content of the soil. Dr. Reginald F. Milton, the consultant biochemist who supervises the analytical work at Haughley, has observed that great fluctuations in plant food take place on the

872

organic farm, and lesser variations occur on the mixed chemical-organic farm. On the exclusively chemical farm the variations are not great.

During the winter the nutrient level of the soil on all 3 farms is about the same. But when the warm weather comes and plants need more nutrients, the plant food level on the organic section increases greatly. In the case of one series of tests, it was found that the phosphorus content of the organic soil doubled between January and July on the organic farm, while it stayed the same on the chemical farm.

Undoubtedly, the cause of these welcome nutrient increases in the organic soil is the natural and bacterial life that exists there. Warm weather stimulates the microorganism into increased activity just at the time when growing plants need the most food. So when you see how your plants growing in humus-rich soil are thriving during the hot months while others are not, you will know that this summer increase in soil nutrients is probably one of the major reasons.

In order to get these important facts, the staff of the Haughley Farms made 25,000 separate soil analyses over the last 5 years. Every month of the year accurate tests are made of many different locations in all fields.

In future years The Soil Association, sponsor of the experiment, hopes to be able to finance additional work in animal feeding, so that observations can be made of the effect of chemical and organic diets on laboratory animals. Such work is necessary, because frequently the chemical tests of food quantity that are so commonly used do not indicate the real worth of that food in supporting animal and human life.

Significance of the Haughley Experiment

Practically all agricultural research is carried on within the narrow confines of small experimental plots, flower pots or test tubes. Such small areas are used to try to eliminate distracting influences and to reduce the cost of carrying on the work. It is not difficult to see that it is impossible to duplicate actual farm conditions in a flower pot or a small test area. You may be able to get information about a specific fertilizer or you may be able to determine a few specific facts about plants or soils, but you can't make an analysis of a whole system of farming on a minute area of ground.

The Haughley Experiment does not have that disadvantage. Its complex of 3 farms, each operated independently, offers scientists the chance to experiment and observe on a truly meaningful scale. The soil can be tilled and planted in the usual manner and livestock can be managed just as it is on the average farm.

Because Haughley is such a large and long-continuing experiment, the scientists and farmers of the world will no doubt look at its results with more than the usual amount of interest.

Chapter 24

HUMUS — THE END PRODUCT

Humus is organic matter which is in a more advanced stage of decomposition than compost in its early stages. In a compost heap, some of the organic matter has turned to humus, but the remaining fraction will complete the decomposition process after it has been placed in the soil. Organic matter in the soil, in the early stages of decomposition, cannot be called humus. It must still be called organic matter. The process in which organic matter turns to humus is called *humification*.

In defining humus, the definition will be more clearly understood if we break it down into its component parts, and treat each one in detail.

The great noticeable difference between humus and organic matter is that the latter is rough looking material, such as coarse plant matter, while in the humus form we find something that has turned into a more uniform looking substance. Humus, in scientific terminology, is called an amorphous substance, or something which is of no determinate shape. It is of no specified character. It is not organized. It has no regular or uniform internal structure. The word *amorphous*, we can see therefore, goes deeper than merely being a fine material, not fibrous in texture.

874

| NATURAL SOIL | SAME SOIL MINUS ORGANIC MATTER | ORGANIC MATTER |

In scientific wording, humus is termed an amorphous substance, something without a definite shape or specified character. In comparison with organic matter, humus is much more uniform. Organic matter becomes humus by complete decomposition.

Humus takes in a vast mixture of compounds, most of which are unknown in formula, broken down to a fine state, and its structure is not definite or uniform.

Colloidal Properties

Humus to a certain extent is colloidal. For all practical purposes we might say that something is colloidal when it is in an extremely fine condition. But in more scientific terms we say that the colloidal state of matter refers to substances which are in a state of subdivision which lies in a zone between the molecular and the microscopic size.

The Winston Dictionary gives the following with regard to the word colloid: "A substance, ordinarily regarded as insoluble, in the form of particles so small as to be indistinguishable to the eye, which remain suspended indefinitely in a suitable medium." Colloidal particles are considered to be between one and 100 millimicrons in size.

1 MICRON = 1/1000 of a millimeter = .000039 inches.
1 MILLIMICRON = 1/1000 of a micron = .000000039 inches = 39/1,000,000,000 inches.

Examples of colloidal matter are paints which consist of pigments ground to a very fine size, homogenized milk in which the butterfat is in the colloidal state, and silt, a component of soil, which is in a colloidal state. In this state, matter behaves entirely differently than when in the larger aggregates.

875

All portions of humus may not be colloidal. Dr. Selman Waksman, in his book *Humus* says that colloidal particles in humus "probably give rise to electrochemical phenomena through which the nutritive elements present in insoluble forms in soil are solubilized and rendered available to plants."

Note that in the dictionary definition a colloid is referred to as a substance which is ordinarily regarded as insoluble, but that Waksman indicates that the colloidal particles in humus, have an effect on nutrients present in the soil that transforms them into soluble substances.

By solubility is meant the ability of a substance to dissolve totally in water. Table salt and sugar are common examples of soluble substances. A chemical fertilizer is in a soluble form, which means it is "available" to the plant immediately through its roots. A plant feeds from the soil's solution, although some of its food supply comes from the air through the activity of soil organisms. Organic matter is said to be insoluble, but actual results show that as soon as it begins to decompose, a process takes place which brings nutrients into the plant's roots.

In review of the factors in the definition of humus covered thus far, we can say that humus is an amorphous, partly colloidal substance.

Different Compounds

Humus is a heterogeneous complex or aggregate which represents a mixture of a large number of different compounds. The word heterogeneous means *opposite* or *unlike in character, quality or structure*. It is the opposite of the word *homogeneous* which we used in referring to coal, which means uniform, or composed of similar parts. In other words humus is both *heterogeneous* and *amorphous*. Coal is *homogeneous* and *amorphous*. Referring back to the definition of the word *amorphous*, it is something of no determinate shape. Both coal and humus are indeterminate in shape. It must be of no specified kind of character and must not be organized. It must have no regular or uniform internal structure. These qualifications apply to both coal and humus.

But where coal and humus differ, to make one homogeneous and the other heterogeneous, is in the fact that humus is far more complex in its make-up. You can understand it more readily if we bring a substance like table salt into the discussion. This is a crystalline, non-amorphous substance.

(Both coal and humus are amorphous.) Table salt always has the same simple formula—namely sodium chloride, which means one part sodium and one part chlorine, but the formula of coal varies considerably depending on the particular deposit. However, in each such deposit the formula is more or less the same. But in humus there is a total lack of uniformity. It is truly a heterogeneous substance, and depends on the kind of materials out of which it is formed. And in this respect we must bear in mind that humus comes not only from the remains of plants or animal matter, but also from the dead bodies of the soil microorganisms—the bacteria, fungi, etc., that took part in its decomposition.

Although humus is extremely variable and heterogeneous, it has its own definitely defined characteristics which differ widely from other natural organic substances. It varies according to how the organic matter of which it is composed originated. In early chemical research on the subject, certain acids under the general classification of humic acids were vaguely referred to as composing humus without much scientific foundation. Fantastic names were given to them. But practically all of this work has been discredited.

Modern research has shown that the following compounds, among others, may be found in humus:

Acrylic acid, acrotonic acid, a-mono-hydroxy-stearic acid, benzoic acid, agroceric acid, oxalic acid, succinic acid, lignoceric acid, humoceric acid, paraffinic acid, saccharic acid, di-hydroxy-stearic acid, resin acids, metaoxytoluic acid, parahydroxybenzoic acid, the aldehydes such as vanillin, tri-thiobenzaldehyde, salicylic aldehyde, etc. These are all known as organic compounds, consisting for the most part of variable amounts of carbon, hydrogen, oxygen, and sometimes nitrogen.

Let us examine the make-up of a few of the compounds mentioned above:

Acrylic Acid $= CH_2\ CH,\ COOH$
      C stands for carbon
      H stands for hydrogen
      O stands for oxygen
Benzoic Acid $= C_6H_5,\ COOH$
Oxalic Acid $= (COOH)_2,\ +\ _2H_2O$
Succinic Acid $= COOH\ (CH_2)\ _2COOH$
Paraffinic Acid $= C_{24}\ H_{48}\ O_2$
Saccharic Acid $= COOH,\ (CHOH)_4\ CO,\ OH$

These are all organic compounds which are in the carbo-hydrate group. Compounds which contain only carbon, oxygen and hydrogen are called carbohydrates. There are other organic compounds in humus, consisting of nitrogen, phosphorus and sulphur, in addition to carbon, hydrogen and oxygen, and these are usually proteins. The phosphorus and sulphur in them are minerals. But, although the carbohydrates in humus are not made up of minerals, and the proteins contain only the minerals phosphorus and sulphur, humus is never dis-associated from minerals. Little is known about exactly how the minerals are interlocked with the organic compounds in humus, but there is evidence to show that each does not exist by itself in chemical purity. You will see what is meant by examining an analysis of humus given in the book, *Green Manuring Principles and Practice,* by Adrian J. Pieters (John Wiley and Sons, 1927) :

Carbon	44.12%
Hydrogen	6.00%
Oxygen	35.16%
Nitrogen	8.12%
Ash	6.60%
	100.00%

The ash, which results upon the burning out of the organic matter, consists of minerals—elements such as calcium, phos-phorus, boron, zinc, magnesium, manganese, etc.

This analysis would tend to show that humus contains minerals. While they can isolate acids from the humus, the total humus is made up of both organic and inorganic com-pounds. As previously stated, the term organic matter is a misnomer, in the strict sense. Corn cobs, pea vine residues, sawdust, etc., although referred to as organic matter, contain also inorganic matter. One would imagine that in the crucibles of nature's reducing processes, when the organic matter is finally refined into humus that a pure product would result, that one would have a clear line of demarcation between organic and inorganic matter. But that does not happen. In nature, evidently, organic is never separated from inorganic. One needs the other, and is so saturated with the other that it takes the best skills of the chemist to separate them. Per-haps they exert a sort of mutual catalystic action one upon the other, each doing something important for the other. (A *catalyst* is a substance that initiates or accelerates chemical action between two or more other substances without itself combining with either of them or undergoing any permanent change.)

Millar and Turk in their book *Fundamentals of Soil Science* (John Wiley and Sons, 1951) : state "Although humus is considered organic, it probably contains various inorganic elements which are an integral part of the complex."

The ash of humus consists of major and minor elements. If we remove the major ones, such as calcium, phosphorus, potash, iron, sulphur, etc., we will find only the very tiniest fraction left—the trace mineral elements—the manganese, the zinc, copper, iodine, tungsten, molybdenum, etc. But we know how important each and every one is, even though it must be present in only 2 or 3 parts per million of matter. For example, if there is a manganese deficiency, and not much is required, tomato and bean plants will be dwarfed. A lack of zinc will produce mottled leaves on citrus trees. A want of copper will lower the sugar content of beets.

In review therefore, thus far, we find that humus is

1. an amorphous substance
2. some of which is colloidal
3. and is of heterogeneous, or complex make-up.

SOURCE OF HUMUS

Humus consists of compounds that are of plant, animal or microbial origin. In other words the source material out of which humus is synthesized is organic matter.

The process of decomposition from organic matter to humus is one of microbial and chemical action. The microbial process may be referred to as a biological one and includes action of bacteria, fungi, yeasts, algae, actinomycetes, protozoa, enzymes, etc. The chemical action comprises hydrolysis: (a chemical reaction produced by decomposition of a compound, its elements taking up those of water), oxidation and reduction: (separating of an element from other elements combined with it). In this process, simple compounds are formed which can function directly or indirectly as nutrients. In organic matter, before its decomposition, there is nothing that can feed a plant.

The humus eventually becomes oxidized to carbonic acid, water, nitric acid and other simple substances serving as food for plants.

In the process of humification, the substances are undergoing decomposition, but true humus consists of those portions of the original organic matter which is resistant to further decomposition.

To some persons humus is humus and that's all there is to it. But that is *not* all there is to it. To know the true value of humus as a factor in making plants grow we must delve below the surface and find out a thing or two about its activities. Mere quantity may not mean too much. We must realize that we do not want humus for its mere presence. We want it for what it can do for the soil and for plants.

When we place either raw organic matter, or what we term finished compost into the soil, decay begins to take place. If there were no decomposition these substances would be of little value in the soil. As it decays, nitrogen and other substances are released when there is sufficient organic matter for a continuous process of decomposition to go on; there is always a goodly stream of nitrogen coming from it. There is a dynamic quality, a movement from the organic matter that is required, if it is to be of any value. Were all the organic matter to be applied to the soil in the most advanced stages of decay, there would be no nitrogen available from this source.

Prof. Sidney B. Haskell, Director of the Massachusetts Agricultural Experiment Station, in his book *Farm Fertility* (Harpers, 1923) says:

"The benefit comes not so much from the character of the final product as from the process of decay taking place in the soil itself. Organic matter to be functional in the soil must decay in the soil; and decaying, the supply must be constantly renewed. Otherwise we either have a barren condition of the soil, brought about by too great a decay of this humus and failure to replace it, or an equally unfavorable condition in which the soil organic matter is dead and inert, like so much peat, or in extreme cases similar in its inertness to coal itself." Thus we have the terms living and dead humus.

A. F. Gustafson, *Nitrogen and Organic Matter in the Soil*, (Cornell, March, 1941) says:

"It is the newly decomposed organic matter on which crops depend mainly for their nitrogen."

In this publication he gives an interesting example of the difference between two soils. An Ontario loam contained 3 per cent organic matter. The Volusia silt loam had 5.2 per cent. But yet the latter, which had about 70 per cent more organic matter, yielded less in crops. The author says that one of the reasons is that the organic matter in the Ontario loam was more active. He states, "Much of that in the Volusia is so inactive that one might regard it as being in a sense embalmed." He advises the liberal addition to it of green manure, leguminous crops, the results of which should not be harvested, but plowed in.

Dynamic Qualities

Here we can see that if we wish to produce the most dynamic qualities in the new organic matter, much would depend on the kind of organic matter we plow in. If we put peat into the soil, the dynamic movement of nutrients from it will be very slow. Humus, whether it is in the form of coal or of fresh organic matter represents stored energy, but if it is to be of any value, it must give it off.

It has been found also that when fresh organic matter was added to a soil there was an acceleration in the rate of decomposition of the existing soil organic matter. It probably has something to do with the stimulation of the soil bacteria, somewhat akin to giving them a shot in the arm. There are peculiarities in the rhythm and timing of decomposition. Another example is a virgin soil which is first put under the plow. The rate of decay of organic matter is very fast at first, but soon it slows down. Evidently the soil bacteria require continued stimulation. This stimulation brings about that dynamic quality of which this lesson is the subject.

In the tropics the movement is faster than in the temperate zone, and thus there is always an urgent call for fresh organic matter. The 4 conditions that make it ideal for microorganisms to do their share in the processes of decomposition are temperature, moisture, acidity and aeration. The higher temperatures in the tropics overstimulate bacteria.

Coming back to our general subject, here is an interesting quotation from *Farm Soils—Their Management and Fertilization* by Edmund L. Worthen (John Wiley and Sons—1941) :

"While the fresh, active organic-matter content of a soil is an important criterion of its degree of fertility, an unproductive soil may contain a considerable quantity of humus, even enough to produce a dark color. Organic matter in the form of humus contains a smaller proportion of the more essential plant-food elements than does fresh organic matter, and is in such an advanced stage of decomposition that it is very ineffective. It is sometimes referred to as the inactive form of organic matter. It not only has little chemical effect, but it is less beneficial than fresh organic matter in improving the physical condition of the soil, or in stimulating activities of the beneficial soil organisms."

Degraff and Haystead *(The Business of Farming*—University of Oklahoma Press) say:

"The more there is of organic matter in the soil and the more rapid its decomposition, the more rapidly plants will grow." Note the expression "the more rapid its decomposition." There must be this dynamic movement for humus to exert its full value. It is of little use if it does not break down. Another writer refers to it as the organic balance—the balance between the constant addition and the constant subtraction of humus.

We should bear in mind that organic matter as such is much more dynamic than the humus which it produces. When you apply fresh organic matter to the land there should begin at once a strong movement of decomposition if conditions are right. Of course, the rate for a thin-stemmed legume plant will be much faster than for a whole corn cob. This process begins as soon as the organic matter is covered with earth. If left on the soil surface, the rate of decay will be much slower. When some of the organic matter turns to humus there will be a slower rate of decay. The humus much more slowly begins to break apart so as to give some of its nutrients to the soil solution.

Adrian J. Pieters in his *Green Manuring* (John Wiley & Sons—1927) compares humus from a new and from an old soil. The new soil contained 8.12 per cent nitrogen, the old, $6\frac{1}{2}$ per cent. The new soil also contained much more in the way of minerals, which indicates that it is not only nitrogen that is given off in the stream from fresh humus. The fact is that the whole array of minerals is held in the organic matter and a fast decomposition releases more of it for use by plants. A great part of the soil phosphorus, for example, is held in the organic matter. In a study of *Iowa Soils* (Pearson and Simonson), it was found that between 27 and 72 per cent of the total phosphorus present was in the organic matter.

Quoting from Lyon and Buckman *Nature and Properties of Soils*—(Courtesy of the Macmillan Co., copyright 1950): "In recent years, Baumann by his researchers has shown freshly precipitated organic matter to possess properties which are largely colloidal in nature (very fine). Among these characteristics are high water capacity, great absorptive power for certain salts, ready mixture with other colloids, power to decompose salts, great shrinkage on drying, and coagulation in the presence of electrolytes." These characteristics would not be present, or would be present to a much lesser extent, in older humus. All of these powers are part of the formula of dynamism. It speaks of action and fast movement.

During the decay of organic matter certain acid substances are produced which have a solvent action on minerals, thus making them more soluble, and available to plants. One of the principal acids is carbonic acid. These acids are produced with the aid of microorganisms—bacteria, fungi, etc. A certain amount of carbon dioxide is important to the production of crop yields. It saturates the soil water, forming an acid solution which has a solvent action on the minerals in the soil, making them available for plant use. Thus we see the principal reason for keeping a fresh supply of organic matter on hand in the soil.

Humus Formation

In the process of humus formation when the decomposition gets to a certain point it slows down. A certain portion becomes resistant to the activities of microorganisms, and remains in an undecomposed state. There is a point then where there is a hold-up in the decomposition for a period of time. Under some conditions the decomposition process stops altogether and eventually peat or coal is produced. This is where the soil becomes more or less permanently covered with water, and asphyxiation occurs. If there is little addition of organic matter from year to year in a soil, after a while, it will contain humus that is old and which lacks the required dynamic quality. That is what happens in farms and gardens where too much dependence is placed upon chemical fertilizers.

In cases where anaerobic conditions exist, that is, where air is lacking, there is a slower decomposition, but in considering this point there is a difference whether the anaerobic conditions exist in a composting process outside of the soil, or whether it is in the soil itself. In an aerobic decay there is an oxidation which, roughly speaking, is a "burning out" process. If it occurs in the soil, as the nutrients stream out of the humus, they are captured and held to a certain extent by the soil. But if this oxidation occurs in an ordinary compost heap, much of it dissipates itself into the atmosphere. In analyses of compost made by both processes it never fails that the anaerobic compost has much more nitrogen and other nutrients.

But in the soil, we want an aerobic condition. Anaerobic decomposition in composting destroys less, so that more is available for dynamic decay in the soil. But of course it is more difficult and costly to maintain anaerobic conditions in a composting process, and that is the problem. It is a good thing to know the correct theory even though we cannot always practice it. Ideally, anaerobic conditions in compost making are the best. In the soil, conditions should be aerobic.

FERMENTATION OR PUTREFACTION AND DECAY?

Two processes are significant on the path of life which leads to the formation of organic matter. One is an upbuilding process which all matter undergoes when it is organized by the living bodies of plants, animals and man. The other is a breaking down process which impairs and transforms "life" matter after it has been used up and fulfilled its task for the building up, growth and maintenance of the living organism. In nourishment we have a special case, where outside matter (food) is broken down through digestive action and transformed into forms of matter to be used "inside" for the growth and maintenance of the body. This, however, is not a complete breaking down but a fermentation. Enzymes are chemical substances which support and direct this fermentation, for instance in the stomach and small intestine. There are also fermentations taking place in nature, in plants, under the influence of yeasts and bacteria. Fermentation is therefore a third process which stands in the middle between the building up and breaking down of organic matter as a kind of "mediator." A typical "fermentation" is for example the transformation of sugar into alcohol and carbon dioxide under the influence of yeast. Another fermentation takes place when wheat or other flours are transformed into bread dough, also through yeast. This process is interrupted at a certain level, namely through the baking of the bread. Should it be permitted to reach its ultimate state, alcohol would be formed out of the starch. As a matter of fact, when we digest bread a certain amount of alcohol is formed in the stomach.

Fermentation we therefore call a transformation of

Sheet composted wheat straw encourages the microbial life of the soil. Each spoonful of soil contains billions of living organisms which aid organic matter decomposition and the resulting supply of humus. Inset shows a colony of soil fungi.

organic matter (especially carbohydrates) so that it can remain and play a role in the organic process, supporting life. Another example of a fermentation process is the hydrolyzation of starch resulting in the formation of sugar. In addition to yeasts, certain molds also aid fermentation. It is of special interest to all industries making use of processes of fermentation to control and direct these processes in such a way that only favorable products result. They try, through controlling these procedures, to eliminate all disturbing factors such as "wild" yeasts. Their cultures are inoculated with selected strains of yeast in order to obtain the proper results (cf. the manufacturing of cheese, wine, beer, vinegar).

Decay is the final process when living matter "dies" and falls apart into its components, which are excreted from an organism and not immediately used in the resultant form. Manure, i.e., any product which is excreted through the bowel movement of an animal or human body, is the final product of the digestive action, of no more use for the building up of the said organism. It is, however, still rich in highly organized organic matter, proteins, sugar, peptones, and undergoes a further decomposition outside in nature towards the simplest forms of organic matter, namely, into minerals, respectively salts, ammonia and carbon dioxide. When these forms are reached the end products are no longer fit for organic up-building. They will be lost unless they are taken up again by plants and organized anew.

The decomposition of manure as well as of any organic matter (including the dead bodies of plants, animals, etc.), may follow a disorderly course. Putrefaction is a mere "decay" which can be just a chemical disintegration of animal matter, proteins especially, or it can also be fostered by certain bacteria which thrive on the products of a partial decay. Such putrefaction is characterized, in general, by a foul odor, by producing slimy, smeary masses, if moisture is present. Poisonous products such as ptomaines, mercaptans and hydrogen sulphide are formed. In the end, these products will hinder any life process. Under certain abnormal circumstances a putrefaction can also take place even in the intestinal tract, gas formation being one of the symptoms. Decaying manure, as well as plant material and animal bodies, undergoes putrefaction and fermentation at random according to chance conditions of heat, moisture, and the influence of microorganisms which may exist under these accidental conditions.

It is in the interest of the farmer and gardener to control these conditions as well as the wine, beer, cheese, and alcohol manufacturers control their processes. Should the random decay go so far that finally salts, carbon dioxide, ammonia and free nitrogen result, then all organic matter is lost, because these end products are washed away or escape into the air. Resultant by-products such as methane gas (marsh gas), hydrogen sulphide would even hinder the development of life. The decay must, therefore, be arrested in time and directed toward producing a kind of material which is stable rather than unstable. In other words, before the breaking down is complete new upbuilding processes have to be introduced. Humus is the stable product which results if the decay is checked in time and upbuilding microorganisms turn the wheel of life before it is too late.

Secret of Composting Methods

This is the "secret" of composting methods: to introduce such conditions of life that no final decay or putrefaction can occur, but that the micro-life of the soil resumes its activity, bringing about a complicated yet stable structure or organic matter. Humus is not so much a definite chemical formula but rather a *state* of *existence* of transformed organic matter

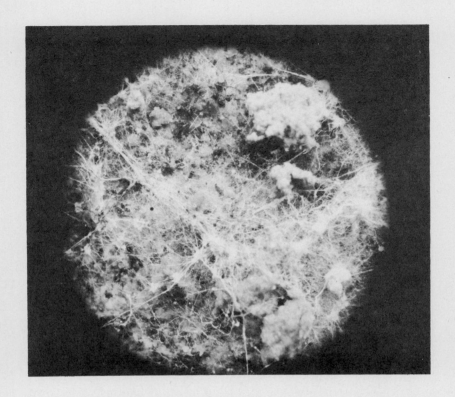

The micro-life of the soil is both intense and extremely complicated. While certain bacteria live only upon decay and putrefaction, thereby helping to break down raw organic matter, others serve to improve soil structure or combat harmful organisms. Seen above are thread-like mycelia from fungi which bind soil particles together.

in connection with soil, soil life, moisture and air. It is a balanced state of matter, almost a living organism or condition in itself.

Certain bacteria live only upon decay or putrefaction, they only break down. In this class belong, for instance, all bacteria which form ammonia or nitrites. Ammonia and nitrites are unstable nitrogen compounds, apt to fall apart into free nitrogen, water and oxygen if not fixed in salts. The most stable forms of nitrogen compounds, on the contrary, are nitrates. A gardener who has a lot of ammonia or nitrites in his compost or soil will eventually lose them unless growing crops can make immediate use of them. The one who has nitrates in his compost and soil will keep them.

The nitrogen cycle in nature best illustrates this principle. We ask the patience of our readers in carefully studying the following schedule in order to get a vivid picture of the situation in his farm or garden:

1. Upbuilding process in plants and animals forms proteins.

2. Proteins break down into peptones, amino acids, finally to ammonia from decaying plants; the proteins from animals result in urea, which is excreted.

3. Urea bacteria in liquid and other manures from ammonia; this if not fixed is apt to be lost.

4. Nitrosomonas bacteria produce nitrites. These, if not immediately transformed, may be lost.

5. Nitrobacter and similar bacteria transform nitrites into stable *nitrates*. We speak, therefore, of denitrifying processes (No. 3 and No. 4, losses), and of nitrifying processes and/or nitrogen fixation (No. 5 and No. 6).

6. (a) Nitrates in the form of potassium salts remain more or less fixed in a humus soil in "digested," i.e. properly decomposed manure and compost, namely when these remain in a humus state.

(b) Nitrates are absorbed by other bacteria and form bacterial proteins and remain as long as the bacteria life of nitrogen fixers is going on. Afterward these bacteria proteins break down, undergo the same changes, from ammonia to nitrites to nitrates again, until the latter are absorbed by plants or nitrogen is lost.

(c) Nitrogen is absorbed directly from the atmosphere by the nitrogen fixing organisms which live in symbiosis with legume roots, besides those bacteria which fix nitrogen directly.

Remember: any putrefaction will lead to losses unless checked by nitrogen fixing organisms in compost, manure and soils. The presence of nitrite forming bacteria, if not checked, can be very disadvantageous to the soil and compost. Their action, called denitrification, leads to the permanent loss of nitrogen. These bacteria live mainly in moist, water-logged, peat soils and on the bottom of compost heaps, as described above, when air is excluded. Bac. denitrificans, Achromobacterium, Psuedomonas, Bact. pyocyaneum, belong in this group.

They are robbers of the fertility of the soil. We quote from "Elementary Bacteriology," by Joseph E. & Ethelyn O. Greaves, M.S., Ph.D., W. B. Saunders Company, 1946, page 225:

"Denitrifiers need large quantities of organic food and develop best in the presence of the fresh plant and animal debris. From the standpoint of production it would thus be unwise for the farmer to use heavy dressings of nitrate and fresh manure, or to plow under with the nitrates green-manuring crops. Partly decayed barnyard or green manures do not appear to favor denitrification."

In other words, proper composting methods counteract the denitrification process even better than the above mentioned "partial" decay. Greaves says, therefore, with good reason: "we find this microbe (the denitrifier) a robber by force of circumstance imposed upon him by the farmer's injudicious handling of his soil."

Azotobacter, on the contrary, is the master nitrogen fixer. For each grain of sugar (carbohydrates) in manure or other organic matter, which it digests, it fixes 10 to 15 mg of nitrogen. This, together with the other non-symbiotic nitrogen fixers in the soil, increase the nitrogen content of soil from 15 to 35 pounds per acre annually. If organic matter is added the increase reaches 40 pounds per acre and more. With over 375 million acres under cultivation, this means a yearly gain in nitrogen of 2.8 to 7.5 million tons (the latter with improved organic methods) just by natural methods, and deriving only from one source which does not even include the legume bacteria fixation.

Other Processes

Another process occurs in the decomposition of starches, sugars and cellulose (lignin). All of these do not contain nitrogen as the proteins do but they also follow a cycle of decomposition leading to the production of carbon dioxide, which is lost in the surrounding air. Under aerobic conditions, i.e. with access of air, the carbon dioxide is formed. Under anaerobic conditions, i.e. without access to air, more complicated compounds, without oxygen, result, such as organic acids, and even methane gas or inert products, including carbon. A carbonization process is responsible for the production of peat, inert hemicelluloses which do not ordinarily enter the life cycle again. The latter happens when organic matter decays on the inside and bottom of a compost heap, where there is no air and lots of moisture. Many of you readers have certainly observed methane gas or blackish-brown or greenish, foul-smelling masses inside the lower part of heaps. There you had a typical putrefaction, the products of which are about the opposite of a good humus fermentation. This can be avoided by proper and sufficient aeration and control of moisture. Anaerobic bacteria belonging to the Clostridium family work there. Such strata in a heap develop gas, and, on account of their acidity (mineral and organic), they do not allow the nitrogen fixers to grow which, for their part, prefer an almost neutral medium.

Not all of the carbonic acid (carbon dioxide) is necessarily lost in a compost fermentation. It is lost when it can escape freely—in the case of a loose, scattered material which is not protected and covered. A heap should be trodden down enough to procure a spongy, porous structure and covered with a layer of earth. Then the carbon dioxide is retained and made available for such microorganisms, bacteria, fungi, as can assimilate it. Azotobacter, for instance, which fixes nitrogen to nitrates, produces 1.3 its own weight in carbon dioxide during a 24 hour period.

Overheating of Materials

Another rapid process of decomposition, chiefly of cellulose and starch, takes place when organic materials become overheated. Here thermophile cellulose digesters, which thrive at temperatures of 120 to 145 degrees Fahrenheit, do a quick job. This hot fermentation is a more or less slow "burning" process. Molds will grow, for instance, the greyish white molds you frequently see in hot, dry horse manure or compost heaps made of dry weeds, loosely piled up and not covered. Here aerobic, mostly sporing bacteria act, bringing about a quick fermentation at the expense of considerable losses of nitrogen and carbon dioxide. A powdery, dusty, loose product results which is easily absorbed by the soil, but it is not humus and is not in a stable form.

Again we see the need of putting on the brakes which, in the case of this process, is done by treading the material down so as to exclude part of the air, and by increasing the moisture (watering). Frequently, when horse manure and compost heaps heat up, there is nothing left but to turn the heap and set it up again. At this point, we should not hesitate and wait

890

Bacteria used to compost garbage multiply rapidly in these heaps, but proper hand-ling prevents overheating. Temperature reaches a desirable 150 to 160 degrees Fahrenheit. Tractor-powered loader stirs the heap, helps give bacteria ample air.

until everything is burned up. We have often checked our heaps with a thermometer. The temperature should remain below 115 degrees Fahrenheit.

Importance of Balance

What we really want to establish is a balance between decomposition, putrefaction, fermentation and a new upbuilding process before a final disintegration occurs. Humus in its truest definition is this stable state which holds everything together—a directed, balanced fermentation (in a broader sense) versus decay and putrefaction.

The benefits of such a balanced state are obvious. Cellulose digesters, for example, liberate sugars and carbon dioxide. Azotobacter uses them up and in turn fixes nitrogen. In a heap, or soil, of too acid a reaction Azotobacter will not grow—only in a soil near the neutral reaction. One group of organisms will prepare the path for the next one if we only take care to maintain proper conditions. We quote from the interesting chapter on the carbon style in Greaves' (pp. 213 and 214):

891

"The cellulose ferments break the plant residues into less complex organic compounds which are decomposed by other microorganisms with the generation of large quantities of organic acids. These acids react with the minerals of the soil and render them available to higher plants. This very likely explains the beneficial results when raw rock phosphate and stable manure are used on phosphorus-poor soil. The fermentation of the cellulose yields acids which render soluble the phosphorus. However, the production of acids may at times become excessive, thus giving rise to the sour humus of moors and heaths.

"The cellulose ferments also perform direct beneficial functions in the soil, for instance in the liberating of plant food which is bound up in the residues of plants. They are the organisms which decompose the cellulose of straw so it can be utilized by the Azotobacter in the fixation of atmospheric nitrogen. More recent investigators have shown that under suitable conditions the Azotobacter may fix 325 mg. of nitrogen for every 100 gm. of straw decomposed. At this rate there would be a gain of 7 pounds of nitrogen for every ton of straw utilized. This, in addition to other beneficial effects, the farmer loses when he burns his straw. The cellulose ferments are being used in the synthetic production of manure. Investigators at Rothamsted have shown that if a straw heap is treated with the correct proportion of ammonia and inoculated with cultures of *Spirocheta cytophaga* it changes into a substance having the appearance of a well-rotted manure."

There is for instance the phosphate cycle. People who have not carefully studied the organic methods criticize them and say: Well, you get organic matter all right, but you still have to add potassium and phosphate fertilizers; compost and manures cannot take care of that.

Experimenters at the Organic Experimental Farm in Allentown, Pa., have analyzed a great number of compost and manure samples, fresh material as well as old, some samples deriving from heaps one, two or more years old. If properly handled, older heaps can contain a lot of phosphates, more than fresh ones. These are available phosphates, easily absorbed by plant roots. In a fresh heap with "raw" material we may have a lot of phosphorus compounds; these also exist in the interlayers of earth, rock, gravel. Granite rock pieces are rich in potassium, so are plants, wood shavings and sawdust. These are also phosphoproteins, nucleoproteins, lecithin, all rich in phosphates but not in an available form. All these forms of phosphate are rendered soluble, transformed by bacteria, no matter whether they derive from inorganic or organic sources. The phosphate transforming organisms need carbon dioxide. Water charged with carbon dioxide, is an almost universal solvent of original rock particles; in conjunction with the micro-life it aids in the liberation of magnesium, iron, boron, phosphorus, manganese, aluminum, potassium (hence the importance of interlayering a compost heap with layers of earth, thin enough so that each particle is accessible to the life process). In composts the transformation of phosphates is rapid and almost complete. We quote from Greaves' again, page 245:

"Moreover, soil organisms form, among other products, formic, acetic, lactic, butyric, and other acids, the kind and quantity of each depending upon the specific microorganisms and upon the substances on which they act. These substances are certain to come in contact with some insoluble plant food which they may render soluble. This may be concentrated by the soil microbes in their bodies which are especially rich in phosphorus. The phosphorus, on the death of its host, is probably returned to the soil in a readily available form."

It is calculated that phosphate losses in the United States total an amount annually which would fill a train of standard box cars reaching from Seattle to Boston, representing 7 to 12 times the world's production of rock phosphates. The organic gardener and farmer can help to reduce these losses considerably by introducing the proper cycle in his composting methods.

THE ROLE OF NITROGEN

Organic matter is the means by which nitrogen is carried in the soil. As the organic matter decays the nitrogen is set free in a form that is available to plants. All the other minerals are also contained in the organic matter and gradually become available as nutrients to plants, but in this lesson we will deal only with nitrogen, because in the question of organic matter it is mainly a problem of nitrogen. Minerals are present in the rock fragments of the soil. The organic farmer can obtain all his minerals from phosphate, potash and basalt rocks, etc., but for him nitrogen is obtainable only in organic matter. Rarely do rocks contain nitrogen. He can, of course, obtain nitrogen from dried blood, bone meal, tankage, etc., but in farming, rarely is money spent for such expensive fertilizers. Adequate nitrogen may be obtained by the farmer from reasonable amounts of organic matter applied to the soil each year.

Nitrogen is an extremely important element in farming and gardening. Without it, productivity of the soil will decline. High productivity is interrelated with the supply of organic matter in a soil. A deficiency of one usually indicates a deficiency of the other. Nitrogen is necessary to the functioning of every cell of the plant, and is needed for rapid growth. It is directly responsible for the vegetative growth of plants above ground. And with a good supply of it, maturity of the plant will come earlier. A lack of nitrogen is indicated by a lightening of the green color of leaves. A great lack of it will show up in the yellowing of the leaves. Of all nutrient deficiencies in arable soils, that of nitrogen is most common. But an excessive supply of it will not only retard the growth period but will reduce the plant's resistance to disease, and produce an inferior quality of crop, which will show up in poor keeping and shipping abilities. It waterlogs the plant, causing an over succulency. This is where the organic method is superior. The organic matter, unless a tremendous excess is applied to the soil, gradually feeds the nitrogen to the plants as required, rarely overfeeding them. It is a known fact that organic matter decays slowly, thus not releasing the nitrogen too quickly. The organic matter thus is a valuable storehouse of nitrogen, maintaining an automatic supply for the entire growing season. But with chemical fertilizers, a too enthusiastic hand can sometimes give the soil an over-supply which will lead to all the troubles described above.

A very common error is found in most agricultural textbooks and publications dealing with the subject of organic matter. They usually state that on the average, 5 per cent of organic matter consists of nitrogen. This statement bothered me for a long time because I could see from actual analyses of various kinds of organic matter that this could not possibly be true. At the most, organic matter contains up to two per cent of nitrogen. Finally the basis of this error dawned upon me. What was meant by these agricultural teachers was that *humus* contained 5 per cent nitrogen. But there is a big difference between organic matter and humus. It is due to a loose and careless handling of the terms *organic matter* and *humus* that this error occurs again and again.

Here, therefore, is a general rule which I have never seen

in any agricultural textbook or publication, but which is true nevertheless. No matter how much or how little nitrogen there is in any kind of organic matter to begin with, when it turns to humus, the latter's nitrogen content will be about 5 per cent.

As to the possible reason for the common error which exists in the minds of agronomists, that organic matter contains 5 per cent nitrogen, there may be several explanations. First, it may be due to the fact that their work is 99.999 per cent with chemical fertilizers, and although they speak of the need for organic matter in farming they do not seem to have the strength to convince the typical farmer as to its value. In their work, discussions in regard to organic matter lack a punch, remaining in the realms of the theoretic, and there is therefore not much dealing with it.

Secondly, it is possible that in the mind of the average agronomist the expression *organic matter* may mean humus. Perhaps the agronomist, when referring to a specific type of organic matter such as alfalfa hay, may use the term *organic materials* as against *organic matter*, but I think such handling of terms would be confusing. We should consider *humus* as the product that comes into being on the decay of organic matter, and *organic matter* as the specific material which is at the beginning of that process. In other words, the terms *organic matter*, or *organic materials* should be considered as one and the same thing.

Protein Compounds

Nitrogen is not present, either in the soil or in humus in a free condition. If it were, it would be rapidly decomposed by soil organisms and much of it become lost to growing crops. Nitrogen is present in humus in the form of protein compounds which are highly resistant to microbial dissolution, thus releasing its nitrogen slowly. In raw organic matter, if not carefully handled, much of the nitrogen can become dissipated into the atmosphere in the form of ammonia, which is a compound of nitrogen and which results from the first stage in the breakdown of protein. This is the great value of humus —its ability to hoard its nitrogen for release to plant roots as needed.

About 30 to 35 per cent of humus consists of protein. Proteins contain about 50 to 55 per cent of carbon, 15 to 19 per cent of nitrogen, 6 to 7 per cent hydrogen and 21 to 23 per cent oxygen, with small amounts of sulphur and occasionally some phosphorus. (Carbohydrates, that is, sugars, starches and cellulose, contain only carbon, hydrogen and oxygen.) In other words, proteins containing all the elements of carbohydrates plus nitrogen, sulphur and sometimes phosphorus.

Generally speaking it is considered that about 16 per cent or one-sixth of protein is nitrogen and therefore when the amount of nitrogen in a substance is known, the protein is figured out by multiplying it by 6.25. (16 by 6.25-100). Not all the nitrogen is in the protein. Small quantities are found in other compounds contained in humus, but these are small in amount.

The release of nitrogen in humus is effected as follows: The protein first decomposes into its amino acids. The next step is the formation of ammonium compounds. Then bacteria break these down into nitrites. There are certain bacteria whose function in the soil is to do this, and only *they* can do it. Then other groups of bacteria turn the nitrites into nitrates, which is the form of nitrogen that plant roots can take in. Sometimes where air is lacking and the decomposition is anaerobic, other compounds besides amino acids form, which give off putrefactive odors. This usually occurs in protein-rich materials.

Organic vs. Chemical Nitrogen

Organic forms of nitrogen are more stable in the soil and become available for plant growth more gradually than nitrogen from chemical fertilizers. When concentrated chemical nitrogen is applied to the soil it produces a "shot-in-the-arm" effect to plant growth. The plants are subjected to too much nitrogen at one time. Then, if a sudden heavy rainstorm drenches the field, the chemical form of nitrogen is, to a large extent, washed out, and the plants become starved for the lack of this element.

Many highly concentrated nitrogen fertilizers are toxic in their effect on earthworms, but it is, probably not the nitrogen that does it. Usually, like cyanamid, it is some other toxic substance that is a carrier for the nitrogen that not only is *not* needed by plants, but remains and accumulates in the soil, to its detriment.

Regarding the difference in quality as between the nitrogen contained in organic and inorganic matter I would like to quote Sir Albert Howard, who in an article *The Nitrogen Problem*, in the January 1947 issue of *Organic Gardening*, said: "The disadvantage of artificial manures like sulphate of ammonia is that the nitrogen is supplied as an inorganic dead chemical. The result is a bastard protein which leads to disease and the loss of the power-of reproduction. This is shown: (1) by the way our dairy herds are afflicted by disease and by inability to bear more than a quarter of the calves they might, and (2) by the way our new varieties of plants run out."

There is an important point involved here. In chemistry we deal with compounds. Compounds are a combination of two or more elements, like nitrogen, oxygen, sulphur, etc. Water is a compound consisting of hydrogen and oxygen and it can be broken down into its separate elements, the building blocks. At times we organic practitioners have let our enthusiasm run away with us. In our fervor we have violated a few of the basic rules of chemistry. We have said that the nitrogen which is in organic matter is different than the nitrogen in a chemical fertilizer. But this is not so. Nitrogen is always nitrogen and phosphorus is always phosphorus. It is like saying that 6 is always 6 and 8 is always 8. There can be no such thing as a synthetic nitrogen. Man cannot bring nitrogen into being.

Protein is a different story. It consists of a maximum of 6 elements—carbon, hydrogen, oxygen, nitrogen, sulphur and phosphorus. There can be different proportions of each one of these 6. Mathematics can be so fantastic that it has been said that over 6 billion different combinations of these elements are known. In other words there are over 6 billion different kinds of protein—so you can see that it is possible for a great variation, and even for a bastard protein to creep in here and there. There are delicate relationships in the formation of compounds. For example water is made up of two parts of hydrogen and one of oxygen. But in hydrogen peroxide the molecule is made up of the same two elements and yet it is a poison. It consists of two atoms of hydrogen and two of oxygen. Only one atom of oxygen more, and yet it can kill.

It must be admitted, therefore, that in the possible combinations of the 6 elements that make up protein there may be some that spell inferior quality.

We can see that protein is like humus. It has no uniform formula, but varies according to how it originated. If it has an artificial chemical origin, it is greatly possible that the atoms may arrange themselves differently within the molecule than if the nitrogen is of organic origin. Nature has a way of arranging them based on an evolution of millions of years.

Man, who only recently came upon the scene, cannot hope to duplicate the chemistry of Nature. In fact no man in any laboratory has ever been able to make protein—even an inferior kind. He has been able to extract nitrogen from the air. But protein is the beginning of life. It is protoplasm and the making of it is in the hands of a power higher than man's.

Dr. Selman Waksman, in his book *Humus* (Williams and Wilkins) item 1082, page 484 cites 3 researches to show the importance of the nature of protein in the soil in improving its ability to feed plant roots. It would seem logical that given defective protein we will have defective plants. In a recent 10 year period in the Middle West the protein content of the grains declined 10 per cent. This is a terrific reduction for such a short period of time. The question is—did the quality of the protein also decline? If it did, it might be an explanation for the alarming recent increases in the degenerative diseases, for protein builds body tissue. Defective protein—defective body tissue. Defective body tissue may be more susceptible to cancer.

Nitrogen is important, but the way it is held in the protein molecule may be *the* one factor which may control the fate of mankind.

In closing, I would like to quote Dr. George D. Scarseth of the American Farm Research Association of Lafayette, Indiana, who, in 1947 in a bulletin entitled *Organic Matter and our Food Supply,* said:

"Protein foods are nitrogen carrying foods. Every farmer knows that nitrogen and soil organic matter are closely related. Every farmer knows that a soil high in organic matter is also a very productive soil. Every farmer also knows that legumes like clover, alfalfa and sweet clover add valuable organic matter to the soil. The farmers also know that the organic matter from these legumes is better than the organic matter from non-legumes, because clover makes nitrogen into chemical compounds out of the free nitrogen in the air."

Incidentally, materials high in nitrogen content are extremely important in composting, for nitrogen (protein) is the principal food of the bacteria which engage in the decay processes. Their bodies are highly proteinaceous. When the raw materials of composting include highly nitrogenous materials such as hen manure and alfalfa hay the composting is accelerated and the quality of the compost better.

THE ROLE OF CARBON DIOXIDE

Many writers on this subject favor the idea that the improvement of the soil, by addition of properly made compost, constitutes the principal factor by which better plant growth is achieved. However, the condition of the atmosphere which surrounds the aerial parts of the plant is just as important as the condition of the soil in which the subterranean parts of the plant are located. No matter how perfect the medium is in which the roots of a plant are placed, without a proper environment for the leaves to function in, no plant can be expected to lead a normal and healthy life.

It is an accepted fact, proven by scientific experiment, that carbon dioxide is as necessary to the life and growth of a plant as oxygen is necessary to animal life. The plant needs a constant supply of carbon dioxide. This is supplied by the air which surrounds the leaves of the plant. As air is more or less in constant motion a fresh supply of CO_2 is always available. But it might be interesting to know that the proportion of CO_2 to air is small—3 parts per 10,000 by volume—so that a constant supply of fresh air is quite necessary for the plant in order to thrive.

Now, since the world contains a large amount of plant life, one would begin to wonder if, sometime, the CO_2 supply would not disappear. However, nature has provided for a continuous supply of CO_2. All dead organic matter decays and ferments back to the simple elements it was built up from, mainly CO_2, water and traces of mineral salts.

This brings us back to our main topic: the role of CO_2 in composting. Besides improving the soil, compost is a material that is at just the proper stage for conversion into a ready supply of CO_2 for the plant. Edwin C. Miller, in his book *Plant Physiology*, records the work of several experimenters studying the effects of an increased supply of CO_2 above normal atmospheric conditions on the growth of plants. In most cases, they discovered that plant growth was increased and that the plants were in a healthier state when the supply of CO_2 was greater than the normal 3 parts per 10,000 by volume. It was noted also that several of the experimenters remarked that an increase in CO_2 concentration could be produced by proper manuring with organic fertilizers. As an added thought, it would seem logical to me to suppose that the good effects caused by loosening the soil near plants releases CO_2 which has been trapped in the earth. Also the removing of weeds allows more CO_2 to be used by the cultivated plants.

The increase in CO_2 concentration may also cause fewer insects on plants where compost is used. Interested persons have noticed that in volcanoes where the concentration of CO_2 is very high no insects can live.

Chapter 25

QUESTIONS AND ANSWERS ON COMPOST

A COMPOST CLINIC

Heating

Q. My heap does not seem to heat up at all. What is the reason for this?

A. The most common cause of compost heap "failures" is a lack of nitrogen. A heap which doesn't heat up or decay quickly is usually made from material which is low in nitrogen, since nitrogen is essential as a source of energy for the bacteria and fungi which do the composting work. Thus it is advisable to add nitrogen supplements such as bone meal, cottonseed meal, tankage, manure or blood meal.

Activators

Q. How do activators help compost?

A. So-called bacterial activators—"canned" cultures of bacteria—have been tested by several universities, including the University of California and Michigan State U. Their general conclusion is that these products do little or nothing to speed up the composting process. This conclusion was confirmed by experiments at the Organic Experimental Farm. The necessary bacteria will be found existing naturally in the composting materials, and none need be added. Since, however, the bacteria derive their energy from nitrogenous materials, it is essential that this food be present in sufficient amounts.

900

Acid Leaves

Q. Will large amounts of leaves make my compost too acid for general garden use?

A. *All leaves are acid, some more than others. It is possible that large amounts of them may make compost too acid for most garden uses. This condition may be counteracted easily with additions of ground limestone.*

Turning the Heap

Q. I would like to get away from turning the compost heap. How can this be done?

A. *The compost heap need not be turned at all if a sufficient number of earthworms are introduced just after the heat of fermentation has subsided. Sufficient moisture, nitrogen and aeration will also expedite the decay process without turning.*

Weeds

Q. I find many weeds growing out of my composted garden areas. How may this be prevented?

A. *The high heat of the well-made compost heap should be sufficient to destroy all weed seeds which could otherwise sprout up in the garden after compost is applied. Be sure that the compost is fully decomposed before applying it. This may mean turning it several times, to make sure all material is exposed to the inner heat, or earthworms may be introduced to facilitate decay.*

Which Leaves for Compost or Mulch?

Q. Are the leaves of such trees as magnolia, avocado, camphor tree, eucalyptus, pepper tree and walnut suitable for composting or mulching?

A. *The leaves of all trees are a valuable source of organic matter and minerals. Those of the eucalyptus, camphor and walnut should be exposed to the weather for a time before using them in the compost heap. In weathering, the aromatic oils, alkaloids, and other components which might interfere with the organisms of decomposition will be leached out. If the leaves are ground by being put through a shredder, leaf grinder or similar equipment, they can be used directly as a mulch and will be suitable more readily for adding to the compost heap as green matter.*

Air Space in Good Soil

Q. Just how does better soil tilth improve plant growth?

A. *As most farmers and gardeners know, loose and fluffy soils work more easily, take less power or effort to plow and cultivate. The greatest help to plant growth, though, comes from the extra pore spaces in soils with good tilth.*

These open pores, or spaces in the soil, help surplus water drain off, enable such soil to dry sooner after heavy rains. At the same time, the pores also hold back some of the water, and help provide needed moisture during dry weather. Soils in good tilth are less parched or subject to drought damage than hard, compact soil.

Finally, the pores allow air to move through the soil, helping to furnish food for growing plants, and encouraging normal, healthful bacterial action and organic matter decomposition.

Applying Compost

Q. What is the best way to apply compost?

A. *For general application, the soil should be stirred or turned thoroughly. Then the compost is added to the top 4 inches of soil. For flower and vegetable gardening, it is best to pan the compost through a half-inch sieve. Coarse material remaining may then be put into another compost heap. Where compost is desired to aid a growing crop, it should be mixed with soil and applied as a mulch. In this way roots will not be disturbed and the top-dressing will gradually work itself down to plants.*

How Much Compost?

Q. For general garden fertility, how much compost should I use each year?

A. *For best results, compost should be applied liberally, perhaps from 1 to 3 inches in thickness per year. Of course, you can get by with as little as half an inch of compost, but in gardening with small plots, it should be applied heavily. There is no danger of burning because of overuse, such is always the case with chemical fertilizers. You can apply compost either once or twice a year. The amount would depend, of course, on the fertility of your soil and how it is being used.*

Plant and Animal Matter

Q. Kindly restate the principles underlying the mixture of plant and animal matter in the compost process. I realize that living things like bacteria require energy and growth food or carbohydrates and proteins just as we do ourselves. What else is there involved?

A. You have stated the most essential fact. There is moreover the actual bacterial content of manure which produces such action in the compost as activators are expected to supply. The important thing is however the proper proportion. Both Sir Albert Howard and J. I. Rodale have experimented with different materials and found the 1:3 ratio of animal matter to plant matter the sound one. If you used, let us say, 100 pounds of rich hoof and horn dust which would amount to perhaps 15 pounds of nitrogen with 300 pounds of plant matter to get full action, there would be too much growth food and too little energy food for the growing bacteria and the horn dust would not be digested. As a result, much of it would go off into the air, some would attract flies, since in the absence of plant matter bacterial growth would be unfinished.

Effect of pH on Plants

Q. What is pH, and how does it affect my plants?

A. Soil pH is a way of expressing the amount of acidity or alkalinity. The pH scale runs from 0 to 14. The 0 end of the scale is the acid end, while the 14 is on the alkalinity extreme. The neutral point is 7.0, lower than that is acid and higher is alkaline. In general, most common vegetables, field crops, fruits and flowers do best on soils that have a pH of 6.5 to 7.0—that is, slightly acid to neutral. If soils have plenty of humus, most plants will do well even if the soil has a lower or higher pH. A few plants, such as azaleas, camellias and gardenias do best on a quite acid soil. If soil is too acid, crushed limestone should be applied. Wood ashes, marl or ground oyster shells are also effective. All of these can be added in compost.

When liming, it's best not to add all the required limestone at one time. Overliming is easiest on a light sandy soil, whereas soils rich in organic matter tend to resist injurious overliming. For gardens, limestone is best applied in compost or just before spading so that it can be worked into the soil. Limestone may be applied to shrubs, trees and flower beds and worked into the soil as needed.

Soils which are too alkaline may be brought back to a favorable pH range by the addition of organic matter. Organic matter contains acid-forming material and produces acids directly on decomposition. These acids combine with any excess alkali thus neutralizing it.

Providing Trace Elements

Q. Within recent years, agricultural scientists have "discovered" and emphasized the importance of *trace elements*. In applying the organic method, how can I be certain of supplying my soil enough of all of these trace elements?

A. *Trace elements, the principal ones being boron, calcium*, chlorine, copper, iron, manganese, and zinc, are needed in* very small amounts *for plant nutrition. Therefore, applications of these trace elements may easily prove toxic. Soils low in organic matter frequently suffer from a lack of these elements, which are found in sufficient quantities in normal soils. Following the organic method, and testing annually for organic matter content, should assure you of an adequate supply of trace elements.*

Practical on Farm Scale

Q. Using 100 per cent organic methods is frequently called *practical only in small gardens*—not in large-scale agriculture or in growing the nation's tremendous food supply. How can the organic method be *possible* on the *farm scale?*

A. *The organic method is indeed not only possible, but practical on a farm scale. This has been proven time and time again by successful organic farmers. Very briefly, the additions of farm manures, rock powders, green manures, turned under crop residues, a rotation plan, and careful soil management, are the keys to organic farming. In most farm crops, only a small portion of the total plant is used for food. If the remainder of the crop is returned to the soil, along with the addition of rock powders and other easily-available organic materials, crops will not suffer from nutrient deficiencies.*

Materials to Compost

Q. I have a wonderful chance to experiment with organic gardening on soil that has never been cultivated and that cur-

---

* Because calcium is needed in much larger quantities than the other trace elements, some soil experts classify it as a major nutrient, along with nitrogen, phosphorus, and potassium. Calcium is usually supplied by lime applications, which are also used as soil-sweeteners.

rently supports nothing but coarse weeds—and sparsely at that. The soil is very acid, mostly grey sand. I wish to get started at once with composting. I have access to seaweed, leaves, chicken manure and sphagnum. Will the following materials be all right to use for composting: waste berries from the cranberry bogs we operate, clam shells and rotted logs? Could I make satisfactory compost by layering it in an unused ditch? (There would be walls of soil on two sides of the heap.)

A. The materials in question, namely cranberries, shells and logs would be satisfactory for composting. With all the material you have available, it would seem worthwhile for you to obtain a compost shredder. We have found this machine a great aid to quick composting methods. Of course, it would be necessary for you to have the clam shells ground before placing in the heap. Building your compost in a ditch is not a good idea, since it would be very difficult to turn the compost in order to hasten decomposition.

Maggots in Compost

Q. How can I control maggots in my compost pile?

A. The maggots in your compost are probably the larvae of the ordinary house fly, and undoubtedly originated from eggs which were deposited by flies on your heap. As a matter of public health, it is desirable to eliminate flies, if possible, or at least reduce their numbers to a minimum. It would therefore be desirable to clean out the composter and begin over again. It may be possible to control the number of maggots (and flies) by keeping your composting material covered with a layer of soil or well-rotted material such as peat, humus, or compost from a previous year.

Eliminating Tank Odor

Q. I have constructed a manure pit, or rather a manure tank, for collecting all the manure from my hog raising project. It is an underground tank measuring 6 feet deep, 6 feet wide and 6 feet long. It takes about 3 or 4 months to fill it. The problem is that when we pump it out into a tank wagon and spread it on the fields, it makes a terrific stench. After it gets about half full, the tank itself puts out quite a lot of very strong odor, although it only has 3 openings in it. How could I eliminate the odor?

A. Perhaps the 3 or 4 months period that it takes to fill the tank is too long a time and allows for too much decaying. One suggestion would be to cut the time in half instead of waiting until the tank is filled, pump it out and spread it, after about a month and a half or two months. In that way, you might eliminate the stench from the tank. Another recommendation is to add some green matter to the tank itself and see if that cuts down the odor at all. Hog manure is generally relatively watery and poor in nitrogen but rich in phosphoric acid. It decomposes slowly and must be ranked as a "cold" manure, but can be used like other manure to make compost. Therefore, the addition of green matter would improve its value as a fertilizer.

Handling Straw for Compost

Q. Can you suggest how oat straw and stubble may best be handled for use in composting?

A. As for handling straw, it is best to mow down the grain stubble after the combine passes and to rake the clippings and the combined straw together and take them in with a hay loader. Set your mower at the same height you would use to mow hay. The straw would be easier to compost if you run it through your hay chopper as you suggest.

Value of Cork

Q. Does cork have any fertilizer value? Should it be composted? I tore down a meat cooler and in the deal I am to dispose of the cork.

A. Natural cork, as such, has no value whatsoever as a fertilizer. Occasionally it is used as a mulch where, because of the tannic acid in cork, it is of value where increased acidity is required in the soil. It is our understanding that cork has been used as a mulch for azaleas, laurel, and other acid-loving plants. Ground cork, however, is quite expensive when compared to other materials used for this purpose, and should not be considered for garden use unless quantities are available at no cost.

Coal Ashes

Q. I have been told to put the ashes from a coal stove on my garden and flower beds. What can you tell me about this? Are coal ashes good for a garden or not?

A. *Coal ashes, hard or soft, should never be used, either in the garden or on the farm. They contain dangerous, soluble compounds containing sulphur which has been shown to be an important factor in causing cancer. Above a small amount, it is toxic. Some soft coals contain too much iron, which also becomes toxic. Soft coal ashes have as much as 10 per cent sulphur trioxide and when water comes in contact with it, it turns to sulphuric acid. Readers have often told of coal ashes preventing or retarding plant growth. Use wood ashes instead in the garden and compost heap—unless your soil is highly alkaline.*

Iron Rust in Compost

Q. Can you tell me whether there is any advantage in putting large amounts of iron rust in compost or in the soil where vegetables and fruits are grown?

A. *Plants use only traces of iron which serves as a catalyst in the manufacture of the green pigment, chlorophyll. Large amounts of iron are not necessary in the compost or in the soil.*

Weeds in Composted Plants

Q. I must be doing something wrong as I have so many weeds growing among my composted plants. Can you help me?

A. *In order to be certain that weed seeds are killed, two precautions can be taken. First when the two turns of the heap are made one must see that what has been on the outside of the heap, gets into the center of it where the heat is sufficiently high to kill the seeds. If this is done twice, then all the material will have a chance at some time or other to be in the center. Secondly, where the material is not turned, earthworms should be used for that purpose. They chew up the material. After a weed seed has passed through the digestive system of a worm it has lost all ability to grow.*

The ideal method would be to combine one and two, that is, make the two turns and use earthworms. On our farm where we have been applying compost for 6 years, the weed problem is getting less and less serious each year.

Chicken Feathers for Compost

Q. Do feathers in a compost heap have any fertilizing value? Late last fall, I added about two barrels of them to my compost pile, and when I used the compost this fall, the feathers had been completely decomposed.

A. *Feathers are similar to silk and wool in that they contain considerable amounts of nitrogen. That is their main value, which is about equal to that of good hoof and horn meal or horn dust. An analysis of feathers revealed that they contained 15.3 per cent of nitrogen. Feathers decay very rapidly in a compost heap, but must be kept unusually moist to do so. It should be remembered that many plants will suffer from an abundance of nitrogen, so add plenty of plant matter to the compost, and perhaps some lime, rock powders or other low-nitrogenous materials to offset the feathers.*

Changes In Manure

Q. What decomposition changes take place in manure?

A. *The decomposition changes which take place in manure are briefly as follows:*

1. *Decomposition of urinary nitrogen. The first change is the formation of ammonia in urine which is lost unless the manure is kept moist and compact.*

2. *Decomposition of insoluble nitrogen. Next the insoluble nitrogen contained in the solid parts of the excrement undergoes putrefactive changes with the formation of ammonia.*

3. *Conversion of soluble into insoluble nitrogen. The ammonia and other soluble compounds of nitrogen are used in considerable amounts as food for the bacteria in the manure and are stored in their bodily substance in insoluble form. This nitrogen becomes available when the bacteria die and undergo decomposition.*

4. *Formation of free nitrogen. Under certain conditions ammonia and nitrates are decomposed with the formation of free nitrogen which escapes into the atmosphere and is thus lost permanently.*

5. *Decomposition of nitrogen-free compounds. The fibrous parts of the manure which are made up largely of cellulose, lignin, and other complex carbohydrates are eventually broken down with the escape of the carbon into the atmosphere in the form of carbon dioxide, and hydrogen in the form of water. These elements, carbon and hydrogen, escape in such amounts that*

from ¼ to ½ of the original dry matter in the manure is lost. This is the reason for the great shrinkage in bulk during decomposition.

Animal Matter

Q. To what extent does organic matter which has decayed without animal activator or fertilizer provide nutrients and not merely a sponge to hold water?

A. *Many people who have been making compost for many years believe that good results are not obtained without animal manure. Animal matter contains hormones which help plants to grow. It is helpful even if it is present in only extremely small quantities. Sir Albert Howard says in his* Agricultural Testament:

"When san hemp is grown for green-manuring or for seed in India, satisfactory results are only obtained if the crop is manured with cattle manure or humus." Again he says on the same subject: "In Ceylon particularly, attempts have been made to prepare humus without animal wastes. The results have not fulfilled expectation. The breaking down of such resistant material as the leaves and prunings of tea is then unsatisfactory: the organisms which synthesize humus are not properly fed: the residues of these organisms which form an important part of the final humus lack the contributions of the animal. No one has yet succeeded in establishing an efficient and permanent system of agriculture without live stock. There is no reason therefore to suppose that the tea industry will prove an exception to what, after all, is a rule in Nature."

Sheep Manure

Q. Can sheep manure purchased from a fertilizer house be used for making compost?

A. *Yes. Sheep manure is generally dry and rich in nitrogen and potassium as indicated in an earlier chapter on manure. When properly aerated in the compost heap, sheep manure undergoes decomposition quite rapidly, and heats quickly.*

Poultry Droppings

Q. How would you use droppings from poultry in the compost heap?

A. *Droppings from poultry are either pure manure on a dropping board or a mixture of manure and litter on the floor.*

It is well to mix the pure manure with water when adding it to the heap as it will then better mix with the plant materials in the heap and cause more rapid decay than when applied as a layer in dried form. Chicken manure contains more nitrogen than any of the other manures and a one inch layer would be enough if the layer system is used. When mixed with litter, a thicker layer can be used depending upon the amount and nature of the litter.

Dog Manure

Q. We have the excrements from 7 dogs. Can these be used for composting? How should we go about it?

A. Dog manure can be used in the compost heap; in fact, it is the richest in phosphorus if the dogs are fed with proper care and given their share of bones. It would be advisable to use with it a mixture of leaves and green matter such as grass clippings, garden and kitchen refuse, and other plant wastes. Citrus peels and other fruit wastes are rich in potash and should be used. It may be wise to arrange the heap so that it cannot attract dogs, which can best be accomplished by using a suitable enclosure.

Rabbit Manure

Q. Can rabbit manure be used in making compost?

A. Rabbit manure has the same value as other manures in making compost. The rabbit manure contains organisms which cause decay without producing heat and is thus classed as a cold manure.

The Same Compost

Q. Do you think it is possible to get your ground for vegetables too rich with finished compost?

Does compost apply the same to all vegetables, or is there a difference in mixture?

A. The same compost is generally used for all vegetables because it is a balanced food, but it is applied in varying amounts. It would be inadvisable to plant vegetables into pure compost. Only very few vegetables such as tomatoes, melons, and cucumbers would succeed.

All the other vegetables which are relatively slow-growing compared with those named should have the compost mixed with the topsoil before planting them. Some crops, like beans and egg plants, also peppers, tomatoes, potatoes, and cucum-

bers will take well to further top-dressing applied around the time when flowers appear.

If you keep composting your garden according to plant needs, which you can easily judge by results, you will find that after a period of 4 or 5 years your garden gets in such good shape that further composting will not show immediate results. It is nevertheless digested by the soil and adds organic matter. A soil rich in humus needs, of course, less compost than a highly depleted or sandy soil.

Heating of Compost

Q. I tried making my first compost heap early in August using, however, old instead of new manure. No heating or appreciable sinking has taken place. What do I do now? Obviously it is hard to remake by separating the ingredients as applied.

A. *Where old manure is used, the heating usually does not take place as it does when fresh animal matter is employed. You state that it would be difficult to remake the heap by separating the ingredients; that is, the green matter and the manure. But this is not necessary. There are different methods of making composts. There is the ordinary way, by which the ingredients are charged into it in layers, that is, 6 inches of green matter and then two inches of manure. In this case the heap must be turned twice. In another method, the green matter and manure are thoroughly mixed and shredded together.*

Since your materials are already mixed, it is advisable to use it to make a new heap, adding some new fresh manure or some dried blood.

Deficiencies and Compost

Q. There is a basic principle involved in organic gardening, which is not yet clear to me. In the production of organic compost all the materials used, directly or indirectly, come from impoverished soils, except possibly where sea vegetation is used in place of manure. The plants raised on our soils in their present condition are of necessity deficient in their mineral and vitamin content. When used in compost and put back into deficient soil they leave the soil still deficient. Manure from animals when fed on these plants must, for the same reason, be deficient as plant food sources. The parts of animals' bodies when used as part of a compost suffer from the same cause. How then does organic fertilizing bring the soil back to a perfect condition in terms of plant food content?

A. Plants as well as animals are gatherers of soil minerals. The analysis of leaves shows that their mineral content is high above that of the surrounding ground. Likewise a recent article in Soil Science *on earthworm castings made it plain that these are much higher in most minerals than the surrounding soil. By adding organic material and by encouraging earthworms, you usually increase the fertility accordingly.*

However, we suggest also the use of phosphate rock, limestone and dolomite for the purpose of adding minerals that otherwise would be lacking. But, in general, you know, of course, that compost is not only readily available plant food, but also concentrated when compared with the materials that go into the heap originally.

Where it is believed that some kind of soil deficiency exists, then it is advisable to bring in mild soil amendments from regions other than your own—for example, raw ground phosphate rock and limestone, dried blood and bone meal, kelp frond, seaweed, etc. The use of a large quantity of leaves also becomes important in such a case because the roots of trees go down sometimes 20 to 25 feet and bring up valuable minerals from unexhausted areas.

Ground Rock

Q. What are the values of ground rock materials?

A. Soil is derived from parent rock material by the weathering and disintegrating forces of nature acting over thousands of years. All the mineral constituents normally present in the soil are therefore also present in the natural rock from which it was formed. If the soil becomes depleted of certain of these mineral elements through leaching or erosion, or made unavailable by the extended use of chemical fertilizers, then it would seem only reasonable to go to the parent rock material for the replacement of these elements.

Although it usually takes nature about 100 years to make one-quarter inch of soil, modern grinding machinery can pulverize rock materials to such fineness that it is available for plant assimilation in relatively short periods of time. It would therefore now be practical to use these finely ground rock materials to supplement mineral losses in the soil. Such natural rock materials as phosphate and potash rock, dolomite and regular limestone, marl, feldspar, marble, granite and many others, when finely ground will add valuable mineral constituents to the soil.

Fruit Drop

Q. I have some apple trees which produce promising fruit, but they fall off the trees before they are ripe.

A. *Premature dropping of fruit is due to a mineral deficiency in the soil, or to insect damage. Remineralize your soil with phosphate rock and potash rock, and then give the trees a good dressing of compost as far as the drip line.*

Heating

Q. I made a compost according to the Indore Process in March but so far it has failed to heat. I have not turned it yet. As I had no green vegetation at this time, I used fallen leaves which I had used as a mulch the past winter. Should I have used these leaves?

A. *The leaves were perfectly all right, but apparently 1 of 3 factors did not come into play:*

1. *There was not enough nitrogen to produce growth food for the bacteria. Perhaps the manure was old.*

2. *The heap may not have been moist enough.*

3. *The heap could have been either too compact or even too loose. I am inclined to think that the first cause might be responsible and if I were you I should add some more nitrogenous material and rebuild the heap.*

Compost Ingredients

Q. My husband and I are planning on building a compost heap this spring. Our manure has a large amount of hay mixed with it. The manure consists of goat, chicken, goose, duck and horse droppings. We have some wood ashes and some coarsely ground limestone. Please advise me about the use of this material.

A. *You have all the necessary ingredients for an excellent compost heap and the fact that the manure and hay are already mixed together is an added advantage. Lay this material down about as you would if the manure and vegetable waste were separate. When you get about 8 inches of the mixed hay and manure add a light layer of fresh manure for heating and some earth, wood ashes, and ground limestone and repeat the process until your heap is 5 feet high. Remember to water the heap while you build it.*

Shredding Plant Materials

Q. What is the advantage of grinding or shredding plant materials before putting them in the compost heap?

A. *The grinding or shredding of plant materials to be composted is a good practice because it hastens the composting process. The finer the materials are, the more surface they will expose to the soil organisms in the compost heap, whose activities convert plant and animal residues into compost.*

Carpet Waste Value

Q. I work in a carpet mill, and have access to a lot of lint made up of nylon, rayon, wool, plastic, etc. Would this be helpful to my soil or would it be harmful?

A. *We have long recommended the use of wool wastes which are often very high in nitrogen. If included in the compost that is teeming with bacteria, the wastes break down rather easily, provided the heap is kept moist enough. It is always a good idea to mix some manure in with the dry materials in order to supply bacterial life and to hasten the compost process. There are no reported research experiments using nylon, rayon or plastic waste materials; so, it would be best to use those materials in experimental quantities only at first, until you know for sure that they are suitable.*

Using Dried Manure

Q. As it is almost impossible to get the natural manure, would the hydrated, or dried, cow manure be all right to use in the garden and in the compost pile? I am gathering all waste from the garden and leaves, and was wondering if the hydrated manure would serve to hasten the work of decomposing this.

All summer I bury all my garbage in a spot in my garden as I gather the crops. Am I doing right?

I use no commercial fertilizer as I think it's ruining everything.

A. *Dried cow manure can be used in the garden as well as in the compost heap. On the garden apply at least 100 pounds to 1000 square feet. If possible triple the amount for the best results.*

Garbage can be dug into shallow ditches in the garden. It can also be used in the compost heap. Cover the garbage with a sprinkling of soil. An application of natural organic fertilizers in the heap will hasten the breakdown of the materials. There are several good bacterial activators on the market that hasten decomposition of raw materials.

To build up the fertility and proper balance it is necessary to add nitrogen, phosphate and potash to the soil as required by results of soil testing. These elements are obtained from compost, natural rock phosphate and potash rock. The natural rocks contain many other elements needed, including the trace minerals.

Use Kelps in Compost

Q. Can the kelps (brown algae which live in the sea) be added to the compost heap? I have access to quantities of kelp and would like to make use of it if there is any value in doing so.

A. *The kelps are excellent composting materials and are good sources of potash and iodine. The potash content of kelps, depending on the species, varies from 1 to 5 per cent. The giant kelp,* Macrocystis pyrifera, *is a perennial which can be harvested several times a year. Potash content of its dry tissue is about 1.5 per cent. Kelps also contain iodine in sufficient amounts for plant needs.*

Composting Poultry Feathers and Cuttings

Q. A friend in the broiler poultry business dresses about 200 birds every week. The cuttings and feathers are hauled away by truck. I know this could be turned into compost. How would you go about this weekly process?

A. *It is definitely advantageous to use the chicken feathers and cuttings in compost-making. After putting a layer of green material about 6 inches high on the ground, you can follow this with another layer, about 2 or 3 inches high, of the chicken cuttings and feathers. This will replace the layer of manure ordinarily suggested.*

An analysis of feathers shows that they contain 15.30 per cent nitrogen. Feathers decay very rapidly in a compost heap, but must be kept unusually moist in order to do so. It is necessary to remember, however, that an excess of nitrogen is not desirable for most crops. Therefore, our recommendation would be to compost these materials and not apply them directly to the soil.

Recognizing Nematodes

Q. How do I know if my soil is infested with nematodes?

A. *Since nematodes or eel worms are generally minute (most are microscopic) their presence must usually be determined by recognizing the damage they do. The majority of plant-parasitic nematodes are root parasites and do not cause specific symptoms of injury on above-ground parts of plants. Instead, these eel-shaped organisms head straight for any plant root nearby, pierce the root and feed on it or lay their eggs in it. This causes numerous small knots to form along the root. As a result, the plant loses nourishment from the roots, becomes stunted or dies. Nematode-infected succulent plants have a tendency to wilt more quickly than healthy plants, while yellowing of foliage and "die-back" of branches or shoots may also be common with such infections.*

Nematodes are best combated by liberal organic fertilizing, the beneficial fungi in humus, crop rotation, trap cropping and the use of resistant plant varieties.

Garden Cover Crop

Q. What is a good cover crop for the home garden?

A. *One suggested winter cover is a seed mixture of one pound of Italian rye grass and two pounds of crimson clover for each 1,000 square feet of garden space. Sow from mid-August to mid-September. Winter oats, barley or rye, seeded at a rate of 4 to 6 pounds to 1,000 square feet, may make better growth and cover when seeded late. If fall and winter vegetables remain in the garden, seed cover crop between the rows. Plow under winter cover crops in the spring, usually by May 1, before they make much growth.*

Overcoming Excess Alkalinity

Q. Both the pH and lime content of my soil are too high. Each year my land is becoming less productive. What can I do to correct this condition?

A. *Increasing your soil's organic content is the only sure way to correct excess alkalinity, and it is a positive way. Grow green manure crops, aerate your soil and collect all organic wastes you can find and spread them on your land. Include as many highly acid materials as possible.*

Faster Composting

Q. Right now, it takes us almost 6 months to make compost. We don't have any power equipment, but were hoping you could tell us some way of making compost in a shorter time.

A. *We definitely believe that compost can be made quickly —without the use of special equipment or chemical activators. Here's how:*

When making the speed compost heap, be sure to mix materials such as grass clippings, vegetable tops, weeds, etc., with materials high in nitrogen (manure, cotton gin wastes, dried blood, feathers and tankage).

All material should be moist to start with, and the heap should be kept wet enough so that no part of it dries out. A brief watering for the first 3 days should be sufficient.

Turn the heap often. The fastest working bacteria thrive in the presence of air, and turning the heap is the best way to aerate it. Initially, every 3 or 4 days is not too often. Remember, speed compost heaps don't have to be large. A ton of compost occupies a space only 4 feet square and 4 feet high.

City Garden Suggestions

Q. I have a small city garden plot. How do I get enough organic materials, time, etc., to make practicing the organic method feasible?

A. *You may buy organic fertilizers at the same place you could buy chemical fertilizers—at garden centers, hardware stores, or nurseries and greenhouses. Each year, more and more organic products are appearing on commercial shelves. Your time is your own, and only you can decide how much of it you want to devote to your city garden. The key to a good city garden is simplicity. It is far better to grow several varieties each of a few select plants, than a great number of different plants. Plants you select should be resistant to smoke, soot, gasoline fumes, shade, and other city problems. And, of course, by following the organic method, plants will be stronger and better able to stand the rigors of city life.*

Trace Elements

Q. If soils lack the trace mineral elements such as boron, manganese, copper or cobalt is it advisable to buy these elements and correct the deficiency with it?

A. *No. That is a dangerous procedure, because the amount*

of these trace elements needed is usually small, perhaps 5 parts per million. Ten parts per million could damage crops. It is best to correct the deficiency by applying organic matter, compost, phosphate rock, lime, granite dust or sludge.

Higher Food Value

Q. Aside from the argument that chemicals are not good for the soil, the contention repeatedly made is that there is no difference in the foods grown by any method with any fertilizers. Is there any factual evidence of higher food quality through crops grown organically?

A. Yes. Repeated tests, both at our own experimental farm and at other test sites, reveal that organically-grown foods do contain higher concentrates of certain vitamins than chemically-grown foods, otherwise grown under the same conditions. In a recent test planting of peppers, organically-fertilized plots showed 137.4 milligrams per 100 grams vitamin C content, while chemical plots averaged only 116.9 milligrams per 100 grams. Repetitions of this test showed that organically-fertilized peppers were always higher in vitamin C than their chemical counterparts.

One of our advertisers, who sells organic oranges fertilized by organic compost only, has had tests conducted by an independent laboratory which showed that the organic oranges contained as much as 30 per cent more vitamin C than average oranges sold over commercial counters.

Further evidence of the vitamin variation of vegetables can be found in the preceding chapters on Compost and The Health of Animals and Man (Chapter 17) and The Value of Compost (Chapter 23).

Chemicals and Organics?

Q. Several specialists and agricultural publications have advocated *combining* organic methods with chemical fertilizing and other practices for best results. Do you agree with this?

A. No. Even though the incorporation of organic methods into chemical gardening and farming will greatly improve general results, 100 per cent organic methods are far superior. Additions of chemicals can prove toxic to soil life and plants. They tend to produce an "off-flavor" in vegetables, and can never achieve the perfect balance of soil nutrition which is inherent in natural fertilizers.

918

Speeding Leaf Composting

Q. I've been collecting leaves for some time now and piling them up in a heap at the rear of my lot. What can I do to speed up the composting process?

A. *First, if you have a rotary mower, you'll be amazed to learn how quickly by using it you can shred leaves, weeds, straw, hay and garden wastes of almost any kind. You'll be even more amazed to find out how fast these materials will turn into compost once they are shredded. All that's necessary is to spread the material (leaves, etc.) on the ground and run over it with the mower or mower attachment. If the material is piled rather high, simply depress the mower handle and push the machine forward until the cutting blades are positioned directly over the pile; then slowly lower the blades into the pile. Rotary mowers with side exit ports create a neat pile of shredded material after only a few minutes of operation. A large cardboard carton or side of a building can be used as a backstop to pile the material.*

But if you don't have a rotary mower or shredder—or even if you do—it's still important to add some nitrogen-rich material such as fresh or dried manure, dried blood or compost made previously, or a small amount of rich soil, because the nitrogen in these materials is an essential food for the decomposing bacteria.

Best Time for Composting

Q. What is the best time to make compost?

A. *Strictly speaking, compost can be made successfully any time of the year, but there are certain times when composting is done easier or more efficiently.*

The summer and fall months are usually the most active composting period, primarily because material for composting is available then. Weeds are growing at their thickest, leaves are falling from the trees, grass clippings are accumulating and various farm crop residues can be had for the asking.

Since compost can be used at any time and is almost a permanent fertilizer, it doesn't make much difference when you make it.

Using Coffee Wastes

Q. I have available at very little cost a practically unlimited amount of coffee grains secured directly from a processing plant. The grains are still wet from the processing and form mold very rapidly.

Can you suggest ways in which this organic matter can be used both by itself and in conjunction with other organic matter? Can its use be overdone? Does the mold formation harm plants?

A. Coffee wastes are practical additions to the compost heap. For good balance, they should be part of a mixture of various plant wastes, animal matter, earth, etc., and not used in excessive proportion. Heat and bacterial action in the composting process will take care of the mold-forming tendency. This material would also be suitable for mulching, again preferably along with other mulch ingredients. Dried coffee grounds contain about two per cent nitrogen, .36 per cent phosphoric acid, and .67 per cent potash.

Pea Vines in Compost

Q. I'm interested in farming organically. I can get quantities of pea vines to make compost or for any other type of fertilizing, but someone said they are of no value. Is that true? If not, how are they best used?

A. "Someone" is quite wrong. Pea wastes are of several kinds, mainly available in quantities in the cannery regions. Apart from the high feeding value of any legume crop, pea shells and vines should be returned to the land in some form. If they can be fed and thus be used as manure residue, they are best employed. If they show diseases, they can be burned and the ashes used for fertilizing. Pea pod ash contains almost 3 per cent phosphoric acid and 27 per cent potash. If without disease, they can be composted with great ease since their nitrogen content, which is highest in green pods and vines, tends to produce a quick break-down.

Value of Leaves

Q. What fertilizer values have the leaves of our common trees?

A. Many trees are deep rooted and absorb minerals from the lower soil levels. These minerals are translocated into the leaves and dropped in the fall. In this way nature replenishes many of the nutrient elements which are leached out of the surface layers of the soil.

Bulletin No. 92 of the Clemson Agricultural College of

Clemson, South Carolina, shows that forest leaves which they tested contained .76 per cent of nitrogen, .26 per cent of phosphorus and .42 per cent of potash per ton of leaves. Besides this, leaves are known to contain rare trace elements and are wonderful for the organic matter which they contain which enables them to absorb and hold more water and improve the physical condition of the soil where they are used.

According to another study apple leaves when fully mature and before falling may contain nearly 3 per cent nitrogen, 6 per cent phosphorus and 12 per cent potash.

Bulletin 395 of the Massachusetts Agricultural Experiment Station contained a study showing that mixed leaves contained .60 per cent nitrogen, .17 per cent phosphoric acid, .13 per cent potash, 1.28 per cent calcium oxide, and .31 per cent magnesium oxide.

Fertilizing Evergreens

Q. Please give some information on feeding evergreens.

A. *Well-rotted compost or manure is probably the best fertilizer for evergreens.*

These plants thrive best in an acid soil. The soil should be free from lime, rich in humus and provided with good drainage.

Mulch heavily with leaves, preferably with oak leaves because they last longer and contribute more to the acid condition.

An occasional top-dressing of well-rotted manure can be given, but if the soil is well supplied with humus and if a plentiful leaf mulch is maintained, any special feeding is best done with fertilizers of an acid-forming nature.

After the plants have become established, the soil surrounding them should be disturbed as little as possible, for the roots are very near the surface. It is known that there is a definite mycorrhizal association between the feeder roots of most of the evergreen plants and shrubs and certain fungi.

Sometimes a balanced organic food or one rich in nitrogen is given to stimulate growth. This should be dug into the soil, and the area well watered; or it may be applied in solution; or it may be applied in crow-bar holes driven at two-foot intervals down to the feeding roots, starting the holes at least 18 inches from the trunk.

Legumes for Soil Improvement

Q. How do legumes help build soil fertility? What are some of the principal legumes and how are these best used?

A. *Leguminous crops are active nitrogen gatherers. According to the USDA, they furnish more nitrogen to our crops than farm manures and fertilizers combined. This comes primarily from the air through a process called nitrogen-fixation. Certain bacteria attach themselves to the legume's roots and form nodules which are rich in nitrogen, one of the main constituents of protein essential to plant and animal growth. Leguminous crops are therefore adding extra fertility to the soil because they encourage bacteria which make atmospheric nitrogen available for plants in the soil. As they sink their roots down, legumes not only aerate the soil, but add valuable organic matter to it, besides bringing minerals to the surface. Because of their high nitrogen content, plowing under the leguminous green-manure crops is no shock to the soil.*

Alfalfa is one of the most practical and widely-grown legumes. Others include alsike and crimson clover, hairy vetch, lespedeza and burr clover. Such plants as soybeans, cowpeas, velvet and field peas, and peanuts—although legumes—are not usually grown for green-manuring purposes because they do not develop deep root systems, as do the others.

Legumes may be selected according to special conditions, grown as winter or summer cover crops, often planted as practical mixed crops with various grains. The State Experiment Station or County Agent can best advise which legumes are suited to your soil area and climate range. The best time for incorporating them into the soil is just before blooming, since then the plants are most leafy and richest in nitrogen.

Differences in Lime

Q. Please tell me the difference between ground limestone and agricultural lime. What does agricultural lime come from? And what action does it have on the soil and plants? Also, what does limestone do to the soil and plants?

A. *Agricultural lime is sometimes confused with ground limestone. In a strict sense, the term applies to any limestone used for agricultural purposes, and can contain slaked lime or hydrated lime. Any bag labeled "agricultural lime" should, therefore, be further inspected before purchasing.*

We recommend the ground limestone, not the hydrated, slaked or quicklime.

Ground limestone contains calcium carbonate, and does not burn the soil. It is the most economical type to use.

When limestone is burned it turns into calcium oxide or quicklime which is much too fierce in its action. It kills micro-organisms and would not be a harmonious element in the biologic life of the soil.

Lime is used on the land because it neutralizes or alkalizes the soil, making conditions proper for the working of bacteria. The lime also furnishes calcium and small amounts of minerals. It tends to aerate and flocculate or granulate the soil and make it crumbly. It ventilates the soil to allow seepage of surface moisture to the plant roots. In sandy soil it tends to bind the sand particles to a more consistent body. After liming, it requires less harrowing to break down clods after plowing.

Limed lands give greater yields and better quality crops. It will help to break down recently applied organic matter. Many plants are diseased because they grow in hard-packed soil. Lime helps to correct this handicap. The use of lime helps to eliminate acid-loving weeds.

Tests show that the use of lime makes roots go deeper and reach levels rich in subsoil minerals. It increases the availability of plant food.

When organic matter decays in soil, acids form. Lime used as a neutralizer cuts acidity; blocks iron and aluminum which otherwise would react with and tie up in unavailable forms the soluble phosphates applied; lowers the solubility of manganese which might otherwise be toxic to plants; stimulates microbes in the soil to decompose organic matter and stimulate nitrogen-fixing bacteria.

Varied Organic Matter

Q. Is there any value to getting organic matter from other than my own grounds?

A. By all means bring in organic matter from other sources, unless it is severely diseased. Green matter raised on different soils may supply trace minerals your plants are lacking and not receiving adequately from your own limited material. In addition, organic matter from other places may hold eggs of beneficial insects that prey on your worst beetles and worms.

Old Cow Manure

Q. I have manure that has been in a pile for about 3 years. Should this be composted or can it be applied to the soil as it is?

A. The manure which has been in a heap for 3 years should be well composted. Its value as a fertilizer will depend upon such circumstances as size of the heap, amount of rainfall to which it has been exposed, extent to which oxidation has taken place, and the like. This decomposed manure can be applied directly to the soil.

Hog Manure

Q. Can hog manure be used for making compost, and will it heat like other manures?

A. Hog manure is relatively watery, relatively poor in nitrogen but rich in phosphoric acid. It decomposes slowly, and must be ranked as a cold *manure. It can be used like other manures in making compost.*

Compost Without Manure

Q. I do not have manure and have no way of getting any. I would thank you for any advice on making compost without manure.

A. If animal manures are not available, it is well to cut or shred the plant materials as finely as possible so as to expose a maximum amount of surface to the organisms of decay. The heap of such finely ground plant materials, as soon as the heat has subsided, may be inoculated with earthworms which have been especially bred for the compost heap and soils rich in organic matter. These worms will supply the manure and various animal excretions needed. Or the heap may be inoculated with special strains of composting bacteria which will help break the plant material down in a short time, providing conditions are kept favorable for the fermentation processes. It may be well also to include in the compost heap such animal residues as bone meal, dried blood, dried meat meal, dried fish and dried manure if available.

Eggshells for House Plants

Q. I have a neighbor who claims house plants (especially roses) will grow better if an eggshell is left over night in a flower pot on top of the soil, and that this will make a big improvement in the growth of the plant. Why is that?

A. Your neighbor's idea is partly right. In addition to their principal ingredient, calcium, eggshells contain over one per cent nitrogen and about 0.4 per cent phosphoric acid. These are all, of course, important nutrients for any plants—includ-

ing house plants. However, much better than the overnight shell-placing method would be crushing or grinding the egg-shells and adding this to the plants' soil or fertilizing mixture. Shells are also a good material for inclusion in the compost heap. Since the calcium provides lime, it should be noted that plants requiring definitely acid soil do not call for such treatment.

Compost and the pH of the Soil

Q. How does compost affect the pH of the soil, and in what way does it influence this condition for better plant growth?

A. *Humus functions as a buffer in the soil. Garden and crop plants are far less dependent upon a specific pH, or acid-alkaline status, in the soil when there is an abundant supply of humus. For example, potatoes require a distinctly acid soil when the humus content is low. In less acid or neutral soils low in humus, potatoes are highly susceptible to potato scab.*

When to Apply Compost?

Q. When should compost be added to the soil, before or after planting?

A. *If possible, compost should be added before planting so that it can be worked into the surface layer of the soil without injuring the plant rootlets. It is a good practice also to mulch the soil lightly with compost after the seedlings are an inch or two high. This mulch will help hold the soil against erosion and will discourage the growth of weeds.*

Back Yard Compost

Q. I am interested in the making of compost, but have only a city back yard garden. I can never have a large compost pile, but I do want to turn my garden waste, kitchen parings, lawn clippings and all organic waste into organic manure.

A. *The best method is to dig in such materials as dried blood and bone meal, which can be purchased from fertilizer dealers. It would then be advisable also each year to dig under such material as grass clippings, etc.; thus the soil would get animal as well as plant matter.*

Soil in the Compost Heap

Q. What is the purpose of soil in the compost heap and how is it correctly used?

A. Soil serves as a base to neutralize acids and to absorb the volatile decomposition products. Each layer of the compost heap should have a soil cover not to exceed one-eighth of an inch in thickness. This is hardly more than a film of soil, but it is exceedingly important. Too much soil in the heap interferes with proper aeration and greatly slows down the rate of decomposition.

Making a compost heap is simple indeed, but it is extremely important that it be formulated with as much care as the baker uses in making a choice cake. An improperly made heap usually results in only partly decomposed plant and animal residues. Such incompletely made compost lacks some of the "plant magic" inherent in properly made compost.

Better Than Nothing

Q. Is there any benefit to be obtained by using pulverized sheep manure in my compost pile?

A. Pulverized sheep manure is dehydrated and in the heat developed by the process it is sterilized. If, however, you find it impossible to obtain fresh manure, it is better than not to use any manure at all.

Different Composts

Q. Are all composts of equal value as organic fertilizers?

A. All composts add to the soil the much needed organic matter, but differ in plant nutrients according to the plant and animal residues used in making the compost heap. To make compost having the highest fertilizer value it is well to collect a wide variety of plant materials from different sources, including leaves of deep-rooted trees and natural ground rock powders.

Earthworms for Composting

Q. Which type of earthworm is best for use in a compost pit—domesticated, hybrid, red wigglers or brown-nosed angle?

A. The first 3 varieties mentioned are all manure worms. By brown-nosed angle worm you probably mean the regular type of night crawler. (Worms surely do have picturesque names.)

In order for manure worms to thrive they must live in manure. Sometimes they do well in rich compost that has as much nitrogen as manure. In general, manure worms are best for use in compost heaps. They can be raised either indoors or outdoors, an advantage in the North where winters are cold. Some Florida worm breeders, though, have switched to angle worms or night crawlers. They are larger and more accustomed to working in actual soil. And they are preferred by fishermen.

Many people who breed worms find that sales of bait to fishermen are an important sideline. It helps to have the kind of worms the fishermen want.

Deficiency in Tomatoes

Q. My tomato plants do not appear healthy. The plants are making poor growth and the tips of the leaves at the top of the plants are very yellowish in color. The stems are hard and are deep purple in color.

A. *The symptoms you describe indicate nitrogen deficiency. Apply organic matter which consists of leguminous material (clover, alfalfa, etc.). If the ground is not needed for planting this year perhaps you should grow a cover crop of legumes. After the crop is well established, apply a liberal covering of manure, finely ground raw limestone and finely pulverized phosphate rock. Work the cover crop and other materials added into the surface layer of soil. This practice will increase the nitrogen content, directly through the decomposition of the legume crop and indirectly through rapid increases in the biological activity of the soil organisms, resulting in greater nitrogen fixation from the air.*

Using Tobacco Stems

Q. I would like to know your opinion as to the use of tobacco stems, in large quantity, on citrus grove land.

A. *Tobacco stems or tobacco dust should not be used in concentrated amounts as a mulch. This organic matter may eliminate insects, but it may also kill off beneficial insects, earthworms and soil organisms that convert organic matter into humus. Tobacco materials, mixed with other organic matter in moderation, may be used in mulching or in sheet composting without this danger.*

Improving Alkaline Soil

Q. Is it advisable to use ammonium sulphate to acidify a highly alkaline soil?

A. We do not recommend the use of ammonium sulphate under any circumstances for increasing the acidity of your soil. The harm done to soil organisms will more than cancel any benefits of lessened alkalinity. Instead, add as much green matter or manure to your soil as you can. The green matter acts as a neutralizer, reducing high alkalinity. An acid peat is most effective.

Earth for Composting

Q. Those who have farms can probably not imagine the small city fellow who has no land to draw on for reserves. When I make my compost heap I am always in need of earth. Where shall I get it?

A. When you consider that your compost goes back into your garden you need not be so stingy with your garden earth. Use some of it, possibly digging it out of the walks between your beds or rows, and get it enriched through the composting process. Then you put it back into the garden and see things grow a bit faster. Nothing is lost. You simply practice rotation in a new manner.

Suburban Composter

Q. Could I make a compost heap in a new galvanized garbage can? I have only a small backyard and not much room.

A. A garbage can could be made into an ideal composter. Punch holes in the bottom and in the sides as well as the lid. Place about 4 inches of fertile soil in the bottom of the can. Then layer your material in the same way as for a large heap in the garden. Such a composter is not objectionable even in the best residential parts of the city. If desired, plants can be grown and trained over the can so that it becomes converted into a mound of green leaves.

Any of the great number of organic materials which may be composted in larger heaps are available for use in this manner.

A Composting Problem

Q. Perhaps you can help us with our composting problem. The first year we made compost according to instructions. The second year we tried the short-cut way, and learned our lesson. We found that in order to be worked into the soil the compost must be well decomposed. When the soil is surface mulched during the growing season, it is perhaps best to fall plow or till since the soil seems to be in need of extra air—or at least it is not just right after a long spell of surface mulching.

A. Finished compost is excellent to use on growing plants or when you must plant immediately after applying. Half-finished compost, however, has certain beneficial properties when added to soil which will not be planted immediately. One of these is that nitrogen is fixed from the air by the organisms which are decaying the organic matter. You might be able to compare it to the case of a person receiving predigested foods or foods with plenty of roughage.

Compost Activator

Q. Can old compost and rotted manure be used to hasten the decomposition of a new compost pile?

A. Yes. Compost from an old heap is an excellent activator with which to inoculate a new heap. Manure contains many of the same decomposition microorganisms that compost does and in addition, contains animal hormones that increase decomposition.

What is Green Matter?

Q. In the compost references, there is frequently one dealing with green matter. What do you mean by this expression?

A. By "green matter" we mean really all substances deriving from plants. The better expression would be "plant matter." It includes, first, the left-overs from the kitchen, second, the weeds and culls from vegetable and flower gardening, third, weeds and grass clippings from lawns, meadows, roadsides, etc., and fourth, special plant material gathered for composting, for instance, cannery refuse, spoiled silage, cotton gin refuse, hay, straw, and finally, leaves. These materials contain various minerals, but also large amounts of carbohydrates; they supply therefore energy food for the growing bacteria and are, in the process of being digested, broken down into compost, if also "animal matter" is supplied which adds nitrogen or growth food.

Preparing Compost for Lawn

Q. You've said that compost should be applied to a lawn in the autumn. How should it be prepared, so it won't detract from the appearance of the lawn?

A. Since ordinary compost is much too lumpy for use on lawns, it should be thoroughly ground up. You can use a shredder or a rotary mower for this purpose. If you do not have access to this equipment, place the compost on a wide board and work it back and forth with a hoe until it is shredded very fine. Then work it through a sieve (about ½-inch mesh), the coarser residue being applied to the vegetable patch, or being worked through the sieve again. Organic fertilizers should always be applied in fall; never in spring or winter.

Compost in Basement

Q. We deposit household garbage in boxes in our basement and employ earthworms to assist in the conversion of this material to humus. The garbage is placed in layers 2 or 3 inches deep and covered with a thin layer of sifted compost. We lay newspapers on the compost to conserve moisture. We are concerned because thousands of tiny white bugs have appeared in and around the material. We have been told they are "springtails" but the name does not mean anything to us. Can you tell us what they are, where they come from, and how we may get rid of them?

A. The insects which you rightly call "springtails" are often also known as "silver fish." These insects live in damp places, but feed mostly on paper. I have no doubt that the paper which you use on your compost is entirely responsible for their occurrence. I suggest you use some other mulch to preserve the moisture in your compost heap. A layer of sawdust would serve your purpose and eliminate the "springtails."

Sods and Compost

Q. You mention a compost made from sod. How do you make such compost and wherein does it differ from the Indore method?

A. For gardening purposes we often need a good humus soil that is not too rich in manure. Old-fashioned growers used to prepare such humus by stripping the sod from a pasture and laying the rolls or pieces upside down, building a compost heap consisting of green matter and earth only. No manure was added. As a result, the heap breaks down rather slowly, since the bacteria do not find much nitrogen for their development. They cannot grow so fast as when animal matter is added. The sod heaps will therefore require at least a year until they are broken down. Weed seeds and disease organisms and insect larvae are usually still alive. It is therefore good practice to allow chickens to pick over this kind of compost.

If you add manure in the building process, the heap will heat up, seeds and insect larvae will be destroyed, and the resulting humus will not only be more quickly obtained, but also be richer in plant food. The Indore method applies therefore manure or other animal matter right when the heap is made.

Composting Tops of Glads

Q. Can you tell me how to compost tops from 10,000 gladioli? It takes us 3 years to compost them, so we have been burning them.

A. The best and fastest way to compost the tops would be to shred them before placing them in the heap. Shredding would greatly hasten the decomposition process.

Compost, Not Fire

Q. Organic materials, no doubt, contain elements which if isolated and used separately might be poisonous to the soil, even though they are organic in origin. Take the case of saltpeter which is contained in manure. Many years ago the farmers had a process by which they obtained saltpeter out of manure.

Or take the case of vegetable potash. Some factories take organic material such as seaweed and extract potash out of it for sale. How would such potash compare with chemical potash and how with the seaweed itself in the compost heap?

A. With regard to saltpeter, we can regard this as nothing more than the final result of the mineralization of humus, which under certain circumstances is formed in the soil by natural agency and certainly does the plants no harm.

The question of potash from seaweed is rather different. This operation is not a natural one but the result of burning. The final product, potassium carbonate, often does harm as well as good. Too much of it always ruins the soil texture.

It is always better to deal with these organic materials through the compost heap, from which we get a natural product rather than the unnatural which results from fire.

Corn Cobs

Q. Can corn cobs be used as a mulch or as a raw material for compost?

A. Finely ground corn cobs make an excellent mulch and may be used as part of the green material in the compost heap.

*They may be purchased in this finely ground condition, and
often are used in this form as chicken house litter. Corn cobs
may be ground with any type of cutter, as an ensilage cutter,
cutter type of plant shredder, or hammermill if thoroughly
dry. Corn cobs contain in addition to organic matter 0.02
per cent calcium, 0.04 per cent nitrogen, 0.08 per cent phosphoric acid, and 0.55 per cent potassium.*

Compost Without Turning

Q. I have plenty of material for making compost, and
would like to compost my entire five acre plot. Would I get the
same results if I just pile the materials together and allow them
to remain until they are decomposed?

*A. No. Good compost can be made without turning by
hand if the materials are carefully layered in the heap which
is well-ventilated and has the right moisture content. When
the heat of fermentation has subsided, add earthworms to do
the turning.*

Cotton Combings

Q. Can cotton combings and cotton be used as plant material in the compost heap?

*A. Cotton and cotton combings may be used in the com-
post heap as part of the green matter. In addition to organic
matter they contain 1.32 per cent nitrogen, 0.45 per cent phosphoric acid, 0.36 per cent potash as well as certain trace
elements.*

Earthworms in the Compost Heap

Q. When can earthworms be used for turning the compost
heap?

*A. Earthworms, particularly the manure worm, may be
placed in the compost heap as soon as the heat of fermentation
has disappeared. This can be done by opening the heap here
and there and placing 50 to 100 earthworms in each opening.
They will multiply rapidly and will penetrate the entire heap
and play an important part in converting the plant and animal
residues into compost. When earthworms are used it is not
necessary to turn the heap, although it will require a somewhat
longer time to complete the composting processes.*

Compost for Blueberries

Q. Will you please advise me what materials may be used
to make compost for blueberry land?

A. Blueberries require an acid soil for normal growth and development. Compost for blueberries should be made of plant materials which should include up to 20 per cent sawdust and 10 per cent oak (finely ground, if possible) leaves with such other plant materials as may be available. Instead of using soil in the compost heap, use acid peat. Omit lime or other alkaline soil amendments from the heap.

Compost Pit for Wet Soils

Q. How would you suggest building a compost heap or pit in regions where the water table is within a foot or so of the surface?

A. Proper composting does not take place in the heap if it is so wet that it becomes soggy or sodden. In extreme cases, it is suggested that a pit be made with a cement bottom and rim to shut out excessive water. Before building the heap in such a pit, the cement floor should be covered with from 4 to 6 inches of fertile soil. Upon this soil the heap should then be constructed in the regular way.

Will Heavy Stems Compost?

Q. Will the heavy stems of brussels sprouts, cabbage, and pelargonium break down in the compost heap?

A. Yes, they will break down in a reasonable length of time because they are more or less succulent and watery, that is, the cells of these types of plants are not highly lignified. They are not woody, in other words. Such material like heavy twigs would not break down easily. The stalks of field corn are more fibrous and will take long to decay unless the heap where they are layered is kept unusually wet. Where large quantities of corn stalks, twigs, etc., are to be composted it would be best to put them through a shredder first.

Toadstools in the Compost Heap

Q. Would it be advisable to incorporate the toadstools in my compost heap which are growing in large numbers under my willow trees?

A. Toadstools are especially good for the compost heap as they usually contain copper as well as other of the minor elements.

Composting at the South Pole

Q. Can compost be made in extremely cold climates, such as the South Pole? What, for example, is done with garbage?

A. Getting rid of garbage at the South Pole station has been a knotty problem, but it has finally been solved by, of all things, a compost heap! Ordinary garbage disposal methods didn't work down there. There are no rivers to dump garbage in. Using tractors to haul it miles away would use up too much fuel. But an ordinary compost heap wouldn't work either, because of the extreme cold. So the Navy men dug out with bulldozer a pit 100 yards long and 4 feet deep. They filled it with burnable rubbish and scrap metal and set fire to it. The resulting black ash absorbed the heat of the sun and made things warm enough for bacteria to work. Garbage thrown into the pit gradually composted. In winter, when the sun goes down, the compost idea doesn't work and garbage must be burned.

Slaughterhouse Blood

Q. I can get any amount of blood from a slaughterhouse and wonder if it is good for the compost. It comes from cows and pigs. What should I do with the blood?

A. The blood is wonderful as a source of nitrogen and will activate the breakdown of the plant material easily, if the heap is kept at its regular moisture. Care must be taken to keep dogs and flies off and it is therefore suggested that you use special care with the outside earth covering, which will also prevent odors in the first stage.

If your plant matter can be cut, so that it packs more easily, you can soak the whole material with blood. If the material is stalky or strawy so that blood will run through, you want to be careful again that you wet the plant matter well with blood and that the earth sprinklings are sufficiently heavy to check the running off of blood.

Collecting Compost Materials

Q. Is it preferable to make the heap as the material is collected or to collect the material and then build the heap in one operation?

A. Whatever section of the heap you are building, you should always have enough material to get the proper height so that heating takes place.

You can make small additions to the heap, building on lengthwise, but you want to keep in mind that collected material that has broken down is not yet a complete compost. That it becomes only through the addition of manure or a suitable substitute, that supplies nitrogen, and an addition of phosphate rock or bone meal to add phosphorus, plus the sprinklings of lime and earth.

If you have enough material to add a small section to the standard heap, go ahead and keep on adding the other required things; if not, save enough material and then build a new heap. In either case, the building process will amount to one separate operation.

Pine Bark for Compost

Q. We have unlimited supply of *pine bark* from a local pulp mill and a good source of oak leaves. *Would the bark make good compost?* Would it be desirable to invent a method of pulverizing the bark if it is suitable? Some of the bark has stood for 6 or 7 years in a pile 4 to 6 feet deep and seems to be partly decayed. Would this bark be better than bark fresh from the log?

A. *The pine bark that you mention would be the equivalent of sawdust or wood shavings provided it is pulverized in some way. If you used it without breaking it up fine, it would be very resistant to decay.*

There is a piece of equipment called a bog machine which would make a very fine sawdust-like material or even finer of this bark. The park system of the city of Miami has one and uses it for breaking down palm fronds. They then use this broken down material as a bedding for cows and it is later composted.

There is no doubt that partially decayed bark would be better and decay more readily than new bark.

Bark Under Compost

Q. Would it be good sense to use bark under the soil to hold moisture and then work compost in the topsoil over the bark?

A. *It would not be advisable to use the bark in the soil in the manner you suggest because it will interfere with the bacterial activities in connection with growing crops unless you would put it in a place where you would not grow crops for a few years.*

Charcoal

Q. Is charcoal suitable for compost heaps?

A. *Charcoal is not suitable. It was formerly an organic*

substance but in the charred form this wood is dead. The bacteria have a most difficult time with it. Scientists have proved that a piece of properly charred wood is often capable of withstanding decay for centuries. Do not use charcoal in the compost heap.

Dishwater

Q. It has been recommended that farmers should take their dish water and throw it on their compost heaps. Would that be advisable in view of the strong acids that are contained in soaps?

A. It is not recommended that dish water be thrown on the compost heaps, as this often contains a lot of greasy matter which interferes with the air supply.

Peat Moss Litter

Q. How would peat moss from a chick brooder be to use on my garden?

A. Peat moss from a chick brooder would be very good for the garden, but the inclusion of the chick droppings makes it advisable to compost this litter first before using it. This is especially important with chicken droppings because they have a tendency to burn if used raw.

Location of Heap

Q. I am starting a compost heap and would like your advice as to whether or not it would be better to pick out an open spot where the sun hits it all day long or would I have better results in a shady spot?

A. Compost heaps, if possible should be put in shady spots rather than in open sunlight. It is also advisable to have it protected at least from the north and if possible, from the east and west sides by either hedges, a protective hill-side or some other means.

Muck and Peat

Q. Can you tell me what difference exists between muck and peat?

A. Both substances are the remains of vegetation that has collected in swamps or otherwise moist localities under exclusion of air. The amount of organic matter in the form of carbons present is therefore greater than in any other comparable substance. The fertilizing value of both peat and muck depends to a large extent, first, on the plants which make up the substance and, second, on the amount of sand or clay mixed in.

By peat one properly designates the substance consisting largely of vegetable matter; while muck is either peat decomposed to such an extent that no stems, flowers, leaves, etc., can be recognized or peat which has become mixed with a great enough amount of soil particles to give it an earthy quality.

As a rule, peat is more acid than muck, though the acidity depends both on the plant material from which the substance was originally formed and on the nature of the subsoil as well as the ground water. In English books muck may mean almost anything from manure to compost.

Oyster Shell Flour

Q. Is oyster shell flour as good as ground limestone for the compost pile?

A. Oyster shell flour is just about as good as ground limestone. Both ground limestone and oyster shells consist of about 90 to 95 per cent calcium carbonate. The balance represents various other elements, which vary. For example, lime may be richer in magnesium than oyster shells. On the other hand, the latter, coming from the ocean, would be richer in iodine and other sea-going elements. It would not be a bad idea to alternate using at one time lime and at another time oyster shell flour, if obtainable. In the goiter belt regions, such as Ohio and Michigan, where the soil lacks iodine, oyster shell flour would be especially recommended. The Indians used to accumulate a lot of oyster shells around their camps and knew its value as a fertilizer.

Waste Paper in Compost

Q. You mention that a certain amount of waste paper can be put in the compost pile. Is this simply for bulk and aeration or does paper have mineral value?

A. Regarding waste paper, we do not think that a deliberate effort should be made to put paper into the compost heap, but sometimes where it cannot be helped and some paper does get into the heap, it will not cause much trouble. Paper has been treated with chemicals in bleaching and has poisonous elements in the printing ink but the quantities are so small that it is nothing to worry about.

Peat Moss or Peat Humus

Q. Are peat moss and peat humus alike in fertilizer or soil-improving value? How should each be used?

A. *Peat humus and peat moss are not the same thing. The peat humus contains fertilizer value, whereas peat moss is merely a filler, giving the soil structure and enabling it to retain moisture. It helps in aerating the soil.*

Naturally, if you put too much of the peat moss into the soil, you might reach a point where it would interfere with the growing of plants. On the other hand, peat humus, which contains much organic material, can be used more freely, but there is a danger of using too much, which you would have to tell by observation. A dressing of one inch should be plenty.

Tool for Turning Compost

Q. What is the best tool to use in order to turn the compost heaps?

A. *A five-tine digging fork.*

Weight of Compost

Q. How can you tell the weight of a compost heap?

A. *Sir Albert Howard has stated that one cubic yard of compost (27 cubic feet) weighs a half ton. There is some variation based on materials used.*

Keep Heap from Tree

Q. Can I make a compost heap under a tree?

A. *No. It is best to keep it somewhat away, at least beyond the drip-line of the branches, so that the tree roots do not penetrate the compost heap.*

Water for Garden or Compost

Q. Is there any evidence as to the difference in the value of rain water for garden watering as compared with water from the city water main?

The Bible speaks of "clear shining after rain." It seems reasonable that such water might have greater value than water from the city main.

A. *Rain water is much more valuable for gardening as compared with other waters. Rain drops gather up particles* of dust and microorganisms in their fall through the air. There is much valuable material which comes into the soil through rain, which includes many mineral elements. Municipal water systems use chemical safeguards which are not good for the soil. For that matter they are not good for the persons who drink them either, but they are the lesser of the two evils as far as drinking water is concerned. Pond water, for the same reason is better than tap water, except where there may be factories polluting them.

Handling Seaweed

Q. How should seaweed be handled in making compost?

A. *Seaweed decays readily. Be sure that you wash all of the salt off it. The action of salt on soil is rather sharp. It is very interesting to note that the Germans who have allowed the ocean to come in and flood much soil in Holland have set that land back at least 5 years. Because of the salts in the water, no crop will be able to grow successfully for at least that length of time. Seaweed is a wonderful fertilizer, but we should caution you about giving it a thorough washing.*

Improving Clay Soil

Q. What is needed to change half clay soil into a good rich soil in the shortest time?

A. *It could be done by incorporating as much compost as possible in it. The answer is compost and compost and compost. If the place is not too big, you can put a lot of peat moss in, in addition to compost.*

Some people put sand into a clay soil to get it more porous. That is satisfactory, but it would not be advisable to include coal ashes, which so many persons do in cases like yours, as coal ashes contain strong substances which are not good for the soil. The more compost or humus you can put into the soil, the better.

You might also grow a green manure crop such as rye grass and plow it under in the fall.

Fall or Spring Spading

Q. If I spade in compost in my vegetable garden this fall, will further spading be necessary next spring, or what is the proper procedure before seeding?

A. Spading in compost in the fall does not require another spading in the spring except when the soil is very sticky and cakes. Working with a hoe in spring would be sufficient in most cases.

Steam from Heaps

Q. Is steam coming from compost heap a bad sign?

A. No. It may be expected during the first stage when the internal temperature of the heap goes up to 150 degrees Fahrenheit.

Defining Organic Fertilizers

Q. What are organic fertilizers?

A. An organic fertilizer is one which is made from plant and animal residues. These may be fresh residues, or residues which have accumulated and have been preserved for long periods of time, as peat, marl, and limestone.

Natural Fertilizer Definition

Q. What is a natural fertilizer?

A. A natural fertilizer is one made of some natural earth product which may be processed mechanically but is not treated with acids or other substances to increase its solubility. Phosphate rock, finely pulverized, is a natural fertilizer.

Chemical Fertilizers Explained

Q. What is usually meant by an artificial fertilizer or, more commonly, a chemical fertilizer?

A. An artificial chemical fertilizer is one which is made of some earth product and a strong acid. As an example may be mentioned superphosphate which is made by treating phosphate rock with sulphuric acid. A hundred pound bag of superphosphate includes 50 pounds of phosphate rock and 50 pounds of sulphuric acid.

Raw Organic Fertilizer

Q. What is meant by a raw organic fertilizer?

A. A raw organic fertilizer is one that is made of raw (unfermented) plant and animal residues. Or it may be made of raw organic matter to which have been added such materials as pulverized phosphate rock, potash rock, oyster shell flour, and seaweed which contains most of the elements which are apt to have been leached out of the soil.

Raw Material and Compost

Q. Can a raw organic fertilizer be used exactly like compost?

A. *No. A raw organic fertilizer should be placed on the soil some time before a crop is to be planted. It can be put on the soil as a winter mulch where it will be fairly well composted by spring. Or it should be worked into the soil lightly some months before planting time. During the growing season it could be applied on the top of the soil as a mulch.*

Using Cooked Bones

Q. Are cooked and roasted bones of value to the soil? If so, how should they be applied?

A. *Cooked and roasted bones are of value to the soil, but must be ground up instead of being composted whole. This material should not be applied to the soil without being broken down. If you have a grinding machine, you can utilize these bones; otherwise, it might be more economical to purchase the bone meal.*

Molasses as Fertilizer

Q. Would you recommend using a cheap black-strap molasses in the irrigating water as a source of organic matter? It is the same molasses that is being used to feed cattle. The molasses appears to contain many trace elements. Would the molasses be helpful to the soil?

A. *We would be slow to recommend adding large amounts of molasses to the soil, as it must be regarded as an unfermented material. When raw organic materials are added to the soil, the bacteria which break them down use the available minerals in the soil and may create temporary deficiencies in the soil and thus interfere with the proper development of the crop plants.*

A small amount of this material for trace elements might be added with the winter mulch in late summer or fall or to the materials in the compost heap.

Bone Meal Rich in Phosphorus

Q. What is the value of bone meal in the compost heap or in the soil?

A. *Bone meal is used especially where phosphorus is desired, as its phosphorus content is very high. Bone meal contains only about one per cent nitrogen. If dried blood is used along with bone meal, a good fertilizer is at hand. It might be better to add the bone meal to the compost heap, or to the winter mulch in late summer rather than to the soil at planting time. This will allow time for breaking down the bone meal to forms available to plants.*

Blood Meal Value

Q. Do you recommend dried blood or blood meal as an organic fertilizer?

A. *Dried blood is an excellent material for making compost and for enriching the soil. It contains about 12 per cent nitrogen and from 1 to 5 per cent phosphate. It contains other nutrients as well.*

Kiln Dust Use

Q. Do not regard kiln dust a suitable organic fertilizer?

A. *Not if it contains appreciable amounts of sulphur. Otherwise it would seem to be an excellent soil builder as it contains the oxides of quite a number of plant nutrient elements.*

Leather Wastes Usable

Q. Of what value is leather dust as an organic fertilizer?

A. *Leather dust is a good, compostable material. Its chemical composition varies according to its origin and the nature of the processing to which it has been subjected. The nitrogen content varies from 5.5 to 12 per cent. It also contains considerable amounts of phosphorus, since the ash contains from 2 to 3 per cent phosphorus. In the compost heap, leather dust develops a rather high temperature.*

Horn Dust High in Nitrogen

Q. Can horn dust be used as an organic fertilizer?

A. *Yes. Horn dust contains from 10 to 15 per cent nitrogen in available forms and a relatively high percentage of phosphorus. Horn dust should be applied at the rate of from 3 to 5 pounds per 100 square feet of soil. It will not burn the plants and tends to lighten and loosen the soil.*

Sludge Fertilizer Value

Q. What fertilizing values has the sludge of a city disposal plant?

A. The analysis of the sewage sludge of Allentown, Pa., may be given as a typical digested sewage. This sewage contains 59.95 per cent water, 19.53 per cent organic matter, and 21.52 per cent ash. Its N-P-K formula is 3.12 nitrogen—0.11 phosphorus—0.035 potassium. It also contains trace elements. For instance, it contains 0.00015 per cent copper.

Contribution of Rock Fertilizer

Q. Why are powdered rocks regarded as such valuable soil builders?

A. Powdered rocks contain a large number of the elements which are absolutely essential for normal and healthy plant growth. Some of these, the trace elements, are especially necessary to normal, healthy, disease-free, and pest-free plants. The point is that these powdered natural rocks contain the elements which have been leached out of our agricultural soils during the past 50 to 100 years of modern, although not too intelligent, farming and gardening.

Phosphate Rock Content

Q. What plant nutrients are contained in phosphate rock?

A. The available phosphate rocks contain from 30 to 40 per cent phosphoric acid, from 30 to 50 per cent lime; small amounts of such minor elements as iron, sulphur, and magnesium; and as many as 20 or more trace elements.

Rocks Rich in Potash

Q. What rocks contain potash in natural form?

A. The most common potash-rocks are glauconite or "green earth," and granites. These rocks contain from 3 to 15 per cent potash, small amounts of the other major and minor elements; and a long list of trace elements.

Fertilizer Value of Grains

Q. Various grains have been suggested as organic fertilizers. What fertilizer value have some of the most common grains?

A. The mineral content of some common seeds and grains are given in the accompanying table.

These seeds (ground up) should follow the rules applying to raw organic matter.

Mineral Content of Seeds and Grains

Seed	Calcium %	Phosphorus %	Potassium %	Sodium %	Chlorine %	Sulphur %	Magnesium %	Iron %	Manganese Mg. per lb.	Copper Mg. per lb.
Barley	0.06	0.37	0.49	0.06	0.15	0.15	0.13	0.0008	8.0	5.8
Beans, field	0.15	0.57	1.27	0.09	0.04	0.23	0.17	0.0012	8.4	4.5
Beans, Lima	0.09	0.37	1.70	0.03	0.03	0.20	0.18	0.010	7.3	3.7
Corn, dent	0.02	0.28	0.28	0.01	0.06	0.12	0.10	0.003	2.6	1.8
Cottonseed	0.14	0.70	1.11	0.29		0.24	0.32	0.014	5.5	22.7
Cow pea seed	0.11	0.46	1.30	0.27	0.04	0.25	0.26	0.036	18.2	2.0
Flax seed	0.26	0.55	0.59			0.06	0.40	0.009	26.0	
Kafir grain	0.02	0.31	0.34	0.06	0.10	0.16	0.15	0.001	7.4	3.0
Millet seed	0.05	0.30	0.43				0.16			
Milo grain	0.03	0.28	0.36				0.22	0.005	5.9	7.8
Oats kernels	0.08	0.46	0.39	0.05	0.09	0.20	0.15	0.010	16.8	3.6
Oat grain	0.09	0.34	0.43	0.09	0.12	0.21	0.14	0.007	19.9	3.8
Peanuts—No Hulls	0.06	0.44	0.54	0.56	0.02	0.25	0.18			
Rice, brown	0.04	0.25		0.08				0.001	9.2	1.2
Rice, grain	0.08	0.32	0.34	0.09	0.09		0.14			
Rye grain	0.10	0.33	0.47	0.04	0.02	0.16	0.12	0.008	37.0	3.4
Soy bean seed	0.25	0.59	1.50	0.22	0.03	0.22	0.28	0.008	13.4	7.1
Sunflower seed		0.55	0.66					0.003	9.8	
Sunflower seed, Hulled	0.20	0.96	0.92	0.03	0.01	0.02	0.38			
Wheat grain	0.04	0.39	0.42	0.06	0.08	0.20	0.14	0.006	19.9	3.7

Nutrients in Leaves

Q. What fertilizer values have the leaves of our common trees?

A. *Many trees are deep rooted and absorb minerals from the lower soil levels. These minerals are translocated into the leaves and dropped in the fall. In this way nature replenishes many of the nutrient elements which are leached out of the surface layers of the soil. The nitrogen, phosphoric acid, and potash content of some common leaves are given in the following table:*

Materials	Nitrogen %	Phosphoric Acid P_2O_5 %	Potash K_2O %
Peach Leaves	.9	.15	.60
Oak Leaves	.8	.35	.15
Grape Leaves	.45	.1	.35
Pear Leaves	.7	.12	.4
Apple Leaves	1.00	.15	.35
Cherry Leaves	.6	.11	.72
Raspberry Leaves	1.35	.27	.63
Garden Pea Vines	.25	.05	.7
Red Clover, Green	.55	.13	.5
Vetch Hay	2.8	.75	2.3
Alfalfa Hay	2.45	.5	2.10
Corn Stalks	.75	.40	.9
Immature Grass	1.00	.5	1.2

QUESTIONS AND ANSWERS ABOUT CHEMICAL FERTILIZERS

Effect of Acid Fertilizers

Q. What will a highly soluble acid fertilizer do to the soil?

A. *The soil must be regarded as a living organism. An acid fertilizer, because of its acids, dissolves the cementing material, made from the dead bodies of soil organisms which holds the rock particles together to form soil crumbs. It spoils the friability of the soil. On the surface of the soil such cement-free particles settle to form a compact, more or less water-impervious layer. This compact surface layer of rock particles encourages rain water to run off rather than to enter the soil.*

Artificial Formula Incomplete

Q. Is a formula like 5-10-5 to be regarded as a complete fertilizer?

A. *No. This fertilizer contains the indicated amounts of nitrogen, phosphoric acid, and potash but may lack entirely the essential minor and trace elements.*

Soil Reaction to Chemicals

Q. How does a highly soluble fertilizer like 5-10-5 or superphosphate affect the soil?

A. *A highly soluble fertilizer goes into solution in the soil water rapidly so that much of it may be leached away without benefiting the plants at all. But the sodium in the fertilizer like sodium nitrate tends to accumulate in the soil where it combines with carbonic acid to form washing soda, sodium carbonate. This chemical causes the soil to assume a cement-like hardness.*

Other minerals, when present in large concentrations, percolate into the subsoil where they interact with the colloidal clay to form impervious layers of precipitates called hardpans.

Hardpans and Production

Q. How do hardpans affect crop production?

A. *Hardpans seal the topsoil off from the subsoil. Water cannot pass downward into the subsoil, and water from the water table cannot rise to the topsoil in which the plants are growing. Many plants cannot live when their roots are kept too wet. Then too, the subsoil below the hardpans is anaerobic and rapidly becomes acid. In such anaerobic acid soils, the soil organism population changes radically and in ways which are unfavorable to crop plants.*

Soil Life Killed

Q. In what way does a highly soluble artificial fertilizer harm soil organisms?

A. *Such highly soluble chemicals as chlorides and sulphates are poisonous to the beneficial soil organisms, but in small amounts act as stimulants. These chemicals stimulate the beneficial soil bacteria to such increased growth and reproduction that they use up the organic matter in the soil as food faster than it can be returned by present agricultural practices.*

When chemical residues accumulate in the soil, the micro-organisms may be killed off by hydrolysis (water-removing). The high salt concentration in the soil water will pull water from the bacterial or fungal cells, causing them to collapse and die. Earthworms will also be poisoned by swallowing soil and humus particles coated with chemical residues.

Fertilizers and Food Value

Q. Will the type of fertilizer used influence the amount of vitamins produced by the plants?

A. *Several Experiment Stations have found that supplying citrus fruits with a large amount of highly soluble nitrogen will lower the vitamin C content of oranges. Other vitamins have been experimented with successfully as well.*

Significance of Diseases and Pests

Q. Would you regard susceptibility of plants to diseases and insects as hunger signs?

A. *Yes. Plants which are incomplete in minerals may appear normal externally, but their incompleteness is revealed by the ravages of fungi and insects. Such scavengers do not find organically raised foods to their liking. They will take a few bites of it and then settle down to strip the crops having an oversupply of carbohydrates caused by excessive fertilizing. It is for this reason that disease-producing fungi and insects are regarded as nature's censors. They separate the wheat from the chaff, the nutritious from the deficient.*

Chemicals and Plant Disease

Q. Is it possible that when artificial fertilizers are used, the crops are more susceptible to disease?

A. *Chemical fertilizers rob plants of some natural immunity by killing off the policemen microorganisms in the soil. Many plant diseases have already been considerably checked when antibiotic-producing bacteria or fungi thrived around the roots.*

When plants are supplied with much nitrogen and only a medium amount of phosphate, plants will most easily contract mosaic infections also. Most resistance is obtained if there is a small supply of nitrogen and plenty of phosphate. Fungus and bacterial diseases have then been related to high nitrogen fertilization, as well as to a lack of trace elements.

More or Less Protein?

Q. Will artificial fertilizers produce the same amount of protein in crops that organic fertilizers will?

A. *It has been found that fertilizers that provide quickly soluble nitrogen will lower the capacity of hybrid corn, in particular, to produce seeds with high-protein content.*

Trace Element Deficiency in Crops

Q. Why will crops grown on land continually doped with artificial fertilizers often be deficient in trace elements?

A. *To explain this principle will mean delving into a little physics and chemistry, but you will then easily see the unbalanced nutrition created in artificially fertilized plants.*

The colloidal humus particles are the convoys that transfer most of the minerals from the soil solution to the root hairs. Each humus particle is negatively charged and will of course attract the positive elements such as potassium, sodium, calcium, magnesium, manganese, aluminum, boron, iron, copper, and other metals.

When sodium nitrate, for instance, is dumped into the soil year after year in large doses, a radical change takes place on the humus particles. The very numerous sodium ions (atomic particles) will eventually crowd out the other ions, making them practically unavailable for plant use. The humus becomes coated with sodium, glutting the root hairs with the excess. Finally the plant is unable to pick up some of the minerals that it really needs.

Change in Soil Population

Q. Do artificial fertilizers change the soil organism population?

A. *Yes. Many artificial fertilizers contain acids, as sulphuric acid and hydrochloric acid, which will increase the acidity of the soil. Changes in the soil acidity (pH) are accompanied by changes in the kinds of organisms which can live in the soil. Such changes often are sufficient to interfere greatly with the profitable growth of crop plants. For this reason, the artificial fertilizer people tell their customers to increase the organic matter content of the soil, thus offsetting the deleterious effects of these acids; also to use lime.*

Effect on Nitrogen-Fixing Bacteria

Q. How do nitrogen-containing fertilizers like sodium nitrate and cyanamid affect the nitrogen-fixing soil bacteria?

A. *About 78 per cent of the atmosphere is made up of gaseous nitrogen. Living soil contains enough nitrogen-fixing bacteria to fix enough atmospheric nitrogen to supply abundantly the needs of crop plants. In the presence of soluble nitrates, these bacteria use the nitrogen which man has provided in his artificial fertilizers and fix absolutely none from the atmosphere.*

Aeration Cut by Synthetics

Q. Are artificial fertilizers responsible for poor aeration of the soil?

A. *There are several ways by which artificial fertilizers will reduce aeration of soils. Earthworms, whose numerous burrowings make the soil more porous, are killed. The acid fertilizers will also destroy the cementing materials which bind rock particles together to form crumbs. Lastly, hardpans result which seal off the lower soil levels, keeping them more or less completely anaerobic.*

Young Plants Burned

Q. Why will chemicals burn especially young, growing plants?

A. *The burning is caused by salts pulling water out of the plant cells. When this happens they collapse and the plant turns brown and dies. Older plants have more resistance to this type of burning.*

Phosphate Rock Label

Q. On the label of some raw phosphate rock, I read that it contains 30 per cent phosphoric acid. Does this not mean that the rock has been treated with an acid, and would be harmful to soil life and earthworms?

A. *Due to the influence of the chemical fertilizer people, all fertilizing materials must be analyzed and the contents stated on the bag in regard to the available nutrient elements. The phosphoric acid on the label does not mean that the rock material actually contains this acid. What it really means is that the phosphate if converted to the acid form would have that content of phosphoric acid.*

949

In other words, in stating an analysis of phosphate, the fertilizer law requires that all phosphate fertilizers be expressed in the percentage of phosphoric acid or equivalent phosphorus pentoxide. Similarly, potash is expressed in the equivalent of potassium oxide (K_2O).

Nitrate of Soda Drawback

Q. Since nitrate of soda is a natural product, that is, not manufactured but mined as such, why do you object to it?

A. *In the first place it is too soluble and forces an unbalanced nourishment on the plant, crowding out other essential elements. Secondly, the plant can take the nitrate, but uses very little of the soda because it is a minor element. Thus the soda piles up in the soil and hardens it.*

Farm Composting

Q. To do the most good, compost must be practical to use on a large farm. I would like some information on just how this can be accomplished. Most reports describe results obtained from one or two applications of compost *2 to 3 inches* thick. *Now this seems impossible to accomplish on a farm.* If we were to cover an acre only one inch thick it would take nearly 3500 cubic feet of compost. Now what I would like to know is just *how much does an acre need and how often does it have to be applied to get good results?*

Now in applying barnyard manure, tests show that best results are obtained by using *12 to 20 tons per acre* once every 5 years. Now if we were to get better results by applying the same amount of compost we would need *the finished compost of at least two pits once every few years per acre.* I get this by figuring compost at 61 cubic feet per ton and each pit containing better than 1000 cubic feet. Of course it would take the products of two working pits to make one pit of finished compost. This would give me 16 tons of compost to the acre of land. Now if I had 60 acres under cultivation and made the above application once every 5 years I would have to compost 12 acres on an average every year. If it takes two pits for each acre a total of 24 pits would be needed to do the job.

Now I do not know just what strength or how heavy an application is needed, but if the above set of figures seems correct it would be a rather large undertaking but probably the results would more than repay the efforts. What is your opinion on the above?

A. Naturally, gardeners can make sufficient compost to apply it 2 or 3 inches thick, but on a farm scale when we apply compost at the rate of 10 tons to the acre, you can barely see it. It isn't even consistently half an inch thick, but the soil feels it through its biologic action.

The pit idea of making compost, the way our pits are constructed, would probably apply to a farm of not over 50 acres, but on larger places, there might be batteries of pits. However, in England there is a machine that helps to make compost, which practically has mechanized the compost heaps, and Mr. Sykes, who has written for the magazine from time to time, has used it successfully for making compost for a farm of over 700 acres.

On a farm the compost is usually placed in the corn acreage and a little with a legume. In other words, as you said yourself, perhaps once in 4 years the land would get some compost. There is much to be done yet in the way of learning to apply the "organic" method on the large scale.

The proper handling of manure and sheet composting is, of course, basic to a farm compost program.

Farming with Compost

Q. Mixed stable manure was listed as having 0.50 per cent nitrogen, 0.26 per cent phosphorus and 0.63 per cent potash. How would each of the following types of compost rate in plant food percentages: corn fodder, straw, grass, clover?

It is generally considered that an application of more than 20 tons manure per acre is unwise because the added amount above 20 tons does not seem to effect a further increase in yield. How much compost is needed for maximum yields?

A. If the stable manure is fresh and if the liquid matter is included, the nitrogen content would be definitely higher, also the other constituents. Corn fodder is richer in potash than in nitrogen and phosphorus; so is straw. Clover, when fresh, and young grass are higher in nitrogen than when dried or during the seeding stage. Much depends on the soil in which they were grown, and a general analysis does not mean anything. *By mixing the various materials, chopping down corn fodder and straw, if possible, and adding some manure in the fresh state, you will get excellent compost.*

In truck gardens, sometimes 40 tons of compost are used to the acre in the course of one year, but much depends on what you are planning to grow. You would not put compost on with the small grains. Twenty tons of compost or even of composted manure are quite all right for corn, tobacco, etc. There always remains a residual effect.

So many of the official recommendations seem to take account mainly of immediate cash returns. When a crop does not increase in proportion to the organic material added they advise against adding more, even if perhaps the material is available and should be disposed of. What about the benefit that the soil is going to derive from extra organic matter? What about its looseness and water-holding capacity, its earlier warming, its ease of cultivation and other similar effects that cannot be computed in outright dollars?

If a farmer can plow or disk because his soil is rich in organics he may get a crop where another farmer will fail. By composting and adding organics the farmer makes himself more independent of uncontrollable conditions. Nor let us forget the quality aspect of crops. A premium is paid for compost-grown crops because they are richer in nutrient values. Thus, even if there is no startling sudden increase in quantity, but only a sustained fertility not otherwise to be had, there is always an improvement in quality. This means, for example, that more animals can be fed on the same area, which in turn means greater manure production, which in turn means constant improvement of farm land.

Composting Citrus Orchards

Q. Do citrus trees respond favorably to the use of compost?

A. *Citrus trees grow satisfactorily in any well-drained soil, although they succeed best in a medium loam which is rich in humus. An increasing number of growers are using organic fertilizers exclusively, particularly compost, to fertilize their citrus orchards.*

Citrus trees are mycorrhizal feeders and respond so well to organic fertilizers that growers no longer need to use the poisonous sprays and dusts to control diseases and insect pests. It is important to maintain a high level of organic matter in the soil. Cover crops disked into the soil in such a way that the feeder roots are not injured is a good practice.

Sheet Composting for Citrus Grove

Q. Can we use the sheet composting method on our 22 acres of oranges and grapefruit in southern Texas? It is difficult to make compost in bins because of limited water. However, when we irrigate there is a supply of water under the trees. Our rainfall is about 16 inches a year. There is a good stand of Johnson grass and yellow clover. When would be the right time of the year to sheet compost?

A. Sheet composting would work well in your citrus grove. When your cover crop is mature, spread whatever organic matter and manure you have available under the trees and disk it in. It would be best to do this just before you are ready to irrigate. Then you would not have the problem of keeping the decaying matter wet. For a permanent planting like a grove, it is all right to allow organic matter to decompose while a crop is growing. Mulches would also be practical for your grove, if you have enough material.

Another fertilization practice applicable to orchards is the ring method of compost-making. The compost ingredients are built up in rings around the trees to a height of about two feet. You then have actual compost heaps under each tree. Organic matter would retain its moisture better if more of it is kept in one spot, as in the ring method.

Recognizing and Correcting Hardpans

Q. Our new farm land has a very low spot, quite large, which collects all the drainage from the surrounding area. We were told that this is probably a hardpan condition. Can you tell us just what this is, how it is formed, and what we may do to overcome it?

A. Hardpans are impervious horizontal layers in the soil that exist anywhere from 6 inches to about 2 feet below the surface. A true hardpan is formed by the cementing together of the soil grains into a hard, stone-like mass which is impervious to water. Another common condition is a similar layer in the subsoil caused by the pore spaces becoming filled with fine clay particles. Such "tight clay" subsoils, called claypans, are generally associated with an extremely acid condition.

When hard or claypans exist, the surface soil is completely cut off from the subsoil; no new minerals are added to the lower section; plant roots, often unable to penetrate these layers, usually grow down to them, then extend horizontally over the hard top. This results in shallow-rooted plants that suffer from lack of nutrient elements otherwise available in the subsoil and from unavailable water during dry periods.

If your land is characterized by poor drainage, with water standing in ponds after a rain or with considerable run-off, you have good reason to suspect the presence of hardpans.

The best method of breaking up hardpans is by subsoiling (cutting into the soil with a chisel plow or subsoiler); by incorporating large amounts of organic matter into the soil to make it more loose and friable; by planting deep-rooted cover crops, improving the soil aeration, and encouraging earthworms, a valuable aid in both subsoiling and aerating.

Cover Crop Choice

Q. My soil erodes badly. What is the best cover crop to hold the soil?

A. *If you are troubled with soil erosion, kudzu beans have been proven to be extremely valuable in holding the soil on steep slopes, or where erosion has been found to be severe. The kudzu bean spreads rapidly over the soil, making a very dense growth which protects the soil from wind and water. Kudzu is a valuable soil-improving and forage crop adopted in the Southeast. It is a perennial, leguminous vine brought to this country from Japan. Owing to its vigorous root system and fine growth, kudzu is particularly effective in stopping erosion in gullies and on steep hillsides.*

Controlling Wire Worms

Q. My garden was swarming with wire worms last year. How can I avoid being overrun with them this summer?

A. *Wire worms are the larvae of click beetles, and live in acid soils which are not properly aerated. As a matter of fact, they are good indicators that the soil has become acid through improper aeration. Wire worms often occur in great numbers in an old sod, where they live on grass roots. The soil under the sod is poorly aerated and somewhat acid.*

To control wire worms, aerate the soil and enrich it with compost. Soil organisms in the compost will bring the insect under control. It is poor practice to plant a cultivated crop in a field that has had sod on it for a long time.

Aeration of the soil can be increased by breaking the hardpans in the subsoil. On a farm scale, this is best done by use of a subsoiler, by planting deep-rooted cover crops, and by increasing the organic matter in the soil so that it will contain a numerous population of earthworms, who also specialize in subsoiling and aerating.

Method for Large Orchards

Q. Is the organic method practical in big orchards?

A. *Absolutely. Figure out the tremendous cost of chemical fertilizers and sprays and the cost of the equipment to apply the sprays. Add to that the cost of counteracting other evils of the chemical method such as sprays to prevent fruit from falling, cost of hand pollination because the bees have been sprayed out of the picture and you will see how much money there is left for making compost.*

Cesspool Overflow

Q. I have a large cesspool about 30 feet back of my house, which catches everything from the home. This cesspool has an overflow pipe running down a hill about 200 yards from the house. The overflow from the barn meets this overflow pipe about 100 yards from the end.

If I put a 500-gallon tank at the end of this line, will I be able to use this overflow safely for watering my garden and my compost pile?

A. *By no means use this water on the garden. It contains undecayed elements that would be dangerous. Apply it to the compost heap and be sure it is thoroughly composted.*

Reducing Soil Alkalinity

Q. I find that the soil in my garden has a pH of slightly over 7 and I have learned that some crops require a slightly acid soil.

Can you recommend any treatment, consistent with the principles of organic gardening, that would slightly reduce the alkalinity of my soil?

I have heard that magnesium sulphate, ammonium sulphate, aluminum sulphate and tannic acid may be used for this purpose.

I would be glad to have your comments on these chemicals, particularly as to their relation to the principles of organic gardening, and also any recommendations you wish to make in regard to soil acidification.

A. *Your solutions would be to put plenty of compost into the soil made in your case without using lime or wood ashes. But many plants require an alkaline condition. For them you would have to use lime.*

We certainly would not recommend any of the chemicals that you suggest, as some of them are notoriously bad actors in the soil. Ammonium sulphate is actually recommended by the government for killing earthworms.

Also any chemicals, which are sulphates, give rise to bacteria of a destructive kind which destroy beneficial fungi in the soil.

Sawdust and leaves are mildly acid but it is never advisable to put raw materials like this into the soil, but to compost them first.

Improving Muck Soil

Q. What is the best way to handle muck land in organic farming?

A. *Muck land is rich in organic matter, but even so it can become quite infertile after being cropped for many years. Minerals are what is needed most, and can be supplied through ground rock fertilizers, like phosphate rock and granite dust. However, adding more organic matter can also be of help, as the humus in muck soil is often old and leached out so that it does not give life to the soil like manure or compost.*

Trouble with Monoculture

Q. How can we prevent disease or insect damage under the present system of raising single crops?

A. *Your problems of preventing insect and disease infestations are more difficult if you raise only a single crop, year after year. The answer, in part, to that question is that if your soil fertility is built up, insect attacks will be less troublesome. However, by rotating crops you will also do a lot to eliminate insect trouble. Author Edward Faulkner in Elyria, Ohio, has done some excellent work with truck crops grown under natural conditions. You might also be interested in his book,* Soil Development, *which is available from the University of Oklahoma Press in Norman, Oklahoma.*

Speeding Straw Decay

Q. How can I hasten the decay or rotting of a large straw stack, so that it is suitable for mulching or sheet composting?

A. *A good way to hasten the decay of a straw stack is to make holes in it with a rod and pour in quite considerable quantities of manure water or water filtered through a com-*

post heap. Such water will supply the bacteria and nitrogen that the straw needs to decay properly and quickly.

Grubs in the Compost Heap

Q. This year we have found white grubs in our compost heap and leaf mold. Can you identify these and tell us what can be done about them?

A. *The white grubs sometimes seen in a compost heap are usually those of the common fly and may be ignored. Most of these do not hatch because flies are rarely found around well-made composts, especially where care is taken to see that a layer of earth at least two inches thick completely covers the heap. If white grubs are in the interior of the pile, the heat will kill them off—as it will with other insect eggs. When a compost heap is turned, see that the outside layers are placed on the inside, thus destroying such grubs.*

Chapter 26

COMPOST AND THE LAW

Making compost on a garden or farm scale violates, of itself, no law whatever. While individual states vary somewhat in regulations *related* to composting, no state in all 50 of the nation legally prohibits the practice as such.

It would, of course, be an indefensible contradiction of the basic principle of soil conservation for a government at any level to restrain or prevent the return of needed organic matter to the land. At the same time, where actual danger to health results from *malpractice*—or, in other words, from improperly made compost—the responsibility of government is clear. Here, then, is where some of the regulations relative to compost-making appear. A number of others are primarily concerned with the commercial production and sale of compost.

TWO MAIN RESTRICTIONS

Through a state-by-state survey, it was found that practically all composting limitations or restrictions fall into one or the other of the two categories just mentioned: commercial manufacture and distribution, and public health danger.

Nearly every state has what is generally termed a "Commercial Fertilizer Law." In part, these stipulate requirements for registration, grading, labeling and selling all products intended "to supply food for plants or to increase crops produced by land." In order for such products to meet the law and be sold in most states, they must be registered with the agriculture department, show that they maintain various minimums of plant nutrients (NPK), and be labeled in accord with the particular state's code, usually to include a guaranteed analysis of these major fertilizer values. Other provisions in most states limit the percentage of inert matter permitted, instruct that any toxic or "injurious" ingredients included be identified, their quantities listed, and adequate directions for use and warnings against misuse be given.

Regulations such as these apply, of course, only where a product is manufactured or processed *to be sold*. Making compost for your own use is *not* governed by the "fertilizer law" in any state. If you plan to distribute a compost product commercially, your wisest first step is to check with the agriculture department in your own state to determine its requirements. Some states do not consider compost—along with various other materials such as limestone, gypsum and manure—as a "commercial fertilizer" at all. A number of them direct that these be called "soil amendments," "soils-improvement mixtures," "manipulated manures" or a similar designation, and insist that they be tagged as "not a plant food product." Again, it is important to emphasize that any state's fertilizer-law provisions control only products actually marketed. None of them affects preparation and use of compost or other fertilizer material for yourself.

Protecting Public Health

The other half of the legal aspect to composting concerns itself with avoiding any "health hazards" which may be involved. This segment is of far more significant and frequent consequence to the usual home gardener or farmer making compost than the legislation regarding fertilizer trade. Yet, *there need never be any difficulty or conflict at all regarding the health-protective statutes anywhere*. The one important thing to keep in mind is that *properly made* compost breaks no rules, endangers no one's health, and legally offends nobody.

Along with adequate care in his compost-making, the organic gardener should give thought to the placement of his heap, bin or pit. Courtesy and good judgment shown to neighbors should follow naturally. This compost pit of building tiles, made by E. S. Bennett of Ottawa, Kansas, is an example of considerate planning.

Quite the contrary, as shown clearly throughout this book, it is of irrefutable value to all plants and soils—and therefore *beneficial* to everyone who derives life from the land.

Almost all states have sections within their Sanitation or Health Codes dealing with waste disposal and public welfare as it may be affected by this. Most often, the latter is called a "nuisance" regulation. It is essential to understand that by a "nuisance" these laws do *not* mean something which is simply "annoying" or an arbitrary "bother" to anyone. In this instance, the legal terminology specifically designates a "nuisance" to mean a condition *dangerous to health* or a likely hazard to personal or public well-being.

A look at one state's wording may help make this clear. The Texas General Sanitation Law (1945) defines a nuisance as: "Any object, place or condition which constitutes a possible and probable medium of transmission of diseases to or between human beings."

Under the provisions of most of these statutes, the state may restrict a composting project or prosecute a violator (to the extent of the particular state's edict) if any of the following conditions, for example, were found to exist:

1. Sewage, human excreta, waste water, garbage or other organic wastes deposited, stored, discharged or exposed in such a way as to be a potential instrument in the transmission of disease.

2. Storage or disposal of any wastes whatever in such manner as to cause pollution of any water supply or contaminate surrounding land to the extent of endangering the public health.

3. Human wastes, bodies of dead animals, refuse, etc., kept or left within certain distances (usually about 300 to 500 feet) of any street or highway so as to create a nuisance (threat to health).

4. Any wastes, garbage, manure, etc., maintained in such a way as to become a breeding place for flies, mosquitoes or other disease-carrying insects, so as to cause infection of such pests, or so as to attract and harbor rats, mice and so forth.

Your home garden or farm composting *will not* create any of these conditions if it is handled with even a moderate amount of care and attention. Following any of the recommended methods (see Composting Methods for the Gardener and Composting Methods for the Farmer) will make certain that:

1. There can be no "transmission of disease" through your compost. Using any heap or pit composting method correctly, the heat promptly generated brings temperatures more than high enough to kill all pathogenic organisms (disease-causing bacteria) which may—or may not—be present in the raw materials being composted.

2. There can be no "pollution of any water supply or contamination of surrounding land." Properly made, no part of a compost heap ever enters a water supply, pond, lake, river, etc. Neither can it "contaminate" any type of soil, adjacent or otherwise, since any harmful bacteria are readily destroyed in the composting process.

3. Regardless of *where* compost is made, it cannot be-

Without being an eyesore, this brick compost pit serves its utilitarian purpose for city-gardener E. W. Crandall. Placed conveniently against a terrace wall, and partly screened by bushes, it can be kept neat and unobtrusive. Proper composting prevents odors, insect or animal attraction, and all other needless health hazards.

come a "nuisance" of any sort, especially in the legal sense of creating a threat to health, when the practice is correctly followed. Naturally, it is only sensible for a gardener or farmer to use good judgment and courtesy in the placement of his heap. Almost invariably, it is to his own advantage to keep it a reasonable distance from any thoroughfare. In heavily populated areas he should, of course, be considerate of a neighbor's landscape or home as well as of any business establishments and public buildings. A well-kept compost heap *does not* produce objectionable odors of any kind—so there can be no contention on that point. Neither is there ever any need for it to be an eyesore. As for animal bodies, few composters include them. Those who do must be adequately cautious to see that they are incorporated properly and do not lead to any potential complaint or danger.

4. Made right, no compost draws flies nor any other insects, rodents, or animals. The conditions favorable

to attracting, breeding or infecting such pests are contrary to those established in composting correctly. The heat, layering and rapid decomposition of the organic matter being composted are biologically unfavorable to insect life, while these same factors, along with a proper layer system, cover or enclosure, very effectively prevent any animal attraction.

Control Mostly Local

Practically every state leaves the general application of its health laws in the hands of local authorities. Each city or town has, usually, a board of health and a health inspector. Seeing that the regulations are upheld, attending to complaints and making inspections and rulings are their responsibilities. Ordinances and usage in different communities may vary slightly, but in general the legal pointers regarding composting adhere quite closely to what has been discussed.

Recourse to Court

A gardener or farmer who has a complaint placed against him in connection with his compost is not compelled to accept the decision of a health board or inspector. His legal rights entitle him to take the matter to court. If his composting is done properly, if he believes it violates none of the specific legislation of his area (especially any of the infractions detailed here), he certainly may seek a court's opinion.

Frequently, a complaint is the result of a cantankerous neighbor or an over-zealous inspector. Where this is the case— and there actually is no breach of the law nor of reasonable consideration for others—he would serve his own interests and those of other gardeners in his community best by appealing to a court. A considerable number in many sections of the country have done this successfully.

COMPOST GOES TO COURT

In 1952, for example, a case came to the Dearborn, Michigan, Municipal Court, concerning whether a compost box was a nuisance. The definition of the court stated that a nuisance meant something "detrimental to the health and safety of the neighbors." It was the City Health Department that seemed to have a desire for a ruling on the desirability of compost piles in general. One of the witnesses was Mrs. George Bouton,

Director of the Detroit Garden Center and Instructor for the University of Michigan in gardening, because for several years she had advocated composting to her pupils, and the owner of the compost pile in question was one of her pupils.

The judge wanted the case to be settled out of court, but there was quite a violent argument between the two neighbors, especially on the question of adding garbage to the compost box, so that the case had to come formally to the court for adjudication.

The opposition could not prove that there were rats in the vicinity of the box caused by the garbage. Mrs. Bouton testified that she had been composting for 25 to 30 years and that she had received excellent results in her gardening because of it, admitting that she had put into her compost box such things as tomatoes, cabbage leaves and other vegetable garbage from her household.

The judge would not rule on the case until he, himself, went to see the compost box, the alleged atrocity, which was a nice-looking wooden affair screened by sunflowers and covered with vines. The week following he issued his verdict— "Not guilty of maintaining a nuisance."

REPORTS FROM STATES

In the state-by-state survey made to determine the laws and interpretations pertaining to composting throughout the country, many interesting facts and sidelights were discovered. Replies from very cooperative agriculture and health departments across the nation—and, in fact, even beyond the Pacific to the State of Hawaii—proved helpful in preparing this summary.

Some of the information and ideas included can be passed along by quoting portions of several of these responses:

Alabama

General public health laws give boards of health legal authority to abate public health nuisances of any kind. The public health significance of a composting process would probably hinge upon the production of flies, rats, or other disease vectors. If a public nuisance were created, whether or not it was a public health nuisance, people affected would have legal recourse either by injunctive processes or perhaps in some instances there might be grounds for damage suits.

963

Municipalities in the State have adopted various ordinances dealing with the keeping of livestock, the handling and disposal of manures and other wastes. These municipal ordinances apply primarily to urban areas and to some extent to the police jurisdiction area surrounding incorporated cities.

California

The sale of fertilizing materials in California is subject to the provisions of the Agricultural Code of California. Fertilizing materials are classified by contents into 5 names, i.e., commercial fertilizers, agricultural minerals, manures, auxiliary plant chemicals, and soil amendments. Organic refuse or vegetable waste usually comes within the class known as soil amendments.

We consider that compost means mixtures of vegetable wastes to which superphosphate and nitrogenous fertilizers were added to aid decomposition and to provide feed for nitrifying bacteria. Such a mixture of material and organic substances occurring from this type of composting are classified as agricultural minerals or commercial fertilizers depending on the analysis. Both of these classifications require registration of the specific materials and labeling.

There are no laws or regulations, to our knowledge, that pertain to sale of rotted or aged vegetable waste to which no plant food material was added. Any material sold as compost which is a mixture of added material and organic substances must be labeled with the information required and must meet the plant food guarantee required on the label.

Florida

Nuisances injurious to health: Filth, the contents of cesspools, offal, garbage, foul water, dye-water, refuse from manufactories, urine, stable manure, decayed animal or vegetable matter, or other offensive substance detrimental to health, thrown, placed or allowed to remain in or upon any private premises, street, avenue, alley, sidewalk, gutter, public reservation or open lot within any incorporated city or unincorporated town or village of the state, are declared nuisances injurious to health, and any person who shall commit, create or maintain the aforesaid nuisances, or any of them, shall upon conviction be fined not less than 5 nor more than 25 dollars for every such offense.

Georgia

Please be advised that Georgia has no specific laws covering home manufacture of compost.

Hawaii

As far as we know, there are no state laws, Health Department regulations or county ordinances at present for the control of compost-making in the new State of Hawaii.

The composting of the city's garbage has been discussed, but has not been attempted or studied.

Mr. Archie E. Erickson of the Oahu Prison in Honolulu has a study project on compost-making at the prison that has been going on for a number of years and is actively engaged in this work at the present time.

Illinois

At the present time there are no state laws devoted to the regulation of composting in Illinois. In Illinois, statutes provide municipal officials with authority for the regulation and disposal of refuse. The statutes prohibit the discharge of refuse from one community within a mile of the corporate limits of another community. In addition, county and township boards of health are authorized to make all regulations which may be necessary for the promotion of health or the suppression of disease within their jurisdiction.

Louisiana

The only law that pertains to this activity, to our knowledge, is the one dealing with fertilizer grades that can be registered.

Maine

To my knowledge there are no legal restrictions in this state pertaining to the production and use of garden composts.

Minnesota

Please be advised that the Minnesota Department of Agriculture does not have any regulations in regard to compost-making, however our Minnesota fertilizer law does have rules and regulations relating to the definition, labeling and distribution of soil conditioners. Composts may or may not come within these rules and regulations, depending upon the claims which are to be made.

Mississippi

Under the general and discretionary powers accorded by the statute, the State Board of Health has had no occasion to refer to composting except in reference to the use of human excreta and undigested sludge for fertilizing purposes.

It is entirely possible that composting at any given time might be carried out by either individuals or industrial operations to the point of constituting a health menace. The general and discretionary powers to take action in the public interest is clear in this regard. Up to the present time, however, we have no record of any specific action occasioned by the act of composting itself. All the references which bear indirectly in this regard relate to the industrial type of waste disposal in connection with various aspects of animal husbandry or waste disposal processing plants. These wastes, of course, should have been used in composting.

It is entirely possible, and even probable, that local ordinances, particularly of municipalities, may carry some specific prohibition against compost piles or other restrictions of a similar nature which might be ruled to include composting. To our knowledge, there has been no action occasioned in this area from the simple act of composting itself.

It would appear, therefore, that properly operated composting procedures for home gardeners or farmers would not constitute a public health menace.

New Mexico

The New Mexico State College at College Park, New Mexico, is the official agriculture agency of the State of New Mexico. In this respect, they make analyses on all fertilizer products that are labeled. This is required for a permit for the sale of labeled fertilizers in the state, and the agricultural inspection division of the College should be contacted if further information is desired.

Where composting of municipal sewage sludges is involved, heat treatment is necessary for safe use as a general fertilizer. Otherwise, the New Mexico Department of Public Health recommends that sewage sludge not be used for fertilizing home vegetable gardens or for commercial truck crops.

This is particularly true where vegetables or fruits are eaten in the raw state.

On the other hand, we encourage the use of sewage sludge as a soil builder and fertilizer for lawns, shrubbery, and other crops. Wide use of air-dried sewage sludge is being made in the State of New Mexico for fertilizing municipal parks and golf courses.

New Jersey

There is nothing in the New Jersey Statutes explicitly dealing with compost-making. We do have sanitary regulations dealing with the piling up of vegetation and/or other materials in such a manner as to constitute a nuisance.

Most of the problems that arise in connection with this matter come about as a result of people including garbage and other items that would permit the attraction of flies and rodents. Strictly speaking, a compost pile properly handled should not present any problem.

North Carolina

The North Carolina Fertilizer Law sets forth the legal aspects of your proposition, to such extent as falls within the jurisdiction of this Department.

You will observe that in the main the law applies to the registration, labeling and sale of composts. Involved also are considerations that the components of such products result in a commodity fully suitable for the purposes inferred.

North Dakota

We are not aware of any Village or Municipal Ordinances that specifically refer to composting. In this relatively dry atmosphere here in North Dakota the practice is generally not in use.

Ordinances are very specific in that the storage of organic matter that may feed or harbor rats or produce flies is illegal.

Oregon

The state of Oregon has no laws, rules, or regulations concerning the use of composting as a means of solid waste disposal.

Pennsylvania

We are not aware of any local or state ordinances or regulations which pertain specifically to composting. However, the majority of local governments have regulations pertaining to control of nuisances resulting from the improper storage and disposal of refuse. Backyard composting improperly conducted would be under the effect of this type of regulation.

Rhode Island

We in this department, have never considered compost as a fertilizer. Therefore, it does not come under the Rhode Island Fertilizer Law.

We and our "technical advisor," Professor John B. Smith, Head of the Department of Agricultural Chemistry at the University of Rhode Island, are of the opinion that compost supplies organic matter, and improves soil structure, etc., but that additional fertilizer is required for good crop growth.

However, some organic gardeners disagree and recommend sufficient compost to make fertilizers unnecessary.

Nevertheless, we do not include it under our definition of fertilizer unless fertilizer elements are claimed.

South Carolina

To my knowledge we have no laws or regulations pertaining to compost-making in this state. In most instances which I am familiar with the homeowner simply piles leaves, grass and other litter in a pile and adds a little commercial fertilizer or nitrogen material or phosphate just to decompose it. I feel sure, however, if this pile of waste began to create undesirable odors, the local health authorities would object and require them to move it or else treat it.

If any commercial concern begins to market compost-making claims for nitrogen, phosphoric acid and potash, then it would come under the fertilizer laws of this state and would be required to be labeled and the tax, inspection and registration fee charged.

South Dakota

Please be advised that there appears to be two specific areas which may have some legal application to compost-making. These requirements are: (1) that fly-breeding areas may be declared as a public nuisance and (2) if a compost pile has drainage into a receiving water or into sub-surface waters this may constitute water pollution control and therefore be subject to regulations and laws.

Except for these above suggested limitations, compost-making is not controlled in South Dakota.

Texas

The regulation of compost-making in the municipalities in this State would come within the jurisdiction of local authority. There possibly could be local municipal ordinances of which we are not cognizant.

The State does not regulate the composting of organic materials as such. However, there have been instances in which this activity has created conditions that come within the scope of the Texas General Sanitation Law.

Utah

The Utah Fertilizer Materials Law would not apply to the manufacture of compost, but such materials would be subject to the law after their manufacture and before distribution within the state.

There are no laws which deal directly with the manufacture of compost products within the State of Utah; however, such a process as composting may be subject to the public nuisance section of the Utah Code. This section empowers cities to "declare what shall be a nuisance and abate the same, and impose fines on persons who may create, continue or suffer nuisances to exist."

Vermont

The Vermont laws do not specifically mention compost-making but it is very likely that the laws on waste disposal may be related at least indirectly. There is a law which prevents any "dead animal or any animal substance" to be left unburied within 500 feet of a dwelling or highway. This would clearly indicate that there could not be any "animal substance" in a compost pile. Also the law on pollution control would prohibit the accumulation of compost or refuse where it could impair the quality of a source of water supply.

The laws also protect the practice of cultivating or using the soil "in the ordinary methods of agriculture if human excretement is not used thereon."

There is also a state law which gives a town health officer authority to make inspections and issue orders where he has any reason to suspect that anything exists which may be detrimental to public health. I believe that in the process of compost-making it would be necessary to take proper precautions to carry on the process correctly so that the question of nuisance conditions or potential health hazards would not become a source of continuous complaint to town health officers.

West Virginia

In the State of West Virginia we do not have a separate law governing composting. In the event composting or compost-making should create a nuisance or create a health hazard, then the situation is controlled or abated under the provisions of our general law governing the disposal of waste or offensive material.

A few of our cities and towns have ordinances pertaining to composting.

Wisconsin

This state does not have provisions at state level concerning the topic of compost. It is within the governing right of local communities to establish ordinances for the regulation of composting. Thus, it is possible that some Wisconsin communities may be regulating the matter. Certainly any gardener proposing to compost waste material should check with his local government to determine if there is a regulation to be followed.

A LAWYER'S OPINION

There can be no real conflict between the law and organiculture. The law has for its primary and most important object the welfare and well-being of humanity. Organiculture seeks the same object. So, basically, it is impossible for these two fields of human endeavor which have such a common aim to be really opposed to each other.

And yet we find this question frequently posed: "Has a representative of a Board of Health the authority to prevent a citizen from building a compost heap in connection with making organic fertilizer for his garden?" This cannot be answered with a categorical yes or no. But the writer will try to suggest an answer to this question which will be a practical solution to the problem based on the principle that a lawyer's true function is to keep people out of trouble with

In Loveland, Ohio, gardener Milton Smith not only chose a desirable site for his cinder-block compost area, he added an unusual decorative touch. As seen here, two of the corners are topped by very attractive (and practical) strawberry barrels.

the law rather than to get them out after they are involved with it.

We start out with a basic proposition of the law, i.e., that I have the right to use my land in any way I please. But this is immediately subject to the qualification found in the legal maxim "Sic utere tuo ut alienum non laedas" (Enjoy your own property in such a manner as not to injure that of another person).

Now, we organiculturists can see nothing harmful to anyone in a compost heap and the law has recognized it as a garden necessity so every gardener should be permitted to maintain one. As long ago as 1871 a Connecticut court had this to say:

"It is essential to the successful cultivation of a farm that the manure produced from the droppings of cattle and swine fed upon the products of the farm, *and composted with earth and vegetable matter taken from the land,* should be used to supply the drain made upon the soil in the production of crops, which would otherwise become impoverished and barren."

(Haslem vs Lockwood 37 Conn. 500)

Why then is there any basis for this apparent conflict between the law and organiculture? It is because to the ordinary citizen a compost pile suggests something unwholesome, unsightly and noisome. He cannot distinguish between a compost pile and the messy manure piles which all of us have seen at one time or another. If there is any basis for complaint against a compost heap it will be because of its effect on your neighbor's sensibilities—either olfactory or ocular.

If you build your compost heap so that it becomes smelly or in such a place that it constantly forces itself upon the attention of passersby or your neighbors, then you are inviting trouble with the authorities. I must pause at this point to observe most strongly that *a compost heap which is giving off foul odors persistently has violated the first law of composting.* In all the literature on composting you will find a constant reiteration that a properly built compost heap will be almost odorless. So aside from any legal consequences, you are most surely going against organic principles if your compost heap is foul smelling.

The writer has thoroughly searched the laws in his own state and can find no specific prohibition against compost piles and will venture to say that no such prohibitions exist in other jurisdictions. A compost pile has no intrinsic objectionableness. As pointed out above, the courts have recognized composting as an essential part of good husbandry and good husbandry is the backbone of a nation. The objection to composting can only be found when it is not properly managed, resulting in foul odors or unpleasant appearance. When this happens it falls afoul of the law by becoming subject to the general prohibition against nuisance found in all jurisdictions and violates the legal maxim quoted above.

In every well-ordered society the state must act as umpire to the extent of preventing one man from using his property or rights so as to prevent others from making a corresponding full and free use of their property and rights. The owner's right to maintain a nuisance on his own property is limited by the rights of other people not to be jeopardized or prejudiced by its proximity.

Accordingly, there exists in the state the so-called "police-power" which is an inherent right on the part of government to prevent misuses of property which are unfair to adjoining owners. So it is the opinion of this writer that your compost pile can be legally attacked only on the grounds that it is a "nuisance." But it is not a nuisance *per se* and your own actions will determine whether or not it really is a nuisance. The declaration by a board of health that a particular thing is a nuisance will not make it such, if in law it is not a nuisance and the question of nuisance is still open to determination in the courts. They and not the board of health have the final word in condemning a compost pile, in which case your compost pile will be "Exhibit A" in the evidence and it should escape condemnation if you have properly built and maintained it.

So much for the law applicable to the question. We now face the problem of resolving or reconciling any apparent conflict. How can we maintain our compost piles and still not run afoul of the law? The answer is fairly simple—obey the basic laws of organiculture and you will at the same time obey the law of the land.

First, follow the complete directions for making a compost pile. If this is done, you will have a heap which will give off very little odor at first and will quickly lose all noticeable odor. You thus remove the first and probably the greatest objection that your neighbors might have to your composting— foul odors. Secondly, build your heap in the most inconspicuous part of your land, as far removed from the vision of neighbors or passersby as it is possible for you to do. Unless your plot is a very large one (in which case you are probably out in the country where a board of health will never bother you), it will not add many steps to your labors if you build your heap in a corner or in a pit. Having put your heap as far out of sight as is possible, why not further withdraw it from attention by letting some fast-growing vine or, better still, a melon or cucumber vine, clamber over it? This will make an excellent camouflage and may reward you with some fruit.

The health officials are not likely to go out of their way to bother with your compost pile. They have too many far more important duties to attend to. They will probably never take any positive action against a composter unless they are prodded by complaints from neighbors. Even then you will be given an opportunity to correct the condition complained of before being hauled into court and if the complaint is justifiable then common sense dictates that you do so.

But suppose that despite all your efforts to follow the rules of good organic gardening and good taste you are still opposed by a board of health official. What then? There is nothing else for you to do but fight it out in the courts. The board of health is not the last word in the matter and you are entitled to your day in court to have your right to garden organically tested out. If you are composting in the prescribed manner and are maintaining your compost heap in such a way that no neighbor can reasonably complain because of odor or unsightliness, you are not violating the law. No one could seriously contest your right to have a garden on your own land and all that goes with its proper maintenance. Subject to the limitations herein expressed you have every right in the world to maintain a compost heap on your land and you should defend your right to do so if it is ever unjustly attacked.

—VINCENT C. TYMANN

HEALTH AND COMPOST

In the British Medical Journal of September 29, 1956 there is a review of the wonderful book by H. B. Gotaas, entitled *Composting, Sanitary Disposal and Reclamation of Organic Wastes* (World Health Organization, Geneva), and I will quote a portion of it:

"The high temperatures that develop in large aerobic heaps of compost are above the thermal death point of the common pathogens (disease producers) and parasites, and Gotaas states that 'the magnitude and duration of the high temperatures, as well as the antibiosis which is characteristic of a mixed population of microorganisms, provide a sound basis for believing that no pathogens, parasites or parasitic ova survive the aerobic composting process.' The efficient mixing of refuse aids greatly in ensuring that all the material composted is subjected to temperatures of about 60 degrees centigrade, long enough to destroy pathogens and weed seeds, and greatly reduces the number of flies which breed in compost heaps that are poorly made and not mixed. There are no recorded cases of disease arising from the use of habitation waste in agriculture in Great Britain."

In spite of the well-known fact that properly made compost heaps offer no threat to the health of the community, there have been many over-ambitious health officers who have forced their removal from peoples' gardens, on the grounds that they spread disease. The sad part of it is that by doing this the health inspector is actually contributing to the causation of disease, because many persons are using compost to grow healthier vegetables — vegetables that contain more vitamins.

Another proof that being in the vicinity of compost is not unhealthy was in a visit I made to a compost making plant in the city of San Salvador in Central America. Here there were dozens of workers in an indoor compost factory under tropical conditions. What could be a better example!

There was an interesting experience in connection with the health of the workers in the larger plant. A physician connected with the public health felt that working in this compost plant would be dangerous to the health of the workers. For 4 years, therefore, he came regularly to observe, but was amazed to find that in the entire period not one cut or wound of a worker developed into an infection, and that the general health of the workers was excellent—much better than the average of workers generally in El Salvador. The management feels that there are antibiotics in the compost particles floating in the air, that are breathed in by the workers.

THE PRINCIPLE OF EMINENT DOMAIN

There is a certain term that is applied, in the study of civics and government, to the public interest. It is called *eminent domain*. What is this principle? It is that the public as a group is more important than the public as an individual. To give one example: Suppose you live in a home which has been in your family for 6 generations. It has sacred memories and nostalgic associations. But the government has decided that in the public interest a road must run through that house. Nothing can prevent it from carrying out its purpose, but of course you will be given a fair price for your property.

Another example: Suppose you live in a built up area of a city and build a compost heap in your back yard. The Board of Health may tell you that you will have to do away with it as they say it is a health menace and may bring disease to your neighbors. They apply the principle of *eminent domain*. The freedom of action of one individual must be subordinated to the general interest of the community. In this case the Board of Health is absolutely wrong. A correctly made compost heap is no health menace and will not draw flies. Those health boards are actuated by the fact that a manure heap may draw flies, but there is all the difference in the world between a manure pile and a well-made compost heap.

There are two ways to correct the situation. One—education. If you have been the victim of such action by a Health Board give us the name of the official in charge and we will go to work on him with the necessary literature to show him that health boards should actually encourage the making of compost heaps. In the long run it will bring community health. Two—court action. Your health officer is not the court of last resort in this democratic country of ours, but unfortunately it will cost you money. I believe that the average judge will preserve to you your sacred right of making a compost heap.

Chapter 27

BOOKS AND PUBLICATIONS ON COMPOSTING

The following is a list of complete books, reference texts, periodical publications and other articles or bulletins which discuss various aspects of composting. A considerable number of these have been used in preparing the material for this book. The listing is included as an aid to readers who may seek sources of additional or more technical information.

Accumulation of Soil Organic Matter from Wood Chips. M. Salomon. *Soil Science Society of America: Proceedings,* v. 17, pp. 114-18

Aerobic Decomposition of Organic Waste Material—Interim Report No. 3. Michigan State University, East Lansing

Agriculture: A New Approach. P. H. Hainsworth. Faber and Faber, Ltd., London. 248 pp.

An Agricultural Testament. Sir Albert Howard. Oxford University Press, New York. 253 pp.

Artificial Manures, or the Conservation and Use of Organic Matter for Soil Improvement. Arthur Beaumont. Orange Judd, New York. 155 pp.

Basic Problems in Organic Matter Transformations. F. E. Broadbent. *Soil Science,* v. 79, pp. 107-14

Bibliography on Disposal of Organic Refuse by Composting. University of California College of Engineering, Sanitary Engineering Research Projects, Berkeley

Bio-Dynamic Farming and Gardening. Ehrenfried Pfeiffer. Anthroposophic Press, New York. 240 pp.

Bio-Dynamics (quarterly). Bio-Dynamic Farming and Gardening Association, Chester, N. Y.

Cato: On Agriculture. Translated by William D. Hooper and revised by H. B. Ash. W. Heinemann, Ltd., London. 542 pp.

Changes in the Content of Certain Vitamins in Organic Materials Decomposing Under Aerobic and Anaerobic Conditions. Journal Series, New Jersey Experiment Station, Rutgers University, New Brunswick

Changes in the Erodibility of Soils Brought About by the Application of Organic Matter. *Soil Science Society of America: Proceedings*, v. 2, pp. 85-96

Changes Occurring in the Organic Matter During the Decomposition of Compost Heaps. M. R. F. Ashworth. *Journal of Agricultural Science*, v. 32, pp. 360-70

Chemicals, Humus and the Soil. Donald P. Hopkins. Chemical Publishing Company, New York. 358 pp.

Columella: On Agriculture. Translated by H. B. Ash. Harvard University Press, Cambridge. 3 volumes

Comparison of Different Methods of Composting Waste Materials. C. N. Acharya. *Indian Journal of Agricultural Science*, v. 9, pp. 565-72

Complete Study of Farm Uses for Organic Wastes. S. J. Toth and W. H. Kelly. *New Jersey Agriculture*, July, 1956. Rutgers University, New Brunswick.

Compost. F. H. Billington and Ben Easey. C. T. Branford Company, Boston. 104 pp.

Compost. J. P. J. Van Vuren. South Africa Agriculture Department Bulletin 310. 39 pp.

The Compost Gardener. F. H. King. Organic Gardening Library, Emmaus, Pa. 100 pp.

Compost—How to Make It. Edited by J. I. Rodale. Organic Gardening, Emmaus, Pa. 63 pp.

Composting. Harold B. Gotaas. World Health Organization, United Nations, New York. 205 pp.

Composting and Mulching. F. B. Smith and G. D. Thornton. Florida Agricultural Experiment Station Bulletin 602. 4 pp.

Composting: An Expanding Frontier for Industrial Waste Treatment. Robert Rodale. *Industrial Wastes,* July-August 1957.

Composting of Municipal Refuse and Some European Composting Operations. Pennsylvania State University, University Park, Pa.

Composting of Organic Wastes—An Annotated Bibliography. John S. Wiley. Public Health Service, Savannah, Ga.

Compost Magazine (bimonthly). New Zealand Organic Compost Society, Inc., Christchurch, New Zealand.

Compost Making for Gardens. D. Hall. *Royal Horticultural Society Journal,* v. 65, pp. 75-6

Compost Manufacturers Manual: the Practice of Large-Scale Composting. Ehrenfried Pfeiffer. Pfeiffer Foundation, Philadelphia. 137 pp.

Composts. E. J. Russell. *Journal of the Ministry of Agriculture,* v. 46, pp. 751-8

Compost Science (quarterly). Rodale Press, Emmaus, Pa.

Composts for Mushroom Culture. L. R. Kneebone. *Market Growers Journal,* v. 84, pp. 16-17

Controlled Humus Production by Separate Sludge Digestion and Drying. L. L. Langford. *Water and Sewage Works,* v. 101, pp. 503-6; v. 102, pp. 36-41, 125-9

Cover Crops, Green Manures and Mulches in Management and Conservation of the Soil. Z. C. Foster. Hawaii Agricultural Extension Circular 337. 7 pp.

Darwin on Humus and the Earthworm. Introduction by Sir Albert Howard. Faber and Faber, Ltd., London. 153 pp.

Digester Converts Sawdust into Humus. *Civil Engineering,* v. 26, p. 270

Disposal of Cannery Waste in Ohio. Prof. H. D. Brown. Ohio State University, Columbus

Does Cropping Affect Soil Organic Matter? K. W. Flach and M. G. Kline. *New York Agricultural Experiment Station Farm Research,* v. 20, p. 13

Does Nitrogen Applied to Crop Residues Produce More Humus? F. E. Allison. *Soil Science Society of America: Proceedings,* v. 19, pp. 210-11

The Earth's Face and Human Destiny. Ehrenfried Pfeiffer. Rodale Press, Emmaus, Pa. 183 pp.

The Earth's Green Carpet. Louise E. Howard. Faber and Faber, Ltd., London. 260 pp.

Earthworms: Their Intensive Propagation. Thomas J. Barrett. Earthmaster Publications, El Monte, Calif. 60 pp.

Effect of Erosion on Losses of Soil Organic Matter. C. S. Slater and E. A. Carleton. *Soil Science Society of America: Proceedings,* v. 3, pp. 123-8

Effect of Fertilizers and Organic Materials on the Cation-Exchange Capacity of an Irrigated Soil. P. F. Pratt. *Soil Science,* v. 83, pp. 85-9

Effect of Green Manure Crops of Varying Carbon-Nitrogen Ratios Upon Nitrogen Availability and Soil Organic Matter Content. L. A. Pinck and others. *American Society of Agronomy Journal,* v. 40, pp. 237-48

Effect of Organic Matter on Phosphate Availability. J. D. Dalton and others. *Soil Science,* v. 73, pp. 173-81

Effect of Stubble Mulching on Number and Activity of Earthworms. S. P. Teotia and others. Nebraska Agricultural Experiment Station Research Bulletin 165. 20 pp.

Effect of the Addition of Organic Materials on the Decomposition of an Organic Soil. C. W. Bingeman and others. *Soil Science Society of America: Proceedings,* v. 17, pp. 34-8

Effect of Various Exchangeable Cation Ratios on Kinds of Fungi Developing During Decomposition of Organic Residues in Soil. J. P. Martin and D. G. Aldrich. *Soil Science Society of America: Proceedings,* v. 18, pp. 160-4

Encyclopedia of Organic Gardening. J. I. Rodale and Staff. Rodale Books, Inc., Emmaus, Pa. 1145 pp.

Evaluation of Composted Fertilizers by Microbiological Methods of Analysis. Charles B. Davey. *Wisconsin Academy of Sciences, Arts and Letters,* v. 43, pp. 93-6

Factors that Influence Clod Structure and Erodibility of Soil by Wind—Organic Matter at Various Stages of Decomposition. W. S. Chepil. *Soil Science,* v. 80, pp. 413-21

Farmers of 40 Centuries. F. H. King. Organic Gardening Press, Emmaus, Pa. 384 pp.

Farm Fertility. Sidney B. Haskell. Harper and Bros., New York. 243 pp.

Farming and Gardening for Health and Disease. Sir Albert Howard. Faber and Faber, Ltd., London. 282 pp.

Farming and Gardening in the Bible. Alastair I. MacKay. Rodale Press, Emmaus, Pa. 280 pp.

Farming with Nature. Joseph A. Cocannouer. University of Oklahoma Press, Norman. 147 pp.

Farm Manures. Charles Thorne. Orange Judd Company, New York. 242 pp.

Farm Soils, Their Management and Fertilization. Edmund L. Worthen and Samuel R. Aldrich. John Wiley and Sons, New York. 439 pp.

Fertility Farming. Newman Turner. Faber and Faber, Ltd., London. 264 pp.

Fertility from Town Wastes. J. C. Wylie. Faber and Faber, Ltd., London. 224 pp.

Fertilizer or Organic Material for Soil Improvement. M. S. Anderson. Water Conservation Research Branch, U. S. Department of Agriculture, Beltsville, Md.

Food, Farming and the Future. Friend Sykes. Rodale Press, Emmaus, Pa. 294 pp.

The Formation of Vegetable Molds Through the Action of Worms. Charles Darwin. D. Appleton and Company, New York. 326 pp.

From My Experience. Louis Bromfield. Harper and Bros., New York. 355 pp.

Garbage Composts and Related Disposal Methods. M. S. Anderson. Agricultural Research Service, U. S. Department of Agriculture, Beltsville, Md.

The Gardener and *The Farmer* (monthly). Newman Turner Publications, Ltd., London, England.

Gardening with Nature. Leonard Wickenden. Devin-Adair, New York. 392 pp.

Gardening Without Digging. A. Guest. Faber and Faber, Ltd., London.

General Recommendations Regarding Methods for Wood Waste Utilization. Forest Products Laboratory, Forest Service, U. S. Department of Agriculture, Madison, Wis.

Green Manuring. Adrian J. Pieters. John Wiley and Sons, New York. 127 pp.

Grow a Garden. Ehrenfried Pfeiffer and Erika Riese. Anthroposophic Press, New York. 118 pp.

Guild Gardening. George H. Copley.

A Handbook of Organic Fertilizers. Association of British Organic Fertilizers, Ltd., London. 84 pp.

The Haughley Experiment. Dr. E. P. Dark. *Medical Journal of Australia,* Oct. 25, 1958

The Healthy Hunzas. J. I. Rodale. Rodale Press, Emmaus, Pa. 263 pp.

How to Have a Country Homestead that Pays for Itself. Organic Gardening and Farming Staff. Organic Gardening, Emmaus, Pa. 64 pp.

How to Have a Green Thumb Without an Aching Back. Ruth Stout. Exposition Press, New York. 164 pp.

Humus and Decay—A Survey of Composting. F. M. Newell. Daniel, New York. 40 pp.

Humus and the Farmer. Friend Sykes. Rodale Press, Emmaus, Pa. 416 pp.

Humus: Origin, Chemical Composition and Importance in Nature. Selman A. Waksman. Williams and Wilkins Company, Baltimore. 562 pp.

Influence of Organic Matter on Aeration and Structure of Soil. J. H. Quastel. *Soil Science*, v. 73, pp. 419-26

Influence of Rate of Plant Residue Addition in Accelerating the Decomposition of Soil Organic Matter. M. J. Hallam and W. V. Bartholomew. *Soil Science Society of America: Proceedings*, v. 17, pp. 365-8

Influence of Straw and Straw-Fertilizer Composts on the Uptake of Fertilizer Phosphorus by Plants. W. H. Fuller and D. R. Nielsen. *Soil Science Society of America: Proceedings*, v. 21, pp. 278-82

Industrial Waste Treatment. Hayes H. Black. *Sewage and Industrial Wastes*, v. 26

Intensive Gardening. Rosa Dalziel O'Brien. Faber and Faber, Ltd., London. 183 pp.

John Innes Composts. W. J. C. Lawrence. *Royal Horticultural Society Journal*, v. 67, pp. 86-91

Laboratory Study of the Decomposition of Vegetable Debris in Relation to the Formation of Raw Humus. D. R. Johnston. *Plant and Soil*, v. 4, pp. 345-69

Lack of Natural Fertilizers is Basic Hindrance to Organic Farming. M. A. Bachtel. Ohio Agricultural Experiment Station Farm and Home Research Bulletin 282, p. 44

Leaves and What They Do. Heinrich Meyer. Organic Gardening Library.

Life from the Soil. H. F. White and S. Hicks. Longmans, Melbourne, Australia. 317 pp.

Living by the Land. John C. Gifford. Glade House, Coral Gables, Fla. 139 pp.

The Living Soil. Lady Eve Balfour. Devin-Adair, New York. 270 pp.

Look to the Land. Lord Northbourne. Dent, London. 206 pp.

Make Friends with Your Land. Leonard Wickenden. Devin-Adair, New York. 144 pp.

Making Compost in 14 Days. Organic Gardening Library

Making Manures from Organic Residues. L. C. Olsen. Georgia Agricultural Experiment Press Bulletin 604, p. 1

Malabar Farm. Louis Bromfield. Harper and Bros., New York. 405 pp.

Manual of Organic Materials. Organic Gardening Library. 64 pp.

The Manufacture of Humus by the Indore Process. Sir Albert Howard. *Royal Society of Arts Journal*, v. 84, pp. 26-59

Manures and Fertilizers. British Ministry of Agriculture and Fisheries. Chemical Publishing Company, New York.

A Microbiologist Looks at Soil Organic Matter. Selman A. Waksman. *Soil Science Society of America: Proceedings*, v. 7, pp. 16-21

Mother Earth (quarterly). Journal of the Soil Association, London, England.

Mulch Farming, Practice with a Future. *Agricultural Research*, v. 2, pp. 10-11

Mushrooms from Sawdust. S. S. Block. *Chemical and Engineering News*, v. 34, p. 2108

Natural Gardening. J. E. B. Maunsell. Faber and Faber, Ltd., London. 128 pp.

Nature and Properties of Soils. T. L. Lyon and H. O. Buckman. Macmillan, New York. 591 pp.

The New Organic Method. J. I. Rodale. Organic Gardening Library.

Nitrogen and Organic Matter in the Soil. A. E. Gustason. McGraw Hill, New York. 424 pp.

Note on the Available Nitrogen of Composts from Waste Materials. G. E. G. Mattingly. *International Society of Soil Science Commission*, v. 2, pp. 68-70

Nutrition and the Soil. Dr. Lionel Picton, O.B.E. Devin-Adair, New York. 400 pp.

Organic Gardening and Farming (monthly). Rodale Press, Emmaus, Pa.

Organic Farming. Hugh Corley. Faber and Faber, Ltd., London. 200 pp.

The Organic Front. J. I. Rodale. Rodale Press, Emmaus, Pa. 200 pp.

Organic Gardening. J. I. Rodale. Hanover House, Garden City, N. Y. 224 pp.

Organic Husbandry: A Symposium. J. S. Blackburn. Biotechnic Press, Ltd., London. 160 pp.

Organic Matter and Our Food Supply. Dr. George D. Scarseth. American Farm Research Association Bulletin, 1947, Lafayette, Ind.

Organic Matter for the Garden. D. Comin. Ohio Agricultural Experiment Station Farm and Home Research Bulletin 247, pp. 131-8

Organic Matter Improves the Soil. R. E. Taylor and others. Wisconsin Agricultural Experiment Station Bulletin 516. 16 pp.

The Organic Merry-Go-Round. J. I. Rodale. Rodale Press, Emmaus, Pa. 64 pp.

Organic Method on the Farm. J. I. Rodale. 128 pp.

Organic Surface Cultivation. Gerard Smith. Ward Lock and Company, Ltd., London. 192 pp.

Our Garden Soils. Charles E. Kellogg. Macmillan, New York. 232 pp.

Our Soils and Their Management. Roy L. Donahue. Interstate Printers and Publishers, Danville, Ill. 446 pp.

Out of the Earth. Louis Bromfield. Harper and Bros., New York. 305 pp.

Pay Dirt. J. I. Rodale. Devin-Adair, New York. 252 pp.

Permanence of Organic Matter Added to Soil. H. H. Mann and T. W. Barnes. *Journal of Agricultural Science*, v. 48, pp. 160-3

Photosynthesis Reclamation of Organic Wastes. Harold B. Gotaas, William J. Oswald and Harvey F. Ludwig. *Scientific Monthly*, December, 1954

Pleasant Valley. Louis Bromfield. Harper and Bros., New York. 300 pp.

Plough and Pasture: the Early History of Farming. E. Cecil Curwen and Gudmund Hatt. Henry Schuman, New York. 329 pp.

Practical Organic Gardening. Ben Easey. Faber and Faber, Ltd., London. 312 pp.

Preparation and Use of Composts, Night Soil, Green Manures, and Unusual Fertilizing Materials in Japan. C. L. W. Swanson. *Agronomy Journal*, v. 41, pp. 275-82

Qualitative Studies of Soil Microorganisms; Effect of Decomposition of Various Crop Plants on the Nutritional Groups of

Soil Bacteria. J. W. Ronatt and A. G. Lockhead. *Soil Science,* v. 80, pp. 147-54

Questions and Answers on Compost. Edited by J. I. Rodale and Heinrich Meyer. Organic Gardening Library

Quick-Return Method of Composting. May E. Bruce. 92 pp.

Rate of Application of Organic Matter in Relation to Soil Aggregation. G. M. Browning and F. M. Milam. *Soil Science Society of America: Proceedings,* v. 6, pp. 96-7

Reclamation of Municipal Refuse by Composting. Sanitary Engineering Research Project. University of California, Berkeley. 89 pp.

Role of Organic Matter in Soil Fertility. N. R. Dhar. *Soil Science,* v. 80, p. 166

Russian Comfrey. Lawrence D. Hills. Faber and Faber, Ltd., London. 167 pp.

Sawdust Composts in Soil Improvement. J. R. Baker and S. Dunn. *Plant and Soil,* v. 6, pp. 113-28

Sawdust Composts: Their Preparation and Effect on Plant Growth. C. B. Davey. *Soil Science Society of America: Proceedings,* v. 17, pp. 59-60

Seaweed Excellent Organic Supplement. Dr. Francis J. Weiss. *Journal of Agricultural and Food Chemistry,* 1954

Seedlings. Evelyn Speiden. Organic Gardening Library, Emmaus, Pa. 95 pp.

Sir Albert Howard in India. Louise E. Howard. Faber and Faber, Ltd., London. 272 pp.

Soil Aggregation as Influenced by the Growth of Mold Species, Kind of Soil, and Organic Matter. C. M. Gilmour and others. *Soil Science Society of America: Proceedings,* v. 13, pp. 292-6

The Soil and Health. Sir Albert Howard. Devin-Adair, New York. 320 pp.

Soil Block Gardening. J. L. H. Chase and A. J. Pouncy. Faber and Faber, Ltd., London. 139 pp.

Soil Chemistry. M. Y. Shawarbi. John Wiley and Sons, New York. 420 pp.

Soil Development. Edward Faulkner. University of Oklahoma Press, Norman. 232 pp.

Soil Fertility and Animal Health. Dr. William A. Albrecht

Soil Fertility and Sewage. Johannes P. J. Van Vuren. Faber and Faber, Ltd., London. 236 pp.

Soil Fertility, Renewal and Preservation. Ehrenfried Pfeiffer. Faber and Faber, Ltd., London. 196 pp.

Soil Humus and Health. W. E. Shewell-Cooper. J. Gifford, Ltd., London. 84 pp.

Soils and Fertilizers. Firman Bear. John Wiley and Sons, New York. 420 pp.

Soil—the 1957 Yearbook of Agriculture. U. S. Department of Agriculture, Washington. 784 pp.

Some Engineering Aspects of High Rate Organic Wastes. John R. Snell. Michigan Associates, East Lansing.

Stimulation of Seedling Plants by Organic Matter. J. R. Piland and L. G. Willis. *American Society of Agronomy Journal,* v. 29, pp. 324-31

Stone Mulching in the Garden. J. I. Rodale. Rodale Press, Emmaus, Pa. 164 pp.

The Story of Microbes. Albert Schatz and Sarah R. Riedman. Harper and Bros., New York. 172 pp.

Studies in Tropical Soils, Organic Transformations in Soils, Compost and Peat. D. W. Duthie. *Journal of Agricultural Science,* v. 27, pp. 162-77

Studies of High-Rate Composting of Garbage and Refuse. John S. Wiley. U. S. Department of Health, Education and Welfare, Savannah, Ga.

This Farming Business. Friend Sykes. Faber and Faber, Ltd., London. 160 pp.

Titans of the Soil—Great Builders of Agriculture. Edward Jerome Dies. University of North Carolina, Chapel Hill. 213 pp.

Topsoil and Civilization. Tom Dale and Vernon Gill Carter. University of Oklahoma Press, Norman

Trampling Out the Vintage. Joseph A. Cocannouer. University of Oklahoma Press, Norman. 220 pp.

The Treatment of Animal Waste. W. Weaver. Institute of Public Cleansing, London. 111 pp.

Types of Composted Fertilizers Used in Forest Nurseries. S. H. Wilde and others. *Soil Science Society of America: Proceedings,* v. 12, pp. 508-10

Use of Organic Materials in Long-Term Experiment. E. R. Parker and W. W. Jones. *California Citrograph,* v. 36, pp. 314-16

The Use of Sawdust for Mulches and Soil Improvement. U. S. Department of Agriculture Circular No. 891, Washington

The Use of Sludge as a Soil Conditioner. Editorial Department, Organic Gardening and Farming, Emmaus, Pa. 16 pp.

The Use of Town Wastes in Agriculture. H. M. Stationery Office, London. 24 pp.

The Uses of Mulches. William A. Albrecht

Utilization and Disposal of Poultry By-Products and Wastes. Marketing Research Report No. 143, U. S. Department of Agriculture, Washington

Utilization of Town and Country Wastes, Garbage and Sewage. Auckland and Suburban Drainage League, Auckland, N. Z. 62 pp.

The Value of Industrial Wastes in the Garden and on the Farm. Editorial Department, Organic Gardening and Farming, Emmaus, Pa. 41 pp.

The War in the Soil. Sir Albert Howard. Organic Gardening, Emmaus, Pa. 96 pp.

The Waste Products of Agriculture: Their Utilization as Humus. Sir Albert Howard. Oxford University Press, New York. 167 pp.

Weed-Free Compost and Seedbeds for Turf. J. A. De France. Rhode Island Agricultural Experiment Station Miscellaneous Publication 31. 15 pp.

Wheel of Health. Dr. G. T. Wrench. C. W. Daniel Company, Ltd., London. 146 pp.

Woodchips, Sawdust and Sewage Sludge for Soil Improvement. *Connecticut Agricultural Experiment Station Frontiers of Plant Science,* v. 6, pp. 4-5

The Work of Sir Robert McCarrison. Edited by H. M. Sinclair. Faber and Faber, Ltd., London. 327 pp.

INDEX

formula for, 60
lawn mower (rotary) as
   shredder, 61
leaves as basic material, 60
manure in, 59
moisture in, 60
rock fertilizers in, 61-62
shredding of organic materials,
   58-61
temperature of heap, 61
turning of material, 61
Frazer method, of compost-making,
   665
"Frit," see Glass
Fruit(s), directions for growing
   indoors, 368
   citrus, analysis of wastes, 837
   premature dropping of, 913
Fruit trees: citrus, fertilizing of,
   379-380
   mulching of, 545-548
   treated with compost, 360
   549-550, 952-953
   malnutrition, 302-304
   nitrogen for, 376-377
   use of compost for, 317, 367-368,
   373 (illus.)
Fucus, in compost, 192
Fungi. See also Actinomycetes,
   Mycorrhizal fungi, Myxomycetes
   action of, in Indore compost
   heap, 54-55
   in soil, 33
   mycelia of, 887 (illus.)
   of soil, 885 (illus.)
   producers of soil aggregates,
   857
   role in decomposition, 657

Garbage, as fertilizer, 915
   analysis of, 670-671
   composition of, 642-643, 669-673
   disposal of, 638-639, 641-642
   at South Pole, 933-934
   by incineration, 683-684
   by municipal compost-making,
   686-687
   effect of home grinding on
   municipal plant, 668
   for compost-making, 18, 129
   (illus.), 153
   ground, treated by anaerobic
   digestion, 668
   moisture in, 645, 652
   shrinkage during decomposition,
   654
   temperature of, 645

Garbage compost, analysis of,
   672-673, 673 (table)
   composition of, 669-673
Garbage trenching, European
   method, 154
Garden, treated with compost,
   579 (illus.)
   when to plant, 292
Gardenias, potting mixture for,
   385
Gardening, by organic method,
   history of, 17-18
   in California, 548-550
Garden tractors, use in green
   manuring, 70
Gas, production in anaerobic
   digester, 413-414, 414
   (table)
Gasometer, for manure gas plant,
   415 (illus.), 416, 417 (illus.)
Geraniums, use of compost for,
   337-338
Gladioli, use of compost for,
   312 (illus.), 338
Gladioli tops, in compost, 931
Glass, use of as fertilizer, 806-807
Glauconite potash mineral, 161
Gloxinias, use of compost for,
   338-339
Granite dust, in compost, 155-157
Grape pomace, analysis of, 813,
   839
Grape wastes, in composts, 157
Grapes, use of compost for, 360
Grass clippings, in compost,
   157-160
Grasses, effect of fertilizer on,
   869-870
Greeks, compost known to, 10
Greenbugs, 576
Green manure, toxic substances in,
   31
   trace elements in, 407-410
   use on farm, 399-401
Green manuring, 68-75
   advantages of, 70-71
   cover crops in, 68-69, 71-75
   polysaccharides in, 75
   use of garden tractors, 70
   use of rotary tillers, 70
Green matter, see Plant waste
Greensand, in compost, 160-162
Grinders, for compost-making,
   239-250
   dealers in, 278-279
   tractor-powered type, 250
Grinding, in experimental compost-
   making, 697-698

995

toxicity of excessive amounts
in soil, 865-867
varying amounts in vegetables,
595-596
Mixers, for large-scale compost-
making, 259-261, 260 (illus.)
Mock orange, use of compost for,
348-349
Moisture, amount in compost-
making, 21-22, 41, 48, 83-84,
107, 108, 111, 701-702
in municipal compost-making,
690
effect on microorganisms, 34
in 14-day compost-making, 60
Molasses, as fertilizer, 941
Monasteries, medieval, compost-
making advised by monks,
11-12
Muck, 15, 17, 936-937, 956
Mulch, application of, in dry
areas, 119
for roses, 350
green, 158-160
use of bark, 826
of sawdust, 127
Mulching, vertical, 467-472
conservation of water by,
468-469, 469 (illus.)
earthworms in channels, 470
in drainage system, 471
in dry soil, 470-471
machine for, 467-468, 472
space between channels,
471-472
types of mulch used, 468, 469
Mulch till planter, 272-273
Mushrooms, use of compost for,
361-362
Mycorrhizal fungi, effect on pine
trees, 376
on plants, 576
Myxomycetes, in decomposition of
organic materials, 861

Narcissi, use of compost for, 341
Neem cake, 867
Nematodes, effect of fungi, 582-583
of sugar waste, 841
in adobe, 539
in roses, 353
signs of infestation, 916
New Zealand box, 57, 101, 102,
223-225, 224 (illus.),
225 (illus.)
Night soil, in anaerobic digesters,
259

in compost-making, 726-727,
732-733, 753
Nitrate of soda, as fertilizer, 950
Nitrates, amount produced in
garbage compost, 673
(table)
in compost, 110-111, 113
in experiments on compost,
703-705, 704 (table)
in the nitrogen cycle, 888
unstable, as cause of
methemoglobinemia in
human beings, 391
Nitrites, in compost, 113, 703-705,
704 (table)
in the nitrogen cycle, 888
toxicity of, 36
Nitrogen activators, 139-141
Nitrogen, added to wood wastes,
820-821, 828
Nitrogen, amounts converted to
nitrate in garbage compost,
673 (table)
amounts in organic materials,
132-137
changes in experimental
compost-making, 703-706
conservation of, in relation to
carbon-nitrogen ratio,
647 (table)
deficiency of, in fruit trees, 302,
303
in vegetables, 295-296
excessive amounts, in
vegetables, 391-392
for fruit trees, 376-377
in animal manure, 173, 180
in garbage compost, 672, 673
in humus, 878
in leaves, 169, 945
in organic wastes, 834-835
in poultry manure, 183
in proteins, 895-896, 898
in raw garbage, 670
in wood wastes, 831
loss of, from compost, 21
from farm manure, 421
prevention of, in poultry
house, 184
need for, in compost heap, 101
organic versus chemical forms,
896-897
role in plant growth, 356,
893-894
Nitrogen cycle, in decomposition,
887-888
Northern United States, compost
calendar for, 304-306

1004